THE LIFE AND WORKS
OF THE LANCASHIRE NOVELIST
WILLIAM HARRISON AINSWORTH,
1805-1882

THE LIFE AND WORKS OF THE LANCASHIRE NOVELIST WILLIAM HARRISON AINSWORTH, 1805-1882

Stephen James Carver

Studies in British Literature
Volume 75

The Edwin Mellen Press
Lewiston•Queenston•Lampeter

Library of Congress Cataloging-in-Publication Data

Carver, Stephen James.
  The life and works of the Lancashire novelist William Harrison Ainsworth, 1850-1882 / Stephen James Carver.
      p. cm. -- (Studies in British literature ; v. 75)
  Includes bibliographical references and index.
  ISBN 0-7734-6633-9 (hc)
    1. Ainsworth, William Harrison, 1805-1882. 2. Novelists, English--19th century--Biography. 3. Lancashire (England)--Biography. I. Title. II. Series.

PR4003.C37 2003
823'.8--dc21
  [B]

                                                                      2003056248

This is volume 75 in the continuing series
Studies in British Literature
Volume 75 ISBN 0-7734-6633-9
SBL Series ISBN 0-88946-927-X

A CIP catalog record for this book is available from the British Library

The Edwin Mellen Press   The Edwin Mellen Press
Box 450   Box 67
Lewiston, New York   Queenston, Ontario
USA 14092-0450   CANADA L0S 1L0

The Edwin Mellen Press, Ltd.
Lampeter, Ceredigion, Wales
UNITED KINGDOM SA48 8LT

Printed in the United States of America

For Chiharu, who has lived with this project as long as I have and to whom it equally belongs

TABLE OF CONTENTS

ACKNOWLEDGEMENTS

I would like to begin by particularly thanking Professor Victor Sage and Professor Roger Sales of the University of East Anglia, whose help and advice at all stages of this project allowed it to develop and succeed. For additional support and guidance over the years, my thanks go also to Professor Lorna Sage; Dr. Robert Clark; Dr. Ivy Garlitz; Dr. Tim Marshall; and Dr. Allan Lloyd Smith, also of UEA; Professor Chris Baldick of Goldsmith's College; Professor David Punter of the University of Bristol; Dr William Hughes of Bath Spa University College; Dr Glyn White of the University of Central Lancashire; Charles Jannuzi of Fukui University; Dr Chiharu Yoshioka; Daniel Capie; Mark Dunham; Nigel Herwin; Sian Marks; Mark Underwood; and Louise Young. A special thanks also to Irene and Walter Carver (Mum and Dad). I would also like to offer my thanks to all the students who have allowed me to test my ideas from this project in nineteenth century literature seminars, and for all their valuable and challenging feedback. I must similarly thank all those who attended my presentations on Ainsworth at the *Legacies of Walpole: The Gothic After Otranto*, International Gothic Association Conference, St Mary's University College, Strawberry Hill (1997); *The Victorian Gothic Colloquium*, UEA (1998); and the *G.W.M. Reynolds: Popular Culture, Literature and Radicalism in the Nineteenth-century* Conference, University of Birmingham (2000) for their interest in my work, their often invaluable advice and moral support. I have also had the backing of a United Nations of friends throughout this project, and I would like to take the opportunity of expressing my gratitude and affection for all of them here: you know who you are. I must also acknowledge the assistance of the following individuals and organisations: Sarah Gooderson, who edited this book; Miranda Buchanan and Andrea Greengrass of Wordwise Edit for putting it all together; Ryan Tebbit and his colleagues at the British Library for providing microfilms of *December Tales* and *Considerations on the best means of affording Immediate Relief to the Operative Classes*, as well as for their numerous other assistance over the years; D.W. Riley F.L.A, Keeper of Printed Books at the John Rylands University Library of Manchester, for allowing me complete access to their rare Ainsworth material; Dora Rayson and her colleagues at the Archives Section, Local Studies Unit, Manchester Central Library for their help during my work on the Aston and Crossley papers; Claire Howlin, and the staff and students of Moberly Hall, the University of Manchester, for making my long stay in their city such a pleasant one; and finally to everyone at the UEA Library for all their help over the years. I hope the present work lives up to everyone's expectations and justifies their collective faith in its author.

CHRONOLOGY

1805   William Harrison Ainsworth born in Manchester, February 4, the first child of Thomas Ainsworth, solicitor, and Ann Harrison.

1806   Birth of brother, Thomas Gilbert Ainsworth, October 4 (destined for a long life of mental illness).

1817   Enters Manchester Free Grammar School.

1819   Peterloo Massacre. St Peter's Field, Manchester, was close to the Ainsworth's family home in King Street.

1820   Writes and produces first plays at a 'Private Theatre' in the King Street cellar, in which he also acts.

1821   *The Rivals: A Serio-Comic Tragedy* published in *Arliss's Pocket Magazine* under pseudonym 'T. Hall'. T. Hall writes 17 articles, including a well-received piece on his discovery of the seventeenth century dramatist 'William Aynesworthe', whose work is quoted at length and favourably compared to that of 'Richard Clitheroe', another invention.

1822   Leaves school, begins study of law. Begins corresponding with Charles Lamb. First book published, a collection of poems under the pseudonym 'Cheviot Ticheburn' which is dedicated to Lamb.

1823   Publication of *December Tales*, a collection of literary articles and short stories previously printed in *The London Magazine*, *The Edinburgh Magazine*, *Arliss's Pocket Magazine* and *The European*.

1824   Produces new periodical, *The Boeotian*, which runs for six issues. Death of father. Leaves Manchester for London to study law.

1825   Meets Lamb. Letter to James Crossley, March 25: 'Little Charles Lamb sends me constant invitations. I met Mrs. Shelley at his house the other evening. She is very handsome; I am going to the theatre with her some evening.'

1826   Qualifies as a solicitor. Publication of *Sir John Chiverton* (written in collaboration with J.P. Aston). John Ebers publishes Ainsworth's pamphlet: *Considerations on the best means of affording Immediate Relief to the Operative Classes in the Manufacturing Districts*. Presented to Sir Walter Scott at Pall Mall. Marries Anne Francis 'Fanny' Ebers, October 11. Sets up shop as a 'Publisher and Bookseller'.

1827   Birth of first child, Fanny.

1828   Publishes an Annual, *The Christmas Box*, which includes 'The Bonnets of Bonnie Dundee' by Scott. Visits France and Germany.

1829   Birth of daughter, Emily. Abandons publishing.

1830   Resumes legal practice. Birth of third child, Anne Blanche. Tours Italy. Begins association with the new *Fraser's* Magazine.

1834   *Rookwood* published in three volumes by Richard Bentley; critical success and popular fame nothing short of meteoric. Novel dramatised for the Adelphi. Thackeray reviews novel in the June *Fraser's*, where Ainsworth is highly praised, mostly at the expense of Lytton. Meets and befriends Dickens at his open-house at Kensal Lodge; introduces Dickens to John Macrone, George Cruikshank and John Forster.

1835   Separation from wife.

1836   Persuades Macrone to publish Browning's early work, *Sordello*. Death of Macrone.

1837   *Crichton.*

1838   Death of wife, March 6, aged 33. Visits Manchester with Dickens and Forster.

1839   *Jack Sheppard* published, out-sells *Oliver Twist*; eight dramatic versions produced. Novel attacked by Forster and Thackeray. A moral panic, the 'Newgate controversy', breaks out around Ainsworth, Dickens and Lytton. Becomes editor of *Bentley's Miscellany* in March, after Dickens' resignation. (Contributions during Ainsworth's editorship include Poe's *Fall of the House of Usher* and Longfellow's *Wreck of the Hesperus*.)

1840   Serial publication of *Guy Fawkes*. *The Tower of London*.

1841   *Old St. Paul's* serialised in *The Sunday Times*. Resigns editorship of *Bentley's* in December.

1842   *Ainsworth's Magazine* begins in February; prints 'A few words to the Public about Richard Bentley' by Cruikshank, which engenders a protracted war of words between Ainsworth and Bentley's champion, 'Father Prout' (Francis Mahony). *The Miser's Daughter*. Begins serial publication of *Windsor Castle*. Death of mother.

1843   Begins serialisation of *Modern Chivalry* (of which authorship remains uncertain, probably written by Catherine Gore). Sells *Ainsworth's Magazine*.

1844   *Saint James's* (the last novel to be illustrated by Cruikshank). Begins serialisation of *Auriol* under title of *Revelations of London*. In the collection of critical essays, *A New Spirit of the Age*, edited by Richard H. Horne, Ainsworth's work is described as: 'generally dull, except when it is revolting'. It concludes that Ainsworth is: 'usually spared in public, because [he is] so much esteemed and regarded in private'.

1845   Purchases the *New Monthly Magazine* for £3,250. Credited as one of the pilots of the 'Victoria' in Poe's 'Balloon Hoax'. Regains possession of *Ainsworth's Magazine*. Begins long-running quarrel with *The Athenaeum*, concerning a disagreement regarding the affairs of the Archaeological Society.

1847   Buys back copyright of romances from Bentley. Serial publication of *James the Second*.

1848   Serial publication of *The Lancashire Witches*. Thackeray parodies the storm scene from *Jack Sheppard* in *Vanity Fair* ('The night attack', chapter 6; this is removed from the revised edition of 1853, and omitted from all subsequent editions.)

1849   Visits France and Spain. Re-issues cheap collected editions of earlier works.

1851   Begins serial publication of semi-autobiographical work, *The Life and Adventures of Mervyn Clitheroe* (not a financial success, and left unfinished until 1858).

1852   Mostly spent in France and Germany.

1853   Serial publication of *The Star Chamber* and *The Flitch of Bacon*. Moves to Brighton.

1854   *Ainsworth's Magazine* ceases publication; purchases *Bentley's Miscellany* for £1,700.

1855   Serial publication of *The Spendthrift. Ballads.*

1856   Granted a Civil List Pension of £100 p.a. on the recommendation of Lord Palmerston. (Later writing to Crossley: 'It was a great misfortune to me that Disraeli went out. He would have given me something better than a pension.')

1857   Thackeray plans a Kensal Lodge reunion dinner for Dickens, Ainsworth, Maclise and himself, but Ainsworth and Dickens both excuse themselves and the event never takes place.

1858   *Mervyn Clitheroe*.

1859   Serial publication of *Ovingdean Grange. The Combat of the Thirty*. Discovers and markets 'Ouida' (Louise de la Ramée).

1860   Serialises Mrs Henry Wood's *East Lynne* in the *New Monthly*. Financial problems: sells family house in King Street, Manchester.

1861   *The Constable of the Tower*.

1862   *The Lord Mayor of London*.

1863   Tours Switzerland and Italy. Begins serial publication of *Cardinal Pole*.

1864   Sells 'Beech Hill', his other Manchester home at Chetham Hill. *John Law*. Spends summer in Europe. Begins serial publication of *The Spanish Match* under the title of *The House of Seven Chimneys*.

1865   Ireland. Serial publication of *The Constable de Bourbon. Auriol*.

1866   *Old Court* serialised.

1867   'Retires' to Tunbridge Wells, marking the end of his open-house policy and social career of expansive dinner parties. The weight of the books in the library of the new house cause the ceiling below to collapse. Serial publication of *Myddleton Pomfret*, his last story to appear in *Bentley's*. Birth of daughter, Clara, by Sarah Wells, probably illegitimate although biographer S.M. Ellis refers to a 'private marriage' but is obviously deliberately vague regarding dates.

1868   Sells *Bentley's Miscellany* back to Bentley. Allies himself to new weekly, *Bow Bells* (formerly *Reynolds's Miscellany*), in which many of the later, rather inferior, historical romances appeared thereafter. Serial publication of *The South-Sea Bubble*.

1869   *Hilary St. Ives* (like *Mervyn Clitheroe*, this is one of the few novels with a contemporary setting). Moves to Hurstpierpoint in the South Downs with his two unmarried daughters, but spends much of his time with his brother in the house he had bought for him in Reigate. Ellis relates the following anecdote, told by Percy Fitzgerald:

> 'I recall a dinner at Teddington, in the sixties, given by Frederic Chapman, the publisher, at which were Forster and Browning. The latter said humorously, "A sad, forlorn-looking being stopped me today, and reminded me of old times. He presently resolved himself into – whom do you think? Harrison Ainsworth!"
>
> "Good Heavens!" cried Forster, "is he still alive?"'

1870   Resigns editorship of the *New Monthly*. Serial publication of *Talbot Harland*.

1871   *Tower Hill*. Death of Bentley. George Cruikshank writes to *The Times* claiming to be the 'originator' of eight of Ainsworth's early novels, but as he also claimed credit for the plot of *Oliver Twist* he is not taken overly seriously.

1872   *Boscobel*. Letter to Crossley, January 25: 'How do you like Forster's *Life of Dickens*? I have only dipped into the book, but I see he only tells half the story.'

1873   *The Good Old Times* (entitled *The Manchester Rebels of the Fatal '45* in subsequent editions).

1874   *Merry England*. Serial publication of *The Goldsmith's Wife*.

1875   *Preston Fight*. Letter to James Penderel-Brodhurst, aspiring author: 'I do not advise you to enter upon a literary career. It is a very hazardous profession ... I am certain you will find your old avocation [the law] more profitable than literature.'

1876   Death of brother. *The Leaguer of Lathom*; *Chetwynd Calverley*.

1877   *The Fall of Somerset*.

1878   *Beatrice Tyldesley*.

1879   *Beau Nash*. Moves to Reigate.

1880   Routledge publishes new editions of the majority of the novels. Visits Germany for health reasons.

1881   *Stanley Brereton*, the final work, serialised in *The Bolton Weekly Journal*. Honoured at a Lord Mayor's banquet in Manchester Town Hall, September 15, 'As an expression of the high esteem in which he is held by his Fellow townsmen and of his services to Literature'. *Punch* affectionately describes Ainsworth as: 'the greatest axe-and-neck-romancer of our time', September 21.

1882   Dies of a heart attack, Reigate, January 5. Buried in family vault at Kensal Green Cemetery.

PREFACE

> His swift narrative and vivid scene setting made him extremely
> popular, with enormous sales in the mid-century, but his
> reputation has not been sustained.
>
> *The Oxford Companion to English Literature* (1996)[1]

William Harrison Ainsworth has been, for the best part of 170 years, the victim of

convention. It is a critical cliché to concur with *The Oxford Companion to English*

Literature that Ainsworth is, as an author, worthy of mention but not of sustained

study. He is 'chiefly remembered', if at all, for one or two novels, seldom read

even within the academy, and for titles which are familiar only through the

frequency with which they may be encountered upon the dusty shelves of second-

hand book dealers.[2] Ainsworth becomes, in such readings, a phenomenon but not

a substance: he is a writer effectively stripped of his texts, essentially an

abstracted reputation which can be read only obliquely through temporary fame

and volume of sales rather than by direct access to the writings upon which both

rest. His works are abstracted to titles, and these known only by their associations

– 'pernicious' Newgate literature, heavily costumed historical romance or

provincial melodrama – rather than their contents. Ironically, therefore, 'his

---

[1] 'Ainsworth, William Harrison (1805–82)', in *The Oxford Companion to English Literature*, ed.
Margaret Drabble, (Oxford: Oxford University Press, 1996), p. 12.
[2] 'Ainsworth, William Harrison (1805–82)', in *Chambers Biographical Dictionary*, ed. Melanie
Parry (Edinburgh: Chambers, 1997), p. 25.

reputation' *has* been sustained, though only at the expense of 'his' writings: Ainsworth is not so much the 'forgotten man' of nineteenth century letters, as the briefly glimpsed signifier of a 'forgotten' oeuvre.

The consequent difficulties a reader may face when approaching Ainsworth are compounded by the striking lack of both scholarly reprints of the author's works, and the dearth of critical studies that treat of the novels in more than a passing fashion. It is to be hoped that the current volume, which addresses the absence of the latter, will stimulate the production of the former. Given the vast output of Ainsworth – thirty-nine novels, fictionalising the best part of 400 years of political, religious, monarchical and, distinctively, Northern, history, in addition to a corpus of unreprinted short fiction and journalism – it is astonishing to record that the most recent volume to be published on the author was Worth's survey *William Harrison Ainsworth*, aimed primarily at the undergraduate reader and issued thirty-one years ago.[3] Beyond this, the critical reader may be tantalised only with the substance of a chapter on 'Gothic, History and the Middle Classes' in David Punter's seminal *The Literature of Terror* (1980, reprinted 1996), with sporadic references in surveys of Victorian popular and historical fiction, and through Marie-Claire Hamard's 1991 article 'William Harrison Ainsworth, romancier historique'.[4] With these few exceptions, it is conventional to pass over Ainsworth with little more than an acknowledgement, as if the mere recollection of a name might function satisfactorily as a signifier of a literary career that remains all but unknown. Dr Carver's protracted period of research into the author, his contemporaries and their culture, realised in the present volume, is thus a much-needed survey of a neglected corpus and a timely addition to a critical debate which deserves reviving.

---

[3] One must note also, here, the unpublished – and thus, for the general reader, less readily accessible – dissertations by Ruth M. Faurot (1953), Jack I. Biles (1954), James Paton (1954), Beatrice Ricks (1954) and Llewellyn Ligocki (1968). Full details are given in the Bibliography.

[4] Ainsworth is, of course, depicted elsewhere as the inspiration, contemporary , or parallel of a number of more celebrated authors of the period, including Browning and Dickens. See, for example, Michael Meredith, 'A Fine Distancing: Browning's Debt to William Harrison Ainsworth', *Browning Society Notes*, 21 (1991–2).

In the present volume, Dr Carver is perhaps the inheritor of the generic specificity represented by Professor Punter's work as much as he is the developer of the textual breadth aspired to by Professor Worth. Laudably, Dr Carver's study resists the temptation to focus only on the novels of positive reputation, represented primarily in the public consciousness by the North-Country romances of Ainsworth's later career, albeit with some acknowledgement of the author's success as a writer of earlier, and more-metropolitan, fictional histories. This is the best that might be gained from the antecedent of Professor Worth's survey, though Dr Carver works not merely with a broader textual compass than his predecessor but also with a greater depth of documentary and epistolary support, and with reference to the critical insight of literary scholarship at the opening of the twenty-first century.

It is through the opening chapter's consideration of Ainsworth's earliest writings – the juvenilia, *December Tales* and *Sir John Chiverton* – that the generic aspect of Dr Carver's book becomes intimate to the volume's overall project of revisiting and widening access to the author's fiction. Ainsworth, in Dr Carver's reading, becomes once more a participant in a mode of fiction popularly associated with Sir Walter Scott, an inheritance which the *Waverley* novelist himself indulgently acknowledged. In itself, this generic insight clarifies the Lancashire author's apparent anachronism, and his seeming aloofness from the voguishness of mid- to late-century literary taste in particular. It raises, however, a problem of critical discrimination, also. Scott is a canonical and respectable writer, even where the literary establishment strives to deny the continued existence of anything as exclusive as a single canon, and yet Scott undeniably fictionalised rogues as well as knights, and ghostly legends in addition to Caledonian histories. Ainsworth, doing much the same thing, albeit for almost fifty years after Scott's death, gains no such acclamation by critic, reviewer or contemporary novelist, all of whom seem in retrospect to be more or less contemptuous of the tastes of the reading public who bought or borrowed the Lancashire novelist's fiction throughout the nineteenth century. If degrees of taste are the major issue here, then the apparent distastefulness of demotic appeal may be a secondary, yet still potent, issue in the dismissal of Ainsworth.

There is arguably a residual public thirst for the spectacle of Gothic throughout the nineteenth century, just as there is an underlying drive towards melodrama and sentiment in the Victorian theatre. Such are things of popular taste, and popular taste is not always in accord with the opinions of contemporary reviewers – or, indeed, the literary critics of a later century. Ainsworth's fictions, from the Newgate stylistics of *Rookwood* and *Jack Sheppard*, to the romance and emotion of the London histories of *Guy Fawkes*, *The Tower of London* and *Old Saint Paul's*, and finally the folk-histories of the North Country, as Dr Carver argues, may be seen to be linked by a common thread of Gothic scenery and melodramatic characterisation, a context virtually unacknowledged by recent criticism. As Robert Mighall suggests, the Gothic is characterised by history and by spatiality, just as much as by the presence of supernatural agencies.[5] So, too, may history – or the fictionalisation of history – be characterised by a spectacle and characterisation that might elsewhere be termed Gothic. This, though, is a Gothic that does not fit easily into the criteria demanded of it by twentieth century criticism: it is first and foremost a stylistic gesture, a conditioner of the spectacle of history, rather than a signifier which may give easy access to the anxieties of the present encoded in the past. It is thus small wonder, as Dr Carver observes, that Ainsworth has been dismissed by the orthodoxies which are empowered to comment upon, and indeed define, what ought to be classed as historical fiction after Lukács.

The problematic that has to be faced when reading Ainsworth's fiction is, therefore, that the author has unwittingly committed a double sin. On the one hand his works exhibit an apparently excessive conformity – he has given the public, the reading public that lies for the most part outside of the institutions of letters, what it wants, and his insistence on so doing has led to the dismissal of his

---

[5] Robert Mighall, *A Geography of Victorian Gothic Fiction* (Oxford: Oxford University Press, 1999), pp. xiv-xv.

writings as formulaic. On the other hand, these works for all their alleged homogeneity fail to conform to the neat pigeonholing of political expediency and purposefulness that are demanded by criticism of the historical novel after Lukács, or the generic rigidities which were required by the critical institutions of an age less epistemologically fluid, less discursively aware, than the present. It is a problematic that has perpetuated the critical stagnation of research into this popular author, and which may arguably elsewhere be a factor in the casual dismissal of other writers who lack the notoriety which has arguably maintained Ainsworth's precarious foothold in the academy.

The present volume is thus an important landmark in the critical rehabilitation of William Harrison Ainsworth, and is likely to function as the touchstone to which subsequent analyses refer. The present volume is more than this, though. It forwards, in an accessible form, a representative selection of the author's works, and contextualises them through letters and reviews that have in many cases never been previously brought before a wide readership. The volume further presents a fascinating insight into the nineteenth century culture of editorship and publishing that implicated Ainsworth together with Dickens, Forster, Thackeray and Bulwer-Lytton, to name but four, in frequently turbulent as well as productive relationships. There is as much here for the general scholar of the nineteenth century, therefore, as there is for the Ainsworth specialist, the Gothicist, or the reader of historical fictions. Dr Carver's book, as this latter observation suggests, has already moved the critical debate on Ainsworth beyond the conventions that have for the most part limited its development. Dr Carver's admirable book is, indeed, a worthy starting point for a renewed – and lively – debate.

William Hughes

Bath Spa University College
January 2003

INTRODUCTION

I. Contemporary reception: the pre and early Victorian critical heritage

'Some books are undeservedly forgotten', wrote W.H. Auden, 'None are undeservedly remembered.'[1] Yet the subject of this present study has been very undeservedly forgotten. The years have not been kind to the memory of William Harrison Ainsworth, a prolific English novelist once held in such high regard that many of his contemporaries viewed him as a natural successor to Sir Walter Scott, a flamboyant editor who numbered among his close friends the literary elite of the first half of the nineteenth century and Charles Dickens's only serious commercial rival until the late 1840s, but whose name is now as obscure as it was once famous.

I first came to Ainsworth during the preliminary stages of a research project on the publisher Henry Colburn. The more I immersed myself in early Victorian critical writing, the more intrigued I became at the usually incidental references to Ainsworth, being invariably negative, if not downright abusive in overall tone. He was, nonetheless, apparently intrinsically linked to a positive legion of literary celebrities: Colburn, Charles Lamb, Leigh Hunt, Sir Walter Scott, J.G. Lockhart, Edward Bulwer-Lytton, Richard Bentley, William Makepeace Thackeray, R.H. Horne, John Forster, Charles Dickens; the list was

---

[1] W.H. Auden, 'Reading', *The Dyer's Hand and Other Essays* (London: Faber and Faber, 1963), 10.

endless. So who was this mysterious figure? I trawled the local second-hand booksellers, returning in triumph with a battered Everyman edition of *Rookwood*, an Odhams *Tower of London* (both pre-war), and a wonderfully lurid-looking 1980s paperback copy of *The Lancashire Witches*. After reading the first two chapters of *Rookwood*, as Luke Bradley clasped the mummified hand of his dead mother with such passion that it came away in his own, I had a new project. This was *grand guignol* English gothic from a historical moment when we are often told that nothing much of any significance was being written, as if English literature was in a state of abeyance, mourning Scott and waiting for Dickens, while the gothic had temporarily expired with *Melmoth the Wanderer* in 1820. *Rookwood*, written in 1834, was beginning to read like a literary missing link. I never developed the Colburn project.

Ainsworth's romances were hugely popular amongst the serial-reading middle classes in the 1830s and 40s, although his melodramatic excesses were a constant source of ridicule among his literary peers. As popular fashion changed therefore, Ainsworth's novels did not survive as canonised works of Victorian literature, but instead faded largely from critical view. Ainsworth's creative vision was an idiosyncratic one, and in many ways he was punished by the literary establishment as a result, assisted, indirectly, by his own refusal to conform to the moral and aesthetic standards of the Victorian novel. If we look beyond the traditional critical dismissals of Ainsworth's writing however, what is revealed is a virtually unexplored resource of kinetic, generically hybrid and singular texts which deserve attention in their own right as significant works of literature while also contributing further to an understanding of the development of the English novel in the immediately post-Romantic period.

A cover story appearing in the May 22 issue of [G.W.M.] *Reynolds's Miscellany of Romance, General Literature, Science, and Art* in 1847 named, 'The three most popular writers in England' as, unsurprisingly, 'Mr. Charles

Dickens, Sir E. Bulwer Lytton, and Mr. William Harrison Ainsworth'.[2] Of this august Victorian triumvirate, only Dickens has endured in the national memory. Lytton is of course not unknown; an academic revival would seem to be in the offing while many devotees of the esoteric are at the very least familiar with his occult romances *Zanoni* (1842), and *A Strange Story* (1862). But few indeed these days have read, or even heard of, William Harrison Ainsworth, the author of *Rookwood*, *The Tower of London*, *The Lancashire Witches* & co.

Based on contemporary sales, the *Reynolds's* assessment of the popularity of these writers was an accurate one. Sceptics might argue that some allowance needs to be made for the partisan nature of literary London in this assessment of authorial celebrity. It is possible, for example, that the Chartist Reynolds admired Lytton's early radicalism, while there are many echoes of the influence of Ainsworth's urban gothic in *The Mysteries of London*. Both Lytton and Ainsworth were also regular targets of abuse from Thackeray via the influential Tory journal, *Fraser's Magazine*; Lytton and William Maginn were old enemies, but Ainsworth, one of the original 'Fraserians', had fallen from grace during the Newgate controversy, a moral panic which followed the success of his novel *Jack Sheppard* in 1839. So, it is possible that, according to *Reynolds's* editor, 'My enemy's enemy is my friend', despite the fact that Ainsworth was superficially a Tory.

Since the arrival of *The Posthumous Papers of the Pickwick Club* slightly over a decade previously, it would have been unthinkable to exclude Dickens from such a roll of honour (although he and Reynolds disliked each other intensely); he had also carefully distanced himself from Ainsworth in particular after the Newgate fiction scandal. As early as 1838 Ainsworth, who had been more than a little influential in Dickens's erstwhile career, was already cheerfully deferring to the superior literary stature of his younger friend and colleague; for example, in arranging a visit to Manchester with Dickens and Forster, Ainsworth

---

[2] *Reynolds's Miscellany*, May 22 1847.

had written to the proprietor of *The Temple Inn*: 'I need not enlarge upon the merits of Mr. Dickens; as, by common consent, he has been installed in the throne of letters, vacated by Scott.'[3] This was praise indeed, coming from the author who had almost assumed the fallen mantle of the Enchanter of the North himself, after the popular success and critical acclaim attendant on the publication of *Rookwood* in 1834. 1846–7 also saw the serialisation of *Dombey and Son*, marking the beginning of Dickens's technical maturity as a novelist and often cited as the first of his truly great works of literature. At the time of the *Reynolds's* article, Lytton and Ainsworth were also at the height of their creative powers, and the following year Lytton wrote what many twentieth century experts on the historical novel regard as the last, great exponent of the form, *Harold*, while Ainsworth similarly produced his masterpiece, *The Lancashire Witches*. 1848 was truly a period of revolution; as Raymond Williams wrote in his introduction to *Dombey and Son*:

> *Dombey and Son* first appeared in book form in 1848. It was a year of outstanding importance in English and European history. It was also an exceptional period in the development of the English novel. Within some twenty months not only *Dombey and Son* but *Vanity Fair*, *Wuthering Heights*, *Jane Eyre*, *Mary Barton*, *Tancred*, and *The Tenant of Wildfell Hall* were first published. There has been no higher point in the whole history of English fiction. Several times before, there had been major individual novelists. Now, as it were suddenly, there was a generation.[4]

Dickens's art heralded this next generation, but if 1847 was a transitional year for him in terms of a new sense of thematic and stylistic control over the more spontaneous excesses of his earlier serial writing, it also marked the beginning of the end of the critical reputations of both of the eminent authors with whom he shared the current literary laurels, at least according to *Reynolds's Miscellany*.

Ainsworth was not part of this 'exceptional period' but was one of its more distinguished antecedents. The eldest son of a prominent Manchester lawyer,

---

[3] William Harrison Ainsworth, letter to Hugh Beaver, December 12 1838, James Crossley Papers, (Archives Section, Local Studies Unit), Central Library, Manchester.
[4] Raymond Williams, introduction, *Dombey and Son*, by Charles Dickens (1848 London: Penguin, 1998), 11.

Thomas Ainsworth and Ann Harrison, the daughter of a Unitarian Minister, Ainsworth was born in 1805 and was a man of Regency sensibilities as much, if not more, than he was ever what we might nowadays label a Victorian.[5] By the age of 16 he was already contributing short fiction to *Arliss's Pocket Magazine*, *The Edinburgh Magazine* and *The European*; at 17 he was corresponding with Charles Lamb and had published a volume of poetry; the next year saw the publication of a collection of short stories and literary essays, *December Tales* (1823), and the year after that the launch of his own journal, *The Boetian*, which ran for six issues. In 1825, aged just 20, Ainsworth travelled to London to be presented to literary society by Lamb. The first novel, a little gothic number entitled *Sir John Chiverton* (co-written with school friend J.P. Aston), was published in 1826, catching the eye of Sir Walter Scott himself. Ainsworth was presented to Scott that year and, having married and moved to London to set up shop as a publisher and bookseller, he charmed Scott enough for the ailing author of *Waverley* to contribute the ballad 'The Bonnets of Bonnie Dundee' to one of his projects, *The Christmas Box* of 1828. There followed the birth of three daughters (Fanny, Emily and Anne Blanche), a brief return to legal practice and some time spent in Europe, before Ainsworth became famous virtually overnight with the publication of his novel *Rookwood, A Romance* in 1834.

 Rookwood was an *Otranto*-esque novel which removed the familiar, by then clichéd, codes of the traditional gothic narrative from a fictionalised version of medieval mainland Europe and relocated them firmly in the heart of eighteenth century England. This bold stroke was given an extra bit of dash and some further historical orientation by the inclusion of the story of the famous English highwayman Dick Turpin. The publication of *Rookwood* in three volumes by Richard Bentley propelled Ainsworth towards popular literary celebrity with all the alacrity of Black Bess herself. 'His story is one that never flags', ran *The Quarterly Review*, adding, 'we expect much from this writer'. *The Spectator*

---

[5] Ainsworth had a younger brother, Thomas Gilbert (1806–1876), a promising scholar who was doomed to a life of mental illness as the result of a head injury sustained whilst riding.

similarly praised the sheer energy of the work as, 'Written with great vigour and wonderful variety', while *The Atlas* proclaimed that, 'It is long since such a work as this has been produced – the author exhibits ability of no ordinary kind.'[6] *The Atlas* review alludes to *Rookwood's* allegiance not only to the literary gothic of the previous century but also to the picaresque, particularly *The Beggar's Opera*, Defoe's criminal biographies, Fielding's *Jonathan Wild*, Schiller's *The Robbers* and, more recently, Lytton's positively refined yet contentious novels of highwaymen and homicide, *Paul Clifford* (1830) and *Eugene Aram* (1832). This was Newgate writing.

Ainsworth was certainly not the first to engage with writing the underworld or to fictionalise notorious criminals; behind his version of Turpin, and later Jack Sheppard and Jonathan Wild, stand those above mentioned, among others real, imagined or both. What is interesting about Ainsworth's interpretation is the immense popular impact it achieved on publication, the cult that grew around his image of the highwayman, and the attendant moral panic that eventually, inevitably, followed. Martin and Aytoun's Bon Gaultier Ballads capture the criminal romance craze perfectly, for example, in an outrageous parody of Wordsworth's address to Milton:

> Turpin, thou should'st be living at this hour: England hath need of thee.
>
> Great men have been among us – names that lend A lustre to our calling – better none: Maclaine, Duval, Dick Turpin, Barrington, Blueskin and others, who called Sheppard friend.[7]

Ainsworth had followed *Rookwood* with the more conventional historical novel *Crichton* (1837), which was politely received by some critics and the general public but lacked the impact of *Rookwood*. In need of another popular success, Ainsworth returned to Newgate one more time with the serialisation of *Jack*

---

[6] Quoted from S.M. Ellis, *William Harrison Ainsworth and his Friends*, 2 vols, vol. 1 (London: John Lane, 1911), 256.

[7] Bon Gaultier (Sir Theodore Martin & Professor William Edmondstoune Aytoun), 'Illustrations of the Thieves' Literature – No. 1, Flowers of Hemp, or, the Newgate Garland', *Tait's Edinburgh Magazine*, April 1841: 215–23.

Sheppard in *Bentley's Miscellany* in 1839, being the story of another eighteenth century criminal, famous for his daring prison escapes. Although *Jack Sheppard* ran concurrently with Dickens's *Oliver Twist* there was no doubt that this was the more popular of the two serials, with Ainsworth's Sheppard becoming as iconic as his Dick Turpin. 'The success of Jack is pretty certain', he was able to write to his friend James Crossley in the Autumn of 1839, 'they are bringing him out at half the theatres in London'.[8] And they were: Mrs Keeley's interpretation of the role at the Adelphi was legendary. The triumph was short-lived however, as a moral panic, known as the Newgate controversy, erupted around the novel, and its author became something of a literary pariah restricting his work thereafter to more conventional historical novels. *The Lancashire Witches* of 1848 was really his last significant contribution to English literature. In 1856 he was awarded a Civil List Pension of £100 p.a. on the recommendation of Lord Palmerston, which is rather symbolic of an old war horse being put out to pasture.

Although Lytton lived until 1873 and Ainsworth until 1882, both dying almost with pen in hand (Lytton's last novel, *Kenelm Chillingly* was published in the year of his death, and Ainsworth's final work, *Stanley Brereton*, was serialised in 1881), their later work never again reached the vast audience that they had both commanded in the 1830s and 40s. Ainsworth's descent into the state of literary limbo where his ghost presently resides was particularly pronounced. *The Lancashire Witches* was his last major critical success. Although he retained his original fans, who grew older with their favourite author and found, perhaps, something reassuring in his continued production of historical romance, Ainsworth was no longer attracting a new audience and his work, increasingly out of step with changes in Victorian taste, began to move inexorably towards the critical void. Ainsworth's name, at once popular and notorious, faded from the pages of literary history, his style of writing superseded by the rising generation of Victorian realists and his popular status supplanted by the increasingly politicised

---

[8] Ainsworth, letter to James Crossley, October 8 1839.

sensationalism of Reynolds and the gothic soap operas of James Malcolm Rymer and Thomas Peckett Prest.

The shifting sands of popular fashion can be identified quite clearly in Mayhew's *London Labour and the London Poor* (1849–50). In the section entitled 'The Literature of Costermongers', the great social explorer explains that:

> It may appear anomalous to speak of the literature of an uneducated body, but even costermongers have their tastes for books. They are very fond of hearing one read aloud to them, and listen very attentively ... What they love best to listen to – and, indeed, what they are most eager for – are Reynolds's periodicals, especially the 'Mysteries of the Court'. 'They've got tired of Lloyd's[9] blood-stained stories', said one man, who was in the habit of reading to them, 'and I'm satisfied that, of all London, Reynolds is the most popular man among them. They stuck to him in Trafalgar-square, and would again. They all say he's "a trump", and Feargus O'Connor's another trump with them.'[10]

While the article concludes that:

> The tales of robbery and bloodshed, of heroic, eloquent, and gentlemanly highwaymen, or of gipsies turning out to be nobles, now interest the costermongers but little, although they found great delight in such stories a few years back. Works relating to Courts, potentates, or 'harristocrats', are the most relished by these rude people.[11]

The above description undoubtedly signals Ainsworth and his imitators, in particular it signals the plot of *Rookwood*, being the well from which the popular craze for penny dreadful tales of highwaymen had sprung with its resurrection of the spirit of Dick Turpin. But Turpin and Jack Sheppard are by this point no longer working class icons, they have now been replaced by the more tangible figures of O'Connor and Reynolds as the working class find a political voice in Chartism.

---

[9] Edward Lloyd, publisher of *The History of Pirates, Smugglers, & c. of All Nations* (1835), *The Calendar of Horrors* (1835, interestingly in association with Thomas Peckett Prest, creator of, among others, Sweeney Todd, who made Lloyd's fortune but was left to die in poverty), and *The History of and Lives of the Most Notorious Highwaymen, Footpads and Robbers of Every Description* (1836–7).
[10] Henry Mayhew, *London Labour and the London Poor*, ed. Victor Neuburg (1851 London: Penguin, 1985), 25.
[11] *Ibid.*, 27.

Ainsworth's fictionalised outlaws were political in the sense of the individual freedom they represented to audiences from both the emergent industrial bourgeoisie and the new urban proletariat, and there were contemporary comparisons made in some quarters to the dangers of Chartism, for example Ainsworth's Edwardian biographer S.M. Ellis quotes the following remark from Mary Russell Mitford upon reading *Jack Sheppard*: 'all the Chartists in the land are less dangerous than this nightmare of a book'.[12] Nonetheless, the Tory Ainsworth's only cause was a by then rather out-dated Jacobitism and he made no pretence (as had Lytton in *Paul Clifford*), of a direct understanding of the working class, criminal underworld. In an interview given to Edmund Yates of *The World* magazine in 1878, Ainsworth answered the question, 'Did you interview thieves and Gypsies to gain authentic knowledge of "flash patter"?' (underworld slang) by admitting that:

> [I] Never had anything to do with the scoundrels in my life. I got my slang in a much easier way. I picked up the Memoirs of one James Hardy Vaux a returned transport. The book was full of adventures, and had at the end a kind of slang dictionary. Out of this I got all my 'patter'.[13]

Ainsworth's correspondence similarly reveals that he was quite aware that he was writing for the popular market, to which he owed his living, once writing to Crossley that 'the truth is, to write for the mob, you must not write too weak. The newspaper level is the true line to take.'[14]

The initial stage of Ainsworth's nineteenth century cultivation of the grossly 'popular' invites comparison with twentieth century cinema. Ainsworth's project, his commercial acumen and his rise and fall, were not in many ways dissimilar, for example, to the British film company Hammer, an uncharacteristically successful, if slightly embarrassing part of the domestic industry, which won the Queen's Award for Industry in 1968 in recognition of the

---

[12] Quoted from Ellis, vol. 1, 376.
[13] Edmund Yates, 'Celebrities at Home. No. LXXXXIV. Mr. W. Harrison Ainsworth at Little Rockley', *The World*, March 27 1878. See Chapter Three for a discussion of 'flash' dialogue.
[14] Ainsworth, letter to Crossley, April 7 1838.

company's unprecedented international success. Both Ainsworth and Hammer had dynamically resurrected the flagging, clichéd and unpopular English gothic tradition at just the right cultural moment (Ainsworth with *Rookwood* in 1834 and Hammer with the movies *The Curse of Frankenstein* 1957 and *Dracula* 1958), and success in both cases allowed them access to an establishment that more usually shunned such popular narratives. Equally, the products of both ultimately failed as a direct result of their authors' apparent inability to evolve creatively. While independent film makers were pushing the boundaries of the genre in response to the political climate of the 1960s in movies such as George A. Romero's *Night of the Living Dead* (1968), a stark, violent film with a black leading man and a contemporary setting, Hammer was still producing period vampire movies. While Reynolds gleefully placed Henry Holford the pot-boy under the arse of Queen Victoria in the first volume of *The Mysteries of London* (hiding beneath a sofa in Buckingham Palace, before sneaking into the Throne Room itself and very symbolically sitting upon the throne therein[15]), Ainsworth was still writing royalist, historical novels like *Windsor Castle,* where, as John Moore wrote in a twentieth century introduction to a Literary Heritage series reprint of the same: 'The kings were kingly and majestic, the queens were queenly and beautiful; and whether the historians had assigned them to the pigeon-hole labelled "Good" or the one labelled "Bad", they were always in a sense Great.'[16]

It should be noted, however, that when Ainsworth attempted to deviate from his established formula which he did, for example, in the mischievously self-satirising *The Life and Adventures of Mervyn Clitheroe* in 1851, his fans would rebel, sales would dramatically fall and financial necessity would invariably give birth to another costume melodrama. Taken together, this new body of work comprises a history of the English monarchy from Henry VIII to George III. In *The Historical Novel and Popular Politics*, Nicholas Rance rather uncharitably

---

[15] G.W.M. Reynolds, *The Mysteries of London*, ed. Trefor Thomas (1844–56 Keele: Keele UP, 1996), 97–101.
[16] John Moore, introduction, *Windsor Castle*, by W.H. Ainsworth (1843 London: Heron, 1968), 11.

describes one of the better examples of this vast catalogue, *The Tower of London*, as an 'incongruous merging of historical romance and guide book'.[17] As these works became increasingly peripheral to English fiction they remained popular in the United States (although unlicensed editions meant that the author never saw a penny), as the following piece of surviving fan mail demonstrates:

To Mr. Ainsworth from Mr. Latrobe,

Permit me, as a stranger to you, to express the pleasure with which I have read the very excellent series of historical romances by which you have so admirably illustrated many of the localities and edifices of England, together with the manners, customs, and superstitions of their most interesting epochs … I am an American residing in the city of Baltimore, Maryland, The United States, visiting England for the first time … In my visits to Windsor Castle and the Tower of London, your volumes … were my companions, and vastly enhanced the pleasure of the visits.

Yours very respectfully
Benjamin H. Latrobe.[18]

Ainsworth can be seen here to be part of what is nowadays referred to as the 'heritage industry'. This may also explain why the only academic work specifically on Ainsworth produced to date has come from North America in the form of a handful of unpublished doctoral dissertations all written in the early 1950s, one more in 1968, and George J. Worth's monograph in the Twayne English Authors series in 1972. By this point only scholars in America would consider Ainsworth worthy of inclusion in a series devoted to prominent English authors; the country of his birth had long since rejected and then forgotten him. With the exception of Worth (who goes back to *Sir John Chiverton*), the researchers are primarily concerned with Ainsworth as a historical novelist, paying little or no attention to anything written before *The Tower of London* in 1840.

---

[17] Nicholas Rance, *The Historical Novel and Popular Politics in Nineteenth Century England* (London: Vision, 1975), 41.
[18] Benjamin H. Latrobe, letter to Ainsworth, November 30 1871.

12

Ainsworth's status here as a popular writer who was disproportionately successful before tastes changed, while also a member of the early Victorian literary establishment in part explains his problematic critical legacy. Although the trend in literary criticism has always been to overlook Ainsworth as something of a popular hack, scholars of popular culture and the penny-a-line authors of the penny dreadfuls are just as likely to overlook Ainsworth because of his connections with Dickens and Bentley. In the seminal *Fiction for the Working Man* for example, Louis James does not tarry overlong with Ainsworth as he is, along with Dickens, an 'upper-class writer' whose work was plagiarised by entrepreneurial publishers 'catering for lower-class' and 'new town' readers.[19] Literary history seems to have lost this author somewhere between the polar extremes of high and low culture.

While Dickens was still working hard to capitalise on the success of *Pickwick*, Ainsworth had written that:

> I met Lockhart[20] the other day looking quite the old man – and very much shaken with rheumatism. He is so much altered that I scarcely knew him. Of course you have read his last volume of the life of Scott. I have been greatly delighted with it … I am sorry to hear what you say about *Nicholas Nickleby*. I feared it was not so well adapted for general popularity as the *Pickwick* – though in reality far better. But the truth is, to write for the mob, you must not write too weak. The newspaper level is the true line to take. In proportion as Dickens departs from this, he will decline in popular favour. Of this I am certain. I think, however, he has so much tact that he will yet retrieve himself … I asked Lockhart what he thought of the *Pickwick*. He said he thought 'it was all very well' – 'but', with one of his usual laughs, 'damned low!'[21]

This is an interesting letter for several reasons, most notably the statement of difference between Ainsworth and Dickens (who were still extremely close at this point, both personally and professionally), and the necessity of placing business before art. There is also Ainsworth's characteristic acknowledgement of

---

[19] Louis James, *Fiction for the Working Man: 1830–50* (London: Penguin, 1973), 29.
[20] John Gibson Lockhart (1794–1854). Journalist and biographer, author of *Memoirs of the Life of Sir Walter Scott* ((Edinburgh: Robert Cadell, 1838).
[21] Ainsworth, letter to Crossley, April 7 1838.

Dickens's skill as an author; *Nicholas Nickleby* may not be so successful as the 'low' (popular) *Pickwick Papers* in terms of sales, but it is the superior work.

Ainsworth's connection with Lockhart and his contemporaries is also significant. In 1822, Ainsworth's short story 'The Falls of Ohiopyle' had appeared in *The London Magazine*, in print alongside the work of fellow former pupil of the Manchester Free Grammar School Thomas De Quincey, as well as Hood, Hazlitt and Charles Lamb, *The Essays of Elia* then making their first appearance in the same periodical. Ainsworth wrote to Lamb and a friendship developed between the two men. Lamb acted as an editor of Ainsworth's first book, *Poems by Cheviot Ticheburn* (1822), and the collection is dedicated to him. When Ainsworth left Manchester to study law in London after the death of his father in 1824, it was Lamb who presented him to the city's most prominent ladies and gentlemen of letters. The 19-year-old Ainsworth was even introduced to the society of Mary Shelley herself. His response was to ask the author of *Frankenstein* on a date, writing to Crossley that, 'Little Charles Lamb sends me constant invitations. I met Mrs. Shelley at his house the other evening. She is very handsome; I am going to the theatre with her some evening. I have met Barry Cornwall[22] and others there.'[23] Whether or not the two ever walked out together is regrettably not recorded.

Ainsworth was also one of the original 'Fraserians', and a sketch of this eminent group assembled at 215, Regent Street in 1834 by Daniel Maclise places Ainsworth in the company of, among others, Fraser and Maginn, Thackeray, Southey, Carlyle, D'Orsay, and Lockhart; the author of the newly published and hugely popular *Rookwood* is shown seated next to an ageing Coleridge.

In addition, Ainsworth was a close friend of Charles Dickens. When they met is slightly unclear, but in *The Life of Charles Dickens* John Forster writes that he met Dickens for the first time 'at the house of our common friend Mr.

---

[22] Bryan W. Procter (1787–1874) poet, dramatist and biographer.
[23] Ainsworth, letter to Crossley, March 25 1825.

Ainsworth'[24] at the end of 1836. Ainsworth's biographer claims that Ainsworth knew Dickens as early as 1834 and that it was he who introduced the then parliamentary reporter for *The Morning Chronicle* to his own publisher, John Macrone, and illustrator, George Cruikshank, while Peter Ackroyd admits that the precise chronology of these meetings is not known, while stating that 'it seems likely that their joint publisher, Macrone, at some point introduced them.'[25] As Cruikshank and Macrone make up with Dickens the triad behind *Sketches by Boz*, whether they introduced Ainsworth to Dickens or *vice versa* is of some considerable historical importance. As Forster claims Ainsworth as already a mutual friend when he first meets Dickens at Kensal Lodge, and further as Ainsworth (being seven years senior to Dickens) was obviously a literary player in London from *at least* the first appearance of *Fraser's Magazine* in February 1830, I am inclined to favour Ellis's version of events in this case. It is beyond doubt however that it was through Ainsworth's legendary social gatherings that Dickens met some of his closest friends; in addition to Forster, Cruikshank and Macrone, he also met D'Orsay, Maclise, Talfourd and Lytton at Kensal Lodge. What is also certain is the friendship that existed between Dickens, Forster and Ainsworth in the late 1830s, Forster claiming in the section of his *Life of Dickens* entitled 'During and after "Nickleby", 1838 and 1839' that:

> A friend now especially welcome, also, was the novelist, Mr. Ainsworth, who shared with us incessantly for the three following years in the companionship which began at his house; with whom we visited, during two of those years, friends of art and letters in his native Manchester, from among whom Dickens brought away his Brothers Cheeryble, and to whose sympathy in tastes and pursuits, accomplishments in literature, open-hearted generous ways, and cordial hospitality, many of the pleasures of later years were due.[26]

After the critically hysterical Newgate controversy of 1839 (engendered in part by the success of Ainsworth's *Jack Sheppard*) threatened to implicate the author of

---

[24] John Forster, *The Life of Charles Dickens*, ed. J.W.T. Ley (1874 London: Cecil Palmer, 1928), 363. Forster is referring to Kensal Lodge, on the Harrow Road near Willesden, which was Ainsworth's home between 1835 and 1841
[25] Peter Ackroyd, *Dickens* (London: Sinclair Stevenson, 1990), 204.
[26] Forster, 383.

Oliver Twist, Dickens and Forster dropped their great friend like a poisonous snake. Ainsworth's only recorded comment on Forster's biography of Dickens was in a letter to Crossley. 'I see he only tells half the story', was all he wrote.[27] Yet before this characteristic act of public and private distancing on the part of Dickens and his professional guardian, Forster, the two writers were as thick as thieves.

These equally mercurial personalities had much in common: both had a passion for theatre, loved riding and taking absurdly long walks in the countryside; they were also both workaholics, while remaining incredibly convivial, celebrating every professional achievement with a huge dinner. In these respects they were very much of the same generation; as Ackroyd observes, both were 'part of that eminently social, gregarious, energetic, vivacious group which we have come to call "Early Victorians"'.[28] The evidence left by these young incarnations, letters, contemporary accounts and reminiscences, paint a dynamic picture of enormous enthusiasm and confidence. The following chain of letters from Ainsworth to Crossley, for example, covers a visit to his native Manchester by Dickens and Forster:

October 25, 1838.

I am sure it will give you pleasure to receive this note, handed to you, as it will be, by my friend Mr. Charles Dickens, and I am equally sure that it will give you pleasure to show him any attention in your power during his stay in Manchester. I rather suspect that he is reconnoitring for character; and, perhaps, you may aid his researches; but, at all events, you can help him to the best glass of wine in Manchester, and that will materially assist his judgement in coming to a conclusion of the habits of my townsmen … I greatly regret that I cannot accompany him. Apropos of accompaniments, I forgot to mention that Mr. Browne, the artist, who illustrates *Nicholas*, will travel with Dickens so that I must beg you to extend your hospitality to him. Pray let them see the Club – and taste its cookery.[29]

---

[27] Ainsworth, letter to Crossley, January 25 1872.
[28] Ackroyd, 204.
[29] Ainsworth, letter to Crossley, October 25 1838.

October 30, 1838.

It appears you are to have a meeting of literary men in Manchester. I have given Dickens a letter to you, and now I wish to add a special introduction for my friend Forster, who you will know by reputation. This is Dickens' most intimate friend, as well as mine, and he visits Manchester in order to see it in company with Dickens.[30]

October 31, 1838.

Dickens' object is to see the interior of a Cotton mill – I fancy with reference to some of his publications.[31]

November 11, 1838.

Dickens and Forster called on me on Sunday to give me an account of their expedition to Manchester and to bring me their two Olivers, Twist and Cromwell – have you read *Oliver Twist*? … Dickens is an excellent fellow, I am glad you like him.[32]

While Dickens sent the following invitation to J.P. Hartley in 1839:

This is my birthday … I took it into my head yesterday to get up an impromptu dinner on this auspicious occasion – only my own folks, Leigh Hunt, Ainsworth, and Forster. I know you can't dine here in consequence of the tempestuous weather on the Covent Garden shores, but if you will come in when you have done Trinculizing, you will delight me greatly, and add in no inconsiderable degree to the 'conviviality' of the meeting.

Lord bless my soul! twenty-seven years old. Who'd have thought it? I *never* did![33]

Dickens's birthday was February 7, but his attitude to Ainsworth was greatly changed by the end of his twenty-seventh year, after *Jack Sheppard* had out-sold *Oliver Twist* and Dickens found his reputation attached to the supposedly socially pernicious Newgate school of writing, where thieves and outlaws like Dick Turpin

---

[30] Ainsworth, letter to Crossley, October 30 1838.
[31] Ainsworth, letter to Crossley, October 31 1838.
[32] Ainsworth, letter to Crossley, November 11 1838
[33] Charles Dickens, letter to J.P. Hartley, February 7 1839, *The Letters of Charles Dickens*, Madeline House and Graham Storey (eds), 8 vols, vol. 1 (Oxford: Clarendon Press, 1969), 506.

were presented as heroes of literature, then dramatised and disseminated to the working classes via the penny theatres.

Ainsworth's relationship with Thackeray had a similar trajectory. Thackeray was probably the fiercest critic of Newgate writing, and of Ainsworth in particular, yet the two men had started out the closest of friends. This can be clearly seen from Thackeray's correspondence. Writing to John Macrone in 1837, Thackeray, still a struggling journalist, asks the publisher to: 'Give Ainsworth a shake of the hand he has praised me so much that I must love him ever after.'[34] The friendship managed to survive the Newgate controversy, but not Thackeray's fame after *Vanity Fair*, although his correspondence does betray a certain level of rather arrogant paranoia. 'There are no end of quarrels in this wicked Vanity Fair, and my feet are perpetually in hot water', he writes to his confidante Mrs Carmichael-Smyth:

> Jerrold hates me, Ainsworth hates me, Dickens mistrusts me, Forster says I am as false as hell, and Bulwer curses me – he is the only one who has any reason – yes the others have a good one too as times go. I was the most popular man in the craft until within abt. 12 months – and behold I've begun to succeed. It makes me very sad at heart though, this envy and meanness – in the great sages & teachers of the world. Am I envious and mean too I wonder? These fellows think so I know. Amen. God knows only. I scarcely understand any motive for any action of my own or anybody else's –[35]

By the following year, Ainsworth has become a figure of fun:

> As for Ainsworth he is more hairy than ever. He begins to sprout at his underlip now and curls all over really its not unlike him. He was at dinner where I was yesterday, and made an observation about Harvey sauce O with such emphasis and solemnity. I burst out laughing but Jack Shepherd didn't know at what.[36]

---

[34] William Makepeace Thackeray, 'To John Macrone', January 1837, letter 106 of *The Letters and Private Papers of William Makepeace Thackeray*, ed. Gordon N. Ray, vol. 1 (London: Oxford UP, 1945), 328.
[35] Thackeray, 'To Mrs. Carmichael-Smyth', July 2 1847, letter 409 of *The Letters*, vol. 2, 308–309.
[36] Thackeray, 'To Edward Fitzgerald', March–May 1848, letter 458 of *The Letters*, vol. 2, 366.

Ainsworth was certainly always a good target for the author of *The Book of Snobs*, as he did tend to leave his flank completely exposed.[37] Thackeray, however, always referred to Ainsworth as his 'old friend' (however horrible he was in print), writing rather innocently to Mrs Carmichael-Smyth that, 'there has been a sort of coolness since I have got on in the world & he has got off'.[38]

By the end of 1839 Ainsworth had finished with his Newgate novels. Although the controversy continued to rage around him, like the storm which begins *Jack Sheppard*, for many years to come. From the first appearance of *Jack Sheppard*, Ainsworth was considered the primary architect of the public's enthusiasm for housebreakers and highwaymen. For example, in the second edition of *Memoirs of Extraordinary Popular Delusions and the Madness of Crowds* (1852, in the chapter entitled, 'Popular Admiration of Great Thieves'), Charles Mackay notes that:

> Since the publication of the first edition of this volume, Jack Sheppard's adventures have been revived. A novel upon the real or fabulous history of the burglar has afforded, by its extraordinary popularity, a further exemplification of the allegations in the text. The *Sixth Report of the Inspector of Prisons for the Northern Districts of England* contains a mass of information upon the pernicious effect of such romances, and of the dramas founded upon them.

In this lengthy footnote, Mackay then extracts from this report at length, obviously pleased that statistical fact has vindicated his original argument of 1841:

> J.L. (aged 14) 'The first time I was ever at the theatre was to see *Jack Sheppard* ... I then went many times. I took the money from my mother out of her pocket as she was sitting down, and I beside her ... I got a great love for the theatre, and stole from people often to get there. *I thought this Jack Sheppard was a clever fellow* for making his escape and robbing his master. *If I could get out of gaol, I think I should be as clever as him;* but after all his exploits, he got done at last. I have had the book out of a library at Dole Field. I had paid twopence a book for three volumes. I also got *Richard Turpin*, in two volumes, and paid

---

[37] The best example would be his advertisement for the new *Ainsworth's Magazine*, which boasted contributors 'not only of talent but of rank', which Thackeray savaged in 'Immense Opportunity', *Punch*, July 5, 1845.

[38] Thackeray, 'To Mrs. Carmichael-Smyth', January 23 1857, letter 1288 of *The Letters*, vol. 4, 13.

the same. I have seen *Oliver Twist*, and I think the Artful Dodger is very like some of the boys here. I am here for picking a pocket of 25*l*.'[39]

Mackay concludes, in the best Gradgrindian fashion, that 'The Inspector's *Report on Juvenile Delinquency at Liverpool* contains much matter of the same kind; but sufficient has been already quoted to shew the injurious effects of the deification of great thieves by thoughtless novelists.'[40] Ainsworth is not named, but these remarks are unquestionably directed at his novel, although it should be noted that it was the theatrical adaptations consumed by the new urban working class that were considered the social problem. It is also worth remarking that these comments appeared 13 years after the original novel was written. What is apparent again and again, as one reconstructs the critical annihilation of Ainsworth, is that the bourgeois establishment neither forgave nor forgot.

II. The Victorian reaction

Although *Jack Sheppard* remained enormously popular with Ainsworth's audience, the controversy surrounding this very success damned him to permanent exclusion from literary society. As Frank Chandler succinctly put it in his *Literature of Roguery*, 'the forces of literature rose in revolt',[41] and Ainsworth was quickly black-balled at the Trinity Club and compelled to decline his nomination at the Athenaeum Club 'having been given to understand that I should meet with formidable opposition from a hostile party'.[42] Ironically, although Dickens continued to write about aspects of criminality for the rest of his life, Ainsworth never again made an ordinary criminal the central figure in a novel and the planned biographies of Dick Turpin and Claude Duval were never written. Had he not abandoned the form that he had effectively originated but rather moderated the

---

[39] Charles Mackay, *Memoirs of Extraordinary Popular Delusions and the Madness of Crowds*, 2nd edn (1851 London: Wordsworth, 1995), 636.
[40] *Ibid.*, 637.
[41] Frank W. Chandler, *The Literature of Roguery*, 2 vols, vol. 2 (Boston: Houghton & Mifflin, 1907), 358.
[42] Ainsworth, letter to Lady Blessington. Quoted from Ellis, vol. 1, 377.

moral message to suit the times as Dickens had done, Ainsworth would have likely remained at the cutting edge of Victorian literature for a little while longer. In an article probably written by Thackeray, the most enthusiastic critic of Newgate writing, entitled 'Mr. Punch's Literary Recipes', it can be seen how closely related the works of Ainsworth and Dickens were (mistakenly) seen to be in the public arena, and how easily a Newgate narrative might be altered to achieve literary respectability:

> *The ingredients of Oliver Twist and Jack Sheppard*:
>
> Take a small boy, charity, factory, carpenter's apprentice, or otherwise, as occasion may serve – stew him well down in vice – garnish largely with oaths and flash songs – boil him in a cauldron of crime and improbabilities. Season equally with good and bad qualities – infuse petty larceny, affection, benevolence and burglary, honour and housebreaking, amiability and arson – boil all gently. Stew down a mad mother – a gang of robbers – several pistols – a bloody knife. Serve up with a couple of murders – and season with a hanging-match.
>
> N.B. Alter the ingredients to a beadle and a workhouse – the scenes may be the same, but the whole flavour of vice will be lost, and the boy will turn out a perfect pattern – strongly recommended for weak stomachs.[43]

The endnote of course acknowledges the difference between these writers, there being many a true word said in jest, but Dickens's purpose is presented as both cynical and sentimental, rather than as ideologically distinct. How different the two stories *were*, however, is immediately apparent if we consider how incongruous Dickens's gothic villain, Monks, appears to be in *Oliver Twist* as compared with Jonathan Wild in Ainsworth's *Jack Sheppard*. Whereas Monks seems to have wandered in from an eighteenth century text, the equally gothic Wild is essential to Ainsworth's narrative. The politics of *Oliver Twist* ally it much more with Lytton's *Paul Clifford*, and to rope it together with Ainsworth's nostalgic portrayals of individual freedom is a gross mis-reading. Ainsworth's previous eulogy to Dick Turpin, *Rookwood*, recalls the German students who ran away to the Black Forest to become bandits after reading Schiller; for him, the outlaw

---

[43] 'Mr. Punch's Literary Recipes', *Punch* August 7 1841. Probably written by Thackeray.

was always MacHeath and never William Sikes. In the end, Ainsworth instead left the field open to his contemporaries and returned to the safer realm of the historical romance, but his close relationship with Dickens was effectively at an end.

Down, but not yet out, Ainsworth had assumed the editorship of *Bentley's Miscellany* at the end of 1839, taking up the post after Dickens's resignation. Given Ainsworth's present fall from grace this was a fortuitous appointment, although it does mark the end of any real friendship between the two novelists. Dickens and Forster had obviously manoeuvred Ainsworth into position as the successor to his abandoned project with Bentley, as a guilty husband might engineer a meeting between an eligible bachelor and his rejected wife and family:

> I reap no gain from parting from you, nor will any conveyance of your property be required, for in this respect you have always been literally Bentley's Miscellany and never mine.[44]

Dickens was probably also hoping to leave 'My Child', as he referred to the magazine, under the management of a devil he knew at least until the completion of the serialisation of *Oliver Twist*. This is how he sold the idea:

> The object I have in view is, to entreat you to see Mr. Bentley without an instant's delay, and to offer yourself as the future Editor of the Miscellany. I think such a connexion would not prove unpleasant to you (who have time to devote to it) and that it is of vital importance to the publication. I need not say that that a great proportion of those who were friendly to me as Editor will be more friendly to you than to any other man – that you will have my warmest wishes and best assistance whenever I can render it in any way – and that you will moreover have the assistance of a very influential body of friends, all anxious and willing to oblige you, personally, on every possible occasion.
>
> As you can confide in my feelings of friendship towards yourself, and as you may naturally suppose that I have yet some lingering interest in the well-being of a periodical which has cost me so much time and so many anxious hours, and in which poor Oliver first saw the light, I urge you most strongly not to neglect this opportunity. I should be really grieved to see it go down; I am quite sure – on all the considerations I have mentioned, and taking into account also, the successful connexion with it, you have just begun – that no man is so

---

[44] Charles Dickens, 'Familiar Epistle from a Parent to a Child', *Bentley's Miscellany* March 1839. Quoted from Forster 117.

likely to keep it up as you – and I feel confident that if you offer your assistance frankly and without reserve at this critical period of its existence, you will do Mr. Bentley the greatest service (while you do that which is not disagreeable to yourself) that you could by [any] possibility render him.

Do not neglect this advice my dear Ainsworth, or lose an hour.[45]

Dickens also needed to pacify Bentley and his solicitors while he extricated himself from a now much-regretted contract of which one complete novel was still outstanding. Ainsworth was apparently initially reluctant, but eventually acquiesced for a salary of £51 per month. Bentley was duly mollified, although he later vindictively claimed that Ainsworth was 'forced upon me'.[46] A few weeks later a rumour began to circulate that Dickens's breach with his publisher was a result of interference by the ever-unpopular Forster, causing Dickens to write a very severe letter to Ainsworth where he all but directly accuses his old friend of originating the slander himself. Forster omits these events in his *Life of Charles Dickens*, probably because Ainsworth was still alive when he published, and the pages covering this period in Dickens's diary have been removed. In his typically Utopian spin on Ainsworth's life, Ellis later wrote that 'Happily this disagreeable affair did not cause any breach of the intimate friendship existing between Dickens and Ainsworth', and points out that Ainsworth later became the Godfather of Henry Fielding Dickens,[47] but in truth the relationship between Dickens and Ainsworth had permanently fractured. This is quite apparent in Dickens's later correspondence with R.H. Horne regarding *Jack Sheppard* and his annoyance at being included in the Newgate school:

I am by some jolter-headed enemies most unjustly and untruly charged with having written a book after Mr. Ainsworth's fashion. Unto these jolter-heads and their intensely concentrated humbug, I shall take an early opportunity of temperately replying. If this opportunity had presented itself and I had made this vindication, I could have no objection to set my hand to what I know to be true concerning the late lamented John Sheppard, but I feel a great repugnance

---

[45] Charles Dickens, letter to W.H. Ainsworth, January 28 1839, *The Letters of Charles Dickens* vol. 1, 498–9.
[46] Ackroyd, 279.
[47] Ellis, vol. 1, 389.

to do so now, lest it should seem an ungenerous and unmanly way of disavowing any sympathy with that school, and a means of shielding myself.[48]

The footnote in *Sketches by Boz* praising *Rookwood* was also deleted from the 1839 edition and the preface to the 1841 edition of *Oliver Twist* offered a further opportunity for Dickens to explain to his public and his peers how different his literary aims were, in fact, from those of Ainsworth. Because *Jack Sheppard* and *Oliver Twist* ran concurrently in *Bentley's Miscellany*, both concerning young boys drawn into the London underworld and also illustrated by George Cruikshank, the two serials had become thematically connected in the popular as well as the critical psyche. This Dickens now addressed:

> The greater part of this Tale was originally published in a magazine. When I completed it, and put it forth in its present form, it was objected to on some high moral grounds in some high moral quarters.
>
> It was, it seemed, a coarse and shocking circumstance, that some of the characters in these pages are chosen from the roost criminal and degraded in London's population; that Sikes is a thief and Fagin a receiver of stolen goods; that the boys are pickpockets, and the girl is a prostitute ... What manner of life is that which is described in these pages, as the everyday existence of a Thief? What charms has it for the young and ill-disposed, what allurements for the most jolter-headed of juveniles? Here are no canterings on moonlit heaths, no merry-makings in the snuggest of all possible caverns, none of the attractions of dress, no embroidery, no lace, no jackboots, no crimson coats and ruffles, none of the dash and freedom with which 'the road' has been time out of mind invested.[49]

Dickens has previously noted the appeal of MacHeath's lifestyle as 'rather to be envied than otherwise', but he allows Gay this figure, and also Lytton *Paul Clifford*, with some reservations, because of their political purpose; the satire of *The Beggar's Opera* hardly requires explanation, and the then radical Lytton was arguing allegorically for the reform of English Law. Similarly, Defoe's Newgate biographies are cited 'for precedents'. Defoe, as Paul J. deGategno has argued, used Jack Sheppard and Jonathan Wild as symbols of disruptive, self-motivated

---

[48] Charles Dickens, letter to R.H. Horne, February 1840, *The Letters of Charles Dickens* vol. 2, 20.
[49] Charles Dickens, preface, *Oliver Twist; or, The Parish Boy's Progress*, Collected Works (1841 London: Odhams, 1897).

free enterprise against his strong commitment to the emerging mercantile system in which he believed so passionately.[50] The damning references to the romanticising of 'the road' are therefore reserved solely for the work of old friend Ainsworth.

Even though he prudently avoided any more Newgate writing for the rest of his literary career (in his long life, Ainsworth produced no less than 43 novels, 2 volumes of poetry and a collection of short stories as well as numerous contributions to numerous periodicals, also variously owning and editing *Bentley's Miscellany*, *Ainsworth's Magazine* and *The New Monthly Magazine* between 1839 and 1870), it is virtually impossible to find any reference to his work written from the Newgate episode to date which does not damn him by invoking the memory of that moral panic. For example, in a review appearing in *Graham's Magazine* of March 1841, ostensibly on the historical novel *The Tower of London*, the ever-bitchy Edgar Allan Poe begins: 'The authorship of this work does a little, and but a little, more credit to Mr. Ainsworth than that of "Jack Sheppard". It is in no spirit of cavilling that we say that it is rarely our lot to review a work more utterly destitute of every ingredient requisite to a good romance', and concludes 'Such libels on humanity, such provocations to crime, such worthless, inane, disgraceful romances as "Jack Sheppard" and its successors, are a blot on our literature and a curse to our land.'[51] Six months later he took exactly the same tack with a review of *Guy Fawkes* for the same journal, this time expanding his critique to encompass Ainsworth's penchant for antiquarian dialogue and detail with such comments on this 'chicanery' as, 'The turgid pretension of the style annoys, and the elaborately-interwoven pedantry irritates, insults, and disgusts ... Of all vanities the vanity of the unlettered pedant is the most sickening, and the most transparent.'[52] Poe also returned to this charge

---

[50] Paul J. deGategno, 'Daniel Defoe's Newgate Biographies: An Economic Crisis', *CLIO* 13 (1984), 157–70.

[51] Quoted from Edgar Allan Poe, *The Science Fiction of Edgar Allan Poe*, ed. Harold Beaver (London: Penguin, 1987), 371.

[52] Poe, *The Essays and Reviews of Edgar Allan Poe*, ed. G.R. Thompson (New York: Penguin, 1984), 102–103.

by casting Ainsworth as one of the pilots of the *Victoria* in his 'The Balloon-Hoax' of 1844, where Ainsworth, *in propria persona*, is used to parody his own melodramatic prose style in 'Mr. Ainsworth's MS':

> The waters give up no voice to the heavens. The immense flaming ocean writhes and is tortured uncomplainingly. The mountainous surges suggest the idea of innumerable dumb gigantic fiends struggling in impotent agony.[53]

Unlike the satirical attacks of Thackeray, this particular burlesque, if anything, actually enhanced Ainsworth's reputation and he is said to have been delighted. As Harold Beaver notes: 'who but Ainsworth – romantic visionary on high – contributes that bold, creative stroke: of making a bid for North America?'[54] From this episode we may begin reasonably to deduce the following: the critics loathed Ainsworth, but his public loved him.

This is nowhere more apparent than in R.H. Horne's collection of essays *The New Spirit of the Age* (1844), written because:

> Nearly twenty years have now elapsed since the publication of Hazlitt's 'Spirit of the Age', and a new set of men, several of them animated by a new spirit, have obtained eminent positions in the public mind.[55]

Richard Henry (or Hengist) Horne (1803–84), was a poet, essayist and adventurer, serving in the Mexican Navy during the war of independence and, in the 1850s, joining the Australian gold rush; his *Australian Autobiography and Australian Facts and Prospects* (1859) gives an account of his experiences abroad. He had written for *The Athenaeum* (a magazine at war with Ainsworth in the 1840s regarding a bitter public dispute about the affairs of the Archaeological Society), and is chiefly remembered for the epic poem *Orion* (1843). He was a close friend of Dickens and was later one of his ghost writers on *Household Words*; he also counted among his inner circle Robert and Elizabeth Barrett Browning, both of whom contributed to *A New Spirit of the Age*. As Hazlitt's *Contemporary*

---

[53] Poe, 'The Balloon-Hoax' (1844), *The Science Fiction of Edgar Allan Poe*, 120.
[54] Harold Beaver, note, *The Science Fiction of Edgar Allan Poe*, 371.
[55] R.H. Horne, preface, *A New Spirit of the Age*, 2 vols, vol. 1 (London: Smith, Elder and Co, 1844).

Portraits had characterised the Romantics, Horne's book was intended to identify and establish a new canon for the next generation of British writers; Dickens, of course, is the perfect embodiment of the new age:

> Mr. Dickens is manifestly the product of his age. He is a genuine emanation from its aggregate and entire spirit. He is not an imitator of any.[56]

Horne's redefinition of English literature begins quite appropriately with this long essay on Charles Dickens where, using comparisons with the grotesque realism of Hogarth, the misnomer that Dickens was a Newgate novelist is again explained for anyone that may still be confused or misinformed:

> Mr. Dickens is one of those happily constituted individuals who can 'touch pitch without soiling his fingers'; the peculiarity, in his case, being that he can do so without gloves; and, grasping its clinging blackness with both hands, shall yet retain no soil, no ugly memory. That he is at home in a wood – in green lanes and all sweet pastoral scenes – who can doubt it that has ever dwelt among them? But he has also been through the back slums of many a St. Giles's.[57]

On the matter of any superficial similarity of form and language between Dickens the moralist and satirist unsullied in the underworld and the narrative of a 'flash Newgate Calendar hero' it is patiently explained that:

> The secret was fully understood, and admirably practised by Sir E.L. Bulwer in his novel of 'Paul Clifford'; it was grievously misunderstood, except in the matter of dialect, by Mr. Ainsworth in his 'Jack Sheppard', which was full of unredeemed crimes, but being told without any offensive language, did its evil work of popularity, and has now gone to its cradle in the cross-roads of literature, and should be henceforth hushed up by all who have – as so many have – a personal regard for its author.[58]

As we can almost hear the last words of Mr Kurtz whispering in the void, 'the secret' is to show, as unflinchingly as propriety allows, a scene of violence or depravity in the realistic manner of Hogarth. That is for an illustrative, moral purpose. The only positive nod in the direction of Ainsworth, who seems to write

---

[56] Horne, vol. 1, 13.
[57] *Ibid.*
[58] *Ibid.*, 14.

only for popular entertainment, is an acknowledgement of a certain linguistic realism, along with an awkward attempt at a personal compliment, reiterated later in the unilaterally vicious chapter devoted to him in the same work, regarding the esteem in which the subject is held socially, presumably as an affable host rather than as an author. Note also the metonymic shift as the outlaw text, like its namesake, is buried at the crossroads in the traditional manner befitting an executed felon.

Such opening remarks do not bode well for Ainsworth although, surprisingly, his friends Lytton and G.P.R. James, with whom he shared many stylistic similarities, are treated with considerable respect in their subsequent entries. The creator of *Paul Clifford* and therefore the father of the contemporary Newgate novel is presented as:

> one of the most prolific authors of our time; and his various accomplishments, habits of research, and extraordinary industry, no less than his genius, will entitle him to the rank he holds as one of the most successful, in that branch of literature in which he eminently excels.[59]

While the author of *The Brigand* is introduced with:

> Of all historical novelists, Scott justly occupies the first place. If he did not create that kind of composition, he was the first who brought it into general favour ... It is not too much to say that the most successful of those who have trodden the same track in England is G.P.R. James. There is no writer, of his particular class, now living, so familiar to the public at large; not one who has drawn so extensively upon sources not always accessible to the readers of novels; not one who has laboured with such unremitting diligence, and such uniform popularity. If he has never greatly succeeded, we know no instance in which he has greatly failed.[60]

George Payne Rainsford James (1799–1860) was even more prolific than Ainsworth. Given the nature of this author's mass production of rather monotonous historical romances, we might wonder at Horne's endorsement of his position in the literary hierarchy compared with the complete rejection of Ainsworth's

---

[59] *Ibid.*, vol. 2, 189.
[60] *Ibid.*, vol. 1, 219.

art, especially as James's 100-strong collected works include such titles as *The Robber*, *The Brigand*, *The Smuggler*, *The Convict*, *The Gypsy*, and *The King's Highway*. Again, it is a question of the moral gaze:

> All his works, without distinction, are pervaded by moral feeling. There is a soul of true goodness in them – no maudlin affectation of virtue, but a manly rectitude of aim which they derive direct from the heart of the writer.[61]

Charles Mackay had evoked the legend of Robin Hood to demonstrate the ethical shortcomings of the likes of Jack Sheppard (either as a reasonably well-documented criminal in the historical record or as the fictionalised hero of a novel or play). James, whose novel *Forest Days* concerns Robin Hood, was, like Lytton, much more interested in portraying the plight of a morally good man driven outside society by tyranny or injustice. He also generally set his tales a safe distance from both England and the nineteenth century. The action of *The Brigand* (1841), for example, takes place in the Savoyard Alps and Paris of the sixteenth century. The hero of the piece, Corse de Leon, the brigand of the title, is much more in sympathy with the robbers of Schiller and Lytton than with those of Ainsworth. Early in the text he explains his philosophical and legal position thus:

> 'Is not God's law the best?' exclaimed the brigand. 'God gave the eagle his law, and therefore that law is right. It is because man's law is not God's law that I stand here upon the mountain. Were laws equal and just, there would be few found to resist them. While they are unequal and unjust, the poor-hearted may submit and tremble; the powerless may yield and suffer: the bold, the free, the strong, and the determined fall back upon the law of God, and wage war against the injustice of man.'[62]

This echoes the Godwinian rhetoric of Lytton's *Paul Clifford*, although Lytton was addressing the contemporary state of the criminal justice system in England rather than sixteenth century France, his commitment to social reform having much in common with the Dickensian project.

---

[61] *Ibid.*, 231.
[62] G.P.R. James, *Corse de Leon; or, The Brigand* (New York: Farmer and Daggers, 1845), 17.

In *A New Spirit of the Age* it is significantly apparent that Ainsworth has failed the test of the times. He is immediately separated from Lytton and James in the opening paragraph of the chapter which bears his name with:

> From the historical novel and romance, as re-originated in modern times, by Madame de Genlis and Sir Walter Scott, and adopted with such high success by Sir E.L. Bulwer, and with such extensive popularity by Mr. James, there has of late years sprung up a sort of lower or less historical romance, in which the chief part of the history consisted in old dates, old names, old houses, and old clothes.[63]

Ainsworth is merely a 'reviver of old clothes' in this analysis. His novel *Old St. Paul's* (1841), is presented as a poor plagiarism of Defoe's *Journal of the Plague Year* and is: 'generally dull, except when it is revolting', and, 'The truth must be told', the unidentified author exclaims.[64] The truth seems to be much more to do with the perpetuation of the moral crusade against the individual author than a more serious consideration of undoubtedly important contemporary fiction (the paradox being that Horne still has to include Ainsworth in his canon). This truth is very apparent as the Newgate scandal is once more regurgitated and again the drop falls on Ainsworth:

> With regard to the Newgate narrative of 'Jack Sheppard' and the extraordinarily extensive notoriety it obtained for the writer, upon the residuum of which he founded his popularity, so much just severity has already been administered from criticism and from the opinion of the intellectual portion of the public, and its position has been so fully settled, that we are glad to pass over it without further animadversion.
>
> The present popularity of Mr. Ainsworth could not have risen out of its own materials. His so-called historical romance of 'Windsor Castle' is not to be regarded as a work of literature open to serious criticism. It is a picture book, and full of very pretty pictures. Also full of catalogues of numberless suits of clothes. Such a passion, indeed, has he for describing clothes, that he frequently gives us two suits with a single body, one being concealed under the other ... As to plot or story it does not pretend to any.[65]

---

[63] Horne, vol. 2, 217.

[64] *Ibid.*, vol. 1, 220.

[65] *Ibid.*, vol. 2, 219–20.

Like Poe's opportunist and partisan review, and a legion of others, the commentary on one text is prefaced by *Jack Sheppard*. The Newgate controversy invades the textual surface like a virus. After this, the critic has *carte blanche* to say anything, however vicious, ill-informed or downright libellous. The quip quoted above regarding Ainsworth's penchant for costume detail becomes doubly dreadful here, as the antiquarian authenticity of G.P.R. James has already been praised in the previous volume. Even more unsettling for the author's career is an endnote explaining that the previous article was a 'joint-production' of four reviewers, each of whom were relieved of the assignment when their highly critical intentions had became apparent to the editor who, in turn, explains that Ainsworth is 'usually spared in public, because so much esteemed and regarded in private'.[66] This can hardly have offered much consolation, especially to an author who prided himself, not without foundation, upon his antiquarian knowledge and research skills.

To engage with Ainsworth is to engage with a positive mountain of similar assassinations of character and creation, which eventually yield only to a general indifference after the 1930s. The most common research encounter with Ainsworth's name is usually in the form of a brief, often brutal dismissal of his work, very alike in language and tone to Horne's remarks of 1844. Even allowing for the fact that Ainsworth was a Tory and thus swimming against the overall tide of Victorian Liberalism, such lexical violence directed against one particular author, especially one so obviously connected with the literary giants of his day, remains excessive.

III. Late Victorian views

A generation after Horne's book had been and gone the tone had still not moderated. In J. Hain Friswell's collection of critical essays, *Modern Men of Letters Honestly Criticised* (1870), the chapter devoted to Ainsworth begins:

---

[66] *Ibid.*, vol. 2, 222.

> Let us start with an opinion, fearlessly expressed as it is earnestly felt, that the existence of this writer is an event to be deplored; and the fact that he is able to assume that he is a Man of Letters who has been of service to his country, and that he has received from the hands of a Prime Minister, himself a Man of Letters, the reward of £100 a year pension for literary services, is a disgrace to this bewildered and Philistine nation.[67]

Honestly criticised? Perhaps not. Friswell continues the trend of pillorying Ainsworth on moral grounds, often sacrificing the historical truth that he claims to value so highly in order to make a point. In a reference to a plot device in Ainsworth's *Talbot Harland* (which Friswell insists upon calling 'Claude Duval' to emphasise the Newgate connection),[68] the critic makes the following appeal to historical verisimilitude: 'Claude Duval shot by the Duke of Buckingham! – (Ha, ha! what says Dame History to *that*?)'.[69] This is the wild style of the saloon bar rant, and Friswell gets it wrong several times as his enthusiasm runs away with his pen. For example, his assertion that, 'Early in his life, the success of Dickens gave him a good opening as playing second to that author',[70] rather puts the cart before the horse, and more worryingly contributes to the misapprehension that the early works of Dickens predate those of Ainsworth whereas the reverse was in fact the case.

As always in these critical attacks (for attacks they are, the level of personal abuse is often quite shocking), Ainsworth's work is presented in comparison with that of Dickens, a conjunction which makes it very easy to dismiss the former without any attempt at detailed analysis. This is of course a question of class. It may be much more useful to consider the popular narratives of Ainsworth in parallel with those of Reynolds, Rymer and Prest, but his social and professional rank placed him more obviously next to Dickens, Thackeray and Lytton while his texts sit more comfortably alongside the literature of

---

[67] J. Hain Friswell, *Modern Men of Letters Honestly Criticised* (London: Hodder and Stoughton, 1870), 257.
[68] Claude Duval (1643–1670) was a French highwayman who tried his luck in England and who was revered by the lower orders in much the same way as Dick Turpin in the next century.
[69] Friswell, 60.
[70] *Ibid.*, 263.

costermongers. Any contemporary references to popular culture are generally intended to be abusive: Friswell at one point writing that Ainsworth's serials now sell for a penny as opposed to the Newgate days when: 'one paid half-a-crown for his rubbish'.[71] The hysterical language of Friswell's assault seems to reflect an inner turmoil brought about by the conflict between his expectations of what is high-brow and what is low in literature, and the possibility that there may very well be a point of intersection, characterised indeed by Ainsworth himself. The opening lament regarding the author's Civil List pension signals a particular bone of contention; Friswell simply cannot reconcile this to his world view: '[Ainsworth] has sent so many boys to prison that Government has forbidden his plays to be acted with one hand and has pensioned him with the other.'[72] Friswell is referring here to the Lord Chamberlain's refusal to license any more plays based upon *Jack Sheppard* after the Courvoisier murder case of 1840; he did not revoke licences already issued and theatrical managers avoided the prohibition by simply re-titling their productions to omit direct reference to Sheppard. To suggest a Government ban is therefore an exaggeration as theatrical adaptations of the Sheppard story were still being produced until the end of the century.[73] Friswell also attributes the plays directly to Ainsworth (who definitely inspired a fair few but never wrote one), while similarly stating with a kind of blue book certainty that there is a direct connection between this type of fiction and juvenile crime, an early example of the 'Effects' theory of popular culture so important to the contemporary critics of Newgate writing, as well as a legion of other moral crusades occurring before or since the days of *Jack Sheppard* at the Adelphi.

Having begun with the Civil List/Newgate dichotomy, Friswell concludes with it, by now assuming that the works of Ainsworth and Lytton are somehow indistinguishable and therefore interchangeable:

---

[71] *Ibid.,*, 259.
[72] *Ibid.*, 261.
[73] See the memoirs of H. Chance Newton, *Crime and the Drama or, Dark Deeds Dramatised* (London: Stanley Paul & Co, 1927) for a useful history of 'All the Jack Sheppards'.

Mr. Ainsworth is, we believe, as Lord Lytton is, we know, a wealthy man through this literature; but if every farthing each has received from his books, pensions and all, were a hundred-pound note, and employed in building reformatories for boy-thieves, the unhappy man could not undo the evil his perverted taste, vulgar admiration, and his fatal itch of writing to pander to the savage instincts of the thief and robber, has caused, and will yet cause, in years to come.[74]

Leaving aside the fact that Ainsworth was never a wealthy man, here then is another typical dismissal, recalling the critiques of Thackeray, Dickens, Poe, Horne and Mackay among many others, where literature, politics and primitive sociology converge via the language of the pulpit and a scandal, long dead, is resurrected in lieu of anything more original, interesting or true. Friswell's justification for this is tenuous, being based entirely on the brief presence of the French highwayman Claude Duval as one of the secondary *dramatis personae* in *Talbot Harland*, which had recently concluded as a serial in *Bow Bells*. The *actual* justification is rather the body of critical literature already in place regarding the Newgate controversy, attached to Ainsworth's name as a cultural code and therefore perceived to be an additional if invisible text appended to whatever narrative the author has just produced, as in Poe's two virtually identical reviews for *Graham's* where the historical novels allegedly under consideration are barely mentioned in favour of references to *Jack Sheppard*. So closely, in fact, does Friswell follow Horne's model of 26 years previously that Horne's description of Ainsworth's historical fiction as a 'romance of old clothes' is regurgitated, unacknowledged, as 'a mere list of the frippery of the wardrobe'.[75]

If Oscar Wilde was correct in his assertion that 'there is only one thing in the world worse than being talked about, and that is not being talked about',[76] then some comfort might be drawn from Ainsworth's appearance in such a collection of articles, as by 1870 (the year that Dickens died), he might easily have been overlooked. The extent to which Ainsworth had faded from the public view by

---

[74] Friswell, 270.
[75] *Ibid.*, 266.
[76] Oscar Wilde, *The Picture of Dorian Gray* (1891 Oxford: OUP, 1998), 2.

this point can be seen from the following anecdote, related to S.M. Ellis by Percy Fitzgerald:

> I recall a dinner at Teddington, in the sixties, given by Frederic Chapman, the publisher, at which were Forster and Browning. The latter said humorously,
>
> 'A sad, forlorn-looking being stopped me today, and reminded me of old times. He presently resolved himself into – whom do you think? Harrison Ainsworth!'
>
> 'Good Heavens!' cried Forster, 'is he still alive?'[77]

Under such an apparent veil of anonymity, Friswell's recourse to Ainsworth and the Newgate argument is at first glance rather surprising, if not downright anachronistic, yet I find myself wondering if Friswell's somewhat desperate protestations reflect a realisation that his age demands such a scapegoat more than ever to offset increasingly loud calls for middle class social culpability and urban reform. Another possibility is that Ainsworth's later novels were less obscure than Ellis and Fitzgerald (and later George J. Worth) have suggested. Ainsworth certainly experienced something of a renaissance towards the end of his life, culminating in civic honours in his home town of Manchester in 1881, and his inclusion in Friswell's assessment of contemporary literature, however negative the comments, suggests that there was still an audience to address regarding the historical novels, albeit rather smaller than it had been in the 1830s and 40s. The Fitzgerald anecdote therefore demonstrates Ainsworth's distance from high literature (as embodied by John Forster and Robert Browning), while taking no account of the popular sphere where his work still found a certain amount of favour. Most obviously, we notice in Friswell how easily the received image of the author is passed from one critic to another, without apparently passing through the brain of either.

---

[77] Ellis, vol. 2, 264. Fitzgerald was a latter-life friend of Dickens and the author of *The Life of Charles Dickens* (London: Chatto & Windus, 1905) and *Memories of Charles Dickens* (London: Arrowsmith Bristol, 1913). He was also Sir Henry Irving's biographer.

IV. Modern judgements

Unsurprisingly, the above trend continues into the next century. One does not need to search very hard to find many similar, and rather throwaway, dismissals of Ainsworth that feed off one another, often with little apparent knowledge of the original texts. Llewellyn Ligocki cites the following example.[78] In an article on Ainsworth published in *The Dickensian*, Leo Mason concludes with:

> History through the eyes of romance is the essence of Ainsworth at his best – *The Lancashire Witches, Tower of London, Old St. Paul's*, are romantic histories and will no doubt endure. *Rookwood, Jack Sheppard*, and the like are historical romances and must take their chances as such.[79]

This loosely paraphrases, without credit, Malcolm Elwin's concluding comments on Ainsworth in *Victorian Wallflowers* that:

> several of his novels – particularly *Tower of London* and *Old St. Paul's*, in spite of the absurd antics of the hero of the latter – have undoubtedly the quality of durability. No writer could hope to surpass either as romantic histories of their particular subjects. *Rookwood, Jack Sheppard*, and *Crichton* are of a different class; they are historical romances instead of romantic histories and must take their chances as such.[80]

The fact that Mason appears to misunderstand Elwin's significant point regarding the difference between historical romance and romantic histories by transposing the categories further suggests a basic lack of familiarity with any of the texts mentioned including, possibly, even Elwin's. In turn, Elwin's chapter on Ainsworth relies heavily on Ellis's biography (which has its own share of positive discrimination and bibliographical inaccuracy), although not always accurately. In short, the regress continues.

Elwin's work, it should however be noted, is considerably more favourable towards Ainsworth than most. *Victorian Wallflowers*, as the title suggests, is concerned with 'unjustly neglected writers' of the nineteenth century,

---

[78] Llewellyn Ligocki, 'William Harrison Ainsworth's Use of History: The Tower of London and Other Tudor Novels', Diss., University of Kansas, 1964, 8.

[79] Leo Mason, 'William Harrison Ainsworth', *The Dickensian* XXXV (1939), 160–61.

[80] Malcolm Elwin, *Victorian Wallflowers* (London: Jonathan Cape, 1934), 175–6.

and is therefore something of a reflection of *A New Spirit of the Age*.[81] The changing fashions of literary history are apparent here as Wilkie Collins is included in Elwin's second eleven. Elwin argues that the charge that Ainsworth's novels were poorly plotted is rather an example of the serial form in general and suggests that Dickens may stand similarly accused. He also takes on Horne, writing that: 'His [Ainsworth's] faults as a craftsman are manifold and easy to seek. Horne might have found sample material for derisive criticism, without satisfying his desire to be scurrilous with cheap sneers at an excusable eccentricity.'[82] Ultimately though, Elwin concludes that Ainsworth's life is considerably more interesting than his work: 'Of all the Victorian novelists, his literary life is among the most important and the most interesting. With regard to his writings, he certainly contributed little or nothing to the development of the novel.'[83] An opinion I find myself incapable of sharing.

A few years after *Victorian Wallflowers* was written, the paper restrictions of the Second World War caused *Rookwood* to be dropped from the Everyman's Library and, apart from a couple of Collins *Pocket Classic* reissues of the early historical novels in the 1950s and the paperback perseverance of *The Lancashire Witches*, Ainsworth's contribution to English literature, significant or otherwise, had left the bookshelves of England forever. R.H. Horne's critique of the same, however, was proving more durable, his total dismissal of Ainsworth's novels travelling full circle in Andrew Sanders's post-Lukácsian reassessment *The Victorian Historical Novel, 1840–1880* (1978):

> In Horne's terms, Ainsworth was little more than a reviver of old clothes, and his novels were destructive of the real potential of historical fiction. In considering whether or not that potential was ever realised in the Victorian novel, it is essential to look beyond the model that Ainsworth left.[84]

---

[81] *Ibid.*, 14.
[82] *Ibid.*, 173.
[83] *Ibid.*, 172.
[84] Andrew Sanders, *The Victorian Historical Novel, 1840–1880* (London: Macmillan, 1978), 46.

So Horne is quoted once again. To engage with Ainsworth is to engage with this distorted critical heritage. Ainsworth continues, after approximately a century and a half, to be defined only by a contempt for his work held by successive generations of the critical establishment.

Sanders's otherwise excellent study does however reflect a trend towards the academic rehabilitation of Lytton, whose work and reputation, unlike Ainsworth's, had continued to lead a precarious parallel existence alongside that of his better known contemporaries, often kept in print by scholars not of literature but of the occult. Leafing through back copies of magazines devoted to paranormal phenomena from the 1960s to date, such as *The Fortean Times*, *Man, Myth and Magic* and *Encounters* one might be forgiven for believing Lytton to be the early Victorian equivalent of Aleister Crowley, the legacy continuing in such books as J.H. Brennan's *Occult Reich* (1974) and Alec Maclellan's *The Lost World of Agharti: The Mystery of Vril Power* (1982), with a foreword by Eric Von Danniken. In his article 'Journey to the Centre of the Earth', Russell Warren offers a credulous account of the current beliefs about Lytton held beyond the walls of university departments of literature:

> Lytton was a strange, shadowy figure, heavily involved with ritual magic and the occult ... He was also a Rosicrucian of some status. Because Lytton was so clearly involved in the occult underworld of Victorian England, it was assumed by many that his extraordinary novel *The Coming Race* was based on some arcane knowledge to which he had access.[85]

One of the many who wanted to believe, we are told, was Adolf Hitler. Warren also refers to the popular story that Lytton was a descendant of the alchemist, Dr John Bulwer, who really had discovered the *elixir vitae*, 'enabling him to live well into his nineties', demonstrating a widely held belief among people who believe everything they see on *The X-Files* that not only *The Coming Race* but *Zanoni* and *A Strange Story* are based on fact. Whether despite or because of such bizarre readings, Lytton's work has increasingly attracted more serious academic attention,

---

[85] Russell Warren, 'Journey to the Centre of the Earth', *Encounters*, December 1994, 62.

most recently seen in the work of Marie Roberts, his influence on English literature no longer considered questionable owing to his status as a popular or sensational author. Although Malcolm Elwin suggested that Ainsworth's work was similarly ripe for reappraisal in 1934, this has not yet happened; neither are there rumours that his novel *Auriol or The Elixir of Life* was factual despite its author's longevity. In consequence, there have been no Oxford World's Classics editions of his novels, no cheap Penguin paperbacks, no BBC costume dramas, no adaptations on Radio 4, no Hollywood movies in glorious Technicolor, not even a scratchy, pre-war, black and white film version of *Jack Sheppard* starring Tod Slaughter as Jonathan Wild. In Lucy Moore's recent and acclaimed study of the life and legend of Jack Sheppard, *The Thieves' Opera* (1997), Ainsworth's novel appears to be considered less influential in terms of what is left of the popular myth than the rather silly British movie of 1968 *Where's Jack?* starring Tommy Steele as the lad himself.

Literary history has then unquestionably decided that the fiction of William Harrison Ainsworth is a bit of a bad joke, the conventional approach being that he is something akin to the Edward D. Wood, Jr of nineteenth century English literature.[86] Even what we might term his apologists tend to confirm this view, often apparently quite accidentally, by being drawn too easily into the critical tradition. George J. Worth notes in his monograph for example that: 'Ainsworth's efforts at historical verisimilitude in his dialogue are frequently painful',[87] while Jack Biles's study, 'William Harrison Ainsworth: His Artistry

---

[86] Edward D. Wood, Jr (1903–1967), independent Hollywood writer, producer, director, occasional actor and transvestite whose private life was considered by the majority of members of the industry which he loved to be much more interesting than his movies. Responsible for ultra-low-budget B-pictures such as *Glen or Glenda* (1953), *Bride of the Monster* (1955) and, probably his best known work, *Plan 9 from Outer Space* (1956), voted the 'worst film ever made' by New York film critics in 1980, Wood's work was a laughing stock in his own lifetime and he died in a pointless tragedy of alcoholism, poverty and despair. His films later achieved cult status among the post-punk generation, eventually leading to a serious reappraisal of his work as an independent, genre *auteur* by film historians. In many ways, Wood is the muse of all projects such as mine. An American biopic based upon Wood's friendship with Bela Lugosi, written and directed by Tim Burton, won an Academy Award in 1994. See Rudolph Grey, *Nightmare of Ecstasy: The Life and Art of Edward D. Wood, Jr* (Los Angeles: Feral House, 1992).
[87] George J. Worth, *William Harrison Ainsworth* (New York: Twayne, 1972), 111.

and Significance' (a somewhat strange attempt to read Ainsworth aesthetically), rather farcically bases a significant proportion of the argument around a novel that Ainsworth didn't actually write, *Nell Gwynne*, thereby unintentionally making a case which favours the talents of one of Ainsworth's opportunist and anonymous impersonators over the original.[88] Nevertheless, as one of the nineteenth century's most prolific, flamboyant and paradoxical novelists, Ainsworth deserves more than a casual dismissal or an ill-informed footnote. It would seem then that to explore his writing and the influence of his work upon the literature of his age it is essential, to paraphrase Andrew Sanders, to look beyond the model that the critics left.

V. An age in transition

By way of dubious mitigation, J. Hain Friswell suggested that it was not so much Ainsworth who should ultimately be held responsible for his 'perverted taste' but 'the times in which he was born'. Appealing to the Victorians' unanimous disdain for the Regency, Friswell is therefore able to segregate Ainsworth from his more socially acceptable contemporaries, shelving his work instead alongside such *chroniques scandaleuses* as Pierce Egan's *Life in London* (1821) and Harriette Wilson's *Memoirs* (1825).[89] Sir Walter Scott, remarking in his journal upon Ainsworth's first novel, *Sir John Chiverton* (1826), called its young co-writer an 'imitator'.[90] Georg Lukács later added the prefix 'incompetent' in *The Historical*

---

[88] Jack I. Biles, appendix, 'William Harrison Ainsworth: His Artistry and Significance', diss., Emory University, 1954. Biles puts a lot of energy into authenticating this text, concluding that Ainsworth produced this book exclusively for the US market in 1847 to avoid a repeat performance of the Newgate controversy. Had he had access to the Ainsworth papers, where he would have found no evidence at all of *Nell Gwynne* and only the most perfunctory reference to an American audience, along with more knowledge of the sheer volume of plagiarisms of popular authors produced on both sides of the Atlantic at that time, he would not have made such a fundamental error.
[89] Friswell, 258.
[90] Sir Walter Scott, journal entry, October 18 1826, *The Journal of Sir Walter Scott*, ed. W.E.K. Anderson (Oxford: Clarendon Press, 1972), 213–15.

Novel[91] and David Punter, in his overview of the gothic tradition, *The Literature of Terror*, wrote of *Rookwood* and *Jack Sheppard* that:

> They are important only as another link in the uneven chain which leads from Godwin, via Lytton, on to Reynolds and Dickens, and which thus produces a form of Gothic connected with the proletarian and the contemporary.[92]

The vexed question of exactly *where* we should place Ainsworth in terms of social and literary history is obviously inter-dependent upon his critical position. Some level of reorientation is definitely required.

Professor Punter's appraisal is, I believe, the most interesting and accurate. In choosing to compare Ainsworth's work with that of Scott for example, as the author of *Waverley* did himself in his much-quoted musings 'on my imitators', or to appeal to the standard set by Dickens, as did Horne, is to set up a potentially erroneous and ultimately misleading dialectic. In such a basic model, figures like Ainsworth, and indeed Lytton, are forever trapped between Scylla and Charybdis. Ian Duncan, in his persuasive study *Modern Romance and Transformations of the Novel*, begins his thesis by noting that, 'We have lacked an effective account of the transition from Scott to Dickens ... whose careers were separated by only four years.' Duncan's elegant and sophisticated analysis takes little account however of Scott's immediate successors during this period:

> the historical novel after Scott offers a weaker lineage of literal imitation in the examples of Bulwer, Ainsworth and G.P.R. James ... Lukács' claim, that the historical novel declined into a 'special genre' and that the true legacy of Scott's work is to be found in the mid nineteenth century social novel, is more to the purpose.[93]

Contemporary critics also considered this period to be something of a cultural desert. In the *Athenaeum* review of *Jack Sheppard*, it is suggested that after the

---

[91] Georg Lukács, *The Historical Novel*, trans. Hannah and Stanley Mitchell (London: Merlin, 1962), 53.
[92] David Punter, *The Literature of Terror: A History of Gothic Fictions from 1765 to the Present Day*, 2nd edn, 2 vols, vol 1 (London: Longman, 1996), 157.
[93] Ian Duncan, *Modern Romance and Transformations of the Novel* (Cambridge: Cambridge UP, 1992), 18. Duncan also recommends Sanders for an account of Scott's successors.

creative and intellectual intensity of the Romantic generation, a fallow interval is to be expected; under the influence of: 'that great and universal stimulus which the French revolution afforded to genius in all its departments', a 'miraculous harvest of intellect was produced', and, therefore, 'a corresponding poverty of the exhausted soil may be but a natural consequence'. The author of the piece looks to Dickens as a possible source of rejuvenation.[94] For my purposes, Punter's uneven chain offers the most room for exploration as his work on gothic fiction (perhaps because of the very nature of the form) is less prone to the imposition of an English, class-based hierarchy of high and low literature and popular culture. In order to re-read an author such as Ainsworth, we must abandon the precise and linear dictionary definitions of Regency and Victorian, and Romantic and Realist while also peeking beneath the feet of the twin giants of Scott and Dickens as they stride across literary history. Punter's version of the evolution of the gothic from Scott to Reynolds at least acknowledges a period of stylistic, theoretical, narratological and, often, downright opportunist transition between the fag-end of Romanticism and the rise of the novel as the dominant art form of the new, industrial middle class in England. Contrary to common opinion, paradigms do not shift without a clutch.

My intention is therefore in part to take issue with what Stephen M. Parrish has described as the 'Whig Interpretation of Literature',[95] being a linear version of literary history which is no longer a satisfactory scholarly model. I suggest that the transitional period highlighted by both Punter and Duncan, the liminal space between the death of Scott and the rise of Dickens as the undisputed national author, is a period of fascinating creative flux in English literary history (rather than a dead-end), which is crucial to the development of the novel in particular. Rather than taking the four years between the death of Scott in 1832 and the first appearance of *Pickwick* in 1836 as the crucial period, as does Duncan,

---

[94] 'Jack Sheppard: a Romance', rev. of *Jack Sheppard*, by W.H. Ainsworth, *Athenaeum*, October 26 1839, 805.
[95] Stephen M. Parrish, 'The Whig Interpretation of Literature', *Text*, 4 (1988), 343–50.

42

I would further suggest that the Victorian, representational norm and the primacy of the novel as the main expression of literary culture is not completely in place until 1848 when, as has been noted above, Ainsworth produces his final, major work. Massively popular though *Pickwick* was, it should be remembered that Dickens was still effectively in his literary apprenticeship at this point, and was just beginning his transition from a reporter to an author of fiction, and was apparently more concerned with succeeding as an editor; his early serials reflect this uncertainty of development as he experiments with the different forms of the day, such as the historical romance and the Newgate novel.[96] Then, Ainsworth was an early mentor and already established as a famous novelist. In this period then of literary uncertainty, given the generic hybridisation he often applied to his narratives in addition to the moral hysteria generated around much of his early work, his admitted stylistic quirks, melodramatic excesses and downright disasters and, finally, his dramatic reversal of literary fortune, might not Ainsworth have a legitimate claim to being the master of this maelstrom?

If we then read Ainsworth through a new lens we can observe more closely the inconsistencies in his contemporary, critical assassination. When Scott read *Sir John Chiverton*, he saw an imitation of the style: 'Which I was born to introduce/Refined it first, and showd its use',[97] which he noted at length in two adjacent and somewhat paranoiac journal entries on his perceived competition, based upon his own analysis of historical writing and the gothic. Ainsworth's first novel ran to only two tiny editions in 1826 and is an extremely rare book; although it has considerably more in common with the gothic fiction of Horace Walpole than the *Waverley* novels, Scott's interpretation has endured, being considerably easier to access. Ainsworth's historical project was, in actuality, diametrically opposed to that of Scott. From this perspective, we can suddenly see quite clearly that Ainsworth's novels take elements from the eighteenth century

[96] See Kathryn Chittick, *Dickens and the 1830s* (Cambridge: Cambridge UP, 1990), for an excellent account of Dickens's early career and its cultural context.
[97] Scott, *The Journal of Sir Walter Scott*, 214

traditions of the gothic and the picaresque and actually redefine them to suit his own, rapidly changing age; in this sense there is almost a subversion of Scott taking place which has often been misinterpreted and misrepresented as merely clumsy impersonation. Friswell's comparisons between Ainsworth, Egan and Wilson also acquire a different meaning within this frame. To compare Ainsworth's urban romance *Jack Sheppard* to *Life in London* unconditionally is as erroneous as the direct comparisons with *Oliver Twist* and *Barnaby Rudge*, but to suggest that there are elements of both in this work, a playful, innocent, Egan-like portrayal of criminals and rogues as characters in tandem with a grotesque, Dickensian urban realism, begins to reveal a rather unique and undervalued contribution to the development of Victorian representation.

Using this model, the eclectic nature of Ainsworth's prose becomes symptomatic of a dynamic period in literary history when older forms of narrative were resurrected, redefined and revitalised, rather than a simply chaotic one. Lytton, for example (another obvious author of transitional literature), tried his prolific hand at almost every style of novel during this period; while Ainsworth's most exciting writing tended to blend alchemically different genre devices within a single text. As the author explained in the Preface to the 1849 edition of *Rookwood*:

> I resolved to attempt a story in the bygone style of Mrs. Radcliffe (which had always inexpressible charms for me), substituting an old English squire, an old English manorial residence, and an old English highwayman, for the Italian marchese, the castle, and the brigand of the great mistress of Romance.[98]

And so he did. *Rookwood* is an enthusiastic amalgam of gothic, picaresque and historical romance, updated and transplanted to England, complete with comic songs and the blood and thunder of melodrama, all luridly illustrated by George Cruikshank. *Rookwood* perfectly suits such a period of transition: written two ·years after the first Reform Act and during the brief reign of William IV, *between*

---

[98] Ainsworth, preface, *Rookwood, A Romance*, Collected Works (1834 London: George Routledge and Sons, 1881).

Regency and Victorian, it also has an infectious, even innocent, creative exuberance which carries it along (the author claiming, quite honestly in all probability, that the 'Ride to York' episode was written in a single, nocturnal sitting).

What follows is a consideration of the life and fiction of Ainsworth, paying particular attention to those texts produced during this period of social, political and creative flux, from the juvenilia of the 1820s (which has been largely over-looked by his American researchers), via the Newgate novels and historical gothics of the 1830s and 40s to his belated public acknowledgement as the 'Lancashire Novelist' shortly before his death. Given the sheer volume of Ainsworth's works, many of the later novels being hurriedly written and rather repetitious, it is necessary to be selective.[99] Chapter One offers an analysis of some of Ainsworth's sub-*Blackwood's* short stories from *Arliss's Pocket Magazine* and *The European* (1821–23) as exponents of the contemporary literary environment and therefore primary influences, and also as heralds of the young author's later writing. This chapter concludes with a reading of Ainsworth's first sustained narrative, the jointly-written novel *Sir John Chiverton* (1826), as a transitional piece between the juvenilia and the novels, and as an introduction to the much misinterpreted relationship between Ainsworth and Scott engendered by Scott's reaction to this novel. Chapter Two examines Ainsworth's gothic project using the novel that made his name, *Rookwood* (1834), considered as a generic hybrid of the gothic, the historic, and the Newgate narrative and as a reaction to the legacy of Scott. Chapter Three is devoted to *Jack Sheppard* (1839), the Newgate controversy, and the author's relationship to popular culture and his fall from fashionable grace. Chapter Four considers Ainsworth's use of British political history as a development of a very personal dramatic project in which

---

[99] Ellis's biography offers a detailed account of Ainsworth's editorial career and George J. Worth's monograph gives a reasonable overview of all the historical novels. I intend to present a broader view of Ainsworth's fiction, including the material written in the 1820s, and also to provide a more honest biography than did Ellis, who was writing much closer to the events and, as the Edwardian gentleman that he was, chose to omit certain details that might cause embarrassment or offence to living friends and relations of his principal subjects.

historical determinism becomes a hybrid form of epic tragedy, which again attracts disproportionate critical ire. The fifth chapter concentrates on Ainsworth's masterpiece *The Lancashire Witches* (1848), its proto-feminist possibilities, and his subsequent Lancashire novels; the sixth and final chapter considers Ainsworth's later years and writing. Given that Ainsworth was intimately connected with the literary elite of Great Britain throughout his life, I have adopted a loosely biographical frame throughout. The story behind the accepted version of Ainsworth's critical assassination is also central to my argument, as this author was pilloried because of *what* he wrote, not *how* he wrote it: the charge of 'bad writing' becoming a convenient way for his voice to be silenced by the Victorian establishment.

It is not my intention to argue that Ainsworth's works are great literature, or to attempt to paper over some often very obvious cracks in their construction, but merely to demonstrate that what is often too readily dismissed as merely pulp fiction exerts a greater influence on contemporary literature than many authors and scholars might care to acknowledge. While admitting that the pulp fiction of any age, whether Newgate novels, penny dreadfuls, 'dime' novels, horror comics or exploitation movies, can often be derivative, poorly-written or just downright silly, they can also, at their best, touch the sublime in the most unlikely of scenarios. At his best, Ainsworth's story-telling could be magical; at his worst, he was usually fun to read, if often unintentionally. As he cheerfully admitted, again in his retrospective preface to *Rookwood*:

> If the design of Romance be, what it has been held, the exposition of a useful truth by means of an interesting story, I fear I have but imperfectly fulfilled the office imposed upon me; having, as I will freely confess, had, throughout, an eye rather to the reader's amusement than his edification.[100]

Ainsworth is a paradox. His social position rendered him too high for low culture while his fictional output created the opposite effect. As literary criticism has been more harsh on this author than on any other of his age, Ainsworth's work, more

---

[100] Ainsworth, preface, *Rookwood*.

than any of his contemporaries', is thus the reflection of the Victorian, literary novel cast in the black and lurid tarn, a figure Dickens once felt he must define his own work *against*. Ainsworth is an outlaw in literary history, yet the evidence I shall present to the reader suggests that, in the words of Dick Turpin: 'England, sir, has reason to be proud of her highwaymen.'[101]

---

[101] Ainsworth, *Rookwood* 53.

CHAPTER ONE

Blood and Thunder: A Gothic Apprenticeship

I. Essential juvenilia, 1821–1823

Over a decade before *Rookwood* made its author famous, if not notorious, and Dickens published *Sketches by Boz*, the then still teenage Ainsworth was already contributing poetry, essays, short fiction and drama to a variety of the small periodicals that existed within the shadow of *Blackwood's Edinburgh Magazine*. His first published work appeared in *Arliss's Pocket Magazine* in 1821 when Ainsworth was aged 16, and he continued to recycle his material (the same story often reappearing somewhere else under a different title) in magazines such as *The Edinburgh Magazine*, *The New Monthly Magazine*, *The Manchester Iris*, *The European*, and *The London Magazine*, which numbered Hood, De Quincey, Hazlitt and Lamb among its contributors, throughout the early 1820s until he eventually started his own magazine, *The Boeotian*, which ran for six issues in 1824. These juvenilia were mostly collected in two volumes, the now lost *Poems by Cheviot Ticheburne* (1822)[1] and the almost equally obscure *December Tales* (1823).

---

[1] Ainsworth, *Poems by Cheviot Ticheburne* (London: John Arliss, 1822). S.M. Ellis refers to a copy in the King's Street Library, Manchester, but it apparently did not survive the Second World War and the subsequent move to St Peter's Square. There is still, as Ellis also noted, no copy in the British Library. Ellis, vol. 1, 85.

The characteristics central to almost every novel Ainsworth subsequently wrote, his antiquarianism, theatricality, gothic affiliations and graphic use of violence, can be traced directly back to his earliest fiction. Recalling J. Hain Friswell's analysis that the 'yeasty and lively age' in which Ainsworth grew up was largely responsible for his literary preoccupations (which could hardly be otherwise), it should be remembered that, in addition to the cultural features listed by the Victorian critic ('a long war, deeds of violence at sea and on land, the press gang, cheating lawyers, bad laws, a debauched king and court'), this was equally the age of the Romantic revival.[2]

Perhaps exceeding, however, the influences of the British and European Romantics (most notably Coleridge, Byron and Scott), Ainsworth was also inspired by a lesser-known writer, James Crossley (1800–83) of Halifax, who joined the legal firm of Thomas Ainsworth and John Sudlow of Manchester as an articled clerk in 1817, where he eventually became a partner. He and Ainsworth met when the former was a young clerk and became friends owing to a mutual love of literature and history. Crossley was something of a literary and antiquarian dilettante, and as a young man contributed widely to the newspapers and journals of the day, including *Blackwood's* and the *Quarterly Review*. This early promise was never really fulfilled, although he later edited numerous volumes for the Chetham Society (of which he eventually became President) including the works of Sir Thomas Browne and Pott's *Discoverie of Witches in Lancashire,* and counted among his friends some of the most distinguished literary figures of his age. He never left Manchester, but he and Ainsworth remained life-long friends, corresponding, often on a daily basis, from 1822 to Ainsworth's death in 1882. As Ainsworth's lawyer, Crossley managed to keep his impetuous friend relatively financially stable (often lending him money against future fees from writing) and as his friend, fellow antiquarian and bibliophile (possessing a private library of over 100,000 books), he provided much of Ainsworth's primary reference material and many project ideas, including *The Lancashire Witches*, which is

---

[2] Friswell, 258.

dedicated to him in acknowledgement of his contribution to the work. He never married.

Ainsworth's recorded recollections of his childhood often describe an early love of literature. He cites the tall stories of his father as a direct influence on the Dick Turpin section of *Rookwood* in the 1849 preface, and the reading room of the Chetham Library, which is described with reverence in the semi-autobiographical *Mervyn Clitheroe*, was his sanctuary from the polluted, over-crowded streets of central Manchester:

> The reading room was most congenial to study. Antique, with a coved and groined ceiling, deeply-embayed windows filled with painted glass, which threw a mellow and subdued light around, walls wainscoted with black oak, a high, carved mantel-piece, above which hung the portrait of the munificent founder, an austere-looking man, 'frosty but kindly, like a lusty winter', chairs of ancient make, with leathern seats and backs, old oak tables, and quaint old reading-desks in nooks – such was the room, and such its furniture.[3]

Crossley, a collector of antiquarian books who was already writing for *Blackwood's* and the *Quarterly Review*, apparently recognising a kindred spirit in his employer's son, encouraged and directed the young Ainsworth's reading. In many ways, he continued to do this for Ainsworth's entire career. In their correspondence Ainsworth constantly defers to his friend's historical and literary expertise, while also frequently consulting Crossley's ever-expanding private library and encyclopaedic knowledge of regional history for ideas and information. Although Crossley's youthful literary potential was never realised, he often seems to be writing through Ainsworth, and his influence cannot be over-stated.[4] It is also through his diligence that Ainsworth's letters have survived, although regrettably Crossley's side of the story has been lost to us.

---

[3] Ainsworth, *The Life and Adventures of Mervyn Clitheroe*, (1858) Works (1881), 63. The Chetham Library, Long Millgate, Manchester, was founded by Humphrey Chetham in 1653 and is the oldest public library in England, the building dating back to 1421. From the publication of *Rookwood*, Ainsworth always sent the Chief Librarian a first edition of his latest work, and considered taking up the post himself in 1876. Ainsworth cast Humphrey Chetham as the romantic lead in *Guy Fawkes* in 1841.
[4] See Chapter Five of this present work for details of Crossley's contribution to *The Lancashire Witches*.

Given the enormous influence Ainsworth was later to have on Victorian popular theatre, it was in every way quite appropriate that he should begin his authorial career with a drama, *Ghiotto; or Treason Discovered.*[5] Originally entitled *The Fatal Revenge* and described by its teenaged author as 'a new Melo-Dramatic Spectacle', Punter sees the influence of Charles Maturin in *Ghiotto*, while Ellis detects echoes of Marlowe's *Doctor Faustus*; both agree, however, that the author's literary origins are obvious from this piece. In *Ghiotto*, a primitive pastiche of revenge tragedy is overlaid with a gothic style resembling that of Lewis or Maturin, the Elizabethan penchant for bloodshed, melodrama and rhetoric implicit in this form having much in common with the less subtle, more hysteric, un-Radcliffian branch of eighteenth century gothic fiction. As any reader already familiar with Ainsworth's literary style knows, storms feature very prominently as harbingers of particularly monumental narrative events (both Poe and Thackeray lampooned this tendency), such as the death of Sir Ranulph Rookwood or the beginning of the history of Jack Sheppard. *Ghiotto*, naturally and appropriately then, begins with a thunderstorm, the elemental turmoil without reflecting the mental state of the protagonist, Ghiotto (a character who has much in common with Shakespeare's Macbeth and Middleton's De Flores), within. The effect (which obviously owes much to Shakespeare as well as, perhaps, contemporary accounts of the Napoleonic wars) is nonetheless impressive, especially when the age of the author is considered, as Ghiotto employs the violence of the elements to drive himself into the bloodthirsty frenzy necessary to commit murder by developing an elegant martial metaphor:

---

[5] Originally entitled *Giotto; or the Fatal Revenge*, *Arliss's Pocket Magazine*, VIII, 1821, 181–9, 250–57. This was published a month *after* Ainsworth's other juvenile melodrama, *The Rivals*, but was actually written first. As to the significance of naming his villain after the founder of modern painting, creator of the *Stefaneschi Altar* in the Vatican and supervisor of Florence Cathedral, I assume that the young author is thinking of Giotto's Catholic Otherness in the gothic tradition rather than his naturalism.

GHIOTTO: Rave on, ye elements! Ye thunders roll!
Flash on, strange fire, ethereal visitant.
Thy blaze breaks on the startled eye, and vanishes,
Like the false visions of the meteor Hope,
And, like them, bare and desolate leaves the spot
Which it has blasted with destructive force.
The loud peals now burst anigh, now murmur from afar,
As if the viewless spirits that control
The elements, and on the lightnings ride,
Held their high carnival, in joyance wild,
O'er the destruction of a sentenced world.
It suiteth well my nature! Some there are
(And men esteemed of worth and valour high)
Men who in the cannon's mouth would storm the breach,
And where death widest waves his fleshless hand,
Would strive to stand the foremost; and where'er,
In all his horrid forms, gaunt Danger stalks
Over the bloody field, still follow on,
Nor heed the sweeping ball, the hissing shot,
Nor the death scattering shell; yet fear to cope
With such a night as this; and fear to see
Nature's sublimest workings. But, to *me*
More pleasing is the sound of the hoarse thunder
Than strains of sweetest music; far more lovely
To watch the blaze of quivering lightning play,
Than all the pomp and splendour that adorns
The glittering festival ...[6]

A character in love with the beauty of destruction: this is true blood and thunder, with Ghiotto's opening monologue setting the standard for all Ainsworth's wonderful, melodramatic villains as yet waiting in the wings of history and imagination. Like the devil, there is a piece of Ghiotto in all of them. In this case, the brief action is set in the Spanish court and centred around the rivalry of the cousins Ghiotto and Manfred (another significant act of naming of course). Ghiotto loves the lady Isabinda who, in turn, loves Manfred. Enraged by rejection, Ghiotto schemes to have the lovers banished and discreetly murdered, but the plot miscarries when one of his hired assassins, Orsino, mistakes the other, Hugo, for Manfred and stabs him. The dying Hugo confesses before the king and implicates

---

[6] Ainsworth, *Ghiotto*, 182.

Ghiotto, and the elemental motif of the opening scene continues to the final curtain as Orsino, preparing to swear an oath upon his master's innocence, is struck dead by a bolt of lightning. When Ghiotto declaims Hugo's dying accusation with: 'By the blue heaven he lied!' the lights go out and he is challenged to swear his innocence upon the corpse:

> MANFRED: Approach cold Hugo's body, place thy hand
> Upon his breast, then take thy God to witness,
> That thou art innocent of this dire charge.

When Ghiotto reluctantly complies, fresh blood begins to flow from Hugo's wound and the corpse opens its eyes and stares in mute accusation and, unlike Banquo's ghost, everybody sees this and Ghiotto is immediately condemned. He denies his captors their final vengeance by killing himself while imprisoned and awaiting execution:

> GHIOTTO: Ha! am I caught; and shall the goaded lion,
> Fast in the hunters' toils, derided die?
> Shall this racked form be stretched upon a wheel,
> Which once I thought to plant upon a throne?
> This head, which nature for a crown designed,
> Be severed from this body by the axe,
> The agonising axe? Never! oh, never!
> While I possess this friend! A friend more dear
> Than India's mines of gold.
> *(Stabs himself with a dagger.)*
> And as for thee, thou loathed object, Manfred!
> Cause of my hate, and fountain of my crimes,
> This legacy I leave thee – Hate! hate! hate!
> May curses everlasting be thy meed!
> But, ha! hell drags me down! I come! Oh! Oh!
>
> *(Dies.)*
>
> MANFRED: There lies ambition and desire of greatness;
> That was his fault.
> Let us avoid the rocks
> On which was shattered this majestic ship.[7]

---

[7] *Ibid.*, 257.

Already, hindsight shows us future echoes of *Rookwood* and *The Tower of London* here. While Manfred (a name lifted from both Walpole and Byron) the virtuous hero is left to offer the moral of the tale in a neat little metaphor, a more vivid, indelible impression is left by Ghiotto's monomaniac obsession, cursing his rival with his dying breath as his soul is drawn down to hell. This seems based upon Sir Rashleigh Osbaldistone's death speech from Scott's *Rob Roy* of 1817:

> He raised himself in his chair, though the damps and chill of death were already on his brow, and spoke with a firmness which seemed beyond his strength. 'Cousin Francis', he said, 'draw near to me.' I approached him as he requested. – 'I wish you only to know that the pangs of death do not alter one iota of my feelings towards you. I hate you!' he said, the expression of rage throwing a hideous glare into the eyes which were soon to be closed forever – 'I hate you with a hatred as intense, now while I lie bleeding and dying before you, as if my foot trod on your neck.'[8]

When the play was performed before friends and family the previous Autumn, Ainsworth cast himself as Ghiotto, his brother Gilbert taking the role of Manfred.[9] Their parents' reaction to the production was not recorded.

Joking apart, the youthful author's choice of role demonstrates his immediate grasp of a central melodramatic device, one that would serve him well for his entire literary career: that the villain is the engine that drives the plot, not the hero, who needs must be rather passive, if not downright stupid. Michael R. Booth offers the following definition:

> The villain thinks, chooses, initiates action, alters his plans, makes new ones; the hero is merely the punching-bag of the villain's brain, the pawn on his chessboard. The villain is a remarkably purposeful man: revenge on the hero, the acquisition of his money and property, and the possession, (sometimes the death) of the heroine are his objectives, and with relentless single-mindedness he pursues them. The hero is confused, muddled, and extraordinarily gullible; sometimes he plots counteraction but frequently this is ineffective and he has to be helped out by the comic man. Sheer chance or some catastrophe of nature are often the only things that save him … In the villain the darkness and violence of melodrama are incarnate. From the point of view of ability the

---

[8] Scott, *Rob Roy* (1817), Waverley Novels, 498.
[9] Ainsworth, hand-written playbill, October 1 1820. The play was performed in the basement of the family house in King's Street.

villain should certainly be hero. In melodrama he is a king, but a king who must die.[10]

This is, of course, the common feature that unites the gothic tradition with the distinctively *English* melodrama which developed in the early nineteenth century and flourished until at least the Great War, being a form, as Booth also notes, that was at its most popular among the urban working classes. This is also a formula that may be usefully applied to almost everything Ainsworth subsequently wrote and is therefore crucial, in terms of both dramatic technique and audience, to an understanding and appreciation not only of his fiction but of his numerous critical detractors. As Peter Brooks has successfully argued with reference to Balzac and James, melodrama 'belongs in our cultural and critical repertory' and offers a way of reading 'great writers who could not be wholly constrained within a realist aesthetic'. In Brooks's terms, Ainsworth's earliest work already clearly exhibits a 'melodramatic imagination'.[11]

Ainsworth's other adolescent contributions to the genre, also published in *Arliss's*, were two shorter pieces entitled *The Rivals: a Serio-Comic Tragedy*,[12] and *The Cut Finger, A Tragedy in One Act*[13] which are equally worthy of note because of the obviously satirical nature of dialogue and situation. The play *The Rivals* is only two pages long and is obviously an intended parody. In what might be more appropriately described as this sketch, Janvan, King of Bedoea, and his prime minister, Stephens Antesblan, both court the affections of Billingtonia, the fishmonger's daughter in what was presumably conceived as a *risqué* reference to the antipathy between George IV and Lord Liverpool, with the Queen consort cast as a Billingsgate fish-wife. The principals mostly insult one another, with Shakespearean pastiche often gleefully degenerating into modern slang with crashing

[10] Michael R. Booth, *English Melodrama* (London: Herbert Jenkins, 1965), 18.
[11] Peter Brooks, preface, *The Melodramatic Imagination: Balzac, Henry James, Melodrama, and the Mode of Excess*, 2nd edn (New Haven: Yale UP, 1995).
[12] *Arliss's*, VII, 1821, 292–4.
[13] *Ibid.*, IX, 1822.

bathos. The effect is only slightly different from that of the companion piece, *Ghiotto*:

STEPHENS: Usurper off! what are you doing there!

JANVAN: Traitor begone! what shall Bedoea's prince
Yield aught to thee, or in his project wince?
Quickly begone, or in a porter vat
Drowned shalt thou be, I swear it, and that's flat.

STEPHENS: Tyrant unjust I scorn thy threats and thee,
And that I'll have this maid thou soon shalt see.
Now if thou stirrest but to give command,
By Heaven, thou diest by this powerful hand.

(Draws.)

JANVAN: *(laughs):* And dost thou think my sword's less sharp than thine?
Its edge less cutting and its point less fine?
Behold it now *(draws)* and if thou dar'st to fight,
Thus feel my valour and approve my might.

(They fight.)[14]

The rivals of course kill each other, and the distraught Billingtonia drinks poisoned gin and dies.

The Cut Finger is a more sophisticated piece of comedy, and S.M. Ellis considered it the best of Ainsworth's *Arliss's* period. This is a premature burial plot, where the corpse, Mrs Botherem, is awakened from a cataleptic sleep when Boreall, sexton, thief and resurrection man, exhumes her.[15] While robbing the body before selling it to a surgeon, Boreall cuts off one of Mrs Botherem's fingers to steal a ring and the shock revives her and she runs shrieking from the churchyard. Boreall gives chase, complaining indignantly that the natural order of life, death and commerce has been transgressed:

BOREALL: The body's gone. I shall be ruined. If the other bodies should learn this trick, and walk off too, what shall we do? – We shall never have any more business. But I'll be hanged if I'll be bilked in this manner. I'll after her, and

---

[14] Ainsworth, *The Rivals*, 294.
[15] Ainsworth is probably playing cheekily upon his own regional identity here: 'Boreall' suggesting 'boreal' (from the Greek *Boreas*), meaning 'of the North'. Boreall's deadpan humour belongs to a great tradition of Mancunian comedy. Les Dawson, for example, began his career in the night clubs of Deansgate.

claim her wherever I find her. I'll get a search warrant, and officer. *(Catches sight of the corpse.)* Stop, ghost! stop, ghost! – Stop, body! stop, ghost! – watch! watch! watch! ... I say you are my property. I am natural guardian of the churchyard; so come back, and be buried in peace like an honest Christian, or I'll get a warrant – Watch! watch! watch![16]

Mrs Botherem manages to make her way home, only to discover her supposedly grief-stricken husband already in the arms of another woman. Mrs Botherem attacks the lovers just as the sexton arrives and nobody survives the ensuing carnage. In addition to being a smart satire of tragic melodrama (the codes of excess already present in the form are tweaked here just enough to create farce), *The Cut Finger* also presents an interesting version of the necrophiliac-as-chorus (an archetypal framing device much more familiar to consumers of twentieth century horror fiction) in the form of the sexton, Boreall. I am thinking here particularly of the ghoulish introductions of 'The Crypt Keeper', 'The Vault Keeper' and 'The Old Witch' in William M. Gaines's EC horror comics, *Tales from the Crypt*, *The Vault of Horror* and *The Haunt of Fear*, printed in America in the early 1950s and killed off by a moral panic and nervous industry self-regulation, much like Ainsworth's Newgate fiction. Unlike previous gothic framing narratives, usually presented by someone of professional authority, such as a doctor, lawyer or detective, these were gruesome, cadaverous story-tellers who revelled in the suffering of others (occasionally joining in), inhabited mausoleums and all had very black senses of humour. One might also recall Alfred Hitchcock's camp introductions to his TV show of the early 1960s. This format has been so liberally adopted by TV companies that the majority of genre fans consider the 'links' to be more interesting than the actual stories. Six years before the Burke and Hare murders came to light in Edinburgh, Boreall also represents a contemporary response to the Georgian epidemic of body-snatching:

BOREALL: Ah! Egad – here is a coffin in an exquisite state of decay, that I'll carefully dry, and sell to my friend the tobacconist; – 'twill scarcely require any grinding to make excellent snuff. But, since the tyranny of the law chooses to consider it as a crime, I'll allow no more bodies to be taken from this

---

[16] Ainsworth, *The Cut Finger*. Quoted, from Ellis, vol. 1, 72.

ground, although I consider them a part of my lawful income. I'll desist for the future from my patriotic exertions. Yes, patriotic. How could the surgeons study anatomy if they could not dissect, and if they could not study anatomy, how could they perform operations on the living?[17]

The sexton of *Rookwood*, Peter Bradley, is recognisably a lineal descendant of Boreall's. Both have a macabre sense of humour, absolutely no scruples and a penchant for chanting morbid ballads as they dig. Like Bradley, Boreall enters singing:

BOREALL: How merrily lives a sexton old.
He sings and he shovels away!
His purse was light, tho' his spade was bright.
Yet he carolled so loud and gay.[18]

Rookwood opens in a vault, with two figures seated upon coffins in lieu of chairs, one of whom, Peter Bradley, is singing a creepy song: 'in a strange sepulchral tone, not inappropriate, however, to his subject', before page four.[19] These characters are very different to Reynolds's Resurrection Man, by way of comparison, who is presented as a cold craftsman of the black economy, his work done with the right tools and without either humour or gothic effect:

The Resurrection Man provided himself with a stout chisel, the handle of which was covered with leather, and with a mallet, the ends of which were also protected with pieces of the same material. Thus the former instrument when struck by the latter emitted but little noise.[20]

He might as well be repairing a wall as stealing a cadaver. We can see here quite clearly the differences between Ainsworth's sensibilities and those of the later Victorians. His work is an essential stop on the road to the grotesque realism of Reynolds and Dickens, but direct comparisons (as often employed by literary critics) can be misleading and erroneous if taken too far. Being slightly older, Ainsworth's Regency self was never all that far beneath the surface of his texts although, with the exception of the somewhat aberrant novel *Mervyn Clitheroe*

---

[17] *Ibid*. It is fun to think of the number of readers who would have been snuff takers.
[18] Ainsworth, *The Cut Finger*. Quoted from Ellis, vol. 1, 71.
[19] Ainsworth, *Rookwood*, 3.
[20] Reynolds, 'The Exhumation', *Mysteries of London*, 164.

58

(which mercilessly sends up believers in the occult), Ainsworth's childhood ability to see the funny side of melodramatic excess did not continue into adulthood and in his later fiction melodrama became a very serious matter indeed. Violence, on the other hand, always remained somewhere between realism and slapstick.

During the *Arliss's* period, for example, Ainsworth also used his sense of humour and his growing knowledge of sixteenth and seventeenth century literature and history to fake a forgotten dramatist whose work he claimed to have discovered, 'William Aynesworthe', under his own pseudonym of 'Thomas Hall', to whom he attributed, among other things, *Ghiotto* and *Venice, or the Fall of the Foscaris*. T. Hall's series *Horae Dramaticae* is a commentary on six plays by Aynesworthe with extracts. The language is compared with that of Aynesworthe's contemporary 'Richard Clitheroe', another invention (and ancestor of Mervyn). An anachronistic allusion to the Javanese upas tree in *Venice* gave the game away, but in the same year Ainsworth fooled the editor of the *New Monthly* with an article on 'The Writings of Richard Clitheroe'. Ainsworth's version of the Foscari story predates Byron's *The Two Foscari* by approximately six months. When Byron's project was announced, the *Edinburgh Magazine* ran an extract from Ainsworth's play with the editorial comment that: 'We cannot say what kind of production will issue from the pen of Lord Byron; but if he excels the one of which we have here given a few specimens, we will allow that he has done wonders.'[21] Again, the young author makes liberal use of thunderstorms and Shakespeare.

While the fledging author was steeped in this heady atmosphere of evolving gothic melodrama and Crossley's especially beloved collection of Elizabethan and Jacobean poetry and drama, his other major influence was undoubtedly the sensational short fiction springing from the new generation of monthly magazines, most notably *Blackwood's Edinburgh Magazine*. Current

---

[21] *Edinburgh Magazine*, IX, 1821.

advances in papermaking and printing technology allowed copy to be produced faster and at a lower cost than ever before, while the growth of the industrial middle classes created the perfect market for instruction and entertainment. The age of Grub Street appeared to be over, superseded, wrote Morrison and Baldick, by 'a new phase of modern British fiction in which the opportunist sensationalism of the monthly magazines assumed an unprecedented importance'.[22] This was an exciting time to be a reader and a writer.

Crossley was already contributing critical articles to *Blackwood's* before the age of 20, so it is probable that it was he who introduced Ainsworth to the 'Maga'. The morbid intensity of the tales of terror that characterised *Blackwood's* fictional component in its heyday (1817–34) would have been paradise to someone of Ainsworth's gothic sensibilities, and his own short stories reflect the tastes of the time. Unfortunately, Ainsworth's contributions to what we now regard as the *Blackwood's* style of writing appeared in the wrong place, albeit at the right time. The 'Writings of Richard Clitheroe' hoax appears to have disqualified him from the pages of *Blackwood's* principal competitor, Henry Colburn's *New Monthly Magazine*, as nothing more appears therein by Ainsworth until 1845, being the year that he bought the magazine for £3,250; he also contributed material to *Blackwood's* hated Whig rivals, *The Edinburgh Review* and *The London Magazine*. It is also very possible that his innocent affiliations with the seditious *European Magazine* (known for its affiliation to the Catholic cause) would not have pleased the arrogant ultra-Toryism of William Blackwood and colleagues. Nevertheless, and with characteristic precocity, Ainsworth visited Edinburgh in August 1822, recording his one and only meeting with Blackwood (who obviously thought much more highly of Crossley than his unsolicited visitor) in a letter to Crossley. The language employed to describe No. 17 Prince's Street and its inhabitants is not unlike that of many of the stories produced from within at the time:

---

[22] Robert Morrison and Chris Baldick, eds, introduction, *The Vampyre and Other Tales of the Macabre*, by John Polidori (Oxford: Oxford UP, 1997).

In the middle of the second chamber, I saw a man advancing to meet me – 'his face was deathly pale, but his nose was beaming bright' – this man of the inexpressible visage – for never before saw I such a one, with those funny teeth of his, that queer one eyebrow up and the other down, with gray streaming locks, – it certainly looked very astonishing. This, you will suppose, was Blackwood.[23]

The subsequent meeting with this apparition was obviously rather strained, although Ainsworth did meet and befriend J.G. Lockhart on this occasion. The same letter concludes with a brief account of a much more satisfactory meeting with Archibald Constable and the staff of the *Edinburgh Review*, demonstrating, as the Tory Ainsworth nailed his colours to the mast of a sinking ship, how little he cared about politics compared to his love of literature and his desire for publication; this feature continues in the ideologically ambivalent nature of his later histories which, rather than striving for narrative objectivity, tended to side with the victim in any given political scenario, hence the sympathy for the Protestantism of Lady Jane Grey in *The Tower of London* and the Catholicism of Guy Fawkes in the novel of the same name, both of which were written concurrently in 1840–41.

Although Ainsworth was not then a *Blackwood's* writer, he was, as many were at that time, writing in the manner of *Blackwood's*. As Leigh Hunt wrote:

A man who does not contribute his quota of grim stories now-a-days seems hardly to be free of the republic of letters. He is bound to wear a death's head, as part of his insignia. If he does not frighten every body, he is no body.[24]

Ainsworth, a disciple of the graphic gothic descriptions of Matthew Lewis rather than the restraint of Anne Radcliffe, was quick to embrace this new trend of explicit representations of terror; like his affinity for melodrama, this technique would serve him well in years to come, his historical romances always

---

[23] Ainsworth, letter to Crossley, August 22 1822.
[24] Leigh Hunt, 'A Tale for a Chimney Corner', *The Indicator*, X, 1819, 73. Cited by Morrison and Baldick, eds, introduction, *Tales of Terror from Blackwood's Magazine* (Oxford: Oxford UP, 1995).

disturbingly accurate in their portrayals of violence, horror and death. As Morrison and Baldick explain:

> The usual tone of these stories is one of clinical observation (although without the customary detachment) rather than of genteel trepidation, and for the most part the terrors are unflinchingly 'witnessed', not ambiguously evoked: here there are fewer phantoms or rumours of phantoms than actual drownings, suicides, murders, executions, and death agonies, veiled only by the thinnest layer of euphemism and moralising.[25]

This clinical observation, usually in the first person (like the voice of a disembowelled surgeon naming each vital organ as it plops out), places the reader behind these same horrified eyes, and the narrative is therefore constructed to convey the most exaggerated emotional intensity. This was the secret, understood so well by Edgar Allan Poe with seismic consequences for the development of the short story in English. In addition, obviously, to his successful employment of this common principle in his own fiction, Poe also illustrates the device in his wonderful burlesque, 'How to Write a Blackwood Article', where the humour of the piece enhances rather than trivialises what he understood as *Blackwood's* significant contribution to literature by employing the same gallows humour which underpins so much of the most extreme, tasteless stories of the period, including his own. The piece is presented as an interview between William Blackwood and the hack writer Signora Psyche Zenobia (Suky Snobbs), where the great man explains the technique which has taken the 'Maga' to the top:

> And then there was 'The Man in the Bell',[26] a paper by-the-by, Miss Zenobia, which I cannot sufficiently recommend to your attention. It is the history of a young person who goes to sleep under the clapper of a church bell, and is awakened by its tolling for a funeral. The sound drives him mad, and, accordingly, pulling out his tablets, he gives a record of his sensations. Sensations are the great things after all. Should you ever be drowned or hung, be sure to make a note of your sensations – they will be worth to you ten guineas a sheet. If you wish to write forcibly, Miss Zenobia, pay minute attention to the sensations.[27]

---

[25] Morrison and Baldick, introduction, *Tales of Terror*.
[26] William Maginn, 'The Man in the Bell', *Blackwood's Edinburgh Magazine*, November 1821.
[27] Poe, 'How to Write A Blackwood Article' (1838) *The Complete Tales and Poems of Edgar Allan Poe*, ed. Edward H. O'Neill (New York: Dorset, 1989), 236.

Miss Zenobia assures him that she will, and proceeds to get herself decapitated by the minute hand of an Edinburgh church clock, her sensations precisely recorded, as her eyes pop out into the gutter, in a story fittingly entitled 'A Predicament' (1838).

The first of Ainsworth's 'quota of grim stories' was a nasty little tale entitled 'The Baron's Bridal' by 'W.H.A.', being the first of many contributions to *The European Magazine* and appearing in the issue for December 1821, and reprinted in *Arliss's* the following year as 'The Spectre Bride', a title which hints at the influence of Washington Irving's 'The Specter Bridegroom' from *The Sketch Book of Geoffrey Crayon, Gent* (1819). Ostensibly, these stories are not dissimilar. Both are *phantasmagoria* set in a fairytale, feudal Germany, and both plots are concerned with the courtship of a nobleman's daughter by a mysterious, possibly preternatural stranger. In Irving's original, itself a version of a European folk story, the intended husband of the Lady Von Landshort is murdered by bandits *en route* to his wedding. Being a gentleman, his dying wish is that his best friend, Starkenfaust, should continue to the castle and present the groom's apologies for not keeping his appointment with the lady, adding that his spirit will not rest until this is done. Arriving at the wedding banquet, Starkenfaust is mistaken for the groom, whom nobody has ever seen, and is placed in a rather awkward position which he resolves by pretending to be the ghost of the groom and leaving to attend his own funeral. By this point, Starkenfaust and the lady have fallen hopelessly in love and the 'ghost' returns each night to stand outside his beloved's window. They elope and the Baron reasonably assumes that his daughter has been taken, like Persephone, to the underworld. They return, all is revealed and every one lives happily ever after.[28] Ainsworth's spin on the mysterious lover *leitmotif* is to take a very similar scenario to Irving's witty little tale, and then cheekily marry his Baron's daughter to a *real* monster: the handsome stranger revealed to be the ancestor of all gothic immortals, the

---

[28] Washington Irving, 'The Specter Bridegroom' (1819) *The Legend of Sleepy Hollow and Other Stories*, ed. Lauriat Lane, Jr (New York: Airmont, 1964), 56–69.

63

'Wandering Jew'. First he steals her heart, then he takes her soul. The language of the matrimonial *finale* positively luxuriates in unnecessary cruelty, and the entire purpose of the story is suddenly and shockingly exposed as nothing more or less than the description of the destruction of innocence by pure, unadulterated evil:

The evening arrived; and already as the hall clock struck eight, Clotilda was on her road to the chapel. It was a dark, gloomy night, thick masses of dun clouds sailed across the firmament, and the roar of the winter wind echoed awfully through the forest trees. She reached the appointed place; a figure was in waiting for her – it advanced – and discovered the features of the stranger. 'Why! This is well, my bride', he exclaimed, with a sneer; 'and well will I repay thy fondness. Follow me.' They proceeded together in silence through the winding avenues of the chapel, until they reached the adjoining cemetery. Here they paused for an instant; and the stranger, in a softened tone, said, 'But one hour more, and the struggle will be over. And yet this heart of incarnate malice can feel, when it devotes so young, so pure a spirit to the grave. But it must – it must be', he proceeded, as the memory of her past love rushed on her mind; 'for the fiend whom I obey has so willed it. Poor girl, I am leading thee indeed to our nuptials; but the priest will be death, thy parents the mouldering skeletons that rot in heaps around; and the witnesses of our union, the lazy worms that revel on the carious bones of the dead. Come, my young bride, the priest is impatient for his victim.' As they proceeded, a dim blue light moved swiftly before them, and displayed at the extremity of the churchyard the portals of a vault. It was open, and they entered it in silence. The hollow wind came rushing through the gloomy abode of the dead; and on every side were piled the mouldering remnants of coffins, which dropped piece by piece upon the damp earth. Every step they took was on a dead body; and the bleached bones rattled horribly beneath their feet. In the centre of the vault rose a heap of unburied skeletons, whereon was seated a figure too awful even for the darkest imagination to conceive. As they approached it, the hollow vault rung with a hellish peal of laughter; and every mouldering corpse seemed endued with unearthly life. The stranger paused, and as he grasped his victim in his hand, one sigh burst from his heart – one tear glistened in his eye. It was but for an instant; the figure frowned awfully at his vacillation, and waved his gaunt hand.

The stranger advanced; he made certain mystic circles in the air, uttered unearthly words, and paused in excess of terror. Of a sudden he raised his voice, and wildly exclaimed – 'spouse of the spirit of darkness, a few moments are yet thine; that thou may'st know to whom thou hast consigned thyself. I am the undying spirit of the wretch who curst his Saviour on the cross. He looked at me in the closing hour of his existence, and that look hath not yet passed away, for I am curst above all earth. I am eternally condemned to hell! And must cater for my master's taste 'till the world is parched as is a scroll, and the heavens and the earth have passed away. I am he of whom thou may'st have read, and of whose feats thou may'st have heard. A million souls has my master condemned me to ensnare, and then my penance is accomplished, and I may know the repose of the grave. Thou art the thousandth soul that I have damned. I saw thee in thine hour of purity, and I marked thee at once for my home. Thy father did I murder for his temerity, and permitted to warn thee of thy fate; and thyself have I beguiled for thy simplicity. Ha! The spell works bravely, and thou shall soon see, my sweet one, to whom thou hast linked thine undying fortunes, for as long as the seasons shall move on their course of nature – as long as the lightning shall flash, and the thunders roll, thy penance shall be eternal. Look below! And see to what thou art destined.' She looked, the vault split in a thousand different directions; the earth yawned asunder; and the roar of mighty waters was heard. A living ocean of molten fire glowed in the abyss beneath her, and blending with the shrieks of the damned, and the triumphant shouts of the fiends, rendered horror more horrible than imagination. Ten millions of souls were writhing in the fiery flames, and as boiling billows dashed them against the blackened rocks of adamant, they cursed with the blasphemies of despair; and each curse echoed in thunder across the wave. The stranger rushed towards his victim. For an instant he held her over the burning vista, looked fondly in her face, and wept as he were a child. This was but the impulse of a moment; again he grasped her in his arms, dashed her from him with fury; and as her last parting glance was cast in kindness on his face, shouted aloud, 'not mine is the crime, but the religion that thou professest; for is it not said that there is a fire of eternity prepared for the souls of the wicked; and hast not thou incurred its torments?' She, poor girl, heard not, heeded not the shouts of the blasphemer. Her delicate form bounded from rock to rock, over billow, and over foam; as she fell, the ocean lashed itself as it were in triumph to receive her soul, and as she sunk deep in the burning pit, ten thousand voices reverberated from the bottomless abyss, 'Spirit of evil! Here indeed is an eternity of torments prepared for thee; for here the worm never dies, and the fire is never quenched.'[29]

And so the story ends, utterly devoid of hope, with the heroine irredeemably damned for all eternity while her destroyer remains unrepentant, unpunished and at liberty to continue his terrible employment. Ainsworth's final description of hell has overwhelmed the narrative, blatantly exploiting common, Western religious belief to generate horror by touching the (collective) Christian nerve and maximising the effect with the use of Biblical language and imagery, ending with Mark 9:44, 'Where their worm dieth not, and the fire is not quenched.' The influence of the gothic is very apparent here, particularly that of Maturin (this is,

---

[29] Ainsworth, 'The Spectre Bride', *Arliss's*, IX, 1822.

of course, Melmoth and Isidora in microcosm), the final scene also recalling the halls of Eblis (Satan) from William Beckford's *Vathek: An Arabian Tale* (1786), the death of Ambrosio from *The Monk*, and 'The Wanderer's Dream', the penultimate chapter of *Melmoth*; we might also remember the conclusion of 'The Vampyre' (1819) by John Polidori: 'The guardians hastened to protect Miss Aubrey; but when they arrived, it was too late. Lord Ruthven had disappeared, and Aubrey's sister had glutted the thirst of a VAMPYRE!'[30] Like his literary predecessors, Ainsworth was well aware of, and willing to exploit dramatically, the obvious relationship between Christian doctrine, by necessity supernatural, and the gothic narrative. What Ainsworth specifically adds to that branch of the gothic which acknowledges the miraculous (in opposition to the version offered by Radcliffe and Scott), is the extreme degree to which he pushes his descriptions of the demonic landscape.

'The Spectre Bride' operates successfully through a chain of negations: hell is the opposite of heaven, the devil is the anti-Christ, the *unreal* (magical, supernatural, gothic), the antithesis of the *real* (natural, rational, realist), and the text itself a dark reflection of a light-hearted story by Irving. Ainsworth exploits the simple point that the door to the miraculous has to swing both ways, and, as the sacred reveals itself in a moment of epiphany, then so must the profane. There is no representational ambiguity in this frame, and the gothic epiphany results not from the collision of an apparently uncanny event with a series of possible explanations,[31] but from the rather intriguing combination of clinical description and eternal damnation, the author's first serious use of the *Blackwood's* technique being to combine it with a fantastic situation. Like Lewis and Maturin, Ainsworth used what was already implicit in Christian myth. As with the codes of melodrama and the use of graphic descriptions of violence, the supernatural and the destruction of innocence were to be recurrent themes in Ainsworth's writing,

---

[30] John Polidori, 'The Vampyre', Morrison and Baldick, *The Vampyre and other Tales*, 23.
[31] See Victor Sage, 'Empire Gothic: Explanation and Epiphany in Conan Doyle, Kipling and Chesterton', *Creepers, British Horror and Fantasy in the Twentieth Century*, ed. Clive Bloom (London: Pluto, 1993), 14.

all of which he would later impose upon his rather unique model of English history.

While 'The Spectre Bride' was undoubtedly a transitional piece, situated stylistically between the works of Lewis and Maturin on one hand and the *Blackwood's* stable on the other, what followed tended increasingly towards the latter position, Ainsworth's stories charting a parallel course to those of James Hogg, John Galt, John Howison, and William Maginn (whose dread-filled stories dominated *Blackwood's* at that time) in smaller, rival magazines. Ainsworth's adoption of this relatively new vogue for horror (rather than the still popular, traditional gothic form) is apparent from the alterations of style and content in his next story, 'The Half-Hangit', which appeared quietly first in *The Manchester Iris* in September 1822 and was re-issued as his penultimate contribution to *The European* the following July, along with several other original stories. As the title suggests, 'The Half-Hangit' is a tale of the gallows, specifically it is a vivid, immediate account of the entire experience of the trial, the condemned cell and the drop, doubly dreadful as it is told by a man falsely convicted of murder. The *Blackwood's* version of this story, 'Le Revenant', by the mysterious Henry Thompson is the famous one; it caused a huge stir when it appeared: Charles Lamb wrote to his editor that it was 'MOST AFFECTING'[32] and both Poe and Dickens were indebted to it, with obvious echoes of Thompson's disturbingly intimate portrayal of the condemned cell present in 'A Visit to Newgate' by 'Boz', and his trial scene influencing Fagin's in *Oliver Twist*; for Poe it was a matter of sensationalism, for Dickens, realism.[33] 'The Half-Hangit', however, pre-dates 'Le Revenant' by five years.

---

[32] Morrison and Baldick, *Tales of Terror*, 289n. Lamb had himself written a similar, if more light-hearted, version of this idea in a piece originally written for *The Reflector* in 1811 entitled 'On the Inconveniences Resulting from being Hanged', which later became an episode of *The Pawnbroker's Daughter*.

[33] See H.P. Sucksmith, 'The Secret of Immediacy: Dickens's Debt to the Tale of Terror in *Blackwood's*', *Nineteenth-Century Fiction*, 26 (1971), 151–7.

In Ainsworth's story, an impoverished school teacher describes how he came across a dying man while taking his customary evening walk in the countryside. The stranger has been violently assaulted and left for dead, and he dies in the narrator's arms: 'He grasped my hand – the blood gushed out in torrents from his side – he shivered all over – his limbs stretched out – and with his eyes wide open, and as I thought fixed upon me – he expired.'[34] (It is a common superstition that to catch the eye of a stranger at the moment of his or her death is a very bad omen indeed.) This horror is compounded by the creeping realisation in the teacher's mind that he is the only, obvious suspect, whether it be murder or suicide. The real killers, two of the victim's servants, return meanwhile to bury the corpse, finding instead an ideal scapegoat. The teacher is tied up and left overnight next to the corpse; after the death and the fear of a false accusation and probable conviction, the third 'nasty epiphany' is a description of a hellish, delirious nightmare:

> I heard a groan behind me, I turned to look, a cloud burst open, and a pale beam of the moon shot down upon the face of the murdered man – it was terrible – his eyes were open, but fixed and stoney, and his countenance was livid and corrupt. I turned away in horror, and endeavoured to escape – my footsteps slipped, and I fell headlong down a steep precipice. Every limb seemed to have suffered dislocation, and yet I could not die. My dream now took a different turn: methought a legion of skeletons sprung up beside me, the glare of their torches danced before my eyes; they raised me unresisting in their bony arms, and bore me on a steed as pale and terrible as themselves over wastes and moors, which nothing but imagination can conceive, and at last dropped me into a cave of inconceivable depths; then I seemed to lose all recollection – my brain began to whirl round, and I fainted.[35]

This escalation of narrative pace, leading to the ultimate epiphany of violent death, betrays once more Ainsworth's debt to the techniques of Matthew Lewis. We are in the realm of 'The Spectre Bride' here, only this time the vision of hell is entirely internal and psychological, anticipating very much the direction which the gothic will take in the nineteenth century. The experience is depicted as increasingly

---

[34] Ainsworth, 'The Half-Hangit', *The European Magazine*, July 1823, 398.
[35] *Ibid.*, 400.

surreal throughout, the protagonist never quite believing that this could possibly be happening, before the realisation that it *is* intrudes: 'Often was I tempted to doubt the reality of every thing around me, and I began to think myself the sport of some delusion.'[36] After the feverish nightmare, he awakes in prison, accused of murder and: 'My story was treated, as I expected it, as an improbable fiction; and all to whom I related it laughed at me.'[37]

The trial is similarly internalised by degrees, beginning with a detached account of the prosecution and the hopeless defence (the defendant is poor, the victim was rich and he was caught literally red-handed), but ending with a very lonely description of the inevitable sentence:

> I was found guilty. A deadly stillness now prevailed all around. My breath began to grow short. The judge slowly placed on his head his black cap – the eye of each gazer became fixed with intense emotion. He passed sentence upon me. [38] I heard his words, but I scarcely knew their import; they sounded like a death-bell on a summer's eve. My senses became bewildered – I was cut deeply to the brain. I endeavoured to kneel, to pray; my limbs forgot their office, every thing fled, and I was carried away fainting.[39]

Once again, the scene is punctuated by unconsciousness. The Judge assuming the black cap is a powerful image in the English collective memory. We do not need to hear the sentence; Dickens does not relate it in Fagin's case either and the condemned man merely: 'gazed stupidly about him.'[40] Only later, back in his cell, does the awful realisation begin to intrude:

> I was sentenced – my hours were numbered. I had three days to live – horrible reflection; as these and other wilder thoughts flashed across my soul, my reason tottered. At one time rage and fury would almost choke me; I clashed my chains together, foamed at the mouth, and endeavoured to dash out my brains against the wall of my prison; the next moment I wept like an infant, and

---

[36] *Ibid.*, 403.

[37] *Ibid.*, 401.

[38] A sentence passed and carried out 460 times in England and Wales between 1821 and 1825. See V.A.C. Gatrell, *The Hanging Tree: Execution and the English People, 1770–1868* (Oxford: Oxford UP, 1994), 617.

[39] Ainsworth, 'The Half-Hangit', 402.

[40] Dickens, *Oliver Twist*, 305.

falling with my face upon the ground seemed ready to breathe out my soul in the dreadful grief which agitated me.[41]

The horror and suspense of the condemned man's precognition of his own terrible, inevitable, unnecessary death to a certain extent foreshadows both Thompson's and Dickens's later descriptions. 'Le Revenant' (literally 'the ghost', or someone returned from the dead) tells us that: 'I could not feel – though I tried to make myself feel it – that I was going to DIE. In the midst of this, I heard the chime of the chapel clock begin to strike; and I thought, Lord take pity on me, a wretch! – it could not be three quarters after seven yet!'[42] This is much like Dickens's later, journalistic account of the same, much-repeated situation:

> The deep bell of St Paul's strikes – one! He heard it; it has roused him. Seven hours left! He paces the narrow limits of his cell with rapid strides, cold drops of terror starting on his forehead, and every muscle of his frame quivering with agony. Seven hours! He falls upon his knees and clasps his hands to pray. Hush! what sound was that? He starts upon his feet. It cannot be two yet. Hark! Two quarters have struck; – the third – the fourth. It is! Six hours left ... A period of unconsciousness succeeds. He wakes, cold and wretched ... He is the condemned felon again, guilty and despairing; and in two hours more he will be dead.[43]

In 'Fagin's Last Night Alive' (the penultimate chapter of *Oliver Twist*), Dickens adds the dimension of delirium and terror to the experience as Fagin pathetically begs Oliver to help him escape. Importantly, all three pieces subvert the traditionally euphemistic accounts of condemned men and women facing their deaths bravely, albeit possibly for rather different reasons; all are sensational accounts, and if only Dickens intends any real sociological comment, each is equally honest. As V.A.C. Gatrell reminds us in his remarkable book, *The Hanging Tree*: 'most felons went to their deaths in quaking terror ... and the man who did contrive to conduct himself bravely was often actually drunk out of his mind'.[44] On the eve of execution, clumsy suicide attempts often took place, and

---

[41] Ainsworth, 'The Half-Hangit', 402.
[42] Henry Thompson, 'Le Revenant' (1827), Morrison and Baldick, *Tales of Terror*, 84.
[43] Dickens, 'A Visit to Newgate' (1836), *Sketches by Boz*, Works, 136.
[44] Gatrell, 37.

for every one who died bravely on the scaffold, scores lost control of all bodily functions and had to be carried, screaming, thrashing and dribbling urine and faeces, to their doom. 'Now that sexual taboos have fallen, what was and is entailed by death by execution may be one of the last agreed obscenities', writes Gatrell.[45] By the time he wrote his two Newgate novels Ainsworth was using the euphemisms himself. In a L'envoi to *Rookwood*, we are reassured that Dick Turpin's 'firmness deserted him not at the last' and:

> When he mounted the fatal tree his left leg trembled; he stamped it impatiently down, and, after a brief chat with the hangman, threw himself suddenly and resolutely from the ladder. His sufferings would appear to have been slight: as he himself sang,
>
>> He died, not as other men, by *degrees*,
>> But *at once*, without wincing, and quite at his ease![46]

There is obviously no room for realism when creating heroes. With even more emotional detachment on the part of his author, Jack Sheppard was 'launched into eternity', being a very common press euphemism at the time.[47] In 'The Half-Hangit' however, the hanging is disturbingly vivid:

> I shuddered dreadfully – the use of my limbs again forsook me – and, had it not been for the assistance which was timely offered me I should have fallen ... I gazed timorously around – it was a beautiful morning, but all seemed black and dark to me ... There was a dead weight upon my heart, and I felt very sick; a thick damp sat upon my brow, and all my limbs felt nerveless. I drew my breath by gasps, and my whole frame heaved with emotion ... I stood upon the boards, and cast my eyes around, but I could dimly see – all floated a confused mass around me – it seemed one ever-moving sea of human heads that swelled and foamed, and rolled up to swallow and devour, and I shrunk in horror ... the

---

[45] *Ibid.*, 29.
[46] Ainsworth, L'envoi, *Rookwood*.
[47] Ainsworth, *Jack Sheppard* (1839), Works, 343. In his article 'Going to see a man hanged', Thackeray describes the act of execution as sending 'this wretched guilty soul into the presence of God'. Thackeray, *Tales, Sketches Etc*, Collected Works (London, Caxton, 1920), 261, reprinted from *Fraser's* July 1840, 261. Descriptions only become more generally explicit after public hanging was abolished in 1868. For example, execution reports were one of the staple components of the necrophiliac *Illustrated Police News* (along with murders, suicides, the discovery of decomposing corpses and attacks by wild animals in the British Empire of Otherness). The *IPN* report of the hanging of the 'Whitechapel Murderer' Henry Wainwright describes such minute particulars as the quivering of the rope. 'Newgate – Tuesday morning', *The Illustrated Police News*, January 1876.

cord was fastened round my neck – the clergyman recommended my soul to Heaven, and departed. The jailor delivered to me a handkerchief to let fall when I was prepared, and left me; and it was then, and only then, that I became alive to the terrors of my situation. I was like one suddenly aroused from a fit of intoxication. I had before an idea of it, but it was a bare idea ... It was an age – it was horrible – the cord of agony was screwed to its tightest – the least move would have cracked it: it was insupportable. But Oh! that moment. The handkerchief had been given me to let fall when I was prepared; and thus I was to become, in a manner, my own executioner. Terrible thought . I half resolved to retain it, and let death come when it would, but I could not bear to wait ... the handkerchief dropped – the boards fell – ! I felt the dreadful jerk through my whole frame – the blood rushed to my head. I felt the veins distend terribly in my temples – my eyes seemed starting out of their sockets, and there were strong shooting pains in the back of my ears. I tried to breathe – a choking sensation ensured. I became convulsed – my hands felt dreadfully painful. I clutched at the air – the convulsions increased. I thought the veins would burst in my brow. I felt that my eyes protruded dreadfully. I heaved for breath again, but the passage was completely obstructed. I shivered all over – my pains became less intense – and I was soon insensible.[48]

Dickens and Thompson as well as Thackeray in 'Going to See a Man Hanged' stop short of describing the actual *hangings*. For Ainsworth, the agony of expectation is matched by the physical agony of death by strangulation. Admittedly, Ainsworth is anticipating Mr Blackwood's advice to Miss Psyche Zenobia here, but the point is I think that he was describing a very common circumstance in contemporary England, which was still, as Peter Linebaugh designated it, a 'Thanatocracy',[49] rather than the fantastic tortures often devised in *Blackwood's*, such as the plight of Maginn's 'The Man in the Bell' or the victim of William Mudford's 'The Iron Shroud'. Ainsworth's narrator is of course cut down at the last minute when one of the murderers confesses, but his lover, Helen, like Romeo, has already died and the narrative concludes bitterly as a now emotionally empty man yearns for the death that was once so fearful. In this aspect, 'The Half-Hangit' again betrays a melodramatic root which Thompson and Dickens manage to avoid. While Ainsworth's language is often artificially tragic

---

[48] Ainsworth, 'The Half-Hangit', 404.
[49] See Peter Linebaugh, *The London Hanged, Crime and Society in the Eighteenth Century* (London: Penguin, 1991), Chapter 2.

and melodramatic ('if misery and solitude of soul be things to be vain of, I may indulge in vanity to the fill. Alas!' he begins, rather at odds with his later ultra-realism), Thompson's is shockingly matter of fact. 'Now *I* am in a situation to speak, from experience, upon that very interesting question – the sensations attendant upon a passage from life to death. I have been HANGED, and I am ALIVE', explains 'Le Revenant' in his opening paragraph.[50]

Ainsworth's character is also innocent (another dimension of the horror and suspense), and the author's attitude to capital punishment remains ambivalent; would the execution have been morally justified if it were the two murderers on the gallows? It would be misleading to ascribe an intentional political moral to this story, the author's purpose is more one of straightforward exploitation, although it remains significant by virtue of its chronology and its unflinching representation of death by hanging, a subject that would continue to preoccupy the Victorians (politically and pornographically) but was rarely described in detail. Even Thackeray admitted, in the essay 'Going to see a man hanged', that 'I am not ashamed to say that I could look no more, but shut my eyes as the last dreadful act was going on which sent this wretched guilty soul into the presence of God.'[51] Ainsworth rarely looks away, unless he has a specific purpose in doing so: although Dick Turpin and Jack Sheppard are allowed equally tasteful exits, there is no shortage of explicitly violent death occurring around the heroes in both texts. 'The Half-Hangit', however, signals the beginnings of the author's preoccupation with criminality and the State, and remains one of the most realistic depictions of capital punishment in English literature crossing, as it does, the line of demarcation between fiction and fact as, at the time it was written, people were being publicly hanged every week.[52] Principally, 'The Half-Hangit', like 'The Spectre Bride', offers another key to Ainsworth's writing. Again there is a hybridisation, potentially a conflict, of different forms of narrative where

---

[50] Thompson, 'Le Revenant', 73.
[51] W.M. Thackeray, 'Going to see a man hanged', *Tales, Sketches Etc*, Works, 261.
[52] I have found no direct evidence that Ainsworth ever attended a public execution but, given the regularity of such events, it is unlikely that he did not.

traditional relationships dissolve and recombine before our eyes. These stories are at once very gothic in the sense of eighteenth century romance and very modern, in terms of violence, immediacy of language and overall sensationalism. In Ian Duncan's terms, these stories could be seen to be a minor example of the process of transition from the *romance* to the *novel* that was starting to take place during this period.[53] What Poe (who, as is well known, reworked several of the classic *Blackwood's* tales in his own *Tales of the Grotesque and Arabesque*) and Dickens were later able to do with such material was effectively to stabilise it, both morally and aesthetically. Ainsworth and his work comes from the necessary and preceding maelstrom of ideas and experiment, where such stylistic mix-and-matching was commonplace. Although 'The Spectre Bride' and 'The Half-Hangit' nevertheless represent Ainsworth's best work during this period, both are surprisingly absent from Ainsworth's collection of his own magazine contributions of 1823, *December Tales*. As this was a prose collection, the mini-melodramas were probably intended to be published in a separate volume, as were the poems (or perhaps they were inappropriately frivolous given the sombre tone of the other essays and stories), but as to the omission of 'The Spectre Bride' and 'The Half-Hangit', it is tempting to suspect that they were simply too extreme for 1823.

II. The best of the rest: *December Tales*, 1823

With the exception of the above, *December Tales* usefully brings together all of Ainsworth's prose from this remarkably prolific period of enthusiastic literary production. Ainsworth's creative output between 1821 and 1823 was as large as it was energetic, and this material is often very difficult to locate and identify even if one is fortunate enough to discover an intact copy of *Arliss's* or *The European*.[54] For the same reason that it is foolish to attempt an overview of all of Ainsworth's

---

[53] See Ian Duncan, *Modern Romance and Transformations of the Novel.*
[54] For such reasons I have had to concede defeat with regard to the poems of Cheviot Ticheburne.

74

novels, it is not my intention to offer a detailed examination of every one of his early short stories; some are more successful than others, and many of his significant themes and literary devices have already been considered. Nonetheless, there are some interesting pieces in this collection, one or two of which would definitely have stood the test of time as gothic tales if only they had appeared in better known and more widely circulated organs.

It is interesting to note that in *December Tales* Cheviot Ticheburne is supplanted by the English Catholic poet Chidiock Tichborne, who was horribly executed for his part in a plot to assassinate Elizabeth I. Tichborne's poem of farewell is attached as an epigraph to the opening story, 'Mary Stukeley', which effectively establishes an atmosphere of melancholy that unites the entire collection:

My prime of youth is but a frost of cares,
My feast of joy is but one dish of pain;
My crop of corn is but a field of tares,
And all my goods is but vain hope of gain:
The day is fled – and yet I saw no sun,
And now I live – and now my life is done![55]

The final image of a living death (written by a condemned man) is present as a controlling metaphor throughout the stories and essays, which are collectively entitled so as to suggest an ending rather than a beginning – the death of the year; and the narrative voice moves easily into morbid introspection: 'Death is your only sure balance in which to weigh the real worth and importance of individuals' muses the youthful author in the essay 'The Church-Yard' while in the guise of an old man, aware that he is close to death, and reminiscing about his childhood: 'Ah! those were happy days.'[56] A nostalgia for an almost prelapsarian past before all innocent hopes were blighted is a recurrent motif, and the tales are generally

---

[55] Chidiock Tichborne, 'My prime of youth is but a froste of cares' (1586), quoted from Ainsworth, *December Tales*, 1. Ainsworth has standardised the early modern English spelling. Tichborne's punishment was to be disembowelled while still alive. This poem of farewell and his speech from the scaffold became quite famous.
[56] Ainsworth, 'The Church-Yard', *December Tales* (London: G. & B.W. Whitaker, 1823), 84–8.

presented directly as the first person narratives of elderly men, usually in a state of guilt or despair, or they are travellers' tales, which are much the same as the former but framed by a worldly-wise narrator. The essays, 'The Church-Yard', 'The Theatre' and 'Recollections' seem similarly fictive in light of the affected age and experience of the author. The story of 'R' at the conclusion of 'The Church-Yard' also marks a subtle blurring of fact and fiction within the piece, which begins as a description of a favourite walk around the Rostherne, Ainsworth's mother's native village, and concludes with a gothic anecdote.

'The Church-Yard' follows the thoughts of the narrator as he wanders through a forest of headstones, immediately establishing his romantic credentials and affiliation to the graveyard school of poetry with the reflection: 'Am I wrong in saying, that this is the place – the school – the theatre for a poet?'[57] The effect of the cemetery, and the sublimity of the surrounding landscape, is epiphanic; as the sun sets: 'sinking and reddening on hill, and plain, and valley: – it is then that the soul, emancipated from earthly thoughts and earthly hopes, holds closer sympathy with the scenes around, and holier visionings flit before the mind'. The received revelation is a Romantic, neoplatonist consideration of the relationship between death, 'your only sure balance', and the art of the poet:

> Is it not here that the casualties of rank and station are destroyed? – and is it not the work of the poet, also, to overlook these accidental distinguishments? – to develop the rise of simple and unadorned loveliness? – and to see, and properly to estimate, the intrinsic excellence of things and actions?[58]

In addition to this essay on the transcendental aesthetic, and in parallel with the Christian discourse of authority represented by the sombre image of the church, there is also an intrusion of the pagan belief system of an earlier, pre-Christian age. The long, opening description of the hallowed landscape is punctuated by 'the white-washed cottage and barn, with the horse-shoe nailed over the door, the lingering relic of drooping faith in demonology'.[59] 'Demonology' rather than

---

[57] *Ibid.*, 83.
[58] *Ibid.*
[59] *Ibid.*, 82.

'superstition' is interesting here, suggesting that Ainsworth had already read Scott's *Letters on Demonology and Witchcraft* and understood its potential as a guide to gothic technique as well as an examination of seventeenth century belief systems.

Just as the landscape is infected with this hint of the supernatural, albeit qualified as simple superstition, the text is penetrated by a supernatural narrative at its conclusion, the story of 'R.'

> R- fell in love – a thing of common occurrence and slight moment with most men; but it was otherwise with him: his constitution was delicate, and his feelings sensitive beyond the conception of any but his intimates; to such a being, to love as he loved, was an exertion of energies almost alarming. He succeeded – the object of his adoration loved him – the day was fixed for their marriage – before it came, she died, and R-'s fond ties were broken. From that hour, all his time was spent in retracing the walks they had taken together. There was a rose tree, which she had planted, and R- watched over it with incessant care; for 'he was the slave of sympathy'. I found him near it one day: he said to me – 'You see that tree – I shall live as long as it; no longer!' He would not be persuaded that it was a mere whim of his imagination. Two months after this, he died. I passed through the garden – the tree was withered.[60]

My grandmother used to tell stories like this. The narrator acknowledges that: 'I am perfectly sensible not half my readers will believe this story', completing with a flourish the rival frames of explanation that coexist within the narrative: R- was emotionally over-sensitive, in combination with a dangerously delicate constitution, and the withered rose could be nothing but mere coincidence; equally the episode could be a preternatural 'instance of the strong power of the imagination over the mental and physical faculties'.[61] The narrator is merely a witness, he leaves the matter to his audience to judge. The textual effect is nonetheless arresting, the realist narrative has been rendered suddenly unstable by the *unrealist*.

---

[60] *Ibid.*, 89.
[61] *Ibid.*, 90.

With the exception of the essays, 'The Theatre' and 'Recollections', and the stories 'The Falls of Ohiopyle' and 'The Englisher's Story', all the pieces that make up *December Tales* are in one way or another gothic. 'Mary Stukeley' is the confession of a bigamist who has been unable to silence his guilt by prolonged debauchery; in 'The Falls of Ohiopyle' an American frontiersman tells of how he awoke from a near-fatal accident to find himself in an Edenic valley, and of how he subsequently fell in love with the angelic woman who nursed him back to health. This version of America is consistent with the idealised reports of the time, where every man could be self-sufficient on his own plot of land. *December Tales* slightly predates Crèvecoeur and Emerson, but Ainsworth had probably been reading Franklin. Jack Biles, with reference to an attempt by Ainsworth to describe the tropical splendour of Jamaica (a country he never visited), in *Hilary St. Ives*, suggests that Ainsworth was at his best when depicting a familiar landscape and at his worst when he was not. 'The Falls of Ohiopyle' definitely belong in the latter category.[62] 'The Test of Affection' is that of a Scottish landowner who fakes his own death in order to test the fidelity of his prospective beneficiaries, and then scares them away by pretending to be his own ghost when they fail; the frame here is gothic, which is subverted by the realism of the macabre joke. Ironically then, the gothic form is transgressed by realism. Finally, 'The Wanderings of an Immortal' is the morally ambivalent confession of a man who sold his soul for eternal life to revenge himself upon his enemies, and now has an eternity to repent. In a particularly lurid passage, the narrator experiences the agony of drowning without dying and is forced to breathe sea water while yearning for the merciful oblivion now denied him by heaven:

> I was dashed about in the water till I was exhausted: I could no longer take my breath, and began to sink: I struggled hard to keep up, but the tempest subsided, and I was no longer borne up by the force of the waves. I descended – they were the most horrible moments of my life. I gasped for breath, but my mouth and throat were instantly filled with water, and the passage totally obstructed; the air confined in my lungs endeavoured in vain to force an outlet; I felt a tightness at the inside of my ears; the external pressure of the water on

---

[62] Biles, 81–2.

all sides of my body was very painful, and my eyes felt as if a cord were tied tightly round my brows. At last, by a dreadful convulsion of my whole body, the air was expelled through my windpipe, and forced its way through the water with a gurgling sound: – again the same sensations recurred – and again the same convulsion. Then I cursed the hour when I had obtained the fatal possession which hindered me from perishing. Ardently did I long for death to free me from the sufferings which I endured. In a short time I was exhausted, the convulsions became more frequent but less powerful, and I gradually lost all sense and feeling.[63]

This is another classic *Blackwood's* moment, taking, like 'The Spectre Bride', its inspiration from *Melmoth*. This is developed actually to include the sensations of an *undeath*, something Maturin never explores so graphically. Written about a year before 'The Half-Hangit', this description is obviously recycled in the later execution scene. There is unfortunately little else of much interest in this story. In common with Ainsworth's subsequent attempt at the subject of immortality, *Auriol, or The Elixir of Life*, there are some interesting ideas in play, but the rich concept of immortality is chronically underdeveloped, especially when compared to the similar stories of Godwin, Maturin and Lytton. Ainsworth's immortal simply does not wander enough, and this imperfect clone of *Melmoth* is certainly not in the same league as 'The Spectre Bride'. There are also three sea stories. The melodramatic 'The Englisher's Story' is told to the framing narrator by a transient who once left his love to go to sea, only to discover too late that his best friend on board was in fact the girl he left behind in disguise:

The barbarian lifted his sword to strike me; when my friend, whom I had not seen during the action, sprang between us, and received the stroke which was meant for me. I caught him as he fell; but that dying shriek – that last expiring glance – that soft pressure – told me all: – it was Eleanor![64]

In 'The Mutiny' a passenger awakes to the awful realisation that he is the last person left alive on the ship; while in 'The Sea Spirit' the ghost of a mutineer is forced to re-enact endlessly his death by drowning at the hands of his captain's wife, driven insane at witnessing the death of her husband, in what is probably the

---

[63] Ainsworth, 'The Wanderings of an Immortal', *December Tales*, 141.
[64] Ainsworth, 'The Englisher's Story', *December Tales*, 63.

most interesting piece in the entire collection, and which will be considered in detail at the conclusion of this present section.

The narrative of social transgression that would later so scandalise Ainsworth's contemporaries is already strongly spoken in these early stories. *December Tales* is Ainsworth's manifesto of the marvellous, a commitment to the language of the darkly fantastic at the beginning of his literary career, and seemingly a commitment to what Rosemary Jackson has described as 'all that is not said, all that is unsayable, through realistic forms',[65] while actually exploiting realist description to increase the horror. Inspiration, then, came to the author first via the dying embers of what he described in 'Recollections' as 'the romances of horrors' (the eighteenth century gothic romance), which he then combined and confronted with explicit and disturbing realism.[66]

On a similar, subversive trajectory the author's later fictionalised affinity with Catholicism, present in *Rookwood* (1834), *Guy Fawkes* (1841), and his Jacobite novels, most notably *James II* (1848), *Boscobel* (1872), *The Manchester Rebels* (1873) and *Preston Fight* (1875), which led to the 'prevalent belief that Ainsworth was himself a member of the Old Faith'[67] as Ellis put it, can also be traced to this manifesto, immediately indicated by the epigraph from Tichborne. 'I am sometimes almost inclined to regret the dissolution of the monasteries', he writes in 'Recollections IV', continuing in a carefully qualified way that might justify his biographer's assertion that: 'he lived and died a member of the Church of England',[68] to explain that his interest lies with the imaginative freedom that Catholicism seems to offer, not with the doctrine itself:

> This is, however, but the mere outstraying of imagination, which judgement admits not the thought of. The re-establishment of papacy, the return of superstition, and of the long exploded infallibility and supreme power of the Vatican, is what no one could with patience contemplate.

---

[65] Rosemary Jackson, *Fantasy: The Literature of Subversion* (London: Routledge, 1981), 26.
[66] Ainsworth, 'Recollections', *December Tales*, 212.
[67] Ellis, vol. 2, 280.
[68] *Ibid.*

> Yet there are moments when sterner reason is subjugated to wild fancy, when the paths of probability are deserted, to ramble on and often to overstep the verge of possibility; when we seek no foundations for our speculations but our own chance ideas, and on so slight a bottom fear not to raise our vast and airy edifices. So it is with me. I am an inveterate castle builder; and splendid and beautiful, in my own estimation, at least, are the fäery scenes which rise to my imagination.[69]

Given the author's admiration for Mrs Radcliffe, it could be argued that he uses 'superstitious' Catholicism in much the same way as the great mistress of romance, as an Other in which mad monks and villainous, foreign aristocrats terrorise innocent young things in blatant opposition to English, Protestant and positivist superiority. But Ainsworth's Guy Fawkes is no Montoni, Schedoni or Marquis de Montalt, instead he is sympathetically portrayed as heroic, iconic and that most dangerous of things to the English elite: a Catholic martyr. Unlike Maturin, and indeed Scott, Ainsworth was not an intentionally political writer however; to the storyteller that he essentially was, Catholicism and Jacobitism were, in turn, magical and romantic, and represented a fantastic and chivalrous space that he chose, unlike Radcliffe, to ally to English history rather than to the safety of a fictionalised, medieval Europe. *December Tales* offers a clear statement of intent with regard to Ainsworth's much misunderstood theological ambiguity.

The confessional rhetoric of 'Mary Stukeley', the opening *December Tale*, is however firmly Protestant, allying it to James Hogg's *The Private Memoirs and Confessions of a Justified Sinner* (1824). It therefore leads not to absolution but to psychologically paralysing despair and may be, in part, a reflection of the tension between Ainsworth's early adoption of Jacobite and Tory principles despite a family background of strict Nonconformity and Whiggism. Ainsworth's mother's family, the Harrisons, had been intimately connected with the Nonconformists since the doctrine was established in Manchester in the late seventeenth century. As a child, he attended services at the Cross Street Chapel, the first

---

[69] Ainsworth, 'Recollections IV', *December Tales*, 216.

Nonconformist Chapel in Manchester (built in 1693), where his grandfather, the formidable Rev. Ralph Harrison, had once been a minister. 'Mary Stukeley' is also a narrative of sexual tension, guilt and desire, as the author, having already sacrificed a virgin to Satan in 'The Spectre Bride' and tackled the taboo surrounding death by hanging in 'The Half-Hangit', engages with the subject of polygamy.

The final line of the stanza that forms the epigraph, 'And now I live – and now my life is done!' can be read as a metaphor for the ultimate despair of Calvinist self-scrutiny, which Victor Sage has described as, 'The idea of being buried alive in your mind at the very height of happiness and confidence'.[70] The narrator and central protagonist of 'Mary Stukeley' is trapped in a ghastly living death of his own guilt, and his opening statement that: 'if ever individual was subject to the influence of a prevailing destiny … I am that one' is immediately over-written by his essentially Puritan conscience:

> But I have no wish to extenuate my faults or crimes, with the flimsy excuse that my actions were controlled by some unknown but powerfully operating cause, compelling me to pursue a pre-ordained course of existence: on the contrary, I am persuaded that such a doctrine is wholly inconsistent with the principles of religion, and subversive of morality: no; I feel – I know that I was free from the first to choose between good and evil.[71]

The Protestant conscience, being its own moral arbiter and thus having nowhere else to go, must ultimately be its own god or devil, its own heaven or hell; thus: 'my heart, once the habitation of the tenderest emotions' becomes 'a wilderness and place of burning sorrow'.

These superlatives of self-loathing preface a confession of sexual desire over bourgeois decorum and decency. On the eve of his marriage to the innocent and virtuous Mary Stukeley, the young man tells of how his passions were aroused by the sudden appearance of a mysterious woman in the woods, just as Robert Wringhim meets the mysterious Gil-Martin in Hogg's *Confessions*:

---

[70] Victor Sage, *Horror Fiction in the Protestant Tradition* (London: Macmillan, 1988), 76.
[71] Ainsworth, 'Mary Stukeley', *December Tales*, 2

> She was above the middle size, of a commanding appearance, and the most expressive countenance I think I ever beheld. She was not, perhaps, what many might call beautiful, but I never knew any one who possessed so much the power of interesting at a first look. Her face was rather pale, but the features were striking, and her dark eye threw a vivid intelligence over their expression. Her black hair was curled in ringlets that clustered about her temples, and one lock waved down upon a beautifully shaped neck.[72]

This is the language of sexual attraction, the woman's unfastened hair further suggesting a wantonness that is apparently absent from an earlier, and much briefer description of Mary. The libertine possibilities of the stranger, and her status as a fallen woman of some kind are next developed, completely eclipsing the safer favours of Mary:

> There was perceivable too a lurking trace of the darker passions, which seemed to be disguised under an habitually assumed look of softness. By her dress, she appeared below the middle station of society; but there was a dignity, an ease in her manner, which repelled the idea. I certainly, for the time, forgot the subject of which I had been thinking – even Mary's image slipped from my mind.[73]

The stranger trips, affording the opportunity of not only a meeting but of physical contact. This creates in the young man an arousal which he describes in terms which are sexually sublime, being both sensual and frightening, potentially overwhelming and obviously new. Although engaged, this is his first real libidinous response to a woman, who had previously appeared to him collectively as merely 'females' which, given the agrarian setting, makes them sound like cattle:

> I offered her my arm, which, after some excuses and apologies she accepted. I really cannot tell how it was, but I felt a strange emotion at being thus situated. I was pleased – (I certainly ought not then to have been pleased, at least peculiarly pleased, by the society of any woman but one) – I said I was pleased, but it was a pleasure mixed with something like fear. There was something unaccountable about her, at least I thought so, which prevented me

---

[72] *Ibid.*, 8.
[73] *Ibid.*

from feeling so at ease as I had always been with other females ... I seemed to be in a dream – a dream, the awakening from which has been terrible.[74]

The confession must by definition be retrospective, a later self commenting upon the immediate actions and experiences of an earlier, but the narrator here still relives the excitement of that initial encounter with a certain amount of pleasure, however much he attempts to justify himself by appeal to an increasingly unstable emotional state: 'It may be mentioned, as an instance of my absence of mind whilst in her company, that I forgot to think, far less to inquire, where we were going.' It is as if a battle is going on between mind and body, and the intellect is losing. As the narrator's state becomes increasingly autonomic, the natural surroundings produce a sensuous epiphany in a lengthy passage which could easily lie at the mid-point of a pastoral scale which has the poetry of Wordsworth on one axis and the prose of D.H. Lawrence on the other. The scene is sticky with sexual metaphors:

> The earth sank in a kind of natural basin, the sides of which were covered with the highest green, and enamelled with the loveliest of flowers: harebells, daisies ... and innumerable others, of all colours, gushed out in profusion. Water-lilies waved their graceful heads on the brink of a spring that bubbled from the bottom of the spot, and oozing away through the long grass and weeds which impeded its progress, trickled down its narrow channel with almost imperceptible murmurings.[75]

The wood becomes enchanted, the man bewitched, and his original fiancée an irritation:

> The magic of the spot ... the perfume of the air, the witching hour, joined with a strange feeling of inquietude, the cause of which I feared to search into, overpowered my senses and unhinged my faculties. A thought of Mary intruded itself on me, for the first time: I felt it an intrusion, and strove to banish it.[76]

This remarkable scene now reaches its climax:

---

[74] *Ibid.*, 9–10.
[75] *Ibid.*, 11.
[76] *Ibid.*

Meanwhile my companion had remained silent … plucking a flower from the ground, she offered it to me. I snatched at it: I caught her hand in mine; she smiled, and I was at her feet![77]

This moment of release is also the moment of the fall. They are observed: 'I was startled by the approach of a footstep. I looked up, and to my confusion, beheld the brother of Mary.' Already enemies, lover and voyeur argue and a duel is arranged. Suffering at the prospect of either dying by the hand of, or killing, his future brother-in-law and, worse, from the guilty yet defensive reflection that: 'I had been seduced', the narrator's situation degenerates further when he is told by his seductress that Stukeley is dead and that he is wanted for the murder. She gives him a horse and some money and sends him to a safe house in the city.

The scene now shifts to 'a small, dirty, uncomfortable house' in London, where the young man and the woman, who now 'desires to be called Eliza', hide out, chaperoned, somewhat intriguingly, by a working class couple. At this juncture the real murderer of Mary's brother is not known, although both hint that they suspect the other. She says, 'Whether you are guilty or not, you know best' while he: 'could scarcely think that accident alone had produced the meeting which had led to such important consequences'. Her motives in shielding him are unclear, and his feelings towards her as an object of physical attraction (the cause of much of his present grief) and his deliverer, are ambivalent in the extreme. Spiritually, he retains his love of Mary, who is now unattainable; he remains, however, fascinated by the enigmatic Eliza:

There certainly was something in her that excited not mere interest: it was not admiration, for she was rather to be feared than admired; it was something which powerfully attracted my thoughts towards, and kept her idea almost continually in view … Her behaviour was contrary to my expectation, particularly delicate, and seemingly that of a woman accustomed to the higher ranks of society. Let it not be imagined that any affection for her existed in my breast: all feelings of that nature were swallowed up in the attachment which, although hopeless, I still nourished for Mary.[78]

---

[77] *Ibid.*
[78] *Ibid.*, 18–19.

Again, the image of the fallen woman is evoked. The implications unspoken in placing a middle class woman in a working class, and therefore debased, environment sexualise Eliza in a way that must, by social convention, be denied the chaste betrothed, so rightly named Mary.

This unhealthy relationship is inevitably brought to a crisis by the intervention of external forces, the arrival of the law, which cause a violent outburst of emotion from the hitherto restrained Eliza:

> 'No, no ... it must not be so. I cannot lose you thus. I love you: promise to me that I shall be your wife, and I will save you.' 'No, never: I will perish first!' was my answer; for I could not bear the thought of ruining, by one blow, all my hopes of being united to Mary. The officers were approaching the door. 'Decide', said my companion; 'in a moment it will be too late.' The thought of my situation, of the ignominious death to which I should probably be doomed, rushed into my mind. I shuddered at the prospect, and, almost fainting with agitation, I promised.[79]

Just like the episode in the wood, there is a building, rhythmic intensity in the narrative. The drama of escape is then succeeded by a rather embarrassed silence, like the awkwardness following sex between strangers. Alone now in a cellar:

> We sat down, and for sometime continued silent, and without looking at each other. At last, I turned my eyes towards her. She looked at me with a fixed and steady gaze, as if to pierce into the recesses of my soul. She rose; she advanced to me – 'Do you remember your promise?'[80]

Blackmail appears imminent, but instead Eliza appears to shift from her predatory role towards a noble one, although her motives remain ambivalent having already shown in the forest that she is intellectually independent and able to manipulate psychologically through her conversation:

> Her discourse was interesting, fluent and animated, perhaps too much so, for it was interspersed with remarks whose general truth and pungency scarcely atoned for their freedom and boldness, which I did not altogether admire: perhaps she perceived this, for she changed the style of her conversation, and I began to listen to her with considerable delight.[81]

---

[79] *Ibid.*, 21.
[80] *Ibid.*
[81] *Ibid.*, 9.

86

Again, one is reminded of the smooth-talking, empathic Gil-Martin who is, of course, the devil. When the object of her obsessive affections replies that he does indeed remember his promise, adding that he is 'ready to fulfil it', she responds with the impassioned cry:

> 'Think not that I am so vile a one; that, though a wretched and erring woman, I am so swallowed up in selfishness; that I have lost all feeling; that, though I love and avow it to you, I would make you mine, by compelling you to sacrifice all that is dear to you.' Her voice faltered; she turned away: in a moment after, collecting herself, she added, 'I release you from your promise.' She sank upon a chair, and wept.[82]

Whether this is a genuine change of heart, or a performance worthy of the Old Vic is left unclear. It does however achieve what must be considered to be the desired result as far as Eliza is concerned, if not also that of the narrator and his audience, because he is compelled to surrender by his own, conventional moral code:

> I was now placed in a situation most embarrassing to me … Was I to consider myself as released from my engagement, and inflict misery upon one who had watched over me, and taken so deep an interest in my fate? … To be the husband of Mary seemed almost out of reach of possibility. I walked up to Eliza; I took her hand. It is useless to relate our conversation. We were married.[83]

The erotic excitement of this situation is furthered enhanced by the following reflection that: 'I was married, to whom? strange as it may appear, I never knew.' Wracked with doubts the young man may have been, yet 'Eliza was a woman, certainly of very superior talents'. With a terrible irony, of course, the real murderer of Mary's brother is apprehended three days after this marriage.

So far, the narrative may have tested social boundaries but it has yet actually to transgress. The breach occurs when the narrator returns home to claim his property after four months of apparently pleasant married life. Once more he is tempted, and once more he falls:

---

[82] *Ibid.*, 22.
[83] *Ibid.*

It was a little past sunset when I passed the residence of Mary ... I fastened my horse to the stump of an old tree, and sprang over the wall. I was surprised by a faint shriek. I turned round; in a moment I held Mary in my arms.[84]

Again, the physical thrill of the moment overcomes reason after an internal struggle where both states temporarily coexist before passion prevails:

With what mingled feelings I pressed her to my breast! Joy, almost amounting to rapture, at again clasping the object of my affection; sorrow, shame, and disappointment embittered the meeting ... Why should I delay to complete my narration? – I loved her. Some months passed over, and we were married.[85]

And so morality fractures and the narrator's inward journey towards isolation and despair truly begins. The cause of this major moral lapse, the narrator's own unmediated desire, remains to him other and unknowable:

I know not what it was that thus far blunted the stings of conscience; but after this second marriage, I was miserable. In vain I found myself beloved and esteemed by all around me. I could not esteem: I could not do otherwise than hate myself ... my spirits sunk; I was haunted by fearful visions; and I was weary of my existence. Mary perceived it, and inquired anxiously into the cause of it. I evaded her questions for a considerable time; at last, I confessed the whole to her.[86]

But the confession of a Protestant can receive no absolution: 'From that moment on her health declined.'

Mary dies and the elemental Eliza has disappeared as suddenly as she appeared. The bigamist is left trapped within his own conscience, an outcast in an irredeemable agony of despair. Nothing will silence this guilt; even relating his story in the compulsive manner of the Ancient Mariner will achieve nothing:

I have long been a wanderer; I have sought for rest, but in vain; the burning sting of remorse has rankled in my breast, and life has long been a burden to me ... Perhaps it might have been as well if oblivion had been suffered to fall over the events contained in this imperfect narrative, instead of adding another to the already countless records of human follies, and of human crimes: but it may serve to shew the evil effects which ensue from the first false step. They cannot be foretold, and are irremediable ... I have been loved, and now I am

---

[84] *Ibid.*, 26.
[85] *Ibid.*, 26.
[86] *Ibid.*, 27.

unknown and uncared for. I had friends, and am desolate. I have striven to bury my sorrow in the whirl of giddy pleasure; but pleasure has lost its excitement, and is succeeded by languor and disappointment … apathy and despair are all that I can expect.[87]

This pessimistic closure concludes the confession, and the confessor's own existence, not with a bang but a whimper: 'She [Eliza] will, with him, be forgotten.' This third person exit makes the narrator so isolated that he has finally even detached from his self. The moral of the story of course restores social normality, *I am telling you so that you may avoid a similar fate*, which superficially renders 'Mary Stukeley' a cautionary tale of uncontrolled passions, while also being at once both an exploration of the destructive nature of the Protestant and internalised conscience, and an erotic fantasy where the male hero gets to have sex with Justine *and* Juliette.

The final story of *December Tales*, 'The Sea Spirit',[88] is a traveller's tale worthy of Kipling or Conrad, and which demonstrates a maturity of style absent from the melodramatic nautical hokum of the other sea stories in the collection. Although the gothic was the favourite form of early English melodrama, the legacy of the recent wars with France ensured that patriotic, military tales of land and sea soon found easy purchase upon the popular stage, the combination of xenophobic nationalism and the public idolisation of soldiers and sailors being easily translatable to the melodramatic absolutes of hero and villain, good versus evil. While borrowing from this form to a certain extent (which was hugely popular and relatively fresh in the early 1820s), Ainsworth is much more interested in hydrophobia than xenophobia and for him the sea is a terrible and isolating force; this is a factor in both 'The Mutiny' and 'The Wanderings of an Immortal', while 'The Englisher's Story' is a more straightforward use of melodrama. In 'The Sea Spirit', the elemental mystery of the ocean drives the tale, in the form of an elegantly framed ghost story both set and told at sea.

---

[87] *Ibid.*, 28.
[88] The last of Ainsworth's contributions to *Arliss's*, originally entitled 'The Lady Sprite' *Arliss's*, IX, 1822.

As is the case with so many of Ainsworth's stories this one begins with a storm, and the passengers and crew of an unnamed ship on an unnamed ocean are forced to take to the boats on the opening page. The unidentified narrator, presumably a passenger, shifts his narrative to the captain's lifeboat. Provisions are running dangerously low and the survivors are starving, and the narrative flirts with the possibility of breaking the ultimate taboo of cannibalism:

> Our provisions were exhausted, and famine stared us in the face. We chewed the soft leather of our shoes, to deaden the sense of hunger, for every morsel of food had been consumed. One of our number died. He was to be thrown over into the sea. Two sailors laid hold of the body to perform that last sad office to it. A sudden thought seemed to seize their minds; they hesitated and looked around. It was dreadful; no one spoke, yet every one knew what was meant. The sailors laid the body down; some horrid feeling seemed to agitate every breast, but it could not burst forth in words. It was the deep silence of every one in the boat, the motion of the eye, a certain pervading feeling, which told each man why the body was again placed in the boat, instead of its being committed to its watery grave.[89]

Time stands still, the storm, still raging, fades. This silent tension is broken by the reassertion of moral authority. The Captain speaks, the storm returns and the spell is lifted. This story is not to be told:

> At last the captain spoke; but his voice could scarce be heard, amid the raging of the contending elements. 'Why is not the body thrown into the sea?' he said; 'will ye keep him here to rot and decay? or do you wish to satisfy your hunger on the carcass of your fellow?' He laid hold of the body, and speaking to a sailor, they lifted it over the side of the boat, and it disappeared.[90]

After this uncharacteristic but highly effective moment of suspense on the part of the author, the survivors sight an island and are, for the present, saved. Both island and surrounding ocean are portrayed as a sublime landscape, which dehumanises and demonises the shipwrecked sailors, their camp fire turning the sea the colour of blood:

> The scene in the evening, when the mists began to gather around, was highly picturesque. The flame rose in high and curling flashes, threw its red glare over

---

[89] Ainsworth, 'The Sea Spirit', *December Tales*, 154.
[90] *Ibid.*

the island, and blazed against the rocks. As it increased, it was reflected on the waves, and extended in a long red blaze over the water. My companions, as they moved about in the light, which shewed more plainly their hard and deep marked features, seemed like some strange and fearful beings, performing their unhallowed rites.[91]

The scene eerily set, the unhallowed rites do indeed summon a demon, as a terrified sailor runs into the camp exclaiming, 'I have seen a ghost!'

'Sailors', notes the narrator, 'are generally superstitious', but this point is raised not to explain the reported uncanny event in rational terms, but to heighten the atmosphere of panic growing in the camp. As before: 'the captain only preserved his composure unmoved', and it is he who, if not actually offering an alternative explanation, rejects the possibility of ghosts and monsters. Nevertheless the witness insists that, while beach-combing on a secluded part of the island as night fell:

Here, as he was picking up some shell fish, which lay at his feet, his attention was engaged by a slight noise, and looking up, he perceived, to his horror, the figure of a man, which seemed to skim along the surface of the water, and was followed by a female form who pursued him, and whom he strove, but in vain, to avoid. The woman overtook him, and with a tremendous laugh, plunged him into the waves. In a moment after, the apparition disappeared, and he saw it no more.[92]

When this vision is related, even the Captain 'seemed inwardly troubled', establishing a secondary mystery. After a nervous night and another day spent scavenging, the Captain unexpectedly breaks his silence and, as night once again draws in, he begins to tell his story while his men huddle around the camp fire and control of the narrative is passed over to him, like Marlow in Conrad's *Heart of Darkness*:

'When I was a cabin boy on board the Thunderproof ', said the captain, who, as orator, was stationed in the centre of the assembly, 'a plot was concerted by the greater part of the crew, to murder the captain and take possession of the vessel. I, with several others who were unconcerned in the scheme, knew nothing of it till the moment of its execution. We were suddenly seized and

---

[91] *Ibid.*, 156–7.
[92] *Ibid.*, 157–8.

pinioned; and the captain, after being severely wounded, was thrown overboard. His wife was in the ship, and hearing the noise, came on deck.'

'The villain who had concerted the plot, caught her in his arms; she struggled, and escaping his grasp, ran to the ship's side, where stumbling, she was again seized. Perceiving herself in the wretch's power, she desisted from her endeavours to free herself; and he, deceived by her apparent submission, relaxed his hold. At this moment she caught him in her grasp, and with a violent effort, sprang over the ship's side, dragging the ruffian along with her. We heard them fall into the water; we heard the shrill and heart-rending scream of her victim, as he received his well merited punishment. We were afterwards unbound; perhaps the villains considered us too few and too insignificant to excite alarm among them. They did not long enjoy the fruits of their crimes. The vessel was wrecked, and I and two others alone escaped; and since that time, the seas near that spot have been considered as haunted by the spirits of the victims and the murderers. Doubtless, it was near this island that the events took place.'[93]

Having little choice, their Captain having been returned by fate to the scene of a childhood horror along with his crew, the sailors wait and watch. The narrative is returned to the original teller, who waits in suspense with the rest:

Hour after hour passed; but we neither saw nor heard any thing to justify our fears. The disagreeableness of the situation made the time seem much longer than it was in reality. We began to grow uneasy of waiting for spirits, and some spoke of giving up the watch. Still we delayed, when, on the surface of the ocean, far off, a dim light appeared. Certainly it would be highly indecorous in me to speak aught reflecting on the courage of British sailors; but, nathless, I will venture to affirm, that the hair of every individual stood in a more upright and porcupine position than they were wont to do. The appearance presently assumed a more definite form; it seemed the likeness of a woman, and we perceived, with feelings by no means pleasant, that it approached the shore. A second figure was perceived in the act of avoiding the first. It fled towards the shore, and was pursued with incredible speed by the other. It had almost reached the shore, when it was overtaken by the female form. She seized on the hair of his head, dragged him round, and with a laugh, that curdled the blood in my veins, seemingly plunged her victim in the waves, and disappeared. My companions were petrified with terror, and the captain lay senseless on the ground. At last we regained some degree of self-possession, and raising the captain, with much difficulty restored him to the use of his faculties. But the impression made upon him by the scene was so strong, that it was a considerable time before he perfectly recovered from the effects of it. He

---

[93] *Ibid.*, 161–2.

declared that he knew the features of the figures as well as he knew any one living.[94]

Having witnessed this eternally recurrent cycle of vengeance and punishment, the shipwrecked sailors decide to leave the cursed island and take their chances on the open sea. They are rescued, but the narrator concludes that he will not tempt fate twice by taking to sea again.

This excellent, unassuming little ghost story is an example of what Ainsworth was capable of in terms of control and originality when he didn't let his influences run away with his text, avoiding in this case the excesses of gothic and nautical melodrama. The framing narrative complements the heart of the tale, the Captain's anecdote, and the roles of the two tellers interchange subtly in terms of both narrative device and character agency as the stern, rational captain who stops the unholy act of cannibalism and makes light of the possibility of ghosts, finally chooses to tell his own story, and then falls into a state of shock when his supposition about the haunted island is confirmed. At this stage, the original narrator maintains a level of plausibility by his complicity in the vision, the admission of his own fear and the unconvincing attempt to mitigate this by appeal to the assumed bravery of British sailors, acting in mediation between the inner space of the Captain's mind and the outer world of the witnesses. 'The Sea Spirit' is the Captain's story, the first narrative voice is therefore free to establish the mysterious mood and scene which the sometimes violent, sometimes eerily calm, ocean setting offers. Within this frame the Captain, a powerful authority figure, is forced to regress and confront a terrible experience from his past when he was young, helpless and at the beginning of his seafaring career, a cabin boy being the lowliest rank on the ship. This tale also functions as a metaphoric parable about a sailor's fear of death by drowning, while also engaging on a deeper level with the unknown, uncontrollable power of the sea itself, so central to British military and economic power and supposedly under their command; their arrogance, or naivety, shown in the naming of the ship *Thunderproof*, which was wrecked in a

[94] *Ibid.*, 162–4.

storm regardless. The Captain may be able to order his men to let the body fall and quite possibly starve, but he is as powerless to control the sea as, when still a child, he was forced to witness a mutiny. The elemental force of the ocean becomes the elemental force of the supernatural, a 'Twilight Zone' which temporarily suspends the natural and quantifiable so that (from the epigraph): 'Heaven's music, which is order, seems unstrung.' The framing narrator tells his tale retrospectively, from the stability of an English drawing room, but he is now left with the unwanted knowledge that this stability is illusory, and even though he concludes that: 'none of us wish to tempt like dangers', he, like the Captain, can never really be free of the horror he has witnessed. He too has travelled too far and touched the Heart of Darkness.

With an already characteristic flamboyance, Ainsworth could not resist some valedictory remarks in a L'envoi to *December Tales*, concluding that:

> I feel a kind of reluctance to leave this volume, trifling and insignificant as it is, without a shake of the hand, and a parting 'good-bye'. The fondness of an author for his works is indeed excessive, and it is not without feelings of regret that he lays down his pen, after adding the finishing stroke to his production. His chance of fame is slight indeed. Longevity is denied to his labours. The philosopher, politician, divine, or scholar, may endure for ages. What has been well said, and established in the walks of science, needs not repetition, and is preserved in the works of its author. But, with the writer of amusing volumes, it fares differently. New novelties spring up; to be read, he must have allurements of style; and as style rapidly changes, his writings please no longer. Farewell then to these (at least) harmless amusements of my solitary hours. That they amuse his readers, is the highest ambition of the writer.[95]

As well as demonstrating a grasp of popular fashion that would uncannily reflect the fate of his own literary reputation in the years to come, while also stating, as he often did in later life, that he wrote to entertain rather than edify, this typically youthful piece of ostentation betrays a genuine affection for this, Ainsworth's second book, which was not carried over into maturity. When a bibliography of the author's work was being compiled by Crossley for a civic banquet in his honour towards the end of his life, Ainsworth wrote specifically requesting that

---

[95] Ainsworth, L'envoi, *December Tales*, 230.

Sir John Chiverton should be omitted.[96] His *Poems, December Tales* and *Auriol* were also absent from this list, the author choosing publicly to begin his literary career with the publication of *Rookwood* in 1834. Given the often supernatural, not to mention gruesome, nature of his vast back catalogue of historical novels, I assume that his intention was based on simple embarrassment rather than an intentional rejection of his gothic roots. *December Tales* was not reprinted, and Ainsworth did not produce many more short stories after this period, pursuing instead (after a failed attempt at publishing in the late 1820s) the more lucrative form of the serial romance. These juvenilia do however offer an important insight into Ainsworth's influences and some unrealised potential hinted at, for example, in the style of 'The Sea Spirit', but abandoned in favour of a much louder narrative voice and an increasing (financially necessary) allegiance to the successful formula of the historical romance. Collectively, this early body of work represents Ainsworth's literary apprenticeship, and he would not have subsequently arrived at the gates of Rookwood Place and the Bloody Tower without first acquainting himself fully with the techniques of the gothic, the melodrama and the sensational magazine story.

In many standard literary histories,[97] the gothic novel is presented as a genre inaugurated by Horace Walpole's *The Castle of Otranto* (1765), and which flourished, particularly in the work of Radcliffe and Lewis, in the 1790s before effectively dying out after *Frankenstein* in the early 1820s, with Maturin's *Melmoth the Wanderer* (1820) generally cited as the last significant gothic novel, the clichéd, repetitive and rather silly form by then very fair game for Austen's satire, *Northanger Abbey* (1818). Needless to say, as Chris Baldick points out in his introduction to the Oxford edition of *Melmoth*, Maturin's masterpiece was not the last of anything: 'Gothic fiction', he continues, 'lingered on in James Hogg's

---

[96] See Appendix A.

[97] The current Penguin *Dictionary of Literary Terms and Literary Theory* describes the gothic novel as, 'A type of romance very popular from the 1760s onwards until the 1820s.' ed. J.A. Cuddon (London, Penguin: 1991). This chronology endorses the cover notes to the ever-popular Penguin collection, *Three Gothic Novels*, ed. Peter Fairclough (London: Penguin, 1968).

Private Memoirs and Confessions of a Justified Sinner (1824) and soon revived in the work of Poe.'[98] Ainsworth's short fiction, written not exactly in the manner of the eighteenth century gothic romance, yet not precisely in the *Blackwood's* style either is, as always with the work of this author, somewhere in the middle. As we shall see, elements of the second wave of gothic fiction, the nineteenth century style from, let us say, Poe in the late 1830s to Bram Stoker's *Dracula* in 1897, are incubated in Ainsworth's novels of the 1830s and 40s, where the codes of the gothic and the melodrama so prevalent in his earliest work are refined and then imposed upon the Victorian discourse of history.

III. The first novel: *Sir John Chiverton*, 1826

Less than a year after the publication of *December Tales* (which apparently passed without notice into almost immediate obscurity), Ainsworth's pleasant life of literary dalliance, dilettantism and dandyism was rudely interrupted by the sudden and unexpected death of his father, aged 46, on June 20 1824. The eldest son of Thomas Ainsworth suddenly found himself the heir to the senior partnership in the legal firm of Ainsworth, Crossley and Sudlow, a role for which he was totally unprepared, unqualified and generally unsuited. Despite having always been appalled by the prospect of a career in law, Ainsworth rose to the challenge of his new responsibilities as head of the family business and belatedly applied himself to the study of the law, moving to London at the end of the year to complete his legal training. He took with him the manuscript of an incomplete novel, written in collaboration with a friend from the Manchester Free Grammar School, John Partington Aston. Aston (1805–82) was the son of a Manchester liquor merchant. He attended Manchester Free Grammar School in the same year as Ainsworth, later clerking for Thomas Ainsworth. He became Ainsworth's closest friend in Manchester during the Summer of 1822 while Crossley was working in London.

---

[98] Chris Baldick, introduction, *Melmoth the Wanderer* by Charles Maturin, ed. Douglas Grant (1820 Oxford: Oxford UP, 1989).

They collaborated on several juvenile literary projects (of which Ainsworth appears to have been the more enthusiastic of the two), culminating in the novel of *Sir John Chiverton* (1826). Unlike Ainsworth, Aston preferred to pursue a successful legal career and there appears to have been no contact between them after 1828 as Ainsworth began to establish himself in London.

Having already corresponded at length with Charles Lamb, Ainsworth was now able to meet him face to face. Through his friendship with Lamb, Ainsworth was introduced to the literary society of London, meeting among others Mary Shelley, Henry Colburn and his hero Leigh Hunt;[99] he was also able to develop the friendship with Scott's son-in-law Lockhart tentatively begun in Edinburgh a couple of years previously. Crossley's family also lived in London, and Ainsworth politely shared his time between the Crossley household and the gatherings at Colebrooke Cottage. His letters home suggest that the Crossleys attempted to moderate his renewed enthusiasm for the literary lifestyle by constantly reminding him of his professional responsibilities. They didn't have much hope against Elia and his friends, and were rather suspicious of Ainsworth after he attempted to seduce one of their housemaids. In a series of letters written to Crossley around Christmas 1824, Ainsworth, reading *Harriette Wilson's Memoirs*, describes his affection for this 'Cockney Aphrodite':

> A lovely girl, short, plump, taper-waisted, and dark-eyed – i' faith a very goodly appearance. You know dark eyes have always been my bane, and these were truly beautiful for a girl 'in her line' – bright, large, and laughing, and so full of kindness that, as Elkington says, it were cruel to disappoint them. Well, on Sunday last I slipped out of the room when your father and some more of his old cronies were at their wine, and got hold of this little girl. She promised to meet me the following evening, and kept her word – but now comes the serious part of the joke. In addition to the little frisky one before mentioned, your father has a cursed superannuated old cook, who being too old for any enjoyment herself, has determined to destroy that of others. This damned old bitch by some means got to hear of it, and communicated the pleasing

---

[99] 'When we were at school reading *The Indicator* ... we used to think that if we could ever write essays or verses like Leigh Hunt, we should have reached the utmost height of our ambition.' Ainsworth, quoted from Ellis, vol. 1, 75.

intelligence to your father and Master George, [Crossley's younger brother] with whom I am presently at issue.[100]

Nevertheless, Ainsworth did somehow manage to pass the bar in February 1826, just before his twenty-first birthday.

As an antidote to the tedium of Chambers, Ainsworth indulged his pleasure for the Opera.[101] This pursuit brought him into the company of the flamboyant lessee of the King's Theatre opera house in the Haymarket, John Ebers, also librarian of the Old Bond Street Library, publisher and father of two charming daughters. The two men became friends and Ainsworth was soon writing for Eber's magazine *The Literary Souvenir*, as well as contributing a political pamphlet to Eber's catalogue entitled *Considerations on the best means of affording Immediate Relief to the Operative Classes in the Manufacturing Districts* dedicated to Robert Peel and calling for the repeal of the Corn Laws. This sounds more intriguing than it is in actuality. The argument begins powerfully by suggesting that the horrors experienced by the crowd at Peterloo (which was not far from the Ainsworth's family home in King's Street, Manchester) were 'less operative than the certainty of present and painful suffering', experienced by the urban poor every day, but the author quickly abandons the radical call for state intervention he appears initially to be suggesting in favour of rather insipid suggestions involving charity.[102]

Ebers, ever the opportunist, was also interested in the manuscript of *Sir John Chiverton*, and he began 'puffing it up' in *The Literary Souvenir* while Ainsworth was still revising the text. The law would have to do without him for a while.

There has been some dispute over the authorship of *Sir John Chiverton*. In later life Ainsworth omitted the novel from his own bibliography, while Aston

---

[100] Ainsworth, letter to Crossley, December 1824.
[101] 'You ask me whether we have any characters in Chambers. I answer none. They are all dull, dreary, plodding, unintellectual fellows.' Ainsworth, letter to Crossley, December 1824.
[102] Ainsworth, *Considerations on the best means of affording Immediate Relief to the Operative Classes in the Manufacturing Districts* (London: John Ebers, 1826).

privately claimed sole authorship until Ainsworth's death, whereupon he published his assertion in *The Times*.[103] It seems highly unlikely however that Ainsworth did not play a significant part in the writing, apparent from his surviving correspondence with Aston and the style and content of the text. At the time of publication, the novel was attributed solely to the pen of Ainsworth in very favourable reviews in *The Literary Gazette*, *The Literary Magnet* and *The New Monthly*, but it is most likely that the final text was a revised version of an original project jointly written with Aston some time in 1824. It is difficult to imagine Aston as the sole author of *Sir John Chiverton* (he never wrote another book), and their correspondence leaves the very strong impression that Aston invariably failed to fulfil magazine commitments jointly agreed upon, leaving Ainsworth to do the work; as their subsequent careers demonstrate, Aston preferred the stability of a lawyer's lifestyle and Ainsworth's juvenile literary schemes were more often than not a distraction from his legal studies.

Stylistically, there is much in the text that fits Ainsworth's later *modus operandi*: the use of a historic building for setting, the detail applied to costume, the gothic scenario, the melodramatic plot (orbiting around an unlawful disinheritance) and the use of graphic violence. Equally, there are sections that do not suit his method at all, such as the theological dialogue between Scymel and Wayward in Chapter Four, which is probably attributable to Aston.[104] When Lady Jane defends her religious convictions in the debate with the Catholic bishop Gardiner in Book II, Chapter Ten of *The Tower of London* by Ainsworth for example, her argument is entirely rhetorical; the philosophical arguments of Scymel in *Sir John Chiverton* are much more sophisticated, and indeed radical, than Ainsworth's. Scymel is also an atheist, while Ainsworth's fiction is always concerned with the tension between Protestant and Catholic, or even heaven and hell, and his characters never question basic Christian belief. There are, however,

---

[103] See Appendix A for a detailed account of the debate and the evidence surrounding the authorship of *Sir John Chiverton*.

[104] Ainsworth, private journal, September 1830, quoted from Ellis, vol. 1, 205.

strong hints that Ainsworth himself was an atheist contained in his only known journal, a record of a tour of Italy in 1830 held in the private collection in New York. He writes, for example, of the church of St John Lateran that: 'A man need have active faith to believe all this, and I confess I am somewhat sceptical.' Whether he is referring to the Roman Church or Christianity as a whole is unclear. My belief is that *Sir John Chiverton* was a genuinely collaborative work which was revised for publication by Ainsworth, who certainly had the experience (and the drive), having already published two books and made numerous contributions to numerous magazines.

Whether written all, in part or even not at all by Ainsworth, the publication of *Sir John Chiverton* did bring the young author to the attention of Sir Walter Scott, who was shown the novel by Lockhart. Scott wrote on *Sir John Chiverton* in his journal and, largely as a result of these private comments on the novel, many a critical comparison between the works of these two very different authors has been made from 1826 to date. As Ainsworth was a writer ultimately known for his historical fiction, such comparisons have been unavoidable, in addition to the obvious fact that all early nineteenth century novelists wrote under the shadow of the Enchanter of the North who was, as Hazlitt wrote: 'undoubtedly the most popular writer of the age'.[105] The commonly held critical belief regarding Ainsworth's first novel is that it is a simple attempt to copy Scott, without any real understanding of the techniques of historical fiction supposedly created by the author of *Waverley*. This intelligence is based not so much upon a reading of the actual novel (which, like its two predecessors, went out of print almost immediately and is nowadays extremely rare), but on the oft-quoted reference to it in Scott's journal. Ainsworth was well-liked by Lockhart, who had moved to London at the end of 1825 to take up the editorship of *The Quarterly Review*, and it appears that he was impressed enough by *Sir John Chiverton* to pass a copy on to his formidable father-in-law. Ainsworth was subsequently presented to Scott at

---

[105] William Hazlitt, *The Spirit of the Age: or, Contemporary Portraits* (1825 London: Collins, 1969), 96.

an engagement at the Lockharts' home at Pall Mall, and his hero later contributed an original poem, *The Bonnets of Bonnie Dundee*, to his annual *The Christmas Box* in 1828. Two concurrent entries in Scott's journal however leave no doubt as to his true feelings towards the young novelist, and to his rising generation as a whole:

> *October 17*. Read over *Sir John Chiverton* and *Brambletye House*[106] – novels in what I may surely claim as the stile
>
> 'Which I was born to introduce –
> Refined it first, and showd its use.'
>
> They are both clever books; one in imitation of the days of chivalry; the other dated in the time of the Civil Wars, and introducing historical characters. I read both with great interest during the journey.
>
> I am something like Captain Bobadil[107] who trained up a hundred gentlemen to fight very nearly, if not altogether, as well as myself. And so far I am convinced of this, that I believe were I to publish *Canongate Chronicles*[108] without my name (*nomme de guerre,* I mean) the event would be a corollary to the fable of the peasant who made the real pig squeak against the imitator, while the sapient audience hissed the poor grunter as if inferior to the biped in his own language. The peasant could, indeed, confute the long-eared multitude by showing piggy; but were I to fail as a knight with a white and maiden shield, and then vindicate my claim to attention by putting 'By the Author of *Waverley*' in the title, my good friend *Publicum* would defend itself by stating I had tilted so ill, that my course had not the least resemblance to my former doings, when indisputably I bore away the garland. Therefore I am as firmly and resolutely determined that I will tilt under my own cognizance. The hazard, indeed, remains of being beaten. But there is a prejudice (not an undue one neither) in favour of original patentee; and Joe Manton's[109] name has borne out many a sorry gun-barrel. More of this to-morrow. [110]

---

[106] Written by Horace Smith in 1826. Scott had previously refused to read this because it was set in the same period as *Woodstock*. Ainsworth later described Smith as 'as dull as ditchwater' in a letter to Crossley, April 21 1830.

[107] Ben Jonson, *Every Man in his Humour* (1616). Bobadil was a soldier who claimed to have survived many great battles and presented himself as an expert military strategist. The Captain's Jonsonian humour is his arrogance, and he is ultimately revealed to be a coward and a drunken braggart at the end of the play.

[108] *Chronicles of the Canongate* marks the beginning of the period where Scott resolves to write himself out of debt after the financial collapse of Ballantyne and Co. in 1825–6.

[109] Joe Manton developed the breech-loading rifle much beloved by the British Armed Forces. He lost much money in litigation, and died penniless at the age of 69. The company which bears his name still exists as one of Britain's leading arms manufacturers. Scott evokes Manton as a much imitated original. The symbolism of the gun here is intriguing.

[110] Scott, *The Journal of Sir Walter Scott*, 213–15.

This is an elaborate piece of self-irony, in which Scott himself becomes a potential victim because of his disguised authorship of the *Waverley* novels, which he did not publicly acknowledge as his own until the following year. This is also a somewhat sweeping set of assertions, taking us down the route that concludes, as Sir John Marriot wrote for example: 'The historical novels written before 1814 may be regarded as preparing the way for the advent of Scott. Those that have been written since look back to him with filial piety.'[111] Scott did not invent the historical novel, he rather continued to develop a mode of fiction already well established in literary tradition. What Scott brought to the model left by writers such as Thomas Nashe, John Leland and, most significantly, Daniel Defoe, was a greater balance of fictional narrative and antiquarian detail even if, despite many claims to the contrary by critics and champions alike, his historical accuracy was often no more genuine than the sporran of Rob Roy proudly on display with numerous other relics at Abbotsford.[112] One cannot dispute that Scott's influence on the English novel is enormous, but he was not the sole Logos, despite his attempts to assimilate every other branch of literature to his own. S.M. Ellis, George J. Worth and Andrew Sanders endorse Scott's belief that *Sir John Chiverton* was very derivative of his own work; Ellis characteristically interprets this as a compliment while Sanders reads the journal entries as a statement that: 'Scott was generally depressed by the poor quality of the work of those who attempted to imitate him.'[113] I am not convinced. Scott tended to have an adversarial approach to his contemporaries as a whole; in his introduction to *St Ronan's Well* for example, he refers to Jane Austen as one of his 'formidable competitors'[114] and seems, with regard to his first obvious followers,[115] Ainsworth

---

[111] Sir John Marriot, *English History in English Fiction*, (London: Blackie and Son, 1941), 9.

[112] See Hugh Trevor-Roper's excellent essay, 'The Invention of Tradition: The Highland Tradition of Scotland', *The Invention of Tradition*, ed. Eric Hobsbawm and Terence Ranger (Cambridge: Cambridge UP, 1989), 15–41.

[113] Sanders, 34.

[114] Scott, introduction, *St Ronan's Well* (1824), Waverley Novels.

[115] Although Scott was to have many followers, Ainsworth and Smith predate them by at least three years. George Croly's *Salathiel* and G.P.R. James's *Richlieu* did not appear until 1829, while Lytton's *Last Days of Pompeii* has the same vintage as *Rookwood*, 1834.

and Smith, to be taking a certain amount of pleasure from the sincerest form of flattery and finding reassurance in the fact that the standard hardly matches his own. Despite this, his concluding remarks betray the fact that he feels slightly threatened. Because of his financial problems, he cannot afford to be overtaken in the marketplace he created by writers he believes to be stealing his ideas, hence the reference to Manton, who made little money from his original patent for the breech-loading rifle.

Apparently still preoccupied with these concerns, Scott returns to his 'imitators' the following day:

October 18. – I take up again my remarks on imitations. I am sure I mean the gentlemen no wrong by calling them so, and heartily wish they had followd a better model; but it serves to show me *veluti in speculo*[116] my own errors, or, if you will, those of the *style*. One advantage, I think, I still have over all of them. They may do their fooling with better grace; but I, like Sir Andrew Aguecheek,[117] do it more natural. They have read old books and consult antiquarian collections to get their information; I write because I have long since read such works, and possess, thanks to a strong memory, the information which they have to seek for. This leads to a dragging-in historical details by head and shoulders, so that the interest of the main piece is lost in minute descriptions of events which do not effect its progress. Perhaps I have sind [sic] in this way myself – indeed, I am but too conscious of having considered the plot only as what Bayes calls the means of bringing in fine things; so that in respect to the descriptions, it resembled the string of the showman's box, which he pulls to show in succession Kings, Queens, the Battle of Waterloo, Bonaparte at Saint Helena, Newmarket Races, and White-headed Bob floored by Jemmy from town. All this I may have done, but I have repented of it; and in my better efforts, while I conducted my story through the agency of historical personages and by connecting it with historical incidents, I have endeavoured to weave them pretty closely together, and in future I will study this more. Must not let the background eclipse the principal figures – the frame overpower the picture.

Another thing in my favour is, that my contemporaries steal too openly. Mr. Smith has inserted in *Brambletye House* whole pages from Defoe's *Fire and Plague of London*.

---

[116] 'Just as in a mirror'.

[117] William Shakespeare, *Twelfth Night* (c.1600). Like the allusion to Captain Bobadil, this is a strange character with which to compare oneself. Sir Andrew is a rather pathetic figure, a 'foolish knight' who fails to see that his drinking partner Sir Toby Belch is relieving him of his fortune and who is, like Captain Bobadil, shown to be a blustering coward.

> 'Steal! Foh! A fico for the phrase –
> Convey, the wise it call!'[118]

When *I convey* an incident or so, I am [at] as much pains to avoid detection as if the offence could be indicated in literal fact at the Old Bailey.

But leaving this, hard pressed as I am by these imitators, who must put the thing out of fashion at last, I consider, like a fox at his last shifts, whether there be a way to dodge them, some new device to throw them off, and have a mile or two of free ground, while I have legs and wind left to use it. There is one way to give novelty: to depend for success on the interest of a well-contrived story. But woe's me! That requires thought, consideration, – the writing out a regular plan or plot – above all the adhering to [one] – which I can never do, for the ideas arise as I write, and bear such a disproportioned extent to that which each occupied at the first concoction, that (cocksnowns!) I shall never be able to take the trouble; and yet to make the world stare, and gain a new march ahead of them all!!! Well, something we still will do.

> 'Liberty's in every blow;
> Let us do or die!'[119]

The author of *Waverley* is definitely worried, and this entire entry is an attempt at personal reassurance by virtue of undermining the opposition. The private insecurities apparently reflected in the previous, brittle yet witty comparison between himself and Jonson's Captain Bobadil and Shakespeare's Sir Andrew Aguecheek are suddenly replaced by an appeal to the great Scottish hero Robert the Bruce, the warrior king who drove Edward II from the field at Bannockburn. Scott concludes his 'remarks on imitations' with this morale-building reminder of the Bruce's address to the troops before battle, a martial prayer to the defeat of the new wave of English pretenders to his throne of letters. What is therefore often taken uncritically as an essay on the historical novel is, in point of fact, more of an exercise in the restoration of the great man's own self-confidence.

George J. Worth restores a certain amount of objectivity to the critical debate by noting that although Ainsworth was influenced greatly by Scott, he was 'by no means his slavish imitator.'[120] He does, nonetheless, consider *Sir John*

---

[118] Adapted from Shakespeare, *The Merry Wives of Windsor* (1602): '"Convey," the wise it call. "Steal"? foh! a fico for the phrase!' I.iii 32.
[119] From Bruce's address at Bannockburn (1314).
[120] Worth, 27.

Chiverton to be a historical novel rather than a gothic. Worth here at least puts a more positive spin on Andrew Sanders's method of distinguishing Ainsworth from his contemporaries, the latter suggesting that: 'unlike most other Victorian writers, he had learnt very little indeed from Sir Walter Scott' and that, 'Scott was perhaps fortunate not to have lived to witness Ainsworth's later popular success and esteem.'[121] Sanders also assumes *Sir John Chiverton* to be a historical novel, and a very poor one at that. No-one, from Scott onwards, actually returns to the original text (even Ellis is more preoccupied with Scott's commentary and the disputed authorship than with the actual novel), which is historical only inasmuch as *The Castle of Otranto* or, indeed, Ainsworth's previous short stories could be classed as such. *Sir John Chiverton* is without question a gothic novel and, unlike its literary predecessors, it is firmly located in an English setting.

Sir John Chiverton is set shortly after the Third Crusade (1189–92). Sir John Chiverton has taken possession of the family seat at Chiverton Hall in Lancashire by declaring the rightful owner by inheritance, his sister Ellice, to be mad; he is assisted in his scheme by the atheist physician Dr Walter Scymel and a mute Moor bodyguard named Mahmood Bali. Sir John plans to marry Isabel, the daughter of the powerful knight Sir Gamelyn de Vancouver, to repair his ailing fortunes. Only Ellice's former suitor, Reginald Prestwyche, lately returned from the holy lands, knows the truth and can thwart Sir John and save Ellice and Isabel. Reginald contacts Ellice in a secret cave near the hall where he is hiding, disguised as a peasant, and they attempt to warn Sir Gamelyn that his future son-in-law is not all he seems. Sir John and Scymel allay Sir Gamelyn's misgivings and Reginald is imprisoned in the dungeons of Chiverton Hall. Ellice frees Reginald on the night of the wedding feast of Sir John and Isabel, but is accidentally killed in a fall while fleeing her brother. Unaware of this tragic turn of events, Reginald gatecrashes the banquet disguised as a minstrel just in time to witness the assassinations of Sir John and his accomplice Scymel, who are both poisoned by Mahmood Bali for no adequately explored reason beyond the

---

[121] Sanders, 34.

audience's known prejudice against Islam. Mahmood Bali escapes and the novel ends with a *tableau vivant* of horrified guests gazing at the corpses of Chiverton and Scymel.

There are some superficial resemblances to the style of Scott here, but they are either so underdeveloped as to be completely incompetent (as most critics would have it), or are merely peripheral in terms of overall authorial intention. In particular, there are a few similarities of plot and characterisation between *Sir John Chiverton* and *Kenilworth* (1821). Both Robert Dudley and Sir John Chiverton are leading complicated double lives, publicly noble and privately scheming, involving elaborate strategies of control over innocent maidens; these aristocratic villains are aided by ruthless and highly intelligent henchmen (Richard Varney and Walter Scymel), who are in fact pursuing their own evil agendas. The virtuous heroes Tressilian and Prestwyche (each an ex-suitor of the damsel in deadly distress) fail to save their heroines, and Amy Robsart and Ellice Chiverton are both killed in fulls. These plots are equally the stuff of tragic melodrama, the difference being that Scott's is an interpretation of a factual event (the mysterious death of the first wife of Elizabeth's favourite the Earl of Leicester in 1560), while Ainsworth and Aston's work has no such pretensions towards historical characterisations whereas, in a reversal of Lukácsian theory, *Kenilworth* lists among its central characters, Elizabeth I, Sir Walter Ralegh, Shakespeare, Marlowe, Sidney and Spenser.

Like Scott's novel, *Sir John Chiverton* also has a tremendous sense of *place* and is consequently the first in a long lineage of novels by Ainsworth which took their setting, inspiration and even titles from historic buildings, the best known examples being *The Tower of London* (1840), *Old St. Paul's* (1841) and *Windsor Castle* (1843). But before the scene is set, there is a brief yet still rather leaden attempt to affect the narrative voice of a melancholy antiquarian:

> There is a degree of pleasure, not unmingled with sad and melancholy reflection, in comparing with the records that remain to us of the manners and private life of our distant progenitors, the mouldering and dilapidated remnants

of their habitations, which time and the wasting hand of violence have suffered to survive; the monuments of a people, whose habits, long become obsolete, owe their existence, even in remembrance, to the minute and laborious zeal of the chronologers of the past, and the excursive researcher of antiquarian curiosity. It is gratifying to have somewhat real and tangible to connect us with days and scenes, on which we are wont to look back with the sensations of the landscape gazer, who straining his glances through the gathering twilight, sees in the dim, though it may be beautiful outlines of the indistinct prospect, much to awaken, but little to satisfy his feelings of inquisitive admiration; vainly endeavouring to distinguish, until he almost doubts the reality of the blended mass of wood, and mountains, and gleaming lake, which growing every moment more dim and shapeless, leave it to the power of fantasy to adorn, and fill up the traces so faintly supplied by observation.[122]

The intention here is certainly to sound like Scott, and this mimicry continues as the framing narrative of the worldly-wise historian segues into a long description of Chiverton Hall where the glorious past of the once great building is read in the ruins of the present site:

How different is, alas! the present, though, even yet beautiful appearance of the same spot. The rich and profuse banquets, of which the noble dining hall was once the scene, have given way to the scanty board of poverty; – the songs and harpings of minstrels, the gallant conversation of brilliant companies, – the bright sallies of wit, and tender conceits, which so often those walls have listened to, have faded away, as unsubstantiated and transient as the breath on which they rose.[123]

This of course recall's Scott's conclusion to his description of the majesty of Kenilworth Castle:

We cannot but add, that of this lordly palace, where princes feasted and heroes fought, now in the bloody earnest of storm and siege, and now in the games of chivalry, where beauty dealt the prize which valour won, all is now desolate. The bed of the lake is but a rushy swamp; and the massive ruins of the Castle only serve to show what their splendour once was, and to impress on the musing visitor the transitory value of human possessions, and the happiness of those who enjoy a humble lot in virtuous contentment.[124]

---

[122] Ainsworth and J.P. Aston, *Sir John Chiverton* (London: John Ebers, 1826), 3–4.
[123] *Ibid.*, 12–13.
[124] Scott, *Kenilworth* (1821), Waverley Novels, 139.

In addition to this characteristic, Ozymandiasian musing on the inevitability of change, Scott is such a perfectionist in detailing the original layout of the castle that an architectural plan is appended to the volume. This is again matched in *Sir John Chiverton* by an exact description of the lay of the hall, which was based on an actual building just as, later, Rookwood Place would more than strongly resemble Cuckfield Place, Sussex. In what for Scott would be an unpardonable anachronism, Chiverton Hall was closely modelled upon Hulme Hall, being one of the old 'black and white' Tudor halls of Manchester, the ruins of which were still a popular beauty spot when Ainsworth and Aston were children but were all but gone by the end of the century. In a late nineteenth century chronicle of the Lancashire landscape, the author laments that of the proliferation of old halls still present a century previously:

> Those which stood in the way of the fast-striding bricks and mortar of the eighteenth century, and the beginning of the nineteenth, if not gone entirely, have been utterly sacrificed ... Hulme Hall, which stood upon a rise of the red sandstone rock close to the Irwell, overlooking the great ford to Ordsall – once the seat of the loyal and generous Prestwich family – is remembered by plenty of the living as the point aimed for in summer evenings by those who loved the sight of hedges covered with the white bells of Galatea's lovely convolvulus. Workshops now cover the ground.[125]

The historical exactitude of Scott is therefore already under assault by placing a Tudor building in a very perfunctorily sketched twelfth century setting which moves the *mise en scène* into the timeless dimension of fairytale. To this end, rather than continuing after the manner of Scott, the historical introduction is soon over-written by the discourse of the gothic and the sublime:

> It is with Chiverton Hall, however, in its former state, that our present concern chiefly lies, as it stood some two centuries back. Rising from the summit of a rock, that sprung abruptly from the spreading waters of the river, by which it was guarded on the west, the building approached so near the brink of the precipice, as to afford space only for a narrow foot-path. From the opposite side of the river, the edifice presented its most irregular, though not less beautiful aspect. A projecting semi-oval turret, the lower part of which was used as a chapel, and in the days of papal dominion, had been consecrated to

---

[125] Leo H. Grindon, *Lancashire – Brief Historical and Descriptive Notes* (London, 1882), 72.

the services of the Roman ritual, advanced beyond the buildings that extended from it on either side.[126]

From contemporary accounts of Hulme Hall itself this is a fair description, but the emphasis is no longer upon architectural verisimilitude but on a sense of gothic menace, echoing the famous description of Emily's first view of Udolpho, where the castle seems to grow out of the mountain on which it stands as twilight descends. Chiverton Hall is also dangerously high and the footpath precarious, and we are also reminded that the England of *Sir John Chiverton* is pre-Reformation, Catholic and therefore the realm of the Other. Scott would of course never tolerate this. As he explained in the introductory chapter of *Waverley*:

> Had I, for example, announced in my frontispiece, 'Waverley, a Tale of other Days', must not every novel-reader have anticipated a castle scarce less than that of Udolpho, of which the eastern wing had been long uninhabited, and the keys either lost or consigned to the care of some aged butler or housekeeper, whose trembling steps, about the middle of the second volume, were doomed to guide the hero, or heroine, to the ruinous precincts?[127]

This first novel is, in effect, a precursor to the break-through novel, *Rookwood*, as an attempt to reimpose the codes of the gothic upon an English, historical setting in a way that Scott would never consider, and thought that he had ruled out.

The 'dragging-in [of] historical details by head and shoulders' bemoaned by Scott are therefore not really an issue here, as history has already become abstract and, like the drama that this work essentially is, *Sir John Chiverton* is largely character-driven. The only exception to this is the detailed description of a rather kinky set of carved oak panels in Sir John's chambers, which were in reality the only survivors of Hulme Hall having been removed to Worsley Hall (then the seat of one Lord Ellesmere), and which are gothic in the more literal sense of ornament and design:

> The apartment into which he entered, was a spacious and handsome one. Its windows occupying the entire range of one side of the quadrangle, looked ... into the garden, and the light, partially intercepted by the foliage without, took

---

[126] Ainsworth and Aston, 7.
[127] Scott, *Waverley* (1814), Waverley Novels, 3.

a still deeper tinge, as passing through the richly stained panes, it fell upon the dark wainscoting of the chamber. This was oak, black with age, and loaded with the most elaborate carvings, in which the invention of the artist had been exerted, to produce the quaintest and most grotesque images. Some of these represented demons, some human figures, and not a few were borrowed from the characters usually personated in the sports and mummeries, then in vogue, among the lower classes of the people. An aim in the ludicrous was visible in the grouping of the figures, nor were ideas bordering upon profane scrupulously avoided, in the associations intended to be awakened by these representations. The figure of the mermaid, the symbol of the family, was lavishly displayed, not only among these carvings, but in the ornaments of the cornice, where the ambiguous sea nymph appeared, dressing the streaming locks which flowed in rich gilding around her shoulders.[128]

This I think has more to do with establishing atmosphere than anything else, although the authors' final remark that 'In execution, these representations were superior to those commonly met with at the time, and were probably the work of a German artist', adds a painful note of unintentionally crashing bathos and definitely qualifies as 'dragging-in'. Whether by accident or design, the interior decor reflects the disturbed duality of the male occupants of the castle. Sir John's person, although ostensibly handsome, displays elements of darker emotions which are ever destabilising his otherwise good looks; although he portrays himself a gentleman, he is, not so secretly, a bounder:

The personage who, among this group, must instantly have been distinguished as the principal, as well from the deference paid to him, as from his manner and demeanour, was a man of apparently not more than thirty years of age, and of an aspect, which, at first sight, seemed noble and prepossessing. In stature, he was somewhat above the middle size; well shaped, and rather strong set. His features, though handsome – almost beautiful, were to close examination scarcely attractive, wearing an expression of strong, but suppressed passion. Clusters of dark hair strayed from beneath his jewelled cap, which was adorned by a heron's plume fastened by a clasp of gold. His eyes were bright and black; too much so to be pleasing, and the same sinister cast which dwelt in his features, was communicated to their glance.[129]

As his many detractors would later find so amusing, Ainsworth (for we can assume from his later style that this is he) cannot resist adding a quick description

---

[128] Ainsworth and Aston, 49–50.
[129] *Ibid.*, 14.

of the knight's rich apparel, a tendency that would eventually become a trademark:

> He wore a dress of the fashion generally adopted by the superior classes of the time, consisting of a doublet of dark satin, slashed with salmon coloured silk, fitting tight to his body, and joined to hose of the same materials, puffed out according to the prevailing mode. – His boots were of blue Spanish leather, and a short cloak of deep purple velvet, richly embroidered, and fastened by a massy golden clasp, hung from his shoulders, and completed the ordinary articles of his wearing apparel. – In addition to these, his hands were now clothed with hawking gloves, and his closed fist supported a lordly gerfalcon, completely attired with her embossed hood and knotted jesses, on the varvels attached to which was stamped the figure of a mermaid, the armorial bearing of the family.[130]

The symbolism of the mermaid is of course significant. Like his family crest, Sir John's beauty is treacherous and his intentions deadly. The controlling metaphor at work here, in the portrayal of Sir John, the legend of the mermaid and framed by the figures carved on the walls (representing a mixture of demons and some human beings), is of a physical or moral state somewhere between man and monster.

This is most intensely realised in the figure of the mute, Moor bodyguard, Mahmood Bali, who is first introduced in the chamber of the black oak carvings while Sir John paces about 'evidently under the dominion of violent and conflicting passions':

> At the farther end of the apartment, stood a dark and swarthy Moor, whose ungainly figure was clothed in a costume, partaking in some degree of both the European and Asiatic fashion; his turban and vest of scarlet cloth, belonging to the latter, but the remainder of his dress was in the style of the other retainers of the hall. His arms were folded on his breast; his looks cast down; and from his fixed and motionless demeanour, he might have been mistaken for a statue, had it not been for an occasional glance, when, without changing the position of his head, he threw a disturbed look after Chiverton – a look in which a triumphing hatred was so blended with an almost unearthly sneer, communicating to his unmoved features an expression of feelings unallied with humanity, as to startle even those who were accustomed to it, and fully to justify the suspicions which had taken root among many of the inmates of the

---

[130] *Ibid.*, 15.

hall, that the devil and Mahmood Bali, if not identically the same, were near relations at least.[131]

Sir John's accomplices are both foreigners, Scymel is a Jew, but the Moor's racial Otherness is represented as uncanny. The blatant, if unsurprising, Orientalist description strips him of human characteristics until he is seen as utterly demonic, the mixed cultural styles of his dress serving only to render his appearance more unreal (another image of the mermaid), while also serving to suggest that although his master may think he has his assassin under control he does not, as the look in the demon's eye confirms. We must take the term 'Moor' here as a basic Western stereotype meaning Muslim; the character of Mahmood Bali is presented as bestial (he doesn't even speak) rather than as a representative of a particular race or culture. We might also usefully recall here the embodiment of Western anxieties and cultural myths of the generic Eastern Other in the figure of 'The Malay' in De Quincey's *Confessions*: 'The Malay has been a fearful enemy for months. I have been every night through his means, transported into Asiatic scenes.'[132] The intimation is that he is a slave, captured by Chiverton during the Crusades, which is the only real explanation for his final action, when he ignores Prestwyche (who has been his target throughout the story at the order of his masters) and kills instead Chiverton and Scymel. He is so Other that his motives seem not to need explanation, and he is definitely the incarnation of absolute evil within the text; both Scymel and Sir John never really go too far, Sir John cannot bring himself to kill his sister which is why he declares her insane and Scymel is nearly persuaded to repent by the priest, Father Wayward. The Moor, on the other hand, is more like the eponymous character of *The Terminator* (1984), a ruthless, cold, killing machine who never gives up:

'If there be hatred on earth, deeper than imagination can present, it is mine, for – his name stifles me.' [Sir John tells Scymel in the oak chamber. The object of his hatred is Prestwyche.]

---

[131] *Ibid.*, 53.
[132] Thomas De Quincey, *Confessions of an English Opium Eater*, ed. Alethea Hayter (1821 London: Penguin, 1986), 108.

'If such be your feelings', replied Scymel, coolly, 'can an answer be necessary to you, ask Mahmood Bali – he will answer well, and quickly.'

As both the speakers turned their looks towards the Moor, and as Chiverton was about to repeat the question, Bali, without otherwise changing his posture, or varying the direction of his eyes, raised slightly the hand that grasped his dagger's hilt, until the weapon was drawn about an inch from its sheath, and relaxing his hold, suffered it to drop again into the scabbard. In doing this the metal of the hilt and the sheath struck, producing a slight noise. To the hint, so given, the lurid smile of the Moor served as a comment.[133]

The Moor, then, communicates through violence. His bejewelled dagger also signals his literary and demonic origins: both Medardus in Hoffmann's *Die Elixiere des Teufels* (translated into English in *Blackwood's* in 1824) and Hogg's Gil-Martin carry daggers.

Mahmood Bali's failure to hit Prestwyche with a crossbow bolt also leads to the most interesting episode in an otherwise pedestrian plot. When another henchman, Neil Jaggar, makes fun of him for his poor marksmanship, Mahmood Bali calmly and methodically kills him, taking care to make the death appear accidental. His dagger is the bait:

> [The Moor] ... walking to the edge of the rock, seemed busily engaged in examining and trying with his foot the stability of a large portion of the stone, severed by a narrow fissure from the body of which it originally formed a part. It hung over the waters, projecting beyond the level of the bank, but without any mark which, to an inexperienced eye could suggest its instability. The motions of the Moor were unobserved ... The Moor had walked to some distance, when Jaggar, having finished his communication to the physician, was stumbling away. In passing the spot where Mahmood had lately stood, the dagger of the latter lying, as if accidentally dropped, on the edge of the precipice, struck Neil's sight. The hilt of the weapon studded with gold and enamelled, was a strong temptation to the greedy covetousness of the wretch ... he stepped forward, and stretched out his hand to seize the weapon.

> But ere his fingers had yet closed upon the object of temptation, the uncertain foundation of his footsteps, swayed by his weight from its precarious balance, was precipitated from its bed, and lurching along with it the unhappy Jaggar, was lost in the river, whose waters it cast around in high and foaming sheets.

---

[133] Ainsworth and Aston, 58–9.

The physician and his companions, attracted by the plunge of the stone, and missing Jaggar, hurried down the rude steps ... the first object that presented itself to their eyes, was the mangled and disfigured corpse of Neil Jaggar, the lower extremities of his frame immersed in the water, the rest extended on the sand. The dagger of the Moor lay by him. The physician took it up, with something like a smile, but without any remark to his companions. They drew the body from the water, and extended it on the beach.[134]

This reminds us of the dangerous topography of the castle and the deadly nature of the Moor, while also dropping another hint as to the unspoken relationship which appears to exist between Mahmood Bali and the cynical Scymel, who regards the fatal misfortune of others as a source of personal entertainment. A minor feature, yet also worthy of note, is the sudden, unexpected violence of the moment, which strongly suggests the hand of Ainsworth and also demonstrates his typical use of surprise rather than suspense. Alfred Hitchcock's often told and widely quoted definition of the difference between 'suspense' and 'surprise' in film narrative is a useful referent here, and can be appropriated to explain the dividing line between Radcliffe's and Scott's version of the gothic (suspense), and that of Lewis and later Ainsworth (surprise):

There is a distinct difference between 'suspense' and 'surprise', and yet many pictures continually confuse the two. I'll explain what I mean.

We are now having a very innocent little chat. Let us suppose that there is a bomb underneath this table between us. Nothing happens, and then all of a sudden, 'Boom!' There is an explosion. The public is *surprised*, but prior to this surprise, it has seen an absolutely ordinary scene, of no special consequence. Now, let us take a *suspense* situation. The bomb is underneath the table and the public *knows* it, probably because they have seen the anarchist place it there. The public is *aware* that the bomb is going to explode at one o'clock and there is a clock in the decor. The public can see that it is a quarter to one. In these conditions this same innocuous conversation becomes fascinating because the public is participating in the scene. The audience is longing to warn the characters on the screen: 'You shouldn't be talking about such trivial matters. There's a bomb beneath you and it's about to explode!'

In the first case we have given the public fifteen seconds of *surprise* at the moment of the explosion. In the second we have provided them with fifteen minutes of *suspense*. The conclusion is that whenever possible the public must

---

[134] *Ibid.*, 179–82.

114

be informed. Except when the surprise is a twist, that is, when the unexpected ending is, in itself, the highlight of the story.[135]

Ainsworth will invariably detonate the bomb without warning. There then follows a fascinating dialogue between Dr Scymel and the local Priest and ally of Prestwyche, Father Wayward, conducted over the broken body:

> 'Unhappy wretch', said Wayward, as he contemplated the lifeless mass which lay at his feet ... 'I tremble to think of his fate.' The physician raised his eyes slowly from the object on which they had been fixed, until their line of vision encountered the priest's. 'His fate, say you master Wayward! what need of such inquiry? It lies before you, and may be read in the perishable clod on which corruption is already at work, tracing, though as yet invisibly, the characters of the decree. To redissolve into the elements – to return to the worthless materials from whence he sprung, is the short chapter of the fate of the dead.'

> 'I might think as you do', answered Wayward, 'did the volume seem to me to close with the chapter you speak of. Such, indeed, as you have said, is the fate of the body, corruption is the last scene of its history. But the spirit which quickened and directed, decay cannot triumph over, – it rose not from the elements, nor will return to them.'[136]

We are obviously supposed to side with Wayward's argument here, which is based on his faith over Scymel's 'boasted reason'. Scymel being doubly placed beyond the pale by the assumed cultural insularity and esoteric knowledge of the Jewish people and, further, by his clinical atheism, likening man to machine as did La Mettrie and de Sade which was still a very transgressive philosophical proposition for 1826. He is also following closely in the footsteps of the arch-schemer of *Kenilworth*, Richard Varney, who was: 'one of the few – the very few moral monsters, who contrive to lull to sleep the remorse of their own bosoms, and are drugged into moral insensibility by atheism, as men in extreme agony are lulled by opium',[137] Scymel, however, seems almost moved to repent of his wicked ways, before reaffirming his existential choice with the confidence of *der Übermensch*:

[135] Alfred Hitchcock, interviewed by François Truffaut. François Truffaut and Helen G. Scott, *Hitchcock*, 2nd edn (London: Paladin, 1986), 91.
[136] Ainsworth and Aston, 183.
[137] Scott, *Kenilworth*, 197.

'I grieve deeply that thou, with the time thou hast before thee, for thou art yet young, and with powers of no ordinary standard, shouldst be as the broken reed, or worthless bramble, rather than the stately cedar of the forest' [*Continues Father Wayward*] ... The physician delayed ere he replied. 'I do believe, Wayward, thou meanest me well, albeit I cannot now profit by such intention. Thou hast read me not wholly wrong, better than I deemed any might read me. There has been a time when – but 'tis idle to talk. The life that is before me is fixed; if as thou say'st man has a choice, I have chosen; whether ill or well, I care not – I am content.'[138]

Having moved beyond religion, his final statement of human freedom anticipates Nietzsche's metaphor of eternal recurrence: 'I willed it thus! So shall I will it!'[139] Anti-Semitism also dictates that it was the chief Jewish priests and elders who condemned Christ. By rejecting God, Scymel comes intriguingly close to becoming Him within the narrative, Sir John's schemes being in reality only part of a larger game being played out by Scymel seemingly by way of a moral experiment:

> Scymel leaned against the trunk of a gigantic elm, whose ambitious arms flung a deep shadow over the waters, and was lost in deep reverie.
>
> 'The issue', said he inwardly, 'of my experiment is near. I shall see how far, by pursuing a fixed course, by yielding to no obstacles, and what is more, to no fears, that success may be attained, which I have bitterly learnt the fabled virtue of bigots and fools cannot ensure ...'[140]

Scymel is much more the melodramatic villain than is Sir John, who plays, in Ainsworthian terms, Luke Rookwood to Scymel's Peter Bradley in *Rookwood* or Sir Rowland Trenchard to Jonathan Wild in *Jack Sheppard*. Behind most aristocratic despots in Ainsworth, there tends to be a bourgeois, in fact, controlling everything. Even Queen Mary is just another piece on the Spanish ambassador Simon Renard's board in *The Tower of London*.

---

[138] Ainsworth and Aston, 185.
[139] Friedrich Nietzsche, *Thus Spoke Zarathustra*, trans. R.J. Hollingdale (1885 London: Penguin, 1969), 216.
[140] Ainsworth and Aston, 226.

Ranged against these 'men of death'[141] are the melodramatic hero Reginald Prestwyche and the gothic heroine, Ellice Chiverton. (The 'good old man' is Sir Gamelyn, there is no 'comic man'.) Prestwyche, whose name suggests that he is of Saxon extraction (as well as being an archaic spelling of the family name of the residents of Hulme Hall), is a typical hero of melodrama, returning from abroad to find his fiancée disinherited and determined to save the day:

> 'Brother! do you call him?' exclaimed the youth, 'call him not – think him not a brother; he it was that feigned your death – he that detained my steps in distant lands – he that, to accomplish his own selfish views of ambition, wrests from you your inheritance, and would have made two faithful – they were once too happy hearts, Ellice, – the stepping stones to raise him in his course of darkness ... Alas, Ellice, your heart, pure in its simplicity, knows not how to suspect. The show of kindness dims your eyesight, and makes you blind to the heaviest wrongs. But a day of justice', added he, grasping suddenly the handle of his sword, 'a day will come when the deceiver shall meet his due; when the wrongs he has inflicted shall return on his own head with double weight.'[142]

In a touch that would be Pynchonesquely postmodern 150 years later, the two sworn enemies never actually cross swords.[143] George Jean Nathan defines such an archetype as, 'that character who displays spectacularly all the attributes of courage save forethought, intelligence and modesty',[144] which pretty much covers Prestwyche's case. Scymel also describes Prestwyche perfectly in such terms:

> '... report speaks him brave and well possessed of all becoming acquirements. But he is a rash, hot headed, and romantic dreamer: one that runs into danger for the sake of extricating himself; trusting to his foolish valour in exclusion of his judgement, and listening to explanation only when the mischief done is irreparable ... he can at times assume the appearance of coolness and deliberation, and has, in fact, a sort of mad sagacity, which enables him to come safely through adventures, which better men would have failed in, and wiser men would have left untried.'[145]

---

[141] *Ibid.*, 175.

[142] *Ibid.*, 38–40.

[143] I am thinking here of the eventual meeting of the sworn enemies and half-brothers Tchitcherine and Enzian in Thomas Pynchon's *Gravity's Rainbow* (1973), the author here subverting expectation by letting a central plot line unravel away into nothing at the conclusion of his narrative.

[144] George Jean Nathan, *Another Book on the Theatre* (New York: B. W. Huebsch, 1915), 311.

[145] Ainsworth and Aston, 213.

This is very true: Prestwyche survives the assassination attempts of Mahmood Bali by sheer luck and although apparently a master of disguise he is constantly wrong-footed by the opposition. It is Ellice who finally saves *him*, only to die herself during the rescue, at the point which the narrative abruptly shifts, as Ainsworth's plots so often do, from melodrama (where good will always triumph over evil, no matter how inept the former and wonderfully diabolical the latter) to tragedy. Ellice is, in fact, another 'Spectre Bride': 'Ellice having emerged from the cave, sprung wildly over up the path which Prestwyche had previously ascended. At the very turn, of which she had warned him, the foot of the unfortunate girl slipped. His name was on her lips as she fell. There was a deep sullen plunge.'[146]

The conclusion of *Sir John Chiverton* is as bleak as it is sudden. Prestwyche, unaware that Ellice is already dead, appears at the wedding banquet of Sir John and the lady Isabel disguised as a minstrel and singing a cryptic song that indicates to the groom that the game is up. But before either can draw his sword:

> The eyes of all the company, which had been turned towards the singer, were suddenly directed to Chiverton, and as suddenly averted from the appalling appearance that presented itself. The guests sprung to their feet, and gazed at each other without speaking. All was terror and confusion. Even the physician for a moment shuddered at the object before him: no one ventured to break the silence that prevailed; a silence interrupted only by the exuberant gaiety of the revellers without, that jarred harshly on the ears of the astonished and confounded assembly.[147]

As this point, Scymel realises that he has also been poisoned by the slave and dies with a sardonic smile of acceptance rather than frustration upon his contorted lips. Mahmood Bali escapes (another demonic trait), and the novel concludes with the sounds of merriment from the celebrations in the courtyard still ringing ironically in the ears of the horrified guests at the bridal. When a deal is struck with the devil, the devil will always turn on you.

---

[146] *Ibid.*, 271.
[147] *Ibid.*, 310.

118

Sir John Chiverton was obviously very hurriedly finished. Like the later work *Auriol*, which was dismissed by the author himself as 'merely a fragment of a Romance',[148] *Sir John Chiverton* is a frantic and eclectic collection of potentially interesting yet never quite fully developed ideas, which is in all probability why Ainsworth omitted both texts from the same bibliography of his work compiled for the Manchester Free Grammar School Register in 1869, and updated for the commemorative brochure given out at the Mayor's banquet in 1881. In this sense, it is appropriate not only chronologically but stylistically to include the novel in the group containing Ainsworth's early plays and short stories, which is really what it is, being at best a novella by contemporary standards. Its significance lies in its statements of difference from Scott, as well as its refusal to comply with *all* of the conventions of the gothic and the melodramatic. Although the supernatural devices often present in the short stories are absent from *Sir John Chiverton*, style and content place it firmly in a gothic space rather than the realm of Scott's model of the historical novel; a line of demarcation will become more important in my following chapter.

Nonetheless, after Lockhart published all the extracts from Scott's journal concerning *Sir John Chiverton* in his *Life of Scott* in 1838, Ainsworth (Lockhart made no mention of a second author) was forever remembered as an 'imitator' of Scott, to such an extent that even his obituary in *The Times* referred to Scott's journal entries on *Sir John Chiverton*. Yet in his choice of setting only, was Ainsworth purely a historical novelist.[149] George J. Worth wrote that: 'without the overwhelming example of Scott, Ainsworth would have written a different kind of fiction', adding that, 'Scott himself recognized *Sir John Chiverton*, Ainsworth's first sustained narrative, as derived from his own practice'.[150] This is rather glib, surely without the overwhelming example of Scott *everyone* would have written a

---

[148] Ainsworth, letter to Crossley, December 9 1869.
[149] Ainsworth rarely wrote about his own century; of his 43 novels only 6 have contemporary scenarios: *Mervyn Clitheroe* (1851), *Old Court* (1867), *Myddleton Pomfret* (1868), *Hilary St. Ives* (1870), *Chetwynd Calverley* (1876) and *Stanley Brereton* (1881).
[150] Worth, 27.

different kind of fiction. As we have seen from the *Arliss's* stories and plays and *December Tales*, Ainsworth's primary influences were gothic, a form that, in its original eighteenth century mode, relied upon Medieval European settings. To accept that his work mimics Scott is to necessarily therefore accept that the gothic romance was nothing more than, as Scott himself believed, a primitive form of the more artistically valid historical novel. *Sir John Chiverton* is therefore very possibly the first example in nineteenth century literature of the struggle to establish a new form of English gothic, which could escape the established clichés of the eighteenth century romance while also taking back the form from the model of the historical novel left by Scott. Although primitive in construction, *Sir John Chiverton* and Ainsworth's juvenilia as a whole contain much in terms of literary device which would define his unique, anomalous style of writing for decades to come.

The novelist Hugh Walpole offered a charming explanation of the reality of Scott's influence on Ainsworth. Although he addressed his remarks towards Ainsworth's later Victorian epics, Walpole's definition could be more appropriately applied to the first novel, written as it was by a much younger man:

> [Ainsworth] seized upon all the boyish toys from Scott's nursery – his armour, his male and female dolls, his spells and incantations, his ability to turn the nursery hearth-rug into a tiger and the nursery table into a fortress. Ainsworth indeed assembled diligently a grand collection of fancy-dress, with an especial taste for tinsel and red ink that ran like gore. He learnt from *Kenilworth* and *Waverley* and *Midlothian* the picturesque value of old historic buildings and, gazing round his nursery, caught so warm a glow of excitement from his collection of toys that his voice broke into shrill screams of narrative. He was never weary of his toy theatre and his own honest, thrilled determination to pile horror upon horror for the benefit of his nursery audience has still, after all these years, a sort of touching nature about it – never human nature – but we are pleased at his own pleasure and wish that, just for half an hour, we could be back in the nursery again, watch his manipulation of his little theatre and see the toy dramas – 'The Tower of London', 'Old St. Paul's', 'The Lancashire Witches'. But he made no discoveries, solved none of the problems.[151]

---

[151] Hugh Walpole, 'The historical novel in England since Sir Walter Scott', *Sir Walter Scott Today*, ed. H.J.C. Grierson (London: 1932), 166–7.

Walpole seems to be appropriately implying in part that Ainsworth's style anticipates the popular narratives of *The Boy's Own Paper*, which appeared in 1879. As Walpole concludes, Ainsworth's stories did not have, or pretend to have, the historical insight of Scott, but they did offer an alternative model which became surprisingly influential in nineteenth and twentieth century fiction, based upon a *romantic* reading of Scott. As we shall see, there is also always a sense of adventure in an Ainsworth narrative, an infectious trait that made him a household name in the 1830s and 40s, but with regard to Sir Walter Scott's version of the gothic tradition as merely a branch of the historical, *Sir John Chiverton* was simply a small skirmish – the real battle was joined when Ainsworth forsook the bar in favour of the pen forever eight years later, with the publication of the phenomenally successful novel of the gothic, the historic and the underworld, *Rookwood, A Romance.*

CHAPTER TWO

Fame and Infamy: *Rookwood, A Romance*, 1834[1]

I. Life in London: business, family and *Fraser's*, 1826–1834

It was arguably the influence of John Ebers as much as it was the encouragement of James Crossley and the fiction of the day that compelled Ainsworth to pursue a career in letters. Despite expressing very justifiable doubts about the financial stability of Ebers to his closest friends, both literary and legal (who were in complete agreement), Ainsworth became part of the family, marrying Frances 'Fanny' Ebers at Marylebone Parish Church on October 11 1826. This was a characteristically impetuous decision (his family and friends in Manchester were informed only two days before the event and none of them attended), Ainsworth having previously withdrawn his suit owing to an argument with Ebers over a dowry. He was right to be worried. Private correspondence between Ainsworth, Ebers and Crossley during this period held in the first volume of the Crossley papers (which S.M. Ellis omitted from his biography), shows that a settlement of £300.00 p.a. was agreed upon by Ebers to help support his daughter's family while his son-in-law established himself in business but that this was never paid, much to Ainsworth's perpetual resentment. Nevertheless, as the lessee's son-in-

---

[1] This chapter began life as a paper entitled, 'The Skeleton Hand: Ainsworth's *Rookwood* Resurrected' and was presented at the *Legacies of Walpole: The Gothic After Otranto* International Gothic Association Conference, St Mary's University College, Strawberry Hill, Twickenham, July 1997.

law, Ainsworth was closely connected with the affairs of the King's Theatre during his first few months of married life. This was the era of the Green Room, where the *beau monde* met to drink, network and be presented to the beautiful artistes. Pierce Egan's Tom and Jerry hang around the 'Greeny' at Drury Lane in his *Life in London*, which is by far the best description of the adventures of young bloods and old bucks produced during this period. Like Jerry Hawthorn's friendship with Corinthian Tom, Ainsworth's exposure to the company surrounding his flamboyant father-in-law facilitated the seamless entry of the 21 year old Mancunian into fashionable London society, a process already begun by Lamb and Lockhart. As Egan would put it:

> 'SEEING LIFE', was their object. To keep all sorts of company – to admire an accomplished mind, whenever they found it – to respect and follow notions of real gentility – and to select the most sensible and agreeable persons in society as their companions.[2]

Ebers held the theatre for the seasons 1821 to 1827; it was undoubtedly a glittering social institution under his extravagant regime and Ainsworth made some very useful contacts during his time there, his only real business sense manifested in the creation of 'deadheads' (people who enjoy privileges free of charge), who then publicly supported his new publishing venture by writing favourable notices in return for complimentary seats. Ainsworth's talent was always for social events rather than commerce.

Ainsworth was a terrible businessman. On the advice of Ebers, he abandoned his fledgling legal career and set up shop as a publisher and bookseller, raising capital by selling his share in the lucrative law firm established by his father in Manchester, of which he was the senior partner, confident, apparently, in the business acumen of his father-in-law, who was about to become bankrupt due to his disastrous management of the theatre. Financial certainty was exchanged for chance in a speculation to which neither father or son-in-law had the temperament

---

[2] Pierce Egan, *Life in London or The Day and Night Scenes of Jerry Hawthorn, ESQ. and his elegant friend Corinthian Tom in their Rambles and Sprees through the Metropolis* (1821 London: John Camden Hotten, 1869), 167.

to prosecute successfully. Ebers's circulating library at 27 Old Bond Street was partitioned and Ainsworth began trading on return from his honeymoon. For a while the business was moderately successful and it allowed the proprietor to continue mixing with many famous writers of the day which he enjoyed enormously. 'I am quite in the back parlour of literature',[3] Ainsworth wrote to Crossley on February 3 1827 and, in another letter dated March 12, he enthusiastically explains that:

> My literary acquaintances are become very extensive. Leigh Hunt and I are great friends. As a set-off to him I patronize Dr. Maginn, who is useful in the puffing department. [Charles] Ollier, is another of my cronies ... [George] Croly and I are hand in glove.[4]

The more influential of these gentlemen would have their names added to the free list at the opera. Henry Colburn, on the other hand, had 'warned me against publishing'.[5]

The following year saw the birth of the first of three daughters, Fanny, and the bankruptcy of the child's grandfather; at the end of Ebers's seven years at the theatre the family fortune was gone, his losses amounting to approximately £70,000. This was also a disaster for Ainsworth, as he had lent Ebers several thousand pounds which were never repaid.

Ainsworth intended his business to be of service to literature, cultivating a catalogue of authors whom he respected and whose work may have been rejected in other quarters as not fashionable enough to warrant publication, while innocently running the enterprise according to liberal and gentlemanly principles, always a recipe for disaster. The book that actually kept his family was *The French Cook* by Louis Eustache Ude (once the personal chef to Louis XVI).[6] There were, however, other hits, beginning with a popular annual entitled *Mayfair* which went to a second edition almost immediately in 1827; a second edition of

[3] Ainsworth, letter to Crossley, February 3 1827.
[4] Ainsworth, letter to Crossley, March 12 1827.
[5] Ainsworth, letter to Crossley, November 25 1826.
[6] See Ellis, vol. 1, 163.

Sir John Chiverton; a reprint of Coleridge's *Wallenstein*; *An Autumn in Greece* by Henry Lytton Bulwer; *Lyric Offerings* by Samuel Laman Blanchard; and *Seven Years of the King's Theatre*. The latter was supposedly written by Ebers but in fact ghosted by J.P. Aston, who was in London at the time to enter himself as an attorney and who invented nearly every anecdote. Ainsworth also launched the literary career of Caroline Norton, whose visits to Old Bond Street became so regular and pronounced that scandal was rumoured.[7] Norton was known to be unhappily married, and was writing to achieve financial independence. Ainsworth arranged the publication of her first collection of poetry, *The Sorrows of Rosalie* (1829), but it was actually published by Ebers, who had by that time taken over the business. Ainsworth edited the first edition of the new annual, *The Keepsake*, in 1828, and published his own, *The Christmas Box*, in the same year, which brought him once more into contact with Sir Walter Scott. Scott contributed his ghost story 'The Tapestried Chamber' to *The Keepsake* and the poem 'The Bonnets of Bonnie Dundee' to *The Christmas Box*. As a good friend of Lockhart (who was married to Scott's eldest daughter Sophia), Ainsworth had already met Scott at the Lockharts' family home in Pall Mall. On that occasion having just embarked upon his career in publishing, he was brave enough to ask Scott for a contribution to an annual he was planning. When Scott next visited London in 1828, the Lockharts and the Ainsworths were near neighbours at Sussex Place, Regent's Park so the young editor was able to thank Scott in person and take the opportunity to pay his agreed rate of 20 guineas; Scott's usual fee was somewhere in the region of £500. Scott thought this hilarious and gave the money to his granddaughter, Charlotte, who was playing in the room at the time, demonstrating, perhaps, exactly what he thought of Ainsworth, or *vice versa*.[8] Although not gifted with the thick skin, patience, attention to detail, or the financial sense he was born with, Ainsworth certainly had more front than Brighton.

[7] Caroline Elizabeth Sarah Norton (1808–1877), poet and novelist.
[8] See J.G. Lockhart, *Memoirs of the Life of Sir Walter Scott* (Edinburgh: Robert Cadell, 1838).

By the beginning of 1829 Ainsworth was already thoroughly sick of running a business. As Ellis wrote: 'This second edition of deserting his profession may appear to indicate instability of character, but the truth was his artistic temperament wholly unfitted him for a commercial career.'[9] Once more impetuous, or just downright careless, Ainsworth quickly off-loaded the business on his father-in-law without any real thought for his own legal protection.[10] A second daughter, Emily, was born that year and, despite toying with the idea of a literary project to raise some much-needed capital, Ainsworth resumed his legal practice in 1830, taking chambers at 12 Grafton Street. The first embryonic sign of *Rookwood* appears at this point, in a letter to Crossley where Ainsworth asks: 'Where shall I find a good account of funeral orations? – I don't mean ancient ones, but authentic middle-age speeches delivered over the dead. Do you know where there are any stories of Gipseys?'[11] A third child, Anne Blanche, was also born that year. The Bohemian lifestyle appeared to be over. Well, almost. 1830 also saw the inauguration of *Fraser's Magazine for Town and Country*, the brainchild of William Maginn and Hugh Fraser. With Maginn as the original editor, and Lockhart and Barry Cornwall immediately on board, their young friend from the days of the Old Bond Street bookshop was naturally invited to attend the literary club which formed itself around the premises at 215 Regent Street, being part council of war (against *Blackwood's*), part editorial committee and part Bacchanal. How much copy Ainsworth actually contributed to *Fraser's* is a matter of some doubt,[12] but then Count D'Orsay was a 'Fraserian' and he never contributed anything; as Ellen Moers explains, although many 'Fraserians' were not actively involved in determining the development of the magazine: 'all

---

[9] Ellis, vol. 1, 181.
[10] From his letters it would appear that Ebers owed £12,000 by 1831, of which Ainsworth never saw a penny.
[11] Ainsworth, letter to Crossley, May 1829.
[12] Because much of the material is unsigned, Ainsworth's only verifiable contributions during Maginn's editorship are the short story 'La Guglielmina of Milan', and three poems, 'The Wind and the Wave', 'St. Augustine and the Boy', and 'One Foot in the Stirrup'.

contributed something to its spirit'.[13] This arrangement was of course reciprocal. By 1831, Ainsworth was writing *Rookwood*.

In a preface added to *Rookwood* for the edition of 1849, Ainsworth describes in some detail the construction of his famous romance, omitting only the break in work between the winter of 1831 and the summer of 1833, when his life was effectively annexed by a chaotic hoard of legal, professional and financial problems brought about by his previous business relationship with John Ebers & Co.[14] Like *Sir John Chiverton*, the inspiration for the piece came initially from the gothic charge which the author associated with an ancient building:

> During a visit to Chesterfield, in the autumn of the year 1831, I first conceived the notion of writing this story. Wishing to describe, somewhat minutely, the trim gardens, the picturesque domains, the rook-haunted groves, the gloomy chambers, and gloomier galleries, of an ancient Hall with which I was acquainted. I resolved to attempt a story in the bygone style of Mrs. Radcliffe (which had always inexpressible charms for me), substituting an old English squire, an old English manorial residence, and an old English highwayman, for the Italian marchese, the castle, and the brigand of the great mistress of Romance.[15]

The 'ancient Hall' was Cuckfield Place, Sussex (once described by Shelley as looking 'like bits of Mrs. Radcliffe'), home of the Rev. William Sergison, a client from the Grafton Street practice who had become a close friend. There was also one Ambrose Rookwood among the Gunpowder Plotters of 1605, signalling that Ainsworth's House of Rookwood is one of England's old Roman Catholic families. The Chesterfield connection was the home of the widow of Ainsworth's

---

[13] Ellen Moers, *The Dandy, Brummell to Beerbohm* (New York: Viking, 1960), 190.
[14] Ainsworth had predicted these problems himself in a letter to Ebers written sometime before his marriage in 1826, when he says:
> The arrangement proposed between us can only be affected by your Bankruptcy and you ought to be aware whether your affairs are in such a state as to make such a situation probable. Should (which God forbid) such a thing take place it might be the means of rendering both your daughter and myself completely wretched, and I should certainly consider myself bound in conscience, although the property might be legally safe, to give it up to the Creditor.
This letter is contained in Crossley's papers in Manchester. As Crossley was by then Ainsworth's solicitor, it must have come into his possession during the running legal battle with Ebers. Ever a player, I believe Ebers passed it on himself using the above as proof that Ainsworth agreed to act as his guarantor.
[15] Ainsworth, preface, *Rookwood*.

cousin James, the formidable Mrs Eliza Touchet. Ainsworth's exact relationship with Mrs Touchet is not clear, although she does share her Christian name with the mysterious lover from 'Mary Stukeley'. Ellis wrote of her that she was: 'a talented woman, of brilliant conversational powers, and although fifteen years older than Ainsworth, had very considerable influence over him to the end of his life'.[16] Ainsworth's own references to Eliza during this period are cryptic. Having arranged to visit Crossley alone in Manchester from the beginning of August 1831, Ainsworth got no further than Chesterfield, writing to his friend by way of apology:

> You must excuse me a day or two longer. I meant to have been with you on Tuesday, but I fear it will be the latter end of the week. I will not fix a day, therefore don't expect me till you receive a positive letter to say so. You are a man of feeling – a man of philanthropy, and will overlook my errors, I am sure. Chesterfield has charms for me; *that* you know, and therefore I throw myself on your mercy.[17]

Ellis also read this letter, and suggests that what attracted Ainsworth to Chesterfield was a sympathetic environment for the writing of *Rookwood*. As Eliza moved in when Fanny moved out in 1835, the 'cousins' sharing Kensal Lodge on the Harrow Road until 1841, it is tempting to imagine a similar liaison to that between Lady Blessington and Count D'Orsay, but the relationship was probably platonic, Chesterfield offering an escape from the constant problems with Ebers and an increasingly unsatisfactory marriage, as politely implied by Ellis. As the Kensal Lodge period saw Ainsworth's famous literary dinners, there are some vague references to Eliza in the letters and journals of many of his distinguished guests. Dickens and Forster, for example, seemed to be quite scared of her.

In a continuation of the project experimentally begun in *Sir John Chiverton*, the gothic was coming home. The *Rookwood* preface is Ainsworth's formal statement of the design of the romance as he claims to have perceived the

---

[16] Ellis, vol. 1, 230.
[17] Ainsworth, letter to Crossley, August 7 1831

128

form when he wrote *Rookwood*; he makes the gothic transition implicit in his opening paragraph, explains the cultural and symbolic codes attached to the legend of Dick Turpin and the poetic possibilities of underworld slang (a feature of European romance, whereas 'We, on the contrary, have scarcely any slang songs of merit'), and admits that he had 'an eye rather to the reader's amusement than his edification.' Most importantly:

> The chief object I had in view in making the present essay, was to see how the infusion of a warmer and more genial current into the veins of old Romance would succeed in reviving her fluttering and feeble pulse.[18]

He then suggests that the development of the romance has proved him correct, and that he may claim a certain amount of credit for this revival:

> The attempt has succeeded beyond my most sanguine expectation. Romance, if I am not mistaken, is destined shortly to undergo an important change. Modified by the German and French writers – by Hoffmann, Tieck, Hugo, Dumas, Balzac, and Paul Lacroix (*le Bibliophile Jacob*) – the structure commenced in our own land by Horace Walpole, Monk Lewis, Mrs. Radcliffe, and Maturin, but left imperfect and inharmonious, requires, now that the rubbish which choked up its approach is removed, only the hand of the skilful architect to its entire renovation and perfection.[19]

What is most interesting here is that Scott is omitted, and that Ainsworth looks to the Europeans rather than to the English, with the only exception being a final acknowledgement of the original gothic novelists of the past. The 'important change' was that the *romance* had become the *novel*. This is of course Ian Duncan's thesis, which begins with an example of Boz the entertainer of the 1830s hailed as Mr Dickens 'the national writer' in a banquet in his honour held in Birmingham in 1853, whereas the novel, he explains: 'was scarcely regarded as "Literature" at the beginning of the century'.[20] By 1849, English fiction was dominated by the rising generation of Dickens, Thackeray, the Brontës, Disraeli, Mrs Gaskell, an increasing move towards realism and the concerns of the condition

---

[18] Ainsworth, preface, *Rookwood*.
[19] *Ibid.*
[20] Duncan, 1–2.

of England question. Ainsworth's romances, by comparison, were fast becoming out of step with a Victorian era within which he seems never to have been completely comfortable. The late 1840s also saw the end of the historical romance's domination of the market. In 1848 Lytton, that reliable barometer of public tastes, published his last contribution to the genre, *Harold*. The author of *The Tower of London* could, however, still quite legitimately claim some allegiance with the author of *The Count of Monte Cristo* (but hardly with the author of *La Comédie humaine*) and their mutual literary forefathers of the romantic agony.

In April 1834 however, no-one had ever read anything quite like *Rookwood* and its publication in three volumes by Richard Bentley launched Ainsworth into literary celebrity with the speed of Black Bess clearing a turnstile gate on the Great North Road. For a reading public that was mourning the passing of Scott and weary of 'Tales of Fashionable Life', *Rookwood* was a revelation: a chaotic, wild and energetic narrative which combined claustrophobic, charnel-house gothic horror with the romance and adventure of the outlaw and the open road, accompanied by a bevy of wonderfully morbid ballads and cheerful drinking songs. The effect on both consumers and critics was electric. Within a couple of weeks of publication, Ainsworth wrote to Crossley that:

> The book is doing famously well here – making, in fact, quite a *sensation*. It has been praised in quarters of which you can have no idea – for instance, by Sir James Scarlett[21] and Lord Durham.[22] I have also received a most flattering letter from Bulwer-Lytton, and it has been the means of introducing me to Lady Blessington and her *soirées*. In fact, as Byron says, I went to bed unknown, arose, and found myself famous. Bentley has already begun to speak of a second edition – he wants to advertise in all the papers ... 'The English Victor Hugo' has already appeared as a paragraph.[23]

'The English Victor Hugo' is an indication of the vacuum left by the death of Scott two years previously, a situation that Bentley understood and was able to

---

[21] The Attorney General.
[22] British Ambassador to St Petersburg.
[23] Ainsworth, letter to Crossley, May 6 1834.

exploit successfully. Dickens was still far from qualifying as a novelist and was virtually unknown, and Lytton had made too many enemies. *Fraser's*, for example, took the opportunity to support their man while also using the review to attack Lytton. Thackeray disliked what he considered to be Lytton's pompous and over-ornamental style, while Maginn simply hated him:[24] 'With Mr. Ainsworth all is natural, free, and joyous: with Mr. Bulwer all is forced, constrained and cold. Ainsworth is always thinking of – or rather with his hero: Bulwer is always thinking of himself.' Ainsworth's songs were quoted at length and hailed as the most original feature of the book, towering in standard over the efforts of Lytton in *Paul Clifford* because Lytton had 'no sense of humour'.[25] In the following number, Ainsworth's portrait (the first of many by Daniel Maclise) appeared in *Fraser's* 'Gallery of Illustrious Literary Characters' (No. 50), the subject splendidly vain in the *outré* attire of the dandy of the D'Orsay period, clutching a riding whip and flanked by images of the highwayman, his hair a mass of curls and no doubt sticky with macassar oil. The accompanying caption, written by Maginn himself, wittily remarked that:

> We have not the pleasure of being acquainted with Mrs. Ainsworth, but we are sincerely sorry for her – we deeply commiserate her case. You see what a pretty fellow THE young Novelist of the Season is; how exactly, in fact, he resembles one of the most classically handsome and brilliant of the established lady-killers ... if he escapes scot-free during the first month of the blaze of his romance, he is a lucky as well as a well-grown lad.[26]

This was rather closer to the mark than even Maginn probably intended. Fanny did not participate at all in the social whirl that now surrounded her husband. As he had written to Crossley, an introduction from Lytton had gained him entrance to the inner circle of one of the most colourful women of the Regency, Lady

---

[24] Lytton had savagely caricatured Maginn in *Paul Clifford*, basing the drunken criminal and intellectual charlatan MacGrawler upon *Fraser's* first editor.
[25] 'High Ways and Low Ways; or Ainsworth's Dictionary, with Notes by Turpin', *Fraser's*, IX, June 1834, 724–8. Ellis believed this to be written by Thackeray, but in a reference to the piece in a letter to John Macrone dated June 2 1836 regarding his next novel, *Crichton*, Ainsworth attributes it to John 'Jack' Churchill, who had apparently also offered to 'Fraserize' *Crichton*.
[26] *Fraser's*, X, July 1834.

Marguerite, Countess of Blessington, whose all-male literary *soirées* at Seamore Place, Park Lane, were legendary. Ainsworth, as can be seen from contemporary portraits, strongly resembled D'Orsay and *Miladi* adored him, once famously placing herself on a hearthrug between D'Orsay (her step-son and, it was rumoured, her lover) and Ainsworth and declaring that she was flanked by the 'two handsomest men in London'.[27] Never fully recovered from the successive births of her three children, exhausted by the legal battles between her husband and her father and humiliated by the former's public flirtations with Lady Blessington, Ainsworth's new-found fame seemed only to alienate his wife from him further, and Fanny left to return to her family home in 1835. Her husband moved to Kensal Lodge and, until the end of the decade, was at the heart of literary London; the Lodge ever after known as the site of the most extravagant parties, each guest list an honour-roll of the most distinguished writers, thinkers and politicians of the day. This then was the house that Dick built.

II. The design of Romance: *Rookwood*, Scott and the gothic[28]

Rookwood was one of the most successful novels of the nineteenth century. The fact that it has now been largely forgotten is in part an indication of the dynamic nature of literary production during this period, the star of 1834–5, Ainsworth, being rapidly eclipsed by Dickens in 1836. Chronologically, it exists exactly between the death of Scott and the emergence of Dickens the novelist. Stylistically, *Rookwood* is a wonderfully enthusiastic amalgam: blending gothic with Newgate, historical romance with underworld anti-heroes, 'flash' dialogue

---

[27] See Michael Sadleir, *Blessington – D'Orsay: A Masquerade* (London: Constable, 1933).

[28] It would be digressive, if not downright foolish, to attempt a detailed exploration of Scott and the gothic here. This I leave to Fiona Robertson's excellent study *Legitimate Histories: Scott, Gothic, and the Authorities of Fiction* (Oxford: Clarendon Press, 1994). I am principally concerned with Ainsworth's relationship with Scott. Robertson's opening chapter on what she calls the 'Healthy Text' is worth noting in particular, however, in conjunction with my thoughts on the 'transitional' and contemporary critical readings of Ainsworth where his work is assessed and defined negatively against that of Scott.

and song, all luridly illustrated by George Cruikshank.[29] This was what made *Rookwood* such a novelty in 1834 although, in many ways, the parts could be said to be greater than the whole. The Turpin narrative, for example, the most popular component of the book, was completely peripheral to the rest of the plot and Book IV, 'The Ride to York', was often published separately.

Sir Walter Scott was by now two years dead, having left no apparent successor. If we recall Ainsworth's preface and then consider Ainsworth's gothic juvenilia and the shocking, rather than suspense-laden narrative of *Rookwood*, then dramatically (or rather melodramatically), the novel is much more of a homage to Walpole and Lewis than to Radcliffe and Scott, given Ainsworth's approach to the supernatural and his unrestrained narrative pace. *Rookwood* has a discreet relationship with the work of 'the great mistress of Romance' (as it does with Scott's novels), although Ainsworth does resurrect the standard signifiers of the eighteenth century gothic romance: ancient houses with polluted and disconnected genealogies; lost and disguised relatives; slimy subterranean passageways; incest; necrophilia; revenge; sexual tension; physical and psychological violence; and the ambivalent uncanny. These features are combined with, as the author states, an English setting in the year 1737. Here, the generic hybridisation of the text becomes apparent: *Rookwood* is also a historical romance. Because of this, the accusations of imitation tend to rise like angry bats from the pages of Scott's journal. The usual dismissal of *Rookwood* is, to return to Ainsworth's preface, that 'substituting' is the operative word for his project to drag the gothic novel into an English setting. Keith Hollingsworth writes, for example, that *Rookwood* contains, 'probably no single item of originality'.[30] The decaying estate of Rookwood recalls Scott's Ravenswood from *The Bride of*

---

[29] The first edition was unillustrated, although Edward Hull produced a collection of six prints depicting scenes from Turpin's ride to York (London, Colnaghi, 1834). Cruikshank produced a set of engravings for the fourth edition (London, John Macrone, 1835), inaugurating a very fruitful period of collaborative projects with Ainsworth. In all, Cruikshank illustrated *Rookwood* (1835 edition), *Jack Sheppard* (1839), *The Tower of London* (1840), *Guy Fawkes* (1840), *The Miser's Daughter* (1842), *Windsor Castle* (1843) and *Saint James's* (1844).

[30] Keith Hollingsworth, *The Newgate Novel 1830–1847* (Detroit: Wayne State UP, 1963), 99.

Lammermoor (1819), and *Rookwood's* principal proairetic, the conflict between two half-brothers over the family inheritance and the hand of the fair Miss Mowbray, is also the plot of Scott's *St. Ronan's Well* (1823). This may ostensibly appear rather damning evidence for the prosecution, but there is a rewriting of Scott taking place within *Rookwood* that has little to do with superficial similarities or downright plagiarism. Such a direct connection with Scott at such a charged historical moment offers an opportunity to examine the whole relationship between the gothic and the historical romance. The difference between the style of Ainsworth and Scott in *Rookwood* signals an interesting struggle for the control and direction of the gothic narrative in the nineteenth century.

According to legend, whenever a branch falls from an ancient lime-tree in the grounds of Rookwood Place, a death in the family is sure to follow. Under such ominous circumstances, Sir Piers Rookwood, lord of the manor, dies suddenly, leaving his wife and two sons, one legitimate and one not, to battle over the inheritance against a backdrop of plots, counter-plots, supernatural events, ill omens and ancient prophecy. *Rookwood* opens in the family vault, which sets the tone for the majority of the novel. By the coffin of his mother Susan, Luke Bradley is told by his grandfather, Peter Bradley (the deranged sexton, *à la* Boreall), that he is the son and heir of the recently deceased Sir Piers Rookwood. Peter hints that Susan did not die of natural causes and at that moment her coffin falls from its shelf. In a fit of grief, Luke takes the hand of his dead mother, which comes away in his own, revealing a wedding ring. Luke realises he is not illegitimate and resolves to claim his inheritance as Luke Rookwood, eldest son of Sir Piers, unaware that this entire episode has just been craftily orchestrated by his grandfather. Luke's rival is his half-brother Ranulph, whose mother, the dowager Lady Maud Rookwood, is as scheming and manipulative as the sexton. Another ancient prophecy foretells that two distant branches of the family will unite and control everything. The key to this eventuality appears to be the beautiful Eleanor Mowbray, Ranulph's cousin and the heir of his grandfather Sir Reginald

Rookwood. Eleanor loves Ranulph, but Luke becomes obsessed with her (as Peter Bradley hoped), and rejects his gypsy lover, Sybil Lovel, in order to pursue Eleanor, whom he intends to force into marriage. With the help of the highwayman Dick Turpin,[31] Luke almost succeeds but is tricked into marrying Sybil instead of Eleanor, who has been drugged and spirited away to a gypsy encampment. Sybil frees Eleanor and commits suicide, and Luke is killed by Sybil's grandmother Barbara, who sends him a lock of Sybil's hair laced with poison. Peter Bradley, now revealed as the long-lost brother of Sir Reginald, Alan Rookwood, and Lady Rookwood finally confront each other in the family vault but, 'some secret machinery' entombs then alive while they fight. Ranulph and Eleanor survive and are married. Bizarrely enough, the principal plot co-ordinates of disputed inheritance, Cain and Abel, mysterious, manipulative and disguised relatives and the marital sleight of hand in order to gain property are all, as Hollingsworth has noted, the same as those of Scott's *St. Ronan's Well*.

St. Ronan's Well is a comedy of manners, as the author put it a '*celebrare domestica facta*', written 'from the hope of rivalling the many formidable competitors who have already won deserved honours in this department'.[32] Note that those who are not 'imitators' are 'competitors'. The first volume is an Austenesque, satirical examination of the social dynamics of society folk at the spa of St Ronan's, punctuated by the appearance and then disappearance of the enigmatic traveller Francis Tyrrel. It is eventually revealed in the second volume that Tyrrel has returned to thwart the diabolical schemes of his half-brother, Valentine Bulmer: usurper of the title Earl of Etherington and destroyer of Tyrrel's once-betrothed, Clara Mowbray, whom Bulmer had tricked into marriage some years previously. These highly complex issues are resolved surprisingly tragically with the death of both villain and victim, and Tyrrel's retirement to a Moravian mission, his title and estates unclaimed. The novel was not a success. Scott

---

[31] The author might have initially planned a relationship between these characters akin to that of Francis Osbaldistone and Robert Roy MacGregor in Scott's *Rob Roy* (1817).
[32] Scott, introduction, *St. Ronan's Well*.

himself conceded that *St. Ronan's Well* was not received with much critical enthusiasm 'on the southern side of the Tweed'.[33] *Rookwood* which, as we have noted, *was* a critical success at least in its own day, is not so much a copy of Scott's earlier novel as its negative image. When Scott is light, Ainsworth is dark and, crucially, apparently devoid of any identifiable moral centre, the author's praise for the most part being reserved for the completely unrepentant figure of the highwayman Dick Turpin.

The motivations of Scott's characters are generally either honour or profit. Tyrrel cannot court the now unbalanced Clara because she is already married, albeit by virtue of subterfuge (Bulmer pretended to be Tyrrel as Sybil impersonated Eleanor), but he does not desire vengeance and has little interest in his inheritance, merely wishing to protect Clara from any further psychological molestation. Bulmer regrets his youthful transgression; but he is on the brink of ruin and needs to be seen publicly to marry Clara to gain another estate as laid down in the conditions of a family will. Squire Mowbray distrusts Bulmer but is in his debt and therefore unable to hinder his designs upon his sister, although it is Mowbray who kills Bulmer in a duel at the novel's conclusion, the rules of gentlemanly combat being correctly observed. All of these events are witnessed, and to a certain extent controlled, by the bombastic Mr Touchwood, a disguised yet fundamentally sympathetic relative. The protagonists of *Rookwood*, conversely, exist in a fallen state which they all acknowledge quite prosaically; as the sexton observes:

> 'When did a great man's heir feel sympathy for his decease? When did his widow mourn? When doth any man regret his fellow? Never! He rejoiceth – he maketh glad in his inmost heart – he cannot help it – it is nature. We all pray for – we all delight in each other's destruction. We were created to do so; or why else should we act thus? I never wept for any man's death, but I have often laughed.'[34]

[33] *Ibid.*
[34] Ainsworth, *Rookwood*, 90.

136

In this Hobbesian universe, the only honour is among thieves ('Or where else should you seek it?' says Turpin in *Rookwood*, 'for it has left all other classes of society'[35]), and dark fate dominates all. In such a damned and deterministic environment the primary male players are generally controlled by a will to power comprising, in roughly equal measure, lust, greed and obsessive fantasies of elaborate revenge. In characters such as Luke Bradley and his manipulative grandfather, the disguised sexton, Alan Rookwood (a dark shadow of Touchwood), betrayed and banished by his brother half a century previously, we have the satanic dialectic of power, desire and predestination that was at the heart of the gothic from Walpole's Manfred onwards and downwards.

Ainsworth's early presentation of Luke is as a brooding, romantic hero: brave, athletic and handsome, unjustly disinherited and in pursuit of his rightful title. This is, of course, a common enough plot device. Luke in fact bears the mark of Cain. As the author explains in his preface:

> One wholesome moral, however, may, I trust, be gathered from the perusal of this Tale; namely, that, without due governance of the passions, high aspirations and generous emotions will little avail their possessor. The impersonations of the Tempter, the Tempted, and the Better Influence, may be respectively discovered, by those who care to cull the honey from the flower, in the Sexton, in Luke, and in Sybil.[36]

Luke is in fact the *doppelgänger* of his half-brother, the whiter-than-white Ranulph, another pretender to the mantle of hero; Luke is Ranulph's Other, in a symbolic relationship not unlike that which exists between Ainsworth and Dickens in English literature: 'We are both the slaves of fate', he tells his brother, over the laid-out corpse of their father (*Rookwood* is certainly one of Ainsworth's most necrophiliac texts, which again sets his style against that of Scott's), 'You have received your summons hither – I have had mine. Your father's ghost called you; my mother's spectral hand beckoned me.'[37]

---

[35] *Ibid.*, 135.
[36] *Ibid., preface.*
[37] *Ibid.*, 81.

As with most good villains, Luke's character has more dramatic range than Ranulph's, allowing for a certain unpredictability of action, if not downright ambivalence (like Turpin, who he is siding with in a scrap is often unclear). The reader's expectation, however, that Luke will not live to see the last page while Ranulph will win the day, get the girl and inherit the estate is never really in question after Book III, Chapter Six, when he first sees Eleanor and promptly falls completely into the sexton's trap. His grandfather's endless recourse to prophecy plays upon Luke's desire for power:

'And who is Eleanor Mowbray?' asked Luke, breaking the silence.

'Your cousin. On the mother's side a Rookwood. 'Tis therefore I would urge your union with her. There is a prophecy relating to your house, which seems as though it would be fulfilled in your person and in hers:

> 𝔚hen the stray 𝔕ook shall perch on the topmost bough,
> 𝔗here shall be clamour and screaming, 𝔍 trow;
> 𝔅ut of right, and of rule, of the ancient nest,
> 𝔗he 𝔕ook that with 𝔕ook mates shall hold him possest.'

'I place no faith in such fantasies', replied Luke; 'and yet the lines bear strangely upon my present situation.'

'Their application to yourself and Eleanor Mowbray is unquestionable', replied the sexton.

'It would seem so, indeed', rejoined Luke; and he again sank into abstraction, from which the sexton did not care to arouse him.[38]

Nonetheless, Luke's fatal flaw remains his lust; a lust for power and property, for revenge in the name of his dead mother, but mostly for Eleanor's pale, bourgeois beauty. Were he to accept his social position in life, which of course he can't, he could have married his gypsy lover Sybil and frolicked about like George Borrow in Mumpers' Dingle without any need for magic, murder and monomania.[39]

This is where Ainsworth cuts the mooring line with Scott. Scott is concerned not with evil, violence or the supernatural but in the emotional effect

[38] Prophesy appears in original font. Ainsworth, *Rookwood*, 132.
[39] George Borrow's *Lavengro; The Scholar – The Gypsy – The Priest* (London: John Murray, 1851) is very much the opposite of Luke.

which such experience has on the individual. As he wrote in his *Remarks on Frankenstein*:

> the author's principal object ... is less to produce an effect by means of the marvels of the narrations, than to open new trains and channels of thought, by placing men in supposed situations of an extraordinary and preternatural character, and then describing the mode of feeling and conduct which they are most likely to adopt.[40]

Here Scott shows his allegiance to Radcliffe who, through the sublime, suspense and deferred desire elevated anxiety, as Ian Duncan has written, to a 'metaphysical state'.[41] Scott attempts this technique, for example, in his gothic short story 'The Tapestried Chamber' (1829), where it is not the apparition of Lord Woodville's 'wretched ancestress' that is of importance but the reaction of the seasoned campaigner General Browne to his night in the haunted room.[42] Here it was no more necessary to *show* the ghost than it was for Edward Waverley to witness the Battle of Culloden Moor. The origin of this device is of course the Black Veil incident in Radcliffe's *The Mysteries of Udolpho* (1794). The reference to '*supposed* situations' signals the final removal of the fantastic from the gothic discourse and informs much of Scott's admiration for Radcliffe rather than Walpole or Lewis:

> A principal characteristic of Mrs Radcliffe's romances, is the rule which the author imposed upon herself, that all the circumstances of her narrative, however mysterious, and apparently superhuman, were to be accounted for on natural principles, at the winding up of the story.[43]

Scott has turned the gothic to his own ideal here. The historical romance and the gothic are actually performing the *same* function, at least after the removal of any unpleasantness. Scott's analysis of the direction of the nineteenth century novel is really quite brilliant, anticipating the inward turn towards psychological

---

[40] Scott, 'Remarks on Frankenstein: or, The Modern Prometheus', *Blackwood's Magazine*, II, 1818.

[41] Duncan, 47.

[42] Scott, 'The Tapestried Chamber' (1829), *English Ghost Stories*, M. Cox and R.A. Gilbert (eds) (Oxford: Oxford UP, 1989).

[43] Scott, introduction, *Ballantyne's Novelist's Library*, vol. X (Edinburgh, 1824).

exploration that would characterise the Victorian realist novel and which, behind the veil, the later Victorian gothic would parallel. What is missing from Scott's gothic-as-historical model is the supernatural dimension, as if appealing to the famous words of Henry Tilney: 'Remember that we are English, that we are Christians!'[44] It is useful to note here the similarities between Scott's beliefs regarding gothic fiction and Lukács's hugely influential work on the historical novel; compare Scott's statement on the supernatural to Lukács on the historical:

> What matters … in the historical novel is not the re-telling of great historical events, but the poetic awakening of the people who figured in these events. What matters is that we should re-experience the social and human motives which led men to think, feel and act just as they did in historical reality.[45]

Lukács's partisan criticism (which often denies a work of literature's relationship to other works of literature in favour of his politics, and which shows his contempt for the gothic romance, *Otranto* in particular, as an inferior ancestor of Scott's innovations) remains a powerful argument. Scott undoubtedly represents a major break with the eighteenth century novel, yet was this as emphatic as strict Lukácsians would have us believe?

Ainsworth, on the other hand, returns to the earlier form and engages more directly with the supernatural and the literalisation of prophecy and imagination in the tradition of Walpole; in effect, he breaks from Scott. In this respect, the House of Rookwood is not dissimilar to *The Castle of Otranto*. Manfred, prince of Otranto, has a 'dread of seeing accomplished' an ancient and highly literal prophecy:

> *That the castle and lordship of Otranto should pass from the present family, whenever the real owner should be grown too large to inhabit it.*[46]

---

[44] Jane Austen, *Northanger Abbey*, ed. Anne Henry Ehrenpreis (1818 London: Penguin, 1988), 199.
[45] Lukács, 42.
[46] Horace Walpole *The Castle of Otranto*, *Three Gothic Novels*, ed. Peter Fairclough (1764 London: Penguin, 1968), p. 51.

140

Shortly thereafter, Walpole renders this augury in actuality; leaving Manfred stunned by the physicality of that which should live only in the imagination and, at the same time, irredeemably committed to the predicted course that will destroy himself and his House:

> He fixed his eyes on what he wished in vain to believe a vision; and seemed less attentive to his loss, than buried in meditation on the stupendous object that had occasioned it. He touched, he examined the fatal casque; nor could even the bleeding mangled remains of the young prince divert the eyes of Manfred from the portent before him.[47]

It is a similar reading of visions, omens and uncanny events that determines the direction of *Rookwood's* narrative and its central characters, whether good, bad or indifferent. As with *Otranto*, *Rookwood* opens with an ancient prophecy:

> 'Is it possible you have never heard of the ominous Lime-tree, [the sexton tells Luke] and the fatal bough? Why, 'tis a common tale hereabouts, and has been for centuries … That tree is, in some mysterious manner, connected with the family of Rookwood, and immediately previous to the death of one of that line, a branch is sure to be shed from the parent stem, prognosticating his doom.'[48]

This is also an early indication of Ainsworth's attraction to the device of prophecy as tragic inevitability which later became central to his historical romances,[49] whereby action is predetermined rather than dictated by rational consequence and the mechanisms of probability that we associate with Scott. Similarly, the struggle between Luke and his half-brother Ranulph Rookwood over the unfortunate Miss Eleanor Mowbray is engendered by the sexton's recourse to the prophecy that, 'The Rook that with Rook mates shall hold him possest', (the sexton, as always, playing chess with people rather than pieces). Bulmer's reasons for marrying Clara in *St. Ronan's Well* are purely commercial, the ruling being legal rather than ominous, although the desired outcome is the same as Luke's:

> 'Mr S. Mowbray of Nettlewood's last will and testament, by which I saw, to my astonishment and alarm, that a large and fair estate was bequeathed to the

---

[47] *Ibid.*, 58.
[48] Ainsworth, *Rookwood*, 4.
[49] This is explored in Chapters Four and Five of this present work.

eldest son and heir of the Earl of Etherington, on condition of his forming a matrimonial alliance with a lady of the house of Mowbray, of St Ronan's.'[50]

The rational has again replaced the unreal with a kind of ironic materialism, although the effects appear ostensibly to be similar to those of *Rookwood.*

It is through the patriarchal manipulation of Clara Mowbray that *St. Ronan's Well* could be argued to utilise a gothic archetype, albeit concealed within a novel of social manners. Such is also the case in *Rookwood.* Both novels, although *Rookwood* probably more so, represent a partial retelling of Radcliffe's *The Mysteries of Udolpho* but where the sensibility of the gothic heroine is *not* explored. Equally, the possibility of rape and murder that *threatens* Emily in *Udolpho* actually *happens* to Clara (although codified as a forced marriage and a melancholy death), and very nearly happens to Eleanor, in both cases motivated by the (gothic) compulsion of external pressure becoming private psychopathology. Luke Bradley is driven by his grandfather's desire for revenge on his brother's House and his descendants (Alan Rookwood's obsessions now being imposed on the next generation), and Tyrrel and Bulmer are locked in a terminal embrace because of the twisted legacy of their father and *his* brother. The women remain passive recipients of all this violence, completely marginalised while boys will be boys. In common with *Udolpho*, nonetheless, *Rookwood* and *St. Ronan's Well* dramatise their heroines' descent into the madness of others' design; to enter Rookwood is to enter Udolpho, where visions are made flesh but also where escape and rescue are at least possible, but for Scott's heroine the fall has occurred *before* the present narrative and she is, therefore, already beyond redemption according to the rules of gender and society, and therefore as doomed as damned:

> She started at these words with a faint scream; for slowly, and with a feeble hand, the curtains of the bed opposite to the side at which Cargill sat, were opened, and the figure of Clara Mowbray, her clothes and long hair drenched and dripping with rain, stood in the opening by the bedside. The dying woman sat upright, her eyes starting from their sockets, her lips quivering, her face

---

[50] Scott, *St. Ronan's Well*, 111.

142

pale, her emaciated hands grasping the bed-clothes, as if to support herself, and looking as much aghast as if her confession had called up the apparition of her betrayed friend.

'Hannah Irwin', said Clara, with her usual sweetness of tone, 'my early friend – my unprovoked enemy! – Betake thee to Him who hath pardon for us all, and betake thee with confidence – for I pardon you as freely as if you had never wronged me – as freely as I desire my own pardon. – Farewell – Farewell!'[51]

This defused gothic moment (heralding Clara's textual execution) is also about as far as Scott is willing to go, the apparition resolved into the unfortunate but still breathing figure of his heroine. In *Rookwood*, by comparison, Ainsworth is more apt to push the boundaries of acceptable taste and decency with his gothic bodies:

The Knight of Malta advanced towards the altar. The torch-light reddened upon the huge stone pillars. It fell upon the shrine, and upon the ghastly countenance of Sybil, who stood beside it. Suddenly, as the light approached her, an object, hitherto hidden from view, was revealed. Sybil uttered a prolonged and fearful shriek; the Knight recoiled likewise in horror; and a simultaneous cry of astonishment burst from the lips of the foremost of the group. All crowded forward, and universal consternation prevailed amongst the assemblage. Each one gazed at his neighbour, anxious to learn the occasion of this tumult, and vague fears were communicated to those behind, from the terrified glances which were the only answers returned by their comrades in front.

'Who has dared to bring that body here?' demanded Barbara, in a tone in which anger struggled with apprehension, pointing at the same time to the ghastly corpse of a female, with streaming hair, at the altar's feet. 'Who has dared to do this, I say? Quick! Remove it. What do you stare at? Cravens! Is this the first time you have looked upon a corpse, that you should shrink aghast that you tremble before it? It is a clod – ay, less than a clod. A way with it! Away, I say.'

'Touch it not', cried Luke, lifting a cloud of black hair from off the features; 'it is my mother's body.'[52]

In common with James Hogg, Ainsworth seems fascinated by dead bodies and employs them to outrageous effect. This was once so with Scott the romantic poet, but never Scott the novelist.

---

[51] *Ibid.*, 342.
[52] Ainsworth, *Rookwood*, 213–14.

With regard to their living heroines however, *Udolpho* and *Rookwood* ephemerally converge to the exclusion of Scott, as Radcliffe and Ainsworth both thrust their heroines into this *imaginary* realm of the gothic narrative, to emerge reasonably unscathed in the rational world at the conclusion of their bizarre adventures. Their tormentors, once so apparently powerful, now have no influence or agency at all:

> Montoni, too, often rose to her fancy, such as she had seen him in his days of triumph, bold, spirited and commanding; such also as she had since beheld him in his days of vengeance; and now, only a few short months had passed – and he had no longer the power, or the will to afflict; – he had become a clod of earth, and his life was vanquished like a shadow![53]

Equally, as Eleanor's brother tells her before her idyllic marriage to Ranulph at the conclusion of *Rookwood*, 'all your misfortunes will have occurred *before* marriage', and:

> as in a simple state, after the completion of the sacred rites, the youthful pair walked, arm in arm, amongst their thronging and admiring tenants towards the Hall, many a fervent prayer was breathed that the curse of the House of Rookwood might be averted from their heads; and, not to leave a doubt upon the subject, we can add that these aspirations were not in vain, but that the day, which dawned so brightly, was one of serene and unclouded happiness to its close.[54]

Paradoxically perhaps, it is only Clara, whose experiences never venture outside those of reasoned, if nasty, reality that has to be sacrificed; such is the concession the author must make to reality if fantasy (in this case the fantasy of a happy ending) is to be denied. Scott has taken a gothic plot yet rejected the gothic; if the disadvantages are not to apply, then neither must the advantages.

Although Ainsworth was an enormous admirer of Scott, *Rookwood* can still be read as an act of almost Oedipal rebellion against him; and, thus reacting against his literary parent, where else could he go but to the values of the grandparents? Ainsworth identified an annexation of the gothic by the historical

---

[53] Ann Radcliffe, *The Mysteries of Udolpho*, ed. Bonamy Dobrée (1794 Oxford: Oxford UP, 1966), 580.
[54] Ainsworth, *Rookwood*, 329–30.

novel, and rather playfully stole it back again. This remained true of his later work, where the fundamentally historical novels he produced after the moral panic and concerted critical attacks of the Newgate controversy still made enormous use of gothic atmosphere, in violent and uncanny gestures that could occur at any time in the course of a narrative. Andrew Sanders has written that Ainsworth's novels, 'reveal that, unlike most other Victorian writers, he has learnt very little indeed from Sir Walter Scott',[55] yet this lazy critical tendency to classify Ainsworth as a slavish, but inferior follower of Scott the romantic novelist takes little account of the legacy of Scott the Romantic poet. There is a certain voyeurism in *Rookwood* that indicates that its author had certainly learnt something from *Marmion* if not *Waverley*.

In a somewhat ironic parallel, Scott's wonderful early romantic, narrative poems have become almost as marginalised in literary study as Ainsworth's novels, lingering, just, into twentieth century classrooms but generally ignored in the revival of interest in Scott outside Scotland that occurred in the 1970s; Robin Mayhead wrote in 1973 that:

> Scott's poetry is harder to recommend today than any other branch of his work. The temptation virtually to ignore it is strong. One may make out a seemingly convincing case for relatively weak novels, can make them sound in some way interesting, even though the actual reading of them will show up the case as an exercise in special pleading. The less desirable kind of Scott Revival criticism, indeed, fails in precisely that way. But with the poetry it is quite different. Whereas the not particularly scrupulous account of a poor novel may suggest that the book has a thematic interest, often of a sociological type, constituting a claim for it to be read, Scott's poetry contains very little that can be made to sound inviting.[56]

In looking for a gothic antecedence that might be somehow more appropriate in connecting Scott with Ainsworth, Scott's poetry suddenly sounds very inviting indeed.

---

[55] Andrew Sanders, *The Victorian Historical Novel, 1840–1880* (London: Macmillan, 1978), 33.
[56] Robin Mayhead, *Walter Scott* (Cambridge: Cambridge UP, 1973), 111. Mayhead prefers the poetry of introductory epistles to the six cantos to *Marmion* itself.

By way of illustrative example, there is a ballad by Scott inspired by his work on Matthew Lewis's 'hobgoblin repast' *Tales of Wonder* (1801), entitled 'Glenfinlas: or, Lord Ronald's Coronach' (1802), which spins a yarn worthy of Bill Gaines's *Tales from the Crypt* comics or Sam Raimi's *Evil Dead* trilogy.[57] A 'coronach' is a lamentation for a dead warrior sung by a clan elder, and this one concerns two Highland hunters, passing their night in a secluded hut in 'grey Glenfinlas' deepest nook'. Lord Ronald likes to drink and make merry, while his companion Moy is of a more sombre nature, being cursed with second sight and mourning his dead lover, Morna. Ronald's lover, Mary, is very much alive, and he leaves the hut for a clandestine meeting, never to return. Only his hounds come back, howling 'in melancholy sound.' Alone on the increasingly wild night, Moy plays his Jew's harp until dogs growl and he hears footsteps outside, then:

And by the watch-fire's glimmering light,
Close by the minstrel's side was seen
An huntress maid, in beauty bright,
All dropping wet her robes of green.

All dropping wet her garments seem;
Chill'd was her cheek, her bosom bare,
As, bending o'er the dying gleam,
She wrung the moisture from her hair.[58]

This voluptuous vision claims to be the daughter of the Lord of Glengyle, and is searching for her lost sister in the storm. She tries every womanly wile to seduce Moy and lead him outside to protect her from 'shrieking ghosts', questioning his masculinity when he repeatedly declines. Moy responds with a muddle of magic and Christian incantations, playing a strain 'consecrated to the Virgin Mary', and thereby compelling the visitor to reveal her true form:

Tall wax'd the Spirit's altering form,
Till to the roof her stature grew;

---

[57] A series of kinetic horror movies produced between 1982 and 1992, the first two of which involve a group of lost hikers under siege by demons in a solitary woodland cabin. The video release of the original movie spent several years on the Obscene Publications List and was one of the high-profile 'video nasties'.

[58] Scott, 'Glenfinlas: or, Lord Ronald's Coronach' (1802), *The Poetical Works* (London: Macmillan, 1928), 153–60.

Then, mingling with the rising storm,
With one wild yell away she flew.[59]

The storm becomes a whirlwind, 'But not a lock of Moy's loose hair/Was waxed by wind, or wet by dew.' In this supernatural tempest, from which the pious Moy is protected by his faith, it is not rain that is falling upon Glenfinlas:

The voice of thunder shook the wood,
As ceased the more than mortal yell;
And, spattering foul, a shower of blood
Upon the hissing firebrands fell.

Next dropp'd from high a mangled arm;
The fingers strain'd an half-drawn blade:
And last, the life-blood streaming warm,
Torn from the trunk, a gasping head.[60]

Lord Ronald has returned, at least what's left of him.

Marmion: A Tale of Flodden Field (1808), Scott's most famous poem and a pre-Byronic epic of passion, betrayal and death, is equally extreme. There is a fascination with torture and violence here which has been totally excised from the bard's prose of later years, even those novels which employ many of the devices of the gothic melodrama such as the *Tales of My Landlord*. Unlike 'Glenfinlas', *Marmion* makes little use of the supernatural,[61] yet the poet does linger on the horror of the death of Constance de Beverley, an Inquisitional torture worthy of Lewis's *The Monk*, but not Radcliffe's *The Italian*:

And now that blind old Abbot rose,
To speak the Chapter's doom,
On those the wall was to enclose,
Alive, within the tomb[62]

---

[59] *Ibid.*, 225–8. A similar episode occurs in Ching Siu-Tung's hugely influential genre movie *A Chinese Ghost Story* (1987), when siren-like ghosts are repelled by Buddhist incantations.
[60] Scott, 'Glenfinlas', 237–44.
[61] Although Constance has a prophetic vision of the dissolution of the monasteries under Henry VIII in canto II XXXI, just before her gruesome execution is carried out which, under the circumstances, sounds like a curse.
[62] Scott, *Marmion* (1808), Poetical Works, canto II XXV.

Scott had written about the Inquisition at length in the seventh of his *Letters on Demonology and Witchcraft* of 1830 (which David Punter describes quite properly as 'also a compendium of themes and images used by gothic writers'[63]), and his punishment of Constance, a nun who has broken her vows for love, recalls the punishment of Agnes de Medina, a nun who has broken her vows for love in *The Monk*:

> St. Clare's rules are severe: But grown antiquated and neglected, many of late years have either been forgotten, or changed by universal consent into milder punishments. The penance, adjudged to the crime of Agnes, was most cruel, most inhuman! The Law had been long exploded: Alas! It still existed, and the revengeful Prioress now determined to revive it. This law decreed, that the Offender should be plunged into a private dungeon, expressly constituted to hide from the world for ever the Victim of Cruelty and tyrannic superstition.[64]

Constance is obsessed with the King's (fictitious) favourite Marmion, and follows him disguised as a page (another plot device favoured by both Lewis and Ainsworth). In his pursuit of the beautiful Lady Clare, who is already betrothed to Sir Ralph de Wilton, Marmion enlists the help of Constance to accuse Sir Ralph falsely of treason. Constance foolishly hopes to regain her lover by helping him, but is betrayed and returned to her convent where she is walled up alive. So pitiful are her cries that her executioners flee from the scene, ordering the chapel bells to toll long and loud, ostensibly to mark the passing of a soul into the afterlife but actually to drown out the horrific screams of the dying woman. This terrible sound of frustration and despair enshrouds the entire landscape, even making the hair of the most powerful highland animals stand on end:

> And hundred winding steps convey
> That conclave to the upper day;
> But, ere they breathed the fresher air,
> They heard the shriekings of despair,
> And many a stifled groan:
> With speed their upward way they take,
> (Such speed as age and fear can make,)
> And cross'd themselves for terror's sake,

---

[63] Punter, vol. 1, 141.
[64] Matthew Lewis, *The Monk*, ed. Howard Anderson (1796 Oxford: Oxford UP, 1973), 351.

As hurrying, tottering on:
Even in the vesper's heavenly tone,
They seem'd to hear a dying groan,
And bade the passing knell to toll
For welfare of a parting soul.
Slow o'er the midnight wave it swung,
Northumbrian rocks in answer rung;
To Warkworth cell the echoes roll'd,
His beads the wakeful hermit told,
The Bamborough peasant raised his head,
But slept ere half a prayer he said;
So far was heard the mighty knell,
The stag sprung up on Cheviot Fell,
Spread his broad nostril to the wind,
Listed before, aside, behind,
Then couch'd him down beside the hind,
And quaked among the mountain fern,
To hear that sound so dull and stern.[65]

Scott the historical novelist would defend such an episode as a matter of antiquarian verisimilitude, but here the theme is employed exactly as it was by the eighteenth century gothic novelists. The 'tyrannic superstition' of medieval European Catholicism, the perfect gothic Other of Great British Protestant rationalism, while simultaneously playing upon a titillating, sadistic fascination with horror and violence, will always sell, from gothic novels in the eighteenth century to contemporary horror movies and video games.

Ainsworth similarly exploits such horror at the conclusion of *Rookwood*, when the sexton/Alan Rookwood is accidentally locked within the vault where the story began. Only Luke knows his whereabouts, and as he waits for his grandson he becomes increasingly frantic. *We* know, however, that Luke will never come. He is already dead. With a precision worthy of the best of *Blackwood's*, the author then minutely documents the stages of such a disgusting death, from panic to ineffectual escape attempts, to hallucinations, despair, starvation and, finally, death. It should also be noted that this process is presented as Alan's 'fate',

---

[65] Scott, *Marmion*, II XXXIII.

149

suspending any possibility of rescue and replacing any remaining drama with a grinding inevitability:

> Alan now abandoned himself wholly to despair ... His fate was sealed. Death awaited him. He must anticipate his slow but inevitable stroke, enduring all the grinding horrors of starvation. The contemplation of such an end was madness ... Terrors of a new kind now assailed him. The dead, he fancied, were bursting from their coffins, and he peopled the darkness with grisly phantoms. They were around about him on each side, whirling and rustling, gibbering, groaning, shrieking, laughing, and lamenting. He was stunned, stifled. The air seemed to grow suffocating, pestilential; the wild laughter was redoubled; the horrible troop assailed him; they dragged him along the tomb, and amid their howls he fell, and became insensible ... He arose. He rushed towards the door; he knocked against it with his knuckles till the blood streamed from them; he scratched against it with his nails till they were torn off by the roots. With insane fury he hurled himself against the iron frame; it was in vain ... Physical suffering now began to take the place of his mental tortures. Parched and consumed with a fierce internal fever, he was approached by an unappeasable thirst ... He licked the humid floor; he sought to imbibe the nitrous drops from the walls; but, instead of allaying his thirst, they increased it ... Nor were the pangs of hunger wanting. He had to endure all the horrors of famine, as well as the agonies of quenchless thirst.
>
> In this dreadful state three days and nights passed over Alan's fated head. Nor night nor day had he ... Each hour added to his suffering, and brought with it no relief. During this period of prolonged misery reason often tottered on her throne. He dragged coffins from their recesses, hurled them upon the ground, striving to break them open and drag forth their loathsome contents. Upon other occasions he would weep bitterly and wildly; and once – only once – did he attempt to pray; but he started from his knees with an echo of infernal laughter, as he deemed, ringing in his ears ... At length he became sensible of his approaching dissolution ... Gathering together his remaining strength, he dragged himself towards the niche wherein his brother, Sir Reginald Rookwood, was deposited, and placing his hand upon the coffin, solemnly exclaimed, 'My curse – my dying curse – be upon thee evermore!'
>
> Falling with his face upon the coffin, Alan instantly expired. In this attitude his remains were discovered.[66]

Lady Rookwood has already been crushed to death inside a stone sarcophagus. The 'infernal laughter' may indeed by demonic, or the ghost of Alan's brother, or Alan himself; unusually for Ainsworth, the supernatural element of *Rookwood* is

---

[66] Ainsworth, *Rookwood*, 335–6.

relatively ambiguous. Unlike Radcliffe, he does however prefer competing frames of explanation to any ultimate rational clarification. Like the death of Constance in *Marmion*, the sexton's demise is dwelled upon to a disturbingly meticulous extent. Both authors seem to be enjoying themselves, reminding one with a knowing smile of a tapestry representing Matthew 2:16 hanging in Rookwood Hall, being:

> The record of the patience and industry of a certain Dame Dorothy Rookwood, who flourished some centuries ago, and whose skilful needle had illustrated the slaughter of the Innocents, with a severity of *gusto*, and sanguinary minuteness of detail, truly surprising in a lady so amiable as she was represented to have been.[67]

Contemporary reviewers understood best what was going on in *Rookwood*, specifically that the text should not be taken too seriously (which is also an often misunderstood rule of horror movies and other extreme cinema). Thackeray being in no doubt as to the author's position in the literary hierarchy, punning on Southey's epithet, 'the Lake Poet', and on the pre-Romantic graveyard poets, Parnell, Young, Blair and Gray:

> Our Regina takes still a *quasi*-maternal interest in this young author ... That face (with figure to correspond) sold five hundred extra copies of our magazine two years ago[68] ... We know not whether he has yet determined what school of poetry he intends to patronize ... *we* think he has a decided vocation for the *'sepulchral'*: his immortal ballad of *The Old Oak Coffin* ... revealed in him the existence of a power akin to that of Ezekiel, and was, in sooth, as glorious a vision of dry bones as we can recollect just now. Southey has chosen a domicile on the margin of his favourite lakes to enact the *genius loci*: it is not without reason that Ainsworth has latterly selected a rural residence close by the grand necropolis[69] on the Harrow Road: if 'the cemetery company's directors' have any brains they will vote him £500 a year and create him

---

[67] *Ibid.*, 71.

[68] An allusion to Maclise's portrait in the 'Gallery of Illustrious Literary Characters', *Fraser's*, X, July 1834.

[69] Kensal Green Cemetery, where Ainsworth, his mother and brother were eventually buried.

laureate of the graveyard, with the grass of the enclosed grounds in fee-simple to his Pegasus[70] for ever.[71]

The Old Oak Coffin is one of 30 original songs sung by characters in the novel (a mixture of morbid, prophetic ballads sung mostly by the sexton or the gypsy priestess, and rollicking, trolloping tub-thumpers in praise of famous robbers, usually belted out by a half-drunk Dick Turpin or the very drunk 'Canting Crew', the male gypsy outlaws), which add to the general air of a chaotic stage production that characterises *Rookwood*; *The Beggar's Opera* is certainly a model, in parallel with a wonderfully bizarre gothic musical accompaniment, to which Thackeray wryly alludes. To Thackeray at this point (not yet outraged by the Newgate novel craze that was to follow), Ainsworth is the ultimate graveyard poet, his Muse feeding upon the grass that grows over, and is consequently fertilised by, the bodies of the dead. He has pursued a renewed romantic intensity that Scott flirted with as a poet until supplanted by the superiority of Byron, and has produced a narrative that is in many ways more gothic than the gothic.

III. The Phantom Steed: the outlaw narrative of *Rookwood*

During the fourth book of *Rookwood*, 'The Ride to York' (the focal point of the text while having nothing whatsoever to do with the primary plot), in a chapter entitled 'The Phantom Steed', Dick Turpin becomes aware of a ghostly horseman riding by his side in the midnight mist. Eventually, the apparition resolves itself into the figure of Luke Rookwood. They ride together for a while, then Luke vanishes into the night to resume his by then near-demented pursuit of Eleanor Mowbray. The next time they meet, Turpin absent-mindedly gives him a package he has been holding for Barbara Lovel. It contains a poisoned lock of Sybil's hair,

---

[70] In Greek myth, the Hippocrene spring on Mount Helicon, the home of the Muses, originally sprung from the touch of the winged horse's hoof, Pegasus thereafter being associated with the Muses and therefore creativity. Although Pegasus ascended to heaven, his rider Bellerophon fell to earth and was permanently crippled. It is possible that Thackeray also had this image wryly in mind regarding Ainsworth by 1836. If not, he would have it soon enough.

[71] 'Another Caw from the Rookwood. Turpin out again', rev. *Rookwood*, 4th edn, *Fraser's*, March 1836. Probably written by Thackeray.

which Luke kisses and then promptly dies. This pair of connected events very much symbolises the structure of *Rookwood*, which is in fact *two* texts riding together in parallel before Text B, *The Ride to York* (starring Dick Turpin), completely overwhelms Text A, *Rookwood, A Romance* (a gothic melodrama about the rivalry of the brothers Luke and Ranulph Rookwood); *The Ride to York* being frequently published and performed in the penny gaffs separately, completely divorced from *Rookwood*.

The Turpin narrative does however intersect with the gothic melodrama of *Rookwood* on occasion. As Ainsworth's Turpin is a simple prototype for the later characterisation of Jack Sheppard, so the connection between the gothic narrative and representations of the criminal underworld is beginning to be explored. Turpin, the glorious social outsider, often appears outside nature as well: 'Talking of Dick Turpin, they say, is like speaking of the Devil', says the sexton, 'he's at your elbow ere the word's well out of your mouth.'[72] Turpin is twice taken for an apparition by other characters; when he disguises himself intentionally as the ghost of Sir Piers Rookwood in order to rob the house, and as himself, or at least the self wearing the mask of the highwayman. Here he is mistaken for the devil incarnate in a characteristically Ainsworthian gothic gesture:

'Stay', cried the sexton. 'He is not in pursuit – he takes another course – he wheels to the right. By Heaven! it is the Fiend himself upon a black horse, come for Bowlegged Ben. See, he is there already.'

The horseman had turned, as the sexton stated, careering towards a revolting object at some little distance on the right hand. It was a gibbet, with its grizzly burden. He rode swiftly towards it, and, reigning in his horse, took off his hat, bowing profoundly to the carcass that swung in the morning breeze.

But, before diffusing the image by identifying Turpin, an ambivalent supernatural event occurs, and the author's natural explanation occupies the same space as the sexton's superstitious allusion to an ominous crow, while also mischievously punning on 'blade' to signify the likelihood of the dissection knife as Turpin's ultimate *post mortem* punishment after his inevitable execution:

---

[72] Ainsworth, *Rookwood*, 58.

Just at that moment a gust of air catching the fleshless skeleton, its arms seemed to be waved in reply to the salutation. A solitary crow winged its flight over the horseman's head as he paused. After a moment's halt he wheeled about, and again shouted to Luke, waving his hat.

'As I live', said the latter, 'it is Jack Palmer.'

'Dick Turpin, you mean', rejoined the sexton. 'he has been paying his respects to a brother blade. Ha, ha! Dick will never have the honour of a gibbet; he is too tender of the knife. Did you mark the crow? But here he comes.' And in another instant Turpin was by their side.[73]

Turpin is, in effect, already larger than life; even his human identity seems called into question. Already it is apparent that, in his case at any rate, death is not the end.

Although originally intended as a secondary character, the ghost of Dick Turpin had seized the imagination of the author to the extent that:

The Ride to York was completed in one day and one night ... Well do I remember the fever into which I was thrown during the time of composition. My pen literally scoured over the pages. So thoroughly did I identify myself with the flying highwayman, that, once started, I found it impossible to halt. Animated by kindred enthusiasm, I cleared every obstacle in my path with as much facility as Turpin disposed of the impediments that beset his flight. In his company, I mounted the hill-side, dashed through the bustling village, swept over the desolate heath, threaded the silent street, plunged into the eddying stream, and kept an onward course, without pause, without hindrance, without fatigue. With him I shouted, sang, laughed, exulted, wept. Nor did I retire to rest till, in imagination, I heard the bell of York Minster toll forth the knell of poor Black Bess.[74]

Ainsworth's passion for his subject is still apparent 14 years on, in the richness of the language he uses to recall what must have been his finest hour: on the brink of fame and fortune, darling of the D'Orsay set, and before the collapse of his marriage, the death of his wife and a long legal battle with his in-laws over the custody of his children and the vicious critical attacks of the Newgate controversy. Although we might now regard the publication of *Rookwood* as, in fact, a contributory factor in his later denigration, there is a combination of

---

[73] *Ibid.*, 133.
[74] *Ibid.*, preface. 'The Ride to York' is approximately 35,000 words.

154

conviction and innocence in the author's heart that rejects such an interpretation. Ainsworth's initial enthusiasm had been infectious, and an eighteenth century, chapbook fascination with outlaws that had lain dormant since the days of Defoe became a national craze once more; a fashion that even crossed the boundaries of social class for a time. As Charles Mackay complained in 1841:

> Turpin's fame is unknown to no portion of the male population of England after they have attained the age of ten. His wondrous ride from London to York has endeared him to the imagination of millions; his cruelty in placing an old woman upon a fire, to force her to tell him where she had hidden her money, is regarded as a good joke; and his proud bearing upon the scaffold is looked upon as a virtuous action.[75]

There are so many contemporary accounts of the incident with the fire that it is probably true, the ride to York is purely an invention of Ainsworth's. S.M. Ellis wryly observed that *Rookwood*, 'may be styled another "novel without a hero"',[76] while George J. Worth favoured Luke Rookwood as 'the tortured protagonist'.[77] The brooding, fated Luke is in fact curiously situated dramatically somewhere between the roles of romantic hero and the gothic villain (which were always both sides of the same coin), while the frilly Ranulph Rookwood is the generic melodramatic hero. Dick Turpin, on the other hand, was, as author and audience understood all along, 'an English Adventurer'.[78]

    'Turpin was the hero of my boyhood', the author later admitted,

> I had always a strange passion for highwaymen, and have listened by the hour to their exploits, as narrated by my father, and especially to those of 'Dauntless Dick', that 'chief minion of the moon'.[79] One of Turpin's adventures in particular, the ride to Hough Green, which took deep hold of my fancy, I have recorded in song. When a boy, I have often lingered by the side of the deep old road where this robbery was committed, to cast wistful glances into its mysterious windings; and when night deepened the shadows of the trees, have urged my horse on his journey, from a vague apprehension of a visit from the ghostly highwayman. And then there was the Bollin, with its shelvy banks,

---

[75] Mackay, 634.
[76] Ellis, vol. 1, 239.
[77] Worth, 94.
[78] Ainsworth, *Rookwood*, 47.
[79] 'Let us be Diana's foresters, gentlemen of the shade, minions of the moon.' Shakespeare, *Henry IV, Part 1*, I.ii. 28. This would make Ainsworth's highwayman a Falstaff figure.

which Turpin cleared at a bound; the broad meadows over which he winged his flight; the pleasant bowling-green of the pleasant old inn at Hough, where he produced his watch to the Cheshire squires, with whom he was upon terms of intimacy; all brought something of the gallant robber to mind. No wonder, in after years, in selecting a highwayman for a character in a tale, I should choose my old favourite, Dick Turpin.[80]

Note the romantic fascination of the language, which is at times almost reverential as befitting a description of such superhuman feats as the non-stop ride to Hough Green (which becomes the Ride to York in *Rookwood* and popular history). This honest confession of childhood fancy also demonstrates the coexistence of the oppositional emotional responses to crime and violence that he was able to tap into as an adult author. The avenue of trees gives the young rider the creeps, but his glances are 'wistful' ones for an age now past; having not been blessed with a vision, Ainsworth had to resurrect Turpin himself. The commercial success of *Rookwood* had much to do with this appeal to the imagined freedom of an earlier age. With this creation, or recreation, of the famous Georgian outlaw, Ainsworth was the catalyst for a whole new style of picaresque narrative. Although his contribution to the Newgate genre of the nineteenth century was not the first[81] (Lytton had published *Paul Clifford* in 1830), it was, and is, Ainsworth's romantic version of the outlaw that endures in the popular imagination (first in England and then, particularly, America in the figure of the Western frontier outlaw[82]) rather

---

[80] Ainsworth, preface, *Rookwood*. Written in 1849, after the Newgate Controversy had permanently undermined his literary reputation, Ainsworth refuses to go with the flow and preach about the moral dangers of rendering outlaws heroic in works of fiction.

[81] *Rookwood* is not a pure Newgate novel, the text is a transitional one blending at least three potentially sympathetic genre styles of the previous generation of literature.

[82] Writing of the robbery of the Union Pacific Railroad Company by Butch Cassidy and the 'Wild Bunch' in 1900, Fenin and Everson argue that 'Such exploits vividly aroused popular fantasy, and the traditional sympathy of the American masses for the underdog, fanned by sensational newspaper reports, provided ideal ground for the emergence of the myth of the outlaw. They provided ground, too, for the physical expression of those stark puritanical values implicit in the struggle between good and evil, which have so affected the American unconscious as revealed in the country's folkways and mores.' George N. Fenin and William K. Everson, *The Western: From Silents to the Seventies* (London: Penguin, 1978), 9. Stories from the frontier as well as James Fenimore Cooper's importation and application of the codes of English historical romance (both in the manner of Scott and James and, in the later *Leatherstocking Tales*, Lytton and Ainsworth) to the new values of the New Republic created an enduring image of rough justice and outlaw nobility that could have no place in Victorian England. Notably, Ainsworth's literary reputation remains intact in the United States.

than Lytton's erudite radical, Paul Clifford, or all the inhabitants of Dickens's Victorian underworld, except when, like the Artful Dodger, they were read as if written by Ainsworth.[83]

There were of course many versions of the life and legend of Dick Turpin already in place in English culture by the time of *Rookwood*, ranging from the official record of his pursuit, accidental capture, and trial and execution in York in 1839, to chapbook romances, Newgate Calendars, Defoe's Newgate biographies, *The Beggar's Opera* and a positive legion of folk songs and tall stories among the lower classes. If a fraction of the contemporary reports of Turpin's criminal behaviour is true (particularly during his time with the 'Gregory Gang' in North London in the early 1830s, from which we get the story of the old lady and the fire), then the original was undoubtedly a murderous, self-serving, sadistic, petty and quite mediocre little man. As Hilary and Mary Evans begin their exploration of the cult of the highwayman (of which Dick Turpin must be the quintessential symbol in English folklore):

> They robbed and raped and murdered. They lied and cheated, betrayed and deceived. When it served their purpose, they stole a man's property, used his wife or his daughter, destroyed his home and livelihood, took his life. When they gave, it was only a bribe; when they showed consideration, it was to buy goodwill. If they claimed to have been unjustly treated by society, it was to justify themselves for flouting society's rules; when they claimed to be revenging themselves on society for its injustice, they took their revenge on the weak and innocent more often than on those who had caused the injustice.[84]

Turpin being one of the worst offenders, yet these men, along with the outlaws of the American Frontier, even in their own day, were more often than not portrayed as heroic, if not downright chivalrous. In a ballad popular around the time of his execution entitled 'Turpin's Appeal to the Judge', Turpin was already being portrayed as a Robin Hood figure (another enduring fiction):

---

[83] Charles Mackay cited interviews with child criminals in which the Artful Dodger in particular is viewed as a Jack Sheppard figure in the second edition of *Memoirs of Extraordinary Popular Delusions and the Madness of Crowds* (1852). These are cited in the following chapter of the present work.

[84] Hilary and Mary Evans, *Hero on a Stolen Horse: The highwayman, and his brothers-in-arms the bandit and the bushranger* (London: Frederick Muller, 1977), 1.

I hope, my Lord, you'll pardon me,
I'm not the worst of men.
I the Scripture have fulfilled
though a wicked life I've led,
when the naked I beheld,
I've clothed them and fed.
Sometimes in a coat of winter's pride,
sometimes in a russet grey,
the naked I've clothed, the hungry fed,
and the rich I've sent away.[85]

Turpin's posthumous existence is the exact opposite of Shakespeare's much quoted maxim from Mark Antony's eulogy to Julius Caesar that 'The evil that men do lives after them/The good is oft interred with their bones.'[86] So strong is this perception of the gentleman of the road that the cover notes of a novelisation of a lavish London Weekend Television costume drama made in 1979 can still clam that 'Dick Turpin is a brilliant rider and master swordsman whose belief in liberty and his own rough justice make him an outlaw in the perilous and corrupt world of eighteenth century England ... Turpin rides riotously for freedom on his beloved mare, Black Bess.'[87] In the series, raven-haired Richard O'Sullivan also

[85] Quoted from Peter Linebaugh, *The London Hanged, Crime and Society in the Eighteenth Century* (London: Penguin, 1992), 203–204.

[86] Shakespeare, *Julius Caesar* III.ii 70–71.

[87] Richard Carpenter, cover notes, *Dick Turpin* (London: Fontana, 1979). Proving that 'What goes around comes around', 1979 was the zenith of the punk rock era in Great Britain, and The Sex Pistols had already looked towards eighteenth century pirates, smugglers and even the Gordon Rioters as the ancestors of working class Punk sensibility during (manager) Malcolm McLaren's masterful campaign of media exploitation. Dick Turpin was obviously ripe for remarketing and the TV series was a great success; similarly, who could forget 'Stand and Deliver' (1981) by Adam and the Ants? The character has also been played on the big screen by Golden Age Hollywood cowboy stars Matheson Lang in 1922, Tom Mix in 1925 and Victor McLaglen in 1933; also Louis Hayward in 1951, David Weston (for Disney) in 1965 and Sid James (*Carry On Dick*) in 1974. More recently, Jake Scott's film *Plunkett and Macleane* (1999) has done the rounds, attempting to combine *Carry on Dick* with *Butch Cassidy and the Sundance Kid* while obviously taking as its inspiration the partnership of Dick Turpin and Tom King. Sources from the anonymous authors of Newgate Calendars to cultural historians such as Hilary and Mary Evans agree that this business arrangement, begun when Turpin attempted to rob King, was terminated when he accidentally shot his partner in crime during a scuffle with the landlord of the Green Man inn, Epping, over a stolen horse. King survived for a week and sang like a canary. Legend has it that Turpin vowed vengeance against the landlord, but he never made good his threat. Interestingly, Ainsworth makes this event a matter of prophecy in *Rookwood*: 'I shall never come to the scragging post, unless you turn topsman, Dick Turpin', says King, 'My nativity has been cast, and the stars have declared I am to die by the hand of my best friend – and that's you – eh, Dick?' Ainsworth, *Rookwood*, 255.

played the role *à la* Robin Hood, there was even a Sheriff of Nottingham figure called Captain Spiker. The moral reversal is a common one in such fiction, in a corrupt social system the outlaw must be the honest man, the rebel, the freedom fighter and, by definition, the hero. Although such figures are not necessarily without historical precedent, such as Sandor Rozsa, the 'bandit of the plains', a Hungarian brigand who became a national guerrilla leader in the 1848 Kossuth rebellion, or Pancho Villa, the Mexican bandit turned revolutionary general in the early years of his country's long revolution (1910–40), they are very, *very* rare. So why should such myths persist?

Eric Hobsbawm pursues a possible answer in the concept he designates as 'social banditry':

> The point about social bandits is that they are peasant outlaws whom the lord and the state regard as criminals, but who remain within peasant society, and are considered by their people as heroes, as champions, avengers, fighters for justice, perhaps even leaders of liberation, and in any case men to be admired, helped and supported.[88]

'Banditry is freedom', says Hobsbawm, 'but in peasant society few can be free.'[89] We might also pause to consider the difference between the public perception of this type of outlaw, invariably deemed heroic, as opposed to other sorts of criminal. 'Jack the Ripper', for example, who preyed upon working-class women in the Autumn of 1888, is also part of English myth, but killers such as he will never be regarded as heroic. In the case of the Whitechapel murders, there was, and is, also an unsubstantiated belief that the killer was a medical man, and therefore a member of the privileged middle classes. Dick Turpin's popularity among the rural and urban poor during his own lifetime is well-documented. Turpin was hanged at York on April 10 1739, and contemporary reports of the behaviour of the crowd at the execution suggest, even allowing for broadsheet invention and exaggeration, that he already had the status of a working-class folk hero, one of their own according to Hobsbawm's analysis, much in the manner of

---

[88] E.J. Hobsbawm, *Bandits* (London: Weidenfeld and Nicolson, 1969), 13.
[89] *Ibid.*, 24.

the recently-deceased Reggie Kray or his equally popular contemporary 'Mad' Frankie Fraser. Even if every account is a fiction, the consistency of reports of flamboyance and bravery at the gallows indicates what the general public were willing, and in fact *wanted*, to believe; the body of popular songs alone is a testimony to this act of faith. Contemporary Newgate Calendar accounts describe Turpin's corpse being borne through the streets like a martyred saint before being buried in lime to render it useless for surgical dissection.[90] Richard Turpin was actually the son of an Essex farmer, and was apprenticed to a Whitechapel butcher; hardly a peasant. Nonetheless, he did not prey upon the poor (why should he?), but upon those whom the poor were likely to view as at best socially remote and at worst oppressors. The robbery of a rich merchant or a local landowner therefore symbolically became an act of rebellion.

Hobsbawm argues that it was the surplus male population of impoverished communities, the unmarried and the unemployed, who were most likely to become outlaws. This is fundamentally the assertion of Lytton's novel *Paul Clifford*, a politically radical, Godwinian novel intended as a critique of social and legal injustice in England. This novel is also centred around the figure of a highwayman, and is four years senior to *Rookwood*. As Hollingsworth points out, the body of Newgate fiction produced between 1830 and 1847 is being written and published during the long and turbulent modernisation of English Law, where it evolves from a fundamentally medieval muddle of complex common law, with over 200 capital crimes on the statute books, to a recognisably modern system of justice. Hollingsworth wisely draws a line under the picaresque novels of the eighteenth century (although they undoubtedly influence the genre, the *picaro* is not generally a heroic figure like the Newgate novel outlaw), and takes Lytton's *Paul Clifford* to be the first of what could be reasonably termed 'Newgate novels'. Politically, Hollingsworth finds Lytton much more interesting than Ainsworth, under the assumption that there is no real agenda beyond entertaining the reader and making a profit in the latter's writing. The dates of Hollingsworth's excellent

---

[90] George Theodore Wilkinson, *The Newgate Calendar* (London: Wordsworth, 1997), 195.

study parallel the rise and fall of Peel and the Tory party between the disarray following the Catholic Emancipation Act of 1829 and the repeal of the Corn Laws in 1846. Hollingsworth takes the Newgate period as running from the publication of *Paul Clifford* in 1830 to Thackeray's damning satire of Ainsworth and Sue, 'The Night Attack', in the February instalment of *Vanity Fair* in 1847, while taking Lytton's *Lucretia* (1846) to be the last truly Newgate novel. I broadly agree, while noting that although the form moves increasingly towards the penny gaffs and the penny dreadfuls from the mid nineteenth century onwards, the relationship between the high literature of writers such as Dickens, Thackeray, the popular entertainment of Lytton, G.P.R. James and Ainsworth, and the work of penny-a-liners like G.W.M. Reynolds, J.M. Rymer and Thomas Peckett Prest is considerably more fluid than Hollingsworth believes it to be. Hollingsworth's book is basically concerned with the politics of Lytton and Dickens.

The purpose of the then radical Lytton in writing his Newgate novel had been to attack his own society's criminal justice system; *Paul Clifford* was the first novel to make such a direct assault on the Law in two decades of repeated and largely unsuccessful parliamentary agitation for reform. In his preface to the 1848 edition, Lytton explained his political purpose in producing *Paul Clifford*:

> A child who is cradled in ignominy; whose schoolmaster is the felon;– whose academy is the House of Correction; who breathes an atmosphere in which virtue is poisoned, to which religion does not pierce – becomes less a responsible and reasoning human being than a wild beast which we suffer to range in the wilderness – till it prowls near our homes, and we kill it in self-defence.

> In this respect, the Novel of 'Paul Clifford' is a loud cry to society to mend the circumstance – to redeem the victim.[91]

Unlike Ainsworth's Turpin, Lytton's Clifford is not based upon a real historical figure, although he did study the Newgate Calendars for information concerning highwaymen. If there is any similarity between these characterisations, it is in the

---

[91] Edward George Earle Bulwer-Lytton, preface, *Paul Clifford*, Collected Works (1830 London: George Routledge and Sons, 1863).

move away from the stereotypical descriptions of criminal personality in the Calendar towards the more daring flamboyance of legend. Keith Hollingsworth describes Paul Clifford as: 'the boys' own outlaw'.[92] This fable initially has more in common with Ainsworth's later novel, *Jack Sheppard*: Paul is potentially good, but his youthful innocence is corrupted by evil circumstance, much as Jack Sheppard falls from grace under the controlling influence of the malevolent Jonathan Wild; both maintain their honour among thieves as adults, as does Ainsworth's Turpin. Where the robbers of Lytton and Ainsworth differ is that Clifford, after transportation, is able to start a new life in America as an exemplary member of the community, while Turpin and Sheppard would have no intention of doing any such thing. They accept the Tyburn tree as a necessary, occupational risk. In much the same way that Gay's characters in *The Beggar's Opera* cannot imagine any kind of death other than hanging. 'Who is there worthy of the name of man', says Turpin, 'that would not prefer such a death before a mean, solitary inglorious life?'[93]

The role that Clifford has been created to enact is that of a Godwinian spokesperson against the Law as an instrument of the rich by which they control and subjugate the poor; the metaphor often employed is that of a state of war between the social classes. Godwin had written in 1793 that:

> The superiority of the rich, being thus unmercifully exercised, must inevitably expose them to reprisals; and the poor man will be induced to regard the state of society as a state of war, an unjust combination, not for protecting every man in his rights and securing to him the means of existence, but for engrossing all its advantages to a few favoured individuals and reserving for the portion of the rest want, dependence and misery.[94]

---

[92] Hollingsworth, 68.
[93] Ainsworth, *Rookwood*, 53.
[94] William Godwin, *Enquiry Concerning Political Justice*, ed. Isaac Kramnick (1793 London: Penguin, 1993), 90.

Paul Clifford echoes this with his statement that:

> I come into the world friendless and poor – I find a body of laws hostile to the friendless to the poor! To those laws hostile to me, then, I acknowledge hostility in my turn. Between us are the conditions of war ...[95]

We can note here that the erudite Clifford is not speaking the flash dialogue of Ainsworth's Turpin and Jerry Juniper; he is merely the author's political automaton rather than a serious attempt at the representation of the life of the criminal in the manner that Dickens would later adopt. Clifford in fact has more than a little in common with Carl von Moor from Schiller's landmark of German romanticism, *The Robbers* (1780). Like von Moor (and in a model later adopted by Scott's chosen successor as master *romancier historique* G.P.R. James in *The Brigand* of 1841[96]), Paul Clifford is the terribly brave leader of a gang of outlaws who are content to steal, cheat, fight, whore and drink until the drop inevitably falls beneath their dirty feet while their leader, when not fighting with Shakespearean valour like the poet-warrior that he essentially is, broods existentially upon the moral weight that bears down upon his soul, and decries the social injustice that has reduced such a pious man to the underworld where morals are a luxury for the rich and crime is a necessity for survival. While his nun-raping comrade-in-arms Spiegelberg 'paces up and down in irritation' muttering, von Moor admonishes the hopeful young volunteer Kosinsky thus:

> Has your tutor been telling you tales of Robin Hood?
>
> – They should clap such careless creatures in irons, and send them to the galleys – exciting your childish imagination, and infecting you with delusions of greatness? Do you itch for fame and honour? would you buy immortality with murder and arson? Be warned, ambitious youth! Murderers earn no laurels! Bandits win no triumphs with their victories – only curses, danger, death and shame – do you not see the gibbet on the hilltop there?[97]

---

[95] Lytton, 200.

[96] Scott's encouragement of, and friendship with, James is covered in detail in Lockhart's *Life of Scott* and S.M. Ellis's biography of James, *The Solitary Horseman, or The Life and Adventures of G.P.R. James* (London: The Cayme Press, 1927).

[97] Friedrich Schiller, *The Robbers*, trans. F.J. Lamport (1780 London: Penguin, 1979), III.ii.

He finally surrenders himself so that the reward may be used to help a starving man and his family. Clifford likewise laments that the life of the outlaw is without honour, with an ignoble death as inevitable as a life of crime is to a poor man:

> Your laws are but of two classes; the one makes criminals, the other punishes them. I have suffered by the one – I am about to perish by the other ... Seven years ago I was sent to the house of correction for an offence which I did not commit; I went thither, a boy who had never infringed a single law – I came forth, in a few weeks, a man who was prepared to break all laws! ... your legislation made me what I am! and it now *destroys me, as it has destroyed thousands, for being what it made me!* ... Let those whom the law protects consider it a protector: when did it ever protect me? When did it ever protect the poor man? The government of a state, the institutions of law, profess to provide for all those who 'obey.' Mark! a man hungers do you feed him? He is naked – do you clothe him? If not, you break your covenant, you drive him back to the first law of nature, and you hang him, not because he is guilty, but because you have left him naked and starving![98]

Only Clifford's companion, the libertine Augustus Tomlinson (ironically presented as a philosopher of crime), accepts the reality of the situation over the dreams of Rousseau's *Social Contract*:

> 'Why, look you, dear Lovett', [Clifford's alias] said Augustus, 'we are all blocks of matter, formed from the atoms of custom; – in other words, we are a mechanism, to which habit is the spring. What could I do in an honest career? I am many years older than you. I have lived as a rogue till I have no other nature than roguery ... I am sure I should be the most consummate of rascals were I to affect to be honest ... I must e'en jog on with my old comrades, and in my old ways, till I jog into the noosehempen – or, melancholy alternative, the noose matrimonial!'[99]

As to the rest of the gang: MacGrawler is happy to have a roof over his head, albeit a cave in a forest ('among the early studies of our exemplary hero, the memoirs of Richard Turpin had formed conspicuous portion'[100]), and food in his belly, while Ned is happy with wine, women and song. Clifford, who is more at home in Plato's cave than in Turpin's, is, like von Moor, an exile in the underworld rather than a true outlaw in the sense that Ainsworth prefers to portray

---

[98] Lytton, 392–3.
[99] *Ibid.*, 328.
[100] *Ibid.*, 317.

them. Ainsworth's trick is to move the likes of Spiegelberg and Augustus Tomlinson to centre stage in the guise of the noble robber to see how they might interact with normal society if unrestrained by a pious authority figure like von Moor or Clifford.

Throughout *Rookwood*, Turpin is a wild card: unpredictable, unrepentant, elemental, *free* from conventional social constraint, able to change his identity at will, and ride with supernatural speed, while also able to confront his own mortality and still drink and sing and enjoy himself.[101] If the literary antecedent of Lytton's highwayman is Schiller's robber, then Turpin's is as surely Gay's MacHeath. As Empson wrote in his radical analysis of *The Beggar's Opera*, 'Mock-Pastoral as the Cult of Independence':

> The only way to use the heroic convention was to turn it onto the mock-hero, the rogue ... The rogue so conceived is not merely an object of satire; he is like the hero because he is strong enough to be independent of society (in some sense), and can therefore be the critic of it ... MacHeath means laird of the open ground where he robs people; he is King of the Waste Land.[102]

This reminds us of Hobsbawm's description of the cultural codes of social banditry, both historically and symbolically.

Dick Turpin, 'a sort of hero',[103] enters *Rookwood* in disguise, as is often the case with Ainsworth's more intriguing characters. Set two years before the original outlaw's death, *Rookwood* introduces 'Jack Palmer' in a chapter entitled 'An English Adventurer' with an epigraph from Gay, 'Sure the captain's the finest gentleman on the road',[104] thus ensuring that Palmer's true identity is the worst kept secret in the novel. A drunken discussion promptly ensues between Turpin and the attorney (and the comic relief) Codicil Coates as to the gentlemanly disposition of the highwayman. This dialogue echoes the conversation of thieves

---

[101] A similar attitude towards life and death can be seen in the elegant gangster movies of the Japanese director/actor Kitano Takeshi.
[102] William Empson, *Some Versions of Pastoral* (London: Penguin, 1966), 163.
[103] Ainsworth, *Rookwood*, 338.
[104] John Gay, *The Beggar's Opera*, Bryan Loughrey and T.O. Treadwell (eds) (1728 London, Penguin, 1986), I.iv.

in *The Beggar's Opera*, and the same ironic blending of the honourable codes of the lawful and the lawless citizen applies until there is little difference between the two; it also makes satiric use of the myth of the highwayman (already more than prevalent in English folklore):

JEMMY TWITCHER: But the present time is ours, and nobody alive hath more. Why are the laws levelled at us? Are we more dishonest than the rest of mankind? What we win, gentlemen, is our own by the law of arms, and the right of conquest.

CROOK-FINGERED JACK: Where shall we find such another set of practical philosophers, who to a man are above the fear of death?

WAT DREARY: Sound men, and true!

ROBIN OF BAGSHOT: Of tried courage, and indefatigable industry!

NIMMING NED: Who is there here that would not die for his friend?

HARRY PADDINGTON: Who is there here that would betray him for his interest?

MATT OF THE MINT: Show me a gang of courtiers that can say as much.[105]

This philosophy is endorsed by the outlaw of *Rookwood* when Turpin argues that:

'It is as necessary for a man to be a gentleman before he can turn highwayman, as it is for a doctor to have his diploma, or an attorney his certificate ... What are the distinguishing characteristics of a fine gentleman? perfect knowledge of the world – perfect independence of character – notoriety – command of cash – and inordinate success with the women ... As to money, he wins a purse of a hundred guineas as easily as you would the same sum from the faro table. And wherein lies the difference? only in the name of the game ... Look at a highwayman mounted on his flying steed, with his pistols in his holsters, and his mask upon his face. What can be a more gallant sight? ... England, sir, has reason to be proud of her highwaymen.'[106]

The English Adventurer then entertains the company with a flash ballad commemorating the most notorious thieves of the last hundred years, set to a somewhat recognisable tune (as were the majority of Gay's airs in *The Beggar's Opera*); a useful device that made the songs ideal for the stage, where the audience could sing along. The song is rendered in underworld slang, and the

---

[105] *Ibid.*, II.i.
[106] Ainsworth, *Rookwood*, 52.

references to the robbers are heavily footnoted by the author for the purpose of historical verification. The lyric is naturally celebratory:

A CHAPTER OF HIGHWAYMEN

Of every rascal of every kind,
The most notorious to my mind,
Was the Cavalier Captain, gay JEMMY HIND!
Which nobody can deny.

But the pleasantest coxcomb among them all
For lute, coranto, and madrigal,
Was the galliard Frenchman, CLAUDE DU-VAL!
Which nobody can deny.

And Tobygloak never a coach could rob,
Could lighten a pocket, or empty a fob,
With a neater hand than OLD MOB, OLD MOB!
Which nobody can deny.

Nor did housebreaker ever deal harder knocks
On the stubborn lid of a good strong box,
Than that prince of good fellows, TOM COX, TOM COX!
Which nobody can deny.

A blither fellow on broad highway,
Did never with oath did traveller stay,
Than devil-may-care WILL HOLLOWAY!
Which nobody can deny.

And in roguery nought could exceed the tricks
Of GETTINGS and GREY, and the five or six,
Who trod in the steps of bold NEDDY WICKS!
Which nobody can deny.

Nor could any so handily break a lock
As SHEPPARD, who stood in the Newgate dock,
And nicknamed the gaolers around him "his flock"!
Which nobody can deny.

Nor did highwayman ever before possess
For ease, for security, danger, distress,
Such a mare as DICK TURPIN'S Black Bess! Black Bess!
Which nobody can deny.[107]

---

[107] *Ibid.*, 54–5.

The fun of the recitation is increased by the singer including himself in the lyric. This is the first of many jaunty songs about highwaymen, whereby the singer augments his discourse by continuing to praise their rank and exploits in terms of modern chivalry, often seconded by the endorsements of Ainsworth's prominent authorial voice.[108] The author even compares Turpin to the hero of Trafalgar at one point: 'Rash daring was the main feature of Turpin's character. Like our great Nelson, he knew fear only by name.'[109] 'A Chapter of Highwaymen' exceeds even this suggestion of noble equality, by punning on Jack Sheppard's surname *and* Biblical imagery when giving the outlaw a 'flock'. This parallels Gay's *leitmotif* regarding MacHeath. As Empson explains, when MacHeath sings 'At a tree I shall suffer with pleasure',[110] the 'half-poetical, half-slang word tree applies both to the gibbet and to the cross, where the supreme sacrificial hero suffered, with ecstasy'.[111] In Turpin's song, his subjects may begin as 'rascals' in the first line, but they finish as divine.

In the final analysis, it is the sense of freedom attached to this type of outlaw (whether in their own day or in the realm of fiction), as clearly identified in fact by Hobsbawm and in fiction by Empson, which makes the figure of Dick Turpin so appealing: a manifestation of longing for a lost cultural innocence, for an imagined past of adventure, heroism and social justice sought from within an increasingly urban, industrialised and Utilitarian society, the moonlit heaths forever shrinking, becoming less magical by the year. In the opening account of his native Manchester in the eighteenth century from *Mervyn Clitheroe*, the narrator concludes that:

> The rivers that washed its walls were clear, and abounded in fish. Above all, the atmosphere was pure and wholesome, unpolluted by the smoke of a

---

[108] The most popular being 'Jerry Juniper's Chant', AKA 'Nix my dolls', the chorus, 'Nix my dolls, pals/Fake away!' translating as, 'Never mind my friends, carry on stealing!'
[109] Ainsworth, *Rookwood*, 163.
[110] Gay, Air, XXV II.v.
[111] Empson, 185.

168

thousand factory chimneys. In some respects, therefore, the old town was preferable to the mighty modern city.[112]

In common with many of Scott's most memorable heroes (the Jacobite, Highland warriors rather than the mediocre heroes of Lukácsian theory), such as the rebel chieftain of *Waverley*, Vich Ian Vohr, Ainsworth presents Turpin as the last of his line:

> Turpin was the *ultimus Romanorum*, the last of a race, which (we were almost about to say we regret) is now altogether extinct. Several successors he had, it is true, but no name worthy to be recorded after his own. With him expired the chivalrous spirit, which animated successively the bosoms of so many knights of the road; with him died away the passionate love of enterprise, that high spirit of devotion to the fair sex, which was first breathed upon the highway by the gay, gallant Claude DuVal, the Bayard of the road – *le filou sans peur et sans reproche* – but was extinguished at last by the cord that tied the heroic Turpin to the remorseless tree.[113]

Scott had likewise concluded *Waverley* with the lament that:

> It was my accidental lot, though not born a Highlander ... to reside, during my childhood and youth, among persons of the above description; and now, for the purpose of preserving some idea of the ancient manners of which I have witnessed the almost total extinction, I have embodied in imaginary scenes, and ascribed to fictitious characters, a part of the incidents which I then received from those who were actors in them.[114]

In each case, these ancestors are not *our* ancestors. They can appear in contemporary culture only as ghosts. Like the walls of Ainsworth's Manchester, his nostalgia offers a simple, almost adolescent view of the past compared with Scott's (although Scott's is equally his own idealised invention), where complex moral and social issues are always presented as either black or white. Characters like Dick Turpin are therefore created in a kind of eternal present, being never allowed to grow up; he was still riding to York on the stage of the Gaiety Theatre in 1890, before galloping away to Hollywood in the twentieth century.

---

[112] Ainsworth, *Mervyn Clitheroe*, 8.
[113] Ainsworth, *Rookwood*, 163–4. Again, the fate of the character is inevitable.
[114] Scott, *Waverley*, 340.

The iconic image of the lone rider, the 'hero on a stolen horse' as the Evans sisters succinctly put it in their book of the same name, found easy purchase in the frontier fables that have always been part of American popular culture. As has been previously noted, the obvious example is the Hollywood western, fed in its turn by wild west myths of outlaws with supernatural shooting skills which remained undeconstructed until Clint Eastwood's existential western *Unforgiven* (1992).[115] And when western fantasy gave way to the domestic concerns of postwar reality, such as the pernicious effects of rock 'n' roll, the outlaw was reincarnated as the teenage rebel in the films of James Dean and, most strikingly for our purposes, in Marlon Brando's interpretation of the Triumph-riding Johnny, leader of a the Black Rebel Motorcycle Club in *The Wild One* (1953).[116] A generation later, as the western world experienced the cultural revolution of the 1960s, Dennis Hopper re-stated the romantic cowboy/biker link in *Easy Rider* (1969), in the scene where the two outlaw long-hairs fix a flat on Peter Fonda's Harley while a blacksmith absentmindedly re-shoes a horse in the foreground.[117] More recently, the original Newgate novel outlaws have returned to source in the quirky Cockney gangster movies of Guy Ritchie, *Lock, Stock and Two Smoking Barrels* (1998)[118] and *Snatch* (2000),[119] where dodgy east-end geezers even dialogue in contemporary London flash. In one scene in *Lock Stock and Two Smoking Barrels*, subtitles are even provided.

Meanwhile, back in 1834, the hero on the stolen horse seemed to be just what the public needed. When it was written in *Fraser's* that, 'With Mr. Ainsworth all is natural, free, and joyous: with Mr. Bulwer all is forced, constrained and cold', the reviewer seems to be endorsing a need for escapism

---

[115] *Unforgiven*, dir. Clint Eastwood, perf. Clint Eastwood, Gene Hackman and Morgan Freeman, Warner, 1992.
[116] *The Wild One*, dir. Laslo Benedek, perf. Marlon Brando, Mary Murphy and Lee Marvin, Columbia, 1953.
[117] *Easy Rider*, dir. Dennis Hopper, perf. Peter Fonda, Dennis Hopper and Jack Nicholson, Columbia, 1969.
[118] *Lock, Stock and Two Smoking Barrels*, dir. Guy Ritchie, perf. Jason Flemyng, Dexter Fletcher, Nick Moran and Jason Statham, PolyGram, 1998.
[119] *Snatch*, dir. Guy Ritchie, perf. Jason Statham, Brad Pitt and Vinnie Jones, Columbia, 2000.

which the heroic pantomime of *Rookwood* offers but the earnest political intent of *Paul Clifford* does not. Such critical accolades were not quite unanimous; John Forster (who later led the war against *Jack Sheppard*), wrote in *The Examiner* that:

> Turpin, whom the writer is pleased with loving familiarity to call Dick, is the hero of the tale. Doubtless we shall soon see Thurtell[120] presented in sublime guise, and the drive to Gad's Hill described with all pomp and circumstance. There are people who may like this sort of thing, but we are not of that number ... The author has, we suspect, been misled by the example and success of 'Paul Clifford', but in 'Paul Clifford' the thieves and their dialect serve for illustration, while in 'Rookwood' the highwayman and his slang are presented as if in themselves they had some claim to admiration.[121]

Despite such occasional suggestions of vulgarity, there were no anxieties expressed in print that this novel, or any other like it, could possibly foster criminal intent among the lower orders: a position that was to alter violently with the commencement of Ainsworth's pure Newgate narrative, *Jack Sheppard*, in *Bentley's Miscellany* in 1839. As was so often the case in an Ainsworth narrative, both literally and metaphorically, there was a storm brewing.

---

[120] John Thurtell, son of a mayor of Norwich, friend of George Borrow and murderer of one William Weare, professional gambler, in 1823. Pierce Egan interviewed Thurtell in prison and subsequently wrote two broadsheet accounts of the case.
[121] Forster, *Examiner*, May 18 1834, 323. As Forster became *The Examiner's* literary critic the year before, this review is assumed to be his work.

CHAPTER THREE

Writing the Underworld: *Jack Sheppard, A Romance*, 1839

I. 'A sort of Hogarthian novel'

By 1838 it was all starting to unravel. Despite the consistent sales of *Rookwood* (which went to five editions within the first three years of publication), Ainsworth's aristocratic lifestyle had left his private finances seriously depleted. The death of his estranged wife in early March had also plunged him back into another stressful and expensive legal battle with the Ebers family, this time over the custody of his three daughters. In September, Ainsworth wrote to Crossley, 'I am so bothered that I hardly know which way to turn ... She is giving me all the trouble she can.'[1] 'She' being Fanny's sister Emily, who blamed Ainsworth for her sister's untimely death and had taken the children out of school and was denying Ainsworth any access; by September she and her father had thwarted all Ainsworth's legal attempts even to *see* his children and were planning to retreat to France. From the outset, Ainsworth had privately conceded from bitter experience that, 'I doubt the possibility of my outwitting the Ebers.'[2] Ainsworth did not get his 'little girls' back until Autumn 1839, and then only after John Ebers, described by his son-in-law as 'utterly callous', had got £300 out of him for two years of

---

[1] Ainsworth, letter to Crossley, September 6 1838.
[2] Ainsworth, letter to Crossley, March 25 1838.

retrospective maintenance. Ainsworth survived during this period by borrowing money from Crossley, writing in the Autumn of 1837 that:

> If needful, I can obtain the advance from Bentley. But it will be attended with bother, and a humiliating sense of obligation, which I would gladly avoid … I have many other friends to whom I could apply, but you are the only person to whom I choose to be under such an obligation.[3]

These problems dogged Ainsworth throughout the composition of *Jack Sheppard*, although Ellis, ever the Edwardian gentleman, omits the entire episode from his biography.

Ainsworth had followed *Rookwood* with *Crichton* in 1837, a historical novel charting the adventures of the dashing Scot James ('the admirable') Crichton at the court of Henri III of France, which had been only a partial success. Ellis summed up *Crichton* thus: 'It was a *very* historical romance, and the mass of erudition, the quantity of Latin, and the ultra-profuseness of detail with which it bristled, must have sadly perplexed the great bulk of its less cultured readers. *Crichton* never had the popular appeal of *Rookwood* and its successors.'[4] Like *Rookwood*, *Crichton* had been very well researched and was another split text of original songs and billowing historical footnotes, which unfortunately suffered from a hasty and contrived conclusion which, wrote George J. Worth, 'no amount of architectonic skill can conceal'.[5] With sidekicks, Blount, Ogilvy and a bloody great dog, Crichton's constant humiliation of the French would be considerably more appropriate to a text produced during the Napoleonic wars rather than in the first year of Victoria's reign. The early chapter entitled 'The English bull-dog' really sets the tone, with the Englishman Blount's seeing-off of a crowd of Sorbinists, their puny staffs no match for his absurdly phallic cudgel: 'which was not a vine-wood staff, but a huge English crab-stick, seasoned, knotty and substantial'.[6] The character of Crichton himself was too remote, clean-cut,

---

[3] Ainsworth, letter to Crossley, November 5 1837.
[4] Ellis, vol. 1, 319.
[5] Worth, 56.
[6] Ainsworth, *Crichton* (1837), Works, 37.

aristocratic, perfect and invulnerable to appeal to fans of Dick Turpin. In debt, and with his in-laws using their knowledge of his financial problems to strengthen their case for custody of his children, Ainsworth desperately needed a successful novel. With public pressure upon him to produce another *Rookwood*, all roads lead inexorably to Old Newgate.

The first sign of *Jack Sheppard* comes from a letter written to James Crossley early in 1837:

> I think you will be glad to hear that I propose visiting Manchester for a few days next week, when I hope to spend some pleasant hours with you ... I want to consult you about my new romance which is a tale of the reign of George the first — and as that monarch cuts a conspicuous figure in the story, I shall really be thankful if you can lend me any memoirs, or other matter, relating to him, or put me in the way of finding them. My exact year is 1724. I mention this that you may just direct your thoughts to the period. It is my intention to introduce Jack Sheppard. Have you any history of Old Newgate? or any pictures of that prison. I think it scarcely likely but I must look to you for George the First. It is curious there should be so little known about his habits, manners of which are exactly what I want. But I doubt not but you will be able to afford me information. I need to write, or attempt to write, a sort of Hogarthian novel — describing London at the beginning of the eighteenth century. But all this, and a good deal more, we will talk over when we meet.[7]

Until the end of the following year, the new romance is referred to under the title of *Thames Darrell*, being the hero of the tale, a child of noble birth adopted by Mr Wood the carpenter and named from the river from which he was rescued as a baby, having been thrown in and presumed drowned by his wicked uncle, Sir Rowland Trenchard. Dick Turpin had dominated the author's fancy and divided the text of *Rookwood*, but the character of Jack Sheppard performs a total textual annexation: overwriting Thames Darrell in both central role and title, and the planned historical novel on George I becomes the purest of Ainsworth's Newgate narratives; the only royalty in *Jack Sheppard* being Jonathan Wild, 'the Prince of Robbers', and Baptist Kettleby, the 'Master of the Mint', ruler of the underworld haven of Southwark.

---

[7] Ainsworth, letter to Crossley, May 29 1837.

Only the Hogarthian aspect of the initial design remained intact, the basic plot and moral of *Jack Sheppard* closely following the model of Hogarth's series of twelve engravings, *Industry and Idleness* (1747), both narratives charting the progress of two apprentices, one of whom pursues a life of vice, the other virtue. Ainsworth's original manuscript even included scriptural epigraphs attached to each book, or epoch, as Hogarth had done with each of his 12 plates, but friend and colleague Rev. R.H. Barham ('Thomas Ingoldsby') advised him to omit these because, 'the mixing up of sacred texts with a work of fancy will revolt many persons who would otherwise read it with pleasure, and will afford your enemies such a handle as they will not fail to use powerfully'.[8] *Industry and Idleness* is Hogarth the Foundling Hospital Governor preaching a simple, pious and mercantile orthodoxy to the masses (there is none of the subtle visual symbolism of *Marriage-à-la-mode* here), and every event is portrayed in terms of polarised moral alternatives. The two apprentice weavers (Goodchild and Tom Idle) are shown together at their looms in the opening plate, before going their separate ways in adult life, each episode starkly contrasted: Goodchild has a broadsheet version of the story of Dick Whittington on the wall behind him, Idle has a broadsheet on Moll Flanders;[9] Goodchild worships at a City church, Tom Idle gambles outside in the churchyard, using a grave stone for a gaming table; Goodchild marries the master's daughter and lives in a mansion, Idle lives with a prostitute in a rookery garret; Goodchild has an adoring wife, while Idle is 'betray'd by his Whore',[10] until the men meet face to face again in the tenth plate as magistrate and thief, Goodchild *en route* to the Guildhall and political power, Idle to Newgate then the gallows. The eleventh plate is the famous depiction of

---

[8] R.H. Barham, *Life and Letters*, quoted in Ellis, vol. 1, 375.
[9] In a corresponding episode in *Jack Sheppard*, Thames has copies of the ballads 'St. George for England and True Protestant Gratitude, or Britain's Thanksgiving for the First of August, being the Day of His Majesty's Happy Accession to the Throne' pasted to the wall, while Jack has 'The Thief Catcher's Prophecy' and 'Life and Death of the Darkman's Budge'. Ainsworth, *Jack Sheppard, A Romance* (1839), Works, 58–9. Thames's Orange commitment to his religion reminds the attentive reader that the original John Sheppard was reported to be a Catholic, placing him doubly beyond the pale as both thief and idolater.
[10] William Hogarth, *Industry and Idleness*, Plate 9 (1747).

'The Idle 'Prentice Executed at Tyburn', the crowds of morbid onlookers a brutally parodic reflection of the cheering crowds at the procession in the final plate celebrating 'The Industrious 'Prentice Lord-Mayor of London'. This bourgeois moral fable, that honesty and hard work bring success as surely as the wages of sin are death, was designed primarily for display on workshop walls where impressionable apprentices might contemplate it at length, the scriptural quotation beneath each illustration adding the obvious dimension of a sermon.

Ainsworth's *Jack Sheppard* is the story of two apprentices, Thames Darrell (Goodchild) and Jack Sheppard (Tom Idle); unlike the parallel narratives of Luke Rookwood and Dick Turpin, the stories of Thames and Jack interact quite fluidly. The novel is divided into three books, or epochs, each taking place in a very compressed temporal space like the acts of a play. Epoch the First, 1703, takes place in one night when the main protagonists are new-born babies, and acts as a prologue. Epoch the Second, 1715 (which begins with a chapter entitled 'The Idle Apprentice'), takes place over a few days in June and shows the adolescent Jack's fall from grace into the orbit of the evil thief-taker and criminal mastermind, Jonathan Wild, while Thames rather foolishly falls into the clutches of his evil uncle, Sir Rowland Trenchard, who is Wild's silent partner. Epoch the Third, 1724, encompasses the six months leading up to Jack's capture and execution. It opens with Jack at the height of his success as a criminal (and consequent depths of depravity) as Wild's right hand, and the return of Thames, who escaped his uncle and fled to France where he became a prosperous merchant. Disgusted at a murder which takes place during a robbery arranged by Wild, Jack turns against him and spends much of the remainder of the narrative assisting Thames in the restoration of his family fortune, except when incarcerated, which allows Ainsworth to recreate the daring prison escapes which had guaranteed the original Jack Sheppard his place in the Newgate Calendars. Wild murders Sir Rowland and traps Jack at his mother's graveside. Jack dies bravely on the gallows, Thames's birthright is established and he marries his childhood sweetheart, Winifred, his old master's daughter. We are reassured, in one of Ainsworth's characteristic historical closures, that Wild was convicted and hanged: 'seven months afterwards, with every ignominy, at the very gibbet to which he had brought his victim'.[11]

After many delays *Jack Sheppard* began its serial run in *Bentley's Miscellany* in January 1839. Dickens's serial *Oliver Twist* was at this point coming to a conclusion in the same magazine, and for four months both serials appeared concurrently. As both stories concerned young boys being drawn in to the criminal underworld and shared the graphics of George Cruikshank, *Jack Sheppard* and *Oliver Twist* became implicitly connected in the minds of their original and massive audience. This was compounded when Ainsworth succeeded Dickens as the editor of *Bentley's* in March. From the outset, *Jack Sheppard* was a great success. Immediately after the launch Ainsworth wrote to Crossley that the usually dour publisher Richard Bentley was in 'tip-top spirits'.[12] In October, before its completion in *Bentley's*, *Jack Sheppard* was issued as a novel in three volumes by Bentley, including 27 engravings by Cruikshank and a portrait of the author by R.J. Lane. Sales were enormous, initially exceeding 3,000 copies a week. Ainsworth was also rewarded by the sincerest form of flattery from the penny-a-liners: *The History of Jack Sheppard* (by John Williams, 1839) depicts Jack as a heroic figure who infiltrates the criminal underworld as part of a scheme to restore the rightful inheritance of Edgeworth Bess, a pure and persecuted heroine rather than an aggressive prostitute; *The Eventful Life and Unparalleled Exploits of the Notorious Jack Sheppard* (T. White, 1840) concentrates on the Jacobite intrigues of Mr Kneebone, cramming a brief summary of Sheppard's career into the conclusion, and *The Life and Adventures of Jack Sheppard* (G. Purkess, 1849) simply plagiarises Ainsworth.[13] *Oliver Twist*, published as a novel in November 1838, had always been very popular, but this year belonged to Ainsworth: 'For a time', recalled Henry Vizetelly in *Glances Back Over Seventy*

---

[11] Ainsworth, *Jack Sheppard*, 344.
[12] Ainsworth, letter to Crossley, January 1 1839.
[13] Source: Louis James, 186–7.

Years, 'Dickens' star paled.'[14] 'The success of Jack is pretty certain', Ainsworth told Crossley, 'They are bringing him out in half the theatres in London.'[15]

And so they were. By the end of October there were eight versions running concurrently in London. Ainsworth and Cruikshank publicly supported these unlicensed theatrical adaptations of their work, whereas Dickens, in general, loathed it when it happened to him; Forster reporting in his *Life of Dickens* that:

> I was with him at a representation of his *Oliver Twist* the following month [December 1838] at the Surrey Theatre, when in the middle of the first scene he laid himself down upon the floor in a corner of the box and never rose from it until the drop-scene fell.[16]

Ainsworth, on the other hand, endorsed J.T. Haines's version of *Jack Sheppard* at the Royal Surrey Theatre while Cruikshank acted as an adviser to the set designers and makers. The author's letter to the manager G.B. Davidge praising the production was printed on all programmes and daily newspaper advertisements (for which he received a one-off royalty payment of £20, the only money he ever made directly from any of these dramas although several were still running when he died):

> Sir, – Having, in compliance with your request, witnessed your Rehearsal, and perused the Drama founded on JACK SHEPPARD, in preparation at the Surrey Theatre, I am satisfied it will furnish a complete representation of the Principal Scenes of the Romance; and have, therefore, no hesitation in giving my entire sanction to the performance. The fact of the whole of the Scenery having been superintended by Mr. George Cruikshank, must be a sufficient guarantee to the Public for its excellence and accuracy.[17]

He also furnished W.T. Moncrieff of the Victoria Theatre with an advance copy of the final instalment of the serial for his scriptwriters.

---

[14] Quoted from Philip Collins, *Dickens and Crime* (London: Macmillan, 1965), 257.
[15] Ainsworth, letter to Crossley, October 8 1839.
[16] Forster, 381.
[17] Ainsworth, letter to G.B. Davidge, October 18 1839.

By far the best loved of all these plays was J.B. Buckstone's version at the Adelphi Theatre starring the legendary Mrs Keeley as Jack Sheppard.[18] What made 'Bucky's' production different was his astute inclusion of many of the flash songs from *Rookwood*. Each performance concluded with a raucous encore of 'Nix My Dolly, Pals' by the full cast and the audience, led by Jack, Blueskin (played by the equally famous Paul Bedford), Poll Maggot and Edgeworth Bess (the very lovely Mrs Nailer and Miss Campbell), which had been set to music by G.H. Rodwell, operatic composer and proprietor of the Adelphi. Sir Theodore Martin ('Bon Gaultier') later wrote of this period:

> *Nix My Dolly* travelled everywhere, and made the patter of thieves and burglars 'familiar in our mouths as household words'. It deafened us in the streets, where it was so popular with the organ-grinders and German bands as Sullivan's brightest melodies ever were in later day. It clanged at midday from the steeple of St. Giles, the Edinburgh Cathedral (A fact. That such a subject for cathedral chimes, and in Scotland, too, could ever have been chosen will scarcely be believed. But my astonished ears often heard it.); it was whistled by every dirty guttersnipe, and chanted in drawing-rooms by fair lips, little knowing the meaning of the words they sang.[19]

Once more, Jack Sheppard had become iconic.

In his own day the original John 'Jack' Sheppard had achieved a certain notoriety, not for his crimes (which were unremarkable acts of burglary around Holborn in the early 1720s), but for his increasingly ingenious and cheeky prison escapes. He even broke out of the condemned hold at Newgate and, when recaptured, he was placed in a fortified room in the heart of the gaol known as the 'Castle', chained hand and foot with 300 pound iron fetters, and attached to the stone floor with an iron staple just to be on the safe side. Here he held court like a celebrity in a theatrical Green Room. Hogarth himself was one of the crowds of gentry who paid the turnkeys 1s 6d to visit Jack Sheppard in the Castle at Newgate in 1724, by now famous for his previous escapes, as well as his open

---

[18] Mary Anne Goward, (1804–99).
[19] Quoted from Ellis, vol. 1, 366.

defiance of the thief-taker Jonathan Wild. Hogarth's father-in-law, Sir James Thornhill, also visited Sheppard, and painted a portrait of him that looked more like that of a poet than a house-breaker. Ainsworth cheekily dramatises the scene in his chapter 'How Jack's portrait was painted', placing Thornhill, Hogarth and Gay together. Ainsworth suggests that Jack inspires both *The Beggar's Opera* and *Industry and Idleness*.[20] When Jack became tired of all this attention, he escaped again. Unfortunately, young Jack wasn't very bright when it came to keeping out of prison, and he was recaptured, dead drunk, in an ale house on Newgate Street, still within sight of the prison. He was hanged at Tyburn on November 23, 1724, aged 22. He did not die well; being a small man, the drop did not break his neck and he took a long time to strangle under his own body weight.

Half a dozen or so biographies of Sheppard were in circulation by the day of his execution (as well as numerous broadsheets, ballads and a couple of plays), including two pamphlets often attributed to Defoe, which became, and remain, the principal sources on Sheppard for later writers.[21] His story also seems likely to have inspired Gay's *Opera*: MacHeath, like Sheppard, having two lovers, while Mr Peachum is undoubtedly modelled on Jonathan Wild, of whom Defoe also wrote a short biography after his execution the following year.[22] It has also been suggested, by Lucy Moore most recently, that the Sheppard story was the

[20] See Jenny Uglow, *Hogarth* (London: Faber and Faber, 1998), chapter 5.
[21] *A Narrative of All the Robberies, Escapes, etc. of John Sheppard*, (London: John Applebee, 1724). Sensing the market, Applebee had also published *The History of the remarkable Life of John Sheppard, containing A particular account of his many Robberies and Escapes* (London: John Applebee, 1724) directly after Sheppard's first escape from Newgate. Both these pamphlets have been attributed to Defoe although there is no real supporting evidence that the two men even knew one another. In a recent biography of Jack Sheppard, the author puts Defoe and Applebee at the execution, with a hearse standing by to whisk Sheppard's corpse away for resuscitation, a factoid of which I am more than a little sceptical. Lucy Moore, *The Thieves' Opera* (London: Penguin, 1997), 224.
[22] Daniel Defoe, *The True and Genuine Account of The Life and Actions of The Late Jonathan Wild, Not made up of fiction and fable, but taken from his own mouth, and collected from papers of his own writing* (London, 1725) appended to Henry Fielding, *Miscellanies*, vol III, *The Life of Mr. Jonathan Wild the Great*, ed. David Nokes (1743 London; Penguin, 1986).

inspiration for *Industry and Idleness*, but this is less likely, generic parables of fallen apprentices being by then very common.[23]

The fame of the real Jack Sheppard and Jonathan Wild was an early example of a media-generated fad however, and they were soon forgotten. By the time Fielding resurrected the Jonathan Wild/Robert Walpole comparison of Gay's opera in the third volume of his *Miscellanies* in 1743 it was already a cliché. The popularity of Ainsworth's character and his theatrical clones, seemed to transcend that of the original: after they read the novel, theatre-goers could actually sing along with Jack, Blueskin, and pretty Poll and Bess, weep with Jack as he hugged the earth of his mother's grave, and cheer with a mixture of horror and delight when an angry mob set Jonathan Wild's house ablaze. As Keith Hollingsworth perfectly put it: 'Sheppard was not simply a sensation in fiction, but an extra-literary popular phenomenon.'[24] Even the famous letters sent to the *Kansas City Star* by the notorious outlaws of the American west Frank and Jesse James were signed 'Jack Sheppard'.[25] This phenomenon was to be a problematic one for Ainsworth, as his character stepped from the pages of the essentially bourgeois novel (at £1. 5s a copy), and onto the boards of the working class, penny gaffs.

S.M. Ellis argued that a story based upon such a model as Hogarth's was 'absolutely moral' by definition, being 'simply a prose version of that famous series of pictures by the greatest of moralists'.[26] While Ellis's intention to defend his subject against decades of ridiculous critical condemnation is laudable, this correlation is misleading, despite Ainsworth's obvious use of *Industry and Idleness*. Ainsworth's Jack Sheppard may begin and end as an apparently direct copy of a character from Hogarth's *Moralities*, but the author refuses to contain him within such a basic role, the simple dialectics of Hogarth in moral mode actually having more in common with the two-dimensional, cardboard

---

[23] See Moore, 35. Hogarth in fact based his narrative upon *The London Merchant*, a popular play by George Lillo first performed in 1731.
[24] Hollingsworth, 140.
[25] Clive Bloom, *Cult Fiction: Popular Reading and Pulp Theory* (London: Macmillan, 1996), 86.
[26] Ellis, vol. 1, 373–4.

characterisations of *Rookwood* than the more complex emotional motivations explored in *Jack Sheppard*.

In the post-*Paul Clifford* period, Hogarth was habitually evoked by commentators as a benchmark for what had come to be known as the Newgate school of novelists. Like Thackeray's ambivalent appeals to Fielding however, Victorian sensibilities fostered an unstable relationship with the great Georgian satirist and moralist, agreeing with the message but having a mixed emotional response to the method. For example, R.H. Horne compared the art of his friend Charles Dickens to that of Hogarth in *A New Spirit of the Age*:

> The tragic force, and deep moral warnings, contained in several of the finest works of Hogarth, have been fully recognized by a few great writers, but are not yet recognized sufficiently by the popular sense. But even some of his pictures, which are deservedly among the least popular, from the revolting nature of their subject or treatment, do yet, for the most part, contain manifestations of his great genius. Of this class are the pictures on the 'Progress of Cruelty:' – but who will deny the terrific truth of the last but one of the series. The cruel boy, grown up to cruel manhood, has murdered his mistress, apparently to avoid the trouble attending her being about to become a mother. He has cut her throat at night in a church-yard, and seemingly to have become suddenly paralysed at the completeness of his own deed, which he was too brutally stupid to comprehend till it was really done, two watchmen have arrested him. There lies his victim – motionless, extinct, quite passed away out of the scene, out of the world. Her white visage is a mere wan case that has opened, and the soul has utterly left it. No remains even of bodily pain are traceable, but rather in its vacuity a suggestion of the last nervous consciousness that her life of misery should be ended. The graves, the tombstones, the old church walls are alive and ejaculatory with horror – the man alone stands petrific. There is no bold Turpin, or Jack Sheppard-ing to carry the thing off heroically. Stony-jointed and stupefied, the murderer stands between the two watchmen, who grasp him with a horror which is the mixed effect of his own upon them, and of their scared discovery of the lifeless object before them. It is plain that if the murderer had been a flash Newgate Calendar hero, he could have burst away from them in a moment. But this would not have answered the purpose of the moralist.[27]

Horne then marks the 'point where the comparison with him and Dickens stops'. Although Horne's argument is essentially one of realism over what he views as the cheap, immature romanticism of Ainsworth, he cannot allow that Hogarth's ends necessarily justify his means; he therefore immediately adds that: 'In dealing with repulsive characters and actions, the former sometimes does so in a repulsive manner, not artistically justifiable by any means.' Dickens, conversely, has the 'good taste' never to allow himself to pollute a text or offend his audience with an unnecessarily 'gross expression or unredeemed action'. This, claims Horne, is the cause of Dickens's 'universal popularity'.[28] A similar thesis can be found in an article on Newgate writing in *The Athenaeum*, but with the cynical suggestion that his popularity comes from a mis-reading which favours sensationalism over moral philosophy:

> In thus introducing Mr. Dickens's name, we are far from classing him with his imitators, or ranging his works with the Factory Boys and the Jack Sheppards, – in external appearance so similar. If Boz has depicted scenes of hardened vice, and displayed the peculiar phases of degradation which poverty impresses on the human character under the combinations of a defective civilization, he is guided in his career by a high moral object; and in tracing what is most loathsome and repulsive, he contrives to enlist the best feelings of our nature in his cause, and to engage his readers in the consideration of what lies below the surface. In this respect he approaches his great predecessors, Fielding and Gay; for, though he proceeds by a different path, he arrives at the same end; and, instead of sullying the mind of an intelligent reader, he leaves him wiser and better for the perusal of his tale. But this is precisely the excellence which we suspect the readers of Boz most frequently overlook; and we are certain that it is far less the under-current of philosophy which has sold his book, than the strong flavour of the medium, in which he has disguised the bitterness of its taste.[29]

The Hogarth illustration to which Horne refers is the penultimate plate of *Four Stages of Cruelty* (1751, immediately following the popular prints *Beer Street* and *Gin Lane*), 'Cruelty in Perfection'. It is a nasty picture. The previous two prints show the unloved and unrestrained St Giles pauper Tom Nero maltreating animals as man and boy, and now he has killed his pregnant lover, Ann Gill, a maidservant

---

[27] R.H. Horne, *A New Spirit of the Age*, 2 vols (London: Smith, Elder and Co., 1844), vol. 1, 10–11.

[28] *Ibid.*, 1, 11–12

[29] 'Jack Sheppard: a Romance', rev. of *Jack Sheppard*, by W.H. Ainsworth, *Athenaeum*, October 26 1839, 804.

who had stolen from her mistress at his demand. A kneeling watchman holds a note towards us written by the victim, wherein her conflict between her affection for her employer and her loyalty to her lover is recorded: 'and my Conscience flied in my face as often as I think of wronging her, yet I am bound body and soul to do as you would have me do'. Her throat is cut so deeply that her head is almost severed and her left hand is almost cut off at the wrist, a presumably defensive wound, but she still points towards her fallen hand luggage, a box containing the *Book of Common Prayer* and a treatise entitled 'GOD'S Revenge against Murder'. In the final print, Tom Nero is not shown at the gallows like Tom Idle but instead on the dissection table, his mutilated body replacing that of the woman from the previous image (their physical poses are almost identical), the artist playing upon one of the commonest fears of the criminal. There is an awful sense of consciousness in Hogarth's depiction of the corpse, his mouth open in a mute scream of agony as one surgeon disembowels him while another probes the delicate sinews of his ankles and a third removes his eyes. A figure of obvious authority sits in a throne-like chair directing the operation; he is presumably a chief surgeon but in fact looks most like a judge; like God Himself he looks down from above, suggesting the moral as well as the physical deconstruction of the subject. Beneath the table a dog feeds upon the heart of the corpse. This is 'The Reward of Cruelty', and it's unremittingly appalling to behold.

The destruction of the fallen woman is also a powerful and recurring image in Dickens's work; he was still shocking audiences with his public reading of 'The Death of Nancy' when he died. But both this episode in *Oliver Twist* and its forerunner in *Sketches by Boz*, 'The Hospital Patient', are careful to avoid the naked, human brutality of Hogarth, even though the story is the same as that of 'Cruelty in Perfection', where the victim remains pitifully loyal to the man who will ultimately kill her. Although the simple allegory of Hogarth is delivered with the most microscopic realism, Dickens steers away from the violence at the last moment, leaving the death blow to his readers' imagination and the final prayer of his Magdalene comes in a moment of melodrama:

> She staggered and fell: nearly blinded with the blood that rained down from a deep gash in her forehead; but raising herself, with difficulty, on her knees, drew from her bosom a white handkerchief – Rose Maylie's own – and holding it up, in her folded hands, as high towards Heaven as her feeble strength would allow, breathed one prayer for mercy to her Maker.

> It was a ghastly figure to look upon. The murderer staggering backward to the wall, and shutting out the sight with his hand, seized a heavy club and struck her down.[30]

There is no gothic or Newgate sensationalism here, but little realism either. Thackeray had similarly written that:

> The world does not now tolerate such satire as that of Hogarth and Fielding, and the world no doubt is right in a great part of its squeamishness; for it is good to pretend to the virtue of chastity even though we do not possess it; nay, the very restraint which the hypocrisy lays on a man, is not unapt, in some instances, to profit him ... The same vice exists, only we don't speak about it; the same things are done, but we don't call them by their names. Here lies the chief immorality of Fielding, as we take it ... It is wise that the public modesty should be as prudish as it is; that writers should be forced to chasten their humour, and when it would play with points of life and character which are essentially immoral, that they should be compelled, by the general outcry of incensed public propriety, to be silent altogether.

But, 'Fielding's men and Hogarth's are Dickens' and Cruikshank's, drawn with ten times more skill and force, only the latter humorists dare not talk of what the elder discussed honestly.'[31] Thackeray, Horne and *The Athenaeum* would appear to concur, yet the former's references to 'hypocrisy' and 'honesty' perhaps betray an uncertain desire to return to a freedom of expression now subservient to public morality. A more confident statement appears in the preface to *Pendennis*: 'Since the author of "Tom Jones" was buried, no writer of fiction among us has been permitted to depict to his utmost power a MAN. We must drape him, and give him a certain conventional simper.'[32]

Although Thackeray, unlike Dickens, appeared to feel this lack, he did not break these new Victorian taboos of representation. Ainsworth did, and this was

---

[30] Dickens, *Oliver Twist*, 268.
[31] Thackeray, rev. of a new edition of the Works of Henry Fielding, *The Times*, September 2 1840.
[32] Thackeray, preface, *The History of Pendennis* (1850), Works.

what he really meant by a 'sort of Hogarthian novel'. This was the creation of a Hogarthian *mise en scène*, where it was not the moral message of *The Rake's Progress, Industry and Idleness, The Four Stages of Cruelty, Gin Lane et al.* that Ainsworth took from Hogarth, but his grotesque realism, a form of representation which could be allied with Ainsworth's use of the gothic to portray graphically an English urban environment that was dark, mysterious, threatening and yet strangely erotic.

This project was perfectly complemented by the art of George Cruikshank, whose style (and, after he signed the pledge, sanctimony) was deeply inspired by Hogarth. In a critical review of Cruikshank, Thackeray wrote that: 'With regard to the modern romance of "Jack Sheppard", ... it seems to us that Mr. Cruikshank really created the tale, and that Mr. Ainsworth, as it were, only put words to it.'[33] *The Athenaeum* similarly wrote of *Jack Sheppard* that, 'it [is] doubtful whether the plates were etched for the book, or the book written to illustrate the plates', but for a different reason to Thackeray:

> In these graphic representations are embodied all the inherent coarseness and vulgarity of the subject; and all the horrible and (it is not too strong to say) unnatural excitement which a public, too prudish to relish humour, and too *blasé* to endure true pathos, requires to keep alive and awaken sensation.[34]

Not only is Thackeray's statement somewhat hypocritical, given his sustained attack on the Newgate school in general and on Ainsworth in particular, but it also misses the point that Cruikshank's illustrations (many of which have been razored out of first editions and framed by collectors who apparently agree with Thackeray) and Ainsworth's prose are interdependent textual components. This was understood from the first by the theatrical producers who framed the action with stage sets based on Cruikshank's engravings. The Hogarthian text demands to be a graphic novel, and Cruikshank's final set of engravings, depicting Jack's two escapes from Newgate and his execution, are sequenced like a comic strip,

---

[33] Thackeray, 'George Cruikshank', *Westminster Review*, June 1840.
[34] *Athenaeum*, October 26 1839, 803.

and presented as a series of linear, narrative panels rather than as conventional, single one-page illustrations. The text is also graphically *violent*, with the extravagant, gothic death scenes of *Rookwood* being replaced by an unsettling, Hogarthian realism:

> 'Spare me!' he groaned, looking upwards. 'Spare me!'
>
> Jonathan, however, instead of answering him, searched for his knife, with the intention of severing his wrist. But not finding it, he had again recourse to the bludgeon, and began beating the hand fixed on the upper rail, until by smashing the fingers, he forced it to relinquish its hold. He then stamped upon the hand on the lower banister, until that also relaxed its grip.
>
> Sir Rowland then fell.
>
> A hollow plunge, echoed and re-echoed by the walls, marked his descent into the water.
>
> 'Give me the link', cried Jonathan.
>
> Holding down the light, he perceived that the wounded man had risen to the surface, and was trying to clamber up the slippery sides of the well.
>
> 'Shoot him! Shoot him! Put him out of hish mishery', cried the Jew.
>
> 'What's the use of wasting a shot?' rejoined Jonathan, savagely. 'He can't get out.'[35]

Ainsworth and Cruikshank returned to the period of the gruesome Georgians in every respect, taking precisely those features of the social commentary of Defoe, the picaresque literature of Fielding and the art of Hogarth that the Victorians had edited out.

Humphry House has written, for example, that the underworld environment that Oliver Twist found himself in would have been, in reality, 'drenched in sex',[36] which it cannot ever possibly be in a Dickensian text. Thackeray had used a similar argument to attack Dickens for his unrealistic portrayal of Nancy:

> Boz, who knows life well, knows that his Miss Nancy is the most unreal fantastical personage possible; no more like a thief's mistress than one of Gessner's shepherdesses resembles a real country wench. He dare not tell the truth concerning such young ladies. They have, no doubt, virtues like other human creatures; nay, their position engenders virtues that are not called into

---

[35] Ainsworth, *Jack Sheppard*, 249.
[36] Humphry House, *The Dickens World* (Oxford: Oxford UP, 1960), 217.

exercise among other women. But on these an honest painter of human nature has no right to dwell; not being able to paint the whole portrait, he has no right to present one or two favourable points as characterising the whole: and therefore, in fact, had better leave the picture alone altogether.[37]

This is of course another manifestation of Thackeray's public modesty argument, a Gordian proposition, apparently calling for a literary realism denuded first of any subject which might cause offence to the public morals. Dickens responded that he wished to 'dim the false glitter' of the Newgate romance by 'showing it in its unattractive and repulsive truth', however:

> No less consulting my own taste, than the manners of the age, I endeavoured, while I painted it in all its fallen and degraded aspects, to banish from the lips of the lowest character I introduced, any expression that could possibly offend; and rather to lead to the unavoidable inference that its existence was of the most debased and vicious kind, than to prove it elaborately by words and deeds. In the case of the girl, in particular, I kept this constantly in view.[38]

Dickens describes Nancy as a 'prostitute' in the preface to the third edition of *Oliver Twist*, but he never calls her such in the main text. In the same way, the dialogue is suitably tidied up for the polite ear: 'He [Bill Sikes] then, in cant terms, with which his whole conversation was plentifully besprinkled, but which would be quite unintelligible if they were recorded here, demanded a glass of liquor.'[39] Dickens wanted completely to reject the flash anti-language of 'Nix My Dolls' which, as Martin had reported, was on everybody's lips by the end of 1839, whether they understood the lyrics or not:

> In a box of the stone jug I was born,
> Of a hempen widow the kid forlorn,
> *Fake away.*
> And my father, as I've heard say,
> *Fake away.*
> Was a merchant of capers gay,
> Who cut his last fling with great applause,
> *Nix my doll pals, fake away.*[40]

---

[37] Thackeray, 'Going to see a man hanged', *Fraser's*, August, 1840.
[38] Dickens, preface, *Oliver Twist*.
[39] Dickens, *Oliver Twist*, 137.
[40] Ainsworth, 'Jerry Juniper's Chant', *Rookwood*, 117.

Which can be translated (or more appropriately perhaps *decoded*, given its presentation as a secret language) as:

> I was born in a prison cell,
> My mother was the widow of a hanged man,
> *Carry on stealing.*
> And my father, as I've been told,
> *Carry on stealing.*
> Was an excellent dancer,
> Whose last dance was bravely done from the end of a rope,[41]
> *Never mind my friends, carry on stealing.*

This was exactly the type of thing that Thackeray objected to as both a glorification of criminal behaviour and linguistic vulgarity, and from which Dickens wished to dissociate himself:

> I have read of thieves by the score; seductive fellows (amiable for the most part), faultless in dress, plump in pocket, choice in horse-flesh, bold in bearing, fortunate in gallantry, great at a song, a bottle, a pack of cards or dice-box, and fit companions for the bravest. But I had never met (except in HOGARTH) with the miserable reality.[42]

Dickens's appeal to Hogarth here being the opposite to that of Ainsworth: Dickens admired his realism, Ainsworth his sensationalism.

As Ainsworth's purpose is not that of the moralist or reformer, *Jack Sheppard* is free of the propaganda of *Oliver Twist* just as *Rookwood* had avoided the politics of *Paul Clifford*. In consequence, the similarities of theme and characterisation between *Sheppard* and *Twist* only serve to make the contrasts between them more apparent, ultimately to the professional detriment of Ainsworth. This is particularly evident in the authors' different presentations of underclass women. Whereas Nancy, in the tradition of Ann Gill, is presented as a

---

[41] Another flash term for hanging was 'The dance without music', referring to the spastic death throes of the victim. See Eric Partridge, *A Dictionary of the Underworld* (London: Routledge & Kegan Paul, 1950). Like Pierce Egan, Ainsworth got his slang from 'A New and Comprehensive Vocabulary of the Flash Language', which was appended to James Hardy Vaux's *Memoirs of a Transport* (London, 1819), a book now considered to be one of the earliest works of Australian literature.
[42] Dickens, preface, *Oliver Twist*.

victim, the young whores of *Jack Sheppard* are sexually predatory, as hard as nails and utterly unrepentant. In the crucial scene in 'The Flash Ken' (an underworld gin palace), the young Jack Sheppard is seduced into a life of vice by Blueskin (Joseph Blake, another historical figure), an accomplice of his late father, Tom Sheppard the executed thief, and two legendary Newgate Calendar prostitutes, Edgeworth Bess (Elizabeth Lyon) and Mistress Poll Maggot, while his horrified mother looks on helplessly. Although the following chapter charts Jack's fall from grace under the temptation of the satanic Jonathan Wild, 'The Flash Ken' episode is the more powerful, the prelapsarian Jack succumbing to the charms of not one but two Eves before he makes his pact with the devil. The scene may also be usefully compared not only to Dickens's cautious portrayal of Nancy but to scenes where Oliver and other orphans are drawn into 'the trade' by the crafty indoctrination of Fagin and the menaces of Sikes. Ainsworth begins by foregrounding the sexual nature of the seduction:

> The agonized mother could scarcely repress a scream at the spectacle that met her gaze. There sat Jack, evidently in the last stage of intoxication, with his collar opened, his dress disarranged, a pipe in his mouth, a bowl of punch and a half-emptied rummer before him – there he sat, receiving and returning, or rather attempting to return – for he was almost past consciousness – the blandishments of a couple of females, one of whom had passed her arm round his neck, while the other leaned over the back of his chair, and appeared from her gestures to be whispering soft nonsense into his ear.

> Both these ladies possessed considerable personal attractions. The younger of the two, who was seated next to Jack, and seemed to monopolize his attention, could not be more than seventeen, though her person had all the maturity of twenty. She had delicate oval features; light, laughing blue eyes, a pretty *nez retroussé*, – why have we not the term, since we have the best specimens of the feature? – teeth of pearly whiteness, and a brilliant complexion, set off by rich auburn hair, a very white neck and shoulders – the latter, perhaps, a trifle too much exposed. The name of this damsel was Edgeworth Bess ... The other *bona roba*, known amongst her companions as Mistress Poll Maggot, was a beauty on a much larger scale – in fact, a perfect Amazon. Nevertheless, though nearly six feet high, and correspondingly proportioned, she was a model of symmetry, and boasted, with the frame of a Thalestris or a Trulla, the regular lineaments of the Medicean Venus. A man's laced hat – whether adopted from the caprice of the moment, or habitually worn, we are unable to state – cocked knowingly on her head, harmonized with her masculine

appearance. Mrs. Maggot, as well as her companion, Edgeworth Bess, was showily dressed; nor did either of them disdain the aid supposed to be lent to a fair skin by the contents of the patch-box. On an empty cask, which served him for a chair, and opposite Jack Sheppard, whose rapid progress in depravity afforded him the highest satisfaction, sat Blueskin, encouraging the two women in their odious task, and plying his victim with the glass as often as he deemed it expedient to do so. By this time, he had apparently accomplished all he desired; for moving the bottle out of Jack's reach, he appropriated it entirely to his own use, leaving the devoted lad to the care of the females.[43]

The gaze of Jack's mother serves as an externalisation of his moral conscience. Although the author describes the seduction of the innocent Jack as an 'odious task', it is an offhand reference and he overlooks the more sinister implications of the scene by dwelling instead on the smouldering sexuality of the *ménage à trois*. Like the bite of the vampire, the pens of Hogarth and Ainsworth eroticise women.

Despite his moral purpose, Hogarth's prostitutes have little in common with the penitent, melodramatic Magdalenes of Dickens,[44] the helpless, exploited and anonymous victims of Flora Tristan or the pitiful grotesques of Mrs Gaskell. Although the role of the whore in *Industry and Idleness* and machinations of Poll and Bess are similarly 'odious', the former remains earthy, sexual and empowered. She is first shown in bed with Tom Idle in Plate 7, 'The Idle 'Prentice Return'd from Sea, and in a Garret with a Common Prostitute', examining an item of presumably stolen jewellery, and again in Plate 9, 'The Idle 'Prentice betray'd by his Whore and taken in a Night Cellar with his Accomplice.' Here Hogarth follows the common model of Eve seducing Adam. This was a standard episode in contemporary criminal biography. The author of *The History of Jack Sheppard* writes, for example, that the young Jack was a good journeyman carpenter and: 'had the Character of a very sober and orderly Boy' before 'he commenced a fatal Acquaintance with one *Elizabeth Lyon*, otherwise call'd,

---

[43] Ainsworth, *Jack Sheppard*, 140–41.
[44] 'The Hospital Patient' dies pathetically, hoping that, 'God almighty will forgive me all the wrong I have done, and the life I have led', and wishing that she 'had died a child'. Dickens, *Sketches by Boz* (1836), Works, 155.

Edgeworth Bess ... Now was laid the Foundation of his Ruin.'[45] Similarly, Defoe's *Account of the Life of Jonathan Wild* shows Wild as an honest tradesman imprisoned for a minor debt, meeting 'a jade of some fame' called Mary Milliner and learning a new trade from her: 'a more than common intimacy soon grew between them. Insomuch that she began to teach him a great many new, and to him unknown ways of getting money, and brought him into her own gang.'[46] Notably, Mrs Milliner is in charge of a gang at this point, and Wild goes on to share power with her until leaving to establish his own gang; we are told that they remain on amiable terms like the business people that they were: 'the other trade [prostitution and extortion] was carried on with mutual assistance, as well as to mutual advantage, for some time'.[47] In *Industry and Idleness* Plate 7 Hogarth paraphrases Leviticus 26:36, 'The sound of a shaken leaf shall chase him',[48] showing the spiritual weakness of Tom Idle, who awakes in a state of some shock in the squalid surroundings, we assume after a night of hard drinking has rendered him insensible and, therefore, powerless. When the woman (always defined only by her profession and simply designated as 'common prostitute' and 'whore') sells him out for financial self-interest in Plate 9 the artist offers the punch line of Proverbs 6:26, 'The adulteress will hunt for the precious life.'[49] In both plates she is shown *décolletée* and, as with a figure in a vanity panting, the male viewer is allowed to stand in judgement while also taking pleasure from the sight of the woman's youth and nakedness.

In his description of the two prostitutes (as well as Cruikshank's accompanying illustrations), Ainsworth revels in their beauty (which he compares

---

[45] Defoe? *The History of the remarkable Life of John Sheppard, containing A particular account of his many Robberies and Escapes*, reprinted in full in Philip Rawlings, *Drunks, Whores and Idle Apprentices, Criminal biographies of the eighteenth century* (London: Routledge, 1992), 49.
[46] Defoe, *An Account of the Life of Jonathan Wild*, 231.
[47] *Ibid.*, 232.
[48] 'And upon them that are left alive of you I will send a faintness into their hearts in the lands of their enemies; and the sound of a shaken leaf shall chase them; and they shall flee, as fleeing from a sword; and they shall fall when none pursueth.'
[49] 'For by means of a whorish woman a man is brought to a piece of bread: and the adulteress will hunt for the precious life.'

to the classical) and their unabashed sexuality, comparing the different physiques of the two, their clothes and their behaviour as they indulge in very public sexual foreplay with Jack. As a powerplay, both women are stronger than the inebriated Jack (who can neither stand or even speak properly) and Blueskin, who merely watches. The real struggle is with Mrs Sheppard, who was once as they are now (which both Blueskin and Poll enjoy reminding her), but has now, as an older and reformed woman, lost both her sexual power and matriarchal, criminal authority. The confrontation between the three women is nonetheless a violent one, even though Mrs Sheppard cannot possibly win, as the struggle for Jack's soul is enacted:

> Amid this varied throng – varied in appearance, but alike in character – one object alone, we have said, riveted Mrs. Sheppard's attention and no sooner did she in some degree recover from the shock occasioned by the sight of her son's debased condition, than, regardless of any other consideration except his instant removal from the contaminating society by which he was surrounded, and utterly forgetting the more cautious plan she meant to have adopted, she rushed into the room and summoned him to follow her.
>
> 'Halloa!' cried Jack, looking round, and trying to fix his inebriate gaze upon the speaker, 'who's that?'
>
> 'Your mother', replied Mrs. Sheppard. 'Come home directly, sir.'
>
> 'Mother be – !' returned Jack. 'Who is it, Bess?'
>
> 'How should I know?' replied Edgeworth Bess. 'But if it is your mother, send her about her business.'
>
> 'That I will', replied Jack, 'in the twinkling of a bedpost.'
>
> 'Glad to see you once more in the Mint, Mrs. Sheppard', roared Blueskin, who anticipated some fun. 'Come and sit down by me.'
>
> 'Take a glass of gin, ma'am', cried Poll Maggot, holding up a bottle of spirit; 'it used to be your favourite liquor I've heard.'
>
> 'Jack, my love', cried Mrs. Sheppard, disregarding the taunt, 'come away.'
>
> 'Not I', replied Jack; 'I'm too comfortable where I am. Be off!'
>
> 'Jack!' exclaimed his unhappy parent.
>
> 'Mr. Sheppard, if you please, ma'am', interrupted the lad; 'I allow nobody to call me Jack. Do I, Bess, eh?'
>
> 'Nobody whatever, love', replied Edgeworth Bess; 'nobody but me, dear.'

'And me', insinuated Mrs. Maggot. 'My little fancy man's quite as fond of me as of you, Bess. Ain't you, Jacky darling?'

'Not quite, Poll', returned Mr. Sheppard; 'but I love you next to her, and both of you better than *her*', pointing with the pipe to his mother.

'Oh, heavens!' cried Mrs. Sheppard.

'Bravo!' shouted Blueskin. 'Tom Sheppard never said a better thing than that ho! ho!'

'Jack', cried his mother, wringing her hands in distraction, 'you'll break my heart!'

'Poh! poh!' returned her son; 'women don't so easily break their hearts. Do they, Bess?'

'Certainly not', replied the young lady appealed to, 'especially about their sons.'

'Wretch!' cried Mrs. Sheppard, bitterly.

'I say', retorted Edgeworth Bess, with a very unfeminine imprecation, 'I shan't stand any more of that nonsense. What do you mean by calling me wretch, madam?' she added; marching up to Mrs. Sheppard, and regarding her with an insolent and threatening glance.

'Yes – what do you mean, ma'am?' added Jack, staggering after her.

'Come with me, my love, come – come', cried his mother, seizing his hand, and endeavouring to force him away.

'He shan't go', cried Edgeworth Bess, holding him by the other hand. 'Here, Poll, help me!'

Thus exhorted, Mrs. Maggot lent her powerful aid, and between the two, Jack was speedily relieved from all fears of being carried off against his will. Not content with this exhibition of her prowess, the Amazon lifted him up as easily as if he had been an infant, and placed him upon her shoulders; to the infinite delight of the company, and the increased distress of his mother.

'Now, let's see who'll dare to take him down', she cried.

'Nobody shall', cried Mr. Sheppard from his elevated position. 'I'm my own master now, and I'll do as I please. I'll turn cracksman, like my father – rob old Wood – he has chests full of money, and I know where they're kept – I'll rob him, and give the swag to you, Poll' ... his wretched mother, in spite of her passionate supplications and resistance, was, by Blueskin's command, forcibly ejected from the house, and driven out of the Mint.[50]

---

[50] Ainsworth, *Jack Sheppard*, 141–3.

We can see and *feel* here Jack's separation from his mother and her moral value system. By degrees, the prostitutes take over Mrs Sheppard's role as Jack's mother. First they both appropriate his mother's pet name, while Jack continually appeals to the authority of his new lover ('Who is it, Bess?/Do I, Bess?/Do they, Bess?'), while rejecting his mother; he loves Bess the most, then Poll, and his mother not at all. Eventually, after a physical tug of war where mother and lovers take an arm each, Jack regresses to the point that the masculine Mrs Maggot lifts him up 'as easily as if he had been an infant', while he babbles a promise to steal for her alone, as if she were his fence, or even pimp. Bess, meanwhile, shows how easily she can change from relaxed and sensual (feminine) to threatening (masculine) when Mrs Sheppard finally returns an insult to which Bess responds with a 'very unfeminine imprecation'. In the underworld (whether Defoe's, Hogarth's or Ainsworth's version), gender roles are reversed rendering women dominant and men subservient. To the male moralist, such female empowerment can lead only to temptation and sin, and such an argument thus supports the subjugation of women. Deborah Nord sees Dickens's early depiction of prostitutes as a: 'proto-Victorian middle-class vision that overcomes an unsettling and threatening female sexuality by casting women as victims'.[51] Ainsworth, by contrast, leaves the women in command. The territoriality of Bess and Poll is assured when Mrs Sheppard is thrown out of the borough completely, leaving the two women free to consummate and complete their seduction of the adolescent boy, possibly *together*. Stripping the scenario of a moral interpretation has rendered it pornographic, something that was often potentially present in Hogarth yet never overtly developed.

---

[51] Deborah Epstein Nord, *Walking the Victorian Streets: Women, Representation and the City* (London: Cornell University Press, 1995), 72.

II. Vagabondiana: *Jack Sheppard* and social exploration[52]

With regard to the licentiousness of the underworld of *Jack Sheppard*, Keith
Hollingsworth observes that Ainsworth 'does not realize how fast times have
changed'.[53] If we recall the high Victorian analysis of J. Hain Friswell, what was
seen by the new generation of writers to remain of an underworld text if the moral
gaze of the author was absent was an implied endorsement of Regency values,
which were now considered immoral and therefore socially dangerous. By the
time of Friswell, Ainsworth had even been symbolically stripped of his status as
an early Victorian:

> He is, perhaps, not so much to be blamed, poor man, being a person of small
> attainments and not a very strong intellect, as the times in which he was born.
> In that yeasty and lively age, in which the results of a long war, deeds of
> violence at sea and on land, the press gang, cheating lawyers, bad laws, a
> debauched king and court, a 'frowsy old Floribel', had produced among the
> people a taste for such literature as the 'Memoirs of Harriette Wilson',
> accompanied by books less vicious only in degree, and not quite as bad in
> intention, such as 'Tom and Jerry', 'The Corinthian Club', and the like, – in
> that very lively age people required a literature that teemed with adventure and
> had 'go' in it …[54]

The personal attack had by then become a standard feature of any high-brow
literary commentary on Ainsworth, but this evocation of the libertine heroes of
Pierce Egan is useful. The critical habit of citing *Life in London* and its imitations
in conjunction with Ainsworthian Newgate was a common one; Forster's damning
review of *Jack Sheppard* in *The Examiner*, for instance, suggested that public
decency had not been so threatened since 'the time of Tom and Jerry'.[55]
Interestingly, Ainsworth's London *is* much closer to Egan's than it will ever be to

---

[52] J.T. Smith, Keeper of Prints in the British Museum, coined this term for his book,
*Vagabondiana, or The Anecdotes of Mendicant Wanderers through the Streets of London, with
Portraits of the Most Remarkable* (London, 1817).
[53] Hollingsworth, 138.
[54] J. Hain Friswell, *Modern Men of Letters, Honestly Criticised* (London: Hodder & Stoughton,
1870), 258–9.
[55] Forster, *The Examiner*, November 3 1839.

the version Dickens sells to Victorian society. As Deborah Nord writes of the time
of Tom and Jerry:

> Early Nineteenth century London was a city in transition, no longer Augustan
> and not yet Victorian, no longer the buoyant, bawdy city of Boswell and not
> yet the menacing labyrinth of the later Dickens. In the first three decades of the
> century, and particularly in the aftermath of Waterloo, the nation celebrated
> itself and its metropolis, keeping at bay an awareness of the new social realities
> that would ultimately dominate urban consciousness.[56]

As we have seen, Ainsworth was an equally transitional writer, and his literary
style is very much a product of this period of cultural flux. As such, he is inclined
to look back as much, if not more, as he does forward. Hollingsworth is quite right
to mark *Jack Sheppard* as the point where Ainsworth parts ideological company
with his contemporaries, as demonstrated by the emergent critical theory of
Thackeray, Dickens and their cronies, but this begs the inevitable question, as is
always the case when reading Ainsworth, of whether he had any sort of ideology
at all.

Hollingsworth also reads *Jack Sheppard* and the initial craze among both
working and middle-class audiences as symptomatic of a positive statement of
cultural renewal, indicative of a new sense of optimism where the horrors of the
Bloody Code were now simply the stuff of history:

> The crudest terrors of Newgate, well enough remembered, could be thought of
> as safely in the past. Freedom and opportunity were in the air. A vast public
> could, at such a moment, permit itself to idolize a young thief – could see him
> as a victim of the old system or as a rebel against it ... This general high-
> spirited extravagance would not have been possible twenty years earlier; its
> *raison d'être* would have been lacking twenty years later. Ainsworth provided
> his novel at the right time. The Sheppard mania which followed was an
> uncalculated, uncalculating paean to the end of the bad old days and the arrival
> of a time like morning.[57]

---

[56] Nord, 19.

[57] Hollingsworth, 141. This invites the *Discipline and Punish* interpretations that many disciples of
Michel Foucault and followers of Hollingsworth have tended to impose upon the Newgate novel.
See, for example, Juliet John, introduction, *Cult Criminals: The Newgate Novels, 1830–1847*, 8
vols (London: Routledge, 1998).

In this case, Ainsworth's frequent comparisons between the London of *Jack Sheppard* in the 1720s and that of the capital in 1839 act as a celebration of social progress and the end of a barbarous past. This is hardly a convincing argument. Despite a certain amount of reform of criminal law by 1840, hangings were still public and urban poverty and crime remained epidemic. The criminal underworld and the condemned cells of Dickens were consequently portrayed as contemporary and always disturbingly close:

> They crossed from the Angel into St John's Road; struck down the small street which terminates at Sadler's Wells Theatre; through Exmouth Street and Copice Row; down the little court by the side of the workhouse; across the classic ground which once bore the name of Hockley-in-the-Hole; thence into Little Saffron Hill; and so into Saffron Hill the Great, along which the Dodger scudded at a rapid pace, directing Oliver to follow close at his heels.

> Although Oliver had enough to occupy his attention in keeping sight of his leader, he could not help bestowing a few hasty glances on either side of the way, as he passed along. A dirtier or more wretched place he had never seen. The street was very narrow and muddy, and the air was impregnated with filthy odours. There were a good many small shops; but the only stock in trade appeared to be heaps of children, who, even at that time of night, were crawling in and out at the doors, or screaming from the inside. The sole places that seemed to prosper amid the general blight of the place, were the public houses; and in them, the lowest orders of Irish were wrangling with might and main. Covered ways and yards, which here and there diverged from the main street, disclosed little knots of houses, where drunken men and women were positively wallowing in filth; and from several of the door-ways, great ill-looking fellows were cautiously emerging, bound, to all appearance, on no very well-disposed or harmless errands.[58]

And so Oliver Twist enters London. In language that anticipates Engels's famous description of Allen's Court in Manchester, Oliver is Dante to the Artful Dodger's Virgil; although what separates this inferno from the realm of the virtuous Mr Brownlow, not to mention Dickens's bourgeois audience, is a single turn:

> The coach rattled away, over nearly the same ground as that which Oliver had traversed when he first entered London in company with the Dodger; and,

---

[58] Dickens, *Oliver Twist*, 44.

turning a different way when it reached the Angel at Islington, stopped at length before a neat house, in a quiet shady street near Pentonville.[59]

With the above in mind, the topography of Jack Sheppard's London as described by Ainsworth is not reassuringly separated by history at all, but rather directly linked to the present:

> MRS. SHEPPARD'S habitation terminated a row of old ruinous buildings, called Wheeler's Rents; a dirty thoroughfare, part street, and part lane, running from Mint Street, through a variety of turnings, and along the brink of a deep kennel, skirted by a number of pretty and neglected gardens in the direction of Saint George's Fields. The neighbouring houses were tenanted by the lowest order of insolvent traders, thieves, mendicants, and other worthless and nefarious characters, who fled thither to escape from their creditors, or to avoid the punishment due to their different offences; for we may observe that the Old Mint, although it had been divested of some of its privileges as a sanctuary by a recent statute passed in the reign of William the Third, still presented a safe asylum to the debtor, and even continued to do so until the middle of the reign of George the First, when the crying nature of the evil called loudly for a remedy, and another and more sweeping enactment entirely took away its immunities. In consequence of the encouragement thus offered to dishonesty, and the security afforded to crime, this quarter of the Borough of Southwark was accounted (at the period of our narrative) the grand receptacle of the superfluous villainy of the metropolis. Infested by every description of vagabond and miscreant, it was, perhaps, a few degrees worse than the rookery near Saint Giles's and the desperate neighbourhood of Saffron Hill in our own time.[60]

The underworld is transcendent. Whether the correlative is the *Cour des Miracles* of Hugo's fifteenth century Paris, St Giles in the age of Sheppard, Wild, Hogarth and Defoe, Saffron Hill in 1838, the Whitechapel of Dorian Gray and Jack the Ripper or the post-war Hackney slums of the Kray brothers, the City will always have its rookeries and thieves' kitchens. Ainsworth also *loved* London, and his experience of the metropolis was totally different from that of Dickens. Ainsworth had arrived as an optimistic teenager in an optimistic time, not yet a decade after Waterloo. He was already a published author, comfortably off, and moving effortlessly in both professional and Bohemian social circles while chasing, albeit

---

[59] *Ibid.*, 59.
[60] Ainsworth, *Jack Sheppard*, 10.

often ineptly, both working class and middle class women.[61] There was nothing like the Marshalsea debtors' prison or Warren's blacking warehouse in Ainsworth's past. Neither did he have Dickens's front-line journalistic experience. For Ainsworth, life in London was a great adventure rather than an urban nightmare, and this enthusiasm is reflected in his writing. To understand the city of *Jack Sheppard*, we must thus look to Pierce Egan rather than Charles Dickens for a point of ideological correspondence.

The extraordinarily lavish popular success of *Rookwood* and especially *Jack Sheppard* in the mid to late 1830s must have reminded many of the phenomenon of Egan the Elder's *Life in London* in the previous decade. Egan (1772–1849) was a sporting journalist, already known for his *Boxiana, or, Sketches of Modern Pugilism* (1818–1824), when he began *Life in London* as a monthly serial in 1820, illustrated by the Cruikshank brothers, George and Robert. The work's lengthy subtitle, *The Day and Night Scenes of Jerry Hawthorn, ESQ. and his elegant friend Corinthian Tom in their Rambles and Sprees through the Metropolis*, signals Egan's theme and his textual combination of two central tenets of eighteenth century London writing: the uninitiated tourist following the sophisticated guide, and the *perpetuum mobile* of exhilarating urban experience. 'Seeing Life' is the clarion call, in all its social aspects, from the aristocratic exclusivity of the assembly rooms in St James's to the gin palaces of the East End. This is presented as a suitable sport for the young gentleman, and the city is laid out as a vast text containing all human knowledge available to those who are willing to learn how to decipher it:

> Indeed, The Metropolis is a complete CYCLOPÆDIA, where every man of the most religious or moral habits, attached to any sect, may find something to please his palate, regulate his taste, suit his pocket, enlarge his mind, and make him happy and comfortable. If places of worship give any sort of character to the *goodness* of the Metropolis, between four and five hundred are opened for religious purposes on Sundays. In fact, every SQUARE in the Metropolis is a sort of *map* well worthy of exploring, if riches and titles operate as a source of curiosity to the visitor. There is not a *street* also in London, but what may be

---

[61] See Chapter One.

compared to a large or small volume of intelligence, abounding with anecdote, incident, and peculiarities. A *court* or *alley* must be obscure indeed, if it does not afford some remarks; and even the *poorest* cellar contains some *trait* or other, in unison with the manners and feelings of this great city, that may be put down in the note book, and reviewed, at an after period, with much pleasure and satisfaction.

Then, the grand object of this work is an attempt to portray what is termed 'SEEING LIFE' in all its various bearings upon society, from the *high-mettled* CORINTHIAN of St James's, *swaddled* in luxury, down to the *needy* FLUE-FAKER of Wapping, *born without a shirt*, and not a *bit of scran* in his cup to allay his piteous cravings.[62]

The ludic game is emphasised in the above introduction by the inclusion of class-specific slang terms. This is the flash language of 'Nix My Dolls', and the acquirement of this (mostly) unrecorded language offers the tantalising possibility of unlocking the secrets of the urban Other. This is the Enigma code of the underworld, and was originally made fashionable by Egan, not Ainsworth:

TOM: [Introducing Jerry to Bob Logic] He is now come to see life, and rub off a little of the rust. In effecting this desirable consummation you can materially assist; under so skilful a professor of the flash as you, Bob –

JERRY: Flash! I'm at fault again, Tom.

TOM: Explain, Bob.

LOGIC: Flash, my young friend, or slang as others call it, is the classical language of the Holy Land; in other words, St Giles's Greek.

JERRY: St Giles's Greek; that is a language, doctor, with which I am totally unacquainted, although I was brought up at a Grammar School.

LOGIC: You are not particular in that respect; many great scholars, and better linguists than you, are quite ignorant of it, it being studied more in the Hammer Schools than the Grammar Schools. Flash, my young friend, or slang, as others call it, is a species of cant in which the knowing ones conceal their roguery from the flats; and it is one of the advantages of seeing Life in London, that you may learn to talk to a rogue in his own language, and fight him with his own weapons ... It's the blunt that does it – blunt makes the man, Jerry.

JERRY: Blunt! I'm at fault again.

TOM: Explain, Bob –

---

[62] Egan, 51–2.

LOGIC: Blunt, my dear boy, is – in short what is it not? It's everything now o' days – to be able to flash the screens – sport the rhino show the needful – post the pony – nap the rent – stump the pewter – tip the brads – and down with the dust, is to be once good, great, handsome, accomplished, and everything that's desirable – money, money, is your universal God, – only get into Tip Street, Jerry.[63]

Egan's easy-going, picaresque story, complete with long, discursive Shandyesque footnotes, bawdy illustrations and comic songs was an instantaneous success. Consequently, just like Ainsworth's highwaymen in the 1830s, Tom and Jerry were quickly appropriated by the theatres; the above dialogue, for example, is taken from W.T. Moncrieff's *Tom and Jerry* at the Adelphi. The public craze, which included six highly successful plays (including one by Egan himself) and a bevy of copycat books and serials, lasted about four years at its height, between 1820 and 1823, and Egan finished the saga with a crafty sequel in 1828. During this period in particular flash slang became common cultural currency with the fashionable set.[64]

The later Victorians publicly denounced Egan as obscene, and his work was consigned to the same critical vacuum occupied by Ainsworth, only to be relatively recently reassessed. Deborah Nord writes of *Life in London* that: 'As in contemporary collections of graphic sketches of London scenes and types, contrasts work here only inadvertently as a tool of social criticism and function primarily as a mode of entertainment and a source of delight.'[65] This is true, yet Egan's work is also being increasingly read as a serious forerunner to that of the Victorian social investigators:[66] 'But though backward-looking in its recreational view of urban education and its often unsympathetic attitudes towards those who are "DOWN"', wrote Rick Allen recently, 'this quintessentially Regency work also anticipates the Victorian vogue for exploration of the city's lower depths and

---

[63] From W.T. Moncrieff's version of *Tom and Jerry* at the Adelphi, quoted from Donald A. Low, *The Regency Underworld* (London: J.M. Dent, 1982), 119–20.

[64] Low, 119–22.

[65] Nord, 31–2.

[66] See Roger Sales, 'Pierce Egan and the Representation of London', *Reviewing Romanticism*, ed. Philip Martin and Robin Jarvis (London, Macmillan, 1992).

for the juxtaposition of social polarities.'[67] It is more than probable that Egan and the brothers Cruikshank did actually visit many of the places they wrote about and illustrated.[68] Egan at one points actually places himself in his own text, in an apology to his subscribers on failing to complete the January 1 1821 instalment in an article entitled 'The Author in Distress' wherein he explains that, while out on a late spree with Bob Logic at the *Albany*, 'Upon turning the corner of *Sydney's Alley*, into Leicester-Fields', (somewhat the worse for the drink), 'we were assailed by some *troublesome customers*, and a *turn-up* was the result (as the plate most accurately represents). Bob got a *stinker*, and poor I received a *chancery-suit* upon the *nob*.'[69] As indicated by the author, there is also an accompanying illustration with the caption, 'Peep 'o Day Boys. A Street Row, the Author losing his "Reader", Tom and Jerry "showing fight", and Logic floored', meaning Egan was mugged and lost his journalist's notebook. This is hardly 'On Duty with Inspector Field' (and the author's textual interaction with his own characters is positively postmodern), but there is still more than a shade here of the subsequent missionary/explorer travel narratives of Tristan, Dickens, Engels, Mayhew, and later still, Stead, Mearns, Booth and Rowntree. Egan, like his more po-faced successors who also explored the dark side of the street, still offers the opportunity for a bourgeois audience to experience the underworld voyeuristically, without ever leaving the drawing room: 'The author, in consequence, has chosen for his readers a *Camera Obscura* View of London, not only from its safety, but because it is so *snug*, and also possessing the invaluable advantage of SEEING and not being *seen*.'[70] Where Egan differs is that he goes native; he talks the talk (often descending into incomprehensible flash) and he walks the walk (mixing with an underclass that delights rather than appals him), and the City is presented as the 'young blood's' playground (should they *dare* to

---

[67] Rick Allen, *The Moving Pageant: A Literary Sourcebook on London Street-Life, 1700–1914* (London: Routledge, 1998), 89.
[68] The rumour about town at the time being that Egan was Logic, George Cruikshank Tom and his younger brother Jerry. Low, 107.
[69] Egan, 311.
[70] *Ibid.*, 46.

enter): the image most often adopted being that of a colourful theatrical performance where 'the scene changed as often as pantomime'.[71] This is where *Life in London* collides with *Jack Sheppard*.

Ainsworth the Newgate narrator also consistently refuses to be outraged by underworld culture. Like Tom and Jerry he seeks it out, appreciating the variety and freedom that such (anti)social spaces as the 'Flash Ken' and the 'Old Mint' offer. When he tries to add a moral gloss, it is without conviction:

> 'Well, I'm sure Winifred could never have loved you as well as I do', said Mrs. Maggot.
>
> '*You!*' cried Jack, scornfully. 'Do you compare love – a love all may purchase – with hers? No one has ever loved me.'
>
> 'Except me, dear', insinuated Edgeworth Bess. 'I've been always true to you.'
>
> 'Peace!' retorted Jack, with increased bitterness. 'I'm your dupe no longer.'
>
> 'What the devil's in the wind now, captain?' cried Blueskin, in astonishment.
>
> 'I'll tell you', replied Jack with forced calmness. 'Within the last few minutes, all my guilty life has passed before me. Nine years ago, I was honest – was happy. Nine years ago, I worked in this very house – had a kind indulgent master, whom I robbed – twice robbed, at your instigation, villain; a mistress whom you have murdered; a companion, whose friendship I have for ever forfeited; a mother, whose heart I have wellnigh broken! In this room was my ruin begun: in this room it should be ended.'
>
> 'Come, come, don't take on thus, captain', cried Blueskin, rising, and walking towards him. 'If any one's to blame, it's me. I'm ready to bear it all.'
>
> 'Can you make me honest?' cried Jack. 'Can you make me other than a condemned felon? Can you make me not Jack Sheppard?'
>
> 'No', replied Blueskin; 'and I wouldn't if I could.'[72]

Neither, of course, would Ainsworth. Jack may claim, rather erroneously, that 'Mrs. Wood struck me a blow which made me a robber', extol the virtues of the chaste Winifred Wood over the loose morals of his two lovers, and blame Jonathan Wild for his descent into crime, but both he and his author often fail to convince. From the outset it was made very plain that not only was Jack bad to the

---

[71] *Ibid.*, 321.
[72] Ainsworth, *Jack Sheppard*, 257.

bone, but that life in the Old Mint was much more exciting than it could ever possibly be in Mr Wood's workshop in Drury Lane; a suspicion confirmed as soon as he (and the reader) meets the girls of the 'Flash Ken'.

Given the charges levelled at this text by the self-appointed guardians of public decency, it demands to be noted, however, that the adult Jack Sheppard has a more complex personality than Dick Turpin, within Ainsworth's universe at any rate. In *Jack Sheppard*, Thames Darrell, Jack's best friend and effectively adopted brother, is perfectly good while Jonathan Wild, the grotesque, gothic, melodramatic villain is perfectly evil. Jack inhabits an ambivalent moral space between the two (much as he moves between the alternate lifestyles offered by Drury Lane and Southwark), somewhere between the sacred and the profane. Although the third epoch in particular dwells upon the heroic dimensions of his character, there is a moral ambivalence present that distances Ainsworth's Sheppard from both the Turpin of *Rookwood*, who may be brave but is also unrepentant, morally one-dimensional and fundamentally hedonistic, and Paul Clifford, who is too good to be true and spends much of his time wracked with guilt. The novelist's challenge is to produce a sympathetic criminal, but it apparently cannot be done with any sense of realism, as we have seen from the rhetoric of *Paul Clifford* and the antics of Dick Turpin. When Dickens dismisses such things as 'canterings on moonlit heaths' in his preface to the 1841 edition of *Oliver Twist* (an obvious criticism of Ainsworth), he does not allow that the occupants of his version of Saffron Hill behave in much the same way as those of Ainsworth's Southwark: drinking, smoking, lying, stealing, whoring and killing. The moonlit heath is much more a piece of scenery from *Rookwood* than *Jack Sheppard*.

Unlike the outlaw of *Rookwood*, the process by which Jack is drawn into the criminal underworld is enacted within the text. Directly after the episode in which Jack loses his physical innocence, Jonathan Wild claims Jack and, by implication, his immortal soul, in a suitably symbolic fashion by inciting the youth to pick a pocket in Willesden Church in sight of his mother, who is among the congregation: 'Your son has committed a robbery – here – in these holy walls – he is mine – mine for ever!'[73] Forever? Perhaps not. Jack's deal with the devil is by no means set, and that is the substance of his ambivalent role within the text. He is much more psychologically complex than his counterpart in *Rookwood*, and is socially trapped between two worlds: torn apart between guilt over the insanity and eventual suicide of his mother; his loyalty to his adopted family and his love for Thames and Winifred; the power which Wild has over him; his honourable criminal associates (especially Blueskin); his two lovers, whom he alternately lusts after and despises; and his desire to leave his illegal lifestyle behind against a passion for easy cash, wine, women and loose living. In his more sober moments, however, Jack is both embittered and repentant, but it would seem that this is the only escape he is not capable of performing: 'I'm tired of the life I'm leading', Jack tells Wild during an argument, 'I shall quit it and go abroad', (following Paul Clifford, perhaps); 'Dare to disobey ... neglect my orders, and I will hang you' is the reply.[74] The conflict can only be resolved by his execution.

Having assisted Thames to his birthright and rejected Wild, Jack finally reaches a state of emotional equanimity on the road to Tyburn, although there is a suggestion even then that his criminal notoriety also still appeals:

> He looked around, and as he heard that deafening shout as he felt the influence of those thousand eyes fixed upon him – as he listened to the cheers, all his misgivings if he had any – vanished, and he felt more as if he were marching to a triumph, than proceeding to a shameful death.[75]

His last words, according to Ainsworth, are 'My poor mother! I shall soon join her!' and 'The next instant, he was launched into eternity.'[76] If Jack is indeed to

---

[73] Ainsworth, *Jack Sheppard*, 145. Wild is presented as a satanic figure throughout the narrative: 'If I am the devil', observed Wild, 'as some folks assert, and I myself am not unwilling to believe, you'll find that I differ from the generally received notions of the archfiend, and faithfully execute the commands of those who confide their souls to my custody.' *Ibid.*, 107.

[74] *Ibid.*, 183.

[75] *Ibid.*, 338.

[76] *Ibid.*, 343.

join his mother, then Ainsworth at least allows the fated figure spiritual redemption and resurrection to the life eternal.[77]

Like Jack in the 'Flash Ken' however, the author is easily diverted from his moral purpose. Ainsworth takes great care in contrasting the two brothers, ostensibly appearing to follow closely Hogarth's original narrative from *Industry and Idleness*. Thames is the conventional hero (another Ranulph Rookwood), but Ainsworth's sympathies again return to the criminal, despite the moral fable he is supposedly writing. When the young Jack is described, along with his collection of pulp Newgate paraphernalia, he gleefully grants his audience a sign of what they may expect; here, thank the Lord, or at least the omnipotent narrator, is another Dick Turpin:

> In Darrell's open features, frankness and honour were written in legible characters; while, in Jack's physiognomy, cunning and knavery were as strongly imprinted ... The expression pervading the countenance of the one was vulgarity; of the other, that which is rarely found, except in persons of high birth.[78]

In addition to this reference to the physiognomy of the criminal type and the clue regarding Thames's true social origins, there are also his patriotic hymns in sight of Jack's Newgate Calendars (ironically confirming the argument later used against Ainsworth that such literature corrupts). The point well made, Ainsworth proceeds unequivocally to take the side of the boy who is, by implication, of low birth for the remainder of the novel because, as his readers already know (or believe that they know) from such sources as *Rookwood* and *Life in London*, it is this class of society that has all the fun:

> 'It is', said LOGIC to TOM, 'I am quite satisfied in my mind, the LOWER ORDERS of society who really ENJOY themselves. They eat with a good appetite, *hunger* being the sauce; they *drink* with a zest, in being *thirsty* from their exertions, and not *nice* in their beverage; and as to *dress*, it is not an object of serious consideration with them. Their minds are daily occupied with

---

[77] This is similarly presented as a consolation to the death of Lady Jane Grey in *The Tower of London* and the principal cast of *The Lancashire Witches*. No-one, apparently, goes to hell except the villains.

[78] Ainsworth, *Jack Sheppard*, 59.

work, which they quit with the intention of *enjoying* themselves, and ENJOYMENT is the result; not like the rich, who are out night after night to *kill* TIME, and, what is worse, dissatisfied with almost everything that crosses their path from the dullness of *repetition*.' 'There is too much truth about your argument, I must admit', replied the CORINTHIAN; 'and among all the scenes that we have witnessed together, where the LOWER ORDERS have been taking their *pleasure*, I confess they have appeared ALL HAPPINESS. I am sorry I cannot say as much for the higher ranks of society.'[79]

This is of course the type of sentiment that later made William Acton's medical text *Prostitution, Considered in Its Moral, Social, and Sanitary Aspects* of 1857 a bestseller amongst the middle classes. Bob Logic is here reacting to the most important 'Flash Ken' in Egan's text, the 'All-Max' in East Smithfield (which Egan contrasts with the high citadel of Regency power, Almack's of St James's, which Jerry finds less interesting than its shadow and Bob Logic avoids altogether). Like the pub in the Old Mint in Southwark, the appeal is in the social freedom; gender, race and class are meaningless here, being all part of the same merry dance:

> ALL-MAX was compared by the sailors, something after the old adage of 'any port in a storm.' It required no patronage; – a card of admission was not necessary; – no inquiries were made; – and every *cove* that put in his appearance was quite welcome; colour or country considered no obstacle; and *dress* and ADDRESS completely out of the question. *Ceremonies* were not in use, and, therefore, no struggle took place at ALL-MAX for the master of them. The parties *paired off* according to *fancy*; the eye was pleased in the choice, and nothing thought of about birth and distinction. All was *happiness*, every body free and easy, and freedom of expression allowed to the very echo. The group motley indeed; – Lascars, blacks, jack tars, coal-heavers, dustmen, women of colour, old and young, and a sprinkling of the remnants of once fine girls, &c., were all *jigging* together, provided the *teazer of the catgut* was not *bilked* of his *duce*.[80]

Ainsworth's den of thieves is admittedly less Utopian than this, and *is* class-exclusive. When Egan's trio enters the All-Max the music stops like a scene from an Italian Western (there are assumed to be 'beaks'), until a young tart reassures the clientele (in flash, naturally), that, 'the *gemmen* had only dropped in for to

---

[79] Egan, 320–21.
[80] *Ibid.*, 320.

have a *bit of a spree*'. Ainsworth's ken portrays the underworld as a separate society that strangely mimics the codes of the conventional and the law-abiding, like Milton's conception of heaven and hell, and where strangers, pretenders and defectors (like Mrs Sheppard) are never welcome.

There is, for example, a hierarchy of thieves, with urchins at the bottom and highwaymen at the top:

> Nor was Jack by any means the only stripling in the room. Not far from him was a knot of lads drinking, swearing, and playing at dice as eagerly and as skilfully as any of the older hands. Near to these hopeful youths sat a fence, or receiver, bargaining with a clouter, or pickpocket, for a *suit* – or, to speak in more intelligible language, a watch and seals, two cloaks, commonly called watchcases, and a *wedge-lobb*, otherwise known as a silver snuff box. Next to the receiver was a gang of housebreakers; laughing over their exploits, and planning fresh depredations; and next to the housebreakers came two gallant-looking gentlemen in long periwigs and riding-dresses, and equipped in all other respects for the road, with a roast fowl and a bottle of wine before them.[81]

This subculture remains however, as it does in Egan, *exotic*, particularly sexually. Like Jack Sheppard, Bob Logic has a woman in each arm; in both cases the characters are playing MacHeath, as Egan makes explicit:

> LOGIC (as the Plate represents) ... was listening to the *jargon* of *Black* Sall, who was seated on his right knee, and very liberally treating the *Oxonian* with repeated *chaste* salutes: whilst *Flashy* NANCE (who had *gamoned* more seamen out of their *vills* and power than the ingenuity or palaver of twenty of the most knowing of the frail sisterhood could effect), was occupying LOGIC'S left knee, with her arm round his neck, laughing at the *chaffing* of the '*lady in black*', as she termed her, and also trying to engage the *attention* of LOGIC, who had just desired HAWTHORN to behold the '*fields of Temptation*' by which he was surrounded, and *chanting*, like a second Macheath:
>
> > How happy could I be with either,
> > Were t'other dear charmer away;
> > But while you both *mug* me together,
> > You'll make me a *spooney* (*Hiccoughing*), I say.[82]

---

[81] Ainsworth, *Jack Sheppard* 141.
[82] Egan, 323–4. This is a flash pastiche of Air XXXV of *The Beggar's Opera*, where MacHeath sings:

Logic is crossing many more social boundaries than Jack, however. Jack, his father's son, belongs in this environment and is seen to be returning home (escaping from the straight world), while Logic is a bourgeois tourist dallying outside his own class and racial group. He surrenders to the place completely and disappears into the kaleidoscopic background:

> Our heroes had kept it up so gaily in dancing, drinking, &c., that the friend of the CORINTHIAN thought it was time to be *missing*: but, on mustering the TRIO, LOGIC was not to be found. A jack tar, about *three sheets in the wind*, who had been keeping up the *shindy* the whole of the evening with them, laughing, asked if it was the gentleman in the *green barnacles* their honours wanted, as it was very likely he had taken a voyage to *Africa*, in the *Sally*, or else he was out on a cruise with the *Flashy Nance*; but he would have him beware of *squalls*, as they were not very *sound* in their *rigging!* It was considered useless to look after LOGIC, and a *rattler* was immediately ordered to the door; when JERRY, TOM, and his friend, bid adieu to ALL-MAX.[83]

What is certain is that both Egan's and Ainsworth's characters are all members of the same cast in the same theatre. The City is the drama: a tragi-comic, *bawdy*, burlesque of a production, and the readers its audience.

Where Ainsworth differs from Egan is in his sense of the underworld as a gothic space. For Egan it is the jungle of the dandy on safari, the 'sport in view'.[84] Egan was a sports writer, Ainsworth fundamentally a gothic novelist. This can be seen in Ainsworth's presentation of Newgate itself: London's most infamous lock-up, named from the medieval city's fifth gate in the Temple Bar, on which site originally, and later traditionally, stood the county gaol for London and Middlesex. Ainsworth understood and creatively exploited the cultural resonance

---

> *How happy could I be with either,*
> *Were t'other dear charmer away!*
> *But while you thus tease me together,*
> *To neither a word will I say.*

Logic's final lines translate as, 'But while you both smother me together/you'll make me all soppy I say!' (A dirty *double entendre* based around the fact that Logic gets the hiccups when he's drunk, and in anticipation of his departure upstairs with both women shortly thereafter.)

[83] Egan, 324–5.
[84] *Ibid.*, 46.

of such an institution, and characteristically described it by combing the codes of the folk narrative, the antiquarian and the gothic:

> At the beginning of the twelfth century – whether in the reign of Henry the First or Stephen is uncertain – a fifth gate was added to the four principal entrances of the city of London; then, it is almost needless to say, surrounded by ramparts, moats, and other defences. This gate, called *Newgate*, 'as being latelier builded than the rest', continued, for upwards of three hundred years, to be used as a place of imprisonment for felons and trespassers; at the end of which time, having grown old, ruinous, and 'horribly loathsome', it was rebuilt and enlarged by the executors of the renowned Sir Richard Whittington, *the* Lord Mayor of London.[85]

The above extracted from the introductory paragraph of an entire chapter devoted to the history of the prison in the third book of *Jack Sheppard*, where the influence of the mythic yet historical Dick Whittington is ascribed to a building that is both an ancient monument and a 'horribly loathsome' gothic dungeon. This is recognisably the device that informs the complete construction of later works, *The Tower of London* (1840) and *Old St. Paul's* (1841), becoming something of an authorial trademark thereafter, the titles of Ainsworth's histories often taking the names of historic buildings. The topography of *Jack Sheppard* is bolder, taking in much of Georgian London. The 'Old Newgate' chapter is therefore immediately preceded by a similar account of the London Bethlehem Hospital entitled 'Old Bedlam', being a Hogarthian *tableau vivant* (as this novel so often is), a history and a horror show:

> Old Bethlehem, or Bedlam – every trace of which has been swept away, and the hospital for lunatics removed to Saint George's field – was a vast and magnificent structure … and as Jack passed, he could not help glancing at the wretched inmates. Here was a poor half-naked creature, with a straw crown on his head, and a wooden sceptre in his hand, seated on the ground with all the dignity of a monarch on his throne. There was a mad musician, seemingly rapt in admiration of the notes he was extracting from a child's violin. Here was a terrific figure gnashing his teeth, and howling like a wild beast; – there a lover, with hands clasped together, and eyes turned passionately upwards. In this cell was a huntsman, who had fractured his skull while hunting, and was perpetually hallooing after the hounds; – in that, the most melancholy of all,

---

[85] Ainsworth, *Jack Sheppard*, 217–18.

the grinning gibbering lunatic, the realization of 'moody madness, laughing wild.'[86]

This is of course a pretty fair representation of the eighth plate of Hogarth's *The Rake's Progress* (1733–34), the mock monarch, musician, lover and lunatic of the engraving are all present, and the reader is therefore placed in the subjective position of the young ladies of fashion from Hogarth's original who are there, we must assume, for an afternoon's amusement. Tom and Jerry also visit Newgate; it being the intention of Jerry, and his author, 'not to neglect visiting any place that might afford him information during his stay in London'.[87] Egan knows his audience will not let him avoid the place, but he cannot quite handle it, being somewhat torn between his essentially upbeat approach to the sport of seeing and his own basic humanity when confronted with an execution. Like Thackeray, he turns away. First words fail him: 'It is a truly afflicting scene; and neither the PEN nor the PENCIL, however directed by talent, can do it adequate justice',[88] then he rejects the situation and returns his characters to the colourful ebb and flow of the City:

> Our heroes were offered a complete view of the prison from the top of it; but this offer was declined, in consequence of TOM'S urging the want of time, on account of having some business to transact in the City. The TRIO hastily quitted the gloomy falls of Newgate, once more to join the busy hum and life of society.[89]

Just this once, Egan has strayed too close to the reality of the underworld for comfort. You can feel his relief as he 'hastily' gets his actors away from somewhere where they have no right to be in the first place.

Ainsworth's character are, of course, quite at home in this brutal penal environment; Jonathan Wild actually *lives* in a house in the Old Bailey. Because Ainsworth utilises both gothic and theatrical space, he turns the historical figure of Jonathan Wild into the quintessential villain of a gothic melodrama.

---

[86] *Ibid.*, 212.
[87] *Ibid.*, 315.
[88] *Ibid.*
[89] *Ibid.*, 317.

Ainsworth's Wild anticipates the later villains of the penny dreadfuls and the mid nineteenth century gothic melodramas penned, at their best, by James Rymer and Thomas Peckett Prest and printed and produced by the likes of the notorious Edward Lloyd and George Dibdin Pitt.[90] It would be fun to proclaim Ainsworth's Wild as the missing link between the eighteenth century gothic villain, such as Radcliffe's Montoni, and the outrageously camp creations of Rymer and Prest in the 1840s and 50s, such as Sweeney Todd from *The String of Pearls* and Mr Dalton from Tom Taylor's *The Ticket of Leave Man* (1863), who is a gentleman and philanthropist by day but by night is a thief and assassin known only as 'The Tiger'. Wild is, however, predated by the bloodthirsty pirate villains of the nautical melodramas of the 1820s and early 1830s, such as Black Ralph from *The Dream at Sea* and The Red Rover from the play of the same name (although none of the above is as sadistic as Wild). Ainsworth, however, had been refining this type of character ever since *Ghiotto*. These characters do, however, share a common *raison d'être*, as explained by one of their number in the following comic monologue by Jerome K. Jerome:

> I will, at great expense and inconvenience to myself, murder the good old man, get the hero accused of the crime, and make love to his wife while he is in prison. It will be a risky and laborious business for me, from beginning to end, and can bring me no practical advantage whatever. The girl will call me insulting names, when I pay her a visit, and will push me violently in the chest when I get near her; her golden-haired infant will say I am a bad man, and may even refuse to kiss me. The comic man will cover me with humorous opprobrium; and the villagers will get a day off, and hang about the village pub and hoot me. Everybody will see through my villainy, and I shall be nabbed in the end. I always am. But it is no matter. I will be a villain, ha, ha![91]

Try this model on any melodramatic villain, including those from contemporary cinema; it always fits.

---

[90] Pitt put Sweeney Todd on the stage for the first time at the Britannia Saloon, Hoxton in *The String of Pearls, or: The Fiend of Fleet Street* in 1842. Pitt also produced a version of *Rookwood* at the Victoria Theatre in 1845.

[91] Jerome K. Jerome, *Stage-Land* (London, 1889), quoted from Booth, *English Melodrama*, 20–22.

Quite mad, Wild is also physically grotesque; deconstructed by his violent life he proudly bears the marks of scores of dirty fights like a Prussian officer treasures duelling scars. He seems obsessed with recalling his nasty adventures, each wound a memory, as if his body itself is a gothic text:

> 'I have had a good many desperate engagements in my time, and have generally come off victorious. I bear the marks of some of them about me still', he continued, taking off his wig, and laying bare a bald skull, covered with cicatrices and plates of silver. 'This gash', he added, pointing to one of the larger scars, 'was a wipe from the hanger of Tom Thurland, whom I apprehended for the murder of Mrs. Knap. This wedge of silver', pointing to another, 'which would mend a coffeepot, serves to stop up a breach made by Will Colthurst, who robbed Mr. Hearl on Hounslow-Heath. I secured the dog after he had wounded me … Not a scar but has its history … The hardest bout I ever had was with a woman – Sally Wells, who was afterwards lagged for shoplifting. She attacked me with a carving-knife, and, when I had disarmed her, the jade bit off a couple of fingers from my left hand …'[92]

This mangled appearance reflects a similarly warped internal state of emotional and spiritual corruption. Wild's interest in Jack is part of an obsessive vendetta which he is continuing, beyond the grave, with his father, Tom Sheppard, the man who took the girl he loved, Jack's mother. Wild the collector even has the head of Tom Sheppard on display. Ainsworth makes the character marginally more sinister than his original counterpart (who was undoubtedly a vicious piece of work in his own right) by giving him a private collection of such grisly artefacts, being an external record of his hieroglyphic scars. As Sir Rowland is left alone to explore casually Wild's study, he gradually becomes aware of the horrific nature of the ornaments on display. That such a vicious man as Trenchard is shocked by such macabre trophies demonstrates how far Wild has gone down the left-hand path:

> At first glance, he imagined he must have stumbled upon a museum of rarities, there were so many glass cases, so many open cabinets, ranged against the walls; but the next convinced him that if Jonathan was a virtuoso, his tastes did not run in ordinary channels. Trenchard was tempted to examine the contents of some of these cases, but a closer inspection made him recoil from them in

---

[92] Ainsworth, *Jack Sheppard*, 101–102.

disgust. In the one he approached was gathered together a vast assortment of weapons, each of which, as appeared from the ticket attached to it, had been used as an instrument of destruction. On this side was a razor with which a son had murdered his father; the blade notched, the haft crusted with blood: on that, a bar of iron, bent, and partly broken, with which a husband had beaten out his wife's brains ... Every gibbet at Tyburn and Hounslow appeared to have been plundered of its charnel spoil to enrich the adjoining cabinet, so well was it stored with skulls and bones, all purporting to be the relics of highwaymen famous in their day.[93]

The necrophiliac Wild is consequently the enemy of Ainsworth's more decent criminals; even after death he detains them, particularly Ainsworth's favourites – highwaymen. The horror of this scene reaches its climax with the suggestion that the observer may one day become part of the exhibit: 'So, you're admiring my cabinet, Sir Rowland', he remarked, with a sinister smile; 'it *is* generally admired; and, sometimes by parties who afterwards contribute to the collection themselves, – ha! ha!'[94] Like Sweeney Todd, Wild considers himself an artist. Coincidentally, the skeleton of the actual Jonathan Wild can still be viewed today in the Huntarian Museum at the Royal College of Surgeons. Sir Rowland is in the lair then of a psychopathic killer (rather than the entrepreneur who Defoe almost seemed to admire). He is later murdered by Wild, in probably the most violent scene in the novel, his bloated corpse eventually reappearing not as a trophy but as the evidence which convicts Wild of murder.

Despite the lack of a camp villain in *Life in London*, what unites Egan the contemporary social explorer with Ainsworth the underworld historian is their approach to the lower-class individual. The 'low life' as seen by Egan and Ainsworth are flamboyant, colourful characters (including the bad guys), with equally flamboyant and colourful names and occupations. In the All-Max episode, for example, Corinthian Tom asks the '*covess* of the *ken*' (Mrs Mace, the landlady, whose name is 'robbery' in 'the flash tongue') to name the dancers for him:

---

[93] *Ibid.*, *Jack Sheppard*, 149.
[94] *Ibid.*, 150.

'*Vy*, Sir', replied Mrs *Mace*, 'that *are* black *voman*, who you *sees* dancing with *nasty Bob*, the coal-*vhipper*, is called *African Sall*, because she comes from foreign parts; and that little *mungo* in the corner, holding his arms out, is her child; yet I *doesn't* think *as how*, for all that, SALL has got any husband: but, *La!* sir, it's a poor heart that never rejoices, *an't* it, sir?'[95]

From Ainsworth, we similarly know the names and histories of even his most incidental characters. In *Rookwood*, every one of the 'Canting Crew' has his or her own biography, as do the 'Minters' of *Jack Sheppard*. He also dwells with interest on the celebrity of Jack Sheppard in the Castle of Newgate, where *beau monde* meets *demi monde*:

The door of the Castle was opened by Austin, who, with a look of unusual interest and importance announced to the prisoner that four gentlemen were shortly coming up with the governor to see him – 'four *such* gentlemen', he added, in a tone meant to impress his auditor with a due sense of the honour attended him, 'as you don't meet every day.'

'Is Mr. Wood among them?' asked Jack, eagerly.

'Mr Wood! – no', replied the turnkey. 'Do you think I'd take the trouble to announce *him?* These are persons of consequence, I tell you.'

'Who are they?' inquired Sheppard.

'Why, first', rejoined Austin, 'there's Sir James Thornhill, historical painter to his Majesty, and the greatest artist of the day…'

'I've heard of him', replied Jack, impatiently. 'Who are the others?'

'Let me see. There's a friend of Sir James – a young man, an engraver of masquerade tickets and caricatures – his name, I believe, is Hogarth. Then, there's Mr. Gay, the poet, who wrote the "Captives" … And, lastly, there's Mr. Figg, the noted prize-fighter…'

'Figg's an old friend of mine', rejoined Jack; 'he was my instructor in the small sword and back sword exercise. I'm glad he's come to see me.'

'You don't inquire what brings Sir James Thornhill here?' said Austin.

'Curiosity, I suppose', returned Jack, carelessly.

'No such thing', rejoined the jailer; 'he's coming on business.'

'On what business, in the name of wonder?' asked Sheppard.

To paint your portrait," answered the jailer.

'My portrait!' echoed Jack.

---

[95] Egan, 24.

'By desire of his Majesty', said the jailer, consequentially. 'He has heard of your wonderful escapes, and wishes to see what you're like. There's a feather in your cap! No housebreaker was ever so highly honoured before.'

'And have my escapes really made so much noise as to reach the ear of royalty?' mused Jack. 'I have done nothing – nothing to what I *could* do – what I *will* do!'

'You've done quite enough', rejoined Austin; 'more than you'll ever do again.'[96]

Admittedly Sheppard is here being turned into a subject of passive observation, albeit from the royal box, but he is being offered immortality by the King through Thornhill's portrait and, although the painting has since been lost, again through Ainsworth's novel. Ainsworth also continues the allegiance between the 'bucks' and the 'bruisers' by introducing another 'low-life' character, James Figg the boxer, who is closely associated with Jack. In Egan and Ainsworth, to be 'down-and-out' can be 'down-and-*in*' (they tend to ignore the poor, honest workers), and the bare-knuckle fighter and the daring criminal people with whom to be *seen*. This *risqué* sense of underworld *chic* is not carried over into the discourse of the Victorian social explorers. To them, the *demi-monde* became the simply demographic.

There was no room for the individual in the rhetoric of the select committees, journalists, sociologists and moral crusaders. As Judith Walkowitz writes:

> Whereas Regency dandies of the 1820s like Pierce Egan's characters, Tom and Jerry, had experienced the streets of London as a playground for the upper classes, and interpreted street sights and characters as passing shows, engaged urban investigators of the mid-and late-Victorian era roamed the city with more earnest (if still voyeuristic) intent to explain and resolve social problems. Frederick Engels, Charles Dickens, and Henry Mayhew were the most distinguished among the throng of missionaries and explorers, men who tried to read the 'illegible' city, transforming what appeared to be a chaotic, haphazard environment into a social text that was 'integrated, knowable, and

---

[96] Ainsworth, *Jack Sheppard*, 279–80. This is all true (see Ellis, Uglow and Moore), although these illustrious visitors did not all turn up at once. Thornhill was Serjeant Painter to George I, and the king ordered two studies of Sheppard to be made. Thornhill's portrait of Sheppard has not survived, but we do have a mezzotint engraving taken from the original by G. White.

ordered'. To realize their subject, their travel narratives incorporated a mixture of fact and fancy: a melange of moralised and religious sentiment, imperialist rhetoric, dramatized characterization, graphic descriptions of poverty, and statistics culled from Parliamentary Blue Books.[97]

As Ainsworth's description of the Old Mint in Southwark acknowledged, the urban rookeries had not gone anywhere; if anything, they had become much worse than they had ever been in the eighteenth century. The mid nineteenth century saw the first demonstrable evidence of England's transition from an essentially rural to an urban society, a situation unprecedented in global history, and with the rise of industrialisation the exodus of the rural poor to the expanding cities was accompanied by rapid population growth. This was the age of *Mary Barton* rather than *Jack Sheppard*, and the emergence of the new industrial working class, a culturally displaced group with, seemingly, no identifiably traditional norms and values, confused, appalled and sometimes terrified the middle-class commentators:

> As a stranger passes through masses of human beings which have accumulated round the mills and print works ... he cannot contemplate these 'crowded hives' without feelings of anxiety and apprehension amounting to dismay. The population, like the system to which it belongs, is NEW; but it is hourly increasing in breadth and strength. It is an aggregate of masses, our conceptions of which clothe themselves in terms that express something portentous and fearful ... as of the slow rising and gradual swelling of an ocean which must, at some future and no distant time, bear all the elements of society aloft upon its bosom, and float them Heaven knows whither. There are mighty energies slumbering in these masses ... The manufacturing population is not new in its formation alone: it is new in its habits of thought and action, which have been formed by the circumstances of its condition, with little instruction, and less guidance, from external sources, these men have speedily laid aside all their old habits and associations.[98]

The above being a description of Ainsworth's home town of Manchester in 1842; the distinctive faces of the pantomime dance are now rewritten as an amorphous

---

[97] Judith R. Walkowitz, *The City of Dreadful Delight* (London: Virago, 1992–4), 18
[98] W. Cooke Taylor, *Notes of a Tour in the Manufacturing Districts of Lancashire*, (1842), quoted from E.P. Thompson, *The Making of the English Working Class* (London: Pelican, 1968), 208–209.

'mass', with differentiated individuals no longer in view. The City is a 'hive' not a pantomime, and the population an insect collective, only much bigger. In this new climate of fear and curiosity, the criminal class becomes a problem in need of a solution, with research becoming quantitative and statistical:

> Mr Thomas Narrill, a sergeant of the Bristol Police, was asked – 'What proportion of the vagrants do you think are thieves, that make it a point to take anything for which they find a convenient opportunity?' 'We have found it so invariably.' 'Have you ever seen the children who go about as vagrants turn afterwards from vagrancy to common thieving – thieving wholly or chiefly?' 'We have found it several times.' 'Therefore the suppression of vagrancy or mendicity would be to that extent the suppression of juvenile delinquency?' 'Yes, of course.'

> Mr J. Perry, another witness states: 'I believe vagrancy to be the first step towards the committal of a felony, and I am supported in that belief by the number of juvenile vagrants who are brought before the magistrates as thieves.'

> An officer, appointed specially to take measures against vagrancy in Manchester, was asked, 'Does your experience enable you to state that the large proportion of vagrants are thieves too, whenever they come in the way of thieving?' 'Yes, and I should call the larger proportion there thieves.' 'Then, from what you have observed of them, would you say that the suppression of vagrancy would go a great way to the suppression of a great quantity of depredation?' 'I am sure of it.'

> The same valuable Report furnishes us with a table of the numbers and character of the known depredators and suspected persons frequenting five of the principal towns; from which it appears that in these towns alone there are 28,706 persons of known bad character. According to the average proportion of these to the population, there will be in the other large towns nearly 32,000 persons of a similar character, and upwards of 69,000 of such persons dispersed through the rest of the country. Adding these together, we shall have as many as 130,000 persons of known bad character living in England and Wales, without the walls of the prisons. These, according to the last census, are 19,888, which, added to the 130,000 above enumerated, gives within a fraction of 150,000 individuals for the entire criminal population of the country.[99]

And what, wondered the police, journalists, politicians, churchmen and academics, might be the cause of such 'juvenile delinquency?' Soon, the microscopic gaze turned toward the popular culture of the masses, and in particular towards the criminal romances playing night and day in the cheap

---

[99] Mayhew, 380–81.

theatres. Ainsworth, father of Turpin and Sheppard reborn, did not initially realise how much trouble he was in. As his approach to criminal biography, and his own private life, demonstrates, he was always something of an innocent, despite his liberal use of trapdoors and stage blood.

III. The storm: the Newgate controversy[100]

Four months after *Jack Sheppard* began its serial run, the first part of *Catherine, A Story* appeared in *Fraser's*, credited to the pen of 'Ikey Solomons, Esq., Jr', Ikey Solomons, Esq., Snr being a notorious fence based in Islington in the 1820s whose criminal empire made Jonathan Wild's look like a kindergarten. Solomons was Jewish and is assumed to be the model for Dickens's Fagin; unlike his literary counterpart, Solomons escaped from police custody after being charged with the capital crime of receiving stolen goods, later turning up in New York.[101] *Catherine* was the story of Catherine Hayes, taken from one of the nastiest of the original Newgate Calendars, *The Malefactor's Bloody Register*, in which the wife of a London tradesman plotted his murder with her lover (Thomas Wood, the lodger) and her illegitimate son (Thomas Billings). After getting Mr Hayes very drunk, the two men killed him with an axe and dismembered the body, disposing of it in a pond in Marylebone Fields except for the head, which they threw in the Thames in the hope of making identification impossible. The head turned up however, and was placed on display (first on a pole in a churchyard, and later preserved in a glass of spirits in the hope someone might recognise it). Catherine Hayes claimed her husband was in Portugal, but his friends were suspicious. Eventually, Wood and Billings confessed and the trio were executed, the two men were hanged in chains and the woman was burnt at the stake at Tyburn in May 1726, as a wife

---

[100] The best study by far of this period remains Hollingsworth's, but John Springhall's recent book, *Youth, Popular Culture and Moral Panics* (London: Routledge, 1998) is interesting in its examination of the cyclical nature of moral panics in Britain and America from the early Victorians to date.
[101] See John J. Tobias, *Prince of Fences: The Life and Crimes of Ikey Solomons* (London: Valentine, 1974).

killing her husband was petty treason under law. In a particularly unpleasant twist of fate, the flames caught so quickly that the executioner was not able to strangle the condemned as was customary, and the unfortunate woman was burnt alive. *Catherine* was the work of Thackeray, and the point of such a nasty story was savagely to shame and satirise the whole of the so-called Newgate school (in which he included Dickens) and their audience.

Generally speaking, nobody got the joke, and *Catherine* is most interesting as an example of Thackeray's metamorphosis from journalist to novelist, as the narrative swings wildly between picaresque parody and saloon bar polemics:

> And here, though we are only in the third chapter of this history, we feel almost sick of the characters that appear in it, and the adventures which they are called on to go through. But how can we help ourselves? The public will hear of nothing but rogues; and the only way in which poor authors, who must live, can act honestly by the public and themselves, is to paint such thieves as they are: not dandy, poetical, rosewater thieves; but real downright scoundrels, leading scroundrelly lives, drunken, profligate, dissolute, low; as scoundrels will be. They don't quote Plato, like Eugene Aram; or live like gentlemen, and sing the pleasantest ballads in the world like Jolly Dick Turpin: or prate eternally about *to kalon*, like that precious canting Maltravers,[102] whom we all of us have read about and pitied; or die white-washed saints, like poor 'Biss Dadsy' in 'Oliver Twist'. No, my dear madam you and your daughters have no right to admire and sympathize with any such persons, fictitious or real; you ought to be made cordially to detest, scorn, loathe, abhor, and abominate all people of this kidney. Men of genius like those whose works we have above alluded to, have no business to make these characters interesting or agreeable; to be feeding your morbid fancies or indulging their own, with such monstrous food.[103]

The story, not produced as a book until it appeared in the posthumous collected works of 1869, did contain some wonderful pastiches of *Jack Sheppard* however, anticipating 'The Night Attack' of the original *Vanity Fair*. I offer the following by way of illustrative example:

---

[102] Lytton, *Earnest Maltravers* (1837).
[103] Thackeray, *Catherine, A Story* (1839), Works, 34.

THE THAMES AT MIDNIGHT.

Here follows a description of the THAMES AT MIDNIGHT, in a fine historical style; with an account of Lambeth, Westminster, the Savoy, Baynard's Castle, Arundel House, the Temple; of Old London Bridge, with its twenty arches, 'on which be houses builded, so that it seemeth rather a continual street than a bridge'; of Bankside, and the 'Globe' and the 'Fortune' Theatres; of the ferries across the river, and of the pirates who infest the same – namely, tinklermen, petermen, hebbermen, trawlermen; of the fleet of barges that lay at the Savoy steps; and of the long lines of slime wherries sleeping on the river banks and basking and shining in the moonbeams. A combat on the river is described, that takes place between the crews of a tinklerman's boat and the water-bailiff's. Shouting his war-cry, 'St. Mary Overy *à la rescousse!*' the water-bailiff sprung at the throat of the tinklerman captain. The crews of both vessels, as if aware that the struggle of their chiefs would decide the contest, ceased hostilities, and awaited on their respective poops the issue of the death-shock. It was not long coming. 'Yield, dog!' said the water-bailiff. The tinklerman could not answer – for his throat was grasped too tight in the iron clench of the city champion; but drawing his snickersnee, he plunged it seven times in the bailiff's chest: still the latter fell not. The death-rattle gurgled in the throat of his opponent; his arms fell heavily to his side. Foot to foot, each standing at the side of his boat, stood the brave men – *they were both dead!* 'In the name of St. Clement Danes', said the master, ' give way, my men!' and, thrusting forward his halberd (seven feet long, richly decorated with velvet and brass nails, and having the city arms, argent, a cross gules, and in the first quarter a dagger displayed of the second), he thrust the tinkleman's boat away from his own; and at once the bodies of the captains plunged down, down, down, down in the unfathomable waters.

After this follows another episode. Two masked ladies quarrel at the door of a tavern overlooking the Thames; they turn out to be Stella and Vanessa, who have followed Swift thither; who is in the act of reading 'Gulliver's Travels' to Gay, Arbuthnot, Bolingbroke, and Pope. Two fellows are sitting shuddering under a doorway; to one of them Tom Billings flung a sixpence. He little knew that the names of those two young men were – *Samuel Johnson* and *Richard Savage*.[104]

Neither do Lytton and Dickens escape unscathed. Reynolds is at this point not yet worthy of high-brow satire. At its conclusion, the serial becomes a literary essay on Dickens and Ainsworth; there is also a companion article on *Jack Sheppard* which suggests that the novel, 'and its manifold theatrical adaptations', could turn

---

[104] *Ibid.*, 125–6.

impressionable boys to a life of crime.[105] Although *Catherine* failed to find popular favour either as a satire or a Newgate novel (much to the chagrin of its author), it was to be the first shot of a very long war of words.

Thackeray's opening salvo had as much to do with his personal dislike of Lytton and his own failure, so far, to succeed as an author while what he believed to be at worst immoral and at best rather silly books made their creators both rich and famous. There was, however, soon a concern over Newgate novels being voiced by a more impartial source. When *Jack Sheppard* was released as a novel in October 1839, *The Athenaeum* used the occasion to publish a long article on contemporary literature and the condition of England under the heading of a review of Ainsworth's novel.

The unidentified author[106] of the piece read *Jack Sheppard* and its like as a response to contemporary culture, and argues that a decline in national standards of taste, intellect and morality is distressingly apparent:

> should an ambassador from some far distant country arrive on our shores for the purpose of overreaching us in a convention, we know not where he could find a better clue to the infirmities of the national character, than in the columns of our book advertisements.[107]

The perceived problem being that literature no longer sets the standard, but merely reacts to the popular market: 'in the present age ... writers take their tone from the readers, instead of giving it; and in which more pains are taken to write down to the mediocrity of the purchasing multitude'.[108] Unlike later commentaries

---

[105] 'William Ainsworth and Jack Sheppard', *Fraser's*, February 1840, probably also written by Thackeray. The concluding critical remarks from *Catherine* are usually absent from the complete works but are appended to the present work.

[106] As this is effectively an editorial within a literary review, it is possible that the author may be Charles Wentworth Dilke himself, editor from 1830 to 1846.

[107] *Athenaeum*, October 26 1839, 803.

[108] *Ibid*. The writer is here articulating a concerned response to a relatively recent development in the relationship between Art and Capital. As Raymond Williams has argued: 'from the third and fourth decades of the eighteenth century there had been growing up a large new middle class reading public, the rise in which corresponds very closely with the rise of influence and power of the same class. As a result, the system of patronage had passed into subscription-publishing, and thence into general commercial publishing of the modern kind. These developments affected writers in several ways. There was an advance, for the fortunate ones, in independence and social

on the subject, this article is however careful to avoid abusing the individual author working under such economic circumstances, while giving no quarter with regard to his primary text:

> If we consider Mr. Ainsworth in the usual light of a mere caterer for the public appetite, and as devoting his talents to a popular work either at his own or his publisher's suggestion, we must freely admit his book to be on a level with the usual specimens of the class, and at least as good as the occasion required. It is not his fault that he has fallen upon evil days, and that, like other tradesmen, he must subordinate his own tastes to those of his customers ... Jack Sheppard, then, is a bad book, and what is worse, it is a class of bad books, got up for a bad public; and it is on the last account that we select it for observation, as a specimen of one of those literary peculiarities, which we consider to be signs of the times ... To relieve the tedium of an endless repetition of adventures, where each reflects its brother, and to raise the work above the level of dry extract from the Newgate Calendar, and the newspapers of the day, the hero is involved in a melo-dramatic story of motiveless crime, and impossible folly, connected with personages of high degree; and an attempt is made to invest Sheppard with good qualities, which are incompatible with his character and position.[109]

The previous models of Fielding and Gay are then invoked as examples of the morally and aesthetically appropriate ways of using such material as the criminal biography. The argument remains, however, elitist:

> Writings of this class, it is true, will in all ages be above the general level of the public; too superior for vulgar use, and too exalted for general taste ... without a prompt and exercised intelligence in the reader, without a familiarity with the noble and the beautiful, the irony is lost, the spirit is overlooked, the Beggar's Opera becomes a mere Tom and Jerry, and Jonathan Wild another Jack Sheppard.[110]

Note the familiar connection between Egan and Ainsworth here. Dickens is excepted from the Newgate school, but concern is expressed as to whether he might be popular for the wrong reasons, his readers excited by his 'strong flavour' rather than his 'undercurrent of philosophy.' The cultural critique becomes a

---

status – the writer became a fully-fledged 'professional man'. But the change also meant the institution of 'the market' as the type of a writer's actual relations with society.' Raymond Williams, 'The Romantic Artist', *Culture and Society, 1780–1950* (London: Penguin, 1963), 50.
[109] *Athenaeum*, October 26 1839, 803–804.
[110] *Ibid.*, 804.

224

review only on the final page, where a lengthy section of flash dialogue from 'The Old Mint'[111] is quoted, the essay concluding with a calculated sneer: 'Such is the "elegant and polite literature" which leads authors on their way to fortune and to fame in this the middle of the nineteenth century.'[112] This is probably the first example in print of the type of Leavisite snobbery that has generally excluded popular culture from serious literary study ever since, whereas, as Christopher Pawling wrote in his introduction to the collection *Popular Fiction and Social Change* if: 'one begins to examine literature as a "communicative practice" with social and historical roots, then one cannot afford to ignore those fictional worlds which command the widest public'.[113]

A couple of days later *The Standard*, a daily which reviewed plays rather than books, cites Ainsworth for criticism in an otherwise favourable notice for Buckstone's adaptation at the Adelphi:

> Most persons have heard of Captain Ainsworth's *Life and Death of Jack Sheppard*, and many there are who have had sufficient pertinacity of purpose to wade through the almost endless rubbish, balderdash, twaddle, and vulgarity of which it consists.[114]

Sensing blood in the water, Forster wrote a damning review of *Jack Sheppard* in *The Examiner* the next month, despite the fact that his friendship with Ainsworth had previously been a close one. The novel was: 'in every sense of the word … bad', and (with reference to the mass marketing of the theatrical versions) 'has been recommended to circulation by … disreputable means'. Forster adds that the book could have been simply ignored and that he felt Ainsworth capable of better things, but: 'we think the puffs even more dangerous'. Even worse, Ainsworth had assisted Moncrieff in his adaptation of the novel at the Surrey: 'the very worst specimen of rank garbage thus stewed up'.[115] Ellis argues that this review might

---

[111] Ainsworth, *Jack Sheppard*, 17–19.
[112] *The Athenaeum*, October 26 1839, 805.
[113] Christopher Pawling ed, introduction, *Popular Fiction and Social Change* (London: Macmillan, 1984), 2.
[114] *The Standard*, October 29 1839, 1.
[115] Forster, *The Examiner*, November 3 1839, 691.

have more than a little to do with Forster's idolisation of Dickens and his fury at the sales of *Jack Sheppard* not only exceeding but eclipsing *Oliver Twist* (there had also been a falling out over the editorship of *Bentley's*), and there may well be more truth in this explanation than literary history allows. Hollingsworth also notes that Dickens and Forster despised Moncrieff, who had dramatised both *The Pickwick Papers* and *Nicholas Nickleby* despite objections by the author. As far as Forster saw it, says Hollingsworth, 'Ainsworth was fraternising with the enemy.'[116]

Although Ainsworth wrote to Crossley that: 'Forster's article has been perfectly innocuous, and has done no harm whatever here. In fact, Jack is carrying everything before him,'[117] he must have realised that the moral panic was escalating. The disturbing aspect of which was that, even though it initially did his sales more good than harm, his name was becoming increasingly linked to the debate on crime and the attendant fear of the new urban working classes. The author of the novel was becoming a convenient scapegoat for its theatrical adaptations, which were increasingly believed to be disseminating moral corruption to the masses and inciting the lower-class youth of the day to crime. Forster, for example, leading the argument by suggesting that there was a potential danger to society: 'in the adaptations of the "romance" that are alike rife in the low smoking rooms, the common barbers' shops, the cheap reading places, the private booksellers', and the minor theatres'.[118] Ainsworth's friend Laman Blanchard later attacked this critical backlash in terms of class-based arrogance combined with a fear of the masses:

> Critics, who had always a passion for heroes in fetters before, now found out that housebreakers are disreputable characters. They were in raptures with the old-established brigand still, and the freebooter of foreign extraction; they could hug *Robin Hood* as fondly as ever, and dwell with unhurt morals on the little peccadilloes of *Rob Roy*; nay, they had no objection to ride behind *Turpin* to York any day, and would never feel ashamed of their company; but they

---

[116] Hollingsworth, 144.
[117] Ainsworth, letter to Crossley, November 19 1839.
[118] Forster, *The Examiner*, 691.

shook their heads at *Sheppard*, because low people began to run after him at the theatres; he was a housebreaker![119]

Charles MacKay, after quoting interviews with young offenders corrupted by Newgate fiction, taken from *the Sixth Report of the Inspector of Prisons for the Northern Districts of England* (which singles out stories and plays about Jack Sheppard as especially pernicious), summarises the common argument thus:

> In the penny theatres that abound in the poor and populous districts of London, and which are chiefly frequented by striplings of idle and dissolute habits, tales of thieves and murderers are more admired, and draw more crowded audiences, than any other species of representation. There the footpad, the burglar, and the highwayman are portrayed in their natural colours, and give pleasant lessons in crime to their delighted listeners. There the deepest tragedy and the broadest farce are represented in the career of the murderer and the thief, and are applauded in proportion to their depth and their breadth. There, whenever a crime of unusual atrocity is committed, it is bought out afresh, with all its disgusting incidents copied from the life, for the amusement of those who will one day become its imitators.[120]

He then carefully goes on to differentiate High from Low culture within the more literary 'adventures of noted rogues', which are 'delightful', so that the outlaw creations of Schiller, Scott and Byron may be spared any charges of the corruption of public morals.

Probably the best known expression of such anxiety, and the belief of the bourgeois Christian reformers that the purpose of Art is to edify rather than to entertain is to be found in Mayhew:

> In many of the thoroughfares of London there are shops which have been turned into a kind of temporary theatre (admission one penny), where dancing

---

[119] Samuel Laman Blanchard, 'Memoir of William Harrison Ainsworth', originally written for *The Mirror* in 1842 but often prefixed to *Rookwood*. As things were turning nasty, Percival Banks of *Fraser's* wrote to Ainsworth to offer a favourable review of the novel as, 'I am anxious that it should succeed, and the more especially because I find certain of the dunces and blackguards are against you' (probably referring to Forster and Thackeray). *Punch*, which later enjoyed a good humoured, tit-for-tat satirical game with *Ainsworth's Magazine*, wrote of *Jack Sheppard* that: 'The pen that recorded his adventures played like a sunbeam about him.' See Ellis, vol. 1, 375 for favourable notices. Dickens, although privately vexed at being associated with the Newgate school of writing, kept publicly silent for a couple of years before explaining his political position in the preface to the 1841 edition of *Oliver Twist*, as has already been discussed.
[120] MacKay, 645.

and singing take place every night. Rude pictures of the performers are arranged outside, to give the front a gaudy and attractive look, and at night-time coloured lamps and transparencies are displayed to draw an audience. These places are called by the costers 'Penny Gaffs'; and on a Monday night as many as six performances will take place, each one having its two hundred visitors.

It is impossible to contemplate the ignorance and immorality of so numerous a class as that of the costermongers, without wishing to discover the cause of their degradation. Let anyone curious on this point visit one of these penny shows, and he will wonder that *any* trace of virtue and honesty should remain among the people. Here the stage, instead of being the means for illustrating a moral precept, is turned into a platform to teach the cruellest debauchery. The audience is usually composed of children so young, that these dens become the school-rooms where the guiding morals of life are picked up ...[121]

This so-called 'effects' theory of popular culture persists to this day, despite a lack of any firm evidence beyond a conviction by contemporary subscribers from the world of right-wing politics, religious fundamentalism and pop psychology, that correlation must prove causation; the logic being that if juvenile delinquents go to penny-theatres/read penny dreadfuls/'dime' novels/horror and crime comics/listen to rock 'n' roll/punk rock/gangsta rap/watch 'video nasties'/play violent computer games and so forth, then the penny theatres *etc* cause juvenile delinquency.[122] Unfortunately for the beleaguered Ainsworth, this theory was considered to be borne out when on May 5 1840 Lord William Russell was murdered by his valet, François Courvoisier, who, it was claimed, had stated that the idea for the crime had come to him while reading *Jack Sheppard*.[123] A working-class man had risen

---

[121] Mayhew, 'Of the "Penny Gaff"', *London Labour*, 36–7.

[122] There are numerous cultural studies on the relationship between delinquency and popular culture. Stanley Cohen posited the 'Deviance Amplification Spiral' model to explain the creation of a moral panic by the media in his seminal study *Folk Devils and Moral Panics* (London: McGibbon and Kee, 1977). Roger Sabin offers an excellent overview of the phenomenon in his analysis of Fredric Wertham's book *The Seduction of the Innocent* (London: Museum Press, 1955) and the attendant moral crusade against crime and horror comics, Roger Sabin, *Adult Comics: An Introduction* (London: Routledge, 1993), 157–63. See also Martin Barker and Julian Petley (eds), *Ill Effects: The Media/Violence Debate* (London: Routledge, 1997).

[123] Probably because of the status of the victim and the alleged connection to a popular novel, this was a famous crime. The murderer's likeness remained at Madame Tussaud's Chamber of Horrors well into the twentieth century, alongside Thurtell, Greenacre, Burke and Hare, Kate Webster, Jack the Ripper, Dr Crippen *et al.* It was Courvoisier's execution that Thackeray wrote of in 'Going to see a Man Hanged'.

up against his master after reading a Newgate novel. This was unprecedented. After the killer was condemned, *The Examiner* returned to Forster's original review, which foretold such a disaster and ran a smug editorial which again denounced *Jack Sheppard*:

> In Courvoisier's second confession, which we are more disposed to believe than the first, he ascribes his crimes to the perusal of that detestable book, 'Jack Sheppard'; and certainly it is a publication calculated to familiarize the mind with cruelties and to serve as the cut-throat's manual, or the midnight assassin's *vade-mecum*, in which character we now expect to see it advertised … If ever there was a publication that deserved to be burnt by the common hangman it is 'Jack Sheppard'.[124]

You couldn't *buy* publicity like this. The book continued to sell, while its author became a literary pariah, blackballed at the Trinity Club and forced to withdraw from candidacy for the Athenaeum club because of the likelihood of defeat and further public humiliation. During this period, Ainsworth was editing *Bentley's*, planning his own magazine with Cruikshank and carrying on the monumental task of writing two serials simultaneously, *The Tower of London* and *Guy Fawkes*; Blanchard called them the 'twin-born romances'.[125] In consequence he did not write to Crossley between November 19 1839 and December 7 1840 (he often kept silent during projects, the *Jack Sheppard* letters are an exception), and his opinions on the Newgate controversy are therefore unknown. Only the Courvoisier accusations caused him publicly to break his silence, writing to *The Times* that:

> I have taken means to ascertain the correctness of the report, and I find it utterly without foundation. The wretched man declared he had neither read the work in question nor made any such statement. A Collection of Trials of Noted Malefactors (probably 'The Newgate Calendar') had indeed fallen in his way, but the account of Jack Sheppard contained in this series had not particularly attracted his attention. I am the more anxious to contradict this false and injurious statement because a writer in *The Examiner* of Sunday last, without

---

[124] *Examiner*, June 28 1840, 402.

[125] Blanchard, 'Memoir of William Harrison Ainsworth', *Rookwood*, xxvii.

inquiring into the truth of the matter, has made it the groundwork of a most violent and libellous attack on my romance.[126]

But nobody believed him. The Courvoisier statement was never confirmed or disproved, although it presumably takes more than reading a novel to enable one to cut someone's throat. That no doubt requires another type of inspiration altogether.

After this, what was left of the Newgate novel story largely belongs to Dickens and Lytton. Ainsworth's planned projects on the lives of Dick Turpin and Claude Duval were never, unfortunately, realised, and he prudently moved away from Newgate and into the realm of his own idiosyncratic version of historical fiction.

As Thackeray fired the first shot, it was in every way appropriate that he also fired the last. *Vanity Fair* (1847–8) marks the *coup de grâce* of the Newgate novel, with its wonderful yet throwaway pastiche of the 'Storm Scene' from *Jack Sheppard* (and most of Ainsworth's other novels, where there is always a dramatic thunderstorm bordering on the apocalyptic somewhere in the text) and his liberal use of flash slang. 'The Night Attack' was originally a false beginning to Chapter Six, where the author considers whether or not he should proceed in the style of 'the genteel, or in the romantic, or in the facetious manner'. 'Fancy', he finally announces, 'this chapter having been headed ...'

THE NIGHT ATTACK

The night was dark and wild – the clouds black – black – ink-black. The wild wind tore the chimney-pots from the roofs of the old houses, and sent the tiles whirling and crashing through the desolate streets. No soul braved that tempest – the watchmen shrank into their boxes, whither the searching rain followed them where the crashing thunderbolt fell and destroyed them – one had so been slain opposite the Foundling. A scorched gabardine, a shivered lantern, a staff rent in twain by the flash, were all that remained of stout Will Steadfast. A hackney-coachman had been blown off his coachbox, in Southampton Row – and whither? But the whirlwind tells no tidings of its victim, save his parting scream as he is borne onwards! Horrible night! It was dark, pitch dark; no

---

[126] Ainsworth, letter, *The Times*, July 7 1840.

230

moon. No, no. No moon. Not a star. Not a little feeble, twinkling, solitary star. There had been one at early evening, but he showed his face, shuddering, for a moment in the black heaven, and then retreated back.

One, two, three! It is the signal that Black Vizard had agreed on.

'Mofy! is that your snum?' said a voice from the area. 'I'll gully the dag and bimbole the clicky in a snuffkin.'[127]

'Nuffle your clod, and beladle your glumbanions', said Vizard, with a dreadful oath. 'This way, men; if they screak, out with your snickers and slick! Look to the pewter room, Blowser. You, Mark, to the old gaff's mobus box! and I', added he, in a lower but more horrible voice, 'I will look to Amelia!'

There was a dead silence.

'Ha!' said Vizard, 'was that the click of a pistol?'[128]

When Thackeray revised the novel in 1853, this passage was omitted, and remained absent in all subsequent editions, the author considering it no longer relevant as a contemporary satire. The drop had fallen on the Newgate novel, and the bells of St Sepulchre's had tolled for Ainsworth's career as a serious novelist in particular; a scapegoat was obviously required and the Courvoisier case was simply too damning. Fictional highwaymen and camp villains had not gone anywhere of course, except into the penny magazines and other working class literature where their narratives became the subject of sociological analysis rather than literary debate. Ainsworth's outlaws, underdogs and murderous fiends similarly remained, only now they were members of the British Royal Family, as the author turned his attention towards the political history of the nation, making the Tower of London, rather than Newgate Prison, his gothic castle.

---

[127] A representative bit of flash dialogue from *Jack Sheppard* can be picked at random. For example: "'Jigger closed!' shouted a hoarse voice in reply. "All's bowman, my covey. Fear nothing. We'll be upon the bandogs before they can shake their trotters!'" Ainsworth, *Jack Sheppard*, 17.
[128] Thackeray, *Vanity Fair* (1848 London: Collins, 1949), 59. This passage is generally omitted from the complete works.

CHAPTER FOUR

The Historical Novelist: Prophecy, Passivity and Tragedy

I. Twin-born romances: *Guy Fawkes* and *The Tower of London*, 1840

Despite the *Jack Sheppard* crisis, Ainsworth was now at his creative zenith and January 1840 saw the commencement of two serial romances, *Guy Fawkes: or, The Gunpowder Treason. A Historical Romance* and *The Tower of London, A Historical Romance*, which ran concurrently throughout the year. *Guy Fawkes* ran in *Bentley's* from January to November 1840, appearing as a book in three volumes in July 1841, also published by Bentley. Bentley published *The Tower of London* separately in monthly instalments from January to December 1840, releasing the book in the same month the serial concluded. Both projects were illustrated by Cruikshank. As soon as *The Tower of London* concluded, Ainsworth threw an enormous celebratory dinner at the Sussex Hotel and promptly began the next serial, *Old St. Paul's, A Tale of the Plague and the Fire.*[1] Ainsworth also continued to edit *Bentley's Miscellany* throughout this period. When Dickens had passed the reins to Ainsworth, he concluded his final editorial: 'With hat in hand, I approach side by side with the friend who travelled with me on the old road, and presume to solicit favour and kindness in behalf of him and his new charge, both

---

[1] The Sussex Hotel, Bouverie Street was close to his printers, Bradbury and Evans, and Ainsworth kept a room there where he would often work through the night to meet a deadline before dashing to the printers with the corrected proofs of his latest instalment.

for their sakes and that of the old coachman, Boz.' Friswell made this the feed-line for his oft-quoted witticism that: 'The new whip, having mounted the box, drove straight to Newgate.'[2] Ainsworth's editorship was, however, more dynamic than many critics give him credit for and, besides *Jack Sheppard*, significant contributions during this period include more of Barham's *Ingoldsby Legends*, Longfellow's *Village Blacksmith*, *The Wreck of the Hesperus* and *Voices of the Night* and Poe's *The Fall of the House of Usher*. He resigned the post in December 1841 to begin his own magazine with Cruikshank. Cruikshank was at that point producing a monthly magazine of his own which he called *The Omnibus*; his after-dinner joke at the time was that he had, 'driven his *Omnibus* into *Ainsworth's Magazine*'.

With the 'twin-born romances' of *Guy Fawkes* and *The Tower of London*, Ainsworth began a 40 year run of increasingly formulaic historical romances.[3] Despite the sneers of the literary establishment, these 'romances of old clothes', as R.H. Horne dubbed them, were originally extremely popular and dominated the market for fiction over the next decade, providing his audience with temporary respite from a rapidly changing, increasingly urban and Chartist-ridden present.[4] Ainsworth continued to write these novels until his death, despite a slow but steady decline in the fashion after about 1850. In 1841 *Old St. Paul's* was one of the first romances to appear serially in a national English newspaper; *Stanley Brereton*, his final work of 1881, could only manage *The Bolton Weekly Journal*.

Ainsworth could be a careless writer, often lapsing into unintentional self-parody; as Sheridan observed in *Clio's Protest*, 'easy writing's curst hard reading'. This is why *Windsor Castle* (which was written far too hurriedly as a companion novel to *The Tower of London* in order to launch *Ainsworth's Magazine* in 1842) was such an easy target for R.H. Horne. With this in mind, as

---

[2] Friswell, 263.
[3] 'Twin-born romances' is a term borrowed from Blanchard's Memoir of Ainsworth.
[4] See Rance chapter 1; also John Sutherland, *Victorian Fiction: Writers, Publishers, Readers* (London: Macmillan, 1995) chapter 4.

well as the parameters of this present work and the body of research already produced in America which concentrates on much of Ainsworth's historical fiction (a reflection of America's on-going fascination with English heritage), and the range of my predecessors Mr Ellis and Professor Worth (who attempt to engage with every novel), I shall restrict myself to the first four historical romances written after *Jack Sheppard* as indicative of Ainsworth's unique approach to historical fiction and as representative examples of his art.

Guy Fawkes begins in the Summer of 1605, by which time the gunpowder conspiracy was already reasonably well advanced. The focal point of the text is the attempt to destroy Parliament on November 5 and Robert Catesby's failed insurrection in the North. The story ends in the Spring of 1606 with the execution of the last of the conspirators, the Jesuit Father Henry Garnet. The narrative is divided into three books. 'The Plot' begins with the graphic execution of two seminary priests in Manchester; under King James's anti-Catholic laws, their very presence on English soil was a capital offence. The execution is briefly interrupted by the ravings of the prophetess, Elizabeth Orton, who escapes the pursuivant (an officer appointed by the Privy Council to seek out recusants) and his guards by diving into the Irwell. This scene introduces the novel's two central protagonists, both of whom attempt to save the half-mad woman: Humphrey Chetham, a Protestant nobleman who argues with the arresting authorities on Orton's behalf, and a soldier in Spanish dress who saves her from drowning, Guy Fawkes. Orton dies prophesying her rescuer's death on the scaffold. That's gratitude for you. After this arresting opening, Book the First remains up North, with the action centring around the ancestral seat of the Radcliffes, one of many old Catholic families in Lancashire. Given the spirit of the age, the family lives in constant fear of the Protestant authorities. Sir William Radcliffe broadly supports the conspirators, and his daughter is torn between the love of the innocent Humphrey Chetham (a union divided by faith) and a deep attraction to Guy Fawkes. In a supernatural interlude, Fawkes meets the alchemist Dr John Dee, who raises the spirit of Elizabeth Orton, who once again predicts disaster.

234

Similarly, in a pilgrimage to St Winifred's Well, Fawkes receives a divine vision warning him against the plot. At the end of Book the First, the Radcliffes are discovered to be harbouring the priests Fathers Oldcorne and Garnet, and the conspirators flee to London as Ordsall Hall is sacked by government troops. Book the Second, 'The Discovery', follows the events immediately leading to the failed bombing attempt on November 5, diverting only from the historical record to marry Guy Fawkes to Viviana Radcliffe, who does not approve of the plot and urges him to abandon it. Fawkes, like all the conspirators, is however bound by oath to prosecute the plan. Book the Third, 'The Conspirators', follows the trial of the conspirators and Viviana's attempts to move her husband to repentance. This he does, by her deathbed in the Tower, going to his own execution both bravely and contentedly. The novel concludes, as it began, with the execution of a Catholic priest, Father Garnet.

Like its companion piece, *The Tower of London* is also set during a period of enormous political upheaval. It is chiefly concerned with the political plots and counter-plots to gain control of England after the death of Edward VI: the nine-day reign of Lady Jane Grey, the coronation of Mary I, her marriage to Philip of Spain and the restoration of the Catholic faith in England, along with Sir Thomas Wyat's[5] failed insurrection. The Duke of Northumberland is determined to take power through the coronation of his daughter-in-law, Jane, and consequently to make his son, Lord Guilford Dudley[6], the King. When this fails and Mary I is crowned while Northumberland goes to the block, Dudley's fanatical obsession to regain his former position leads to a doomed attempt at insurrection and the executions of himself and his wife. Meanwhile the Archbishop of Canterbury schemes with the French Ambassador to depose the Catholic Mary and replace her with the Protestant Elizabeth. The arch-plotter is the Spanish Ambassador Simon Renard, who manipulates everybody in order to force the marriage between Mary and Philip of Spain and 'establish the Inquisition in the heart of

---

[5] Ainsworth's spelling of Wyatt.
[6] Ainsworth's spelling of Guildford.

London within six months'.[7] Comic relief is present in the lives and loves of the lower orders (the servants and soldiers who actually run the *Gormenghast*-like citadel), particularly the three giants of the Tower, Og, Gog and Magog (gate-keepers who are rumoured to be illegitimate children of Henry VIII, and who therefore function as a comic opposite to Jane, Mary and Elizabeth), and their friend, the dwarf Xit, whom they torment constantly. There is also a melodramatic sub-plot involving the esquire Cuthbert Cholmondeley, Mistress Cicely (the 'Rose of the Tower'), and Nightgall the Jailer (the camp villain who is sexually obsessed with Cicely). Cicely is an archetypal secondary gothic heroine, her blighted relationship with Cholmondeley closely matching the disastrous romance of Agnes and Raymond in Lewis's *The Monk*. The luckless life of Lady Jane gives the novel its temporal frame. Ainsworth begins with her entry to the Tower as Queen on July 10 1553, and ends with her execution on February 12 the following year. This allows the author the use of two coronations, a royal wedding, several executions and a siege without recourse to undue invention as, he explains in his original preface, he was 'Desirous of exhibiting the Tower in its triple light of a palace, a prison, and a fortress'.[8] In a model a least partially inspired by Hugo's *Notre Dame de Paris* the Tower itself is the focal point of the narrative, a controlling metaphor for the nation's history. In the cases of both novels (one with a Catholic hero, the other Protestant), Ainsworth's scenarios utilise gothic space alongside meticulous antiquarian research and recreation, so that there is always a forgotten prisoner in a rat-infested dungeon beneath the Bloody Tower, and ghosts that walk alone on Tower Hill. Chat Moss (in the seventeenth century a boggy swamp to the West of Manchester) also becomes a terrifying, alien landscape where

---

[7] Ainsworth *The Tower of London, A Historical Romance*, Works, 398. This character's name seems too convenient for him to be a historical figure: *renard* being the French word for *fox*, the manipulative villain of the novel perfectly suiting the expression, 'c'est un fin renard' meaning 'he's a sly fox'. There was, however, a well-documented Spanish Ambassador to Mary's Court named Simon Renard. See Diarmaid MacCulloch, *Thomas Cranmer* (New Haven, Yale UP, 1996), 558 and also J.E. Neale, *Queen Elizabeth I* (London: Pimlico, 1934), chapters 3–5.
[8] Ainsworth, preface, *The Tower of London*.

horses and their riders in pursuit of Guy Fawkes are sucked up by a living morass beneath eerily glowing mist.

At the beginning of *Guy Fawkes*, the hero saves the half-mad prophetess, Elizabeth Orton, from the pursuivant who is overseeing the execution of two Catholic priests in Manchester, from one of whom the old lady had sought a blessing. To aid their escape, Orton leads Fawkes to a secret place on the bank of the river Irwell:

> Descending the eminence, and again entering the lane, which here made a turn, the soldier approached a grassy space, walled in on either side by steep sandstone rocks. At the further extremity of the enclosure, after a moment's search, by the direction of his companion, he found, artfully concealed by overhanging brushwood, the mouth of a small cave. He crept into the excavation, and found it about six feet high, and of considerable depth. The roof was ornamented with Runic characters and other grotesque and half effaced inscriptions, while the sides were embellished with Gothic tracery, amid which the letters I.H.S.,[9] carved in ancient church text, could be easily distinguished. Tradition assigned the cell to the priests of Odin, but it was evident that worshippers at other and holier altars had more recently made it their retreat. Its present occupant had furnished it with a straw pallet, and a small wooden crucifix fixed in a recess in the wall. Gently depositing her upon the pallet, the soldier took a seat beside her on a stone slab at the foot of the bed. He next, at her request, as the cave was rendered almost wholly dark by the overhanging trees, struck a light, and set fire to a candle placed within a lantern.
>
> After a few moments passed in prayer, the recluse begged him to give her the crucifix that she might clasp it to her breast. This done, she became more composed, and prepared to meet her end. Suddenly, as if something had again disturbed her, she opened wide her glazing eyes, and starting up with a dying effort, stretched out her hands.
>
> 'I see him before them!' she cried. 'They examine him – they adjudge him! Ah! he is now in a dungeon! See, the torturers advance! He is placed on the rack – once – twice – thrice – they turn the levers! His joints snap in their sockets – his sinews crack! Mercy! he confesses! He is led to execution. I see him ascend the scaffold!'
>
> 'Whom do you behold?' inquired the soldier, listening to her in astonishment.

---

[9] Representing the Greek capitals IHC: (H, capital *eta*, C, a form of *sigma*) being the first two and last letters of *Iesous* (Jesus). Often misread as *Jesus Hominum Salvator*, 'Jesus Saviour of Men'. This is High Church symbolism, stressing the continuity of the Church of England with Catholicism.

'His face is hidden from me', replied the prophetess; 'but his figure is not unlike your own. Ha! I hear the executioner pronounce his name. How are you called?'

'GUY FAWKES', replied the soldier.

'It is the name I heard', rejoined Elizabeth Orton.

And, sinking backward, she expired.[10]

In this space, different ages seem to converge and coexist in a single moment. The cave is a natural phenomenon and therefore effectively prehistoric, it has been a place of illicit pre-Christian worship (the Anglo-Saxons taking Woden from the Norse god Odin), and the walls share pagan, runic writing with increasingly contemporary signs of Christian habitation, from the ancient Greek symbol for Christ carved on the medieval gothic decorations to the evidence of a very recent Jesuit hiding place. Through the medium of the dying seer, the future (to the reader the past) is also revealed from the edge of eternity. The textual construction of the cave is therefore based upon these various temporal co-ordinates, with each axis an infinity. This is Ainsworth's perception of history at its most elegant, as a fourth dimensional drama with sets that could have been designed by Pugin; a production that is usually critically under-rated due to the author's penchant for melodramatic dialogue.[11]

Similarly, when Jane spends her first night in the Tower, as its monarch rather than its victim, she is drawn to St John's Chapel in the White Tower:

Descending a short spiral wooden staircase, she found herself within one of the aisles of the chapel, and passing between its columns, entered the body of the fane. For some time, she was lost in admiration of this beautiful structure, which, in its style of architecture – the purest Norman – is without an equal. She counted its twelve massive and circular stone pillars, noted their various ornaments and mouldings, and admired their grandeur and simplicity. Returning to the northern aisle, she glanced at its vaulted roof, and was enraptured at the beautiful effect produced by the interweaving arches.[12]

---

[10] Ainsworth *Guy Fawkes: or, The Gunpowder Treason. An Historical Romance*, Works, 11.
[11] Pugin was briefly interested in theatrical set design, notably working on a production of Scott's historical romance *Kenilworth* in 1831.
[12] Ainsworth, *The Tower of London*, 39.

Such an interlude is common in any work by Ainsworth, but the design of *The Tower of London* necessarily includes innumerable such descriptions of ecclesiastical buildings. As Ainsworth positively pestered The Governor of the Tower and the Keeper of the Regalia to visit areas that were then closed to the public while researching the novel, it is probable that Jane's feelings on viewing St John's Chapel for the first time reflect the author's own. The effect is one of Puginesque epiphany, closely following the greatest of all Victorian architects' unrestrained opening remarks in *Contrasts* concerning, 'those stupendous Ecclesiastical Edifices of the Middle Ages', a group to which St John's Chapel surely belongs, being rebuilt by Henry III, to whom we owe Westminster Abbey:

> It is, indeed, a sacred place; and well does the fabric bespeak its destined purpose: the eye is carried up and lost in the height of the vaulting and the intricacy of the aisles; the rich and varied hues of the stained windows, the modulated light, the gleam of the tapers, the richness of the altars, the venerable images of the departed just, – all alike conspire to fill the mind with veneration for the place, and to make it feel the sublimity of Christian worship.[13]

Ainsworth's descriptions of church buildings, his architectural allegory, carry a code that his readers would instantly recognise as Catholic and signal an affirmation of his contemporary Pugin's belief that:

> Such effects as these can only be produced on the mind by buildings, the composition of which has emanated from men who were thoroughly embued with devotion for, and faith in, the religion for whose worship they were erected.[14]

The Tower of London is very much part of the Gothic Revival in architecture as much as it is a continuation of Ainsworth's project to place the literary gothic in an English, historical setting. While Cardinal Newman was prevaricating over Christian architecture, favouring a Utilitarian approach to church building which Pugin interpreted as an outward sign of the spiritual decay of the nation,

---

[13] Augustus Welby Pugin, *Contrasts; or A Parallel Between the Noble Edifices of the Fourteenth and Fifteenth Centuries, and Similar Buildings of the Present Day; Shewing the Present Decay of Taste* (London, 1836), 2.
[14] *Ibid.*

Ainsworth was effectively adding his voice to that of the author of *Contrasts*. Although somewhere between Anglican and atheist, Ainsworth too saw a sublime link between the architecture and the infinite.

Many years later, in 1884, the Victorian essayist and fantasist C. Howard Hinton (1853–1907) produced a pamphlet in London entitled 'What is the Fourth Dimension?' in which he argued that linear time was an illusion, and that all times coexist in eternity. Fourth dimensional patterns within eternity would seem merely random events to third dimensional percipients, but could be 'a tumultuous record of changes and vicissitudes' moving towards inevitable points of convergence, like 'an archway's lines ... an invisible curve rising through the centuries'.[15] For Hinton, history had an architecture. Hinton's theories coincide with Edwin Abbot's *Flatland* (1884), to which he wrote a kind of sequel, 'An Episode of Flatland' in 1907. In another science fiction story entitled 'An Unfinished Communication' (1895), Hinton represents life after death as the freedom to travel in the fourth dimension (time), through the moments of life, 'unlearning' and 're-evaluating.' His fiction and essays were published in two collections, tellingly entitled *Scientific Romances*, the first series in 1886, the second in 1902.[16]

Although much earlier in the century, Ainsworth is reading history in a very similar fashion. Frank W. Chandler wrote of the Newgate fallout that

---

[15] C[harles] Howard Hinton, 'What is the Fourth Dimension?' (London, 1884), 27–8.

[16] Since the theory of relativity it has been orthodox to treat time alongside the other three spatial dimensions, as the fourth dimension of a unified space-time. In the late nineteenth century, physicists such as Helmholtz popularised the work of Riemann that suggested that there might be a fourth spatial dimension, into which things might disappear, only to reappear elsewhere. This idea was enthusiastically adopted by the Theosophists and other Victorian occultists. In addition to the analyses of Abbott and Hinton, the concept is also mentioned in the work of H.G. Wells and Oscar Wilde, and it reappeared in orthodox physics in the work of Kaluza immediately after the Great War. In contemporary quantum physics, the favoured number of dimensions is ten. Hinton's scientific romance in particular can be detected in Kurt Vonnegut's *Slaughterhouse 5* (1969), Peter Ackroyd's *Hawksmoor* (1985) and *From Hell* (1994) by Alan Moore and Eddie Campbell. Hinton's life and theories are documented in the work of the pop mathematician Rudy Rucker.

'Ainsworth himself forsook roguery for historical romance in the vein of Hugo.'[17] If *The Tower of London* in particular has a model it was certainly *Notre Dame de Paris* (1831).[18] The heart of both texts is the buildings themselves, each is a 'book of stone'[19] deciphered by narrators who are at once antiquarians calling for preservation and historians concerned with progress and change. The author can therefore assume the role of Hinton's traveller, and range across the streams of time where they converge, such as historically charged sites of great religious and political power like the great Paris Cathedral and the Tower of London. Hinton's image of the arch is made real, like the Puginesque Ordsall cave on a vaster scale; history is not only written but can be revealed in the gothic architecture of the pointed arches, rib vaults, flying buttresses, and clerestory windows of the ancient fortress, originally built by William the Conqueror and a millennium-old symbol of the English Crown:

> 'There you behold the Tower of London', said Winwike, pointing downwards.
>
> 'And there I read the history of England', replied Renard.
>
> 'If it is written in those towers it is a dark and bloody history', replied the warder.[20]

Consequently almost every room and feature has a story to tell, related peripherally around the central plot by both author and his characters. The third chapter of Book II is solely historical, and the story ranges beyond the Tudor protagonists of the novel to the nineteenth century, from William the Conqueror

---

[17] Chandler, vol. 2, 370.

[18] This was an apt conjunction given the reaction to Hugo's work in England at the time. *The Literary Gazette*, for example, raised the urgent question: 'Are these volumes fit for the youthful eye, or for the girlish ear?' while the *Englishman's Magazine* described the final, necrophiliac embrace of La Esmeralda and Quasimodo as 'an idea ... both unnatural and disgusting'. Quoted from Kenneth Ward Hooker, *The Fortunes of Victor Hugo in England* (New York: Columbia UP, 1938). 38.

[19] Victor Marie Hugo, *Notre Dame de Paris,* trans. I.G. Burnham (1831, London: J.M. Dent, 1965). 175.

[20] Ainsworth, *The Tower of London.* 128.

to the Cato Street conspiracy.[21] Only at the conclusion of the chapter does the novel's plot return to the fore, when Winwike, a senior warder of the Tower, who has been telling Renard the history of the Tower while Ainsworth tells his readers, mentions that Jane Grey, 'passes most of her time … in prayer'. 'She shall either embrace the Romish faith or die by the hand of the executioner', replies Renard. With this narrative device, the weight of the horrible history of the Tower just told suddenly presses very heavily upon the novel's tragic heroine.[22]

The original preface to the work demonstrates the scope of the unique project that the author has set himself:

> It has been, for years, the cherished wish of the writer of the following pages, to make the Tower of London – the proudest monument of antiquity, considered with reference to its historical associations, which this country, or any other possesses – the groundwork of a romance … [endeavouring] to contrive such a series of incidents as should naturally introduce every relic of the old pile – its towers, chapels, halls, chambers, gateways, arches, and draw-bridges – so that no part of it should remain unillustrated.[23]

The minute particulars of the Tower's architecture and history were obsessively researched by both Ainsworth and Cruikshank, who consequently produced their best collaborative work. Cruikshank's illustrations are in perfect sympathy with Ainsworth's text. As the author constructed a parallel narrative of romance and antiquarian detail, the artist produced 40 atmospheric engravings of events in the story and a further 58 woodcuts devoted to purely architectural features. Ainsworth graciously acknowledges in the preface that the novel was produced, 'in conjunction with the inimitable artist whose designs accompany the work'.[24] As always, the author has excelled at hybridisation. Fact and fiction are skilfully blended here, resulting in a cohesive whole so complete in detail that its reputation as an authority on the history of the Tower endured as late as the 1950s.

---

[21] A revolutionary plot in 1820 led by the Spa Fields veteran Arthur Thistlewood (1770–1820). The conspirators planned to assassinate the cabinet and seize power. They were apprehended by soldiers and police in a hayloft in Cato Street, Marylebone, London and Thistlewood and four lieutenants were hanged.

[22] Ainsworth, *The Tower of London*, 142.

[23] Ainsworth, preface, *The Tower of London*.

The Tower of London is, for example, quoted as a work of reference in *A Pageant of History: The Reigns of our Kings and Queens, Famous People and Events in our History*. This glossy, patriotic book was a standard history text for every schoolchild in post-war Britain.[25] *The Tower of London* is also equipped with a full index.

When Edmund Swifte, Keeper of the Crown Jewels, wrote an account of an experience of a haunting in the Tower in *Notes and Queries*, a page reference to Ainsworth's description of the Anne Boleyn room and Cruikshank's accompanying illustration is immediately given, 'For an accurate picture of the *locus in quo* my scene is laid.'[26] As A.L. Rowse noted in *The Tower of London in the History of the Nation*:

> It was this work that formed the impression of the Tower in most people's minds throughout the Victorian Age, as it did mine as a schoolboy in remote Cornwall early this century.[27]

This was both Ainsworth's purpose and achievement. When he began his work, the Tower was an abandoned garrison, closed in most part to the public and mutilated by modern alteration in some areas while practically falling down in others:

> One important object the author would fain hope his labours may achieve. This is the introduction of the public to some parts of the fortress at present closed to them. There seems no reason why admission should not be given, under certain restrictions, to that unequalled specimen of Norman architecture ... They [the rooms and buildings of the Tower] are the property of the nation, and should be open to national inspection.[28]

Sales were enormous and as the romance progressed, month by month, thousands of people visited the monument to trace the places and events depicted

---

[24] *Ibid.*

[25] Gareth Browning, Rowland W. Purton *et al.*, *A Pageant of History: The Reigns of our Kings and Queens, Famous People and Events in our History* (London: Collins, 1958), 164.

[26] Edmund Lenthal Swifte, 'The Reply to the Question "Is there not a ghost story connected with the Tower of London?"' *Notes and Queries*, September 8 1860.

[27] A.L. Rowse, *The Tower of London in the History of the Nation* (London: Weidenfeld & Nicolson, 1972), 250.

[28] Ainsworth, preface, *The Tower of London*.

by Ainsworth's words and Cruikshank's pictures. When the authorial voice lamented the presence of the recently-built Grand Storehouse in Book II ('that frightful structure ... We trust to see it raised to the ground'[29]), persons unknown obligingly torched it the following year. Fortunately this time the blame did not fall upon the author. With the exception of the storehouse, demolition ceased and the Tower was restored as one of the first Victorian museums and as a patriotic symbol in the national psyche at the dawning of the new age of Victoria. The novel was therefore extravagantly dedicated to the queen: 'Finally, beseeching God to bless these realms, and its ever precious jewel, our gracious QUEEN VICTORIA, and the infant princess newly given to us; to save them as the apple of His eye; and to protect them with the target of His power against all ill.'[30]

Notionally, it would seem that Ainsworth has entered the realm of Scott once more, but his approach to the stories of British history remains very different from the model left by the author of *Waverley*. John Moore has aptly described Ainsworth's novels of this period as 'history in gorgeous Technicolour'.[31] Ainsworth was an author who loved melodrama and whose work translated effortlessly to the Victorian stage; the closest correlative to his historical narratives are the costume dramas of the golden age of Hollywood, such as Michael Curtiz's *Private Lives of Elizabeth and Essex* (1939) starring Errol Flynn at his roguish best, Bette Davis at her most regal and Vincent Price at his most villainous.[32] The emphasis is on pageantry, romance and valour, and the *dramatis personae* are the historically famous. Ainsworth's approach to historical fiction therefore endorses Lady Clarinda's assertion in *Crotchet Castle* that: 'history is

---

[29] Ainsworth, *The Tower of London*, 137.
[30] Ainsworth, preface, *The Tower of London*. The 'infant princess' being Victoria, the Princess Royal and later mother of Wilhelm II, the German Kaiser.
[31] Moore, introduction, *Windsor Castle* by W.H. Ainsworth, 16.
[32] *The Private Lives of Elizabeth and Essex*. Dir. Michael Curtiz. Perf. Bette Davies, Errol Flynn, Olivia de Havilland and Vincent Price. Warner Brothers, 1939.

but a tiresome thing in itself; it becomes more agreeable the more romance is mixed up with it'.[33]

Lukácsian and proto-Lukácsian critics as a rule, however, despise romanticism and apparently rarely watch melodramas or old movies. Already prejudiced against *Jack Sheppard*, R.H. Horne and his friends were quick to label Ainsworth's historical fiction in opposition to that of Scott, and therefore worthless:

> From the historical novel and romance, as re-originated, in modern times, by Madame de Genlis and Sir Walter Scott, and adopted with such high success by Sir E.L. Bulwer, and with such extensive popularity by Mr. James, there has of late years sprung up a sort of lower or less historical romance, in which the chief part of the history consisted in old dates, old names, old houses, and old clothes. But dates in themselves are but numerals, names only sounds, houses and streets mere things to be copied from prints and records; and any one may do the same with regard to old coats, and hats, wigs, waistcoats, and boots. Now, we know that 'all flesh is grass', but grass is not flesh, for all that; nor is it of any use to show us hay for humanity.[34]

Whereas the significance of the 'great' writer of historical romance (being everyone presently writing within the form with the exception of Ainsworth, according to Horne's literary overview) is in his ability to:

> throw the soul back into the vitality of the past, to make the imagination dwell with its scenes and walk hand in hand with knowledge; to live with its most eminent men and women, and enter into their feelings and thoughts as well as their abodes, and be sensitive with them of the striking events and ruling influences of the time; to do all this, and to give it a vivid form in words, so as to bring it before the eye, and project it into the sympathies of the modern world, this is to write the truest history no less than the finest historical fiction; this is to be a great historical romancist – something very different from a reviver of old clothes.[35]

Horne's belief in the primacy of the 'vivid form' as opposed to the 'lower' is a Victorian statement of what Lukács would later describe as the 'conscious growth

---

[33] Thomas Love Peacock, *Crotchet Castle*, ed. Raymond Wright (1831 London: Penguin, 1969). 200.
[34] Horne, vol. 2, 217.
[35] *Ibid.*, 218.

of historicism' that characterised, for Lukács, the significance of the historical novel and of Scott in particular.[36]

There were some who did consider Ainsworth's historical novels educational, however. When *Ainsworth's Magazine* was launched, the *Atlas* delivered an endorsement so glowing that it was appended to later advertisements:

> For a romance writer, possessed of such peculiar powers as Mr. Ainsworth brings to his subjects, it was an admirable notion to commence a series of historical illustrative romances, each of which should be made to throw open, as it were, the traditions and the mysteries of some particular locality. Thus, the Tower of London afforded the first specimen of what might be done in that way, and Old St. Paul's, the second: and now, the author announces his intention of commencing immediately Windsor Castle. The indolent circulating-library reader gains something by such works as these. He gets a peep into old architecture and old history; he sees moving around him old characters, whom he has hitherto known only by the echoes of dull books which he has never troubled himself to peruse; he gets a glimpse of the ways and means of antiquary, of the visages and costumes of his ancestors, and makes a current flesh-and-blood acquaintance with people in far-off centuries, of whom he had never before known anything except by name, regarding them rather as inscriptions in an unknown tongue which he should never be called upon to decipher, than as human realities whom he should be thus tempted to sympathise with.[37]

This review actually attributes a similar quality to Ainsworth's historical romances to the prerequisites of R.H. Horne and his successors, although the two reviewers obviously had different classes of audience in mind. The 'indolent circulating-library reader' being most likely to gain by Ainsworth's straightforward patriotism, historical knowledge transmitted by stealth under cover of an action-packed plot. As a literate barrow boy once explained to Henry Mayhew:

> 'Love and murder suits us best, sir; but within these few years I think there's a great deal more liking for deep tragedies among us. They set men a thinking; but then we all consider them too long. Of *Hamlet* we can make neither end nor side; and nine out of ten of us – ay, far more than that – would like it to be

---

[36] Lukács, 22.
[37] *Atlas*, December 19 1841.

confined to the ghost scenes, and the funeral, and the killing off at the last. *Macbeth* would be better liked, if it was only the witches and the fighting.'[38]

Popular culture was, of course, of no interest to Horne and his ghosts.

In the same year that Horne published his essays, V.G. Belinskii similarly wrote that to read a novel by Scott: 'is like living in the age he describes, becoming for a moment a contemporary of the characters he portrays, thinking for a moment their thoughts and feeling their emotions'.[39] This again foreshadows Lukács and his work on the 'classical form of the historical novel':

> Scott thus lets his important figures grow out of the being of the age, he never explains the age from the position of its great representatives, as do the Romantic hero-worshippers. Hence they can never be central figures of the action. For the being of the age can only appear as a broad and many-sided picture if the everyday life of the people, the joys and sorrows, crises and confusions of average human beings are portrayed. The important leading figure, who embodies an historical movement, necessarily does so at a certain level of abstraction.[40]

Ainsworth wrote in almost total opposition to what Lukács described as this: 'renunciation of Romanticism ... a conquest of Romanticism, a higher development of the realist literary traditions of the Enlightenment in keeping with the new times'.[41] Ainsworth's central characters were not the average or mediocre heroes so necessary to Scott's historical project but the kings and queens of England.

The Lukácsian model is seemingly so endemic to literary analysis however, that any work of historical fiction that is not seen to conform is easily rejected as somehow artistically inferior and (particularly if the work was popular) therefore unworthy of anything other than a casual dismissal or a witty remark. Coupled with the curse of Newgate, this is a common and unhelpful approach to Ainsworth, being only partially more accurate than Friswell's suggestion that the

---

[38] Mayhew, 'Habits and Amusements of Costermongers', *London Labour*, 21.
[39] Vissarion Grigorevich Belinskii, *Selected Philosophical Works* (Moscow: Foreign Languages Publishing House, 1956), 259.
[40] Lukács, 39.
[41] *Ibid.*, 33.

author was simply not very intelligent. As an apparent devotee of both Lukács and Horne, Andrew Sanders has written of Ainsworth, for example, that:

> His didacticism is of a peculiarly unimaginative kind, however, for he was not so much concerned with moral teaching as with the value of facts and dates ... Many of his important historical characters are presented with a destructive ambiguity simply because he has not thought out the implications of his plots with sufficient thoroughness ... This ambiguity is equally evident in the treatment of ordinary citizens. In his stories, unlike Scott's, the common people are allowed to express the novelist's prejudices without appearing to have evolved any kind of understanding of what is happening to them. They are rarely more than spectators observing events which they have no power to influence.[42]

The critical implication is even more didactic than Ainsworth's antiquarianism: any historical novel not written in the manner of Scott or Tolstoy, as defined by Lukács's Marxist historicism, is badly written and deserved to be not just ignored but actively *disremembered*. Once again, the comparison with Scott is misleading. As Ainsworth's histories are concerned with the well known stories of equally well known historical figures of title, position and political power, it is actually more useful to compare his work with that of Sophocles or even Shakespeare rather than Scott, which remains the critical norm. Just as theatre audiences know that Oedipus will marry Jocasta and that Richard II will be usurped by Bolingbroke (and cinema audiences that the *Titanic* must sink), Ainsworth and his readers accepted that Lady Jane Grey was only a nine day queen, that Guy Fawkes would never fire the fatal train and that both would be executed. In choosing then to retell such stories, Ainsworth overcame historical determinism by employing the codes of tragedy to his narratives; the central tenet of tragedy being, of course, *inevitability*.

Guy Fawkes and Lady Jane are both tragic heroes. The common charge that Ainsworth's historical characters tend to lack any psychological depth or insight may be ascribed to this dramatic status. Like the predictable ghosts of Tower Hill (in *The Tower of London* the shade of Anne Boleyn always appears

---

[42] Sanders, 37.

like clockwork the night before an execution), these characters are robbed of agency and are instead doomed to act out the fate that history has dictated they must. In the female characters, this disposition is manifested by an almost angelic passivity, in the male, a brooding melancholy.

Guy Fawkes and Lady Jane are therefore often forewarned by Cassandra in her many guises but, like the Trojans, they pay no heed:

> At the moment Jane was crossing the railed plank leading to her galley, a small wherry, rowed by a young man ... passed between the state barges, and drew up at her feet. Before the daring intruder could be removed, an old woman, seated in the stern of the boat, arose and extended her arms towards Jane ... Fixing an imploring glance on the queen, she cried – 'A boon! a Boon!'
>
> 'It is granted', replied Jane, in a kind tone, and pausing. 'What would you?'
>
> 'Preserve you', rejoined the old woman. 'Go not to the Tower.'
>
> 'And wherefore not, good dame?' inquired the queen.
>
> 'Ask me not', returned the old woman – her figure dilating, her eye kindling, and her gesture becoming almost that of command, as she spoke – 'ask me not, but take my warning. Again, I say, go not to the Tower. Danger lurks therein – danger to you, your husband, and to all you hold dear. Return while it is yet time; return to the retirement of Sion House – to the solitudes of Bradgate. Put off those royal robes – restore the crown to her from whom you wrested it, and a long and happy life shall be yours. But set foot within that galley – enter the gates of the Tower – and another year shall not pass over your head.'[43]

This marriage of melodrama and classicism exemplifies Ainsworth's dramatic technique. The old woman is chased away by Lord Guilford Dudley (Jane's ambitious husband, and son of the arch plotter the Duke of Northumberland), as a storm gathers about the Tower. 'Tis a bad omen for Northumberland', mutters the Earl of Pembroke. All the pomp and circumstance of Jane the queen's entry into London in the opening chapter (the 'romance of old clothes' component of the narrative) is therefore overwritten by the dark hand of Fate:

> As soon as she emerged from the gateway with her retinue, the members of the council bent the knee before her. The Duke of Northumberland offered her the keys of the Tower, while the Marquess of Winchester, lord treasurer, tendered her the crown. At this proud moment all Jane's fears were forgotten, and she

---

[43] Ainsworth, *The Tower of London,* 413.

felt herself in reality a queen. At this moment, also, her enemies, Simon Renard and De Noailles, resolved upon her destruction.[44]

The author is now free to explore chiefly the political plots and counter-plots to gain control of England after the death of Edward VI, and to assign his fictional characters secret roles in leading events, much in the manner of Dumas.

Edgar Allan Poe famously, or rather infamously, wrote that: 'the death of a beautiful woman is, unquestionably, the most poetical topic in the world',[45] and this connection between femininity, art and death is similarly present in much of Ainsworth's writing in a line that can be traced directly back to 'The Spectre Bride'. The sufferings of Cicely form part of this design, but it is Ainsworth's principal tragic heroines, such as the Protestant Jane and the Catholic Viviana Radcliffe of *Guy Fawkes*, that most conform to a bourgeois aesthetic of virtuous femininity. They are therefore almost totally submissive to patriarchal authority in the form of their fathers, their husbands and their gods, before being eventually sacrificed upon the altar of history. This is the complete opposite of the independent, sexually aggressive and godless women of *Jack Sheppard* (who survive their narratives), and may be ascribed either to Ainsworth's return to the Victorian fold or to an inevitable consequence of the tragic role. Both Lady Jane and Viviana are the victims of the political machinations of their husband and fathers. Their dilemma is that they know, even if the men choose to ignore all the obvious signs, that they are doomed, but that they cannot break their marriage vows. Viviana constantly argues against the Gunpowder Plot, for example, and certainly knows enough to stop it, but the inevitable process of Ainsworth's vision of history again renders her powerless:

> 'I deny that the oath … you have taken is binding. The deed you have sworn to do is evil, and no vow, however solemnly pronounced, can compel you to commit crime. Avoid this sin – avoid further connexion with those who would work your undoing, and do not stain your soul with guilt from which it will never be cleansed.'

---

[44] *Ibid.*, 17.
[45] Poe, 'The Philosophy of Composition', *Essays and Reviews*, 19.

'You seek in vain to move me', replied Guy Fawkes firmly, 'My purpose is unalterable … Oppression can go no further; nor endurance hold out longer. If this blow be not struck we shall have no longer a religion. And how comes it, Viviana, that you, a zealous Catholic, whose father perished by these very oppressors, and who are yourself in danger from them, can seek to turn me from my purpose?'

'Because I know it is wrongful', she replied. 'I have no desire to avenge the death of my slaughtered father, still less to see our religion furthered by the dreadful means you propose. In his own due season, the Lord will redress our wrongs.'

'The Lord has appointed me one of the ministers of his vengeance', cried Fawkes, in a tone of enthusiasm.

'Do not deceived yourself', returned Viviana, 'it is not by Heaven, but by the powers of darkness, that you are incited to this deed. Do not persevere in this fatal course', she continued, clasping her hands together, and gazing imploringly at his face, 'do not – do not!'

Guy Fawkes continued in the same attitude as before, with his gaze turned upwards, and apparently lost in thought.[46]

Viviana therefore represents the Catholic majority, who would never countenance violence, whatever the ends. She is the conscience of the text, offering a counter argument to armed insurrection. In his preface, the author explains what each of the central characters is intended to represent: Viviana's role is 'To portray the loyal and devout Catholic, such as I conceive the character to have existed at the period'; Catesby is the 'unscrupulous and ambitious plotter, masking his designs under the cloak of religion'; Garnet is the 'subtle, and yet sincere Jesuit'; and Fawkes the 'gloomy and superstitious enthusiast'.[47] The devout extravagance meant by the term 'enthusiast' would suggest a dissenting religion to an early Victorian audience (in balance, it is also applied to the Protestant 'Hot Gospeller' Edward Underhill in *The Tower of London*, a fictional creation who attempts to assassinate Mary and is burnt at the stake on Tower Hill). Radcliffe castigates such 'enthusiasm' in *The Mysteries of Udolpho*, and 'dissent' here implies a material rather than a spiritual attitude, and therefore renders Fawkes as another of Ainsworth's outlaws. Viviana remains loyal however, rejecting the man she really

---

[46] Ainsworth, *Guy Fawkes*, 141.

loves (the bizarrely fictionalised founding father of Elizabethan Manchester, Humphrey Chetham) because of her religious conviction, and dies just before her husband. Viviana's rejection of the Protestant Chetham in favour of Fawkes also reflects a maturity of attitude towards the representation of faith and duty on the part of the author which had been absent in his previous historical outing, *Crichton*. That novel had concluded with the hero announcing that, 'I am not so staunch a Catholic as I fancied myself' in order to marry the Protestant Princess Esclairmonde, because 'Points of faith are easily settled where love plays the umpire.'[48]

Jane, in common with Viviana, is similarly torn between common sense, faith, love and history when Dudley continues to plot after Mary is crowned and Northumberland executed. She quite rationally begs her husband to thank God that they are still alive and to renounce all claim to the throne. Obviously this is an argument that she cannot win, their fate already preordained, but the author ascribes this failure to her devotion to Dudley. He, on the other hand, considers killing her:

'Dudley', replied Jane, falling at his feet – 'by your love for me – by your allegiance to your sovereign – by your duty to your Maker – by every consideration that weighs with you – I implore you to relinquish your design.'

'I have already told you my fixed determination, madam', he returned, repulsing her. 'Act as you think proper.'

Jane arose, and walked slowly towards the door. Dudley laid his hand upon his sword, half drew it, and then thrusting it back into the scabbard, muttered between his ground teeth, 'No, no – let her go. She dares not betray me.'

As Jane reached the door, her strength failed her and she caught against the hangings for support. 'Dudley', she murmured, 'help me – I faint.'

In an instant he was by her side.

'You cannot betray your husband?' he said, catching her in his arms.

'I cannot – I cannot', she murmured, as her head fell upon his bosom.[49]

---

[47] *Ibid.*, preface.
[48] Ainsworth, *Crichton*, 493.
[49] Ainsworth, *The Tower of London*, 270–71.

252

Her husband's decision to put away his sword is an ambiguous statement: he needs his wife alive for his insurrection to have any semblance of legitimacy – she was Edward's named heir, not he.

Given that the Tower of London itself is a perfect gothic castle (complete with moat, secret passages, dungeons, forgotten prisoners, torture chambers, ghosts headsmen and psychotic jailers), and the rise of Bloody Mary such a horrible history, Ainsworth needs little recourse to the supernatural in *The Tower of London*. In *Guy Fawkes* however, Ainsworth represents prophecy as a much more necromantic act, and the deterministic universe of this text reveals Fawkes's destiny through a series of spectacular supernatural signs and portents. Rather than playing on Catholic superstition as the eighteenth century gothic novelists had done (although the faith of the central characters must imply an element of this), Ainsworth presents the supernatural as an obvious companion to Christian belief, as he had done in his earliest short fiction. This can be seen in the vision of Saint Winifred, for example. Such innocence also reflects an increasing nostalgia for a pre-Enlightenment past over an increasingly rationalist and secular present, when science, religion and magic were still epistemologically linked. This is achieved by the inclusion of the character of Dr John Dee: astrologer to Elizabeth I, teacher of Philip Sidney, mathematician, Cabalist, alchemist and, conveniently for Ainsworth, Warden of the Collegiate Church, Manchester between 1596 and 1604 (when he was accused, but not convicted, of witchcraft). The fluidity of the knowledge of the alchemist appealed to Ainsworth, and he used the character again in the unfinished *Auriol* in 1844. This is another example of Ainsworth's oppositional relationship with Scott, who presents alchemists, such as Herman Dousterswivel in *The Antiquary* (1816) and Alasco in *Kenilworth*, as either charlatans or under the 'general control of superstition … professors of this pretended science', and, 'a species of dupe to his own imagination'.[50]

---

[50] Scott, *Kenilworth*, Waverley Novels, 15.

Dee and his associate, Edward Kelley, are introduced in the opening, Manchester section of the novel. His principal scene is a quintessential example of Ainsworth's black art, illustrating how effortlessly and effectively he can make the gothic gesture. Much like the opening scene of *Rookwood*, the action takes place in a charnel house:

> The chamber in which Guy Fawkes found himself was in perfect keeping with the horrible ceremonial about to be performed. In one corner lay a mouldering heap of skulls, bones, and other fragments of mortality; in the other a pile of broken coffins, emptied of their tenants, and reared on end. But what chiefly attracted his attention, was a ghastly collection of human limbs, blackened with pitch, girded round with iron hoops, and hung, like meat in a shambles, against the wall. There were two heads, and, though the features were scarcely distinguishable, owing to the liquid in which they had been immersed, they still retained a terrific expression of agony. Seeing his attention directed to the revolting objects, Kelley informed him they were the quarters of the two priests who had recently been put to death, which had been left there previously to being placed on the church-gates.[51]

Once more, we are reminded of the terrible laws against Catholics. It is Dee's role to provide the early prognostications of Fawkes's doom, which he does with the aid of a magic glass and, most memorably, the reanimated corpse of the prophetess, Elizabeth Orton:

> There was a rushing sound, and a stream of dazzling lightning shot down upon the corpse, which emitted a hollow groan. In obedience to the Doctor's commands, Guy Fawkes had prostrated himself on the ground: but he kept his gaze steadily fixed on the body, which, to his infinite astonishment, slowly arose, until it stood erect upon the frame. There it remained perfectly motionless, with the arms close to the sides, and the habiliments torn and dishevelled. The blue light still retained its position upon the brow, and communicated a horrible glimmer to the features. The spectacle was so dreadful that Guy Fawkes would fain have averted his eyes, but he was unable to do so. Doctor Dee and his companion, meanwhile, continued their invocations, until, as it seemed to Fawkes, the lips of the corpse moved, and an awful voice exclaimed, 'Why have you called me?'
>
> 'Daughter!' replied Doctor Dee, rising, 'in life thou wert endowed with the gift of prophecy. In the grave, that which is to come must be revealed to thee. We would question thee.'

---

[51] Ainsworth, *Guy Fawkes*, 53.

'Speak, and I will answer', replied the corpse.

'Interrogate her, my son', said Dee, addressing Fawkes, 'and be brief, for the time is short. So long only as that flame burns have I power over her.'

'Spirit of Elizabeth Orton', cried Fawkes, 'if indeed thou standest before me, and some demon hath not entered thy frame to delude me, – by all that is holy, and by every blessed saint, I adjure thee to tell me whether the scheme on which I am now engaged for the advantage of the Catholic Church will prosper?'

'Thou art mistaken, Guy Fawkes', returned the corpse. 'Thy scheme is not for the advantage of the Catholic Church.'

'I will not pause to inquire wherefore', continued Fawkes. 'But, grant that the means are violent and wrongful, will the end be successful?'

'The end will be death', replied the corpse.

'To the tyrant – to the oppressors?' demanded Fawkes.

'To the conspirators', was the answer.

'Ha!' ejaculated Fawkes.

'Proceed, if you have ought more to ask', cried Doctor Dee. 'The flame is expiring.'

'Shall we restore the fallen religion?' demanded Fawkes.

But before the words could be pronounced the light vanished, and a heavy sound was heard, as of the body falling on the frame.

'It is over', said Doctor Dee.[52]

Thus Fawkes knows his fate throughout the novel. There are numerous other omens, including an ecstatic vision during the pilgrimage to Saint Winifred's well (a warning from heaven as well as hell).

The Catholic shrine of Saint Winifred's well (also Winefride, Wenefred, Gwenfrewl), in Holywell, North Wales had survived the Reformation and was, at the time the novel is set, an important recusant centre with Jesuits and secular priests in semi-permanent residence. At the time the novel was written, pilgrims still visited the shrine, including several of the founder members of the Oxford movement. The legend is that the virgin Winifred refused the sexual advances of Caradoc, the son of a neighbouring prince, who hacked off her head in displeasure

---

[52] *Ibid.*, 54–5.

when she tried to seek sanctuary in a church. A fountain sprang up where her head fell, and Winifred was resurrected, later becoming abbess of Holywell Priory. The waters of the spring are said to have curative properties. In the novel, Saint Winifred appears to Fawkes in a vision and tells him his plot will fail, being '*not approved by Heaven*'.[53]

The Orton episode is based in part upon a passage in Dee's own memoir, *Relations with Spirits*, a copy of which Ainsworth owned along with several other rare books and manuscripts on the occult, and of which he did not believe a word, judging by his parody of nineteenth century Rosicrucian dreamers such as Lytton in his semi-autobiography *Mervyn Clitheroe* in 1851. Nonetheless, inserting such fantastic events into the nation's history seems still to betray an innocent sense of longing for myth and magic in the face of an increasingly regimented present, while also joining English history to the gothic tradition. In *Guy Fawkes*, prophecy therefore performs a dual role as a code for both tragedy and the gothic. It should also be noted that although Elizabeth/Cassandra is precise regarding the failure of the plot, she is ambivalent on the possibility of the restoration of the 'Old Religion'. This would be an inflammatory issue in 1840, when anti-Catholic feeling was still running high in the wake of recent and contentious legislation. The Test (1673) and Corporation (1661) Acts had only been repealed in 1828, and dissenters' political disqualifications had been removed, Catholic emancipation following a year later. The Test Acts excluded nonconformists from civil and military office. Office holders were required to receive the Anglican communion and swear allegiance to the crown, affirm the monarch's supremacy as head of the Church of England, and repudiate the Catholic doctrine of transubstantiation. The earlier Corporation Act was one of a series of parliamentary measures passed between 1661 and 1665 known collectively as the Clarendon Code after the King's chief minister, Edward Hyde, 1st earl of Clarendon. These acts were designed to re-establish the position of the Anglican Church following the Restoration. The Corporation Act excluded from municipal office anyone refusing

---

[53] *Ibid.*, 84.

to take communion in the Church of England, to swear the oaths of allegiance, supremacy and non-resistance, and to reject the Solemn League of the Covenant (an agreement between the covenanters and the Long Parliament in 1643 in order to secure Scottish military aid against Charles I during the Civil War). Despite the obvious problems associated with imposing religious tests upon candidates for secular office, the Acts were not repealed until 1828. Catholic emancipation, the achievement of full civil and political rights, was delayed until 1828 due to the resistance of George III and the Tories. Only when Irish Nationalist Daniel O'Connell was elected to represent County Clare that year did Wellington and George IV concede to the principle of full Catholic emancipation for fear of serious civil disturbances in Ireland. This became law in 1829.

Under such a yoke of determinism, the passivity of Ainsworth's protagonists is as inevitable as their fate. As his central characters have no practical agency, the author therefore attempts to explore the spiritual dimension of precognition of one's own death. This is a heightened sense of the intellectual state in which all humanity shares, as well as a theme already explored by the author for more gothic purposes in stories such as 'The Half-Hangit' and, most significantly, a Christian allegory. In 'The Half-Hangit', death is an object of horror; 'The Spectre Bride' offers the worst prospect of eternal damnation; Dick Turpin's execution is presented as a glorious, samurai death; and Jack Sheppard's, although the complex symbolism of the triple tree is flirted with by the author, remains a final act of heroism rather than martyrdom. The twin histories, however, are much more self-conscious religious fables where, remarkably, Catholicism and Protestantism are accorded equal respect.

Given the revival of the latent anti-Catholicism of the English, awakened after the Emancipation Act of 1829, the Whig government's concessions to the Irish Catholics throughout the 1830s and the attendant flood of Irish immigrants to the major cities, the preface to *Guy Fawkes* is nothing short of astounding:

> The tyrannical measures adopted against the Roman Catholics in the early part
> of the reign of James the First, when the severe penal enactments against

recusants were revived, and with additional rigour, and which led to the remarkable conspiracy about to be related, have been so forcibly and faithfully described by Doctor Lingard, that the following extract from his history will form a fitting introduction to the present work.

'The oppressive and sanguinary code framed in the reign of Elizabeth, was re-enacted to its full extent, and even improved with additional severities ... The execution of the penal laws enabled the king, by an ingenious comment, to derive considerable profit from his past forbearance. It was pretended that he had never forgiven the penalties of recusancy; he had merely forbidden them to be exacted for a time, in the hope that this indulgence would lead to conformity; but his expectations had been deceived; the obstinacy of the Catholics had grown with the lenity of the sovereign; and, as they were unworthy of further favour, they should now be left to the severity of the law. To their dismay, the legal fine of twenty pounds per lunar month was again demanded, and not only for the time to come, but for the whole period of the suspension; a demand which, by crowding thirteen payments into one, reduced many families of moderate incomes to a state of absolute beggary. Nor was this all. James was surrounded by numbers of his indigent countrymen. Their habits were expensive, their wants many, and their importunities incessant. To satisfy the more clamorous, a new expedient was devised. The king transferred to them his claims on some of the more opulent recusants, against whom they were at liberty to proceed by law, in his name, unless the sufferers should submit to compound, by the grant of an annuity for life, or the immediate payment of a considerable sum. This was at a time when the jealousies between the two nations had reached a height, of which, at the present day, we have but little conception. Had the money been carried to the royal coffers, the recusants would have had sufficient reason to complain; but that Englishmen should be placed by their king at the mercy of foreigners, that they should be stripped of their property to support the extravagance of his Scottish minions, this added indignity to injustice, exacerbated their already wounded feelings, and goaded the most moderate almost to desperation.'[54] From this deplorable state of things, which is by no means over-coloured in the above description, sprang the Gunpowder Plot.[55]

John Lingard (1771–1851) was a Catholic Priest as well as a historian, and spent most of his life in Ainsworth's native Lancashire. His *History* was highly regarded in contemporary scholarly circles due to its author's apparent impartiality, in particular his balanced presentation of the Reformation, and his

---

[54] John Lingard, *The History of England from the First Invasion of the Romans to the Accession of William and Mary*, 10 vols, vol 7 (London: Charles Dolman, 1830), 19. Ainsworth's other principal source was David Jardine's *Criminal Trials* (1835–40).
[55] Ainsworth, preface, *Guy Fawkes*.

meticulous use of original documents. He was also the author of *The Antiquaries of the Anglo-Saxon Church* (1806) and *A New Version of the Four Gospels* (1836). Although a Catholic priest, Lingard the historian had a reputation for intellectual objectivity. Now, like Ainsworth, forgotten, Lingard's version of British history had even rivalled David Hume's *History of England* in his own day. This was praise indeed from the intellectual establishment, as Hume's *History* was long believed to have overcome the partisan politics that so often prejudiced the discipline of history.[56] As John Kenyon has discovered, however, Lingard was nothing of the sort. Lingard's mission had been to write a history which would not offend Protestant tastes while correcting what he saw as the anti-Catholic bias of previous accounts. His method was wonderfully subversive, if rather an affront to academia. He would initially go along with conventional Protestant prejudice, and then rewrite his accounts extensively in subsequent editions to favour the Catholic cause. Kenyon has found the following letter from Lingard, written in 1847 and warning a friend not to bother with his first edition:

> I had then to acquire credit among Protestants, and was therefore extremely cautious – and I believe in that respect successful, for I was held by many to be a moderate, perhaps impartial writer; this made me bolder in the duodecimo edition.[57]

Whether Ainsworth, a good historical scholar in his own right, had spotted this tactic or not, in interpreting Lingard's research to mean that the Catholic population were the principal victims of Early Modern England (admittedly a difficult assertion to dispute, except under the reign of Mary I), and therefore suggesting that the Gunpowder Plot was an act of justified desperation rather than Jesuit-funded terrorism, Ainsworth was taking a potentially greater risk than he ever did in *Jack Sheppard*. As Mark Nicholls notes, the national standard was more usually that:

---

[56] See John Kenyon's excellent study, *The History Men: The Historical Profession in England since the Renaissance* (London: Weidenfeld and Nicolson 1983).
[57] Quoted from Kenyon, 86.

the most vehement criticism of Catholics and Catholicism has come during periods when the critics feared, often with good reason, that the authorities were inclined to treat Catholics leniently. We see this in 1678–80 with the Popish plot, and as late as the 1850's when the final stages in Catholic emancipation were marked by a resurgence of religious xenophobia in traditional bonfire night celebrations throughout the land.[58]

It is therefore surprising that Nicholas Rance has confidently described Ainsworth as 'patriotic and anti-Catholic.'[59] In his own day Ainsworth seems to have had to field the opposite accusation because, like Scott, he often displayed a romantic affection for the Jacobites, leading Ellis to include the following disclaimer in the biography:

> Probably it was the author's high praise of the Penderals, [*Boscobel*, 1872] and other Roman Catholic families who aided Charles II, which originated the prevalent belief that Ainsworth was himself a member of the Old Faith: it may be well to state here that such was not the cause; he lived and died a member of the Church of England.[60]

Even in 1911, we can still see the stigma attached to Catholicism in England. Rance's comment is a characteristic misreading of the companion novel to *Guy Fawkes*, *The Tower of London*, considered in isolation as a condemnation of Mary I rather than as the Protestant half of a balanced pair. Taken together, the twin-born romances justify the author's claim that, 'One doctrine I have endeavoured to enforce throughout – TOLERATION.' This plea for tolerance is also linked to the painful experience of the *Jack Sheppard* controversy, and Ainsworth concludes his loaded preface with:

> From those who have wilfully misinterpreted one of my former productions, and have attributed to it a purpose and an aim utterly foreign to my own intentions, I can scarcely expect fairer treatment for the present work. But to that wider and more discriminating class of readers from whom I have experienced so much favour and support, I confidently commit this volume, certain of meeting with leniency and impartiality.[61]

---

[58] Mark Nicholls, *Investigating Gunpowder Plot* (Manchester: Manchester UP, 1991), 47.
[59] Rance, 41.
[60] Ellis, vol. 2, 280.
[61] Ainsworth, preface, *Guy Fawkes*.

This dedication to his public betrays his increasing isolation from the literary elite and also his growing annoyance with them. His confidence in his audience was well founded, however; *Guy Fawkes* proved to be extremely popular and *The Tower of London* the most successful novel of his career.

Rather than being portrayed then as a religious fanatic, Fawkes the tragic hero is a soldier: a brave and pious man who believes in his political actions ('My part is to act, not talk',[62] he tells a confederate at Radcliffe Hall). His hubris is complicated, because he has sworn a binding oath which he cannot break, despite the warnings of Elizabeth Orton and Saint Winifred: 'You shall swear by the Blessed Trinity, and by the sacrament you propose to receive, never to disclose, directly nor indirectly, by word or circumstance, the matter that shall be proposed to you to keep secret, nor desist from the execution thereof, until the rest shall give you leave.' When Fawkes tells Father Garnet of his vision at the well, the Jesuit sternly reminds him immediately that, 'You cannot desist, my son ... Your oath binds you to the project.' Fawkes agrees, but replies that, 'I am well assured it will not be successful.'[63] This is also rather like Jack Sheppard's unbreakable covenant with Jonathan Wild.

Knowing he is doomed to failure, torture and violent death (as do we), Fawkes's real battle is not against the State, or even Fate, but with himself. His spiritual dilemma is almost Christ-like, and he must struggle internally to reject the worldly (his life, and his love for the beautiful and virtuous Viviana) and accept his fate as a religious martyr. The story of Christ also contains all the essential elements of tragedy: his death was foretold and inevitable, he knew his life was not his own and resisted the temptations of Satan in the wilderness, but his friendship with Mary Magdalene and his cry of agony and despair on the cross

---

[62] Ainsworth, *Guy Fawkes*, 91.
[63] *Ibid.*, 84.

in the ninth hour reveal his basic humanity. Fawkes's material conflict is fundamentally similar:

'Why should I hesitate to declare my feelings? Why should I not tell you that – though blinded to it for so long – I have discovered that I do love you? Why should I hesitate to tell you that I regret this, and lament that we ever met?'

'What mean you?' cried Viviana, with a terrified look.

'I will tell you', replied Fawkes. 'Till I saw you, my thoughts were removed from earth, and fixed on one object. Till I saw you, I asked not to live, but to die the death of a martyr.'

'Die so still', rejoined Viviana. 'Forget me – oh! forget me.'

'I cannot', replied Fawkes, 'I have striven against it. But your image is perpetually before me. Nay, at this very moment, when I am about to set out on the enterprise, you alone detain me.'

'I am glad of it', exclaimed Viviana, fervently. 'Oh that I could prevent you – could save you!'

'Save me!' echoed Fawkes, bitterly. 'You destroy me.'

'How?' she asked.

'Because I am sworn to this project', he rejoined; 'and if I were turned from it, I would perish by my own hand.'

'Oh say not so', replied Viviana, 'but listen to me. Abandon it, and I will devote myself to you.'

Guy Fawkes gazed at her for a moment passionately, and then, covering his face with his hands, appeared torn by conflicting emotions.

Viviana approached him, and pressing his arm, asked in an entreating voice, 'Are you still determined to pursue your dreadful project?'

'I am', replied Fawkes, uncovering his face, and gazing at her; 'but, if I remain here a moment longer, I shall not be able to do so.'

'I will detain you, then', she rejoined, 'and exercise the power I possess over you for your benefit.'

'No!' he replied, vehemently. 'It must not be. Farewell, for ever!'

And breaking from her, he rushed out of the room.

As he gained the passage, he encountered Catesby, who looked abashed at seeing him.

'I have overheard what has passed', said the latter, 'and applaud your resolution. Few men, similarly circumstanced, would have acted as you have done.'

'*You* would not', said Fawkes, coldly.

'Perhaps not', rejoined Catesby. 'But that does not lessen my admiration of your conduct.'

'I am devoted to one object', replied Fawkes, 'and nothing shall turn me from it.'

'Remove yourself instantly from temptation, then', replied Catesby. 'I will meet you at the cellar beneath the Parliament House to-morrow night.'[64]

The crisis faced and decided, rather than resolved, Guy Fawkes rides off to meet his destiny. The following section of the narrative, the second book, is a well-researched presentation of the failed bombing of Parliament (with still a little romance mixed up with it).

In English history, the Gunpowder Plot is as mysterious as the assassination of John F. Kennedy. There are theories ranging from the conspirators as independent fanatics, as members of an international Jesuit plot and even as *agents provocateurs* working for Robert Cecil (Earl of Salisbury and principal secretary to James I), in order to manipulate public opinion against the Catholics and in favour of the new, and less than universally popular, king and who went to their deaths confident of a last-minute reprieve. What is certain is the damage the conspiracy did to the Catholic cause in England and the political advancement of Cecil as a result of his role in the discovery and the subsequent show trials. Much of the mystery revolves around the identity of the author of the famous letter to Lord Mounteagle,[65] which cryptically warned him to find some excuse to avoid Parliament and alerted the new Stuart administration to the imminent danger. The Houses of Parliament were then thoroughly searched, the mine found and guards almost casually placed to await the bombers. Fawkes was caught when he arrived to fire the train. The Government had known of the plot for a full week as a result of this letter. Lingard admitted that all he could do as a historian was either, 'enumerate the different conjectures', or 'relate what seems, from Greenway's manuscript, to have been the opinion of the conspirators

---

[64] *Ibid.*, 226–7.
[65] Ainsworth's speling of Monteagle.

themselves', this possible informer therefore being Francis Tresham, a Catholic landowner on the periphery of the plot.[66] In the most recent popular history published on the plot to date, Antonia Fraser can only restate the problem that 'Candidates for its authorship have included almost all the main players in the drama.'[67] This type of popular history in many ways follows the tradition established by Ainsworth. Note that Fraser too sees history as 'drama'.

Ainsworth attributes the letter to Mounteagle himself, which is as reasonable as any other of the theories. In this version, Mounteagle, who was a moderate Catholic, is aware of the conspiracy, disapproves of it because of the injury it would do to his Church, but must warn the king without implicating himself as an accessory after the fact. Where the evidence exists, such as the records of the imprisonment of the conspirators, the surviving transcripts of their examinations and accounts of their executions, Ainsworth remains very faithful to the original documentation. Although critics are often scathing of this author, *Guy Fawkes* Book the Second *is* a reasonable history lesson.

Ultimately captured, Fawkes undertakes his final, spiritual journey. Characteristically, he begins his captivity like a soldier, and with a wonderful bravado justifies his actions to the King:

> 'Dangerous diseases require desperate remedies ... My sole regret is that I have failed ... My main purpose was to blow back the beggarly Scots to their native mountains', returned Fawkes.
>
> 'This audacity surpasses belief', said James. 'Mutius Scævola, when in the presence of Porsenna, was not more resolute. Hark 'e, villain, if I give you your life, will you disclose the names of your associates?'
>
> 'No', replied Fawkes.[68]

This extraordinary meeting *did* take place and the 'examination' was duly recorded. Ainsworth's dialogue is by all accounts accurate. Mucius Scaevola was

---

[66] Lingard, 32. The Greenway manuscript being a contemporary copy of the sixth examination of Fawkes and the interrogation of Francis Tresham.

[67] Antonia Fraser, *The Gunpowder Plot: Terror and Faith in 1605* (London: Mandarin, 1995), 151.

[68] Ainsworth, *Guy Fawkes*, 260.

a legendary hero of ancient Rome who attempted to assassinate the Etruscan leader, Lars Porsena. Captured and brought before his enemy, Scaevola held his hand over an open fire until it burnt away to show that he would never break under torture. Porsena was so impressed that he released Scaevola and made peace with Rome. Unlike Mucius Scaevola however, Fawkes was immediately put to the torture. The author resists the temptation to make these scenes sensationally graphic, and instead makes the process a redemptive one for his protagonist, again reminding us of Christ's suffering on the cross. Now in the Tower and without hope, Fawkes's situation parallels that of Lady Jane Grey in *The Tower of London*; the episodes depicting their despair, the temptations offered by their captors (Fawkes must name his fellow conspirators, Jane must renounce her faith), and their eventual spiritual equanimity and redemption being originally published concurrently. As his central characters are the doomed heroes of a tragedy, the only positive closure that the author has to offer his audience is the salvation of his heroes' souls. Fawkes is in Purgatory because he pursued the plotter's path despite repeated warnings from heaven. Viviana surrenders herself in order to see her husband, and to make him face his mortal error, but it is only his political conviction that has enabled him to endure as long as he has:

'I came here to urge your repentance. Oh! if you hope that we shall meet again hereafter – if you hope that we shall inherit joys which will requite us for all our troubles, you will employ the brief time left you on earth in imploring forgiveness for your evil intentions.'

'Having had no evil intentions', replied Fawkes, coldly, 'I have no pardon to ask.'

'The Tempter who led you into the commission of sin under the semblance of righteousness, put these thoughts into your heart', replied Viviana. 'You have escaped the commission of an offence which must have deprived you of the joys of heaven, and I am thankful for it. But if you remain impenitent, I shall tremble for your salvation.'

'My account will soon be settled with my Maker', rejoined Fawkes; 'and he will punish or reward me according to my deserts. I have acted according to my conscience, and can never repent that which I believe to be a righteous design.'

'But do you not see you were mistaken', returned Viviana, – 'do you not perceive that the sword which you raised against others has been turned against yourself, – and that the Great Power whom you serve and worship has declared himself against you?'

'You seek in vain to move me', replied Fawkes. 'I am as insensible to your arguments as to the tortures of my enemies.'

'Then Heaven have mercy upon your soul!' she rejoined.

'Look at me, Viviana', cried Fawkes, 'and behold the wreck I am. What has supported me amid my tortures – in this dungeon – in the presence of my relentless foes? – what, but the conscience of having acted rightly? And what will support me on the scaffold except the same conviction?'[69]

Both characters are here also approaching an embodiment of the nineteenth century moral design: they are tortured, their faith tested and they must die before their implicit resurrection to the life eternal; as John Reed argues 'Victorian readers, accustomed to consider earthly existence as probation for eternity, did not find affirmations of the redemptive effects of suffering unusual in their literature.'[70] Fawkes, a national pariah, burnt in effigy for centuries, is therefore finally allowed salvation when he repents by Viviana's deathbed:

'I am now standing on the brink of eternity', she said in a solemn tone, 'and I entreat you earnestly, as you hope to ensure our meeting hereafter, to employ the few days left you in sincere and hearty repentance. You have sinned – sinned deeply, but not beyond the power of redemption. Let me feel that I have saved you, and my last moments will be happy. Oh! by the love I have borne you – by the pangs I have endured for you – by the death I am now dying for you – let me implore you not to lose one moment, but to supplicate a merciful Providence to pardon your offence.'

'I will – I will', rejoined Fawkes in broken accents. 'You have opened my eyes to my error, and I sincerely repent it.'

'Saved!' cried Viviana, raising herself in the bed. Opening her arms, she strained him to her bosom; and for a few moments they mingled their tears together.[71]

Viviana then expires, while Fawkes prays beside her. He is to be hanged, drawn and quartered. As a result of his repentance however, the author explains, 'Guy

---

[69] *Ibid.*, 35.
[70] John R. Reed, *Victorian Conventions* (Ohio: Ohio UP, 1975), 8.
[71] Ainsworth, *Guy Fawkes*, 346–7.

Fawkes's tranquillity of mind did not desert him to the last. On the contrary, as his term of life drew near its close, he became more cheerful and resigned.' Finally:

> As the hangman adjusted the rope, he observed a singular smile illumine the features of his victim.
>
> 'You seem happy', he said.
>
> 'I *am* so', replied Fawkes, earnestly, – 'I see the form of her I loved beckoning me to unfading happiness.'
>
> With this, he stretched out his arms and sprang from the ladder. Before his frame was exposed to the executioner's knife, life was totally extinct.[72]

Like Jack Sheppard (who was, according to Ainsworth's version, killed by a stray bullet during the riot at his execution before he endured the trauma of slow strangulation), Fawkes has an easy death and achieves a rather unusual version of eternal salvation in the arms of Viviana, reflecting popular Victorian fantasies of the domestic as much as religious conviction.

In *The Tower of London*, the character of Lady Jane Grey assumes a similar spiritual trajectory, although from the opposite theological direction. She is Fawkes's Protestant double, and the twin texts are therefore in symmetry: 'My lord, I have lived in the Protestant faith, and in that faith I will die. In these sad times, when the power of your Church is in the ascendant, it is perhaps needful there should be martyrs in ours to prove our sincerity.' As Fawkes is to be a Catholic martyr, Jane is to be a Protestant one.[73] After imprisonment and initial despair, she gains strength from her faith and refuses to recant to save herself or her husband and, rather like Viviana, becomes beautiful and serene through her suffering, supplications and eventual acceptance of her fate:

> Entertaining no hopes of mercy, Jane's whole time was passed in preparation for her end. Except the few hours of refreshment actually required by nature, every moment was devoted to the most intense application, or to fervent prayer. By degrees, all trace of sorrow vanished from her features, and they assumed a spiritualised and almost angelic expression. Lovely as she was

---

[72] *Ibid.*, 354. This scene was later appropriated by Hollywood for the execution of William Wallace in *Braveheart*, dir. Mel Gibson, perf. Mel Gibson, Sophie Marceau and Patrick McGoohan, 20th Century Fox, 1995.

[73] Ainsworth, *The Tower of London*, 181.

before, she looked far more lovely now – or rather her beauty was of a more refined and exalted character. She was frequently visited by the queen's confessor, Feckenham, who used every effort to induce her to renounce her religion – but in vain. When told that the sure way to Her Majesty's favour would be to embrace the faith of Rome – she replied that, anxious as she was to obtain the queen's forgiveness, she could not purchase it at the price of her salvation, and that the only favour she desired was to pass the brief residue of her days unmolested.[74]

While like Fawkes, she becomes actively cheerful as she finally rejects the worldly altogether and faces her own death:

No longer agitated by the affairs of the world, she could suffer with patience, and devote herself wholly to God … And thus she passed her time, in the strictest self-examination, fixing her thoughts above, and withdrawing them as much as possible from earth. The effect was speedily manifest in her altered looks and demeanour. When first brought to the Martin Tower, she was downcast and despairing. Ere three days had passed, she became calm and almost cheerful, and her features resumed their wonted serene and seraphic expression.[75]

She also sees a vision of her dead spouse, as did Fawkes, waiting for her just beyond the scaffold. Where these characters differ is in the actual nature of their martyrdom. At the time of writing *Guy Fawkes*, the redefinition of a traditional folk devil as a Catholic martyr would have been a very dangerous thing for the author (still bloodied from the furore surrounding *Jack Sheppard*) and for the British government. Fawkes's political status therefore remains ambiguous. Viviana, the reasonable Catholic, facilitated his salvation by urging him to abandon his conviction that his war was a just one; Ainsworth's historical frame,

---

[74] *Ibid.*, 174. In a strange passage from *Guy Fawkes*, Viviana is similarly beautified by her suffering and devotions during the pilgrimage to Saint Winifred's well:
An hour before daybreak, the party again assembled in the chapel, where matins were performed; after which, the female devotees, who were clothed in snow-white woollen robes, with wide sleeves and hoods, and having large black crosses woven in front, retired for a short time, and re-appeared, with their feet bared, and hair unbound. Each had a large rosary attached to the cord that bound her waist.
Catesby thought Viviana had never appeared so lovely as in this costume; and as he gazed at her white and delicately formed feet, her small rounded ankles, her dark and abundant tresses falling in showers almost to the ground, he became more deeply enamoured than before. His passionate gaze was, however, unnoticed, as the object of it kept her eyes steadily fixed on the ground. Lady Digby, who was a most beautiful woman, scarcely appeared to less advantage; and, as she walked side by side with Viviana in the procession, the pair attracted universal admiration from all who beheld them. Ainsworth, *Guy Fawkes*, 79.

however, seems to suggest that it was. Lady Jane's martyrdom is, of course, beyond dispute:

> 'Do not question the purpose of the Unquestionable, Angela', replied Jane, severely. 'I am chastened because I deserve it, and for my own good. The wind is tempered to the shorn lamb, and fortitude is given me to bear my afflictions. Nay, they are *not* afflictions. I would not exchange my lot – sad as it seems to you – for that of the happiest and the freest within the realm. When the bondage of earth is once broken – when the flesh has no more power over the spirit – when the gates of Heaven are open for admittance – can the world, or worldly joys, possess further charms? No. These prison walls are no restraint to me. My soul soars upwards, and holds communion with God and with His elect, among whom I hope to be numbered. The scaffold will have no terror for me. I shall mount it as the first step towards Heaven, and shall hail the stroke of the axe as the signal to my spirit to wing its flight to the throne of everlasting joy.'
>
> 'I am rebuked, madam', returned Angela, with a look of admiration. 'Oh! that I might ever hope to obtain such a frame of mind.'
>
> 'You may do so, dear Angela', replied Jane; 'but your lot is cast differently from mine. What is required from me is not required from you. Such strong devotional feelings have been implanted in my breast for a wise purpose, that they usurp the place of all other, and fit me for my high calling. The earnest and hearty believer in the Gospel will gladly embrace death, even if accompanied by the severest tortures, at seasons perilous to his Church, in the conviction that it will be profitable to it. Such have been the deaths of the martyrs of our religion – such shall be my death.'
>
> 'Amen!' exclaimed Angela, fervently.[76]

And thus, the historical romance, for all its peripheral humour, gothic sub-plots and antiquarian detail, is ultimately rendered as an English Morality Play which seeks to redistribute moral value in the narrative of history via the evocation of tragic martyrdom.

Yet these texts were still romances. It is true that the scenario of *The Tower of London* does anticipate the religious purges of Mary I: this is the realisation at the moment of 'deep and mournful silence' felt by the mob at the horrific burning of the outspoken Protestant Edward Underhill; but it is the sly

---

[75] Ainsworth, *The Tower of London*, 388–9.
[76] *Ibid.*, 393.

schemer Simon Renard rather than Mary who is associated with the Inquisition, who is represented as a Gallic/gothic stereotype. Ainsworth's Queen is not the Bloody Mary of English history, typically described for example by Dickens, who wrote of her, taking a shot at Ainsworth along the way, that:

> As BLOODY QUEEN MARY, this woman has become famous, and as BLOODY QUEEN MARY, she will ever be justly remembered with horror and detestation in Great Britain. Her memory has been held in such abhorrence that some writers have arisen in later years to take her part, and to show that she was, upon the whole, quite an amiable and cheerful sovereign! 'By their fruits ye shall know them', said OUR SAVIOUR. The stake and the fire were the fruits of this reign, and you will judge this Queen by nothing else.[77]

In his preface, Ainsworth anticipates and disclaims with:

> To those who conceive that the author has treated the character of Queen Mary with too great leniency, he can only affirm that he has written according to his conviction of the truth. Mary's worst fault as a woman – her sole fault as a sovereign – was her bigotry: and it is time that the cloud which prejudice has cast over her should be dispersed.[78]

This statement (very much echoing the hidden agenda of Lingard) sets the author against Protestant historicism and the stereotypes which accompany it while also, by reference to the taint of bigotry, introducing the thematic of the corrupting possibilities of power, notably irrespective of religious or political persuasion. Like Hugo and Dickens, he will graphically depict the systematic brutality of the ruling classes, but whereas these authors 'put not [their] trust in princes', Ainsworth was not so republican. He also speaks as a patriotic Englishman. Mary is the queen of England, daughter of Henry VIII. She may go on to burn over 300 men, women and children to death, lose Calais and marry Philip of Spain, but the author still attributes to Mary the most Churchillian of speeches during Wyatt's rebellion:

> 'Oh, that I had been born a man!' she cried, 'that with my own hand I might punish these traitors. But they shall find, though they have a woman to deal with, they have no feeble and faint-hearted antagonist. I cannot wield a sword;

[77] Dickens, *A Child's History of England,* Works, 411.
[78] Ainsworth, preface, *The Tower of London.*

but I will stand by those who can … take these orders from me; and they are final. Let the siege go how it may, I will make no terms with the rebels, nor hold further parley with them. Show them no quarter – exterminate them utterly. I no longer regard them as subjects – children; but as aliens – foes. Deal with them as such. And look you yield not this fortress – for by God's grace, *I* will never yield it.'[79]

In this brazen paraphrase of Elizabeth's speech to the troops at Tilbury on the approach of the Armada, we see that in Ainsworth's eyes the monarch is always the parent and protector of the nation, and never truly a villain and a tyrant.

II. Hell on earth: *Old St. Paul's; A Tale of the Plague and the Fire*, 1841

Old St. Paul's continues to follow the narrative codes described above, but nonetheless stands alone in many ways among Ainsworth's catalogue for its sheer scale; the author taking great delight in painting a vivid and reasonably accurate picture of Restoration London, and then destroying his creation with equal aplomb. With equally characteristic vigour, Ainsworth began this new project the instant *The Tower of London* was completed, as can be seen from the following letter to Crossley:

> Chancing to call on Rodd to-day, I heard that you are expected in town at the latter end of this week, and I therefore lose not a moment in letting you know that I have a large party dining with me on Saturday next, the 12th, at the Sussex Hotel, Bouverie Street, Fleet Street, at six o'clock, to celebrate the completion of *The Tower of London;* and I sincerely hope you will be able to join them. You will meet many persons whom you cannot easily see, except under similar circumstances, and I really think if you *are* coming to town, it would be worth coming a day or two earlier to be present at this dinner. You do not tell me what you think of *The Tower* in its complete state. I have worked desperately hard to get it done, as you may suppose … You told me that you have a *second* part of De Foe's *History of the Plague*. Pray bring this with you. I will take the greatest care of it, but it is quite necessary I should see it, as I commence a new Romance with the New Year, under the title of *The Plague of London*. If you have any other tract relating to the period, or to the Fire, I shall feel obliged by the loan of it … Let me have a line to say you will be with me on Saturday. You will meet a great number of people from the Tower.[80]

---

[79] Ainsworth, *The Tower of London*, 322.
[80] Ainsworth, letter to Crossley, December 7 1840.

Guests at this dinner included Dickens, Forster, Maclise, Cruikshank, Blanchard, Sir Thomas Talfourd, Major Elrington (Governor of the Tower), Edmund Swift (Keeper of the Regalia) and John Blackwood, son of the fearful Tory publisher William. John Blackwood wrote home of this occasion, and his letter offers a rare glimpse into the convivial charm of his host:

> There was a great deal of speechmaking, and 'butter me and I'll butter you' seemed to be the principle on which they all went. Talfourd, in giving Ainsworth's health, touched upon the excellence of the company assembled. In coming to the Booksellers he gave a panegyric upon them, and said they could boast the presence of a Longman and a Fraser. Ainsworth whispered to him, and he said, 'But Scotland hath a thief as good; one who is the representative of one who had Scott for his friend and Wilson for his inspired aid – one who did more than any other for the advancement of literature on the other side of the Tweed.' Ainsworth returned, and then went on to toast almost the whole of the company individually. About the centre he gave me, and begged to introduce me to the company as one who, he doubted not, would shortly take a leading part in London publishing. He spoke very handsomely about our father ... George Cruikshank was very good. He sang *Lord Bateman* and some others. The claret and champagne were as plenty as could be wished.[81]

Cruikshank, the vice-chair, also stuck Ainsworth with his half of the bill. Ainsworth was also able to consult with Crossley at length about the new project, the first instalment of which appeared in *The Sunday Times* on January 3, running until December 26 1841. Ainsworth received £1,000 for his labours, the copyright of the work reverting to him upon completion.

This romance unfortunately marks a schism between Ainsworth and Cruikshank, who did not illustrate *Old St. Paul's* although he apparently thought that he was the intended artist. As with Ainsworth's problems with Dickens, Ellis predictably refuses to engage: 'Ainsworth did not arrange for Cruikshank to illustrate *Old St Paul's*; why he did not was a disputed point between the two, and cannot be cleared up now.'[82] The 'disputed point' refers to Cruikshank's

---

[81] Quoted from Margaret Oliphant, *Annals of a Publishing House: William Blackwood and His Sons: Their Magazine and Friends*, 2 vols, vol. 2 (Edinburgh, William Blackwood and Sons, 1898), 260–61.
[82] Ellis, vol. 1, 429.

own public remarks upon his professional relationship with Ainsworth, contained in his pamphlet of 1872, *Artist and Author*, where he asserted, among other things, that it was he and not Ainsworth who originated the ideas for their famous collaborations (claiming also the partial authorship of Dickens's *Oliver Twist* along the way). Cruikshank, as his Victorian biographer Blanchard Jerrold noted, had a tendency to quarrel with everyone with whom he was in business, and in old age such smouldering resentments tended to exaggerate all the imagined wrongs the artist had suffered at the hands of authors and publishers such as Dickens, Ainsworth and Bentley. The success of *The Tower of London* left booksellers clamouring for a similar sequel. As Ainsworth's letter to Crossley shows, he already had one well in preparation. In *Artist and Author*, Cruikshank writes that he suggested 'The Plague and the Fire of London', an idea Ainsworth stole and secretly sold to *The Sunday Times*. The serial was not illustrated, but Ainsworth later engaged John Franklin to produce 20 plates for the three volume edition published by Cunningham. Robert L. Patten has recently published the most detailed account of this muddle in his excellent biography *George Cruikshank's Life, Times, and Art* (1996). Patten speculates that as no written agreement existed and that Cruikshank had merely proposed an idea already in the mind of the author (as the letter to Crossley indicates), Ainsworth saw nothing wrong in following the money. Alternately, suggests Patten, Ainsworth might have believed that Cruikshank's present contracts with Bentley meant that he simply did not have the time to embark immediately on another *Tower of London*-sized project or, perhaps, he was finding Cruikshank's editorial suggestions increasingly intrusive. It would seem to be the case, however, that whatever Ainsworth's reasons for his decision to exclude Cruikshank from the new serial, the first Cruikshank heard of it was when the advertisements appeared, leading him to exclaim to a friend that, 'Ainsworth has deserted me.' In *Artist and Author*, the apparently still outraged Cruikshank wrote that, on hearing that 'another artist [Franklin] was working out my pet subject, which I had nursed in my brains for many years, and which I had long intended to have placed before the public with my own hands', he decided to wash his hands of Ainsworth and start his own periodical, the *Omnibus*.[83] The ageing artist's chronology seems rather unstable here however. After *Old St. Paul's* commenced its serial run, Ainsworth and Cruikshank were still collaborating on the novelisation of *Guy Fawkes*; also, as Patten notes, Cruikshank was committed to Tilt and Bogue for the *Omnibus* by February 1841, so Ainsworth's relationship with Franklin, which commenced in December, had nothing to do with Cruikshank's decision to start his own magazine. The two men also collaborated on *Ainsworth's Magazine* from February 1842 until Ainsworth sold out to his publisher (much to Cruikshank's annoyance) the following year; Cruikshank therefore illustrated *The Miser's Daughter* (of which he also later claimed authorship) and *Saint James's* after the *Old St. Paul's* disagreement. Ainsworth also offered Cruikshank the job of illustrating *Old St. Paul's* before Franklin, but Cruikshank was by then too committed to other projects and declined. His letter of reply is included in Ellis's chapter 'George Cruikshank and His Claims' (which finally takes on *Artist and Author*), and shows that he was still very hurt about Ainsworth's decision to abandon the *Tower of London* sequel and format in favour of *The Sunday Times*:

I do assure you my Dear Ainsworth I sincerely regret – that I cannot join you in this work, but what was I to think – what conclusion was I to come to but that you had *cut* me – at the latter end of last year you announced that *we* were preparing a 'New Work' – in the early part of December last – I saw by an advertisement that – your 'New Work' – was to be published in the 'Sunday Times' – you do not come to me – or send for me nor send me any explanation – I meet you at Dickens's on 'New Years Eve.' You tell me then that you will see me in a few days and explain everything to my satisfaction – I hear nothing from you – in your various notes about the 'Guy Fawkes' you do not even advert to the subject –

I purposely keep myself disengaged refusing many advantageous offers of work – still I hear nothing from you – at length you announced a New Work as a *companion to the 'Tower'* without my name – I then conclude that you do not intend to join *me* in *any* New Work – and therefore determine to do something for myself – *indeed I could hold out no longer* – To show that others besides my self considered that you had left me – I was applied to by Chapman & Hall

---

[83] Robert L. Patten, *George Cruikshank's Life, Times, and Art*, 2 vols, vol. 2 (Cambridge: The Lutterworth Press, 1996), 162.

– to join with them & Mr. Dickens in a speculation – which indeed I promised to do should the one with Mr. Tilt be abandoned – However I have still to hope that when you are disengaged from Mr. Bentley that some arrangements may be made which may tend to our mutual benefit.[84]

Being the most contemporary account of the above dispute, we must draw our own conclusions based upon it, while remembering that Cruikshank's memory became more selective the older he became. Patten surmises from the reference to Bentley here that Ainsworth may have had to avoid another collaboration with Cruikshank to facilitate his escape from the formidable publisher and the *Miscellany* (much as Dickens had previously done). After the success of *The Tower of London*, it would have been difficult to keep Bentley out of a similar deal. Such fallings out were not uncommon in the hectic environment of Victorian publishing, the dramas often rivalling any fiction the protagonists produced. Meanwhile, *Old St. Paul's* was unfolding to a very receptive audience, despite the lack of illustrations.

As Ainsworth's letters to Crossley suggest, it was Crossley's Defoe collection that was the real inspiration for the new project. This is freely acknowledged in Ainsworth's advertisement to the novel of November 30 1841:

THE portion of the ensuing Tale relating to the Grocer of Wood-street, and his manner of victualling his house, and shutting up himself and his family within it during the worst part of the Pestilence of 1665, is founded on a narrative, which I have followed pretty closely in most of its details, contained in a very rare little volume, entitled, '*Preparations against the Plague, both of Soul and Body*', the authorship of which I have no hesitation in assigning to DEFOE. Indeed, I venture to pronounce it his masterpiece. It is strange that this matchless performance should have hitherto escaped attention, and that it should not have been reprinted with some one of the countless impressions of the '*History of the Plague of London*', to which it forms an almost necessary accompaniment. The omission, I trust, will be repaired by Mr. HAZLITT the younger, DEFOE'S last and best editor, in his valuable edition of the works of that great novelist and political writer, now in the course of publication. It may be added, that a case precisely similar to that of the Grocer, and attended with the same happy results, occurred during the plague of Marseilles, in 1720.

---

[84] George Cruikshank, letter to Ainsworth, March 4 1841, quoted from Ellis, vol. 2, 97–9.

For my acquaintance with this narrative, as well as for the suggestion of its application to the present purpose, I am indebted to my friend, Mr. JAMES CROSSLEY, of Manchester.[85]

The attribution of *Due Preparations for the Plague* (1722) to Defoe is an astute piece of literary scholarship, as its authorship is nowadays unquestioned. This gave Ainsworth the idea for Stephen Bloundel, the prosperous puritan grocer who supplies and seals his house, while his principal source of reference was Defoe's *Journal of the Plague Year* (1722). We may also reasonably assume some recourse to contemporary diarists such as Allin, Evelyn and, most notably, Pepys. Defoe's novel is a remarkably immediate account of the Summer of 1665, a sleight of hand supposedly written by a first-hand witness ('H.F.'), but in fact written from contemporary accounts and verifiable records, embellished with anecdotal (fictional) episodes which the author insists are all hearsay. Defoe in fact takes much care to present his *Journal* as a true history, but it is rather a historical novel. In much the same way that the young Walter Scott would later grow up listening to folk-tales, legends and ballads from labourers and servants at the farm of his grandfather Robert Scott at Sandyknowe in the Borders, Defoe, who was five years old in 1665, would have had a head full of tales told by his older relatives and family friends, which were probably bought into focus by the accounts of the outbreak of plague in Marseilles in 1720. Also anticipating Scott, Defoe, through a relatively neutral narrator ('H.F.'s middle class Puritanism is present, but never as morally didactic as the contemporary accounts), examines the effect on basic humanity of such a dehumanising experience. 'H.F.' is not a hero so much as a camera, turned upon an entire city in decay and despair.

Ainsworth's rewrite of Defoe (adding the closure of the Fire of London, which Defoe ignored) was generally applauded by his contemporaries, many of the best of which he appended to the advertisement for the launch of *Ainsworth's Magazine* and the novelised version of *Old St. Paul's*. *Bell's Life of London* notes

---

[85] Ainsworth, advertisement, *Old Saint Paul's; A Tale of The Plague and The Fire*, Works.

the Defoe connection, while allowing that Ainsworth has expanded Defoe's sparse prose style and intriguing anecdotes:

> Although the horrors of the Plague and the Fire have already been described by various writers, and especially by Defoe, Mr. Ainsworth has in these volumes clothed those events in a manner the most exciting. Many of the passages are written with great eloquence; and few of our modern romances possess more sterling clams upon the lovers of this species of composition.

The Courier similarly applauds Ainsworth's talent for weaving an engaging story out of the historical record without taking too many liberties with the facts:

> In this work, Mr. Ainsworth has portrayed many of the horrible incidents of the Great Plague with historical fidelity. He places his principal characters in the midst of that dreadful scourge, and makes the plot depend in a great measure for its progress and development on the circumstances common to the time. The scenes described are all founded on well-authenticated accounts, presented by Mr. Ainsworth with a forcible semblance of reality, which his pen can so well accomplish. These volumes are illustrated by numerous engravings by Mr. Franklin, which correspond in their striking effects with the horror of the scenes depicted.

The Atlas (fans since *Rookwood*) appreciates the horror, as well as the narrative pacing:

> Two of the most appalling events in the history of London have been drawn into the work before us – the Plague and the Fire, and treated in Mr. Ainsworth's usual graphic style. It argues in favour of the skill with which these scourges of the great city are treated, that several of the descriptive passages made us literally shudder. We could not thread the Labyrinth of terror, without a sensation of pain and uneasiness we cannot very easily convey in words. This is probably the very end aimed at in the romance. Mr. Ainsworth does not fatigue his readers with long accounts of places, and scenes, and events. He always mixes up his descriptions with vivid action, and never lets his narrative pause for a moment. This is one of the secrets of his success.

The Observer pays a huge compliment:

> We are glad to meet Mr. Ainsworth again in the region of historical romance, a department of literature in which he has already distinguished himself above almost every author of the day. A better subject than that chosen for his present volumes could not have been selected. It is replete with incidents of the most varied, striking, and affecting character. These Mr. Ainsworth has turned to the

account which every reader of his former works must have been prepared to expect. He has interwoven historical facts into a web of most pleasing fiction, thereby investing history herself with new attraction. Many passages, indeed whole pages of the work, remind us of the simple pathos and truthfulness of Defoe. The plot is natural, and is conducted with great skill to the *dénouement*. 'Old St. Paul's', we understand, has already met with a large sale. It will, with the aid of the illustrations, become one of the most popular of the author's very popular works.

The above indicates that the Newgate taint had been banished by Ainsworth's new direction (at least in the short term), while also demonstrating the immense popularity of Ainsworth's now forgotten fiction. Even old enemy *The Athenaeum* revised its earlier opinions, writing that:

> We prefer the two first volumes of "Old St. Paul's" to any previous work of their author. Treated as a tale of adventure, the test of which is the hold retained on the reader, these volumes have great merit. The reader who has once opened them will hardly be disposed to lay them down again.

Finally, *The Court Journal* paid the highest tribute possible:

> In this tale of the Plague and the Fire, which now appears in a new and embellished form, we recognise all the excellences which have gained for Mr. Ainsworth so high a name on the scroll of historical literature. There is the same centralization of interest; few marked personages; a plot not too transparent, but of great simplicity; easy power, and most natural pathos in the more tragic portions; characteristic dialogue; and over all, a lucid style of expression. Mr. Ainsworth is the Defoe of his day.[86]

While such accolades have vanished into obscurity, R.H. Horne's predictable rejection of this novel endures:

> 'Old St. Paul's, a tale of the Plague and the Fire', is a diluted imitation of some parts of Defoe's 'Plague in London', varied with libertine adventures of Lord Rochester and his associates. It is generally dull, except when it is revolting. There are descriptions of nurses who poison or smother their patients, wretched prisoners roasted alive in their cells, and one felon who thrusts his arms through the red-hot bars, – 'literally' is added, by way of apology.[87]

---

[86] All reviews quoted from the advertisement for 'New Periodical Works Preparing for Publication by Mr. Cunningham, 1, St. Martin's Place, Trafalgar Square', December 1841.
[87] Horne, vol. 2, 404.

The influence of Defoe is now just superficial plagiarism, and Ainsworth's stylised use of violence and horror (praised by *The Atlas*) 'revolting' that is, if we recall Horne's reading of Hogarth and Dickens, without any moral merit. What other readers found impossible to put down is now 'dull'. Once again the literary elite fails to understand a popular narrative. As Mark Kermode has written of the never-ending debate in Britain regarding horror films and censorship, on reading the reports of the British Board of Film Classification in the 1970s and 80s, one often feels that they have been watching a completely different film. This is to a certain extent true. Kermode argues that:

> Gory special effects, constantly the target of attacks by the censors and media pundits alike, work upon disparate audiences in a similarly polarised manner. A key problem in persuading non-horror fans that genre devotees are not a pack of marauding sadists hell-bent on destruction ... lies in the recurrent inability of untrained viewers to see past the special effects, puncture the gaudy surface of the movies, pull apart their rubbery rib-cages and grasp their dark thematic hearts. Essentially a surrealist genre, contemporary horror demands to be read metaphorically rather than literally ... The horror fan understands this, and is thus not only able but positively compelled to 'read' rather than merely 'watch' such movies. The novice, however, sees only the dismembered bodies, hears only the screams and groans, reacts only with revulsion or contempt. Being unable to differentiate between the real and the surreal, they consistently misinterpret horror fans' interaction with texts which mean nothing to them.[88]

Horne, Thackeray, Forster and their disciples obviously belong in the latter camp, the periodical reviewers and, most importantly, Ainsworth's readers belong in the former.

Old St. Paul's certainly operates successfully on considerably more levels than R.H. Horne will ever allow. It is a 'disaster story' worthy of Hollywood, where an all-star cast is introduced merely to be decimated by fire, flood, earthquake, shipwreck, alien invasion or act of God. It is an apocalypse of biblical proportions, laced with love, intrigue, bravery, humour and horror. It takes the narrative codes of *The Tower of London* in particular and renders them in epic terms.

---

[88] Mark Kermode, 'I was a teenage horror fan', Martin Barker and Julian Petley (eds), *Ill Effects: The Media/Violence Debate* (London: Routledge, 1997), 61.

After the success of the previous romance, where else could Ainsworth go? This, in essence, became his problem with most of his subsequent novels. How does the creator go beyond *Revelations*?

Rather than continuing to draw on real figures from the past Ainsworth ostensibly moves towards Scott's type of historical novel, choosing to focus on fictional characters living through major historical events. Again he themes the work around a famous, although this time doomed, monument. There is some level of antiquarianism within the text, but the cathedral assumes a more symbolically representative role in the narrative, alternately a cathedral, a public meeting place, a den of thieves, a pest house and finally an inferno.

Old St. Paul's is divided into six books, each separately dated between April 1665 and September 1666. Manchester man Leonard Holt, the grocer's apprentice, is in love with his master's daughter, Amabel Bloundel. His rival is a young aristocrat, Maurice Wyvil (later revealed to be John Wilmot, 2nd Earl of Rochester), whom she meets in secret in St Paul's Cathedral. Light relief is provided by Bloundel's credulous, hypochondriac servant, Blaize, and his faith in a variety of quack remedies. Often seen on the roof of the cathedral is the crazed ex-Quaker Solomon Eagle, who wears a burning brazier and prophesies the doom of the city. As the plague progresses, the cathedral is turned into a pesthouse and London becomes an eerie wasteland where victims of the illness are preyed upon by unscrupulous and opportunist characters such as the coffin-maker Anselm Chowles and Mother Malmaynes, the plague nurse, who are quite happy to hasten their patients' ends in order to loot their properties. Bloundel decides to seal his family within their house, and Leonard finds himself wandering the wasteland, finally catching, but surviving, the plague. Rochester, meanwhile, tricks Amabel into a phoney marriage and deflowers her. On learning the truth, Amabel falls into a fever from which she does not recover. The beautiful daughter of a blind piper whom Leonard meets on his travels, Nizza Macascree, falls for him and this initially unrequited love grows after Amabel's death. Nizza is actually Lady Isabella Argentine, so marriage seems out of the question. After an interlude of nine months, religious zealots fire the city, and Leonard saves the life of King Charles II during a scheme of his own invention to halt the spread of the fire by demolishing buildings in its path. Leonard is rewarded by a title, and marries Isabella. With the exception of Amabel, the Bloundels survive their ordeals, while Chowles and Malmaynes die horribly in the vaults of St Paul's, burned to death in a sea of molten lead. Leonard lives to see St Paul's rebuilt by Wren.

The Revelation of St. John is as much present as Defoe's *Journal*, the destruction of London being often viewed in biblical terms by protagonists whereas Defoe had tempered these concerns with an examination of, 'a distemper arising from natural causes'.[89] The first book of *Old St. Paul's* opens with a sermon on the day of judgement:

> Stephen Bloundel offered up a long and fervent supplication to the Most High for protection against the devouring pestilence with which the city was then scourged. He acknowledged that this terrible visitation had been justly brought upon it by the wickedness of its inhabitants ... that the sins of London were enormous; that it was filled with strifes, seditions, heresies, murders, drunkenness, revellings, and every kind of abomination; that the ordinances of God were neglected, and all manner of vice openly practised.[90]

Such languages characterises the pious Bloundel, his mind never far from the divine judgement and the moral degeneracy of the age. Ainsworth is also not the first to link the manners of the Restoration Court to the general *zeitgeist*. As Bloundel's friend Dr Hodges laments:

> 'Never was a court so licentious as that of our sovereign, Charles the Second, whose corrupt example is imitated by every one around him, while its baneful influence extends to all classes. Were I to echo the language of the preachers, I should say that it was owing to the wickedness and immorality of the times, that this dreadful judgement of the plague has been inflicted upon us.'[91]

---

[89] Daniel Defoe, *A Journal of the Plague Year, being observations or memorials of the most remarkable occurrences, as well public as private, which happened in London during the last great visitation in 1665. Written by a Citizen who continued all the while in London. Never made public before*, Anthony Burgess, Christopher Bristow (eds) (1722 London, Penguin, 1966), 205.
[90] Ainsworth, *Old St. Paul's*, 1.
[91] *Ibid.*, 66.

This would appeal to the Victorian audience, who can take the moral high ground while enjoying the licentiousness. Although Rochester's poetry is not cited, the debauchery begins well with Rochester and his cronies playing cards for each other's wives while the city falls apart, before being relegated to a subplot like a Restoration comedy being played out in parallel with the primary narrative, suddenly and surprisingly turning nasty at its conclusion. The author seems rather to like Rochester, and seems unsure quite how to treat him. More impressively realised is the image of the fanatical Solomon Eagle, who pours his judgement on the city and the text from the roof of Saint Paul's like an Old Testament prophet:

> His brazier was placed on one of the buttresses, and threw its light on the mighty central tower of the fabric, and on a large clock-face immediately beneath. Solomon Eagle was evidently denouncing the city, but his words were lost in the distance. As he proceeded, a loud clap of thunder pealed overhead.
>
> 'It comes – it comes!' cried the enthusiast, in a voice that could be distinctly heard in the death-like stillness that followed the thunder. 'The wrath of Heaven is at hand.'[92]

This Ezekiel-like figure is taken straight from the pages of Defoe, who had sketched him in thus: 'I suppose the world has heard of the famous Solomon Eagle, an enthusiast. He, though not infected at all but in his head, went about denouncing of judgement upon the city in a frightful manner, sometimes quite naked, and with a pan of burning charcoal on his head. What he said, or pretended, indeed I could not learn.'[93] Solomon Eagle is a much more developed descendant of Elizabeth Orton (*Guy Fawkes*) or Gunnora Braose (*The Tower of London*); his function is to prophesise the fate of an entire city, not just an individual character such as Guy Fawkes or Lady Jane Grey.

The witness to this terrible fate, the death of a city, is Leonard Holt, whose journey through the Inferno the novel principally charts. The reader sees what Holt sees as he experiences each terrible event. As Holt travels through the urban

---

[92] *Ibid.*, 177.
[93] Defoe, *Journal*, 119.

wasteland, much like Defoe's observer, civilisation increasingly unravels before his eyes:

> As Leonard passed Saint Michael's church, in Basinghall-street, he perceived, to his great surprise, that it was lighted up, and at first supposed some service was going on within it, but on approaching he heard strains of lively and most irreverent music issuing from within. Pushing open the door, he entered the sacred edifice, and found it occupied by a party of twenty young men, accompanied by a like number of females, some of whom were playing at dice and cards, some drinking, others singing Bacchanalian melodies, others dancing along the aisles to the notes of a theorbo and spinet. Leonard was so inexpressibly shocked by what he beheld that, unable to contain himself, he mounted the steps of the pulpit, and called to them in a loud voice to desist from their scandalous conduct, and no longer profane the house of God ...

> 'Repentance!' cried another of the assemblage. 'Do you know whom you address? These gentlemen are the brotherhood of Saint Michael, and I am the principal.'[94]

Everywhere Holt goes he encounters chaos, violence and death. The beast that lives beneath the veneer of civilised society is loose. If people fall in the street, passers-by step over them, the nurse Mother Malmaynes and Chowles the coffin-maker rob and murder the sick with impunity, law and order is replaced by mob violence, the churches have closed and the aristocracy has withdrawn into orgy to await the end. In a particularly surreal scene Ainsworth anticipates Poe's 'The Masque of the Red Death' (1842), the cathedral becoming the venue for the *danse macabre*:

> In the midst of the nave ... stood a number of grotesque figures, apparelled in fantastic garbs, and each attended by a skeleton. Some of the latter grisly shapes were playing on tambours, others on psalteries, others on rebecs – every instrument producing the strangest sound imaginable. Viewed through the massive pillars, beneath the dark and ponderous roof, and by the mystic light ... this strange company had a supernatural appearance ... with a wild gibbering laugh that chilled the beholders' blood, one of the tallest and grisliest of the skeletons sprang forward, and beating his drum, the whole ghostly company formed, two-and-two, into a line – a skeleton placing itself on the right of every mortal. In this order, the fantastic procession marched between

---

[94] Ainsworth, *Old St Paul's*, 204–205.

the pillars, the unearthly music playing all the while, and disappeared at the further extremity of the church.[95]

This uncanny vision eventually resolves itself into a party of young, aristocratic revellers, drifting through the streets and laughing at the horror they find there. Many will be dead by the morning, and it is the reality of this episode, rather than its potential unreality, that conveys the ghastliness of the situation.

Old St. Paul's is not so much gothic as darkly carnivalesque. The world is turned upside down here: nurses kill their patients; grocers hoard food; sexual encounters result in death not life; monks blaspheme; and the dead throw their own wakes. Pain, despair, death and decay are celebrated in their every aspect.

The chapter entitled 'The Dance of Death' immediately precedes the heart of the novel, the central image of the plague-pit:

> Leonard ventured to the brink of the pit. But even this precaution could not counteract the horrible effluvia arising from it. It was more than half-filled with dead bodies, and through the putrid and heaving mass many disjointed limbs and ghastly faces could be discerned, the long hair of a woman, and the tiny arms of children, appearing on the surface.

Despite himself, Holt is gripped by the fascination of abomination; like Defoe's observer (who admits that 'I had been pressed in my mind to go'[96]), he must look. What he sees is an epiphany of nightmares:

> It was a horrible sight – so horrible, that it possessed a fascination peculiar to itself, and in spite of his loathing, Leonard lingered to gaze at it. Strange and fantastic thoughts possessed him. He fancied that the legs and arms moved, – that the eyes of some of the corpses opened and glared at him – and that the whole rotting mass was endowed with animation.

Again reality is even worse, he is brought back to his senses by the workman-like dumping of more bodies:

---

[95] *Ibid.*, 187–8.
[96] Defoe, *Journal*, 79.

> So appalled was he by this idea that he turned away, and at the moment beheld a vehicle approaching. It was the dead-cart, charged with a heavy load to increase the already redundant heap.[97]

This is only one of many graphic and dehumanising descriptions of the devastation of disease and, subsequently, fire, throughout the novel. London is rendered as a necropolis and, unlike the Tower of London, even St Paul's is not inviolate; it burns like everything else.

Writing in American university campuses as the Vietnam war dragged on, both Llewellyn Ligocki and George J. Worth have read the stronger of Ainsworth's historical novels as pessimistic allegories of human suffering, violence and cruelty. Ligocki argued that:

> History is a vehicle for Ainsworth to express larger truths about life. History, thus, is the subject of the novels as well as fact. In short, Ainsworth appears to discuss certain historical situations because they represent, in one way or another, the problems of all mankind.[98]

Worth's analysis is similar. Like Ligocki (who was taught by Worth), he interpreted Ainsworth's historical narratives as naturalistic portrayals of a political barbarism of which the human race is still not free:

> By and large, Ainsworth's fictional world was a singularly violent one that was marked by turmoil, cruelty, and intrigue; and this aspect is undeniably a side of his work which must appeal to certain strains of our twentieth-century sensibility ... The interest in these novels is not solely antiquarian. There is, for example, something timely in the story of Leonard Holt, the hero of *Old Saint Paul's*, who endures in 1665 and 1666 experiences not very different in degree from those which would have been his lot had he been at Auschwitz in 1944 or at Hiroshima in 1945.[99]

As Worth has suggested, this image is symbolic of human misery on a scale more recognisable to a modern reader. The mass grave is a twentieth century icon, a code for the industrialised carnage of two world wars and many more besides, for

---

[97] Ainsworth, *Old St. Paul's*, 200–201
[98] Liewellyn Ligocki, 'William Harrison Ainsworth's Use of History: *The Tower of London* and other Tudor Novels' (Diss., University of Kansas, 1968), 12.
[99] Worth, 76.

man-made famines, toxic spills in third world countries and the continuing use of the concentration camp. Whether this was the author's initial intention is questionable, although the violence of his imagery throughout the three historical novels of 1840–41 seems to remind us that there is not a single civilisation, including the British Empire, that is not built upon a foundation of human bones. It is true that *Old St. Paul's* concludes on an image of rebirth, the rebuilding of the cathedral by Wren, but it is the plague-pits that remain longest in the memory.

III. The devil and his works: *Windsor Castle*, 1843 and *Auriol*, 1844

From his earliest compositions, the gothic was never far from the surface of an Ainsworth text. His histories were, as we have seen, not excepted from this influence. In addition to the gothic *mise en scène* so apparent in these novels, Ainsworth in particular returned again and again to the related themes of alchemy and the demonic pact in his writing, spinning them to suit his own approach to historical determinism.

From 'The Spectre Bride' onwards, there is a fascination with the Faustian pact. This is particularly explicit in 'The Wanderings of an Immortal', where the narrator confesses that he employed the black arts to summon Satan himself:

The night advanced. It was time for me to begin my terrible solemnities. I trembled at the thought of what I was about to do. I hesitated whether to proceed; but the hopes of revenge still impelled me on, and I resolved to prosecute my design. It was soon done. The rites were begun; the flame on my lamp blazed clear and bright; I knew the moment was approaching when I should hold communion with beings of another world; perhaps with the prince of darkness himself. I grew faint, a heavy load weighed on my breast, my respiration grew thick and short, my eyes seemed to swell in their sockets, and a cold sweat burst from every pore of my body. The flame wavered – it decreased – it went out. The heavens were darkened: I gazed around, but the gloom was too great for me to see any thing. I looked towards the waterfall, and, amid the mist and obscurity which covered the place of its subterranean outlet, a star shone alone with wild and brilliant lustre. It grew larger – it approached me – it stopped, and a brighter radiance was diffused around. The Evil One stood before me.[100]

In common with 'The Spectre Bride', several influences are apparent here. The star (Lucifer meaning 'morning star', the planet Venus) also signals the presence of summoned spirits in Byron's *Manfred* (1817); there is the devil incarnate from Lewis's *The Monk* (1796), and the sin of Maturin's *Melmoth the Wanderer* (1820), all of whom follow the fortunes of Marlowe's *Doctor Faustus* (c.1594). Although Ainsworth's initial attempts to emulate his heroes can seem rather clumsy pastiches at best, a more sophisticated application was to follow in his historical novels.

Windsor Castle was written in parallel with *The Miser's Daughter*. Ainsworth was working around the clock, a situation lamented by his friends. Mrs Hughes writing to Mrs Southey that:

> Were I an absolute monarch I should for the love I bear him put him in handcuffs, or any confinement which would prevent his writing more than for limited time every day; his present double undertaking appears to me as an act of deliberate suicide, and cannot be accomplished without injury to mind and body, besides the minor consideration that the works must suffer by such undue haste in composition: but he is deaf to the voice of a friend 'charm she never so wisely', so I can only hope I am not a Cassandra.[101]

Windsor Castle was originally intended to appear in monthly parts like *The Tower of London*, its launch date advertised as March 29 1842. This plan was interrupted by the death of Ainsworth's mother, Ann, on March 15, aged 64. Among the many condolences offered by friends, one letter is particularly interesting offering, as it does, an insight into John Forster's rarely seen soft side:

> How deeply I sympathize with the sorrow you are suffering – I hope I need not say. This is the grief that of all others, in this world of grief and losses, falls heaviest on a true-hearted man. So much of all one's life is in it – so many of

---

[100] Ainsworth, *December Tales*, 132–3.

[101] Quoted from Ellis, vol. 2, 55. Mary Ann Hughes (née Watts) was the wife of the Rev. Thomas Hughes, Canon of St Paul's and tutor to the younger sons of George III; she was the mother of the writer John Hughes and grandmother of Thomas Hughes, author of *Tom Brown's Schooldays*. Ainsworth was a regular guest at Mrs Hughes' residence at Kingston Lisle, and *Guy Fawkes* is dedicated to her. Mrs Southey was the wife of the Lakeland poet Robert Southey.

those thoughts of life's beginning which last beyond all others. But you have many consolations, my dear friend, and not the least that you have attended your poor mother to the close, and that she died with your love beside her. Is there anything I can do for you? I imagine that you will defer the *Windsor Castle* this month – but should you not do so, I might be of some assistance to you. I have all my Henry VIII books here, and if you told me some particular thing you wanted – it may be horrible conceit – but somehow I think I might be of some beggarly service to you. At all events, in that or lesser matters, try if for old affection's sake you can discover anything for me to do for you ... I will go to you at any time you wish. Forgive my naming such a thing now, but it is from the fear you may think me careless in the matter of your magazine.

> Ever, my dear Ainsworth,
>   Your affectionate friend,
>
>   JOHN FORSTER.[102]

Ainsworth apparently declined the offer, and *Windsor Castle* ultimately ran in *Ainsworth's Magazine* (the cover price being raised by sixpence), commencing in the July issue 1842, overlapping with *The Miser's Daughter* which was still being serialised, and concluding in June the following year. The French artist Tony Johannot provided the first four illustrations, being replaced by Cruikshank at the completion of *The Miser's Daughter*. W. Alfred Delamotte also contributed 87 woodcuts depicting forest scenes and architectural features (much as Cruikshank had done for *The Tower of London*), and 3 plans: Windsor Great Park in 1529, and the Castle in 1530 and 1843. As R.H. Horne had it: 'It is a picture-book, and full of very pretty pictures.'[103] Like *The Tower of London*, this is a very visually exciting text; unlike the former however, the quality of the narrative rarely matches that of the illustrations. Also in common with *The Tower of London*, *Windsor Castle* was equipped with a full index when published as a three volume novel by Henry Colburn in 1843. Despite the somewhat hasty composition, *Windsor Castle* was another great success, its popularity kept it in print in England (along with *Old St. Paul's*), until the late 1960s, outlasting the technically superior *The Tower of London* by a generation. In its own day, a French translation appeared daily in *Le Messenger* and a play inspired by the

---

[102] Quoted from Ellis, vol. 2, 56.
[103] Horne, vol. 2, 402.

romance, entitled *Herne the Hunter*, played all over London. This is telling, as the 'Herne the Hunter' episodes are undoubtedly the most engaging in the narrative.

Windsor Castle is divided into six short books, the first five take place in 1529, the sixth and final a coda set in 1536 which allows for the conclusion of Anne Boleyn's story and life. Book the Third is a long digression covering the history of the castle itself. The plot of *Windsor Castle* demonstrates the emerging pattern of Ainsworth's historical romances. The main stream follows Henry VIII's attempts to replace his queen Catherine of Aragon (which Ainsworth spells 'Arragon') with Anne Boleyn. Anne is presented as coquettish and, the author explains early on, 'How severely she suffered for it, it is the purpose of this history to relate.'[104] Fictionalised subplots meanwhile follow the lives and loves of various courtiers. The Earl of Surrey loves the 'fair Geraldine', Lady Elizabeth Fitzgerald, but the King opposes the union. The narrative also closely follows the fortunes of the beautiful Mabel Lyndwood, apparently the grandchild of the forester Tristram Lyndwood but really the secret child of Cardinal Wolsey. Sir Thomas Wyat loves Anne Boleyn with an ill-concealed passion that almost gets him executed. Wolsey tries everything he can think of to subvert Henry's plans for Catherine and Anne, using the King's obvious attraction to Mabel to make Anne jealous; when this fails he gives Catherine information regarding Anne's relationship with Wyat to present to Henry. Wolsey's plan again comes to nothing, as we know it must, and he is dismissed from court, dying shortly afterwards. Catherine surrenders to the inevitable, but predicts that Henry will tire of Anne as he has her, and this prophecy is fulfilled at the romance's conclusion when Anne is dumped for Jane Seymour, Anne's infidelities with Sir Henry Norris giving Henry the excuse he needs to have her executed. A supernatural dimension is added to the narrative by the inclusion of the satanic Herne the Hunter, an elemental deity who haunts Windsor Forest with a motley band of followers, often helping mortal characters in wicked designs, in order to gain their

---

[104] Ainsworth, *Windsor Castle, An Historical Romance* (1843), Works, 21.

souls. Herne kidnaps Mabel and Wyat, and the mortals fall in love while imprisoned, but Mabel is drowned during an escape attempt. Henry, Surrey and Richmond expend a lot of energy trying to destroy Herne, but they never do and he remains at large at the end of the story.

As the authors of the *Windsor Castle*-inspired play well knew, Herne is the most interesting character in the narrative. He also represents the author's continuing interest in the Faustian pact, present from his earliest fiction, sketched out in his portrayal of Cosmo Ruggieri, chief astrologer to Catherine de Medicis in *Crichton*, and already surviving his transition to the ostensibly conventional and uncontentious post-Newgate historical romance in the character of the alchemist Dr John Dee from *Guy Fawkes*. Herne the Hunter is a legendary figure dating from the reign of Richard II, although the pagan imagery of the stag's horns worn upon his head suggest a much longer lineage still. Shakespeare uses the legend for laughs in *The Merry Wives of Windsor*, when Falstaff dresses as Herne for an assignation with Mistress Ford by Herne's oak in Windsor Forest, only to be assailed by the Page family dressed as fairies in the culmination of a series of practical jokes played on him by Mistresses Ford and Page. Mrs Page reminds the audience of the legend thus:

> There is an old tale goes that Herne the hunter,
> Sometime a keeper here in Windsor forest,
> Doth all the winter-time, at still midnight,
> Walk round about an oak, with great ragg'd horns;
> And there he blasts the tree, and takes the cattle,
> And makes milch-kine yield blood, and shakes a chain
> In a most hideous and dreadful manner:
> You have heard of such a spirit, and well you know
> The superstitious idle-headed eld
> Received and did deliver to our age
> This tale of Herne the hunter for a truth.[105]

Ainsworth uses this as an epigram for his romance. Herne's oak was still alive in Windsor forest in Ainsworth's day, until it was blown down in 1863 and, as Ellis

---

[105] Shakespeare, *The Merry Wives of Windsor*, IV.iv.

remarks: 'This was just the sort of wild legend that had an irresistible appeal to Ainsworth.'[106] This is quite true, but Herne's role obviously goes deeper.

Shakespeare's text is the first printed reference to Herne although, as with Robin Goodfellow (another horned god), he was tapping into a much older vein of myth and folklore. Ainsworth offers a detailed origin in a chapter entitled 'The Legend of Herne the Hunter', a complete invention which is rightly treated with scepticism by scholars of Herne legends but nonetheless often cited.[107] In Ainsworth's version (as told by Hector Cutbeard), Herne was one of Richard II's keepers of Windsor Forest, highly skilled in all aspects of woodcraft. Attended by Herne one day, the King's horse was gored by a terrified hart, throwing its rider. The enraged deer charged Richard, but Herne threw himself in the animal's path, receiving a mortal wound but killing the hart with his hunting knife. Richard promises to reward Herne by making him head keeper of the forest, but Herne insists he is done for. The Earl of Oxford and the other keepers arrive on the scene, the keepers privately delighted at Herne's imminent demise, one even suggests putting him out of his misery. The king is not impressed, and offers a reward to anyone who can save the man who saved his life. At this point, 'a tall dark man, in a strange garb, and mounted on a black, wild-looking steed, whom no one had hitherto observed' appears and offers to cure Herne.[108] Philip Urswick, the stranger, flays the head of the hart and has the gory skull tied to Herne's head, before having him carried to his hut in the woods, where he explains he must attend the patient for a month. The keepers make a litter for Herne and follow Urswick, muttering all the way that it was a pity the deer had not killed him outright. Urswick suddenly asks the chief keeper Osmond Crooke, Herne's principal rival, what it would be worth to him to stop Herne taking his position:

'Will you swear to grant the first request I may make of you – provided it shall be in your power?' demanded Urswick.

[106] Ellis, vol. 2, 59.
[107] See Eric L. Fitch, *In Search of Herne the Hunter* (London: Capall Bann, 1994); Brian Branston, *The Lost Gods of England* (London: Constable 1994); and Miranda Green's work on Celtic myth and legend.
[108] Ainsworth, *Windsor Castle*, 204.

'Readily', they replied.

'Enough', said Urswick. 'I must keep faith with the King. Herne will recover, but he will lose all his skill as an archer – all his craft as a hunter.'

'If thou canst accomplish this thou art the fiend himself!' cried Osmond, trembling.

'Fiend or not', replied Urswick, with a triumphant laugh – 'ye have made a compact with me, and must fulfil it. Now begone. I must attend the wounded man.'

And the keepers full of secret misgiving, departed.[109]

Herne recovers but, as Urswick promised, all his skills had deserted him. After repeatedly failing at the simplest tasks at the next hunt, Herne is given a week to regain his former talents by Richard, on pain of dismissal. Herne rides wildly into the forest, returning: 'with ghastly looks and a strange appearance – having the links of a rusty chain which he had plucked from a gibbet hanging from his left arm, and the hart's antlered skull, which he had procured from Urswick, fixed like a helm on his head'.[110] He is soon found hanging from an old oak tree, his body disappearing shortly after discovery. A terrible storm blows up, and the fatal oak is struck by lightning. The other keepers now lose their hunting skills, and are told by Urswick that, 'The curse of Herne's blood is upon you', and that they must go to the old oak. The keepers arrive at midnight, and Herne appears before the terrified men, ordering them to return the following night with horse and hound. The weird hunt is assembled, and Herne leads the keepers in a mad dash to the heart of the forest, halting at a huge beech tree:

Herne dismounted and pronounced certain mystic words, accompanying them with strange gestures.

Presently, he became silent and motionless. A flash of fire then burst from the roots of the tree, and the forester Urswick stood before him. But his aspect was more terrible and commanding than it had seemed heretofore to the keepers.

'Welcome, Herne', he cried; 'welcome, lord of the forest. And you his comrades, and soon to be his followers, welcome too. The time is come for the fulfilment of your promise to me. I require you to form a band for Herne the

[109] *Ibid.*, 205.
[110] *Ibid.*, 207.

hunter, and to serve him as leader. Swear to obey him, and the spell that hangs over you shall be broken. If not I leave you to the king's justice.'[111]

An orgy of destruction follows, as many of the king's deer are slaughtered, Herne each night laying the four finest bucks at the foot of the same beech. Travellers' tales eventually reach the ear of the King, and he leads an expedition made up of his keepers and personal guard to the forest at midnight. As the party near Herne's oak, the hunter appears. 'Why dost thou disturb the quietude of night, accursed spirit?' demands Richard:

> 'Because I desire vengeance!' replied Herne, in a hollow voice. 'I was brought to my present woeful condition by Osmond Crooke and his comrades.'
>
> 'But you died by your own hand – did you not?' demanded King Richard.
>
> 'Yea', replied Herne; 'but I was driven to the deed by an infernal spell laid upon me by the malice of the wretches I have denounced. Hang them upon this tree, and I will trouble these woods no longer while thou reignest!'
>
> The king looked round at his keepers. They all remained obdurate, except Roger Barfoot, who, falling on his knees, confessed his guilt, and accused the others.
>
> 'It is enough', cried the king to Herne; 'they shall all suffer for their offence.'
>
> Upon this, a flash of fire enveloped the spirit and his horse, and he vanished.
>
> The king kept his word. Osmond and his comrades were all hanged upon the scathed tree, nor was Herne seen again in the forest while Richard sat upon the throne. But he re-appeared with a new band at the commencement of the rule of Henry the Fourth, and again hunted deer all night. His band was destroyed, but he defied all attempts at capture; and so it has continued to our own time, for not one of the seven monarchs who have held the castle since Richard's day, have been able to drive him from the forest.[112]

Cutbeard is spinning his yarn to a hushed crowed of servants and foresters in the castle kitchen. At the moment he finishes, a deep voice from the darkness responds to his final line with: 'Nor will the present monarch be able to drive him from the forest … As long as Windsor Forest endures, Herne the hunter will haunt it.' This is a wonderful piece of stagecraft. Everybody in the room jumps, and no-one

---

[111] *Ibid.*, 209.
[112] Ainsworth, *Windsor Castle*, 210–11.

recognises the speaker. The 'tall archer' (later hinted to be Herne in person), commends Hector on the telling of his tale, but offers some amendments which snap us back into the present of the text. Herne was bewitched by a lovely damsel, not a weird forester. He carried off a nun, and lived with her in a cave in the forest: 'it was through her that the fiend tempted him. The charms that proved his undoing were fatal to her also, for in a fit of jealousy he slew her. The remorse occasioned by this deed made him destroy himself.'[113] Mabel Lynwood was the very image of Herne's lost love, which could be why he later spirits her away. If it really is Herne himself speaking here, we must take his words to be the true story, but Ainsworth craftily leaves the teller's identity anonymous while the company in the kitchen speculate for us. Herne does appear as a tall archer at the end of the novel, however, so we could backtrack.

In common with most folk tales, everyone seems to know a slightly different version of the legend, but there is one constant. As the Duke of Richmond tells the Earl of Surrey (who also has his own Herne story) early in the narrative: 'the spirit by which the forest is haunted is a wood demon, who assumes the shape of the ghostly hunter, and seeks to tempt or terrify the keepers to sell their souls to him'.[114] Herne is of course another version of Ainsworth's much loved outlaw, much as Jack Sheppard had transmuted into Guy Fawkes, but the implicit satanic overtones of the legend remain most significant.

Herne is one of many incarnations of the Stag Lord Cernunnous, or Carnan, worshipped by Iron Age Celts across Europe. Cernunnous was also known as the Horned God of the Hunt and the Lord of the Forest, and seems to have been imported from the East as he bears a close resemblance to the Hindu Lord of the Animals, Pashupati. He is also associated with Pan, Janus, Tammuz and Damuzi, Osiris and Dionysus and, of course, Herne the hunter. A famous image of Cernunnous can be seen on the Gundestrup Cauldron, a second century BC Celtic artefact discovered in Northern Jutland in 1891 which can be seen at

---

[113] *Ibid.*, 211.
[114] *Ibid.*, 26.

the Musée Lapidaire at Avignon, and his earliest known image is that of the Palaeolithic cave drawings in the Caverne des Trois Frères at Ariege. His main visual signifier is his stag's horns, and he is also frequently depicted holding a serpent with the head of a ram. In Celtic mythology, Cernunnous was the first God of Danu, the Earth Goddess and, although associated with the hunt and fertility, is the lord of life, death and the underworld. His cyclical existence begins with his birth on the Winter Solstice, he marries the Goddess at Beltane (May day) and dies at the Summer Solstice. As Christianity rolled across Europe, the one God driving out the many, the Horned God eventually became the Devil.

Ainsworth, following Shakespeare and Milton, knows that the forest is an allegorical space, and still in communion with the magical where the Christian and the pre-Christian meet. Who Herne and Urswick actually *are* remains obscure. What we do know is that the forest is their realm, despite being the King's land, and that when a character enters, his or her deepest secrets are revealed to the spirits who in turn tempt their victim to gain these dark desires at the expense of the soul:

> When within a few paces of the tree, its enormous rifted trunk became fully revealed to him. But no one was beside it. Wyat then stood still, and cried, in a loud, commanding tone – 'Spirit, I summon thee! – appear!'
>
> At these words, a sound like a peal of thunder rolled overhead, accompanied by screeches of discordant laughter. Other strange and unearthly noises were heard, and amidst the din, a blue, phosphoric light issued from the yawning crevice in the tree, while a tall, gaunt figure, crested with an antlered helm, sprang from it. At the same moment, a swarm of horribly-grotesque, swart objects, looking like imps, appeared amid the branches of the tree, and grinned and gesticulated at Wyat, whose courage remained unshaken during the fearful ordeal. Not so his steed. After rearing and plunging violently, the affrighted animal broke its hold, and darted off into the swamp, where it floundered, and was lost.
>
> 'You have called me, Sir Thomas Wyat', said the demon, in a sepulchral tone; 'I am here. What would you?'
>
> 'My name being known to you, spirit of darkness, my errand should be known also', replied Wyat boldly.

'Your errand *is* known to me', replied the demon. 'You have lost a mistress, and would regain her?'

'I would give my soul to win her back from my kingly rival', cried Wyat.

'I accept your offer', rejoined the spirit. 'Anne Boleyn shall be yours. Your hand upon the compact.'

Wyat stretched forth his hand, and grasped that of the demon. His fingers were compressed, as if by a vice, and he felt himself dragged towards the tree, while a stifling sulphurous vapour rose around him. A black veil fell over his head, and was rapidly twined around his brow in thick folds.

Amid yells of fiendish laughter, he was then lifted from the ground, thrust into the hollow of the tree, and thence, as it seemed to him, conveyed into a deep subterranean cave.[115]

This is Ainsworth at his gothic best, rivalling Lewis, Maturin and even Byron. Herne effortlessly steals every scene in which he appears, much as he steals souls. In common with Herne's ambivalent status (seen in terms of his many legends and the various supernatural terms the author uses to describe him), he later tells Wyat that: 'I am not the malignant being you suppose me; neither am I bent upon fighting the battles of the enemy of mankind against Heaven. I may be leagued with the powers of darkness, but I have no wish to aid them.'[116] The suggestion here is that Herne, if we take him to be possessed by the spirit of the forest rather than simply a reanimated woodsman from the days of Richard II, goes back much further than the Christian notion of heaven and hell. Nonetheless, he wants power over human beings, and everyone he deals with comes to a nasty end. Wyat, of course, does not get either Anne or Mabel (neither of whom survive the narrative), and as he later leads a failed rebellion against Mary I (as told in *The Tower of London*), we know his fate is sealed. Henry Norris also makes a deal for the love of Anne, and ends up in the Tower for his trouble. There is undoubtedly a metaphysical uncertainty about the entire Herne narrative, which is as peripheral to the main plot as was that of Dick Turpin in *Rookwood* but, like Dick Turpin, it is Herne that compels one to keep reading. He also has the last word in the text:

---

[115] *Ibid.*, 90–91.
[116] *Ibid.*, 267.

'There spoke the death-knell of Anne Boleyn!' cried Herne, regarding Henry sternly, and pointing to the Round Tower. 'The bloody deed is done, and thou art free to wed once more. Away to Wolff Hall, and bring thy new consort to Windsor Castle!'[117]

As with his portrayal of all English monarchs, Ainsworth errs on the generous side with regard to their morals, but Herne's last turn leaves us with the suggestion that, with the death of Anne Boleyn, Henry has surrendered his soul to marry Jane Seymour.

Herne returns in a different guise in Ainsworth's incomplete romance *Auriol, or The Elixir of Life*, a tale of alchemy, immortality and satanic pacts that would have been fascinating if adequately completed. *Auriol* is a fragment, is Ainsworth's *Edwin Drood*, and is in consequence overlooked by his few serious critics as, 'carelessly constructed and incomplete',[118] and, 'certainly the most disjointed of Ainsworth's novels'.[119] It was equally dismissed by the author himself as 'merely a fragment of a romance' which he omitted from a bibliography of his work compiled for the Manchester Free Grammar School.[120] In 1845, before the story was completed in *Ainsworth's Magazine*, the author-editor had a falling out with his owner-publisher, John Mortimer, over a £60.00 'editorial honorarium' and promptly resigned his editorship. Legal action was threatened by Mortimer over breach of contract but not pursued, and Ainsworth purchased both *Ainsworth's Magazine* and *The New Monthly Magazine* soon after in another of his impulsive, and highly expensive, literary speculations. *Auriol* did not move on with him, and was not published as a novel until twenty years later; a slim volume with an obviously hurried conclusion and expanded to an acceptable size by the inclusion of two early short stories: 'The Old London Merchant: A Sketch' (which originally appeared in *The Pic-Nic Papers*, edited by Dickens and published by Colburn in 1841) and 'A Night's Adventure in Rome' (from *The*

---

[117] *Ibid.*, 314–15.
[118] Ellis, vol. 2, 110.
[119] Worth, 120.
[120] Ainsworth, letter to Crossley, December 9, 1869.

Book of Beauty, 1835), and containing a handful of wonderful illustrations by 'Phiz' (Hablot K. Browne) from the original serialisation.[121]

Auriol (the Christian name of the central character) was originally entitled *Revelations of London*, which offers the first clue to the author's initial intentions. This title suggests an allegiance to Sue's *Les Mystères de Paris* (1842–43), which was also, of course, the model for Reynolds's *The Mysteries of London* which also began serialisation in 1844. The notoriety of Reynolds's epic work, along with his sequel *The Mysteries of the Courts of London* (1848–56), may well be the reason for Ainsworth's changes of title: first to the enigmatic *Auriol* and, subsequently, the more descriptive *The Elixir of Life*. Ainsworth's original project, in line with his earlier but abandoned Newgate fiction, appears to be the continued, sensational exploration of what Reynolds called 'the city of fearful contrasts' – contemporary London. For the Chartist Reynolds, these contrasts are distilled down to 'WEALTH and POVERTY', and his *Mysteries* are fictionalised indictments of the corrupt nature of the British aristocracy, and this may have also been a feature in Ainsworth's design. It is true that in common with *Jack Sheppard*, *Auriol* begins with the underworld of Tinker, The Sandman and their Captain, the sinister Dog-Fancier (a figure which carries initial suggestions of Ainsworth's Jonathan Wild, but this stereotypical Jewish caricature is perhaps closer to Dickens's Fagin), yet the real villain of the piece is the decadent and downright demonic aristocrat, Rougemont.

---

[121] The text, such as it was, was also given away with *The New Monthly* as the first and, as it turned out, *only* part of a series entitled *The Revelations of London* as a 'gratuitous supplement'. Ellis quotes but decides to leave unaccredited the following comment on this (probably taken from *Punch*):

Says Ainsworth to Colburn,
'A plan in my pate is,
To give my romance as
A supplement, *gratis.*'
Says Colburn to Ainsworth,
''Twill do very nicely,
For that will be charging
Its value precisely.' Ellis, vol. 2, 122.

Auriol is set predominantly in London in 1830 which, with the exception of *The Life and Adventures of Mervyn Clitheroe*, makes it the only near-contemporary novel that Ainsworth ever wrote. Nonetheless, by having apparently immortal characters at his disposal he is able not only to pursue his preoccupation with British history and its relation to his own time, but actively to dramatise the dynamic by having Elizabethans wandering around the England of William IV and commenting on matters of continuity and change. In a monologue more usually performed by the author, for example, the dwarf Old Parr (once the Elizabethan alchemist Dr Lamb's assistant Flapdragon) discourses at length upon the evolution of London:

'I've seen this great city of London pulled down, and built up again – if that's anything. I've seen it grow, and row, till it has reached its present size. You'll scarcely believe me, when I tell you, that I recollect this Rookery of ours – this foul vagabond neighbourhood – an open country field, with hedges round it, and trees. And a lovely spot it was. Broad St. Giles's, at the time I speak of, was a little country village, consisting of a few straggling houses standing by the roadside, and there wasn't a single habitation between it and Covent Garden ... The whole aspect of the place is altered. The Thames itself is unlike the Thames of old. Its waters were as clear and bright above London-bridge as they are now at Kew or Richmond; and its banks, from Whitefriars to Scotland-yard, were edged with gardens ... Remembering, as I do, what the river used to be when enlightened by gay craft and merry company, I can't help wishing its waters less muddy, and those ugly coal-barges, lighters and steamers, away. London is a mighty city, wonderful to behold and examine, inexhaustible in its wealth and power; but in point of beauty, it is not to be compared with the city of Queen Bess's days ... Imagine what my feelings must be, to walk through streets, still called by the old names, but in other respects wholly changed. Oh! If you could but have a glimpse of Old London, you would not be able to endure the modern city. The very atmosphere was different from that which we now breathe, charged with the smoke of myriads of sea-coal fires; and the old picturesque houses had a charm about them, which the present habitations, however commodious, altogether want.'[122]

This pastoral panegyric against the evils of industrialisation (which must have been on many contemporary readers' minds) is delivered to a Dickensian crew of vagabonds who think that their companion is entertaining but as mad as a brush.

---

[122] Ainsworth, *Auriol, or The Elixir of Life*, Works, 51–4.

In common with all other features of this text, this character is structurally unstable: he begins as an incidental character; is later revealed to have achieved eternal life on the same night as Auriol Darcy; and a supernatural connection between the men and the ghost of the alchemist, Lamb, is proposed and then never pursued ('I am constantly haunted by visions of my old master. He seems to hold converse with me – to lead me into strange places'[123]); he often disappears completely from the narrative only to eventually re-emerge as the morally ambivalent, if not utterly motiveless, servant of Rougemont. Plotlines continually unravel before the reader's eyes with the elegance of a postmodern novel. When reading *Auriol*, one must either attend closely to the unwritten or simply lament the fact that one of Ainsworth's final experimental texts remains unfinished.

The framing narrative of *Auriol* is impressive. It begins and ends in the laboratory of the alchemist Dr Lamb on the last night of the sixteenth century, underneath a very ill omen: 'a stream of rosy and quivering light issuing from the north traversed the sky, like the tail of some stupendous comet'.[124] The image of the comet, the falling star, represents dark destiny (throughout the book Auriol laments the intractable nature of his fate), and the 'rosy' hue of the unexplained light is also not without significance. The atmosphere outside the laboratory is carnival, 'Music and singing were heard at every corner', but around Dr Lamb the author effortlessly adopts his characteristically gothic style:

> Immediately before him stood the Southwark Gateway – a square stone building, with a round, embattled turret at each corner, and a flat, leaden roof, planted with a forest of poles, fifteen or sixteen feet high, garnished with human heads.[125]

As with the introduction to *Guy Fawkes*, two Catholics have just been executed, and a relative, Auriol Darcy, is attempting to recover their heads. He is mortally wounded by the gatekeeper, but saved by Lamb's magic. Auriol returns the favour by stealing the old man's *elixir vitae*, as Lamb dies before his eyes. Lamb is

---

[123] *Ibid.*, 58.
[124] *Ibid.*, 1.
[125] *Ibid.*, 4.

undoubtedly intended to represent the notorious Dr John Dee: astrologer to Elizabeth I, teacher of Philip Sidney, mathematician, Cabalist, alchemist and author of *Monas hieroglyphica* (1564), whose influence is directly cited in the first Rosicrucian manifestos: *Fama Fraternitatis* (1614) and *Confessio Fraternitatis* (1615). Ainsworth had already fictionalised Dee and his associate, Edward Kelly, in *Guy Fawkes*, although whom they sided with was unclear. In this previous incarnation, Dee's role was to predict the future; in *Auriol*, however, the Rosicrucian connection adds a new dimension.

What *Melmoth the Wander* was to Catholic emancipation, *Auriol* is to Victorian Lyttonesque Rosicrucianism. Whether this could be deemed what Marie Roberts has designated a 'Rosicrucian novel' is open to question, but the myth of the cult offers Ainsworth a perfect occult folk devil in the character of Rougemont: the man in black who quickly steals the villain's cloak from The Dog-Fancier and plots the plot with a similar dexterity to Jonathan Wild in *Jack Sheppard*.[126] Rougemont, a fitting successor to Herne the hunter, virtually controls everyone and everything in the novel: Auriol and his modern lover Ebba, Thorneycroft (Ebba's father), Ginger the Dog-Fancier and his merry men, even the dwarf. The source of his power lies in the 'Tomb of the Rosicrucian' in the dead hands of his secretly buried ancestor, Cyprian de Rougemont. There is, of course, a price:

> 'Dost hear me, old ancestor?' he cried ... 'I know that thou wert a brother of the Rosy Cross – one of the illuminati – and didst penetrate the mysteries of nature, and enter the region of light. I know also, that thou wert buried in this house with a vast treasure ... Satan appeared to me in a dream last night, and bade me come hither and I should find what I sought. The conditions he proposed were that I should either give him my own soul, or win him that of Auriol Darcy. I assented. I am here.[127]

Rougemont, Auriol and the dwarf all seem to be receiving instructions from a different plane. It could be that Dr Lamb, cheated of immortality by Auriol and

---

[126] See Marie Roberts, *Gothic Immortals, The Fiction of the Brotherhood of the Rosy Cross* (London: Routledge, 1990).
[127] Ainsworth, *Auriol*, 127.

Flapdragon, is exacting a terrible revenge from beyond the grave. Lamb's ghost could even be masquerading as the devil in order to manipulate Rougemont. Sadly, we never find out.

Cyprian de Rougemont would appear to be modelled on the myth of Christian Rosenkreuz. In Rougemont's tomb there lay a corpse, 'unchanged by decay' and clutching a 'large book, bound in black vellum' and, recalling an ancient tome in Lamb's laboratory, 'fastened with brazen clasps'. According to legend, Rosenkreuz's secret burial place was discovered by a member of the fraternity 120 years after his death (aged 106); the corpse was perfectly preserved, and in his hand certain esoteric documents were found. In Ainsworth's universe this figure is explicitly linked to blatant satanism.

As with the relationships between Jonathan Wild and Jack Sheppard and Herne and Wyat, Rougemont also plays Mephistopheles to the hero's Faust although, in Rougemont's case, albeit via some pretty abstract textual shifts, the role is no longer merely metaphorical:

'Some men would call me the devil!' replied Rougemont, carelessly. 'But you know me too well to suppose that I merit such a designation. I offer you wealth. What more could you require?'

'But upon what terms?' demanded Auriol.

'The easiest imaginable', replied the other. 'You shall judge for yourself.'

And as he spoke, he opened a writing-desk upon the table, and took from it a parchment.

'Sit down', he added, 'and read this.'

Auriol complied, and as he scanned the writing he became transfixed with fear and astonishment, while the pocket-book dropped from his grasp.

After a while, he looked up at Rougemont, who was leaning over his shoulder, and whose features were wrinkled with a derisive smile.

'Then you *are* the Fiend?' he cried.

'If you will have it so – certainly', replied the other.

'You are Satan in the form of the man I once knew', cried Auriol. 'Avaunt! I will have no dealings with you.'

'I thought you wiser than to indulge in such idle fears, Darcy', rejoined the other. 'Granting even your silly notion of me to be correct, what need you be alarmed? You are immortal.'

'True', rejoined Auriol thoughtfully; 'but yet –'

'Pshaw!' rejoined the other, 'sign and have done with the matter.'

'By this compact I am bound to deliver a victim – a female victim – whenever you shall require it', cried Auriol.

'Precisely', replied the other.[128]

Having lived presumably relatively happily and forever young for the previous two centuries, Auriol's gambling debts place him easily in the hands of Rougemont, unbeknown to him his arch nemesis. The compact requires the sacrifice of innocents, young women who are foolish enough to fall in love with the weak-willed and decadent immortal. Their fate is as bizarre as it is graphic, and completely unexplained. Thus we return to *Melmoth*. Auriol soon capitulates, engendering a textually retrospective catalogue of corrupted innocence in a chain that is not broken by the novel's 'conclusion.' Rougemont, employing a variety of complex mechanical devices including an electric chair (exploiting, perhaps, the dark side of the emerging age of industrial technology with gadgetry anticipating Leroux's *Phantom of the Opera* and Rohmer's Fu Manchu), outmanoeuvres all opposition at every turn of the plot. During something like a Black Mass, the abducted Ebba meets, 'three female figures, robed in black, hooded and veiled', who identify themselves as 'the victims of Auriol', and is incited by 'a terrible voice' to sign away her soul to save the life of her beloved:

At this injunction, the figure moved slowly towards the table and, to his unspeakable horror, Auriol beheld it take up the pen and write upon the parchment. He bent forward, and saw that the name inscribed thereon was EBBA THORNEYCROFT.

The groan to which he gave utterance was echoed by a roar of diabolical laughter.

---

[128] *Ibid.*, 135.

The figure then moved slowly away, and ranged itself with the other veiled forms.

'All is accomplished', cried the voice. 'Away with him!'[129]

From this point on (originally a cliffhanger ending to the first part of the serial), the narrative becomes increasingly incoherent as it rushes towards a very abrupt ending 40 odd pages later. Auriol disappears, and Thorneycroft's rescue attempt either fails completely or simply ceases to exist depending on our interpretation of the profoundly negative ending. The rescuers are left running around the labyrinthine passages of Rougemont's mansion like laboratory mice with every possible escape frustrated by the godlike and authorial Rougemont:

'Someone must have followed you', groaned Thorneycroft. 'We're watched on all sides.'

'Ay and from above, too', cried the Sandman. 'Look up there!' he added, in accents of alarm.

'What's the matter? What new danger is at hand?' inquired the iron-merchant.

'Look up, I say', cried the Sandman. 'Don't ye see, Tinker/'

'Ay, ay, I see', replied the other. 'The roof's a-coming in upon us. Let's get out o' this as fast as ve can.' And he kicked and pushed against the door, but all his efforts were unavailing to burst it open.

At the same time the Sandman rushed towards the ladder, but before he could mount it all egress by that means was cut off. An immense iron cover worked in a groove was pushed by some unseen machinery over the top of the pit, and enclosed them in it.[130]

And that's the last we see of the lovers' supposed saviours. Auriol, meanwhile, awakens in a dungeon wearing his Elizabethan clothes:

'What can this mean?' he cried. 'Have I endured a long and troubled dream, during which I have fancied myself living through more than two centuries? Oh, Heaven that it may be so! Oh, that the fearful crimes I suppose I have committed have only been enacted in a dream! Oh, that my victims are imaginary! Oh, that Ebba should only prove a lovely phantom of the night!

---

[129] *Ibid.*, 124.
[130] *Ibid.*, 186.

And yet, I could almost wish the rest were real – so that she might exist. I cannot bear to think that she is nothing more than a vision.'[131]

The only suggestion that this is an elaborate attempt to disorient the hero psychologically comes from the presence of Rougemont, who is now shown sympathetically keeping watch over his mad friend in 1599, and an earlier comment from an unidentified observer (either Rougemont, Satan, Lamb or all three) that: 'The scheme works to a miracle.' Auriol is then led to Dr Lamb's laboratory again, back to his own beginning, where he looks from a window across a dark city and fancies, although we cannot be absolutely certain, that he sees Elizabethan landmarks. The last line of Auriol runs: 'After a while he returned from the window, and said to his supposed grandsire, "I am satisfied. I have lived centuries in a few nights."'[132] Or has he? Having accurately listed the kings of England up to and including George IV while in this state, the narrative remains completely contrary.

The novel has totally unravelled. Ebba is damned like 'The Spectre Bride', everybody is trapped in the mansion and, if the clues suggesting that Rougemont has brainwashed Auriol are true, then the villain is triumphant. Alternatively, if this was all a fevered dream, then every character and situation in which the reader has invested interest simply cease to have ever existed. The obscured final image of London by night could equally be either sixteenth or nineteenth century. Narrative closure is not often so emphatically denied.

The pragmatic reading of *Auriol*'s conclusion is that this is what happens when you tack an ending onto the first part of a promising (but abandoned) serial and try to pass it off as a short novel; yet enough of this intriguing misfire does exist, along with the almost equally flawed *Windsor Castle*, to serve as something of a preface to Ainsworth's finest piece of occult writing: *The Lancashire Witches*.

---

[131] *Ibid.*, 188.
[132] *Ibid.*, 201.

CHAPTER FIVE

The Lancashire Novelist

I. A dream of flying: *The Lancashire Witches. A Romance of Pendle Forest,* 1848

Ainsworth's Magazine ran two more historical romances by its editor in the 1840s. *Saint James's or The Court of Queen Anne, An Historical Romance* was serialised between January and December 1844, and published by Mortimer in three volumes the same year. Worth has described this, quite correctly I believe, as: 'A relatively plotless and formless novel.'[1] The usually gushing Ellis similarly remarks that this text: 'is in a very different category to the fine romances written by Ainsworth previously and to two, at least, that followed it; it has but little pretensions to literary merit, and the romantic glamour so characteristic, as a rule, of the author's works is lacking'.[2] Perhaps it was the essentially wishy-washy nature of the reign of Queen Anne, the last Stuart sovereign, which made for such a dreary account of the Tories' successful strategy, led by Harley and St. John, to curb the political influence of the Duke and Duchess of Marlborough. Even Anne's close friend Sarah, Duchess of Marlborough, wrote of her that: 'she certainly ... meant well and was not a fool; but nobody can maintain that she was wise, nor entertaining in conversation. She was in everything what I described her: ignorant in everything

---

[1] Worth, 118.
[2] Ellis, vol. 2, 74–5.

but what the parsons had taught her as a child.'[3] *Saint James's* was the last of Ainsworth's romances to be illustrated by Cruikshank. *Auriol*, such as it was, then followed, and the next completed work was *James the Second, or The Revolution of 1688. An Historical Romance*, which ran from January to December 1847, appearing as a three volume novel published by Henry Colburn the following year. Both serial and novel were illustrated by R.W. Buss. The serial was described as 'edited' by Ainsworth, but the novel was attributed to him alone, despite a false rumour at the time that Crossley was actually the author which resulted in some teasing from Ainsworth. In this team Crossley did the history, Ainsworth the creative writing. This romance deals with the decline and fall of the most unpopular king of England, and his replacement by William of Orange in the Glorious Revolution of 1688, resulting in the removal of his descendants, of whom Ainsworth was so fond, from the royal lineage. In common with the majority of Ainsworth's historical plots, *James the Second* also tells the story of the romance between Charles Moor, a loyal Jacobite, and the Huguenot Sabine Saint Leu. The pair are eventually able to marry when Charles proves that he is the rightful Lord Mauvesin, a title usurped by an impostor who is killed when an angry mob fires the house of the Spanish ambassador in London. A highwayman, Will Davis[4] ('The Golden Farmer'), is sneakily included, but his presence does not save the narrative, which is only marginally more interesting and well-constructed than *Saint James's*. Ainsworth is also often credited with *Modern Chivalry, or a New Orlando Furioso*, which was serialised in *Ainsworth's Magazine* in 1843. This was in fact written by Mrs Catherine Gore and edited by Ainsworth. As I have attempted to indicate in the previous chapter, among this collection of essentially hack writing, it is only the incomplete *Auriol* that gives an

---

[3] Quoted from John Cannon and Ralph Griffith, *The Oxford Illustrated History of the British Monarchy* (Oxford: UP, 2000), 458.

[4] The farmer William Davis (c.1625–1689) was an unusually successful highwayman, and was active for over 40 years before finally being apprehended and executed. He was nicknamed 'The Golden Farmer' by neighbours as he always paid his bills in gold; apparently no-one ever paused to wonder where this gold might be coming from.

indication of the epic romance with which Ainsworth was to conclude this decade: *The Lancashire Witches*.

Ellis wrote that '*The Lancashire Witches* is undoubtedly its author's finest work',[5] a statement endorsed by David Punter.[6] Largely because of a popular fascination with the occult, *The Lancashire Witches* is the only one of Ainsworth's novels to have remained consistently in print to this day, often shelved alongside the worst excesses of Dennis Wheatley and Montague Summers (both of whom it undoubtedly influenced). The novel is also one of the mainstays of the Pennine tourist industry, and is available in many local museums, railway stations and gift shops. As the Dick Turpin narrative of *Rookwood* seamlessly passed into the national myth, Ainsworth's romance of Pendle Forest has supplanted the unusually well-documented history of these unfortunate men and women in Lancashire folklore. This 'classic tale of the supernatural'[7] although generally overlooked by scholars of the gothic, therefore continues to exist quietly both as a popular cultural curio and, rather more erroneously, in an extra-literary sense as a genuine history.

The Lancashire Witches is the first of Ainsworth's Lancashire novels, and it is perhaps because of the author's love for the county of his birth that the novel does not suffer from the obviously hasty, and consequently often clumsy, composition that so often marred Ainsworth's originally interesting ideas. While sharing the Faustian conceit of the Herne the Hunter subplot of *Windsor Castle* and the incomplete *Auriol*, both of which in rushing headlong towards abrupt and unsatisfying conclusions had caused the author much critical ridicule, *The Lancashire Witches* was subject to uncharacteristically detailed preparation. 'My desire', he admitted towards the end of his life, 'has really been to write a

---

[5] Ellis, vol. 2, 143.
[6] Punter, vol. 1, 157.
[7] The marketing slogan for the Granada paperback edition of 1980.

Lancashire novel, a novel that should please the whole county, and I don't care whether it pleased anyone else.'[8]

The Lancashire Witches is set on and around Pendle Hill in early seventeenth century Lancashire, with an introduction set in 1536. The Cistercian monk Borlace Alvetham is falsely accused of witchcraft by his rival, Brother John Paslew, and condemned to a lingering death. Alvetham escapes by selling his soul to Satan, and returns as the warlock Nicholas Demdike during the Pilgrimage of Grace to witness the execution of the now Abbot Paslew for treason. Paslew dies cursing Demdike's daughter and, 'that infant and her progeny became the Lancashire Witches'.[9] The remainder of the narrative is set about a century later, when the ancient witch Mother Demdike wields tremendous supernatural power over the area, her evil family challenged only by the rival witches Mother Chattox and Alice Nutter. The elaborate plot centres around the fate of two lovers, the pious Alizon Device (raised by the Demdike clan, but in fact the long-lost daughter of Alice Nutter) and the young aristocrat Richard Assheton. In Book I Alizon discovers her birth mother is Alice Nutter and resolves to save her soul. Book II chronicles the rivalry between Demdike, Chattox and Nutter, Demdike's attempts to corrupt Alizon and the eventual destruction of Demdike and Chattox in a fire on Pendle Hill. Book III follows Alice Nutter's penitence, a visit from James I, and the final struggle between heaven and hell for the souls of Alice and her daughter. Both are killed in a violent confrontation with Alice's ex-demon familiar, but they die in prayer and the mark of Satan fades from Alice's brow. Richard Assheton, who has been cursed repeatedly by various vindictive witches throughout, pines away and the lovers are buried in a single grave.

---

[8] James Crossley and John Evans (eds), *Specially Revised Accounts of the Recent Banquet to William Harrison Ainsworth, Esq., by Thomas Baker, Mayor of Manchester. As an expression of the high esteem in which he is held by his Fellow-townsmen and of his services to literature* (Manchester: 1881).
[9] Ainsworth, *The Lancashire Witches. A Romance of Pendle Forest*, Works, 62.

The project appears to have commenced in 1845, three years prior to the first published instalment of the serial in *The Sunday Times* on January 1 1848.[10] In dedicating the novel to James Crossley, Ainsworth acknowledges that both the source material and the original idea for the work came from his friend:

> To James Crossley, Esq., (of Manchester), President of the Chetham Society, and the learned editor of 'The Discoverie of Witches in the County of Lancaster', – the groundwork of the following pages, – this romance, undertaken at his suggestion, is inscribed by his old and sincerely attached friend, the author.[11]

This is the quintessential Ainsworth/Crossley project, with each text, Crossley's history and Ainsworth's romance, complementing the other. Ainsworth's references to the new novel in his correspondence with Crossley date from the Chetham Society's 1845 reprint of the Lancaster Castle Assizes clerk Thomas Potts's record of the 1612 trial of the so-called Lancashire witches,[12] and document three years of preparation for what was to become his master work. In late 1845 Ainsworth wrote to Crossley that, 'I have not yet started the *Witches* as I want to commence with effect ... Pray see Rodd about Whitaker and the Witchcraft books.'[13] In May 1846, he wrote, 'I have some intention of running down into Lancashire to see the Witch Country once more ... what say you to another trip?'[14] and, again, in August 1847, 'I shall soon be in Manchester, as I want to pay another visit to Whalley.'[15]

---

[10] The accompanying advertisements were written in a garish 'creepy' font, causing Thackeray to remark that, 'I thought I was drunk when I saw the placards in the street.' Thackeray, 'To Frances Fladgate', January 1848, letter 442 of *The Letters*, vol. 2, 344.

[11] Ainsworth, dedication, *The Lancashire Witches*.

[12] Thomas Potts, *The Wonderfvll Discoverie of Witches in the Covntie of Lancaster. With the Arraignement and Triall of Nineteene notorious WITCHES, at the Affizes and generall Gaole deliuerie, holden at the Caftle of LANCASTER, vpon Munday, the feunteenth of Auguft laft, 1612*, ed. James Crossley (Manchester: The Chetham Society, 1845.)

[13] Dr Whitaker was a historian and collector of rare manuscripts who provided George Ormerod of the Chetham Society with material for the collection *Remains Historical and Literary connected with the palatine counties of Lancaster and Chester* of which Potts's *Discoverie* is a part.

[14] Ainsworth, letter to Crossley, May 5 1846.

[15] Ainsworth, letter to Crossley, August 1847.

These frequent visits to Pendle Hill, the surrounding forest and the ruins of Whalley Abbey were the evolutionary process which were to result in the author's ultimate evocation of a sublime, gothic landscape in his writing:

> This glen was in very ill repute, and was never traversed, even at noonday, without apprehension. Its wild and savage aspect, its horrent precipices, its shaggy woods, its strangely-shaped rocks and tenebrous depths, where every imperfectly-seen object appeared doubly frightful – all combined to invest it with mystery and terror.
>
> No one willingly lingered here, but hurried on, afraid of the sound of his own footsteps. No one dared to gaze at the rocks, lest he should see some hideous hobgoblin peering out of their fissures. No one glanced at the water, for fear some terrible kelpy, with twining snakes for hair and scaly hide, should issue from it, and drag him down to devour him with shark-like teeth.[16]

In Ainsworth's magical forest, notions of fact and fantasy blur within the text just as they seemed to in wild, mysterious reality. As Crossley wrote in his introduction to Potts's *Discoverie*:

> The 'parting genius' of superstition still clings to the hoary hill tops and rugged slopes and mossy water sides, along which the old forest stretched its length, and the voices of ancestral tradition are still heard to speak from the depth of its quiet hollows, and along the course of its gurgling streams. He who visits Pendle will yet find that charms are generally resorted to among the lower orders ... that each small hamlet has its peculiar and gifted personage whom it is dangerous to offend ... that each locality has its haunted house; that apparitions still walk their ghostly rounds.[17]

Leo H. Grindon also wrote of Whalley Abbey that, 'In all Cheshire there is not a locality more desolate, bleak and lonely.'[18] *The Lancashire Witches* succeeds because of this tangible tension between the real and the unreal which surrounds the complex aesthetic of the author's native county. The prologue, which begins with the failure of the Pilgrimage of Grace, as warrior monks wait by a beacon on the summit of Pendle Hill, establishes the symbolic nature of the landscape as a place of fire and violence:

---

[16] Ainsworth, *The Lancashire Witches*, 225–6.
[17] James Crossley, introduction, *The Wonderfvll Discoverie of Witches*, by Thomas Potts.
[18] Grindon, 63.

As the beacon flame increased it lighted up the whole of the extensive table-land on the summit of Pendle Hill; and a long, lurid streak fell on the darkling moss pool near which the wizard had stood. But when it attained its utmost height it revealed the depths of the forest below, and a red reflection, here and there, marked the course of Pendle Water.[19]

The signal beacon, rather than the call to arms it was intended to be, marks the end of the rebellion and foreshadows the fire of the sabbat on the hill at the climax of Book I. This ultimately becomes a funeral pyre for Chattox and Demdike and their gateway to hell, the place of 'oceans of fire, in which miserable souls were forever tossing'[20] and a familiar space within Ainsworth's fiction. The river of blood snaking through the forest is also the line that Nowell, Potts and Assheton follow into the heart of darkness where Old Mother Demdike reigns absolute. The shadow of Pendle Hill also falls across the entire text. The innocent locals find it glorious: '"I love Pendle Hill", cried Nicholas, enthusiastically – "Some folks say Pendle Hill wants grandeur and sublimity, but they themselves must be wanting in taste."'[21] The fallen find it ominous, when Alice looks towards it in a moment of peace: 'One blot alone appeared in the otherwise smiling sky, and this was a great ugly black cloud, lowering over the summit of Pendle Hill',[22] and the Londoner Master Potts loathes it, declaring to Nicholas that: 'I hate your bleak Lancashire hills', thus marking him as a rogue and a scoundrel in Ainsworth's universe.[23] As Mrs Gaskell also understood, Pendle Hill carried a code of magic, mystery and evil, and she employed it as the sublime backdrop to her moral fable of 1850, 'The Heart of John Middleton', a tale set in Sawley, 'where the shadow of Pendle Hill falls at sunrise'.[24] J. Sheridan Le Fanu similarly used it as a setting to his short story 'Dickon the Devil', which begins, 'About thirty years ago I was selected by two rich old maids to visit a property in that part of Lancashire which lies near the

[19] Ainsworth, *The Lancashire Witches*, 9.
[20] *Ibid.*, 481.
[21] *Ibid.*, 220.
[22] *Ibid.*, 408.
[23] *Ibid.*, 220.
[24] Elizabeth Gaskell, 'The Heart of John Middleton', *Cranford and Other Tales*, Collected Works (London: Smith, Elder & Co., 1886), 161.

famous forest of Pendle, with which Mr Ainsworth's "Lancashire Witches" has made us so pleasantly familiar.'[25] The word 'pleasantly' seems complimentarily ironic in this context.

In addition to Potts's *Discoverie* Ainsworth made good use of another Chetham Society publication, *The Journal of Nicholas Assheton*, which was the fourteenth volume of the same series that loosed Thomas Potts once more upon the world. Only the entries covering 1617–18 had survived, fortuitously including an account of the King's visit to Lancashire in 1617 of which Ainsworth made much use, moving the event back five years in time in order to place the witches in the royal presence. Assheton is one of Ainsworth's principal characters, essentially playing Mercutio to his cousin Richard's Romeo, and the vivid accounts of country life in the journal found easy purchase in the sympathetic mind of the author, who obviously felt a great affection for the young squire: 'Oh, Nicholas, Nicholas! I am thoroughly ashamed of you, and regret becoming your historian. You get me into an infinitude of scrapes.'[26] Perhaps because both historian and subject were kindred spirits, Ainsworth's portrait of Assheton is one of his best and, in contrast to his temporal licence, the personality which he ascribes to Assheton appears, on the strength of the journal, to be perfectly accurate. Assheton, writes Ainsworth on introducing the character, 'might be considered a type of the Lancashire squire of the day', expertly combining piety with hedonism and hellraising:

> A precisian in religious notions, and constant in attendance at church and lecture, he put no sort of restraint upon himself, but mixed up fox-hunting, otter-hunting, shooting at the mark ... foot-racing, horse-racing, and, in fact, every other kind of country diversion, not forgetting tippling, cards, and dicing, with daily devotion, discourses, and psalm-singing in the oddest way imaginable.[27]

---

[25] J. Sheridan Le Fanu, 'Dickon the Devil', *Madam Crowl's Ghost and other stories*, ed. M.R. James (London: Wordsworth, 1994), 41.
[26] Ainsworth, *The Lancashire Witches*, 181.
[27] *Ibid.*, 78.

In corroboration, the journal records, in the brief period covered, 16 fox-hunts, 10 stag-hunts, and a further fortnight spent hawking, shooting and fishing. There are also 19 confessions of inebriation, ranging from the merely 'merrie' to 'sicke with drinke'.[28] Sadly, there is no record of a wild dance with the phantom votaress, Isole de Heton, as featured in Ainsworth's account.

In early 1848, Ainsworth wrote to Crossley, 'I hope you like the "Witches". They find favour here; and satisfy the Sunday Times.'[29] Further correspondence suggests that Crossley genuinely approved of the novel, and Ainsworth was also right to claim that the novel found favour with public and publishers alike. He had received £1,000 from *The Sunday Times* for the complete serial (copyright to revert to the author upon completion), which was the same deal he had accepted from them in 1841 for *Old St. Paul's*; that his fee had not risen in seven years is an indication of his increasing commercial stagnation. Nevertheless the serial was a hit, as was the complete novel upon its release the following year. Regrettably the work was not illustrated by Cruikshank, whose style would have perfectly suited the subject. It remained unillustrated until the third edition of 1854 which contained 12 drawings by Sir John Gilbert, all of which contribute to the fairytale qualities that are often apparent in the text by depicting the witches as pointy-hatted, warty old hags with flying broomsticks.

The Lancashire Witches was to be Ainsworth's last major, national success and marks the end of his literary celebrity, at least in the South of England, although a further 28 novels were yet to be written. It is also, however, the first of an irregular series of works devoted to the history of his beloved Lancashire, which would result in the epithet of which he was so proud: that of The Lancashire Novelist.

---

[28] F.R. Raines (ed.), *The Journal of Nicholas Assheton of Downham, in the county of Lancaster, esq. for part of the year 1617, and a part of the year following: interspersed with notes from the life of his contemporary, John Bruen Stapleford, in the county of Chester, esq.* (New York: Johnson Reprint, 1969).
[29] Ainsworth, letter to Crossley, February 15 1848.

There were in fact two notorious cases of supposed witchcraft in Lancashire in the first half of the seventeenth century. The first was prosecuted in 1612, dutifully chronicled by Master Potts, and forms the basis for Ainsworth's novel. The second occurred in 1633 and is similar to the first inasmuch as the most damning testimony came from young children. In this case however, the judges were considerably less credulous than those of 1612 and four of the seven accused were acquitted after the matter was referred to Charles I himself for consideration. The key witness, an 11-year-old boy named Edmund Robinson confessed many years later to having been suborned by his father to give false evidence against women towards whom he bore an unspecified series of grudges. Although three people had been executed no-one was ever brought to justice for perjury.

Robinson's accusations also formed the basis for the other fictional works on the subject. *The Late Lancashire Witches* by Thomas Heywood and Richard Broome of 1634 took much of its supernatural material from Robinson's descriptions, and this play was later partially rewritten by Thomas Shadwell in his comedy of 1681, *The Lancashire Witches, and Tegue O Devilly The Irish Priest*. Shadwell dramatised protagonists from both trials, casting Mother Demdike of 1612 alongside Mother Dickenson of 1633 while setting the story in his own political present. Ainsworth begins his novel with an epigraph from Shadwell in a line lampooning the credulous and/or devious figure of the witch-finder, personified by the lawyer Matthew Hopkins, the infamous 'witch-finder general', active during the Civil War. This epigraph is taken from a speech given by Sir Jeffery Shacklehead, a bumbling Justice of the Peace who bears more than a little resemblance to Ainsworth's representation of the 'rascally attorney' Thomas Potts: 'Is there a justice in Lancashire has so much skill in witches as I have? Nay, I'll speak a proud word; you shall turn me loose against any witch-finder in Europe. I'd make an ass of Hopkins if he were alive.'[30] To Shadwell, Hopkins and

---

[30] Thomas Shadwell, *The Lancashire Witches* (1681), I.

his kind were asses anyway, hence his outrageous lampoon. This was still a dangerous assertion in Shadwell's day but a statement of fact by Ainsworth's. Charles Mackay, for example, chronicles the stupidity of centuries of paranoia and persecution in a retrospective chapter of his *Extraordinary Popular Delusions* entitled 'The Witch Mania', which also includes a couple of pages on the Lancashire witches (referring to this second group of 1633).[31] It is worth noting that the great moralist did not have the same problem with the gothic that he had with Newgate writing, concluding his argument:

> Still, it is consoling to think that the delirium has passed away; that the raging madness has given lace to a milder folly; and that we may now count by units the votaries of a superstition which in former ages numbered its victims by tens of thousands, and its votaries by millions.[32]

Mackay is of course referring to a deluded minority who still believe in witchcraft, but his comments can just as easily apply to purveyors and consumers of occult fiction. Intriguingly, Ainsworth and Shadwell both ridicule the beliefs of the witch-finders of the day while still representing these beliefs as actually true. There are initial suggestions of mesmerism and drug use in the early part of Ainsworth's novel as a frame of explanation, for example when Mistress Nutter, 'fixed a searching look on Jennet, and then raising her hand quickly waved it in her face', causing the little girl to faint when she was about to say something inopportune in public, but the broomsticks come out shortly thereafter.[33]

In 1612, the 'nineteene notorious witches' of Potts's account are made up of three separate cases: the Pendle Forest group, the Samlesbury witches and two independents from Padiham and Windle. The Pendle witches present at the August Assizes at Lancaster Castle were: Anne Whittle, alias Mother Chattox; Elizabeth, James and Alizon Device (this is Potts's spelling and is probably pronounced Davies, which it became in the written reports when the family appeared again in the 1633 case), Anne Redfern (Nance in Ainsworth's version),

---

[31] Mackay, 508–10.
[32] *Ibid.*, 564.
[33] Ainsworth, *The Lancashire Witches*, 176.

Alice Nutter, Katherine Hewitt and John and Jane Bulcock. The famous Old Mother Demdike (Elizabeth Southerns) was not in attendance having died while in custody awaiting trial. Jennet (Janet) Device, the nine-year-old daughter of Elizabeth, was a key witness for the prosecution and was herself not accused. As Potts tellingly writes of the Magistrate Roger Nowell, 'by his great paines taken in the examination of Iennet Deuice, al their practises are now made knowen'.[34] Ironically, Jennet was later hanged in the 1633 fiasco.

Briefly, the Pendle problems began when the licensed beggar Alizon Device was accused of laming by witchcraft one John Law, a peddler from Halifax after a dispute over some pins on the evening of March 18. Law's stroke led to his son's demands for justice and Roger Nowell's examination of the entire Device family and their friends. Demdike, Chattox, Redfern and Alizon Device were immediately detained and despatched to the dungeons at Lancaster. Understandably concerned, friends and relatives held a meeting at Malkin Tower on Good Friday and reports of this 'sabbat' resulted in further arrests. At the Assizes, surprisingly all but Elizabeth Device confessed to witchcraft, consorting with the devil and being attended by familiar spirits and were therefore duly convicted and condemned. We can assume this was tortured out of them. These statements of satanic practices form the body of Potts's account, although Pendle Hill is never mentioned, and Ainsworth takes his inspiration for much of the supernatural events in his novel from these testimonies. The Pendle witches were hanged together at Lancaster castle on Thursday August 20 1612, early victims of James I's Witchcraft Act of 1604 and the increasing influence of the continental Inquisition.

Because of Potts's report, this is the most precisely documented witch trial in English history, but there are still many popular versions of the story which have more in common with the imagination of Ainsworth than with the detailed

---

[34] Potts, 'The Examination and Euidence of IENNET DEVICE', *Discoverie*.

accounts left us by Master Potts. In *The Devil and All His Works* for example, Dennis Wheatley wrote with characteristic seriousness that:

> In Pendle Forest, a lofty ruin known as Malkin Tower was a favourite place for holding sabbats. Two rival witches, Mother Demdike and Mother Chattox, caused so much trouble in the neighbourhood that a local magistrate had them arrested. On the night of Good Friday, 1612, their covens met at the Tower to cast spells, with the object of freeing their leaders ... all that group of witches were seized and went to the stake.[35]

Malkin Tower was, and is, a rather unremarkable farm near Blacko rather than the impregnable, phallic fortress as written by Ainsworth and unproblematically accepted by Wheatley. Contemporary descriptions of the labourer's cottage that housed the Devices confirm that it was never lofty, ruined or otherwise. The rivalry between Demdike and Chattox is also an Ainsworthian plot device rather than part of the original account, and the stake was the European punishment while England employed the gallows. Wheatley, of course, follows Ainsworth's final judgement, which folklore dictated over history. Ainsworth's audience expected a certain execution etiquette where highwaymen hang, aristocrats lose their heads and witches are burned. Similarly, the Rough Lee boundary dispute between Alice Nutter and Roger Nowell, so often cited as the catalyst for the accusations, again comes from the novel.[36] Nowell lived in Read, which is approximately ten miles south west of Rough Lee with several properties in between the two at the time of the chronicled events. Once again, the forgotten novelist has supplanted history.

In addition to the above, Ainsworth has also finally achieved a narrative that has space to develop and contain his unique synthesis of history, romanticism and what we now refer to as magic realism. In his presentation of powerful women, who have by social necessity embraced the word and world of Satan over God, Ainsworth offers his best and, perhaps, the ultimate, romance of fall and

---

[35] Dennis Wheatley, *The Devil and All His Works* (London: Hutchinson, 1971), 247.
[36] See Christina Hole, *Witchcraft in England* (London: B.T. Batsford, 1977).

redemption. His Faustian protagonists are not modelled after those of Goethe or Byron, but return instead, at last, to source: to Eve herself.

In such criticism of *The Lancashire Witches* as we have (my own included), there is a tendency to go down the Shakespearean path with regard to literary witchcraft. Ellis concentrates specifically on the *Macbeth* connection, and I have elsewhere argued that such a reading allows Ainsworth his oft-criticised ambivalence with regard to his blurring of humanism and magic in the text.[37] The above being a response to David Punter's comment on *The Lancashire Witches* that:

> [The] point appears to be to demonstrate, after Scott, the evils consequent upon persecution ... In accordance with this point, the good liberals are all on the side of the witches, and try to defend them against harassment; unfortunately, however, Ainsworth also seems to claim that the witches really *are* witches, which makes the good liberals appear rather foolish.[38]

These issues do not have to be quite as exclusive as Professor Punter suggests however, there being a dramatic tradition in which the real and the magical are allowed to coexist, the one interrogating the other. For example, in his excellent introduction to the Oxford *Macbeth*, Nicholas Brooke has argued convincingly that:

> In *Macbeth* it is the opening by the Weïrd Sisters which proposes a relation between supernatural and natural phenomenon. No amount of quotation from King James's early and credulous *Demonology* will transfer the Sisters from a category of belief into one of verifiable knowledge.[39] The Weïrd Sisters are,

---

[37] See Stephen Carver, 'Abnormal Literature: The early fiction of William Harrison Ainsworth', diss., University of East Anglia, 1999.

[38] Punter, vol. 1, 158.

[39] Medieval England had no Inquisition and the independence of the Church from Papal authority had isolated the country from the intellectual and judicial climate of persecution in Europe, where the *Malleus Maleficarum* of 1486 and an ever-growing canon of Roman Law relating to demonology and witchcraft had long established a general belief in devil-worship. When, for example, Reginald Scot produced his refutation of Satanism in 1584, the *Discoverie of Witchcraft*, his intellectual opponents were all continental scholars who were still basically occupied in refining the tenets of the *Malleus*. Shadwell was satirically to quote these authorities to excess in his *Lancashire Witches*. As Keith Thomas has shown, the irony of the English experience was that in the years immediately following Scot's treatise the concepts formulated by medieval Catholicism were disseminated in England by Protestant writers excited by ideas from abroad, chief among them King James VI of Scotland, author of the *Daemonologie* of 1597. Keith Thomas, *Religion and the Decline of Magic* (London: Penguin, 1971), Chapter 14.

like Ariel and Caliban, essentially creatures of drama, not really naturalistic representations of old women.[40]

The status of witches in English literature is traditionally binary and ambivalent. In *Macbeth*, the primary purpose of the witches is prophecy, 'weird' meaning Destiny or Fate in early modern English. This is a classical device as much as it suggests supernaturalism. They do not seem especially powerful, but they still vanish, 'Into the air; and what seemed corporeal melted/As breath into the wind.'[41] Unlike Macbeth's vision of the dagger or Banquo's ghost, the witches cannot be rationalised as psychological disturbances, although Banquo posits the possibility of such gothic uncertainty with, 'have we eaten on the insane root/That takes the reason prisoner?'.[42] In *Macbeth*, says Brooke, 'illusion mediates between natural and supernatural', and 'offers a thorough analysis of the epistemological relationship between belief and knowledge',[43] rather than merely flattering James I and symbolically capitalising on the recent Gunpowder plot while indulging the King's interest in witchcraft.[44] Dramatic witches can therefore be seen to exist in a space between the world of the stage and the audience, their entrances and exits a combination of smoke and trap doors.

As has been noted, the direct literary antecedents of Ainsworth's novel are both comedy dramas which, as we have seen, in turn belong to a dramatic tradition that can usefully be traced back to Shakespeare's *Macbeth* via, for example, *The Witch*, a comedy by Thomas Middleton (1615–16) and *The Witch of Edmonton*, a tragicomedy by William Rowley, Thomas Dekker and John Ford

---

[40] Nicholas Brooke (ed.), introduction, William Shakespeare, *The Tragedy of Macbeth* (Oxford, UP, 1998).
[41] Shakespeare, *Macbeth*, I.iii 81–2.
[42] *Ibid.*, I.iii 84–5.
[43] Brooke, introduction, *Macbeth*.
[44] See Gary Wills, *Witches and Jesuits, Shakespeare's Macbeth* (Oxford: UP, 1995) for an excellent example of this reading.

(1621).[45] As with Ainsworth's earlier tragic histories, the codes of this novel are also dramatic. Ainsworth makes his link with Shakespeare's Weïrd Sisters explicit, as can be seen by the following incantations, his witches echoing the famous chant that opens the fourth act of *Macbeth*:

> Head of monkey, brain of cat,
> Eye of weasel, tail of rat,
> Juice of mugwort, mastic, myrrh –
> All within the pot I stir.
>
> —
>
> Here is the foam from a mad dog's lips,
> Gathered beneath the moon's eclipse,
> Ashes of a shroud consumed,
> And with deadly vapour fumed;
> These within the mess I cast –
> Stir the cauldron – stir it fast!
>
> —
>
> Here are snakes from out the river,
> Bones of toad, and sea-calf's liver;
> Swine's flesh fattened on her brood,
> Wolf's tooth, hare's foot, weasel's blood,
> Skull of ape and fierce baboon,
> And panther spotted like the moon;
> Feathers of a hornéd owl,
> Daw pie, and other fatal fowl.
> Fruit from the fig tree never sown,
> Seed from cypress never grown.
> All within the mess I cast,
> Stir the cauldron – stir it fast![46]

There are also very recognisably similar songs in Shadwell, and this intertext is also doubled in the tendency of authors to mix up historical characters from the different Lancashire Witch episodes of 1612 and 1633. English literary witches are apparently very closely, if not downright incestuously, related.

---

[45] *The Witch of Edmonton* (c.1621) is a particularly divided text. The witch of the title, Elizabeth Sawyer, is a poor and lonely old woman who turns to the devil because no-one else cares. Persecuted by her neighbours, her demonic pact is an act of desperation to protect herself, and the play often shows a sympathy for the down-trodden and ill-used that would seem at odds with the subject and the times.
[46] Ainsworth, *The Lancashire Witches*, 195.

While Ainsworth's witches are deliberately shown to perform what is basically the same rite as their Shakespearean ancestors, he also links his text to Shadwell's by his choice of epigraph. Shadwell's play was a daring satire on religious bigotry (both Catholic and Anglican), produced at the height of the political battle between Shaftesbury and the Crown for the exclusion of James from the succession. Unlike Ainsworth, this was not a matter of antiquarian interest, and Shadwell had to tread carefully. His play was accused of being 'seditious', 'treasonous' and 'a satyr upon the Church of England', but fortunately Charles II saw the funny side and, as the author records in his highly defensive preface, 'let it live'.[47] Shadwell thus balanced his criticisms of credulous, superstitious members of Church and State unhealthily influenced by continental and Catholic ideas, with representations of supposedly authentic black magic (ironically supported by voluminous references to authorities on the black arts printed as endnotes to each act).[48] Unlike Shakespeare's Weïrd Sisters, whose function is largely that of prophecy, Shadwell's witches are much more proactive, their comedy antics assisting the play's heroines, Theodosia Shacklehead and Isabella Hartfort, in choosing their own husbands, and therefore destinies, rather than those selected as suitable by their fathers. Early in the play, Isabella begins a running conversational battle with her idiot suitor, Sir Timothy Shacklehead (who is incidentally terrified of witches), the first round of which concludes with her boxing his ears when he attempts to kiss her hand; he suspects witchcraft, which is synonymous with any non-feminine assertions of individuality: 'She has piss'd upon a Nettle today, or else the Witches have bewitched her.'[49] The first act notably concludes with the arrival of the witches, who are immediately followed by the *real* lovers of the story, Bellfort and Doubty. In response to their overall

---

[47] Montague Summers, 'Theatrical History', Thomas Shadwell, *The Complete Works*, ed. Montague Summers, 5 vols, vol. 4 (London: The Fortune Press, 1927), 93–8.
[48] As Sir Edward Hartfort laments, 'Our new-fashioned Gentry love the French too well to fight against 'em; they are bred abroad without knowing any thing of our Constitution, and come home tainted with Foppery, slavish Principles, and Popish Religion.' Shadwell, III.
[49] Shadwell, I.

predicament as marriageable daughters, Theodosia and Isabella unite in a wonderfully gender-exclusive statement of feminist principle:

> *Isab.* Well, we are resolved never to marry where we are designed, that's certain. For my part I am a free English woman, and will stand up for my Liberty and property of Choice.[50]
>
> *Theo.* And Faith, Girl, I'll be a mutineer on thy side; I hate the imposition of a Husband, 'tis as bad as Popery.
>
> *Isab.* We will be Husband and Wife to one another, dear *Theodosia*.[51]

The above issue of female emancipation also transcends class in this text. The peasant Mal Spencer, for example, sexually rejected by Sir Edward's retainer, Clod ('a country fellow'), appears shortly thereafter at the Act III sabbat '*Leading Clod in a bridle*'. Here a new witch, Madge, is inducted, and ordered by Satan to: 'Curse Heaven, Plague Mankind, go forth and be a witch.'[52] At the end of each, act-closing sabbat, the witches go out singing with anarchic, alarming and elemental enthusiasm: '*They beat the ground with Vipers, they bark, howl, hiss, cry like Screetch Owles, hollow like Owls, and make many confused noises: The Storm begins.*'[53] Such assertions of female freedom and power are interesting. The dramatic witches of Middleton, Heywood and Shadwell all have enormous fun playing elaborate tricks on the male population. They are also sexually liberated to the point of perversion (in this sense, they are sisters to Ainsworth's underworld women, as well as to the likes of Mal Spencer). In Middleton's play, for example, Hecate and her witches cruise around each night looking for young men. If nobody promising turns up, Hecate will have sex with her son, Firestone, or even the cat, her familiar Malkin:

> HECATE: Thou'rt now about some villainy?
>
> FIRESTONE: Not I forsooth. [*Aside*] Truly the devil's in her, I think.

---

[50] This anticipates her father's later comment that: 'I am a true English-man, I love the Princes Rights and Peoples Liberties, and will defend them both with the last penny in my purse, and the last drop in my veins, and dare defy the witless Plots of Papists.' Shadwell, III. This line was prudently omitted from the original text.

[51] Shadwell, I.

[52] Shadwell, III.

[53] Shadwell, I.

How one villain smells out another straight! There's no knavery but is nosed like a dog and can smell out a dog's meaning. [*To* HECATE] Mother I pray give me leave to ramble abroad tonight with the Nightmare, for I have a great mind to overlay a fat parson's daughter.

HECATE: And who shall lie with me then?

FIRESTONE: The great cat for one night mother. 'Tis but a night – Make shift with him for once.

HECATE: You're a kind son!
But 'tis the nature of you all, I see that.
You had rather hunt after strange women still
Than lie with your own mothers. Get thee gone.[54]

The point I wish to make here is that witches, in their obvious role of gothic Other to patriarchal versions of femininity, are allowed, like a medieval fool, to say and do things that would be completely taboo outside the carnival realm to which such figures belong. Like a playful regiment of Bertha Masons, they torment male authority figures, personify the frustration of the culturally-imprisoned female characters and ultimately facilitate the true desires of such heroines, although they themselves are invariably destroyed in the process, usually by fire. Such a reading may also open up Ainsworth's text to a new vista of political possibility excluded by the Weïrd Sisters, who do not seem especially powerful: they can only torment the master of the *Tiger*, they cannot destroy the ship.

The heart of all good witchcraft stories is the compact with the Devil, the model for which is concisely provided by the Inquisitors Sprenger and Kramer in their *Malleus Maleficarum*:

Now the method of profession is twofold. One is a solemn ceremony, like a solemn vow. The other is private, and can be made to the devil at any hour alone. The first method is when witches meet together in conclave on a set day, and the devil appears to them in the assumed body of a man, and urges them to keep faith with him, promising them worldly prosperity and length of life; and they recommend a novice to his acceptance. And the devil asks whether she will abjure the Faith, and forsake the holy Christian religion and the worship of the Anomalous Woman (for so they call the Most Blessed Virgin MARY), and never venerate the sacraments; and if he finds the novice or disciple willing, then the devil stretches out his hand, and so does the novice, and she swears

---

[54] Thomas Middleton, *The Witch* (c.1616) I.ii. 87–100.

with upraised hand to keep that covenant. And when this is done, the devil at once adds that this is not enough; and when the disciple asks what must be done, the devil demands the following oath of homage to himself: that she give herself to him, body and soul, for ever, and do her utmost to bring others of both sexes into his power. He adds, finally, that she is to make certain unguents from the bones and limbs of children, especially those that have been baptized; by all which means she will be able to fulfil all her wishes with his help.[55]

The Brothers, who fear women as much as they hate them, then move immediately from the theory to the practice, and offer verification of the above based on their own experiences of the seduction into the craft of a young girl in Breisach by her witch-aunt (whom they later burned alive in Strasburg). In common with the earlier gothic writers whom he admired so much, the theme of the satanic pact and eternal damnation held considerable interest for Ainsworth, as we have seen from his earliest fiction.

Ainsworth's narrative is full of deals. In the impressive introduction, when the beacon on Pendle Hill is not fired and the Pilgrimage of Grace collapses before our eyes, the warlock Nicholas Demdike of Worston ('he whose wife is a witch') tells the disgraced Abbot John Paslew that, 'I alone can save thee, and I will on one condition.' Paslew responds by denouncing the wizard as a 'bond-slave of Satan', developing Demdike's infernal credentials further by next wailing that 'It must be the demon in person that speaks thus to me!' as Demdike continues to point out the hopelessness of his situation as a renegade Catholic and an offence to the King. Demdike's response is: 'No matter who I am', which is not a denial, Demdike being both the tempted (in the pre-narrative space) and the tempter.[56] Demdike's origin is soon told, ironically growing out of the last confession of Parslew, when he tells the disguised Demdike of his guilt over denouncing a rival Cistercian monk as a witch in order to further his own career 30 years before. In an episode which would not have been out of place in Scott's *Marmion*, the accused monk, Borlace Alvetham, was walled up within a tiny cell

---

[55] James Sprenger and Heinrich Kramer, *Malleus Maleficarum*, trans. Montague Summers (1486 London: Dover, 1978), 100.
[56] Ainsworth, *The Lancashire Witches*, 15–16.

at Whalley Abbey. Borlace is, of course, Demdike, who recounts his satanic conversion in a passage which recalls the legend of the monk Theophilus, an Anglo-Saxon source of the Faust tradition. The Devil appears before him in his cell, and offers him freedom and revenge in exchange for his soul:

> 'I discerned a tall shadowy figure standing by my side.
> "Thou art mine", he cried, in accents graven forever on my memory; "but I am a generous master, and will give thee a long term of freedom. Thou shalt be avenged upon thine enemy – deeply avenged."
> "Grant this, and I am thine", I replied, a spirit of infernal vengeance possessing me. And I knelt before the fiend.'[57]

Demdike's story also announces the recurring theme of the morally destructive nature of vengeance within the text. Demdike's enemy, the Catholic Abbot Paslew, is presented as the author of the disastrous chain of events that forms the main novel. In addition to facilitating an innocent monk's fall from grace, he also vindictively curses Demdike's child, and we are told:

> As to the infant, upon whom the abbot's malediction fell, it was reserved for the dark destinies shadowed forth in the dread anathema he had uttered; to the development of which the tragic drama about to follow is devoted, and to which the fate of Abbot Paslew forms a necessary and fitting prologue.
> Thus far the veil of the future may be drawn aside. That infant and her progeny became the LANCASHIRE WITCHES.[58]

The deal Demdike had offered Paslew on Pendle Hill was not for his soul, but to baptise his daughter (later Mother Demdike). Already, it is difficult not to sympathise with the witches, which would seem to be the author's intention.

The offers, pacts and general metaphysical horse-trading introduced above continue throughout the text, as a kind of controlling moral metaphor; every major character is, or has been, tempted in the wilderness. In a desire for advancement that mirrors Paslew's confession, Thomas Potts, the self-styled witch-finder, plays upon Jennet Device's envy of her half-sister Alizon's new relationship with Alice Nutter, and tempts her into making an incriminating statement against his enemy:

---

[57] *Ibid.*, 41.
[58] *Ibid.*, 62.

'you may have attended a witch's Sabbath ... If you have seen this, and can recollect the names and faces of the assembly, it would be highly important ... Has it ever occurred to you that Alizon might be addicted to these practices? ... I cannot help thinking she has bewitched Mistress Nutter.'

'Licker, Mistress Nutter has bewitched her', replied Jennet.

'Then you think Mistress Nutter is a witch, eh?' cried Potts eagerly.

'Ey'st neaw tell ye what ey think, mon', rejoined Jennet, doggedly.

'But heae me', cried Potts, 'I have my own suspicions also – nay, more than suspicions.'

'If ye're shure, yo dunno want me', said Jennet.

'But I want a witness', pursued Potts, 'and if you'll serve as one –'

'Whot'll ye gi me?' said Jennet.

'Whatever you like', rejoined Potts.[59]

Discounting the brave but rather painful attempt at phonetic dialect, this type of examination is particularly disquieting if read in conjunction with the actual witness testimonies presented in the original Master Potts's transcripts. There is also the legend of Isole de Heton, the fallen nun and grandmother of Nicholas Demdike, who: 'invoked the powers of darkness, and proffered her soul in return for five years of unimpaired beauty', ageing like Dorian Gray when her time was up.[60] For the witches, the devil's compact is an infinite regress, as they must endlessly provide their master with innocent souls to prolong their own existences: 'Thou who seek'st the demon's aid/Know'st the price that must be paid' chants an 'awful voice' from beneath the ground during the great sabbat at the heart of the novel, to which the appropriate catechetic response from the witches is:

I do. But grant me the aid I crave,
And that thou wishest thou shalt have
Another worshipper is won,
Thine to be when all is done.[61]

---

[59] *Ibid.*, 184.
[60] *Ibid.*, 284–6.
[61] *Ibid.*, 199.

Whether or not they succeed in recruiting Alizon (who Ainsworth has made an adopted Device, beautiful, virtuous and actually of nobler birth) is a constant threat in the novel. Mistress Nutter (such an adept trader, incidentally, that she can cut deals with demons and humans with equal aplomb), along with Mothers Demdike and Chattox, has already sold her soul, but her daughter has not; Alice is determined to protect her, rather paradoxically perhaps, with black magic if necessary, while the satanic Mother Demdike is equally determined to corrupt her. She offers, for example, to give Alizon the aristocratic Richard Assheton as a lover, 'if you will only follow my counsel and do as I bid you', and plans to sacrifice Alizon to Satan to prolong her own life and take revenge on Alice, after Alizon refuses to make a deal in Malkin Tower.[62] The dramatic question constantly raised is whether or not Alizon will fall from grace, owing to the vengeance of Alice's enemies and her own desire for Assheton, or take the place of her damned birth mother in hell. It should by now be apparent that the frame for this narrative is not at all Shakespearean, but rather Miltonic and, by further rewriting *Paradise Lost*, both a return to radical Romanticism and a precursor of Victorian feminism.

It is well known that the Romantics had adopted Satan as the true hero of Milton's epic. In a passage removed from Schiller's *The Robbers*, Karl von Moor asks Spiegelberg if he has read Milton, adding, 'He who could not endure that another should be above him, and who dared to challenge the Almighty to a duel, was he not an extraordinary genius?'[63] In 'The Marriage of Heaven and Hell', Blake famously notes that 'The reason Milton wrote in fetters when he wrote of Angels & God, and at liberty when of Devils & Hell, is because he was a true poet and of the Devil's party without knowing it.'[64] Shelley similarly writes in his *A Defence of Poetry* that:

---

[62] *Ibid.*, 354.
[63] Friedrich Schiller, *The Robbers* (1781), quoted from Mario Praz, *The Romantic Agony*, trans. Angus Davidson, 2nd edn (London: Oxford University Press, 1970), 59.
[64] William Blake 'The Marriage of Heaven and Hell', Plates 5–6 (1790–1793).

Nothing can exceed the energy and magnificence of the character of Satan as expressed in *Paradise Lost*. It is a mistake to suppose that he could ever have been intended for the popular personification of evil – Milton's Devil as a moral being is as far superior to his God.[65]

Finally, upon reading *Paradise Lost* the creature of Mary Shelley's *Frankenstein*, the ultimate Romantic rewriting of Milton, tells his creator that: 'Many times I considered Satan as the fitter emblem of my condition, for often, like him, when I viewed the bliss of my protectors, the bitter gall of envy rose within me.'[66] With the exception of Mary Shelley's elegant re-evaluation of Milton, as explored in the now classic feminist readings of *Frankenstein* by, most notably Mary Poovey, Sandra Gilbert and Susan Gubar, the male Romantics (Blake being the only anomaly) were not as interested in Eve as they were Satan, often taking their implicitly female muse completely for granted. When the Romantic poet stares into a female face, he invariably sees his own, narcissistic reflection. This can be seen quite clearly in Wordsworth's 'Lines written above Tintern Abbey', where the poet sees his own childhood in Dorothy's eyes, not hers:

Of this fair river; thou, my dearest Friend,
My dear, dear Friend, and in thy voice I catch
The language of my former heart, and read
My former pleasures in the shooting lights
Of thy wild eyes. Oh! Yet a little while
May I behold in thee what I was once,
My dear, dear sister![67]

Similarly, debate over the true identity of the subject of the 'Lucy Poems' seems incongruous when we consider that she has none:

She *liv'd* unknown, and few could know
When Lucy ceas'd to be;
But she is in her Grave, and Oh!
The difference to me.[68]

---

[65] Percy Bysshe Shelley, *A Defence of Poetry* (1821).
[66] Mary Shelley, *Frankenstein* (1818), ed. Peter Fairclough, *Three Gothic Novels* (London: Penguin, 1968), 396.
[67] William Wordsworth, 'Lines written above Tintern Abbey' (1798), 116–22.
[68] Wordsworth, 'Song' (1800), 9–12.

Charlotte Brontë also recognised that the female voice seemed to be as absent in Romanticism as it would later be in the Victorian poetry of writers such as Matthew Arnold ('The Buried Life') and Coventry Patmore ('The Angel in the House' and 'The Wife's Tragedy'), and cheekily inverted Wordworth's 'Strange fits of passion I have known' in *Villette* (1853), when Miss Marchmont waits for her lover, who arrives dragged behind his horse and dying. In the original, the male rider and poetic voice imagines: '"O mercy!" to myself I cried/"If Lucy should be dead!"'[69]

Ainsworth is, as always, looking forward as well as back. There is a certain ambivalence in his work with regard to the portrayals of Satan who, in some of his guises, can be taken as vaguely heroic, yet it is the strong women of *The Lancashire Witches* that remain the most interesting characters. Ainsworth's narrative may not have the subtlety and depth of *Frankenstein*, nor the overt feminism of all the three Brontë sisters, but there is a case, as yet unmade, that can place him in the same ideological camp as Mary, Charlotte, Emily and Anne. We have already seen how Ainsworth's underworld women, Poll Maggot and Edgeworth Bess, are radically different from their sacrificial counterparts in Dickens's early fiction; these happy hookers are about the only members of the criminal cast left standing at the conclusion of *Jack Sheppard*. The year of *The Lancashire Witches*, 1848, also saw the publication of fellow Mancunian Elizabeth Gaskell's *Mary Barton*, wherein the fallen woman, Esther, fares no better than Dickens's Nancy had almost a decade previously. Against such a familiar frame, Ainsworth's witches are positively trail-blazing in their self-emancipation. As 'The Old Chevalier' remarks in the story of the same name by Isak Dinesen: 'most women, when they feel free to experiment with life, will go straight to the Witches' Sabbath. I myself respect them for it, and do not think that

---

[69] Wordsworth, 'Strange fits of passion I have known' (1800), 27–8.

I could ever really love a woman who had not, at some time or other, been up on a broomstick.'[70]

Gilbert and Gubar read *Paradise Lost* as a distillation of the endemic, institutional misogyny of Western literary culture, arguing that: 'if Eve is in so many negative ways like Satan the serpentine tempter, why should she not also be akin to Satan the Romantic outlaw'.[71] Eve, therefore, 'is the only character in *Paradise Lost* for whom a rebellion against the hierarchical status quo is as necessary as it is for Satan'.[72] Although Adam is subordinate to God, he is still the master of Eden and Eve. Eve, however, dreams of flying:

> Forthwith up to the clouds
> With him I flew, and underneath beheld
> The earth outstretched immense, a prospect wide
> And various.[73]

Parallels between Satan and Eve abound in *Paradise Lost* and, note Gilbert and Gubar: 'not only is Milton's Satan in certain crucial ways very much *like* women, he is also – enormously attractive to women'.[74]

Ainsworth's novel would seem to offer a similar reading, with his witches representing, in Blakean terms, the various emanations of Eve. In his previous, Maturin-inspired takes on temptation and fall, the protagonists were all flawed male Faustian figures prosecuting the destruction of female innocents, with only 'Mary Stukeley' offering an ambivalently drawn female tempter. In *The Lancashire Witches*, Ainsworth's previously passive female victims become suddenly very active. The Demdike dynasty is one based upon matriarchal rather than patriarchal authority, the implication being that the peasant women have fallen into grace rather than out of it, from a cultural hell of repressive fathers,

---

[70] Isak Dinesen (Karen Blixen), 'The Old Chevalier', *Seven Gothic Tales* (1934 London: Penguin, 1963), 57.
[71] Sandra M. Gilbert and Susan Gubar, *The Madwoman in the Attic* (New Haven: Yale UP, 1979), 201.
[72] Gilbert and Gubar, 202.
[73] John Milton, *Paradise Lost* (1667), V, 86–9.
[74] Gilbert and Gubar, 206.

husband, priests and landlords into a heaven of self-realisation and determination. This can be seen quite clearly in the story of the landed and independent Alice Nutter:

> A proud, poor gentleman was Richard Nutter, her late husband, and his scanty means not enabling him to keep up as large an establishment as he desired, or to be as hospitable as his nature prompted, his temper became soured, and he visited his ill-humours upon his wife, who, devotedly attached to him, to all outward appearance at least, never resented his ill-treatment.
>
> All at once, and without any previous symptoms of ailment, or apparent cause, unless it might be over-fatigue in hunting the day before, Richard Nutter was seized with a strange and violent illness, which after three or four days of acute suffering, brought him to the grave. During his illness he was constantly and zealously tended by his wife; but he displayed great aversion to her, declaring himself bewitched, and that an old woman was ever in the corner of his room, mumbling wicked enchantments against him. But as no such old woman could be seen, these assertions were treated as delirious ravings.[75]

The author adding wryly that: 'Mistress Nutter gave the best proof that she respected her husband's memory by not marrying again.' It is later revealed that Richard Nutter was jealous of his best friend, one Edward Braddyll, and made his wife a prisoner in her home. When she escaped, begging Braddyll for help, he responded by propositioning her sexually. Her husband, aided by John Device (Elizabeth's husband), pursued her, killing Elizabeth's baby daughter in a fit of jealous rage, believing her to be Alice's child. John Device came to a sticky end, drowned in a moss-pool, and Edward Braddyll, like Richard Nutter, succumbed to a painful and mysterious illness. This story also explains Alizon's parentage; she was entrusted to Elizabeth, and believed dead by Alice. Alice tells Alizon that Richard's crime was: 'hidden from the eyes of men', but not the women, who had their revenge.[76]

The innocent Alizon of course represents the young, prelapsarian Eve, and resists all temptations to the dark side, being the only one of Elizabeth Device's family to do so. The witches are Eve 'fallen', free, empowered and unrepentant

---

[75] Ainsworth, *The Lancashire Witches*, 81.
[76] *Ibid.*, 153.

(the dream of flying now a reality), with only Alice becoming a penitent and guilty Eve-figure. The head witch, Mother Demdike, is the ultimate radical feminist, choosing to rule in hell rather than serve in heaven:

> There was nothing human in her countenance, and infernal light gleamed in her strangely set eyes.
>
> 'Saw'st thou ever face like mine?' she cried. 'No, I wot not. But I would rather inspire aversion and terror than love. Love! – foh! I would rather see men shrink from me, and shudder at my approach, than smile upon me and court me. I would rather freeze the blood in their veins, than set it boiling with passion. Ho! Ho!'
>
> 'Thou art a fearful being, indeed!' exclaimed Richard, appalled.
>
> 'Fearful am I?' ejaculated the old witch, with renewed laughter. 'At last thou own'st it. Why, ay, I am fearful. It is my wish to be so. I live to plague mankind – to blight and blast them – to scare them with my looks – to work them mischief.'[77]

The aptly-named 'Mother' Demdike's inhuman and androgynous appearance, coupled with her supreme supernatural power, also casts her as the most overtly satanic-Eve correlative in the text:

> Scarcely had the last notes died away when a light shone through the dark red curtains hanging before a casement in the upper part of the tower. The next moment these were drawn aside, and a face appeared, so frightful, so charged with infernal wickedness and malice, that Richard's blood grew chill at the sight.
>
> Was it man or woman?
>
> The white beard, and the large, broad, masculine character of the countenance, seemed to denote the former, but the garb was that of a female. The face was at once hideous and fantastic – the eyes set across – the mouth awry – the right cheek marked by a mole shining with black hair, and horrible from its contrast to the rest of the visage, and the brow branded as if by a streak of blood. A black thrum cap constituted the old witch's headgear, and from beneath it her hoary hair escaped in long elf-locks … Throwing open the window, she looked forth, and demanded, in harsh imperious tones, 'Who dares to summon Mother Demdike?'[78]

---

[77] *Ibid.*, 307.
[78] *Ibid.*, 305.

As Satan's coupling with Sin in *Paradise Lost* begets death, Mother Demdike's deal with the devil has produced generations of witches. Her tower protected by a wild tempest, through which Richard must battle, the elemental Mother Demdike is also Mother Nature unrestrained, an angry goddess who seems to mock the order imposed on her realm by patriarchal society:

> Fast as Richard rose up the steep hillside, still faster did the black clouds gather over his head. No natural cause could have produced so instantaneous a change in the aspect of the sky, and the young man viewed it with uneasiness, and wished to get out of the thicket in which he was now involved, before the threatened thunderstorm commenced. But the hill was steep and the road bad, being full of loose stones, and crossed in many places by bare roots of trees. Though ordinarily surefooted, Merlin stumbled frequently, and Richard was obliged to slacken his speed. It grew darker and darker, and the storm seemed ready to burst upon him. The smaller birds ceased singing, and screened themselves under the thicket foliage; the pie chattered incessantly; the jay screamed; the bittern flew past, booming heavily in the air; the raven croaked; the heron arose from the river, and speeded off with his long neck stretched out; and the falcon, who had been hovering over him, sweeped sidelong down and sought shelter beneath an impending rock; the rabbit scudded off to his burrow in the brake, and the hare, erecting himself for a moment, as if to listen to the note of danger, crept timorously off into the long dry grass.
>
> It grew so dark at last that the road was difficult to discern, and the dense rows of trees on either side assumed a fantastic appearance in the deep gloom. Richard was now more than halfway up the hill, and the thicket had become more tangled and intricate, and the road narrower and more rugged. All at once Merlin stopped, quivering in every limb, as if in extremity of terror. Before the rider, and right in his path, glared a pair of red fiery orbs, with something dusky and obscure linked to them; but whether man or beast he could not distinguish.
>
> Richard called to it. No answer. He struck spurs into the reeking flanks of his horse. The animal refused to stir. Just then there was a moaning sound in the wood, as of someone in pain. He turned in the direction, shouted, but received no answer. When he looked back the red eyes were gone.
>
> Then Merlin moved forward of his own accord, but ere he had gone far the eyes were visible again, glaring at the rider from the wood. This time they approached, dilating, and increasing in glowing intensity till they scorched him like burning-glasses.[79]

---

[79] *Ibid.*, 303–304.

At this point, Mother Demdike *is* the forest, her spirit possessing every rock, branch and creature. This is the language of fairytale, but we can also read in it a description of hell as uncontrolled, feminine Nature, blasting Richard's horse much as Morgana Le Fey did his namesake in Arthurian legend. The battle between good and evil enacted in this amazing episode is as much a battle between matriarchal Nature and Patriarchal Culture, and deep in the woods Culture has no chance. Richard is, of course, absolutely no match for her. In accordance with Vladimir Propp's model of the folktale, Richard is given a magical agent for protection (a talisman given to him by Alice), which Mother Demdike effortlessly cons out of him, before throwing him in a dungeon with Alizon, whom he has come to rescue.[80]

Alice Nutter is similarly powerful when she first appears in the narrative, and has no trouble outwitting the avaricious magistrate Nowell and the idiot witch-finder Potts. Having tasted the forbidden fruit and the attendant freedom which it offers, she does however ultimately adopt a feminine role with which Victorian readers would find more acceptable, that of guilt-ridden penitent. The original Alice was a mysterious figure from the original trial of whom little is known, which gives the author particularly free reign with the character. As she is independent of the Demdikes and the Devices, she is not subject to the abbot's curse and has thus chosen freely to sign the dreaded parchment in return for the power she is seen to wield at the sabbat at the conventual church, where the other witches: 'bent so lowly at her coming, and rose so reverentially at her bidding'.[81] Alice, however, moves from the 'queen witch' of Book I to the 'penitent' in Book III, brought to feelings of remorse by the love of the pure Alizon:

> For the first time remorse assailed her ... This change of feeling had been produced by her newly-awakened affection for her daughter, long supposed dead, and now restored to her, only to be snatched away again in a manner which added to the sharpness of the loss. She saw herself the sport of the juggling fiend, whose aim was to win over her daughter's soul through her

---

[80] See Vladimir Propp, 'The Function of the Dramatis Personae', XIV, *Morphology of the Folktale*, trans. Laurence Scott (Austin: University of Texas, 1998), 43.
[81] Ainsworth, *The Lancashire Witches*, 198.

instrumentality, and she was resolved, if possible, to defeat his purposes. This, she was aware, could only be accomplished by her own destruction, but even this dread alternative she was prepared to embrace. Alizon's sinless nature and devotion to herself had so wrought upon her that, though she had at first resisted the better impulses kindled within her bosom, in the end they completely overmastered her.

Was it, she asked herself, too late to repent? Was there no way of breaking her compact?[82]

This is essentially a filial version of the Gretchen episode from Goethe's *Faust Part One*. Moving then towards Marlowe, Alice finally finds herself sitting before an hour-glass waiting for eternal death like Doctor Faustus, who admits 'I writ them a bill with mine own blood: the date is expired, this is the time, and he will fetch me.'[83] On her forehead she bears the mark of Satan, and as long as it remains we know she is damned; one cannot help but feel that Stoker had this in mind when Mina was similarly branded by Van Helsing's crucifix in *Dracula* (1897). The finale comes in a highly kinetic battle between Alizon and her mother's former demon familiar over Alice's immortal soul:

'Pray thou, mother!' cried Alizon.

'I cannot', replied the lady.

'I will kill her if she but makes the attempt', howled the demon.

'But try, mother, try!' cried Alizon.

The poor lady dropped on her knees, and raised her hands in humble supplication.

'Heaven forgive me!' she exclaimed.

The demon seized the hour-glass.

'The sand is out, the term has expired; she is mine!' he cried.

'Clasp thy arms tightly round me, my child. He cannot take me from thee', shrieked the agonised woman.

'Release her, Alizon, or I will slay thee likewise', roared the demon.

'Never!' she replied; 'thou canst not overcome me. Ha!' she added, joyfully; 'the brand has disappeared from her brow.'

---

[82] *Ibid.*, 317.
[83] Christopher Marlowe, *The Tragical History of the Life and Death of Doctor Faustus* (c.1589), XIX, 66–7.

'And the writing from the parchment', howled the demon; 'but I will have her notwithstanding.'

And he plunged his claws into Alice Nutter's flesh; but her daughter held her fast.

'Oh, hold me, my child – hold me, or I am lost!' shrieked the lady.

'Be warned, and let her go, or thy life shall pay for hers', cried the demon.

'My life for hers willingly', replied Alizon.

'Then take thy fate', rejoined the evil spirit.

And placing his hand upon her heart, it instantly ceased to beat.

'Mother, thou art saved – saved' exclaimed Alizon, throwing out her arms.

And gazing at her for an instant with a seraphic look, she fell backwards and expired.[84]

Alice is then burned at the stake with all the rest, but her passing is serene and her soul is saved. Whereas Ambrosio, *The Monk*, and Melmoth the Wanderer die horribly and go to hell forever in the manner of Doctor Faustus, Ainsworth's redemptive conclusion returns to Goethe's text in positive contrast to the desolate endings of 'The Spectre Bride' and *Auriol*. In Goethe's words:

Ah, look down,
Thou Rich in heaven's renown,
Turn thou the grace of thy dear face
On the fullness of my bliss;
For now my lover,
Earth's sadness over,
Comes from that world to meet me in this.[85]

As in Ainsworth's tragedy of Guy Fawkes and Viviana Radcliffe, Alizon sacrifices her life for a penitent sinner, and both achieve a state of grace as a result. When Alice and Mother Chattox challenge Mother Demdike on Pendle Hill at the climax of Book I, Alice's reply to Mother Chattox's rabid vow that she will do 'anything to avenge myself upon that murtherous hag', is: 'I do not want

---

[84] Ainsworth, *The Lancashire Witches*, 483–4.
[85] Johann Wolfgang Goethe, *Faust Part Two*, ed. and trans. Philip Wayne (1831 London: Penguin, 1979), V.

vengeance … I want only to save my child.'[86] The rebellion is over, and the hell's angel is once more the angel of the house.

The ostensibly conventional Christian conclusion to *The Lancashire Witches* does little, however, to dispel the overall impression (in common with Shadwell's play) that it can be good to be bad. The story of Alice and Alizon merely confirms that the rewards of virtue are largely spiritual, whereas the witches are seen actively to enjoy their mortal existence. The novel concludes:

> Jennet was the last of the Lancashire Witches. Ever since then witchcraft has taken a new form with the ladies of the county – though their fascination and spells are as potent as ever. Few can now escape them – few desire to do so.

> But to all who are afraid of a bright eye and a blooming cheek, and who desire to adhere to a bachelor's condition – to such I should say, 'Beware the Lancashire Witches.'[87]

Witchcraft is now a metaphor for female sexuality, which is really what it always was historically. While in flippant praise of Lancashire ladies, the author leaves the battle of the sexes raging, also suggesting that the sexual-supernatural power of women that informed his novel may have been transmuted, but that female magic is merely dormant rather than completely absent, at least in his home county.

Ainsworth always sympathised with his outlaws, obviously preferring the social freedom they seemed to symbolise compared to the political norm. His own position as a literary outsider since the Newgate Controversy might well also be read allegorically within the pages of this book. Similarly, it should be noted that *The Lancashire Witches* was written during the year of the final Chartist petition, and many Lancashire Chartists found themselves incarcerated in Lancaster Castle, the place where the Lancashire Witches met their unpleasant end.[88] Finally, and

---

[86] Ainsworth, *The Lancashire Witches*, 352.
[87] *Ibid.*, 492.
[88] See Edmund and Ruth Frow, *Manchester and Salford Chartists* (Manchester: Lancashire Community Press, 1996).

most significantly, Ainsworth's witch-women seem to anticipate what is to come in mid-Victorian women's writing.

Like the traditional gothic narrative, Ainsworth's vogue was now passing. A letter he wrote to his brother-author, the historical novelist G.P.R. James, during this period seems to signal their mutual departure from the mainstream of literature as the new generation of Victorian novelists comes of age:

> My dear James
>
> Anything I can do for you at any time you know you may command, and I shall only be too happy in the opportunity of making kindly mention in *The New Monthly Magazine* of your *Dark Scenes of History*.[89] The times are not propitious to us veterans, and literature generally has within the last two years suffered a tremendous depreciation –
>
> Do you know, I took it into my head you were the author of *Jane Eyre*, but I have altered my opinion since I read a portion of *Shirley*.[90] Currer Bell, whoever he or she may be, has certainly got some of your "trick", and I began to think you were coming upon us in fresh and more questionable shape. But *Shirley* has again perplexed me.
>
> I hope when you are next in town you will come and dine with me. It will really delight me to see you.
>
> Ever cordially yours,
>
> W. Harrison Ainsworth.[91]

Ainsworth, like his beloved outlaws, seems suddenly out of time and place, the last of a line, a fantasist in an age of fact. The last of the original English gothic novelists, soon to be pensioned off by Lord Palmerston. Although baffled by Charlotte Brontë, Ainsworth might, despite his perplexity, have paused to consider the heroines of *Jane Eyre* and *Shirley* in relation to those of his last novel. Consider, for example, little Jane Eyre's instinctive rebellion against Mrs Reed:

> 'What would Uncle Reed say to you if he were alive?' was my scarcely voluntary demand. I say scarcely voluntary, for it seemed as if my tongue

---

[89] G.P.R. James, *Dark Scenes of History* (London: T.C. Newby, 1849). Various historical events are presented as romantic tales, which would appeal to Ainsworth.
[90] *Shirley* had been published the previous month.
[91] Ainsworth, letter to G.P.R. James, November 14, 1849.

pronounced words without my will consenting to their utterance: something spoke out of me over which I had no control.

'What?' said Mrs. Reed under her breath: her usually cold, composed gray eye became troubled with a look of fear; she took her hand from my arm, and gazed at me as if she really did not know whether I were child or fiend. I was now in for it.

'My Uncle Reed is in heaven, and can see all you do and think; and so can papa and mamma; they know how you shut me up all day long, and how you wish me dead.'

Mrs. Reed soon rallied her spirits: she shook me most soundly, she boxed both my ears, and then left me without a word. Bessie supplied the hiatus by a homily of an hour's length, in which she proved beyond a doubt that I was the most wicked and abandoned child ever reared under a roof. I half believed her, for I felt, indeed, only bad feelings surging in my breast.[92]

Jane is here possessed by something which she does not fully understand herself, the devil of dissent, and the notion of the child-fiend (a controlling metaphor developed throughout the novel, Jane forever being described in supernatural or elemental terms) establishes *Jane Eyre* firmly within the Romantic/satanic tradition. In the second round, a couple of pages further on, Jane also realises for the first time that rebellion and revenge can be rather enjoyable, and she experiences the heady pleasures of the satanic:

Ere I had finished this reply, my soul began to expand, to exult, with the strangest sense of freedom, of triumph, I ever felt. It seemed as if an invisible bond had burst, and that I had struggled out into un-hoped-for liberty. Not without cause was this sentiment: Mrs. Reed looked frightened: her work had slipped from her knee; she was lifting up her hands, rocking herself to and fro, and even twisting her face as if she would cry – I was left there alone – winner of the field. It was the hardest battle I had fought, and the first victory I had gained. I stood awhile on the rug, where Mr. Brocklehurst had stood, and enjoyed my conqueror's solitude.[93]

Jane shortly enters Lowood, where her heroic struggle continues, including her rejection of the passive Christianity of Miss Temple and Helen Burns. When the Byronic Mr Rochester formally meets Jane, he famously remarks that:

---

[92] Charlotte Brontë, *Jane Eyre*, ed. Q.D. Leavis (1847 London: Penguin, 1966), 60.
[93] *Ibid.*, 69.

'No wonder you have rather the look of another world – When you came on me in Hay Lane last night, I thought unaccountably of fairy tales, and had half a mind to demand whether you had bewitched my horse.'[94]

Brontë's use of satanic symbolism is obviously much more refined that Ainsworth's tendency towards brute literalism, and she also takes the rebellion much further, leading some critics to evoke comparisons with the dangers of Chartism, much as they had done with regard to *Jack Sheppard*. Currer Bell's 'autobiography', wrote Elizabeth Rigby in *The Quarterly Review*: 'is pre-eminently an anti-Christian composition', adding, 'The tone of mind and thought which has fostered Chartism and rebellion is the same which has also written *Jane Eyre*.'[95] Miss Rigby, a middle class woman happy to be complicit in her own subjugation, also made the connection with rebellious Eve implicit in her review by stating that the daughters of Eve should accept their guilt and know their place: 'She [Jane] has inherited in fullest measure the worst sin of our fallen nature – the sin of pride.' As Gilbert and Gubar note, what disturbed Victorian critics most about Jane Eyre was her refusal to accept her position in the social order, read as 'anti-Christian' and, therefore, satanic:

> Jane Eyre is proud, and therefore she is ungrateful, too. It pleased God to make her an orphan, friendless, and penniless – yet she thanks nobody, and least of all Him, for the food and rainment, the friends, companions, and instructors of her helpless youth – On the contrary, she looks upon all that has been done for her not only as her undoubted right, but as falling far short of it.[96]

'In other words', respond Gilbert and Gubar, 'what horrified the Victorians was Jane's anger.'[97] Without actively selling her soul to Satan (unless we count her marriage to Rochester rather than St John, which is certainly on her own terms), as did Ainsworth's witches, Jane Eyre is fighting in exactly the same revolutionary war as Eve and the hell's angels. 'Humility', says the pious suitor St

---

[94] *Ibid.*, 153.
[95] Elizabeth Rigby, rev. of *Jane Eyre*, by Currer Bell, *The Quarterly Review*, 84, December 1848, 173–4.
[96] *Ibid.*
[97] Gilbert and Gubar, 338.

John, 'is the groundwork of Christian virtues',[98] but we know that Jane will never know her place in the orthodox hierarchy.

In *Shirley*, the other novel by Brontë we know 'perplexed' Ainsworth, Eve's potential omnipotence and present political impotence are further developed by her author, and the feminist revision of the Romantic dialogue with Milton continues: 'Milton was great; but was he good?' wonders Shirley rhetorically, continuing:

'His brain was right; how was his heart? He saw heaven: he looked down on hell. He saw Satan, and Sin his daughter, and Death their horrible offspring. Angels serried before him their battalions – Milton tried to see the first woman; but, Cary, her saw her not.'[99]

Alluding to the episode in Book V of *Paradise Lost* where Eve prepares food for Adam and the archangel Raphael (being only a girl), Shirley explains that: 'It was his cook that he saw.' The independent Shirley, however, sees a different Eve:

'I saw – I now see – a woman-Titan: her robe of blue air spreads to the outskirts of the heath, where yonder flock is grazing; a veil white as an avalanche sweeps from her head to her feet, and arabesques of lightning flame on its borders. Under her breast I see her zone, purple like that horizon: through its blush shines the star of evening. Her steady eyes I cannot picture; they are clear – they are deep as lakes – they are lifted and full of worship – they tremble with the softness of love and the lustre of prayer. Her forehead has the expanse of a cloud, and is paler than the earthly moon, risen long before dark gathers: she reclines her bosom on the ridge of Stilbro' Moor; her mighty hands are joined beneath it. So kneeling, face to face she speaks with God. That Eve is Jehovah's daughter, as Adam was his son.'[100]

Shirley's companion, the shy and retiring Caroline Helstone, thinks they should carry on into Church but Shirley replies: 'Caroline, I will not: I will stay out here with my mother Eve, in these days called Nature. I love her – undying, mighty being! Heaven may have faded from her brow when she fell in paradise; but all

---

[98] Brontë, *Jane Eyre*, 428.
[99] Charlotte Brontë, *Shirley*, Andrew and Judith Hook (eds) (1849 London: Penguin, 1974), 314–15.
[100] *Ibid.*, 315.

that is glorious on earth shines there still.'[101] The vision is interrupted by the symbolically-charged passing of a group of soldiers, bought into the area to quell the Luddite uprising, and by the Moore's foreman, Joe Scott, who quotes St Paul's first Epistle to Timothy as if to remind us how radical Shirley's Eve differs from her biblical counterpart: 'Let the woman learn in silence, with all subjection. I suffer not a woman to teach, nor to usurp authority over the man; but to be in silence. For Adam was first formed, then Eve.'[102]

Shirley's Eve-Titan, which Caroline considers to be pagan, refers to the six sons and six daughters of Uranus (Heaven) and Gaia (Earth), the elder-gods of Greek mythology who were overthrown by Zeus and the gods of Olympus. She has lost heaven but gained the earth, and has to kneel to look God squarely in the eye. Her titanic physical proportion also recalls Milton's Satan after the fall:

Thus Satan talking to his nearest mate
With head uplift above the wave, and eyes
That sparkling blazed; his other parts besides
Prone on the flood, extending long and large
Lay floating many a rood, in bulk as huge
As whom the fables name of monstrous size,
Titanian or Earth-born, that warred on Jove,
Briareos or Typhon, whom the den
By ancient Tarsus held, or that sea-beast
Leviathan, which God of all his works
Created hugest that swim th'ocean stream[103]

Shirley, which is all about rebellion, the Luddite riots during the Napoleonic Wars providing the historical frame, once again returns us to the implicit relationship between Eve and Satan, not as the fallen but as revolutionary heroes. As in the argument between Shirley and Joe, Brontë often reminds us of how the Bible is used to justify the subjugation of women and the exploitation of the working classes under capitalism, Christian orthodoxy making legitimate all forms of social, economic and sexual repression. With regard to the perceived role of

---

[101] *Ibid.*, 316.
[102] *Ibid.*, 322.
[103] Milton, *Paradise Lost*, I, 192–202.

women, Shirley clearly understands the false and fragmentary nature of the male gaze, with particular regard to literature. What Shirley realises needs to be done, under pain of biblical retribution, is to unite and accept all feminine emanations in life and in literature:

> 'If men could see us as we really are, they would be a little amazed; but the cleverest, the acutest men are often under an illusion about women: they do not read them in a true light: they misapprehend them, both for good and evil: their good woman is a queer thing, half doll, half angel; their bad woman almost always a fiend. Then to hear them fall into ecstasies with each other's creations, worshipping the heroine of such a poem – novel – drama, thinking it fine – divine! Fine and divine it may be, but often quite artificial – false as the rose in my best bonnet there. If I spoke all I think on this point; if I gave my real opinion of some first-rate female characters in first-rate works, where should I be? Dead under a cairn of avenging stones in half an hour.'[104]

Ainsworth being, like Milton, a comparative mythologist of sorts, was as guilty of the above as anyone in *The Lancashire Witches*, yet I cannot help but feel that Mother Demdike's first appearance atop Malkin Tower offers us another image of the Eve-Titan, another emanation to place beside Shirley's: Mother Nature unbound, angry and destructive (which we know she can be), rather than nurturing and protective; both belong to a pre-Christian mythology, both look God in the eye, both choose another path.

We know that Ainsworth read Brontë, even if he did not get the point, but we do not know if Brontë read Ainsworth. We do know, however, that the Brontës did not lead the life of romantic isolation that the English heritage industry has sold us. The family had full access to the periodicals of the day and, even if they did not concern themselves overmuch with popular literature, as Yorkshire folk they would have certainly known the legend of the Lancashire Witches. Ainsworth may well not have appreciated the full implications of his narrative, and he also put the genie firmly back into the box at its conclusion, throwing it onto the fire for good measure (as Brontë did Bertha Mason in *Jane Eyre*), but his well-established love of outlaws and powerful women at least

---

[104] Charlotte Brontë, *Shirley*, 343.

allows us to place his work back within the romantic literary tradition that leads us to the ideological concerns of the writers who succeeded him in redefining the satanic and the gothic once more. His women at least do know how to fly.

II. The Lancashire novels

The Lancashire Witches represented Ainsworth at his creative zenith, but as his letter to James suggests, he was well aware by this point in his literary career that his time was passing; his inability to understand Charlotte Brontë's early works a further indication of his rather ever-present literary anachronism. He had also misunderstood Dickens's growing maturity as an artist, writing to Crossley that *Dombey and Son* was: 'infernally bad'.[105] As already noted in the introduction to the present work, this period saw a rising generation of talent changing the face of contemporary literature, while the popular, working class audience was shifting its allegiance towards the politically-charged sensationalism of writers such as G.W.M. Reynolds. Ainsworth's fiction was fast becoming a fossil of another age, although cheap reprints of his early historical romances published by Chapman and Hall in 1849 sold extremely well; *Windsor Castle* alone shifted 30,000 copies. Nonetheless, his decline was becoming apparent and he knew it. Writing to Thackeray in 1849, Mrs Brookfield relates the following, less than flattering, anecdote:

> I am amused at your having Mr. Ainsworth at Paris – he was at Venice when we were there, and was always called 'Tiger or Tig' by Uncle Hallam, who did not know who he was till he came up one day and proffered the hand of fellowship to uncle H. on the ground of their mutual authorship. 'I am Mr. Ainsworth', as if he had been Herschel at the least, and we sat together in the Place St. Mark, eating ices and discussing you, and I recollect saying you had 'such an affectionate nature', which Mr. Ainsworth made me repeat about 3 times, pretending not to hear, and I felt I had thrown pearls before swine and been unnecessarily frank in my praise of you, and began to think he might very possibly have a feeling of jealousy about you as an author, tho' it would be

---

[105] Ainsworth, letter to Crossley, October 29 1847.

ludicrously presumptuous in him – as of all detestable writing his is the worst, I think.[106]

Given Thackeray's treatment of Ainsworth over the years, we can hardly blame him for letting his guard slip once in a while. It is also never easy to be superseded by one's protégés, and for Ainsworth this was becoming a depressingly regular occurrence.

Ainsworth's correspondence with Crossley shows that the next project was to be a sequel to either *Windsor Castle* or *The Tower of London*. It would seem, however, that reading Currer Bell had made some kind of impression on the author of *The Lancashire Witches*, as he followed this with a radical departure from his previous literary style, the downright experimental (by Ainsworth's standards), and semi-autobiographical *The Life and Adventures of Mervyn Clitheroe*: a *bildungsroman* with just a touch of the *roman à clef*.

Mervyn Clitheroe is also set in Ainsworth's native county, but there any similarity with *The Lancashire Witches* ends. Following a contemporary fashion for fictional autobiography (for example *Jane Eyre*, *Pendennis* by Thackeray, *My Novel* by Lytton, and Dickens's *David Copperfield*), Ainsworth for the first time wrote a story set entirely in his own century. The first book of *Mervyn Clitheroe* was serialised by Chapman and Hall between December 1851 and March 1852, covers designed by 'Phiz.' What makes this a particularly significant text is that, as Ainsworth's oldest friends immediately recognised, the central character is very recognisably the author himself. This was confirmed by Ainsworth in a letter to Charles Ollier:

> Having chosen an everyday subject, I have endeavoured to be as natural as possible, and most of the characters and incidents of this part of the story are taken from life and actual occurrences. The schooldays of 'Mervyn' are a mere transcript of what happened to me at the Free Grammar School at Manchester. 'Dr Longdale' and 'Mr Cane' are no exaggeration.[107] 'John Leigh' is

---

[106] 'From Mrs. Brookfield', September 4 1849, letter 624 of *The Letters and Private Papers of William Makepeace Thackeray*, vol. 2, 585.
[107] In reality Dr Jeremiah Smith and Dr Robinson Elsdale.

unchanged even in name.[108] Almost all the incidents at Nethercrofts happened to myself; and the old farmer and his wife stood in the same degree of relationship to me that they are supposed to stand to the autobiographer. My uncle always declared he would make 'a gentleman of me', by which he meant he would leave me the whole of his property, which was very considerable. But he did not do so, or probably I should not have thought it worth while to describe him. The farmhouse and its occupants are, I think, true to nature. And even 'Mrs. Mervyn', who may appear overdrawn, is taken from life, and lives at Kersal Cell ('The Anchorites'), near Manchester.

I have adopted a simple Defoe-ish style as best adapted to the subject; and I rather feared that this homely sort of narrative would not be relished, or appreciated. But you have reassured me – As you may suppose, I have abundant material, which I shall endeavour to work out as I have begun.

Thanking you, my dear Ollier, for your praises, of which I am proud.[109]

The author was obviously enjoying himself, having had, by all accounts, a very happy childhood (cynics might note that a worse one might have furnished a more successful narrative). Other characterisations were equally personal: the reserved and scholarly 'John Brideoake' was very much based upon Ainsworth's brother Gilbert as a youth, although rather poignantly John's fate is happier than the tragic Gilbert's; 'Cuthbert Spring' was based on old friend Gilbert Winter; 'Colonel Clitheroe' was Captain John Ainsworth, the author's uncle; and the plump and balding bibliophile 'Dr Foam' was not a million miles from Crossley. The hero's name itself is a combination of family and familiarity, 'Mervyn' came from the Touchets, and 'Clitheroe' (along with several other character names such as 'Massey', 'Malpas', 'Mobberley' and 'Sale'), is taken from the map of Lancashire and Cheshire. 'Apphia', the story's heroine, was the Christian name of Ainsworth's great-grandmother. Cottonborough was, of course, Manchester, and *Mervyn Clitheroe* is dedicated to: 'My contemporaries at the Manchester School'.

Ainsworth felt that *Mervyn Clitheroe* was 'better than anything I have written. There is novelty, I think, about it.'[110] Friends and critics alike seemed to

---

[108] John Leigh was an old soldier who had lost his right arm at the battle of Bunker Hill; he ran a tuck shop opposite the school gates.
[109] Ainsworth, letter to Charles Ollier, December 3 1851.
[110] Ainsworth, letter to Charles Kent, quoted from Ellis, vol. 2, 179–80.

warm to *Mervyn Clitheroe* (Charles Kent gave it an excellent review in *The Sun* for example), but Ainsworth's audience was not so ready to accept this new direction, wishing instead for another bloodthirsty tale of historical romance, the author writing to his old friend and confidante Mrs Mary Ann Hughes that:

> I am highly gratified to learn from Mrs. Touchet that you think so well of *Mervyn Clitheroe.* Though, in some respects, he resembles his father more than the rest of his brethren, he is so little like *them*, that the public scarcely seem to recognise him as one of the family. I have taken more pains with him than with some of the others, and have tried to make him a very quiet boy, so that no one should be offended by him, but I fear his simplicity and homely character may somewhat stand in his light.[111]

It is noticeable that he once more uses 'homely' to describe his character (as he had to Ollier), betraying his anxiety regarding his radical change of pace; he knew he was taking a chance in daring to develop as a writer in such a competitive marketplace. Ainsworth's disappointment is palpable in his final letter to Crossley on the subject: 'I cannot understand why it has not found favour with the general public, because I have written it carefully, and I think there is interest in the story. But I could not go on at a loss, when that loss might be serious if increased monthly. It is certainly vexatious.'[112] This was the problem, Ainsworth did not live to write so much as write to live by this point. As with *Auriol*, the serial story of *Mervyn Clitheroe* ended abruptly, the fourth issue (March 1852) therefore concluded:

> The First Part of the Adventures of Mervyn Clitheroe – 'part of a whole, yet in itself complete' – is now concluded. Some delays will probably occur in the continuation of the story. The Author regrets it, but the delay is unavoidable on his part. Unforeseen circumstances are likely to compel him to suspend, for a while, his pleasant task; – pleasant, because many of the incidents and characters have been supplied to him by his own personal recollections, while the scenes in which the events are placed have been familiar to him since childhood. Ere long he hopes to meet his friends again; bidding them, meanwhile, a kindly farewell.[113]

---

[111] Ainsworth, letter to Mrs Hughes, January 8 1852.

[112] Ainsworth, letter to Crossley, March 4 1852.

[113] Ainsworth, *The Life and Adventures of Mervyn Clitheroe*, original serial publication (March 1852).

The unforeseen circumstances were that Ainsworth had produced, in commercial if not critical terms, his first 'flop', which must have been a very nasty surprise, especially given his own particular affection for and personal investment in the work. Just as critical pressure had killed off a very promising run of innovative outlaw fiction, public pressure had once more pushed Ainsworth back into the clutches of the historical romance, just as he appeared, along with his contemporaries, to be breaking away into a new creative area. Judging by the standard of *Mervyn Clitheroe*, Ainsworth unfettered would have had a very different literary career if more of his die-hard readers had supported the serial.

Three stereotypical historical romances followed the failure of *Mervyn Clitheroe* – *The Star Chamber* (1854), *The Flitch of Bacon* (1854), and *The Spendthrift* (1857) – before Crossley managed to convince Ainsworth to complete his semi-autobiography. Eight additional numbers, then the complete novel, were published by George Routledge in 1858. This time it was reasonably well-received, but regrettably the author, once bitten twice shy, did not subsequently pursue the new style.

The young Mervyn Clitheroe is effectively an orphan; his mother dies in Chapter One and he has never met his father, who is an officer in India. He is raised by an elderly relative, Mrs Mervyn, whose great-grandfather had died for the Stuart cause in 1715, her grandfather keeping up the family tradition by being killed in the second uprising of 1745. Everyone in Mrs Mervyn's household and social circle can proudly boast of having ancestors executed as Jacobites in various grisly ways: her grandsires both had their heads stuck on spikes in the Cottonborough marketplace and much the same thing happened to the great-grandfather of her butler, Comberbach, who, being a barber, had his head set upon his own pole in 1716: 'as an example to all his brethren of the razor and strap not to meddle with affairs of state'.[114] The barber's son, who had followed in his father's footsteps, later dressed the Young Pretender's peruke during the second

---

[114] *Ibid.*, 5.

uprising; inspired to join cause and avenge his father, he also followed his dad to the block. Mervyn wonders what happened to the heads. He also spends much of his time with his rich great-uncle and aunt, the Mobberleys, at their farm, Nethercrofts, where he meets and falls foul of his arch-nemesis, Mobberley's grandnephew Malpas Sale. Mervyn attends the Free Grammar School, where he befriends the impoverished but brilliant John Brideoake, whose proud mother has fallen upon hard times; Brideoake has a sister, Apphia, whose hand Mervyn spends much of the narrative attempting to win. Mervyn is expected to inherit his great-uncle's property, but is wrongfully accused of killing a much-loved family pet and is disinherited. Mobberley repents and makes a new will, but it is stolen by the bent barber-surgeon Simon Pownall who, along with the gypsies Phaleg and Obed, is apparently an ally of Malpas Sale. Playing both sides off against the middle, Pownall and the gypsies use the secret of the will to threaten Malpas, who is due to inherit the Mobberley estate upon coming of age, and to tease Mervyn. To make matters worse, Malpas has ingratiated his way into the hearts of the Brideoakes and the Mervyns while Mervyn has been travelling in Europe; when news of this reaches Mervyn he is unable to master his temper (his fatal flaw), and writes a hasty and strongly-worded letter to Mrs Mervyn. When he returns to England he is shown the door by both families. Mervyn has a few friends left, and with the help of a disparate group of *Pickwickesque* characters (including the mysterious Major Atherton, who turns out to be his father in disguise, and the dotty occultist Old Hazilrigge), he eventually secures his inheritance. Malpas is killed in a riding accident, and the Brideoakes are revealed to be Jacobite nobility and their fortunes restored. Mrs Brideoake moderates her opinion of Mervyn, and he is finally able to marry Apphia, while best friends John Brideoake and Cuthbert Spring pair off with the daughter and sister of Hazilrigge.

The story of *Mervyn Clitheroe* does read rather like a conventional Ainsworth subplot with its lost inheritance and star-crossed lovers, but without the overall frame of great historical events and personages (which is why his fans felt so short-changed at the time) but, as they say, the devil is in the detail. The story, if clichéd (Worth uses it as an example of a common Ainsworth plot), is certainly well enough executed and written with a warm sense of humour, yet the most interesting features by far are those which give us an insight into the way in which Ainsworth saw himself as a youth, his friends and the city of his birth. This is Ainsworth's portrait of the artist as a young man, at about the age when he wrote *December Tales*:

> Though I had entered upon man's estate, I still possessed a very youthful appearance, and I have seen the upper lip of many a bewitching Andalusian dame more darkly feathered than mine was at the period in question. Some people told me I was handsome, and my tailor (excellent authority, it must be admitted) extolled the symmetry of my figure, and urged me to go into the Life Guards. But these flattering comments did not turn my head. Thus much I may say for myself, and I hope without vanity; I excelled in all manly exercises; I could run, swim, or leap as well as most young men of my day; and I had never met with a horse that I should have hesitated to mount. My habits were so active, and I was endowed with a frame so vigorous, that I scarcely knew what it was to feel fatigue. I was a hard rider, fond of shooting, and of all field sports, and had stalked deer in the Highlands, and speared the wild-boar in the woods of Germany. No one could enjoy better health than I did, and the only time I was ever laid up was owing to an accident, as I shall presently relate. To complete my personal description, I may refer to the passport which I obtained on going abroad, and where I find the following items in my *signalement*: – 'Hair, dark brown, and worn long; eyebrows, arched; eyes, blue; forehead, open; nose, straight; mouth, small; chin, round; visage, oval; complexion, rosy; beard, none; height, five feet eleven inches.' As these particulars were meant to convey some idea of me to foreign authorities, they may possibly serve the same purpose to the reader.[115]

From the numerous society reports of the young dandy as he was, as well as Maclise's equally numerous sketches and portraits, the above can be read as a fair description rather than the mere vanity of middle age. Ainsworth, like his fictional counterpart, had always cut quite a dash. Crossley does not fare quite so well physically, as he appears in the text as he was in the 1850s rather than the 1820s:

> Doctor Foam was a stout little man, with a head like an old piece of polished ivory – so perfectly bald, that I do not think there was a single hair upon it. His eyes were deeply sunk in their sockets, and his chin almost buried in the ample folds of a cravat. He wore a black coat, drab knee-breeches, and brown top-

---

[115] *Ibid.*, 129.

boots. The room smelt terribly of tobacco, as if he had just been smoking. His voice was extraordinarily husky, and he wheezed very much as he spoke; but his manner was affable, and he made me feel easy with him directly. Inquiring after Mrs. Mervyn, he launched out into praises of her, and spoke of her admirable library. I thought he had a good library of his own, as I glanced round the walls, which were covered with well-filled book-shelves; and, noticing the glance, he told me every room in the house was equally full of books, but still he was always adding to his collection; 'though where I'm to put them all I don't know', he continued, with a smile, 'and that reminds me that I've a sale to attend at Tomlinson's to-day. There are several works I have marked (putting a catalogue into his pocket) which I mean to purchase if I can, for there are other collectors besides myself in Cottonborough, and I am often out-bidden now.'[116]

From a photograph of Crossley taken c.1870 and reproduced by Ellis, this is a reasonably close likeness; what gives him away most is his literary learning, his vast private library and his equally vast generosity, to which the author draws our attention repeatedly. Dr Foam takes the young scholar Brideoake under his wing much as Crossley had done Ainsworth. These characterisations and the vivid accounts of such crucial formative places as the Chetham Library and the Free Grammar School make the first book of *Mervyn Clitheroe* essential reference for any biographer of Ainsworth.

Most importantly of all, we have Ainsworth's own description of Manchester at the height of its industrial prosperity, the cityscape dominated by giant warehouses and ostentatiously gothic public buildings, reflecting an obscenely wealthy mercantile class who had left the cramped city centre to their new workforce. The dichotomy of extreme wealth matched by equally extreme poverty is not lost on Ainsworth (who had himself written a political pamphlet on the condition of the Manchester poor); neither is the excessive pollution. As a middle class Mancunian himself however, he does seek to find a balance which is generally absent from better known contemporary accounts of this potent symbol of Victorian industrial capitalism. His description of Mervyn entering the city is well worth quoting in full:

---

[116] *Ibid.*, 65.

What a wondrous town is Cottonborough! How vast – how populous – how ugly – how sombre! Full of toiling slaves, pallid from close confinement and heated air. Full of squalor, vice, misery: yet also full of wealth and all its concomitants – luxury, splendour, enjoyment. The city of coal and iron – the city of the factory and the forge – the city where greater fortunes are amassed, and more quickly, than in any other in the wide world. But how – and at what expense? Ask yon crew of care-worn men, wan women, and sickly children, and they will tell you. Look at yon mighty structure, many-windowed, tall-chimneyed, vomiting forth clouds of smoke, to darken and poison the wholesome air. Listen to the clangour and the whirl of the stupendous and complicated machinery within. Count the hundreds of pale creatures that issue forth from it at meal-times. Mark them well, and say if such employment be healthy. Yet these poor souls earn thrice the wages of the labourer at the plough, and therefore they eagerly pursue their baneful taskwork. Night comes; the mighty mill is brilliantly lighted up, and the gleam from its countless windows is seen afar. It looks like an illuminated palace. Come nearer, and you may hear the clangour and the whirl still going on, and note the steady beat of the huge engine, that, like the heart of a giant, puts all in motion; and you may seethe white faces flitting past, and the young girls and boys still toiling on, sweltering beneath the glaring gas that consumes the vital air. The owner of that mill, and the worker of that vast machinery of flesh and blood, iron and steam – for all are mere machines with him – is rich, and will soon be richer – richer than many a prince. And he will strain the money-getting principle to the utmost, for the power has been given him. And there are a thousand such in Cottonborough. There Mammon has set up his altars: there his ardent votaries are surest of reward. Ugly and black is Cottonborough, shrouded by smoke, tasteless in architecture, boasting little antiquity, and less of picturesque situation; yet not devoid of character strongly impressive, arising from magnitude, dense population, thronged streets, where the heavy wagon with its bales of goods takes place of the carriage, vast warehouses, and a spacious and bust 'Change – the resort of the wealthiest merchants of the realm. Active and energetic are its inhabitants, enterprising, spirited, with but one thought – one motive – one aim, and one end – MONEY. Prosperous is Cottonborough – prosperous beyond all other cities – and long may it continue so; for, with all its ugliness, and all its faults – and they are many – I love it well.

Some such thoughts crossed me as I approached the large and smoky town, though, doubtless, as I now record them, they have got mixed up with impressions subsequently received. And it is only right to add, that, of late years, considerable ameliorations have been made by the millowners, and the hours of labour limited, from which causes the health, condition, and morals of the persons employed, especially the girls and children, have been materially improved. But I could not help contrasting the careworn countenances and emaciated frames of the fustian-jackets I now encountered, with the cheerful, ruddy visages, and hardy limbs of the country people I had left; and I thought how infinitely preferable was the condition of the latter. The women, too, and the young girls – how different were those sallow faces, bleached like their own calico, from the rosy-cheeked, brown-armed damsels of Marston!

I passed through the far-spreading suburbs, consisting for the most part of long rows of mean-looking habitations of red brick, with the occasional bare spaces, which had once been fields, and still retaining a few consumptive bushes of thorn to show where hedges had grown, but otherwise caked over with cinders, or receptacles for rubbish; I passed by many public-houses; several Methodist chapels; an ugly, formal church, part brick, part stone – (a magnificent Roman Catholic temple has since been erected in the same neighbourhood); more rows of red brick houses, but of a better description, and neater, with low iron rails in front, to fence them from the road, and bright brass plates on the doors; huge factories, whose smoke was blackening the air, and blotting out the sun; little streams that ran like frothing ink, and into which the mills and dye-works discharged their steaming and livid waters; and, crossing a bridge over a river, into which all these inky currents poured, I entered the town.

All looked dark, dirty, and disagreeable. When I left Marston – and even a few miles off – the sun was shining brightly; but now imperfectly distinguished through the canopy of smoke, the luminary looked like a great red ball, – as it does through a London November fog. The streets were almost ankle-deep in black sludge, and where the frost had maintained its power, the snow had become the colour of soot. The very houses seemed to wear an unusually dingy aspect, as if the black snow had melted into them, and stained them of its own hue. The fog and smoke appeared to have got down everybody's throat, for almost all the people I met were coughing, and I myself felt affected by the reeky atmosphere, to an extent that made my eyes smart and water. I would have got on faster if I could, but my course was impeded by ponderous waggons laden with heavy bales of cotton, carts, hand carts, and numerous other vehicles, and I was compelled to proceed at a slow pace through the long thoroughfare intersecting the town from south to north. The eye found little pleasurable to rest on, but much that was disagreeable and even distressing; and the ear constantly caught the sharp click of the pattern, and the clamp of the wooden clog – for clogs are much worn in Cottonborough.

Amid the crowd, which was constantly increasing, as the tide poured in towards the centre of the town, there were many haggard faces that told of want and disease, many miserable, famished children, without shoes and stockings, trampling through the mire. Then there were the sots at the doors of the public-houses, with the recruiting-sergeant amongst them, holding out his lures, by which some of them were sure to be taken. Then came another wide thoroughfare, leading to the quays along the banks of the Ater, and to a bridge connecting Cottonborough with its sister town of Spinnyford; but my way not being along it, I passed by a large butchers' shambles, held under a low roof, approached by low brick archways, and delightfully inconvenient; by a great coaching-house, with several stage-coaches before it; by a long range of warehouses, with here and there an old black and white chequered house among them (mementoes of other days, and looking quite beautiful amid so much architectural uniformity, not to say deformity); by another bridge leading to Spinnyford; and leaving the Square and the Exchange, and several other public places unvisited, I descended the eminence on which the fine old Collegiate Church is situated, crossed the Ink, and was right glad some quarter of an hour afterwards to find myself under the roof of the sequestered Anchorite's.[117]

In common with the Manchester of Gaskell's *Mary Barton*, Ainsworth makes much of the contrast between countryside and city life. Although Mervyn asserts his love of this city of contrasts, he cannot help but return again and again to the squalor that surrounds him (the corrosive air, ankle-deep sludge and creeping black snow are also particularly memorable details of industrial and moral pollution as all is sacrificed in pursuit of profit), and he is happy to escape into the preserved Georgian haven of Mrs Mervyn's household. We might also usefully compare 'Cottonborough' to the better known accounts of Manchester from James Kay's *The Moral and Physical Condition of the Working Classes Employed in the Cotton Manufacture in Manchester* (1832), Engels's *The Condition of the Working Class in England* (1844–5), and Dickens's 'Coketown' (Preston), the setting of *Hard Times* (1854); Dickens having first seen the cotton mills of Lancashire on a visit up North in the company of Ainsworth and Forster in November 1838. Kay feared that the diseases of the poor would cross the class divide, while Engels's famous description of Allen's Court below Ducie Bridge in Manchester followed the trend (in common with Kay) of Victorian social explorers to ignore the individual citizens in favour of the city, as already noted in the third chapter of the present work:

The view from this bridge, mercifully concealed from mortals of small stature by a parapet as high as a man, is characteristic for the whole district. At the bottom flows, or rather stagnates, the Irk, a narrow, coal-black, foul-smelling stream, full of *débris* and refuse, which it deposits on the shallower right bank. In dry weather, a long string of the most disgusting, blackish-green, slime pools are left standing on the bank, from the depth of which bubbles of miasmatic gas constantly arise and give forth a stench unendurable even on the bridge forty or fifty feet above the surface of the stream. But besides this, the

---

[117] *Ibid.*, 60–62.

stream itself is checked every few paces by high weirs, behind which slime and refuse accumulate and rot in thick masses. Above the bridge are tanneries, bone mills, and gasworks, from which all drains and refuse find their way into the Irk, which receives further the contents of all the neighbouring sewers and privies. It may be easily imagined, therefore, what sort of residue the stream deposits. Below the bridge you look upon piles of *débris*, the refuse, filth, and offal from the courts on the steep left bank; here each house is packed close behind its neighbour and a piece of each is visible, all black, smoky, crumbling, ancient, with broken panes and window-frames. The background is furnished by old barrack-like factory buildings. On the lower right bank stands a long row of houses and mills; the second house being a ruin without a roof, piled with *débris*; the third stands so low that the lowest floor is uninhabitable, and therefore without windows or doors. Here the background embraces the pauper burial ground, the station of the Liverpool and Leeds railway, and, in the rear of this, the Workhouse, the 'Poor Law Bastille' of Manchester, which, like a citadel looks threateningly down from behind its high walls and parapets on the hilltop, upon the working-people's quarters below.[118]

Engels's political point is well made, yet he offers a soulless sociological scenario, albeit flavoured at times with a positively Swiftian scatology. It is also an outsider's view, and therefore necessarily lacking the social detail, topographical flourishes and affection of Ainsworth's account in *Mervyn Clitheroe*. Dickens's perspective of Coketown/Preston seems to offer a more developed use of the material already apparent in Ainsworth's description of the industrial urban environment and its masters and slaves in his famous opening to Chapter Five of *Hard Times*, 'The Key-note':

It was a town of red brick, or of brick that would have been red if the smoke and ashes had allowed it; but as matters stood it was a town of unnatural red and black like the painted face of a savage.

It was a town of machinery and tall chimneys, out of which interminable serpents of smoke trailed themselves for ever and ever, and never got uncoiled.

It had a black canal in it, and a river that ran purple with ill-smelling dye, and vast piles of building full of windows where there was a rattling and a trembling all day long, and where the piston of the steam-engine worked monotonously up and down, like the head of an elephant in a state of melancholy madness. It contained several large streets all very like one another, and many small streets still more like one another, inhabited by people

---

[118] Friedrich Engels, *The Condition of the Working Class in England*, W.O. Henderson and W.H. Chaloner (trans. and eds) (1844–5 Oxford: Basil Blackwell, 1971), 60–61.

equally like one another, who all went in and out at the same hours, with the same sound upon the same pavements, to do the same work, and to whom every day was the same as yesterday and to-morrow, and every year the counterpart of the last and the next.[119]

Here Dickens's language outdistances anything Ainsworth was likely to produce, and his apparent social reductivism is essential to his anti-Utilitarian argument rather than indicative of an indifferent gaze – we are as much seeing Coketown through the eyes of Gradgrind and Bounderby as we are Dickens at this point, and his subsequent narrative is to be one of the triumph of the individual spirit over the awful uniformity of industrial society. As is well known, Dickens's famous 'Condition of England' novel side-steps the working class movement in favour of an appeal to Christian brotherhood, much as Gaskell had done in *Mary Barton*, where Chartism does not come off much better than the trade unions do in *Hard Times*. Engels was, of course, effectively researching the *Communist Manifesto*. With Ainsworth, as we have seen, it is virtually impossible to identify a stable political agenda in his writing – in this case an advantage for the historian. I would offer 'Cottonborough' as one of the few genuinely objective accounts of Manchester to be found in this period.

We must not leave *Mervyn Clitheroe* however, without noting Ainsworth's radically different approach to the supernatural in this text as compared to the ghostly goings on that characterised the majority of his fictional output. As we have seen, Ainsworth invariably introduces a character into his narratives who is well versed in all arts necromantic, most usually an alchemist or a descendant of alchemists. In *Mervyn Clitheroe* we are offered Norbury Radcliffe Hazelrigge (or 'Old Hazy') of Owlarton Grange, who firmly believes himself to be such a necromancer, but is in fact nothing of the sort. As Mervyn puts it: 'He seems to have the organ of credulity rather extensively developed.'[120] Through a humorous deconstruction of Hazelrigge's dearly held beliefs, Ainsworth appears to enjoy himself negating some of his very own stock supernatural devices.

---

[119] Dickens, *Hard Times* (1854), Works, 17–18.
[120] Ainsworth, *Mervyn Clitheroe*, 180.

Hazelrigge is introduced to Mervyn and his readers upon waking from a prophetic dream not unlike the legend of the lime tree which opens *Rookwood*:

> 'I dreamed that the old yew-tree in the churchyard yonder, with the bench round it, was struck by lightning and withered. This I dreamed last night – three times, sir – and I resolved to drive over this morning, and ascertain, from personal inspection, whether the yew-tree had really sustained any damage from the fiery element.'[121]

The fact that he finds it 'fair and flourishing' does not detract from his earnest reading of the meaning of the vision, citing several authorities from his personal collection of occult books. Mervyn likes him immediately, and makes up a few authorities to provide a more positive interpretation. The detail of the bench surrounding the tree in question should give us a clue to the author's intention here, lawn furniture tending not, on the whole, to act as a gothic signifier. More is to follow. Owlarton Grange also has its very own tapestried chamber, a room which Hazelrigge is convinced is haunted by the miser Old Clotten who was murdered by his servant Jotham Shocklach. The legend being that Shocklach killed Clotten while the latter was counting his money in a priest hole; the secret door shut behind them and Shocklach died slowly in company of his dead master and his fortune. A 'singular old portrait' depicting the pair still hangs in the room. Mervyn spends a night in the haunted room, and the author proceeds to play upon our gothic expectations:

> Once more I was alone in the haunted chamber. Again I glanced at the portraits of the miser and his murderous servant, and, now that I was acquainted with the legend connected with the picture, it impressed me still more powerfully. In consequence, no doubt, of the story I had heard from Old Hazy, superstitious fancies crowded thickly upon me, and all my efforts to shake them off were unavailing. As on the previous night, I drew back the heavy curtain from before the deep bay-window, and allowed the moonlight to stream into the chamber. I took some precautions which I had not deemed needful on the former occasion. Taking my case of duelling-pistols from my portmanteau, I loaded the weapons, and laid them on the table. Then seating myself in an easy-chair, I determined to keep watch, but in spite of my resolutions of vigilance, sleep after awhile stole over my eyelids.

---

[121] *Ibid.*, 178.

How long I slumbered I cannot say, but I was suddenly aroused by a strange and startling noise, which I at once recognised as the ghostly knocking described by Cuthbert Spring. I listened intently. After the lapse of about a minute there was another heavy blow as if dealt by a mallet – a third – a fourth – up to ten; with the same intervals between each.

The unearthly sounds seemed to proceed from the lower part of the wall on the left of the bed. But they did not appear to be stationary. On the contrary, the blows were dealt at various points inside the wainscot.

I am not ashamed to own that I felt appalled. My taper had burnt out, and the wan light of the moon, which must have been struggling with passing clouds, only served to make darkness visible. The further end of the chamber in which the bed stood was plunged in deep shade.

While peering into this obscurity I fancied I saw a figure standing near the bed. It was perfectly motionless, and scarcely distinguishable; but as far as I could make it out, the attire of the phantom – or semblance of attire – was like that worn by Jotham Shocklach, as represented in the portrait – while the features, as far as they could be discerned – were those of the murderous servant. Something like a thin shroud hung over the lower part of the figure, and in its right hand it held a mallet.

Terror completely transfixed me. I strove to speak – but my tongue clove to the roof of my mouth. My limbs refused their office, and I could not grasp my pistols. The figure remained motionless and stationary, half concealed by the dark drapery of the bed, from which it could scarcely be distinguished. As I gazed at it, for I could not withdraw my eyes, it began to glide slowly towards me. No sounds that I could detect attended its progress.

My terror increased. At length the phantom came under the influence of a ray of moonlight streaming athwart the chamber, which lighted up its ghastly and cadaverous features. It then paused; and at that moment I recovered my firmness, for I felt convinced that I had to do with one of mortal mould. Starting to my feet, I demanded of the ghost, in tones that sounded hoarse and strange in my own ears – who it was, – and what it wanted?[122]

After this terrific build-up, the ghost is revealed to be Hazelrigge's spiritual adviser Dr Hooker, the barber-surgeon Simon Pownall in disguise. Mervyn has seen this act before, when Pownall pretended to be the ghost of his Uncle Mobberley in Marston Churchyard at the conclusion of Book I. We might argue that the author has belatedly decided to adopt the technique of Mrs Radcliffe, yet this is unlikely; Ainsworth seems to be writing an early 'thriller', while rewriting

---

[122] *Ibid.*, 219–20.

his previous gothic narratives and, perhaps, moving with the times. There could be ghosts in Early Modern history, but not in Victorian Britain. Pownall, who knows that there is one born every minute, has been posing as an eminent scholar of the black arts in order to trick Hazelrigge out of his fortune. The conclusion to the Owlarton Grange episode is one of pure slapstick, a pastiche in many ways of the episode in *Guy Fawkes* where John Dee raises the spirit of Elizabeth Orton:

> The chief wizard, whom I took to be Simon, produced a wallet from under his cloak, and brought out a human skull and cross-bones, the dried skins of toads, lizards, adders, and other reptiles, and disposed them in a circle round the cloth. While he was thus employed, the second wizard produced a little iron trivet with some combustibles; and these he placed outside the mystic ring.

> The pair of conjurors then marched thrice round the magic circle, and seemed from their gestures to be muttering spells. This done, they paused, and the second wizard, whom I took for Old Hazy, brought forth a large book bound in black parchment, which I at once recognised as the grimoire he had shown me in his sanctum.

> Opening this magical volume, he pronounced some strange sounding words from it, which might be intended as an incantation, while his companion stepped into the magic circle and began to trace certain lines upon it with the points of his fingers.

> By this time my patience having become exhausted, I determined to put an end to the scene. When, therefore, the second wizard summoned some spirit, with a tremendous name, to appear, I did not wait for the response, but rushing forward, and shouting out, 'You have raised a spirit you did not expect!' I snatched the grimoire from the hands, and with the ponderous volume buffeted his companion soundly on the head and shoulders.[123]

Mervyn unfortunately picks the wrong wizard, and soundly drubs poor old Mr Hazelrigge. We cannot say for sure that Ainsworth was lampooning himself and his readers, but the suspicion remains nonetheless. Had he pursued this course, he may well have moved stylistically towards mystery writing, and perhaps have given Wilkie Collins a run for his money. As it is *Mervyn Clitheroe* is unique; it remains a significant anomaly in Ainsworth's bibliography.

---

[123] *Ibid.*, 256.

As *Mervyn Clitheroe* turned out to represent another creative ending rather than a new beginning, it is in every way appropriate that this period also marks the end of Ainsworth's time at Kensal Manor House. He moved to Arundel Terrace, Brighton in 1853, selling his beloved horses and dismissing his servants and ceasing forever to play a part in London literary life. Ainsworth's extravagant lifestyle over the last twelve years at the Manor House had left his finances severely depleted; his magazines had also devalued drastically and were not selling well, while his literary works could no longer command the kind of fees he had become accustomed to in the 1840s. In terms of popular fiction, Ainsworth was now being rapidly eclipsed by the rising stars of writers such as Wilkie Collins, Anthony Trollope and Charles Reade. In the words of his biographer: 'the Fifties mark the close of Ainsworth's meridian in both a literary and a social sense'.[124]

The remaining Lancashire novels were not written until the 1870s. Like Mrs Mervyn's household, *The Manchester Rebels of the Fatal '45* (1873), *Preston Fight* (1875), *The Leaguer of Lathom* (1876) and *Beatrice Tyldesley* (1878) are all pledged to the Jacobite cause.

In later life, Ainsworth's thoughts turned more and more towards his native city, exhibiting a desire to chronicle its history in much the same way that he had so successfully done with London over the long years. As soon as he completed another Jacobite romance, *Boscobel* (1872), the tale of Charles Stuart's attempts to elude Cromwell's forces and escape to France after the Royalists were defeated at the Battle of Worcester in 1651 (in terms of narrative chronology, this is a prequel to *Ovingdean Grange*, 1860), for *The New Monthly Magazine*, Ainsworth wrote to his historical advisor Crossley that:

> I am already casting about for a subject for a new story, and shall be very glad of a suggestion from you.
>
> I have an idea of opening the new tale with a picture of Manchester in 1745, during the stay of Prince Charles. Doctor Byrom and a good many other personages might be introduced, with Colonel Townley, the Deacons, Jenny

---

[124] Ellis, vol. 2, 196.

Dawson, Syddall, and the Jacobite clergy.[125] I think the period is better than 1715. Written in a quiet sort of style, I think a sketch of Manchester in 1745, with the society of the period, would be interesting.

PS. Mention any subject that occurs to you on any period.[126]

This project became *The Manchester Rebels of the Fatal '45*, published in three volumes by the Tinsley Brothers for the pitiful fee of £150; the first edition appeared under the telling title of *The Good Old Times* until it was discovered that a book of the same title was already in print by Anne Manning. *The Manchester Rebels* was dedicated to Ainsworth's old friend from the D'Orsay days, Benjamin Disraeli, 'with every sentiment of respect and admiration'.[127]

Northern Jacobites had already paid dearly for their involvement in the previous uprising of 1715; following Ainsworth's literary chronology, I offer the details of the 'fifteen' in my later remarks on *Preston Fight*. Nonetheless, Manchester raised a regiment and the city was occupied by the Young Pretender Charles Edward Stuart himself. This is in part explained by Manchester's curious civic status. The city had no borough charter, despite its rapid industrial expansion by the standards of the day, and was consequently somewhat isolated from Westminster, the hand of national government being much ignored in turn; it was also bitterly divided by religious factions, and many a family was raised according to Jacobite principles and prepared for another uprising. As Ainsworth shows in his text, influential figures such as the Reverend John Clayton and Dr Byrom ensured that Manchester remained spiritually Jacobite. Charles Edward Stuart landed at Eriskay with a tiny band of followers in June 1745. After an initially muted response from the now cautious Highland clans, he remarkably managed to capture Perth and Edinburgh, declaring the Union dissolved. Charles went on to defeat Sir John Cope at Prestonpans, his now 5,000-strong army beginning to represent a genuine challenge to George II; he crossed the border, took Carlisle

---

[125] Those named being local heroes for their involvement in the ill-fated Manchester Regiment of Charles Edward Stuart.

[126] Ainsworth, letter to Crossley, November 4 1872.

[127] Ainsworth, dedication, *The Manchester Rebels of the Fatal '45* (1873 Manchester: Printwise 1992).

and headed for Lancashire. Despite Charles's enthusiastic welcome in Manchester, the rest of the English Jacobites stayed away and his forces got no further south than Derby, where his officers convinced him to retreat or be soundly defeated. This was a terrible scenario: Charles's choice was between the humiliation of retreat or a potential military disaster. The disaster came anyway, as government troops pursued the retreating army, growing smaller by the day as soldiers deserted in droves, and slaughtered them at the Battle of Culloden in April 1746. Charles escaped to France, where he drank himself to death in 1788. State reprisals were brutal, bloody and absolute, and the Jacobite cause was broken forever. This story forms the backdrop for Scott's seminal historical novel *Waverley*.

The *Manchester Rebels* is Ainsworth's Mancunian version of *Waverley*. The story follows the fortunes of prominent Jacobite citizens and their children. In Book I, while the Young Pretender and his Highland Army march on Manchester, the former argue about the implications of pledging allegiance to the Stuarts once more (remembering the rebellion of 1715), and the latter fall in love with the romance of the cause and each other. Book II, the most interesting and well-crafted section of the narrative, details the occupation of Manchester by Charles Edward Stuart. Books III to V chronicle the rebel army's march to Derby, the retreat, the siege of Carlisle and the final rout; like Scott before him, Ainsworth does not describe the final Battle at Culloden. Book VI follows the defeated heroes, now traitors, to their inevitable fate and they are hanged, drawn and quartered on Kennington Common. The political moral of the narrative, voiced several times by author and characters alike, is that the Prince failed tactically by not attacking Cumberland's forces at Lichfield, and that even a glorious defeat would have been preferable to a retreat without engagement. A subplot deals with the tragic love story of Helen Carnegie and Sergeant Erick Dickson. Erick is sentenced to death by court martial for killing a superior officer, the dastardly Captain Lindsay, who is obsessed with Helen; Helen throws herself in front of the firing squad and dies with her lover. Ainsworth presents Athertone Legh as 'our hero', although the dashing Jacobite Captain Jemmy Dawson seems a more likely contender. In a typical Ainsworth plot device, Legh is really Conway Rawcliffe, dispossessed of his birthright by his wicked uncle Sir Richard when a baby. Conway is the only leading Jacobite character to survive the narrative; he is pardoned by the Duke of Cumberland and marries his beautiful cousin, Constance, the happy couple taking up residence at Rawcliffe Hall. Similarities with the conclusion of *Waverley* should be noted: by saving the life of the English Colonel, Talbot, during the Battle of Prestopans when the Jacobite forces are routed, Waverley secures a pardon for his treason, but his friends are not spared during the Highland clearances which follow the decisive victory of the English Hanovarians at Culloden, and Mac-Ivor and Evan Dhu are executed. Waverley, meanwhile, marries Rose Bradwardine.

By his own admission, what Ainsworth is doing here is retelling the stories of elderly relatives and family friends, upon whom Mrs Mervyn and her friends had already been based in *Mervyn Clitheroe*. *The Manchester Rebels* is therefore the story that is ever present but not told in *Mervyn Clitheroe*. Ainsworth describes the construction of the narrative, its inspiration and historical sources, in his Preface:

> All my early life being spent in Manchester, where I was born, bred, and schooled, I am naturally familiar with the scenes I have attempted to depict in this Tale.

> Little of the old town however, is now left. The liver of antiquity if any such should visit Manchester – will search in vain for those picturesque black and white timber habitations, with pointed gables and latticed windows, that were common enough sixty years ago. Entire streets, embellished by such houses, have been swept away in the course of modern improvement. But I recollect them well. No great effort of imagination was therefore needed to reconstruct the old town as it existed in the middle of the last century.

> When I was a boy, some elderly personages with whom I was acquainted were kind enough to describe to me events connected with Prince Charles's visit to Manchester, and the stories I then heard made a lasting impression upon me. The Jacobite feeling must have been still strong among my old friends, since they expressed much sympathy with the principal personages mentioned in the Tale – for the gallant Colonel Townley, Doctor Deacon and his unfortunate

sons, Jemmy Dawson, whose hapless fate has been so tenderly sung by Shenstone, and, above all, for poor Tom Syddall. The latter, I know not why, unless it be that his head was affixed on the old Exchange; has always been a sort of hero in Manchester.

The historical materials of the story are derived from the CHEVALIER DE JOHNSTONE'S *Memoirs of the Rebellion*, and DR. BERT WARE'S excellent account of Prince Charles's sojourn in the town, appended to the *History of the Manchester Foundations*. But to neither of these authorities do I owe half so much as to Beppy Byrom's delightful Journal, so fortunately discovered among her father's papers at Kersal Cell, and given by DR. PARKINSON in the *Remains of John Byrom*, published some twenty years ago, by the Chetham Society.[128]

The preface is a telling one, the author's nostalgia for the old city is very prominent within the text, comparisons made constantly between Manchester as it was (not only in 1745 but in the author's own Regency youth) and the dirty, industrial metropolis it had become by the second half of the nineteenth century. This nostalgia is further informed by romantic tales recollected from childhood. Whether consciously or no, Ainsworth is again following Scott who had written in a postscript to *Waverley* that:

> It was my accidental lot, though not born a Highlander, (which may be an apology for much bad Gaelic) to reside, during my childhood and youth, among persons of the above description; and now, for the purpose of preserving some idea of the ancient manners of which I have witnessed the almost total extinction, I have embodied in imaginary scenes, and ascribed to fictitious characters, a part of the incidents which I then received from those who were actors in them. Indeed, the most romantic parts of this narrative are precisely those which have a foundation in fact.[129]

Like Scott, Ainsworth has invested much of himself in his work, writing to Crossley at its conclusion: 'No one I think could have written it but myself, and though I am not altogether satisfied with what I have done, I believe that the tale will become popular in Manchester.'[130] The novel was indeed particularly popular in Manchester, Manchester Public Library statistics showing it to have been as popular as Ainsworth's 'classics' such as *The Tower of London, The Lancashire*

---

[128] Ainsworth, preface, *The Manchester Rebels*.
[129] Scott, *Waverley*, 340.
[130] Ainsworth, letter to Crossley, October 10 1873.

Witches, *Old St. Paul's* and *Windsor Castle*. The local journalist Edward Mercer, in a retrospective on Ainsworth, explained this obvious appeal:

> We doubt whether Ainsworth ever told a tale more interesting to a Manchester born reader – As a plot it is smooth and straightforward as the alphabet; as history its main incidents are true; as a description of Manchester and Manchester life at the time it is the more realistic as the scenery is, so to say, allowed to draw itself, and the characters were all real men and women with well-known figures, traits and dispositions. Ainsworth's style is here at its lightest, and its very simplicity adds so much to the verisimilitude of the dialogue that he might have seen and heard all he relates, might have been an actual participator in the events that happen. Perhaps the secret of this is that he was born in the town and personally knew every street in it, and – that he often heard (from lips repeating what eyes had seen and ears had heard) the doings in Manchester at first hand.[131]

Mercer was making much the same argument I offered above regarding *Mervyn Clitheroe*. Although Mercer's description of a 'straightforward' story may be damning by faint praise (recalling a common English Philistine tendency to reject any form of challenging or experimental art in favour of that which is representational and immediately accessible), it is still a point well made; equally, no-one could praise Dickens's *Hard Times* for his linguistic verisimilitude. *The Manchester Rebels* remains, however, strangely out of place in literary history. It reflects Ainsworth's growing sense of age and isolation from contemporary Victorian Britain, and would have been a huge commercial success if it had appeared in print when the historical novel was still in vogue. Almost 60 years after *Waverley*, it is something of an anachronism. As Constance Rawcliffe exclaims to Atherton Legh: 'With such exalted sentiments, 'tis a pity you did not live in the days of chivalry.'[132] She might just as well have been addressing her author.

Ainsworth continued the Lancashire Jacobite project with what was to become *Preston Fight, or The Insurrection of 1715. A Tale*, as always running the idea past Crossley in advance:

---

[131] *Manchester Evening Chronicle*, December 24 1904.
[132] Ainsworth, *The Manchester Rebels*, 94.

I have already commenced a new story which I intend to call *The Last Lord Derwentwater*. It will relate, as you will at once comprehend, to the Rebellion of 1715. 'Preston Fight' may be made very effective I think. Lord Derwentwater, Lord Widdrington, General Forster, and Brigadier Mackintosh are well contrasted. Dr. Hibbert-Ware's *Lancashire during the Rebellion of 1715* will furnish me with ample material. Can you suggest a better title for the new story than the one I have selected?[133]

Ainsworth is again tapping into a rich vein of regional history, backed up once more by the Chetham Society, which had previously published Hibbert-Ware's history.

When George I acceded to the British throne in 1714 he did not immediately endear himself to his subjects; he never bothered to learn English and clearly preferred Hanover to Britain. The last decade of the previous century had already seen Jacobite resistance in both Scotland and Ireland. The Highland uprising collapsed after defeat at the Battle of Killiecrankie in 1689 and James Edward Stuart, the Old Pretender, who had been hanging around in Ireland, finally fled to the continent after his forces were decisively defeated at the Battle of the Boyne in 1690. More alarming for the new monarch, James had tried, unsuccessfully, to invade Scotland with French troops in 1708, and the English Tory party had continued to maintain a flirtatious contact with him across the water. The Hanovarian succession ended any political chance of a peaceful Stuart restoration, and open Jacobite rebellion broke out in 1715. It was a desperate gamble. The cause received no support from Louis XIV, or his successor the Regent Orléans, and the British government, knowing what was coming, suspended habeas corpus and reinforced the army. The original conspirators, mostly Anglican Tories, had already failed in the south when rebel leaders met at Greenrig, near the seat of Lord Derwentwater, hoping to march on Newcastle. Their intention was to raise revolts in the West Country and the north of England, where there remained a concentration of old Catholic families and attendant Jacobite sympathies. Ainsworth had, it will be remembered, already explored this

---

[133] Ainsworth, letter to Crossley, December 21 1874.

political geography in *Guy Fawkes*, and it is also interesting to note that Paul Kléber Monod sees the 'fifteen' as bearing more than a little resemblance to the great northern Catholic rising, the Pilgrimage of Grace (which began *The Lancashire Witches*).[134] Sir William Blackett, a principal plotter, panicked however, and surrendered to the authorities, alerting them to the plan. Not sure how to respond, the insurgents rode rather aimlessly around Northumbria, recruiting when and where they could. Eventually, they entered Scotland, where the Earl of Mar had recently rallied the Highland clans by declaring James III at Braemar, somewhat prematurely as it turned out. Somewhat unsure how to proceed, the insurgents wasted valuable time waiting at the border, trying to decide which way to go: should they march north to support Mar or move into Lancashire and Cheshire? They chose the latter, and marched into Preston, where they met a greatly superior government force under General Wade. Despite inflicting almost ten times as many casualties as they suffered in the ensuing battle, the Jacobite army was sold out by its leaders, who lost heart in the cause and surrendered in much the same way as their successors were to do in 1745, as chronicled in *The Manchester Rebels*. With the tactical acumen that seems to characterise Jacobite actions, James landed in Scotland in January 1716. By February his followers were sick of the sight of him, and he left for France, never to return. Twenty-six English insurgents were executed by the State, including the Earl of Derwentwater, more severe reprisals prevented by an apparent desire not to stir up the Anglican Tory lobby and cause further political instability. Almost 50 estates were confiscated in Lancashire and Cheshire, and two Registration Acts were passed; the first an unsuccessful attempt to facilitate the legal seizure of further recusant property, the second allowing any two Justices of the Peace to administer randomly a loyalty oath to Catholics on pain of imprisonment or heavy fines, a measure which impoverished many Catholic families.

---

[134] Paul Kléber Monod, *Jacobitism and the English People: 1688–1788* (Cambridge: UP 1989), 317.

It is obvious that such a heroic failure would appeal to Ainsworth, doubly so given the location of the final battle. As he wrote in the dedicatory epistle to his cousin, William Francis Ainsworth:

> The hero of my Tale is the ill-fated Earl of Derwentwater – by far the most striking figure in the Northumbrian insurrection. The portrait I have given of him I believe to be in the main correct, though coloured for the purposes of the story. Young, handsome, chivalrous, wealthy, Lord Derwentwater was loyal and devoted to him whom he believed his rightful sovereign.[135]

Preston Fight begins at Dilston Hall, Northumberland, Lord Derwentwater's ancestral seat and depicts an apocryphal secret visit by James Edward Stuart. The narrative follows the historical record reasonably closely from then on, describing the Braemar rising and the subsequent, ill-fated advance to Preston, where Derwentwater and his co-conspirators are taken and sent to London as traitors. The battle itself is a romantic depiction of the kind of military action that the English seem to love, where the underdogs, outnumbered and under-equipped bravely face a superior enemy; we need think only of Agincourt, Rorke's Drift or the Battle of Britain for similar cultural correlatives. As with the inglorious Derby retreat of the second rebellion, blame for the outcome is laid at the door of overly cautious and gutless generals rather than the heroic rank and file, which does not fall far short of the truth. The Earls of Nithsdale and Wintoun escape, Jack Sheppard-style, from the Tower of London, while other Jacobite friends break out of Newgate. The tale concludes with Derwentwater's execution on Tower Hill where, according to legend, the aurora borealis burned blood red that night, becoming known for a period thereafter as 'Lord Derwentwater's Lights'. *Preston Fight* was issued in three volumes by the Tinsley Brothers in May 1875. This time, the fee was only £125.

Ainsworth followed *Preston Fight* with another foray into Lancashire history, returning to the Civil War and the siege of Manchester in 1642 in *The Leaguer of Lathom, A Tale of the Civil War in Lancashire*, again published by the

---

[135] Ainsworth, dedicatory epistle, *Preston Fight, or The Insurrection of 1715. A Tale*, Works.

Tinsley brothers for a modest fee. The author is principally concerned with the brave defence of Latham House against Parliamentary forces by Charlotte de la Tremouille, Countess of Derby, during the absence of her husband. The author also describes the storming of Lancaster and Bolton and the surrender of Warrington. The narrative concludes with the martyrdom of the gallant Cavalier Derby at Bolton in 1651. Ainsworth once again used Chetham Society publications as his primary source here: Seacome's *Memoirs of the House of Stanley* and *Discourse of the War in Lancashire* and *The Memoirs of James, Earl of Derby* by Canon F.R. Raines, to whom the novel is dedicated.

After the unintentionally opportunistic *Chetwynd Calverley* (1876), where the poisoning of the hero of the title's father by his wicked stepmother uncannily mirrors the sensational 'Balham Mystery' surrounding the murder of Charles Bravo at the time of publication (a connection Ainsworth urged the Tinsley Brothers to exploit), and a story of my home town, Norwich, during Kett's Rebellion, *The Fall of Somerset* (1877), Ainsworth returned, once more, to Manchester. His letters reveal that he had two projects in mind, one about the eighteenth century dandy Beau Nash (which became his penultimate novel in 1879), and one based on the Jacobite trials in Manchester in 1694, inspired by two Chetham Society publications: *The Jacobite Trials in Manchester in 1694* (edited by William Beaumont, who had also edited Seacome's histories, and to whom the resulting novel, *Beatrice Tyldesley*, is dedicated) and *Abbott's Journal* (edited by Dr Alexander Goss). Crossley obviously preferred the latter: 'I shall take your advice', wrote Ainsworth, outlining the plan of the new work:

> I shall commence with the Jacobite Trials in Manchester then introduce the assassination and invasion plots, and Sir George Barclay, the Duke of Berwick, and Sir John Fenwick. The arrests, trial, and execution of the latter will form the staple of the story.
>
> I shall give William III at Kensington, and James II at St. Germain.
>
> If I can manage all this satisfactorily I shall do very well.[136]

---

[136] Ainsworth, letter to Crossley, August 20 1877.

A characteristic cessation of correspondence then occurs as Ainsworth shuts himself away to write, broken in the Spring of the following year with this descriptive announcement to his friend:

> I have just finished my new story, *Beatrice Tyldesley* which will be published in the course of the spring. It is partly founded on the Jacobite Trials in Manchester, and I propose to dedicate the work to Mr. Beaumont, if perfectly agreeable to him. One of the principal characters is Colonel Tyldesley of Myerscough, and I have given the trial at Manchester at full length. Beatrice is a cousin of Colonel Tyldesley. In the latter part of the story I have given a picture of James II, with his visit to the Monastery of La Trappe. I think the book will be popular – at all events, in Lancashire, as it refers to so many of the old country families – Of course, Lunt the Informer figures in the story – I will send a copy for review to Mr. Axon of *The Manchester Guardian. The Leaguer of Lathom* has been very successful, and is now republished in a cheap form.[137]

Against the historical background of James II's dispossession, his defeat in Ireland and subsequent retirement to Saint-Germain, and while his adherents attempt without success to restore him to the throne, Ainsworth weaves an uneven secondary love story. The Jacobite Beatrice Tyldesley is maid of honour to Queen Mary of Modena at Saint-Germain, while her lover, the equally Jacobite Walter Crosby, finds himself, through a bizarre set of circumstances, stuck at the court of William and Mary. Eventually, love conquers all and Beatrice and Walter marry. *Beatrice Tyldesley* was serialised in *Bow Bells* (illustrated by Frederick Gilbert) and again published in three volumes by the Tinsley Brothers in April 1878, again for £125. A sixpenny edition was later issued by John Dicks. Thus ended Ainsworth's irregular series of Lancashire novels. They did not pay well, but seem to have been written as much for the author's own pleasure as for profit. As we will see in the following, concluding, chapter, despite the huge success of his earlier works, it was the Lancashire novels of which Ainsworth was most proud.

---

[137] Ainsworth, letter to Crossley, March 9 1878.

CHAPTER SIX

The Greatest Axe-and-Neck Romancer of Our Time

I. Growing old gracefully: 1850–1881

When Ainsworth abandoned *Mervyn Clitheroe* in 1852, it is not unfair to say that his significance as an important English novelist also ended. As Ellis notes in an uncharacteristic moment of melancholy:

> It is a pathetic task to trace the gradual declension of a talented writer to mediocrity, from prosperity to reduced conditions of means; yet such must inevitably be the course of events with an author who, when his pristine powers are becoming exhausted, is compelled by circumstances to continue writing as actively in his advancing years as in the days of his prolific youth.[1]

This is not to dismiss entirely Ainsworth's subsequent literary output – there were of course a few moments of genius remaining (such as *The Manchester Rebels*) – but how deeply must he have dredged his imagination to produce these?

In the early 1850s at least, Ainsworth still maintained enough financial power to expand his magazine holdings significantly. While retaining ownership of *Ainsworth's Magazine* and *The New Monthly Magazine*, Ainsworth's third and final acquisition was the very periodical in which he had made his name in the 1830s, *Bentley's Miscellany*, which he purchased from Bentley for £1,700 in October 1854. Once he had secured this prize, Ainsworth concluded the magazine

---

[1] Ellis, vol. 2, 251–2.

which bore his own name at the end of the year. This was something of a mercy killing, as Ainsworth had maintained *The New Monthly Magazine* at a very high standard at the expense of *Ainsworth's Magazine*, which had become a mere shadow of its former self, unillustrated, plain and yellow-leafed, its content as low in quality as its format; pieces rejected for *The New Monthly Magazine* often found their way to the pages of *Ainsworth's Magazine*. Ainsworth was extremely positive about his new investment, writing to Crossley that: 'I shall have two powerful magazines in my hands. I have given a long price ... but I hope in the end it will fully repay me.'[2] This would not be the case.

1854 also saw the completion of Ainsworth's own serial, *The Flitch of Bacon, or The Custom of Dunmow* in *The New Monthly Magazine*. This is an interesting piece, not in itself but as one of the last of Ainsworth's curious, extraliterary contributions to Victorian culture. *The Flitch of Bacon* is a simple and thoroughly unremarkable story of domesticity, with a plot that anticipates the domestic comedies of post-war Hollywood seen, for example, in the collaborations between Doris Day and Rock Hudson, in which two eighteenth century couples compete for the honour of winning the Dunmow Flitch, a prize of ancient custom awarded to married couples who can prove that theirs is a life of untroubled, marital bliss. For the last 12 months they must have not so much as raised a voice, let alone a hand, to each other, broken any of their vows or ever regretted tying the knot; as Ellis notes, 'Onerous conditions indeed'.[3] In a text most noteworthy by far for its incidental ballads (including the wonderfully morbid 'Old Grindrod's Ghost'), Ainsworth offers the following version of the custom of Dunmow:

> You shall swear by Custom of Confession,
> That you ne'er made nuptial transgression;
> Nor since you were married man and wife
> By household brawls or contentious strife,
> Or otherwise at bed or at board

---

[2] Ainsworth, letter to Crossley, October 19 1854.
[3] Ellis, vol. 2, 197.

Offended each other in deed or word:
Or since the parish clerk said Amen
Wished yourselves unmarried again:
Or in a Twelvemonth and a Day
Repented not in thought any way;
But continued true and in desire
As when you join'd hands in holy quire.
If to these Conditions, without all fear,
Of your own accord you will freely swear:
A whole Gammon of Bacon you shall receive,
And bear it hence with love and good leave;
For this is our Custom of Dunmow well known:–
Though the pleasure be ours, the Bacon's your own.[4]

Having been thoroughly cross-examined by their peers, the happy couple were required to take their oath kneeling upon sharp stones before being borne through the streets by sedan chair, the bacon at the head of the carnival procession. This custom predates the English Reformation; Chaucer's Wife of Bath jokes about it at the expense of her first husband: 'The bacon was nat fet for hem, I trowe,/That som men han in Essex at Dunmowe.'[5] The custom had been last celebrated in 1751. This was exactly the type of dotty old English (Catholic) tradition which Ainsworth adored and, indeed, collected; his correspondence revealing that the Dunmow Flitch had been in abeyance as a potential serial project for at least ten years. The story commenced in *The New Monthly Magazine* in January 1853, concluding in May the following year, being simultaneously published by Routledge in a single volume illustrated by Sir John Gilbert. Ainsworth, betraying an author's unconditional love for the youngest literary offspring, wrote to Charles Kent: 'it seems to me one of the best things I have achieved'.[6] This was something of a critical overstatement, yet this cheerful piece of fluff certainly caught the public imagination on an international scale, the book being translated into French, German, Dutch and Russian; theatrical versions also appeared all

---

[4] Ainsworth, *The Flitch of Bacon, or The Custom of Dunmow. A Tale of English Home*, Works, 4.
[5] Geoffrey Chaucer, *The Wife of Bath's Prologue*, 217–18.
[6] Ainsworth, letter to Charles Kent, June 19 1854.

over Europe and, as the Crimean War raged, both sides were reading Ainsworth. Then things really got out of hand.

The people of Dunmow were so taken with Ainsworth's story that they decided to re-establish their ancient tradition. They of course invited Ainsworth to present the bacon, and he responded with characteristic generosity with a donation put towards the festivities. A notice was placed in local newspapers inviting applicants. Two couples were selected, James and Hanna Barlow of Chipping Ongar, and Ainsworth's friends M. and Mme Tauchnitz of Leipzig; Bernhard Tauchnitz published English classics and Ainsworth was a regular visitor, *The Flitch of Bacon* being dedicated to them as: 'I have never known a more fondly-united couple.'[7] There was some civic opposition to the revival however. The Lord of the Manor denied access to the original site of the festivities (a modest church which was all that remained of the original priory) and the local clergy circulated pamphlets denouncing the ritual as pagan, papist and nonsense. The general public remained enthusiastic however, and the committee in charge of festivities merely moved the event two miles along the road from Little Dunmow to Great Dunmow.

The event took place on July 19 1855 (one of the wettest days of the year) with special trains running visitors from London. Ceremonies began in the Town Hall (which was decked out in flowers for the occasion) with Ainsworth in the chair, presiding over the court. Robert Bell, editor of *The Atlas*, acted for the claimants and Dudley Costello, another distinguished journalist of the day, defended the flitches; the jury consisted of six maidens and six bachelors and the spectators paid five shillings each to attend. Ainsworth opened proceedings with a lengthy speech in which he offered the historical background to the custom, cited other medieval towns in Britain and Europe with similar traditions and quoted at length from various texts which mentioned the tradition, such as *The Vision of Piers Plowman* (Robert de Longland c.1362), *The Wife of Bath's Prologue* and an

---

[7] Ainsworth, dedication, *The Flitch of Bacon*.

anonymous fifteenth century theological poem reproduced in the *Reliquiæ Antiquæ* by the Victorian scholars Wright and Halliwell. He concluded:

> Lover as I am of ancient Customs – anxious as I am to keep alive all traditions of the past, and to see old sports and pastimes practised as they were once practised in Merrie England – desirous as I am of promoting, to the utmost of my power, the harmless recreation of the people – it is a matter of pride and rejoicing to me to be instrumental in reviving such a ceremony as the good old Custom of the Dunmow Flitch of Bacon.[8]

The jurors decided that both couples were entitled to their flitch, the weather cleared and a long procession marched through the town to a marquee in Windmill Field, where a 7,000 strong crowd heard the couples take the oath, kneeling on stones naturally. The rest of the day was given over to a chaotic mixture of sports and drinking. *The Illustrated London News* covered the day in detail, including an illustration showing Ainsworth in the chair at the Town Hall ceremony. This picture could have come out of *The Flitch of Bacon* itself, which in many ways it did, and that day the author was therefore placed effectively, in word and picture, within his own text. The event was restaged two years later, with Ainsworth again in the chair, and has carried on, albeit irregularly, ever since. After 1857 however, organisers had to do without Ainsworth, who tired of his crazes easily. This was to be his last but one major media event.

Ainsworth followed *The Flitch of Bacon* in *The New Monthly Magazine* with *The Spendthrift: A Tale*, chronicling the fall and redemption of Gage de Monthermer of Suffolk during the reign of George II. The serial commenced in January 1855. Gage squanders his fortune gambling, goaded by his evil steward Fairlie, who constantly profits at his master's expense until they virtually exchange social roles. Fairlie has a change of heart on his deathbed and restores the thoroughly repentant Gage's fortunes. Gage marries happily in the end, the

---

[8] Ainsworth, speech given at Great Dunmow Town Hall, July 19 1885. A full account of the festivities and the history behind them can be found in William Andrews, *The History of the Dunmow Flitch of Bacon Custom* (London: 1877), which is dedicated to Ainsworth, and Lascelles Wraxall's account in *Bentley's Miscellany*, August 1855. Ellis also reproduces Ainsworth's speech in full in his biography. See also F.W. Steer, *The History of the Dunmow Flitch Ceremony* (Chelmsford: Essex County Council, 1951).

moral of the story being that: 'A reformed rake makes the best husband',[9] which, it would have to be said, was not so in the author's case. In the words of Ellis: 'The story possesses but little merit, and both plot and incident are weak.'[10] Unfortunately, Ainsworth missed the opportunity to explore the class issues attendant in the fatal relationship between master and servant, or the destructive effects of a gambling addiction; both themes had been much better handled by Reynolds in *The Mysteries of London*. Much more fun was Routledge's publication of an anthology of ballads from Ainsworth's novels the same year, *Ballads: Romantic, Fantastical and Humorous*. The book was well illustrated by John Gilbert, and collected 82 lyrics in the following sections: 'Legendary and Romantic', 'Fantastical', 'Humorous', and 'Translations'. This is now an extremely rare little book, but is well worth seeking out as it demonstrates Ainsworth's minstrel side admirably, and can remind one how nicely done were the majority of his ballads and of his exceptional skill as a translator of French.[11] At the recommendation of the Prime Minister, Lord Palmerston, Ainsworth was granted a Civil List pension of £100 per annum for services to literature. 'It was a great misfortune to me that Disraeli went out', Ainsworth later told Crossley, 'He would have given me something better than a pension.'[12]

Ainsworth ended the decade with the publication (both in *Bentley's Miscellany* and as a separate pamphlet) of an epic poem entitled *The Combat of the Thirty*. This was his own translation from the French of an ancient ballad he had discovered in the Bibliothèque du Roi, detailing the battle between 30 Englishmen and 30 Bretons close to Ploëmel, Brittany in 1350. 'I want to get it known', Ainsworth wrote to Charles Kent, 'and it is difficult to make the public look at a poem nowadays.'[13] 1859 also saw the loss of Ainsworth's old friend, the publisher Charles Ollier, the only man in whom Ainsworth confided almost as

---

[9] Ainsworth, *The Spendthrift: A Tale* (Leipzig: Bernard Tauchnitz, 1856), 335.
[10] Ellis, vol. 2, 223.
[11] My personal favourite, 'Old Grindrod's Ghost', is appended to the present work as a representative example.
[12] Ainsworth, letter to Crossley, October 18 1869
[13] Ainsworth, letter to Charles Kent, October 12 1859.

much as he did Crossley. Leigh Hunt also died that year; Ainsworth wrote of him that he was: 'one of the shrewdest and kindliest of critics – a man who always tried to see good in everything'.[14]

The sixties began with a new romance in *Bentley's Miscellany*, *Ovingdean Grange, A Tale of the South Downs*, which ran from November 1859 to July 1860. Of his later historical romances, *Ovingdean Grange* is one of Ainsworth's better efforts; his descriptions of the sweeping South Downs are particularly effective. The story itself is largely concerned with the escape of Charles II after defeat at the Battle of Worcester in 1651; in terms of historical chronology, *Ovingdean Grange* actually takes up Charles's flight where the later novel *Boscobel* (1872) concludes. Scott's *Woodstock* (1826) covers much the same ground and Ainsworth's plot is often quite similar. In Scott's original story, Alice Lee, daughter of the ageing cavalier Sir Henry, loves Everard, a Parliamentarian, against the backdrop of the protection of the fugitive king; Cromwell turns on Everard, and Charles is able to effect a reconciliation between the lovers and Sir Henry. Ainsworth exchanges Woodstock for Ovingdean Grange, and the sex of the politically estranged lovers (Clavering Maunsel and Dulcia Beard) is reversed; Charles similarly persuades his staunch Royalist protector, Colonel Maunsel, to accept his son's match before escaping to France. The energy of the chases in the story recalls the style of *Guy Fawkes*. Having removed to Brighton, and fallen in love with the South Downs, Ainsworth was looking for a historical narrative in which to place this spectacular country rather than simply rewriting Scott. The legend that Charles had visited Ovingdean Grange gave Ainsworth his plot, although it is highly unlikely that the King would have made such a detour at such a critical time. There is a direct connection with the Grange nonetheless; the Grange was, during the Civil War, owned by one Francis Mansel, owner of the ship, *The Surprise*, on board which Charles made his escape to France. Ainsworth's love of this part of the country is reflected in his dedication: 'To the

---

[14] Ainsworth, letter to Charles Kent, August 4 1859.

Rev. Alfred Stead, Rector of Ovingdean, by One of his Flock'.[15] Ainsworth now walked to Ovingdean Church every Sunday, as he used to attend Willesden Church during his more prosperous days at Kensal Lodge, and every location in *Ovingdean Grange* was familiar to him by his long and much loved walks across the Downs. This then is another very personal piece of writing.

Money was now once more a problem, and Ainsworth was forced to sell the house in which he was born (21 King Street, Manchester) in 1860. He received £5,500 for the property but, with his usual business luck, King Street was soon to become prime real estate as a new business district, which it remains to this day. Had Ainsworth postponed the painful decision for no more than a couple of years he would have made a small fortune. Ainsworth's correspondence also shows that he was very eager to sell his other family house in Manchester, 'Beech Hill', as soon as possible to provide some much needed financial security in increasing old age. One letter in particular tells of his exhaustion due to the strain of constant literary production:

> Under such circumstances, and considering how time is stealing on, you will not wonder at my anxiety to sell the property.
>
> Indeed, it is a matter to me of very serious consequence. For several years I have been obliged to work exceedingly hard, and the strain is almost too much for me, and I may break down. It is only prudent therefore to relax these excessive exertions, but as I now stand I cannot do so. Of course I should be glad to get more for the property, But I will take £3000 for it ... I shall consider what you do for me in this matter as a *great act of friendship*, and I feel sure you will be glad to serve me, and to help lighten my labours ... I would run down to Manchester, but I am so busy that I cannot leave my desk, and I shall not have finished the work I am engaged on at present – *John Law* – before 10th June.[16]

Crossley sold the house for £3,000 in June of that year, which Ainsworth invested in Indian Railway shares.

---

[15] Ainsworth, inscription, *Ovingdean Grange, A Tale of the South Downs* (1860), Works.
[16] Ainsworth, letter to Crossley, March 21 1864.

Ainsworth continued to write at least one serial a year throughout the sixties. *The Constable of the Tower* (*Bentley's Miscellany* 1861) sits between *Windsor Castle* and *The Tower of London* in terms of historical chronology. It begins with the death of Henry VIII and follows the coronation and brief reign of Edward VI; the characters Xit, Og, Gog and Magog from *The Tower of London* are reintroduced. On the domestic front, Ainsworth's youngest daughter Blanche married Captain Francis Swanson, Royal Artillery, in August 1861. The couple had three children: Apphia, Frank and John. Frank died in the Boer War; Apphia married two military men, both of whom were killed in action; John became a Captain in the 27th Worcester Regiment and fortunately lived to collect his pension.

The Lord Mayor of London (*Bentley's Miscellany* 1862) covered much the same ground as *The Spendthrift*, being the story of the reformation of another extravagant eighteenth century rake with the weird and wonderful name of Tradescant Lorimer, son of the Lord Mayor of London. *Cardinal Pole* (*Bentley's Miscellany* 1863) is very much a sequel to *The Tower of London*, dealing as it does with Mary Tudor's marriage to Philip of Spain and sharing many of the same characters. The secondary plot concerns the doomed romance of Osbert Clinton and Constance Tyrrell. *Cardinal Pole* concludes with the death of Mary. In 1862, Ainsworth also placed first editions of his favourite works in the Chetham Library in Manchester, after a request by the Chief Librarian. 'I have been applied to by Mr. Ives[17] of Chetham's Library for my ballads and *The Combat of the Thirty*, both of which I have had great pleasure in sending him', he wrote to Crossley, 'I have also sent him *Rookwood* and *Crichton* – first editions, illustrated, and ere long I mean to send a complete set of my books. The Chetham Library is a proper receptacle for them.'[18] Before *Cardinal Pole* had concluded its serial run, Ainsworth was already working on *John Law* (*Bentley's Miscellany* 1864). John Law was an early eighteenth century Scottish financier who went to the French

---

[17] Librarian, Chetham Library, Manchester.
[18] Ainsworth, letter to Crossley, February 3 1862.

court. He was a brilliant speculator and established the Bank of France until his bubble eventually burst and he died in poverty. Ainsworth follows his life in France, which is told in parallel with the Laborde family, whose fortune and future is ruined by the speculative mania incited by Law's paper money and Mississippi schemes. Ainsworth next penned *The House of the Seven Chimneys* (*Bentley's Miscellany* 1865), detailing the adventures of Charles Stuart, then still Prince of Wales, as he travels to Madrid to claim the hand of the Infanta Maria, fighting brigands and attending balls and bullfights along the way. The title refers to the house where Charles lived, incognito, upon arrival in Madrid; it was changed to *The Spanish Match* when published as a three volume novel by Chapman and Hall at the end of 1865. That year, Ainsworth was delighted to be included in an anthology of Lancashire poetry, edited by Crossley's friend John Harland, writing to Crossley that: 'Nothing could gratify me more than that your friend should include my ballads in his proposed collection.[19] He is quite at liberty to choose as many as he thinks proper. "Grindrod's Ghost" seems peculiarly appropriate to the work.'[20] *Auriol* followed, then one of the worst: *The Constable de Bourbon* (*Bentley's Miscellany* 1866) is reminiscent of *Crichton* and fails to engage in much the same way as the earlier novel. In 1523 Charles de Bourbon, Constable of France, throws in his lot with Emperor Charles V and Henry VIII in an attempt to overthrow his kinsman François I of France; the serial covers the Siege of Marseilles, the Battle of Pavia and concludes with Bourbon's traitor's death during the Sack of Rome in 1527. Ainsworth then leapt from the sixteenth century to the present day, *Old Court* (*Bentley's Miscellany* 1867) being another of his rare fictional forays into contemporary Britain. Worth notes the uneasy combination of genres present in *Old Court*, at once a tale of fashionable life, a gothic novel and a very Victorian melodrama. Sir Hugh Chetwynd and his brother

---

[19] John Harland F.S.A. (ed.), *Modern Songs and Ballads of Lancashire* (London: Whittaker & Co, 1866). This collection contains the following poems by Ainsworth: 'The Mandrake' (from *The Lancashire Witches*), 'Black Bess' (*Rookwood*) and 'Old Grinrod's Ghost' (*The Flitch of Bacon*). This anthology has now been updated by Cliff Hayes and reprinted as *The Best of Old Lancashire in Poetry and Verse* (Manchester: Printwise 1992).

[20] Ainsworth, letter to Crossley, August 10 1865.

Clarence love the same girl. Hugh accidentally kills his brother, and the plot revolves around his plan, in atonement, to bequeath Old Court to his late brother's son. Young Clarence loves Hugh's daughter Lucetta, but she rejects him for Captain Rainald Fanshaw; Clarence eventually pairs off with Fanshaw's sister. The shadowy Vandeleur La Hogue is a witness to the original fratricide. He blackmails Sir Hugh at first, then finally murders him. Old Court burns in the end, with La Hogue trapped inside. A strange story, to say the least. In the same year, an ever decreasing income forced Ainsworth to move house once more. After 14 reasonably happy years in Brighton, he moved to a smaller house in Tunbridge Wells. Life at 1 St. James's Villas was quiet and Ainsworth became increasingly insular; he had few friends locally and was rarely seen in public. Although 'retired', he continued to generate an incredible volume of text. The new house did not have the capacity for his private library; the upstairs was given over almost entirely to books, which eventually brought the ceiling down.

The most significant event of 1867 was, however, the birth of another daughter, Clara. Contemporary records become totally opaque at this point. Clara's mother was Sarah Wells, and although Ellis refers to a 'private marriage (some years earlier)' I have found no record of this. Ms Wells's details are equally mysterious, and Ainsworth's correspondence with Crossley never mentions her.

Ainsworth kept it modern for his last contribution to *Bentley's Miscellany*. *Middleton Pomfret* (1868) is the assumed name of debt-ridden Julian Curzon, who fakes his own suicide by drowning in Lake Windermere (before the eyes of his new bride Sophy no less, the bounder), before sneaking off to India and making a fortune. Curzon/Pomfret returns years later to find Sophy married to the villainous Captain Scrope Musgrave, whom he eventually kills in a duel. If nothing else, Ainsworth had not lost his flair for naming. Almost 30 years after his first serial in *Bentley's Miscellany*, Ainsworth sold the now moribund magazine, for which he had paid £1,700, back to Bentley for a mere £250. An increasing lack of funds had resulted in the necessity of greatly reducing contributors' fees over the last few years, and the talent had gone elsewhere. As had been the case with *Ainsworth's*

Magazine, sales had fallen and *Bentley's Miscellany* was no longer what it had once been; it ceased publication in 1868, the title assimilated by *Temple Bar*.

Although all things must pass, Ainsworth's association with *Bentley's Miscellany* had been impressive. Under his stewardship as an editor and, later, owner the magazine published work by many luminaries of English and American literature: as well as Ainsworth himself and a legion of now forgotten journalists, poets and authors who did not leave footprints in the sands of time, Thackeray, Barham, Poe, Longfellow, 'Ouida' (Louise de la Ramée) and Mrs Henry Wood all wrote for the magazine; Cruikshank, Crowquill and Leech were its most distinguished illustrators. It should also be noted that both 'Ouida' and Mrs Henry Wood were discovered and promoted by Ainsworth.

'Ouida' (from a childhood mis-pronunciation of 'Louise') knew Ainsworth's cousin Dr William Francis Ainsworth, who probably encouraged the young writer to try her luck with one of Ainsworth's magazines. Her first contribution was the short story 'Dashwood's Drag; or the Derby and what came of it', which was published in *Bentley's Miscellany* in 1859; she was only 19 at the time. Ainsworth was so impressed that he published a further 17 stories by 'Ouida' over the next year, writing in his 'Epilogue' of 1860 that:

> We offer not our own opinion, but that of a host of critical commentators, when we say that few periodical writers have suddenly achieved a greater success than the contributor who has chosen the fanciful designation of 'Ouida', whose sketches of society, both in England and on the Continent, are as graceful as they are accurate.[21]

'Accurate' was something of an overstatement, as 'Ouida's' early short fiction was already establishing her intense style of bodice-ripping romanticism, always set against a somewhat artificial background of military and society life. After a succession of stories with titles such as: 'Belles and Blackcock', 'Coaches and Cousinship', 'Two Viscounts', 'The Marquis's Tactics' and 'Taming of the Pythoness', 'Ouida' was ready for a novel. Under the encouragement and tutelage

---

[21] Ainsworth, 'Epilogue', *Bentley's Miscellany*, December 1860.

of Ainsworth, 'Ouida' wrote her first long work for *The New Monthly Magazine*, the serial *Granville de Vigne*, which ran from 1861 to 1863 and is better known to the world as her first novel, the luridly titled *Held in Bondage*. This she followed with *Strathmore* (*The New Monthly Magazine* 1863–1865), then *Idalia* (*The New Monthly Magazine* 1865–1867). The title of the latter was suggested by Ainsworth, who disapproved of her original in a telling editorial note: 'I do not like the title *The Lady of his Dreams*. It might do very well as the title of a poem, especially of the Tennysonian school, which I abominate, but it is too lackadaisical for a novel. If you can find nothing better, give it the name of the hero or heroine.'[22] Here we have another example of what we might term the 'alternative history of English literature', which can be tracked via the life of Ainsworth, where Tennyson is rejected and 'Ouida' embraced, entertainment and popular, if fleeting, fashion always put before art. 'Ouida' was a suitable successor to Ainsworth. She went on to write 45 novels, the most popular being *Under Two Flags* (1867), a tale of the Foreign Legion; she remained popular until the early 1890s. A period of poverty followed until she was granted a Civil List pension, and she died in relative comfort in 1908; like Ainsworth, she is not much read these days.

Mrs Henry Wood (born Ellen Price) contributed short stories to both *Bentley's Miscellany* and *The New Monthly Magazine* anonymously for some years before she became anxious to move on to a sustained long narrative. Ainsworth was resistant at first, but Wood persuaded him by refusing to contribute any further short fiction unless he also accepted a novel; the old charmer is said to have later explained to her that her short stories were so good that he could desire nothing better, and that the magazine could not have survived without them. Ainsworth accepted *East Lynne* as a serial for *The New Monthly Magazine*, and it ran from January 1860 to September 1861. Mixing piety, sentimentality and melodrama in roughly equal measure, the saga of Lady Isobel Vane was something of a slow burner at the time. As *East Lynne* ultimately made

---

[22] Ainsworth, letter to Louise de la Ramé, December 18 1864.

Mrs Wood world famous, it is often forgotten that she could not originally give it away to a publisher in its novelised form. *East Lynne* was first offered to Chapman and Hall, who turned it down flat on the recommendation of their reader, George Meredith, despite Ainsworth's protestations to the contrary. Ainsworth continued to lobby his old publishers and, at his suggestion, Chapman and Hall had another look, and returned the manuscript to Meredith for reconsideration, but it was again dismissed out of hand. Smith and Elder returned *East Lynne* unread, and Bentley finally took it on, the novel going on to be one of the best sellers in the history of the publishing house. Mrs Wood, now suddenly rich and famous, did not forget Ainsworth's support, and she wrote *The Shadow of Ashlydyat* (*The New Monthly Magazine* 1861–1863) especially for him, accepting a fee of only £60, her standard rate pre-*East Lynne*, for the serial rights; she always considered this her finest novel. S.M. Ellis's biography and Ainsworth's surviving correspondence provide numerous examples of Ainsworth's kindness and patience with aspiring authors, lesser authors and simply fans. Throughout his hectic life, he always seemed to make time to thank and encourage, and if at all possible to assist.

Ainsworth concluded the sixties with *Hilary St. Ives* (1869) in *The New Monthly Magazine*. This serial had a contemporary setting, and the devices of the historical romance, melodramatic dialogue, formal courtship, transparent disguises and supernatural occurrences, seem absurdly out of place in the polite society of Victorian Guildford. Extracts from *Mervyn Clitheroe* also appeared in *The Manchester School Register*. Always restless, Ainsworth quit Tunbridge Wells at Christmas and returned to his beloved South Downs, moving to 'Little Rockley' at Hurstpierpoint. Here he lived with his two single daughters, moving between 'Little Rockley' and Hill View Lodge, Reigate, the house he had purchased for his mentally disabled brother, Gilbert. By all accounts, Ainsworth, such a social animal in youth, had no desire to socialise outside his immediate family, and actively shunned the company of locals. He took long lonely walks with his King Charles spaniels, and took pains to avoid people as he slogged across the Downs. This is the figure which Browning described to Forster as a 'sad, forlorn-looking being'.[23] Ainsworth was, however, destined to outlive almost all his contemporaries. On hearing of Dickens's death in 1870, Ainsworth poignantly wrote to Charles Kent that, 'I was greatly shocked by the sudden death of poor Dickens. I have not seen him of late years, but I always hoped that we might meet again, as of old.'[24]

As soon as he cut the mooring line with *Bentley's Miscellany*, Ainsworth threw in his lot with John Dicks's new periodical *Bow Bells*. This was to be the destination of most of the remainder of his literary output. Many of these romances are less than impressive and particularly hard to find as they were often only published as cheap and fragile sixpenny soft-cover novels by Dicks; they have not survived and they are not well known. Ainsworth's first serial therein was *The South Sea Bubble* (1868), something of an English version of *John Law*. Framed by the audacious rise of the South Sea Company and subsequent crash in 1720, Margaret Harpledown establishes her parentage, recovers the will of her murdered father, and marries the love of her life Trevor Craven. *Talbot Harland* appeared in *Bow Bells* next in 1870. This 'Tale of the days of Charles II' was contemporary with J. Hain Friswell's scathing *Modern Men of Letters*, and he singled it out for particular attack owing to the inclusion of the character of the legendary French highwayman, Claude Duval. Had this text been conceived and written in the 1830s it would probably have been a masterful Newgate novel; as it is, Talbot Harland is a dreary hero and 'Claude Duval' turns out to be a fake. In the same year, Ainsworth passed the editorship of *The New Monthly Magazine* to his cousin Francis (he remained proprietor until 1879, when Chapman and Hall took over until the magazine came to an end in 1884). In October, Ainsworth was invited to dinner in Manchester by the trustees of the Grammar School as a distinguished old boy. As the South of England forgot Ainsworth, his native North was increasingly embracing him as something of a regional treasure.

---

[23] See Chapter One.
[24] Ainsworth, letter to Charles Kent, July 7 1870.

Tower Hill, another history which fills in the gaps between *Windsor Castle* and *The Tower of London*, was the next project, appearing serially in *Bow Bells* in 1871. This is something of a return to form, and tells the story of Anne of Cleves and Catherine Howard. Catherine uses her influence over Henry VIII in an attempt to forward the Catholic cause in England, but she is exposed as the lover of Francis Dereham by Archbishop Cranmer and the story ends with her execution on Tower Hill. *Boscobel* (1872) followed, then *The Manchester Rebels* (1873), as already described. *Merry England* (*Bow Bells* 1874) shot back in time to 1381 and the Peasants' Revolt of Wat Tyler and Jack Straw; Chaucer appears as an incidental character. *Merry England* is a powerful story of the feudal class war (interrupted only by the pointless subplot of Editha Tyler, who is in fact of noble birth), and the novel was published in a durable, three volume format by the Tinsley Brothers. With dizzying speed, considering his age, Ainsworth next gave *Bow Bells* the raunchy tale of Jane Shore, *The Goldsmith's Wife* in 1874. Jane Milverton (later Shore) was something of a Nell Gwyn figure in the history of the amours of the English monarchy; although married to the goldsmith Alban Shore, Jane became a mistress of Edward IV. In Ainsworth's version, Jane tries to save the King's sons after his death, but the story of the princes in the Tower is well known and popular (if unsubstantiated) history dictates that they are murdered by order of the Duke of Gloucester on his way to becoming Richard III. We are also treated to the Duke of Clarence's horrible death in a barrel of Malmsey wine.

In 1875 the Chief Librarian of Chetham College, Mr Jones, died and Ainsworth considered applying for the post, writing to Crossley that: 'I really think the office would suit me, and I shall give the matter consideration.'[25] The compulsion to keep writing remained too strong however, and Ainsworth later told Crossley: 'I have ceased to think of the Librarianship of the Chetham Hospital. Don't trouble yourself any more about it', adding, 'I am so fond of the place that I fancied I should like to live there.'[26] In April 1876 Ainsworth's only

---

[25] Ainsworth, letter to Crossley, December 25 1875.
[26] Ainsworth, letter to Crossley, April 9 1876.

sibling, Gilbert, died suddenly aged 69. Ainsworth and Crossley collaborated on a Memoir for *The Manchester Courier*. 'I am certain', wrote Ainsworth, 'if Gilbert had retained his mental powers, he would have been a distinguished writer.'[27] The loss of Gilbert seemed to shock Ainsworth out of his solitary existence however, and he rather bizarrely became a patron of The Sussex Bicycle Association and an enthusiastic early cyclist, flamboyantly presenting signed copies of his works as prizes at race meetings. Ever the old survivor, he continued to write. As detailed in the previous chapter, his next works were, in order: *Preston Fight* (1875), *The Leaguer of Lathom* (1876), *Chetwynd Calverley* (1876), *The Fall of Somerset* (1877) and the final Lancashire novel, *Beatrice Tyldesley* (1878).

In 1878, Ainsworth presented a full length portrait of himself, painted by H.W. Pickersgill in 1841, to his beloved Chetham Library. In the same year, Routledge published the only standard edition of Ainsworth's novels; he sent a set to the Chetham Library. 'I myself regard the series with some surprise', he later confessed to Crossley.[28] This reminded the reading public of his existence enough to warrant a charming little interview in *The World*: 'Celebrities at Home. No. LXXXIV. Mr. W. Harrison Ainsworth at Little Rockley' by Edward Yates. 'Time has dealt kindly with Mr. Harrison Ainsworth', begins Yates, 'and laid its finger but lightly on his handsome head. There is no difficulty in recognising in the well-preserved gentleman of threescore and twelve the Adonis of the D'Orsay period, whom Maclise loved to paint.'[29] Ainsworth now moved to his late brother's house in Reigate, apparently to cohabit with Sarah Wells. Sarah apparently did not encourage visitors, and Ainsworth was forced to meet his few remaining friends at his London club, the Carlton. His health began to decline; later writing to his cousin, Dr James Bower Harrison, Ainsworth explained that:

> For myself, I live here very quietly, but I shall draw nearer London in the summer. I suffer awfully from neuralgic pains. As you will perceive, I cannot

---

[27] Quoted from Ellis, vol. 2, 300.
[28] Ainsworth, letter to Crossley, March 30 1880.
[29] *The World*, March 27 1878.

give a very satisfactory report of myself. My handwriting will show you how desperately shaky I am.[30]

Only two novels remained to be written.

Beau Nash (1879) is a surreally archaic portrait of Bath in the eighteenth century and the doings of the dandy of the title, while also painting a picture of a morally corrupt aristocracy which would not have looked out of place in contemporary newspapers. Mrs Aylmer Mallet, 'the Beauty of Bath', elopes with Sir Thomas Carew. Carew kills Aylmer's husband in a duel and his distraught lover enters a convent as Sister Helena for the remainder of the narrative, eventually dying. Mallet's nephew, Frank Farington, meanwhile courts the contrary Edith Wilmot with the help of his friend Nash. It is most interesting to note that Ainsworth, once a great dandy, all but ends his career with an account of another, Richard 'Beau' Nash (1674–1762). Ainsworth's final work, *Stanley Brereton*, had a modern setting and ran as a serial in *The Bolton Weekly Journal*, a long way down from *The Sunday Times*. Ellis barely mentions this text, but as the last novel we owe the author a few lines. Sir Thomas Starkey elopes to France with a mistress; his wife's cousin, Lionel Darcy, restores family honour by killing Starkey in a duel. Starkey's nephew, Stanley Brereton, inherits the estate and weds Mildred Warburton, who is no better than she should be. In a reflection of earlier events, Mildred runs off with dastardly Darcy, whom Stanley kills in a duel. Stanley takes Mildred back, but she is killed in a riding accident, leaving Stanley to marry Rose Hylton, the girl who truly loves him. Both the above were published in three volumes by Routledge; they are good books, but not great, fossils soon to be buried completely by the modernist movements stirring in Europe. In every sense, Ainsworth was out of time.

II. Man of La Manchester

For the majority of his literary life, Ainsworth was, as we have seen again and again, a pariah, denied the laurels of contemporaries (even when they were deserved) in favour of abuse by Thackeray, Forster, Horne and their imitators.

---

[30] Ainsworth, letter to Dr James Bower Harrison, January 22 1880.

Although he never once laid down the pen in 60 years, Ainsworth's fame and fall were over with quickly and, early ripe, early rot, he never really achieved the approval of his peers that he so earnestly desired. At the very end of his life however, Ainsworth's contribution to English letters was in some small way recognised by the city of his birth, in a public display of love and respect that had so often eluded her prodigal son since the glory days of *Rookwood*.

In July 1881, the Lord Mayor of Manchester, the Right Honourable (and soon to be Sir) Thomas Baker formally invited Ainsworth to a civic banquet in his honour to be held at the Manchester Town Hall. From this moment on, Ainsworth's correspondence becomes a touching flurry of organisation and enthusiasm: who is to be invited, how is he to be presented? The once-dazzling socialite, now sole survivor, of the D'Orsay set was going to throw one last party:

> My Dear Crossley,
>
> Very likely you may have heard that I have agreed to dine with the Mayor of Manchester on *Thursday September 15* – He sent me a very gratifying letter. Mr. Charles Rowley proposed to give some of the illustrations of my works in a little tract to be presented to the guests at the Dinner, but on consideration, I did not like the idea, as it might be misconstrued, but I see no objection to a reprint of your excellent Memoir, containing a list of my work, (which may be completed to date), accompanied by a good photographic portrait.[31]

Many more excited letters about arrangements and correct invitations were to follow. Charles Rowley had recently arranged a similar 'do' for Henry Irving at the Queen's Hotel in Manchester that July. Ainsworth met him for dinner at the Junior Carlton Club and 'was very much pleased with him'.[32] This was a sound judgement of character, for Mr Rowley did not disappoint.

To give the event its full title, the 'Complimentary Dinner to William Harrison Ainsworth, Esq., by Thomas Baker, Mayor of Manchester. As an expression of the high esteem in which he is held by his Fellow-townsmen and of his services to literature' took place on Thursday September 15, 1881, and was

---

[31] Ainsworth, letter to Crossley, July 25 1881.
[32] *Ibid.*

impressively heralded by the Town Hall bells as if welcoming royalty. As the great and the good of Manchester, old friends, new friends, writers and journalists mingled in the reception room, each was presented with a commemorative brochure (Ainsworth's original misgivings having been overruled by the Mayor) designed by one Thomas N. Storer. This beautiful (and exceedingly rare) little booklet, the cover bearing Ainsworth's photograph and his coat of arms, contained a short biography, a bibliography (which omitted *Preston Fight* for some obscure reason) and an original illustration from each of the following works from Ainsworth's heyday: *Rookwood, Crichton, Jack Sheppard, The Tower of London, Old St. Paul's, The Miser's Daughter, Windsor Castle, The Lancashire Witches* and *Mervyn Clitheroe*. Among the guests were members of Ainsworth's family; Crossley; the journalists William Axon (who later wrote a nice little memoir of Ainsworth), John Evans (Manchester journalist and fan) and Edmund Yates (editor of *The World*); local military and religious dignitaries such as Colonel Henry Fishwich and the Rev. Silas Hocking; Charles Sutton, Chief Librarian of the Manchester Free Library; and the cotton merchant John Rylands (whose fortune gave Manchester the incredible gothic library which bears his name on Deansgate). The now forgotten authors Mrs Stanford Harris and Miss Jessie Fothergill represented the literary ladies of Manchester, decorum requiring that they dined separately from the men in the company of Ainsworth's cousin Mabel Harrison and the Lady Mayoress; the women were allowed into the banqueting hall only for the after-dinner speeches.

Although surrounded by leading local politicians, writers and industrialists, Ainsworth must have felt acutely aware of the gaps in the crowd. Whether or not members of his own literary generation would have attended a banquet in his honour is a matter of conjecture as, with the exception of Crossley and the formidable R.H. Horne, Ainsworth had outlived them all, friends and enemies alike. Some had gone early: Laman Blanchard, subeditor of *Ainsworth's Magazine*, had committed suicide after the death of his wife in 1845; the Rev. R.H. Barham ('Ingoldsby') had died the same year and Lady Blessington had followed in 1849; valued school-friend Gilbert Winter ('Cuthbert Spring' in *Mervyn Clitheroe*) died in 1853; Thackeray in 1863; Dickens and Maclise both died in 1870, Bulwer-Lytton following in 1873, Forster in 1876, and Cruikshank in 1878; Disraeli, whose health had been bad for some months, had died recently, on April 18 1881. The Mayor had managed to trace three surviving members of Ainsworth's form and year at the Free Grammar School, the Rev. George Heron, the Rev. John Howard Marsden and Sir Humphrey de Trafford, but all were too infirm to attend. 'We may congratulate ourselves', said the Mayor, 'that Mr. Ainsworth is in a sufficiently hale state of body and mind to be with us to-night to receive our recognition of his great literary abilities.'[33] Four months later Ainsworth joined his friends. Both Ellis and Worth consequently observe an element of pathos in these proceedings. Ellis writes sympathetically of the curse of outliving your friends and your age:

> His joy must have been strangely allied with pathetic, poignant memories of long-past days and long-dead friends; memories of his romantic, happy boyhood, with its dreams and ambitions long since realised and now consummated; and memories of that other dinner, over forty years agone, when, in the height of his fame, he was honoured by his native city conjointly with Dickens. As he gazed around the banquet-table of 1881, the faces he saw were mainly those of a younger and unfamiliar generation; and he and Crossley must have felt like ghosts from another era – even Manchester itself entirely changed since the days of their youth, its narrow streets and picturesque timber houses vanished like a city of dreams.[34]

Worth echoes this opinion, writing that:

> All of Manchester's prominent citizens were there, but what was Ainsworth, whose own generation except for the faithful Crossley was dead and gone, to make of these youngsters? The sad, resigned face, fringed by receding white hair and a white beard, which stares off into space from the front page of the souvenir brochure of the dinner bears no recognisable relationship to the handsome young man whose picture was drawn by Maclise and D'Orsay in the 1820s and 1830s.[35]

---

[33] Crossley and Evans, *Specially Revised Accounts of the Recent Banquet etc.*
[34] Ellis, vol. 2, 336.
[35] Worth, 21–2.

There is undoubtedly some truth to such sentiments, but I do not think they should be overstated. Ainsworth loved people, and made friends as fast as he lost them, adopting, for example, the Manchester journalist John Evans as a result of preparations, charmingly confusing the earnest young correspondent with one of his circle anyway: 'who is Mr. John Evans?' he wrote to Crossley, 'Is he an old friend of mine?'[36] The transcripts of the banquet speeches and proceedings, carefully documented by Crossley and Evans in their *Specially Revised Accounts of the Recent Banquet* ('printed for private circulation only'), also tell a rather different, and more cheerful story.

After the extravagant banquet, formal proceedings began with the Lord Mayor offering a toast to the Queen and the Royal Family, before giving the welcoming address in honour of Ainsworth. It is interesting to note with which great nineteenth century authors the Mayor allies Ainsworth, the explicit link he makes between the author's work and Lancashire and the way in which he describes the historical novels in general; his library statistics also highlight Ainsworth's working-class audience. The warmth of such a welcome must surely have more than balanced any feelings of melancholy that Ainsworth might have initially harboured:

> I have now to ask your attention while I propose the health of the gentleman in whose honour we are met – (applause) – distinguished as being a fellow-citizen with us, his immediate ancestors having for several generations resided within a very short distance of the spot whereon we are now assembled, and distinguished also for the possession of the highest literary ability of any living native of Manchester. (Applause.) My personal acquaintance with Mr. Ainsworth, though it dates back some forty years, has, unfortunately for myself, not been of an intimate character. But the mental intimacy which I have with Scott, and Bulwer, and Southey, and Thackeray, all men of my day whom I did not know, has in his case the vitality of just so much personal knowledge as has enabled me, while I was reading his books, to picture to myself the personal appearance of the author of them. (Hear, hear.) ... The thought, gentlemen, that we should pay some mark of respect to Mr. Ainsworth has passed through the minds of several gentlemen who are now present.

---

[36] Ainsworth, letter to Crossley, August 30 1881. John Evans was a Manchester journalist and fan; he is the author of 'The Early Life of William Harrison Ainsworth', *Manchester Quarterly*, vol. 1, 1882.

(Hear, hear.) My position enables me to-night to give that thought a local habitation and a name. We all knew that our fellow-citizen had through a long life contributed very greatly to the intellectual pleasure of his countrymen, that he made many a heart glad, and that many a reader of his works had risen from the perusal of them refreshed, invigorated, amused, and instructed. (Hear, hear.) It would have been a very easy thing to fill the great hall of this building with admirers of his genius. (Hear, hear.) It would have been very easy to bring here to-night all the eloquence which this city possesses; but this was not my object. It was rather to make this a gathering of local literary men, who had a kindred spirit with our fellow-townsman and the power of appreciating fully his great ability and genius. And while I wished through them to pay a compliment to him, I wished also through him to pay a compliment to them, and to show my sense of literary merit, though it does not attain the popularity of *Guy Fawkes* or *Windsor Castle*. (Applause.) ... It forms no part, gentlemen, of my duty to-night to offer any criticisms upon Mr. Ainsworth's voluminous works. I may, however, remark that he has embodied in them just so much of historical matter to give great interest to his stories; in point of fact, to make them most delightful reading. (Hear, hear, and applause.) He has also done another thing which gives him a claim to the gratitude of every native of this county, by introducing into his works the legends and the characters of past times in this county – (hear, hear) – and by making the folk-lore and speech of Lancashire a distinctive literature. (Applause.) And now, just one other subject. It is fitting that I should say something about the amount of popularity which Mr. Ainsworth's works enjoy in this his native city. (Hear, hear, and cheers.) And on this point I am enabled to speak with some authority. In our Manchester public free libraries there are 250 volumes of Mr. Ainsworth's different works. (Applause.) During the last twelve months those volumes have been read 7660 times – (applause) – mostly by the artisan class of readers. (Hear, hear.) And this means that twenty volumes of his works are being perused in Manchester by readers of the free libraries every day all the year through. (Applause.) My statistics would be incomplete if I did not tell you which of his books are most read. It would be a pleasure to me if I could only read Mr. Ainsworth's mind and know what the conviction is on this point which he entertains. (Hear, hear.) Whether I shall astonish him, or whether the result of my inquiry agrees with the result which prevails in his own mind, I really cannot tell. But I give you six of his most popular works, and in the order in which they are most read. The first is – what? (Laughter.) *The Tower of London*. (Loud applause.) The next is – what? The ladies can tell me. (Laughter.) It is *The Lancashire Witches*. The third is *Old St. Paul's*. Then comes *Windsor Castle*, *The Miser's Daughter*, and *The Manchester Rebels*. (Applause.) I think now, gentlemen, I have said enough to make you agree with me in saying that we may consider ourselves very proud in having such a man as Mr. Harrison Ainsworth among us. (Applause.) We may consider ourselves very proud in having him here tonight to tell him how much we appreciate his genius and his industry. (Applause.) And he, too, will, I think, be gratified to hear that he has given and is giving so much pleasure and instruction to the reading part of the community of England. (Applause.) I have only one more remark to make and then I conclude. A work of fiction which may have been produced in solitude and silence is sent into the world and becomes the means of interesting and enlightening millions. I ask you to drink the health of Mr. William Harrison Ainsworth. (Loud applause.)[37]

The toast was accepted with great enthusiasm, and cheers greeted Ainsworth as he rose to reply.

Ainsworth's speech is one of great joy, and a fitting antidote to the reading previous biographers have imposed upon this event. With characteristic style and grace, he also delivers a eulogy to his old friend Gilbert Winter, before acknowledging his best friend of all, James Crossley, who was of course by his side throughout the evening. One can still feel the intense emotion of the moment in this speech, which I reproduce in full, the pride and the pleasure at finally receiving some recognition for all those years of labour:

> With those ringing cheers in my ear, I scarcely know how to thank you; but I can assure you that I really think this is the most gratifying moment of my life. I feel proud, and beyond measure indebted to my excellent friend the Mayor, for the kindly welcome he has given me. In the course of my life many compliments have been paid me, but none that has gratified me so much as the present one. If, however, a compliment is to be paid me, it is here in Manchester – in my native city – that I would have it. (Hear, hear and applause.) Nothing has delighted me more than to be styled, as I have been, the 'Lancashire novelist.' (Hear, hear.) You have heard it said to-night that the most popular of my works is *The Tower of London*. It may be so, but I can assure you that my desire has really been to write a Lancashire novel, a novel that should please the whole county, and I don't care whether it pleased anyone else. (Applause.) If I really thought that the designation which I have latterly received of the "Lancashire novelist" were justified, I should indeed feel proud. I hope I may deserve it; I hope it may attach to my name. My great ambition has been to connect my name as an author with the city of my birth, and with this aim I have chosen certain subjects that would give me a chance of doing so. I sought to describe the Rebellion of '45 and the visit to Manchester of the unfortunate Prince Charles. With the old city as it existed at the period I was tolerably familiar, from the views I had seen of it, and could conjure up its picturesque black and white houses and other ancient structures, most of which, I grieve to say, have now entirely disappeared. In the days I refer to

---

[37] Crossley and Evans.

there was a very strong Jacobite feeling in Lancashire, and especially amongst the oldest families in Manchester – (hear, hear.) – many of whom were devoted to what they deemed the 'good cause'. Prominent amongst these were Dr. Byrom and his charming daughter Beppy, both of whom had always the strongest attraction for me. Tom Syddall, the Jacobite barber of Manchester – (applause) – was likewise a favourite, as were Dr. Deacon and his sons and Jemmy Dawson. In *Beatrice Tyldesley* I have described the Jacobite trials in Manchester in 1694. In *The Leaguer of Lathom, a tale of the Civil War in Lancashire*, and in *Preston Fight; or, The Insurrection of 1715*, I had other periods to deal with and other parts of the county to depict; and in the locality of *The Lancashire Witches* I had very picturesque and curious scenery to describe, and I strove to do justice to it. (Hear, hear.) But it is in a modern story, portions of which may almost be termed autobiographical, that I have described my early days in Manchester and neighbourhood – my old school fellows and schoolmasters, Dr. Smith and Dr. Elsdale, and I have now had my reward. (Applause.) I have been honoured by the Chief Magistrate of my native city, who has bidden me to a Banquet at which I have been received with a warmth I shall never forget. (Applause.) I thank you again most heartily for the reception you have accorded me. I shall ever look back with pride and pleasure to this day. (Applause.) And now, before sitting down, I would fain say a word respecting a much valued and excellent friend; I allude to Mr. Gilbert Winter, whom I regard as one of the best specimens of the Manchester men of the last generation (applause) – a model of kindly hospitality, a man of business, a man of the strictest honour, and untiring in his zeal to serve a friend. (Applause.) Mr. Gilbert Winter must have been known to many gentlemen now present; and I am sure they will concur in the opinion I have expressed of him. (Hear, hear.) He resided in the house on the Cheetham Road now occupied by another old friend of mine –(applause) – for whom I have an equally strong regard, and whom I am happy to see beside me to-night – I allude to Mr. James Crossley. (Applause.) I need not expatiate on Mr. Crossley's social qualities, on his learning and scholarship, on his varied and extensive reading. It is not an extravagant compliment to say that he may be compared to the great Dr. Johnson himself. (Hear, hear.) As I cannot doubt that the honour paid me by the Mayor is due to my having gained some distinction as a chronicler of Lancashire, I may congratulate myself on obeying the impulse that prompted me to select that particular walk. (Hear, hear.) I believe my task to be well nigh accomplished, and can scarcely hope to write another tale, but should I do so I shall return to the old ground, and strive to maintain the honourable distinction I have acquired as the 'Lancashire novelist'. (Applause.) Mr. Mayor and gentlemen, I am thankful to have lived to see this day. (Applause.)[38]

A standing ovation followed, which must have brought a tear to the eye of all there assembled.

---

[38] *Ibid.*

Crossley appropriately followed, proposing the next toast, 'The Archaeological and Historical Societies of the County Palatine of Lancaster'. His speech was particularly charming (following the time-honoured tradition of opening with a joke), as he strongly hinted at the close relationship between the author and himself when it came to material and inspiration for the novels, without ever once even thinking of taking a little limelight. He also took the party back to the banquet given some 40 years since to celebrate the completion of *The Tower of London*, offering the assembly a unique glimpse into the literary past while reminding them, as had the Mayor, of Ainsworth's stature as a writer in those dear, dead days:

I might say a great deal of these societies with which I have the honour to be connected ... I think the aspect of the toast that I am most called to direct myself to is that which concerns my excellent friend, Mr. Harrison Ainsworth. (Hear, hear.) When, gentlemen, I look upon that long series of novels which he has published, extending, in the good orthodox three-volume form, to somewhere about one hundred volumes, I cannot but consider that there is a possibility of the time arriving when his ample resources may come to an end, for, as the fertility of the most fertile must have its limit, it may be impossible to have always at hand plots and subjects and characters. (Laughter.) When that time does come – when, like the Governors of the Bank of England, who, seeing bullion going out more rapidly than is consistent with financial policy and, perhaps, with financial security, think it necessary to call in some agency which will rectify and readjust the balance – if ever that does happen to Mr. Ainsworth, I may say he cannot do better than direct himself to the societies which are embodied in the toast. (Laughter.) Old Mr. Simeon, of Cambridge, used to encourage his clerical friends by saying, 'My dear Sir, whenever your theological cistern is drawn dry, come to me; I have one hundred skeletons of sermons which are ready at your service, and which will keep you on your legs for a considerable time to come.' (Laughter.) The reverend gentleman's metaphors were rather confused, but still the offer, I have no doubt, gave great satisfaction – (laughter) – and must have been a comfort and consolation to his clerical friends. (Laughter.) Should it be necessary for our excellent friend, Mr. Ainsworth, to direct himself to some assistance of that kind, I can, I think, on behalf of these societies say that we will find him the skeletons of one hundred historical novels – (laughter) – which with his master hand and his creative power can be made instinct with life, and form a very considerable addition to that long procession of heroes and heroines with which he has made us familiar, and which are extensive enough almost to form a literature of themselves, and which certainly will require and undoubtedly deserve – and I recommend it to the attention of Mr. Charles Sutton if he happens to be here –

an Ainsworth Bibliography. (Applause.) I was very forcibly struck on coming
into this room with the recollection of another dinner in honour of Mr.
Ainsworth which took place just forty years ago in London, and at which I had
the good fortune to be present. It was given in celebration of his popular, and
deservedly popular *Tower of London*; and if any one wishes to know how Mr.
Ainsworth looked at that time – for forty years make rather a difference in a
man's personal appearance – I cannot do better than recommend him to look at
the fine contemporary portrait painted by Pickersgill, Senior ... The place
where this London dinner was given was one of those old hotels, spacious and
commodious, which had the reputation of many good dinners ... The inn was a
comfortable one, and excellently adapted for the party ... The chairman on that
occasion was Mr. Serjeant (afterwards Mr. Justice) Talfourd ... and the party
that was congregated on that occasion was a fair and full representation of
those who as authors, as critics, as artists, as publishers, were in the first rank
in the metropolis at that time. Amongst them was, then in the full bloom of
authorship, delighted and delighting, Charles Dickens – and with him his friend
and subsequent biographer – I cannot say successful biographer – John Forster
... Amongst the party were several of that group of Fraserians of whom I
believe Mr. Ainsworth is now the sole survivor, but who still sit around their
table perpetuated and pictured by the admirable sketches of Maclise. Nor was
there wanting on that occasion that capital artist, whose bark will ever

> Attendant sail,
> Pursue the triumph and partake the gale,[39]

with the works of the distinguished authors whom he so admirably illustrated.
Need I say I refer to George Cruikshank? The Chairman, in proposing the toast
of the evening, did full justice to the work which had been the means of calling
that party together; and in his happiest terms gave his estimate of the literary
merits of Mr. Ainsworth. That estimate was a very high one, and it was
enthusiastically seconded and adopted by the party present. My only regret is
that of that speech and of Mr. Ainsworth's grateful response there is at present
no report. Horace deplores the want of the *vates sacer*, but what is the *vates
sacer* to the reporter, without whom wit, wisdom, and eloquence are only born
and spoken to perish. The characteristic of the remaining part of the evening
was the grand geniality and the utter impossibility of anything like a jar. There
were rival authors present, but they did not quarrel; there were hostile critics,
but their challenges were limited to champagne; there were men of different
schools, but they broke down the partition in order to make the harmony
perfect. There was a case of mortal feud, but it was arranged by an armistice
which lasted, at all events, that evening. I believe everybody spoke – whether
accustomed or unaccustomed to public speaking, who was able and capable in
his turn of assisting that grand social exhibition ... The proceedings were

---

[39] 'Say, shall my little bark attendant sail,/Pursue the triumph and partake the gale?' Alexander
Pope, *Essay on Man. Epistle iv* (1734).

carried out with admirable spirit and success to the end. I cannot tell you – I have referred to my diary, but it does not assist me – at what time we broke up; but from inquiries I made I ascertained that every guest present awoke a wiser and better man in the morning, but without the disagreeable headache which generally accompanies that discovery. I have always considered that that meeting settled, by a decisive and conclusive verdict, the position of Mr. Ainsworth amongst the novelists of his time. Mr. Ainsworth has done much excellent work. He has had, and it must have been a great satisfaction to him, the pleasure of seeing the avidity with which his works are read by the sons and grandsons of those by whom they were read when they first appeared. He has also the satisfaction of knowing that he is popular wherever the English language prevails. (Hear, hear.) His works have been translated into at least five of the great European languages. He has received from all sides kindly tributes, many of which he will, no doubt, consider as amongst his best possessions. But it has happened also, by one of those extraordinary chances, I may say, that do occur, that no voice of a collective or public kind, no general voice of tribute has ever reached him from his native town which has now become one of the great cities of the world. It has been reserved for our excellent Mayor, with that instinctive sense of what is just and right and fitting, and with that prompt liberality which has characterised his career as Mayor, to remedy this deficiency. He has afforded Manchester, through this dinner, the opportunity of recognising the claims and merits of one of the worthiest of its sons. (Applause.)[40]

As always, Crossley was content to step back and let his friend get all the glory, yet this event was as much in honour of the much-loved historian as the much-loved novelist; they were, after all, always something of a matched pair.

Several other long speeches followed. H.H. Howorth F.S.A., replying to Crossley's toast, spoke at one point of the timeless qualities of the romantic novelist in the industrial age:

Our smoking climate and our whirling machinery are poor accompaniments to the voices of the Muses; and we are constantly told that here men are too overwhelmed with the ever-pressing present to have much time to look backwards or to look onwards. On every side the literary man has to meet the questions of a successful Philistinism – Does this pay? Are you making a fortune by it? Mr. Mayor, is not this very fact a sufficient justification? Do not we all long beyond measure to escape as much as we can from the pressure and the commonplace of this everyday life of ours to where more poetry and more romance may be found? (Hear, hear.) But if this be granted, we shall still be told that Lancashire does not afford materials for literature – our rough

---

[40] Crossley and Evans.

moorlands and their rough inhabitants were not given to romantic ways. Is this so? May we not claim that the most limpid streams and the most sparkling water come out of the most rugged rocks? (Applause.) ... Gentlemen, whatever walk in literature we adopt, save one, we shall inevitably have one fate. We shall all be found out presently, and superseded; all, I mean, save the poet and the writer of romances, who deal with the evergreen and changeless passions of men and women. It is their good fortune to paint the past and the future in colours that the eye never wearies of looking at – colours mixed with the glamour of old Time. (Applause.)[41]

R.C. Christie, Chancellor of the Diocese, then proposed 'The Literature of the County Palatine of Lancaster'. His speech (which started with a bad joke) also naturally concentrated on Lancashire, and offered a warm welcome to Ainsworth upon his final journey home:

As we looked around we found there was hardly a county in the kingdom which had not been remarkable for one or more men of eminence in art or letters or in science. Some of the counties had achieved what might be called a speciality in the character of their literature. And neither last nor least among them was the county of Lancaster. Here there had been an unusual list of authors, some of whom had pushed their way up through the hard soil, like moorland flowers which grew without the aid of the cultivator, whilst many others were men of the greatest eminence, who had had all the advantages of school and college. They had with them that evening one of the finest existing links connecting past generations with the present. (Applause.) It was a pleasant thing thus to welcome the magician to the scenes of youth, around which his romantic genius had delighted to play during long years of absence from them. Mr. Harrison Ainsworth might well say in the words of Moore:

And doth not a meeting like this make amends
For all the long years I've been wand'ring away,
To see thus around me my youth's early friends,
All smiling and kind as in that happy day?

Although over some of your brows, as o'er mine
The snowfall of Time may be stealing, what then?
Like Alps in the sunset, thus lighted by wine,
They'll wear the gay tinge of youth's roses again.[42]

---

[41] *Ibid.*
[42] 'And doth not a meeting like this' by Thomas Moore from *A Selection of Irish Melodies*, Vol 9 (1824).

J. Fox Turner then proposed 'The Lancashire Witches', and Dr Francis Ainsworth responded; and Mr T.R. Wilkinson proposed 'The Press', before giving a tortuous history of journalism in Manchester and London.

Edmund Yates, who had interviewed Ainsworth for *The World*, and who had basically invited himself by writing to Ainsworth, offered an irreverent little coda to the increasingly dry speeches. In replying to the toast, 'The Press', Yates said that: 'I have had this evening the pleasure of making the acquaintance of after-dinner Manchester; and even in the midst of enjoyment, I would hazard the friendly criticism that though it was eloquent it was not concise', and that, 'One advantage of this I fully appreciate, as the time is so far advanced as to relieve me from any necessity of making a speech.'[43] He then made a speech, playing upon the fact that he had once had a poem rejected by *Ainsworth's Magazine* which apparently had the audience in stitches. Yates concluded:

> It has been a special pleasure to me to be here to-night, and to see the way in which the town of Mr. Ainsworth's birth honours the great Lancashire novelist, for he is not only a friend of many years' standing, but had been a friend of my father before me ... The Mayor of Manchester has set a most praiseworthy example in this departure from the ordinary routine of civic feasts. I think the example is one that ought to be imitated. A banquet with, it might be, something in the form of a testimonial, is a very pleasant way in which literature could be recognised. On the part of my colleagues of the press, I would say that they were ready, whenever called upon, to give up the name of their birthplaces to the mayors of the respective boroughs which had had the honour of giving them birth whenever those dignitaries were prepared to follow the magnificent lead of the chief magistrate of the ancient town of Manchester. (Laughter and cheers.)[44]

E.J. Broadfield, then proposed 'The Mayor and Corporation of Manchester', saying that he felt sure that, 'the Mayor would have no more brilliant day recorded in the history of his mayoralty than that of the Banquet to Mr. Harrison Ainsworth'.[45] The Mayor's response to this toast concluded the speeches.

---

[43] Crossley and Evans.
[44] *Ibid*.
[45] *Ibid*.

Ainsworth's subsequent correspondence suggests that the cheers were ringing in his ears for what remained of his life.

Before leaving Manchester for the last time, Ainsworth took a walk through her dear, dirty streets, saying goodbye as he knew by this point that his health was failing fast; he did this in the company of John Evans (who had very much attached himself to the elderly novelist), who later recalled their perambulations:

> Rambling through some of the principal streets of Manchester with The Lancashire Novelist (a privilege which fell to my lot on two or three days during his last visit to his native city) was a memorable treat. We found, however, much to his expressed regret, 'little of the old town now left', and sought in vain for 'those picturesque black and white timber habitations, with pointed gables and latticed windows', which formed the delight of his boyhood and the subject of some of his happiest descriptions in manhood.[46]

As he strolled along the much altered King Street, did the old man's thoughts drift back in time to where it all began? Was he once more acting out *The Fatal Revenge* with his brother in the family basement, mistiming his lines in a curtain-costume? Did he return to the wild hills of Lancashire where he and Aston composed *Sir John Chiverton*? Did he remember his early poems, *December Tales*, his friendship with Lamb; visiting London for the first time, falling in love, taking Dickens under his wing, the mad, bad days of the Regency? Did he reflect upon his past glories, his meteoric rise, terrible fall and now this final, albeit regional, redemption? Did he wonder whether he had lived a good life? We can only hope that he felt that he had, and that this final moment of glory gave the old survivor of Victorian literature a suitable sense of closure. After attending a service in Manchester Cathedral on Sunday September 18 (and another, more modest dinner with Thomas Baker at his home in Old Trafford), Ainsworth left Manchester forever.

In London, *Punch* remembered the novelist with whom it had shared a love-hate relationship throughout the 1840s and 50s and commemorated the

---

[46] *The Manchester Quarterly*, vol. 1, 1882.

Manchester banquet with the last in a long line of affectionate caricatures. This wonderful drawing by Linley Sambourne depicts the elderly Ainsworth in Elizabethan dress, sitting at his writing desk, the pen of romance in one hand, a short dagger in the other; an axe rests casually against his leg, and a miniature highwayman (a doll perhaps) sits upon a hobby-horse at his feet, flintlock drawn; the caption reads: 'To the greatest axe-and-neck-romancer of our time, who is quite at the head of his profession, we dedicated this block. *Ad Multos Annos!*'[47] This was not far short of the truth and Ainsworth loved it, commending the cartoon to Crossley in a letter that is also careful to remark that an article in Yates's *The World* compares Crossley's scholarship to that of Coleridge.[48]

In gratitude to Thomas Baker, Ainsworth dedicated his last work to him, tellingly inscribing the Routledge edition thus:

My Dear Mr. Mayor,

As I deem the banquet given by you in my honour, in my native city of Manchester, one of the most important events of my life, I shall endeavour to evince my sense of it by inscribing this tale to you. To you, moreover, and to the friends assembled on the occasion, I owe the gratifying title conferred upon me of 'The Lancashire Novelist', and I assure you I feel extremely proud of that distinction. And never surely was there a happier idea, or one more tastefully carried out, than the presentation to each guest at your banquet of an artistic little brochure containing a portrait and memoir of the author you had so greatly honoured, with specimens of the illustrations of his works. As an introduction to this tale I have given a revised report of the banquet that your readers may judge of it.

Your deeply obliged

W. Harrison Ainsworth.[49]

Ainsworth *loved* the Manchester banquet and, with an honest, almost childlike response to praise which he had exhibited all his life (in his long and earnest letters to fans for example), he uses this dedication to blow his own trumpet as much as that of the mayor. It must have been nice to be briefly famous once more.

---

[47] *Punch*, September 21 1881.

[48] Ainsworth, letter to Crossley, September 21 1881.

[49] Ainsworth, dedication, *Stanley Brereton* (London: George Routledge and Sons, 1881).

Nonetheless, Ainsworth also remembered to include Crossley, quite rightly, in the glory, writing to him that, 'this Banquet will form an important festival in your own biography as well as mine'.[50]

There is little else to record of the life of the Lancashire Novelist. His final letter to Crossley was as upbeat, yet as matter of fact, as usual, giving nothing away of his faltering health:

> My Dear Crossley,
>
> I have the pleasure to send you a copy of *Stanley Brereton*, and shall address the packet to the Chetham's Library. Like all the Tauchnitz editions, it is very charmingly printed.
>
> The Mayor was good enough to send me the *Manchester Courier* containing the report of his re-election, at which I am rejoiced – for he is a most excellent fellow. I have written to offer him my hearty congratulations. It certainly is very gratifying to me that he has been complimented on this Banquet and his re-election.
>
> Let me hear what you think of *Stanley Brereton* when you have read the book.
>
> Give my kind regards to Evans, and thank him for sending me the *Guardian*. I hope Routledge's edition will soon be published.
>
> Give my kind regards to Ralph. When he dined with me the other day at the Queen's Hotel, I gave him one of the *best* bottles of claret to be had at the house, but he didn't seem to understand it. Hinde thought the same wine superb.[51]
>
> Always yours
>
> W. Harrison Ainsworth.[52]

The banquet is, of course, still fresh in his mind. Ainsworth's final letter, written just after Christmas, was to his cousin, Dr James Bower Harrison. Here he gives a more honest account of his health, having been plagued since the winter of 1880 with severe neuralgia, bronchitis and insomnia brought on by the constant pain: 'I cannot give a very good report of myself', wrote Ainsworth, 'for the fogs with which we have been troubled during the last week have affected me a good deal,

---

[50] Ainsworth, letter to Crossley, October 31 1881.
[51] Ralph's identity has eluded me, but C.H. Hinde was the Executor of Ainsworth's estate.
[52] Ainsworth, letter to Crossley, November 11 1881.

and I have been obliged to call in Dr. Holman, our chief medical man ... Dr. Holman thought me much wasted since I last saw him, and so I am in no doubt.'[53] Five days later, on January 3 1882, Ainsworth suffered a fatal heart attack and died at home aged 76. He is buried at Kensal Green Cemetery with his mother and his brother, near the sites of his beloved Kensal Lodge and Kensal Manor House and having, among others, Henry Mayhew, Thackeray and Maclise for neighbours. James Crossley was too old to make the journey south for the funeral and he died, aged 83, almost exactly a year after Ainsworth.

---

[53] Ainsworth, letter to Dr James Bower Harrison, December 28 1881.

CONCLUSION

I have spent more time than some might consider healthy with Mr Ainsworth and his work over the last few years, and have found him to be an on the whole fascinating and amiable companion. As is always the case with projects such as this however, I leave my subject feeling that there still remains much to be said. There is another book, I am sure, on Ainsworth's contribution to Victorian journalism alone. His relationship with international writers of historical romance, most notably Alexandre Dumas, also awaits detailed exploration.[1] There is also a case to be made for his influence on the Sensation novels of the 1860s. The above I leave to experts in such areas, which I cannot claim to be.

The aim of my present project has been to reassess the significant works of William Harrison Ainsworth by first moving beyond the critical discourse that literary history has apparently bequeathed. To remain within the established frame of Ainsworth criticism, such as it is, is to regress uncritically to a bourgeois Victorian value system whether one chooses the path of moral and aesthetic condemnation (Horne to Sanders), or moral and aesthetic apology (Ellis to Worth). By approaching his texts as cultural artefacts, which it is absurd to continue to ignore given the vast audience the author commanded between 1834 and 1848 (from *Rookwood* to *The Lancashire Witches*), the trends in nineteenth century fiction he inaugurated and his legacy to the national myth, rather than as

---

[1] The first English translation of *The Count of Monte Cristo* appeared in *Ainsworth's Magazine* in 1845.

works of high literature (which they are not), I have attempted a new analysis which is intended to recontextualise Ainsworth. My intention has been to offer a different reading that is not based entirely upon contemporary comparisons that swing wildly between the gutter and the stars, and to find a more comfortable position for Ainsworth in the history of English literature. As we have seen from the critical orthodoxy, Ainsworth is usually judged in a couple of lines as a minor and rather pathetic author who was never in the same literary league as Sir Walter Scott or Charles Dickens; judged and indeed found guilty. To paraphrase one of Erskine Caldwell's remarks on authorship, Ainsworth was not a great thinker, not a great philosopher, but a story-teller.[2] Although a contemporary of Dickens, and as well-loved by much the same audience, Ainsworth was just part of the popular spirit of his age; Dickens was its visionary. Assessing many nineteenth century English novelists by the standards of the fathers of the nineteenth century English novel is, however, likely to yield similarly redundant conclusions. Every time yet another 'Barsetshire Chronicle' is serialised by the BBC, for example, I wonder how it is that Anthony Trollope has gotten away with it while William Harrison Ainsworth has not.

Neither, as I hope I have demonstrated, is Ainsworth just another fleetingly fashionable and fundamentally commercial hack, a literary dead-end whose fiction is a failed project to be filed away and forgotten somewhere between the periods of Romanticism and Realism. On the contrary, Ainsworth was an adventurer in a vast and largely unexplored narrative continent. He was at his most creatively active during a seismic period in English literature, counting many of its most distinguished figures as close friends, and both his life and works deserve more attention than they currently attract by any serious scholar of early nineteenth century literature. Continue to ignore him at your peril.

---

[2] 'I think that you must remember that a writer is a simple-minded person to begin with and go on that basis. He's not a great mind, he's not a great thinker, he's not a great philosopher, he's a story-teller.' Erskine Caldwell, *The Atlantic Monthly*, July 1958.

The examination of the work of a relatively forgotten novelist most active in the 1830s, Ainsworth in this case, although one might equally choose G.P.R. James for example, Catherine Gore, or even Lytton, can also reveal an often overlooked period of creative dynamism at a cultural moment still often viewed as something of a literary void, waiting to be filled by the Dickensian logos. I have attempted to explore this period using Ainsworth's life and art as the portal to a time that was as colourful as it was chaotic, an intellectual vortex where eighteenth century discourse and genres combined and recombined in a dizzying number of literary experiments, some of which developed aesthetically and theoretically as the century progressed, many of which did not. Rather, then, than backwardly imposing the Dickensian discourse of the *Dombey* period upon *Rookwood et al.* and consequently finding them wanting, or indeed taking the Lukácsian model of the historical narrative as the only valid form of analysis, I have looked towards the codes of the popular narratives of the gothic and the melodrama (interconnecting forms within themselves), the *Blackwood's Magazine* story, and Regency social exploration as other, equally sound, ways to interpret Ainsworth's literary output. This is in many ways a consideration of paraliterature and popular culture as the obvious and necessary ancestor of the mid Victorian novel, yet given the dignity of a literary reading rather than the merely sociological. As my view is that this author's most interesting writing appears between cultural paradigms, I have tried to examine the different influences that come together within an Ainsworthian text, such as the codes of classical tragedy and Elizabethan drama, in addition to British history, folk narrative and the gothic novel. In Ainsworth's writing, the process was on-going at least until *The Lancashire Witches*, where these different narratives finally coexist relatively seamlessly, before suddenly drowning in the wake of the new social realism of a rising generation of English novelists to which Ainsworth did not belong.

In common with all rebellious and self-assured youth, this new generation rejected its parents in favour of its grandparents, as we have seen in the many panegyrics to the likes of Defoe, Fielding and Hogarth by the likes of Thackeray,

Dickens and Forster, and usually at the expense of Ainsworth. It is as if the new age demanded a sacrifice to purge emergent Victorian sensibility of the excesses of the Regency and Romanticism. Because of the Newgate Controversy, Ainsworth was the perfect scapegoat.

By attempting such a reading of Ainsworth, I hope to have at least opened up the possibility that there might be a place in English literature for the author of *Rookwood* after all. I have suggested, for example, that Ainsworth may be the last of the original gothic novelists. Ainsworth began his career in the eighteenth century gothic tradition, and contributed much to the form's development in the nineteenth century through the undoubted influence of *Rookwood* and its successors, at least until the magical realism of *The Lancashire Witches*. Although, with the possible exception of *Jack Sheppard* and the unfinished *Auriol*, Ainsworth cannot easily be proved to have contributed directly to the new vogue of urban, psychological gothic in his own writings, he was certainly an important antecedent. Perhaps he had travelled as far as he was able, being at heart essentially a child of the Regency.

Ainsworth's early romances are also very much the bridging piece between the early gothic, and indeed historical, novels and their popular reinterpretations and revivals, first on the stage and, later, the screen. In common with the majority of modern film-makers, Ainsworth knew he was in the entertainment business and he knew how to deliver. As the poor sales of *Mervyn Clitheroe* demonstrate, you do not alter a successful formula. To this day, rightly or wrongly, the excessively violent, sexy, and melodramatic model of romance Ainsworth pioneered in many ways lives on. It may be unacknowledged, but it endures. When I watch a Hammer version of *Dracula* or *Frankenstein*, for example, or an early Roger Corman gothic from American International, I am invariably reminded of Ainsworth rather than Stoker, Shelley or Poe. The same can be said of the recent Hollywood fashion for historical epics such as

Braveheart and *Titanic*.[3] Like it or not, Mel Gibson and James Cameron were not reading Scott, Tolstoy and Lukács when they directed these movies. Perhaps they should have been, but despite the legion of sophisticated analytical approaches to the gothic and the historical romance to which we have access these days, most readers and viewers (not being blessed with a literary education) just want their gothic to be gory and their history to be glamorous.

On a broader scale, I hope that my work on this individual novelist may have also contributed to the wider study of the gothic, Newgate and historical novels as a whole, inasmuch as it offers an alternative way of reading texts that do not quite conform to a precise set of literary and historical standards, without recourse solely to the theories of popular culture. As I note above, the historical romance as written by Ainsworth, for example, continues to flourish in contemporary cinema, often to the chagrin of critics of film, historians and literary scholars. I believe that my reading of Ainsworth's historical narratives as mixed forms of tragedy, rather than simply failures to understand Scott, may offer some further room for debate on the presentation of history in not only nineteenth but twentieth and twenty-first century film and fiction.

Finally though, my wish is that we might reinstate this author in literary history, and republish a few of his classics so that students, or simply fans, of the nineteenth century novel will have access to *Rookwood, Jack Sheppard, The Tower of London, Old St. Paul's* and *The Lancashire Witches* once more, in order to understand a little more about the creative processes that led to the condition of England novel on the one hand and the costume drama on the other.

It is equally important to note that these creative processes also contributed to our own national myth, a version of England so unconditionally accepted that it is held, as they say, to be self-evident. Like the story of *Frankenstein* (incorporating, among other aspects, Mary Shelley's original text, wild nights at the Villa Diodati, the Fall, Romanticism, the films of Boris Karloff

---

[3] *Titanic*, dir. James Cameron, perf. Leonardo DiCaprio, Kate Winslet and Billy Zane, Warner, 1997.

and Peter Cushing, and genetically modified food), novels such as *Rookwood, The Tower of London* and *The Lancashire Witches* have a complex relationship with what Chris Baldick has called 'modern myths'. Such myths, explains Baldick, are, by definition, anomalous to the most influential anthropological, psychological and literary studies, which all agree that 'myth' is a feature of a lost, preliterate world 'to which modern writers may distantly and ironically allude, but in which they can no longer directly participate.'[4] Ainsworth's myths are, however, like objects in a rear-view mirror: closer than they appear. Dick Turpin's ride to York, the Lancashire Witches cavorting on Pendle Hill, and the ghost of Anne Boleyn wandering across Tower Green, for example, belong to popular English myth so comfortably that the source has become redundant. The only myth to which Ainsworth's name presently remains directly attached is the critical myth of the Victorians, his negative author-function. As only the greatest of magicians can do, Ainsworth has actually made himself disappear. I still hope that there is a magic word that might bring him back.

In his own monograph of Ainsworth, a work I am very aware that I follow, George J. Worth writes in his preface that 'It would be absurd to claim that the purpose of a study like this is the rehabilitation of Ainsworth.'[5] I am afraid I am more ambitious. I can only hope that my own research, however imperfect, may yet reopen the debate regarding Ainsworth's significance in the history of English letters, and that scholars of the Victorian novel, students of literature, historians, and, perhaps most importantly, the people of Manchester and his beloved Lancashire will once more read his work with interest and pleasure, which is all the man himself would ask of us I am sure. Such scholarship is, of course, an endless and dynamic process. When Malcolm Elwin wrote of his 'Victorian Wallflowers' in 1934 he included 'neglected' novelists whom we now, quite justifiably, acknowledge in mainstream literary history, such as: R.D.

---

[4] Chris Baldick, introduction, *In Frankenstein's Shadow: Myth, Monstrosity, and Nineteenth-century Writing* (Oxford: Clarendon Press, 1990).
[5] Worth, preface.

Blackmore, Wilkie Collins, John Forster, Mrs Henry Wood and the Rev. R.H. Barham. Similarly, at the time of writing, G.W.M. Reynolds is finally receiving the academic attention which he deserves, along with several even lesser known Chartist novelists. I therefore conclude by commending the Lancashire Novelist to the world once more, a wallflower no longer, and with the final suggestion that if *Jack Sheppard* ever makes it to the screen Alan Rickman would make a great Jonathan Wild.

APPENDIX A

On the authorship of *Sir John Chiverton.*
A debate from beyond the grave

I offer the following extracts of correspondence, which I unearthed during my research in Manchester, as both an illustration of the disputed authorship of *Sir John Chiverton* and as a reasonable solution.

Ainsworth's correspondence with Aston, and their subsequent career trajectories, suggest strongly that it was Ainsworth rather than Aston who was the enthusiastic young author. Aston was much more the enthusiastic young lawyer, who preferred to put aside childish things such as romance writing upon leaving the Manchester Free Grammar School. It appears that Ainsworth sometimes had to fulfil Aston's part of jointly agreed upon magazine commitments himself, and that the original novel, notably described as '*our* Sir John' in surviving correspondence, was certainly polished by Ainsworth during his time with Ebers. Contemporary reviews citing Ainsworth as the sole author of the novel were not challenged by Aston at the time, while Ainsworth was first keen that the novel should be credited as a joint production between them, before finally omitting it from the Manchester banquet bibliography along with his other juvenilia (of which there is no doubt concerning authorship), preferring his literary career to be seen to begin with the hugely popular *Rookwood* in 1834, while also avoiding any potential arguments with Aston, who was still living in Manchester at the time.

Aston did not publicly claim authorship of the novel until after Ainsworth's death, sparking a sharp debate in the Manchester press. The discovery of William Henville's letter by Ainsworth's executor, C.H. Hinde, does not, of course, establish that Ainsworth had written the text that Henville copied for him but it does demonstrate at the very least a strong editorial input. Ainsworth did not save his letters as did Crossley, which is why we never hear the latter's side of the correspondence, but he did save this one. I suspect he knew that some evidence of his contribution to the novel from Scott's Journal might be required one day.

I. Ainsworth to John Partington Aston

What in the name of all extraordinary things has kept you silent all this week. Did you not promise with a most reliable appearance of truth that you would write with the work agreed upon weekly. Is this the way you fulfil promises. Certainly you are consistent in one aspect. Your correspondence is in a *weakly* way. If you will not write, the duty naturally devolves upon me.[1]

With regard to our *Sir John*. What shall we do with this. I will tell you what I propose. Nobody will buy him in his present state and he would want a great deal of amendment for our present volume. If perfectly agreeable to you I will pay you some reasonable sum for the copyright and publish it at my own expense. The merits of the work will I trust make it sell and if it does we will divide the profits.[2]

I send you a couple of copies of *Sir John Chiverton* first edition …[3]

II. Contemporary reviews

'A young gentleman of Manchester, and a contributor to our pages, is about to favour the world with a Romance entitled, *Sir John Chiverton*.'[4] To read Mr. Ebers's announcement of *Sir John*, one would suppose the author was a 'pocket unknown', or, as Mr. Colburn calls young D'Israeli in his puffs of *Vivian Grey*, a 'new unknown' … This tale, written, as we have already stated,

---

[1] Ainsworth, letter to Aston, March 1 1825.
[2] Ainsworth, letter to Aston, November 27 1825.
[3] Ainsworth, letter to Aston, undated, presumably late July 1826.
[4] Ebers's 'puff', an advance notice of the novel, placed in *The Literary Souvenir* 1826.

by a young gentleman of Manchester, of the name of Ainsworth, reflects great credit upon its author.[5]

This is one of the early works of talent and genius which makes us hope to see many more from the same source ... a rich picturesque illusion surrounds the whole fiction.[6]

III. Ainsworth to James Crossley

Crossley had submitted a proof to Ainsworth of a passage in the 'Manchester School Register' regarding *Sir John Chiverton*, to which the author replied:

I have added a line to the memoir of Aston, which will set the matter right. The interlineation is simply – written in collaboration with W. Harrison Ainsworth – as is the fact.[7]

The following concerns the preparation of a bibliography of Ainsworth's works by Crossley, to be appended to a commemorative brochure being presented to guests attending the Lord Mayor's banquet in Ainsworth's honour, held at Manchester Town Hall, September 15, 1881, 'As an expression of the high esteem in which he is held by his Fellow townsmen and of his services to Literature'.

I anticipate a very pleasant *friendly* dinner at the Town Hall ...

PS. Take care *Sir John Chiverton* is not placed among the list of my works. I saw it in the list sent to me by the Mayor, and struck it out. I should be annoyed if this is neglected.[8]

(A following letter, dated the next day, concludes, 'Don't neglect to strike out Sir John Chiverton.')

The Mayor has sent me proofs of the little pamphlet, which contains a 'chronological list of my works'. This I have approved and returned. It makes no mention of *Sir John Chiverton*. ... By the way, who is Mr. John Evans? Is he an old friend of mine?[9]

---

[5] *The Literary Magnet*, July 1826, quoted from Ellis, vol. 1, 134–5.
[6] *The Literary Gazette*, July 1826, cited by Ellis, vol. 1, 135.
[7] Ainsworth, letter to Crossley dated November 30 1871.
[8] Ainsworth, letter to Crossley, August 26 1881.
[9] Ainsworth, letter to Crossley, August 30 1881. John Evans was a Manchester journalist and fan. Author of 'The Early Life of William Harrison Ainsworth', *Manchester Quarterly*, I, 136–55.

IV. Aston to C.W. Sutton

I had the opportunity last evening, for the first time, of seeing your interesting *List of Lancashire Authors*, in which I met with my name mentioned as 'collaborateur with Mr. W. Harrison Ainsworth in the romance of *Sir John Chiverton*'. I have no wish to be held out as an author at all, but if I must be, I desire that it may be done correctly. Mr. Ainsworth never wrote a line of *Sir John Chiverton*, for which I am solely responsible. I am neither anxious to participate in Mr. Ainsworth's celebrity, nor wishful to throw upon him the credit, or discredit, of my juvenile performances, and if any further 'Additions and Corrections' to your *List* be printed, I trust that the correction I now bring under your notice may be attended to. In the meantime, I should be glad to have it notified to the very respectable club under whose auspices the *List* appears.[10]

V. Aston to *The Times*

THE LATE MR. HARRISON AINSWORTH.

TO THE EDITOR OF THE TIMES

Sir,–

I shall be obliged by the insertion in *The Times* of the following reference to the obituary article on the above gentleman in your issue of the 4th inst., in which it said:– 'While in his teens he wrote and published his romance of "Sir John Cheverton"' (Chiverton), &c. Ainsworth did not write this book, of which I am the author, nor does his name appear on the title-page as the author.[11] In what is described as the second edition (though, in fact, a mere re-issue) his name appears as publisher and only so; nor does 'Sir John Chiverton' appear in the chronological list of Ainsworth's works, printed on the beautifully-illustrated card pamphlet, presented to the guests at the dinner given in September last to Ainsworth by the Mayor of Manchester.

My acquaintance with Ainsworth commenced at the Manchester Free Grammar School, and our intimacy increased when he became a fellow clerk with me in the office Mr. Alexander Kay, the solicitor, to whom he was articled.[12] We were both fond of literary pursuits, or what we considered such, and our conversation generally turned on literary subjects. Hulme-hall, an

---

[10] C.W. Sutton was the author of *A List of Lancashire Authors* (Manchester: 1877). Quoted from Ellis, vol. 1, 137.

[11] Neither does Aston's, the book is anonymously written.

[12] This is incorrect, and demonstrates that Aston's memory was less than reliable. Aston and Ainsworth were never fellow-clerks in Alexander Kay's office, but were in the office of Ainsworth's father; Aston joined Kay's firm after Ainsworth had moved to London. Ainsworth never worked for Kay.

ancient mansion on the late Duke of Bridgewater's estate, was a locality in which we took much interest, and I think it was Ainsworth who suggested to me the writing of a romance in connexion with it. This I did, and hence the production of the work in question, in which the name 'Chiverton Hall' was substituted for 'Hulme-hall'. I communicated the manuscript as the work progressed to Ainsworth, and he attended to its publication. It was originally published by Ebers, but what purports to be the second edition bears Ainsworth's name as publisher in Old Bond-Street, 1827. He had, however, no part in the composition nor do I know that he ever claimed it, and the celebrity he afterwards attained must have rendered the question (had any such existed) of its authorship of very little importance to him.

Our intimacy declined when he established himself in the literary world of London, and I became absorbed in my professional pursuits.

Apologising for this intrusion on your space,

I am, Sir, very respectfully yours,

JOHN P. ASTON

St. James's-chambers,
South King-street,
Manchester,
January 6th.
1882.[13]

VI. *The Manchester Guardian*

DEATH OF MR. JOHN PARTINGTON ASTON.

The obituary concludes:

In early professional life Mr. Aston was not unknown as an anonymous contributor to the popular annuals and periodicals, both in prose and verse. One work, a romance, entitled 'Sir John Chiverton' deserves special mention, being referred to by Sir Walter Scott (as stated in his Life by Lockhart), as one of those literary productions which the great enchanter himself had called into birth.[14]

---

[13] Aston, letter to *The Times*, January 6 1882.
[14] *Manchester Guardian*, May 13 1882.

418

VII. John Evans, *Notes and Queries*

In recently preparing a monograph on the early life of Mr. Harrison Ainsworth, I have had occasion to make a close investigation into the real authorship of the romance in question ... For nearly forty years the authorship had been publicly attributed to Mr. Ainsworth, without any public denial on the part of Mr. Aston until the week after the novelist's death. I believe however that prior to this Mr. Aston had made privately some claim upon the authorship, and, in order to test that claim, Mr. James Crossley, the President of the Chetham Society, submitted a proof to Ainsworth of a passage in the 'Manchester School Register' (vol. iii, pt. i. pp. 112–13) which relates to Mr. Aston. The proof originally stood: 'In early life Mr. Aston was not unknown as an anonymous contributor to the popular annuals and periodicals, both in prose and verse. One work, a romance, entitled "Sir John Chiverton" deserves special mention, being referred to by Sir Walter Scott &c.' In sending the proof in question Mr. Crossley asked Ainsworth to make any necessary corrections before finally going to press, as he (Mr. Crossley) felt a personal interest in having the question settled. The proof was returned, and in the sentence beginning, 'One work, a romance entitled "Sir John Chiverton"', Ainsworth interpolated, in his own handwriting, the very explicit words, 'written in collaboration with Mr. Harrison Ainsworth.' Further, with the corrected proof Mr. Crossley received a letter in which, referring to the authorship of 'Sir John Chiverton,' the novelist remarked to the effect that he had *now* made the matter right.[15]

VIII. William Henville to Ainsworth

C.H. Hinde, Ainsworth's Executor, found the following letter among the deceased's papers and sent a copy to the Editor of the *Manchester Guardian*.

October 14th 1841.

Sir,–

In the years 1823, 1824, and 1825 I had the privileged honour to be engrossing clerk at Mr. Alexander Kay's at Manchester, and of being at that time useful to you as amanuensis in copying and collecting material for your celebrated novel of 'Sir John Chiverton'. When you left Manchester you were kind enough to say that you would do what you could for me in case I should come to London.

---

[15] John Evans, *Notes and Queries*, March 4 1882, quoted in the *Manchester Courier*, May 13 1882. In response to this article, Henry Harwood, a friend of the recently deceased Mr Aston, wrote to the Editor of the *Manchester Guardian* that Aston's original letter to *The Times* was, 'a statement which Mr. Aston only a few weeks ago verbally confirmed by stating that "Mr. Ainsworth did not write a word of it"'. *Manchester Guardian*, May 15 1882.

I shall feel very much obliged by your exerting your powerful interests with any gentleman in the profession on my behalf.

Mr Hinde concluded his own letter with, 'I leave the letter to speak for itself without any further comment.'[16]

---

[16] *Manchester Guardian*, May 18 1882.

APPENDIX B

The original conclusion of *Catherine, A Story* by Thackeray

This long diatribe against Dickens and Ainsworth preceded the final paragraph of Thackeray's serial in *Fraser's Magazine*. It is not included in subsequent editions of *Catherine* in book form or in Thackeray's collected works.

To begin with Mr. Dickens. No man has read that remarkable tale of *Oliver Twist* without being interested in poor Nancy and her murderer; and especially amused and tickled by the gambols of the Artful Dodger and his companions. The power of the writer is so amazing, that the reader at once becomes his captive, and must follow him whithersoever he leads; and to what are we led? Breathless to watch all the crimes of Fagin, tenderly to deplore the errors of Nancy, to have for Bill Sikes a kind of pity and admiration, and an absolute love for the society of the Dodger. All these heroes stepped from the novel on to the stage; and the whole London public, from peers to chimney-sweeps, were interested about a set of ruffians whose occupations are thievery, murder, and prostitution. A most agreeable set of rascals, indeed, who have their virtues, too, but not good company for any man. We had better pass them by in decent silence; for, as no writer can or dare tell the whole truth concerning them, and faithfully explain their vices, there is no need to give *ex-parte* statements of their virtue.

And what came of *Oliver Twist*? The public wanted something more extravagant still, more sympathy for thieves, and so *Jack Sheppard* makes his appearance. Jack and his two wives, and his faithful Blueskin, and his gin-drinking mother, that sweet Magdalen! – with what a wonderful gravity are all their adventures related, with what an honest simplicity and vigour does Jack's biographer record his actions and virtues! We are taught to hate Wild, to be sure; but then it is because he betrays thieves, the rogue! And yet bad, ludicrous, monstrous as the idea of this book is, we read and read, and are interested, too. The author has a wondrous faith, and a most respectful notion of the vastness of his subject. There is not one particle of banter in his composition; good and bad ideas, he hatches all with the same gravity; and is just as earnest in his fine description of the storm on the Thames, and his admirable account of the escape from Newgate; as in the scenes at Whitefriars, and the conversations at Wild's, than which nothing was ever written more curiously unnatural. We are not, however, here criticizing the novels, but simply have to speak of the Newgate part of them, which gives birth to something a great deal worse than bad taste, and familiarises the public with notions of crime. In the dreadful satire of *Jonathan Wild*, no reader is so dull as to make the mistake of admiring, and can overlook the grand and hearty contempt of the author for the character he has described; the bitter wit of the *Beggar's Opera*, too, hits the great, by shewing their similarity with the wretches that figure in the play; and though the latter piece is so brilliant in its mask of gaiety and wit, that a very dull person may not see the dismal reality thus disguised, moral, at least, there is in the satire, for those who will take the trouble to find it. But in the sorrows of Nancy and the exploits of Sheppard, there is no such lurking moral, as far as we have been able to discover; we are asked for downright sympathy in the one case, and are called on in the second to admire the gallantry of a thief. The street-walker may be a virtuous person, and the robber as brave as Wellington; but it is better to leave them alone, and their qualities, good and bad. The pathos of the workhouse scenes in *Oliver Twist*, or the Fleet prison descriptions in *Pickwick*, is genuine and pure as much of this as you please; as tender a hand to the poor, as kindly a word to the unhappy as you will; but in the name of common sense, let us not expend our sympathies on cut-throats, and other such prodigies of evil![1]

---

[1] W.M. Thackeray, 'Catherine, A Story', *Fraser's Magazine*, February 1840, 211.

APPENDIX C

'OLD GRINDROD'S GHOST': A BALLAD*

OLD GRINDROD was hanged on a gibbet high,
    On the spot where the deed was done;
'Twas a desolate place, on the edge of a moor, –
    A place for the timid to shun.

Chains round his middle, and chains round his neck,
    And chains round his ankles were hung:
And there in all weathers, in sunshine and rain,
    Old Grindrod, the murderer, swung.

Old Grindrod had long been the banquet of crows,
    Who flocked on his carcase to batten;
And the unctuous morsels that fell from their feast
    Served the rank weeds beneath him to fatten!

All that's now left of him is a skeleton grim,
    The stoutest to strike with dismay;
So ghastly the sight, that no urchin at night,
    Who can help it, will pass by that way.

As such as had dared, had sadly been scared,
    And soon 'twas the general talk,
That the wretch in his chains, each night took the pains,
    To come down from the gibbet – *and walk!*

The story was told to a Traveller bold,
    At an inn, near the moor, by the Host;
He appeals to each guest, and its truth they attest,
    But the Traveller laughs at the Ghost.

---

* Founded on an incident, related to me, with admirable humour, by my old and much-valued friend, GILBERT WINTER, ESQ., late of Stocks, near Manchester. (Author's original note.)

424

'Now, to show you', quoth he, 'how afraid I must be,
    A rump and a dozen I'll lay;
That before it strikes One, I will go forth alone,
    Old Grindrod a visit to pay.

'To the gibbet I'll go, an this I will do,
    As sure as I stand in my shoes;
Some address I'll devise, and if Grinny replies,
    My wager, of course, I shall lose.'

'Accepted the bet; but the night it is wet',
    Quoth the Host. 'Never mind!' says the Guest;
'From darkness and rain, the adventure will gain,
    To my mind, an additional zest.'

Now midnight had toll'd, and the Traveller bold
    Set out from the inn, all alone;
'Twas a night black as ink, and our friend 'gan to think,
    That uncommonly cold it had grown.

But of nothing afraid, and by nothing delayed;
    Plunging onward through bog and through wood;
Wind and rain in his face, he ne'er slackened his pace,
    Till under the gibbet he stood.

Though dark as could be, yet he thought he could see
    The skeleton hanging on high;
The gibbet it creaked: and the rusty chain squeaked;
    And a screech-owl flew solemnly by.

The heavy rain pattered, the hollow bones clattered,
    The Traveller's teeth chattered – with cold – not with fright
The wind it blew lustily, piercingly, gustily; –
    Certainly not an agreeable night!

'Ho! Grindrod, old fellow!' thus loudly did bellow,
    The Traveller mellow, – 'How are ye, my blade?' –
'I'm cold and I'm dreary; I'm wet and I'm weary;
    But soon I'll be near ye!' the skeleton said.

The grisly bones rattled, and with the chains battled,
    The gibbet appallingly shook;
On the ground something stirr'd, but no more the man heard, –
    To his heels, on the instant, he took.

Over moorland he dashed, and through quagmire he plashed;
    His pace never daring to slack;
Till the hostel he neared, for greatly he feared
    Old Grindrod would leap on his back.

His wager he lost, and a trifle it cost;
    But that which annoyed him the most,
Was to find out too late, that certain as fate,
    The Landlord had acted the ghost.[1]

---

[1] Ainsworth, *The Flitch of Bacon*, Works, 152–4.

THE WORKS OF WILLIAM HARRISON
AINSWORTH

Manuscript Sources

Ainsworth, William Harrison, *Autograph letters of W.H. Ainsworth to James Crossley*, 11 vols, Archives Section. Local Studies Unit, Central Library, Manchester.
Aston, John Partington, *Letters*, 2 vols, Archives Section; Local Studies Unit, Central Library, Manchester.

Published Works[1]

Ainsworth. William Harrison, *Poems by Cheviot Ticheburn* (London: John Arliss, 1822).*
—*Monody on the Death of John Philip Kemble* (Manchester: John Leigh, 1823).*
—*December Tales* (London: G. and B.W. Whitaker, 1823).*
—*The Bœotion* (Manchester: Thomas Sowler, 1824).*
—*Considerations on the best means of affording Immediate Relief to the Operative Classes in the Manufacturing Districts* (London: John Ebers, 1826).*
—*Sir John Chiverton. A Romance.* Written in collaboration with John Partington Aston (London: John Ebers, 1826).*
—*Rookwood, A Romance*, 3 vols (London: Richard Bentley, 1834).
—*Crichton*, 3 vols (London: Richard Bentley, 1837).
—*Jack Sheppard, A Romance*, 3 vols (London; Richard Bentley, 1839).
—*The Tower of London, A Historical Romance* (London: Richard Bentley, 1840).
—*Guy Fawkes, or The Gunpowder Treason. An Historical Romance*, 3 vols (London: Richard Bentley, 1841).

---

[1] *The Original Illustrated Edition of the Novels of William Harrison Ainsworth*, 31 vols (London: George Routledge and Sons, 1881) is the standard edition. Those works marked with an asterisk are not included in this collection. There is no complete uniform edition.

—*Old St Paul's; A Tale of the Plague and the Fire*, 3 vols (London: Hugh Cunningham, 1841).

—*The Miser's Daughter, A Tale*, 3 vols (London: Cunningham and Mortimer, 1842).

—*Windsor Castle, An Historical Romance*, 3 vols (London: Henry Colburn, 1843).

—*St James's or The Court of Queen Anne, An Historical Romance*, 3 vols (London: John Mortimer, 1844).

—*James the Second, or the Revolution of 1688. An Historical Romance*, 3 vols (London: Henry Colburn, 1848).

—*The Lancashire Witches, A Romance of Pendle Forest*, 3 vols (London: Henry Colburn, 1849).

—*The Star Chamber, An Historical Romance*, 2 vols (London: George Routledge & Co., 1854).

—*The Flitch of Bacon, or The Custom of Dunmow. A Tale of English Home* (London: George Routledge & Co., 1854).

—*Ballads: Romantic, Fantastical, and Humorous* (London: George Routledge & Co., 1855).*

—*The Spendthrift, A Tale* (London: George Routledge & Co., 1857).

—*Mervyn Clitheroe* (London: George Routledge & Co., 1858).

—*Ovingdean Grange, A Tale of the South Down*s (London: Routledge. Warne. and Routledge, 1860).

—*The Constable of the Tower, An Historical Romance*, 3 vols (London: Chapman and Hall, 1861).

—*The Lord Mayor of London: or City Life in the Last Century*, 3 vols (London: Chapman and Hall, 1862).

—*Cardinal Pole: or The Days of Philip and Mary. An Historical Romance*, 3 vols (London: Chapman and Hall, 1863).

—*John Law, The Protector*, 3 vols (London: Chapman and Hall, 1864).

—*Auriol, or The Elixir of Life* (London: George Routledge & Sons. 1865.

—*The Spanish Match, or Charles Stuart at Madrid*, 3 vols (London: Chapman and Hall, 1865).

—*The Constable de Bourbon*, 3 vols (London: Chapman and Hall, 1866).

—*Old Court, A Novel*, 3 vols (London: Chapman and Hall, 1867).

—*Myddleton Pomfret, A Novel*, 3 vols (London: Chapman and Hall, 1868).

—*The South-Sea Bubble, A Tale of the Year 1720* (London: John Dicks, 1869).*

—*Hilary St Ives, A Novel*, 3 vols (London: Chapman and Hall, 1870).

—*Talbot Harland, A Tale of the Days of Charles the Second* (London: John Dicks, 1870).*

—*Tower Hill, An Historical Romance* (London: John Dicks, 1871).*

—*Boscobel, or The Royal Oak. A Tale of the Year 1651*, 3 vols (London: Tinsley Brothers, 1872).

—*The Manchester Rebels of the Fatal '45*, 3 vols (London: Tinsley Brothers, 1873).

—*Merry England, or Nobles and Serfs*, 3 vols (London: Tinsley Brothers, 1874).

—*The Goldsmith's Wife, A Tale*, 3 vols (London: Tinsley Brothers, 1875).

—*Preston Fight, or the Insurrection of 1715. A Tale*, 3 vols (London: Tinsley Brothers, 1875).

—*Chetwynd Calverley, A Tale*, 3 vols (London: Tinsley Brothers, 1876).

—*The Leaguer of Lathom, A Tale of the Civil War in Lancashire*, 3 vols (London: Tinsley Brothers, 1876).

—*The Fall of Somerset*, 3 vols (London: Tinsley Brothers, 1877).

—*Beatrice Tyldesley*, 3 vols (London: Tinsley Brothers, 1878).

—*Beau Nash; or Bath in the Eighteenth Century*, 3 vols (London: George Routledge and Sons, 1879).

—*Stanley Brereton*, 3 vols (London: George Routledge and Sons, 1881).

Contributions to other works

Ainsworth. William Harrison, 'The Old London Merchant (Sir Lionel Flamstead)', *The Pic-Nic Papers*, Charles Dickens (ed.) (London: Henry Colburn, 1841).

—'The Astrologer', *Evenings at Haddon Hall*, Baroness de Calabrella (ed.) (London: Henry Colburn, 1846).

—'The Mandrake', 'Black Bess', 'Old Grindrod's Ghost', *Lancashire Lyrics: Modern Songs and Ballads of the County Palantine*, John Harland F.S.A. (ed.) (London. Whittaker & Co., 1866).

—'Memoir of Thomas Gilbert Ainsworth', *The Manchester Grammar School Register* (Manchester, 1871).

Contributions to periodicals

Ainsworth. William Harrison, 'The Rivals: A Serio-Comic Tragedy', *Arliss's Pocket Magazine*, VII, 1821.

—'Venice. or the Fall of the Foscaris', I.i, *Arliss's Pocket Magazine*, VII, 1821.

—'Venice', ii, *Arliss's Pocket Magazine*, VII, 1821.

—Scene from 'Ximenez', *Arliss's Pocket Magazine*, VII, 1821.

—'Scenes from Act II of Venice', *Arliss's Pocket Magazine*, VII, 1821.

—'The Tempest', *Arliss's Pocket Magazine*, VII, 1821.

—'Epigram', *Arliss's Pocket Magazine*, VII, 1821.

—'The Dream', *Arliss's Pocket Magazine*, VII, 1821.

—'Dramatic Scenes. No. 1', *Arliss's Pocket Magazine*, VII, 1821.

—'Evening', *Arliss's Pocket Magazine*, VII, 1821.

—'Ghiotto; or Treason Discovered. A Tragedy in Two Acts', *Arliss's Pocket Magazine*, VIII, 1821.

—'Recollections of a Veteran', *Arliss's Pocket Magazine*, VII, 1821.

—'Farewell Address. spoken at the Theatre. Manchester Feb. 8', *Arliss's Pocket Magazine*, VII, 1821.

—'Sir Albert's Bride', *Arliss's Pocket Magazine*, VII, 1821.

—'The Dying Laird', *Arliss's Pocket Magazine*, VII, 1821.

—'Song', *Arliss's Pocket Magazine*, VII, 1821.

—'Epistle to J.W. Dalby. Esq', *Arliss's Pocket Magazine*, VII, 1821.

—'Translation from Seneca: *Quis Vere Rex?*', *Arliss's Pocket Magazine*, VII, 1821.

—'Gothamburg Transactions. No. 5', *Arliss's Pocket Magazine*, VII, 1821.

—'Letter of Mr. Poker' [also poss. in collaboration with Aston], *Arliss's Pocket Magazine*, VIII, 1821.

—'The Pirate: A Romance', *Arliss's Pocket Magazine*, VIII, 1821.

—'Farewell Address To—', *Arliss's Pocket Magazine*, VIII, 1821.

—'Stanzas', *Arliss's Pocket Magazine*, VIII, 1821.

—'The Spectre Bride [The Baron's Bridal]', *Arliss's Pocket Magazine*, VIII, 1821.

—'Translation from Tibullus. Book IV. Elegy II', *Arliss's Pocket Magazine*, VIII, 1821.

—'An Adventure in the South Seas [The Mutiny]', *Arliss's Pocket Magazine*, VIII, 1821.

—'The Cut Finger. A Tragedy in One Act', *Arliss's Pocket Magazine*, VIII, 1821.

—'Gothamburg Transactions', *Arliss's Pocket Magazine*, VIII, 1821.

—'The Pokerian Controversy', *Arliss's Pocket Magazine*, VIII, 1821.

—'On The Writings of Richard Clitheroe', *The New Monthly Magazine*, 1821.

—'The Baron's Bridal [The Spectre Bride]', *The European Magazine*, 1821.

—'The Scrap Book', *Arliss's Pocket Magazine*, IX, 1822.

—'The Lady Sprite [The Sea Spirit]', *Arliss's Pocket Magazine*, IX, 1822.

—'A Letter to the Editor', *The Edinburgh Magazine*, IX, 1821.

—'Venice or the Fall of the Foscaris', *The Edinburgh Magazine*, IX, 1821.

—'The Emigrant's Return', *The Edinburgh Magazine*, X, 1822.

—'Sonnet', *The Edinburgh Magazine*, X, 1822.

—'Translation from Seneca: *Quis vere Rex?*', *The Edinburgh Magazine*, X, 1822.

—'London Periodicals', *The Edinburgh Magazine*, X, 1822.

—'What shall I write? [The Theatre]', *The Edinburgh Magazine*, X, 1822.

—'*Horae Seniles*: Three parts [Recollections]', *The Edinburgh Magazine*, X, 1822.

—'A December Tale [The Englisher's Story]', *The European Magazine*, 1822.

—'The Imperishable One [The Wanderings of an Immortal]', *The European Magazine*, 1822.

—'Venice', *The European Magazine*, 1822.

—'The Test of Affection', *The European Magazine*, 1822.

—'The Emigrant', *The European Magazine*, 1822.

—'The Reading Room', *The European Magazine*, 1822.

—'Snoring', *The European Magazine*, 1822.

—'The Falls of Ohiopyle', *The London Magazine*, 1822.

—'The Half-Hangit', *The Manchester Iris*, 1822.

—'The Half-Hangit', *The European Magazine*, 1823.

—'*Coenobium Atticum*', *The European Magazine*, 1823.
—'A Tale of Mystery', *The Boeotian*, I, 1824.
—'Marian Seaforth of Pine Hollow', *The Boeotian*, I, 1824.
—'The Ladies' Bazaar at the Exchange', *The Boeotian*, I, 1824.
—'The Fortress of Saguntum', *The Literary Souvenir*, 1825.
—'An Imperfect Portrait', *The Literary Souvenir*, 1825.
—'The Fairy and the Peach Tree', *The Christmas Box*, 1825.
—'Dedicatory Stanzas', *The Keepsake*, 1827.
—'Pocket Books and Keepsakes', *The Keepsake*, 1827.
—'The Cook and the Doctor', *The Keepsake*, 1827.
—'Opera Reminiscences for 1827', *The Keepsake*, 1827.
—'The Ghost Laid', *The Keepsake*, 1828.
—'The Wind and the Wave', *Fraser's Magazine*, 1830.
—'La Guglielmina of Milan', *Fraser's Magazine*, 1834.
—'St. Augustine and the Boy', *Fraser's Magazine*, 1835
—'One Foot in the Stirrup', *Fraser's Magazine*, 1835.
—'A Night's Adventure in Rome', *The Book of Beauty*, 1835).
—'April Fools', *Bentley's Miscellany*, Apr. 1837.
—'Lines on the Portrait of Mrs. Fairlie', *The Book of Beauty*, 1838.
—'Jack Sheppard'. *Bentley's Miscellany*, Jan. 1839–Feb. 1840.
—'Old St. Paul's', *The Sunday Times*, 1841.
—'Beatrice di Tenda [Michele Orombell]', *The Keepsake*, 1841.
—'Guy Fawkes', *Bentley's Miscellany*, Jan. 1840–Nov. 1841.
—'Literary Intelligence', *Bentley's Miscellany*, Jan. 1841.
—'To a Young Italian Lady', *The Keepsake*, 1842.
—'Preliminary Address', *Ainsworth's Magazine*, Feb. 1842.
—'Strawberry Hill', *Ainsworth's Magazine*, 1842.
—'The Miser's Daughter', *Ainsworth's Magazine*, Feb.–Nov. 1842.
—'Our Library Table', *Ainsworth's Magazine*, Feb. 1842.
—'Our Correspondent', *Ainsworth's Magazine*, Mar.–Apr. 1842.
—'L'envoi', *Ainsworth's Magazine*, Apr. 1842.
—[G.P.R.] James's *Morley Ernstein*', *Ainsworth's Magazine*, June 1842.
—'To Our Readers', *Ainsworth's Magazine*, July 1842–Jan. 1844.
—'Windsor Castle', *Ainsworth's Magazine*, July 1842–June 1843.
—'*Miser's Daughter* at the Adelphi', *Ainsworth's Magazine*, Nov. 1842.
—'Saint James's', *Ainsworth's Magazine*, Jan.–Dec. 1844.
—'Reviews of *Martin Chuzzlewit* and *A Christmas Carol*', *Ainsworth's Magazine*, Dec. 1844.
—'[G.P.R.] James's Late Romances', *Ainsworth's Magazine*, Feb. 1844.
—'Pocket ed. of Leigh Hunt's poems', *Ainsworth's Magazine*, May 1844.
—'Revelations of London', *Ainsworth's Magazine*, Oct. 1844–May 1845.
—'[G.P.R.] James's Gipsy and Mary of Burgandy', *Ainsworth's Magazine*, Oct. 1844.
—'British Archaeologists at Canterbury', *Ainsworth's Magazine*, Oct. 1844.

—'[G.P.R. James's] *Agincourt* and *The Huguenot*', *Ainsworth's Magazine*, Jan. 1845.

—'Supper Sages [on Kenealy's *Brallaghan*]', *Ainsworth's Magazine*, Feb. 1845.

—'Condition of Archaeological Association', *Ainsworth's Magazine*, Mar. 1845.

—'The Late Mr. Laman Blanchard', *Ainsworth's Magazine*, Mar. 1845.

—'The D'Orsay Gallery', *Ainsworth's Magazine*, Mar. 1845.

—'Archaeological Society and Athenaeum', *Ainsworth's Magazine*, May 1845

—'Revelations of London. [Auriol]', *The New Monthly Magazine*, July 1845–Jan. 1846).

—'Cecco del Orso', *The New Monthly Magazine*, July 1845.

—'The opera', *The New Monthly Magazine*, July 1845–Aug. 1850.

—'British Archaeological Society. Winchester', *The New Monthly Magazine*, Sep. 1845.

—'Sir Lionel Flamstead', *Ainsworth's Magazine*, Jan. 1846.

—'Laman Blanchard and his writings', *The New Monthly Magazine*, Feb. 1846.

—'Decorations of the opera house', *The New Monthly Magazine*, Mar. 1846.

—'Michele Orombello', *Ainsworth's Magazine*, June 1846.

—'Old Saint Paul's', *Ainsworth's Magazine*, June–Dec. 1846.

—'A Night's Adventure in Rome', *Ainsworth's Magazine*, July 1846.

—'James the Second', *Ainsworth's Magazine*, Jan.–Dec. 1847.

—'Alexandra Dumas and His Romances', *Ainsworth's Magazine*, Mar. 1847.

—'Sketches of Hooton and Hewlett', *The New Monthly Magazine*, Mar. 1847.

—'The opening of the opera', *The New Monthly Magazine*, Mar. 1847.

—'British Archaeological Association', *The New Monthly Magazine*, Aug. 1847.

—'Mr. Lumley and Giuseppe Verdi', *The New Monthly Magazine*, Aug. 1847.

—'The Lancashire Witches', *The Sunday Times*, 1848.

—'Crichton', *Ainsworth's Magazine*, Jan. 1848–Aug. 1849.

—'Subjects in season', *The New Monthly Magazine*, June 1848.

—'Her Majesty's Theatre', *The New Monthly Magazine*, Apr. 1849–June 1850.

—'Royal Italian opera-house', *The New Monthly Magazine*, Apr.–May 1849.

—'Guy Fawkes', *Ainsworth's Magazine*, July 1849–June 1850.

—'The closing of the opera', *The New Monthly Magazine*, Sep. 1849.

—'*Lines, Leaves* [by Mrs A. Tindal]', *Ainsworth's Magazine*, Feb. 1850.

—'The approaching opera season', *The New Monthly Magazine*, Mar. 1850.

—'*Lays of Past Days* [by John Hughes]', *Ainsworth's Magazine*, Apr. 1850.

—'Hughes's *Lays of Past Days*', *The New Monthly Magazine*, May 1850.

—'*La Tempesta* at the opera', *The New Monthly Magazine*, July 1850.

—'Lancashire Witches', *Ainsworth's Magazine*, July 1850–Sep. 1853.

—'Pavilion Hall at Brighton', *The New Monthly Magazine*, Feb. 1851.

—'Royal Academy Exhibition', *The New Monthly Magazine*, May 1851.

—'The great Paris fetes', *The New Monthly Magazine*, Sep. 1851.

—'The Star Chamber', *The Home Companion*, 1853.

—'Bird's-eye view of things in general', *The New Monthly Magazine*, Dec. 1851.

—'Things in general', *The New Monthly Magazine*, Mar. 1852.

—'Frederick Lemaitre and Charles Kean', *The New Monthly Magazine*, Apr. 1852.

—'Royal Academy Exhibition', *The New Monthly Magazine*, May 1852.

—'*Esmond* [by Thackeray]' *The New Monthly Magazine*, Dec. 1852.

—'The epilogue to 1852', *The New Monthly Magazine*, Dec. 1852.

—'Prologue to Vol XCVII', *The New Monthly Magazine*, Jan. 1853.

—'The flitch of bacon', *The New Monthly Magazine*, Jan. 1853–May 1854.

—'Annual picture show', *The New Monthly Magazine*, May 1853.

—'The epilogue of 1853', *The New Monthly Magazine*, Dec. 1853.

—'Prologue to the hundredth volume', *The New Monthly Magazine*, Jan. 1854.

—'The Royal Academy', *The New Monthly Magazine*, May 1854.

—'Things in General', *Bentley's Miscellany*, Jan. 1855.

—'The Spendthrift', *Bentley's Miscellany*, Jan. 1855–Jan. 1857.

—'The Royal Academy Exhibition', *Bentley's Miscellany*, May 1855–May 1858.

—'How we are all getting on', *Bentley's Miscellany*, July 1855.

—'What we are all about', *Bentley's Miscellany*, Jan. 1856.

—'Re-opening of Her Majesty's Theatre', *Bentley's Miscellany*, June 1856.

—'Current Events', *Bentley's Miscellany*, July 1856.

—'The Session and the Season', *Bentley's Miscellany*, Aug. 1856.

—'How the world wags', *Bentley's Miscellany*, Jan. 1857.

—'The opera and the bouffes Parisiens', *Bentley's Miscellany*, June 1857.

—'Notes of the month', *Bentley's Miscellany*, July 1857.

—'Our annual dissertation', *Bentley's Miscellany*, Jan. 1858.

—'Her Majesty's Theatre', *Bentley's Miscellany*, June 1858.

—'The old and the new regime', *Bentley's Miscellany*, June 1858.

—'A glance at 'the situation',' *Bentley's Miscellany*, Jan. 1859.

—'*Combat of the Thirty*; a Breton lay', *Bentley's Miscellany*, Jan.–May 1859.

—'Affairs: Political and Literary', *Bentley's Miscellany*, Mar. 1859.

—'Books and pictures', *Bentley's Miscellany*, Apr. 1859.

—'Pot-pourri of art and literature', *Bentley's Miscellany*, May 1859.

—'At home and abroad', *Bentley's Miscellany*, June 1859.

—'Here and there', *Bentley's Miscellany*, July 1859.

—'Abroad and at home', *Bentley's Miscellany*, Aug. 1859.

—'Is the peace peaceful?' *Bentley's Miscellany*, Sep. 1859.

—'A glance at passing events', *Bentley's Miscellany*, Oct. 1859.

—'Exhibition of fine arts. Paris. 1859', *Bentley's Miscellany*, Oct. 1859.

—'Ovingdean Grange', *Bentley's Miscellany*, Nov. 1859–July 1860.

—'The epilogue to 1859', *Bentley's Miscellany*, Dec. 1859.

—'Before the curtain', *Bentley's Miscellany*, Jan. 1860.

—'Epilogue to Vol XLVIII', *Bentley's Miscellany*, Dec. 1860.

—'The Constable of the Tower', *Bentley's Miscellany*, Feb.–Sep. 1861.

—'The present state of literature', *Bentley's Miscellany*, Mar. 1861.

—'Lord Mayor of London', *Bentley's Miscellany*, Jan.–Nov. 1862.

—'Cardinal Pole', *Bentley's Miscellany*, Dec. 1862–Nov. 1863.

—'John Law', *Bentley's Miscellany*, Nov. 1863–Sep. 1864.

—'House of seven chimneys. [The Spanish Match]', *Bentley's Miscellany*, Nov. 1864–Sep. 1865.

—'Constable de Bourbon', *Bentley's Miscellany*, Nov. 1865–Aug. 1866.

—'Old Court', *Bentley's Miscellany*, Oct. 1866–May 1867.

—'Myddleton Pomfret', *Bentley's Miscellany*, July 1867–Mar. 1868.

—'The South Sea Bubble', *Bow Bells*, 1868.

—'Hilary St. Ives', *The New Monthly Magazine*, 1869.

—'Talbot Harland', *Bow Bells*, 1870.

—'Tower Hill', *Bow Bells*, 1871.

—'Boscobel', *The New Monthly Magazine*, 1872.

—'Merry England', *Bow Bells*, 1874

—'The Goldsmith's Wife', *Bow Bells*, 1874.

—'Chetwynd Calverley', *Bow Bells*, 1876.

—'Memoir of Thomas Gilbert Ainsworth', *The Manchester Courier*, April 1876.

—'The Fall of Somerset', *Bow Bells*, 1877–1878.

—'Beatrice Tyldesley', *Bow Bells*, 1878.

—'Stanley Brereton', *The Bolton Weekly Journal*, 1881.

BIBLIOGRAPHY

Ackroyd, Peter, *Dickens* (London: Sinclair Stevenson, 1990).

Allen, Rick, *The Moving Pageant: A Literary Sourcebook on London Street-Life, 1700–1914* (London: Routledge, 1998).

Alpert, Michael (trans. and ed.), *Two Spanish Picaresque Novels* (London: Penguin, 1969).

Alssid, Michael W., *Thomas Shadwell* (New York: Twayne, 1967).

Anderson, W.E.K. (ed.), *The Journal of Sir Walter Scott* (Oxford: Clarendon Press, 1972).

Andrews, William, *The History of the Dunmow Flitch of Bacon Custom* (London: 1877).

Auden, W.H. *The Dyer's Hand and Other Essays* (London: Faber and Faber, 1963).

Austen, Jane, *Northanger Abbey,* (ed.) Anne Henry Ehrenpreis (London: Penguin, 1988).

Axon, W.E.A., *William Harrison Ainsworth: A Memoir* (London: Gibbings, 1902).

Baldick, Chris, *In Frankenstein's Shadow: Myth, Monstrosity and Nineteenth-century Writing* (Oxford, Clarendon Press, 1990).

—introduction, *Melmoth the Wanderer* by Charles Maturin, ed. Douglas Grant (1820 Oxford: Oxford UP, 1989).

Baker, Joseph Ellis, *The Novel and the Oxford Movement* (New York: Russell and Russell, 1965).

Barker, Martin and Petley, Julian (eds), *Ill Effects: The Media/Violence Debate* (London: Routledge, 1997).

Beaver, Harold (ed.), *The Science Fiction of Edgar Allan Poe* (London: Penguin, 1987).

Belinskii, Vissarion Grigorevich, *Selected Philosophical Works* (Moscow: Foreign Languages Publishing House, 1956).

Bevan, B., 'H.A.', *Contemporary Review*, August 1955.

Biles, Jack I., 'William Harrison Ainsworth: His Artistry and, Significance'. Diss., Emory University, 1954.

Bindman, David, *Hogarth* (London: Thames and Hudson, 1994).

Blanchard, Samuel Laman, 'Memoir of William Harrison Ainsworth', *The Mirror*, 1842.

Bloom, Clive (ed.), *Creepers, British Horror and Fantasy in the Twentieth Century* (London: Pluto, 1993).

—*Cult Fiction: Popular Reading and Pulp Theory* (London: Macmillan, 1996).

Bon Gaultier (Sir Theodore Martin and Professor William Edmondstoune Aytoun), 'Illustrations of the Thieves' Literature – No. 1, Flowers of Hemp, or, the Newgate Garland', *Tait's Edinburgh Magazine*, April 1841.

Borrow, George, *Lavengro; The Scholar – The Gypsy – The Priest* (London: John Murray, 1851).

Booth, Michael R., *English Melodrama* (London: Herbert Jenkins, 1965).

Branston, Brian, *The Lost Gods of England* (London: Constable 1994)

Brennan, J.H., *Occult Reich* (London: Futura, 1974).

Brombert, Victor, *Victor Hugo and the Visionary Novel* (Massachusetts: Harvard University Press, 1984).

Brontë, Charlotte, *Jane Eyre*, ed. Q.D. Leavis (1847 London: Penguin, 1966).

Brontë, Charlotte, *Shirley*, Andrew and Judith Hook (eds) (1849 London: Penguin, 1974).

Brooke, Nicholas, (ed.), introduction, *William Shakespeare, The Tragedy of Macbeth* (Oxford, UP, 1998).

Brooks, Ann, and Haworth, Bryan, *Manchester, 'This Good Old Town'* (Preston: Carnegie Press, 1997).

Brooks, Peter, *The Melodramatic Imagination: Balzac, Henry James, Melodrama, and the Mode of Excess* (New Haven: Yale UP, 1995).

Browning, Gareth, Purton, Rowland W. et al., *A Pageant of History: The Reigns of our Kings and Queens, Famous People and Events in our History* (London: Collins, 1958).

Butler, Elizabeth M., *The Fortunes of Faust* (Stroud: Sutton, 1998).

Cannon, John and Griffith, Ralph, *The Oxford Illustrated History of the British Monarchy* (Oxford: UP, 2000), 458.

Carpenter, Richard, *Dick Turpin* (London: Fontana, 1979).

Carswell, Donald (ed.), *Trial of Guy Fawkes and Others (The Gunpowder Plot)* (London: William Hodge, 1934).

Carver, Stephen, 'Abnormal Literature: The early fiction of William Harrison Ainsworth'. Diss., University of East Anglia, 1999.

Casti, John L., *Paradigms Lost, Images of Man in the Mirror of Science* (London: Cardinal, 1989).

Cavendish, Richard, *Man, Myth and Magic* (London: Purnell, 1970).

Chandler, Frank W., *The Literature of Roguery*, 2 vols (Boston: Houghton and Mifflin, 1907).

Chesney, Kellow, *The Victorian Underworld* (London: Penguin, 1991).

Chittick, Kathryn, *Dickens and the 1830s* (Cambridge: Cambridge UP, 1990).

Clarke, Basil F.L., *Church Builders of the Nineteenth Century: A Study of the Gothic Revival in England* (London: Society for Promoting Christian Knowledge, 1938).

Cohen, Stanley, *Folk Devils and Moral Panics* (London: McGibbon and Kee, 1977).

Collins, Philip, *Dickens and Crime* (London: Macmillan, 1965).

Collins, Rex (ed.), *Classic Victorian and Edwardian Ghost Stories* (London: Wordsworth, 1996).

Corbin, Peter (ed.) *Three Jacobean Witchcraft Plays* (Manchester: Manchester UP, 1986).

Cox, Michael, and Gilbert, R.A. (eds), *English Ghost Stories* (Oxford: Oxford UP, 1989).

Crossley, James (ed.), *Potts's Discovery of Witches In the County of Lancaster, Remains Historical and Literary Connected with the Palantine Counties of Lancaster and Cheshire* (Manchester: The Chetham Society, 1845).

Crossley, James and Evans, John (eds), *Specially Revised Accounts of the Recent Banquet to William Harrison Ainsworth, Esq., by Thomas Baker, Mayor of Manchester. As an expression of the high esteem in which he is held by his Fellow-townsmen and of his services to literature* (Manchester: 1881).

Davies, Godfrey, *The Early Stuarts 1603–1660* (Oxford: Clarendon Press, 1937).

Defoe, Daniel, A *Journal of the Plague Year, being observations or memorials of the most remarkable occurrences, as well public as private, which happened in London during the last great visitation in 1665. Written by a Citizen who continued all the while in London. Never made public before.* Anthony Burgess, Christopher Bristow (eds) (1722 London: Penguin, 1966).

Defoe, Daniel, *The Novels and Miscellaneous Works of Daniel De Foe* (Oxford: Thomas Tegg, 1841).

deGategno, Paul J., 'Daniel Defoe's Newgate Biographies: An Economic Crisis', *CLIO*, 13 (1984).

De Quincey, Thomas, *Confessions of an English Opium Eater*, Alcthca Haytcr (ed.) (1821 London: Penguin, 1986).

de Vries, Leonard, and Van Amstel, Ilonka, *'Orrible Murder, An Anthology of Victorian Crime and Passion Compiled from The Illustrated Police News* (New York: Taplinger, 1971).

Dickens, A.G., *The English Reformation* (Glasgow: Fontana, 1967).

Dickens, Charles, *Collected Works*, 17 vols (London: Odhams, 1897).

Dinesen, Isak (Karen Blixen), *Seven Gothic Tales* (1934 London: Penguin, 1963)

Dunae, Patrick A., 'Penny Dreadfuls: Late Nineteenth-Century Boys' Literature and Crime', *Victorian Studies*, 22, (79).

Duncan, Ian, *Modern Romance and Transformations of the Novel: The Gothic, Scott, Dickens* (Cambridge: Cambridge UP, 1992).

Egan, Pierce, *Life in London or The Day and Night Scenes of Jerry Hawthorn, ESQ. and his elegant friend Corinthian Tom in their Rambles and Sprees through the Metropolis* (London: John Camden Hotten, 1869).

Ellis, S[tewart] M[arsh], *William Harrison Ainsworth and His Friends*, 2 vols (London: John Lane, 1911).

—*The Solitary Horseman, or The Life and Adventures of G.P.R. James* (London: The Cayme Press, 1927).

—and Bleackley, Horace, *Jack Sheppard. With an Epilogue on Jack Sheppard in Literature and Drama* (Edinburgh: William Hodge, 1933).

Elwin, Malcolm, *Victorian Wallflowers* (London: Cape, 1934).

Empson, William, *Some Versions of Pastoral* (London: Penguin, 1966).

Emsley, Clive, *Crime and Society in England, 1750–1900* (London: Longman, 1996).

Engels, Friedrich, *The Condition of the Working Class in England*, W.O. Henderson and W.H. Chaloner (trans. and eds) (1844–5 Oxford: Basil Blackwell, 1971).

Evans, Eric J., *The Forging of the Modern State, Early Industrial Britain 1783–1870* (London: Longman, 1983).

Evans, Hilary and Evans, Mary, *Hero on a Stolen Horse: The highwayman, and his brothers-in-arms the bandit and the bushranger* (London, Frederick Muller, 1977).

Evans, John, 'The Early Life of William Harrison Ainsworth', *Manchester Quarterly*, l, 1882.

Fairclough, Peter (ed.), *Three Gothic Novels* (London: Penguin, 1968).

Faller, Lincoln B., *Crime and Defoe, A New Kind of Writing* (Cambridge: Cambridge UP, 1993).

Faurot, Ruth M., 'The Early Novels of William Harrison Ainsworth'. Diss., University of North Carolina, 1953.

Fenin, George N., and Everson, William K., *The Western: From Silents to the Seventies* (London: Penguin, 1978).

Fielding, Henry, *Jonathan Wild*, David Nokes (ed.) (London: Penguin, 1986).

Fitch, Eric L., *In Search of Herne the Hunter* (London: Capall Bann, 1994).

Fitzgerald, Percy, *Memories of Charles Dickens* (London: Arrowsmith Bristol, 1913).

—*The Life of Charles Dickens* (London: Chatto and Windus, 1905).

Fletcher, Angus, *Allegory, The Theory of a Symbolic Mode* (London: Cornell UP, 1964).

Forster, John, *The Life of Charles Dickens*, J.W.T. Ley (ed.) (London: Cecil Palmer, 1928).

—*Examiner*, May 18 1834.

—*Examiner*, November 3 1839.

Fraser, Antonia, *The Gunpowder Plot: Terror and Faith in 1605* (London: Mandarin, 1995).

Friswell, J. Hain, *Modern Men of Letters, Honestly Criticised* (London: Hodder and Stoughton, 1870).

Frow, Edmund and Ruth, *Manchester and Salford Chartists* (Manchester: Lancashire Community Press, 1996).

439

Gardiner, Samuel Rawson, *What Gunpowder Plot Was* (London: Longmans, Green and Co, 1897).

Gaskell, Elizabeth, *Collected Works* (London: Smith, Elder and Co, 1886).

Gatrell, A.C., *The Hanging Tree: Execution and the English People, 1770–1868* (Oxford: Oxford UP, 1994).

Gay, John, *The Beggar's Opera*, Bryan Loughrey, and T.O. Treadwell (eds) (London: Penguin, 1986).

George, M. Dorothy, *London Life in the Eighteenth Century* (London: Penguin, 1992).

Gilbert, Sandra M. and Gubar, Susan, *The Madwoman in the Attic* (New Haven: Yale UP, 1979), 201.

Godwin, William, *Enquiry Concerning Political Justice*, Isaac Kramnick (ed.) (London: Penguin, 1993).

Goethe, Johann Wolfgang, *Faust*, trans. Philip Wayne, 2 vols (London: Penguin, 1979).

Gore, Catherine, *Modern Chivalry, or a New Orlando Furioso* (London: 1843).

Grey, Rudolph, *Nightmare of Ecstasy: The Life and Art of Edward D. Wood, Jr* (Los Angeles: Feral House, 1992).

Gribble, Francis, 'Harrison Ainsworth', *Fortnightly Review*, 77 (1905).

Grindon, Leo H., *Lancashire – Brief Historical and Descriptive Notes* (London: 1882).

Gross, John, and Pearson, Gabriel, *Dickens and the Twentieth Century* (London: Routledge and Kegan Paul, 1962).

Guy, John, *Tudor England* (Oxford: Oxford UP, 1998).

Hamard, Marie-Claire, 'William Harrison Ainsworth, romancier historique', *Caliban*, 28 (1991).

Harland, John (F.S.A.) (ed.), *Modern Songs and Ballads of Lancashire* (London: Whittaker and Co, 1866). Now updated by Cliff Hayes and reprinted as *The Best of Old Lancashire in Poetry and Verse* (Manchester: Printwise 1992).

Hart, Francis R., *Scott's Novels: The Plotting of Historic Survival* (Charlottesville: Virginia UP, 1966).

Hayden, John O. (ed.), *Scott: The Critical Heritage* (London: Routledge and Kegan Paul, 1970).

Hazlitt, William, *The Spirit of the Age: or, Contemporary Portraits* (London: Collins, 1969).

Heywood, Thomas, *Dramatic Works*, A. Wilson Verity (ed.), 6 vols (New York: Russell and Russell, 1964).

Hinton, C[harles] Howard, 'What is the Fourth Dimension?' (London, 1884).

Hobsbawm, E.J., *Bandits* (London: Weidenfeld and Nicolson, 1969).

—and Terence Ranger (eds), *The Invention of Tradition* (Cambridge: Cambridge UP, 1989).

Hole, Christina, *Witchcraft in Britain* (London: Batsford: 1977).

Hollingsworth, Keith, *The Newgate Novel 1830–47: Bulwer, Ainsworth, Dickens and Thackeray* (Detroit: Wayne State UP, 1963).

Hooker, Kenneth Ward, *The Fortunes of Victor Hugo in England* (New York: Columbia UP, 1938).

Horne, R[ichard] H[engist], *A New Spirit of the Age*, 2 vols (London: Smith, Elder and Co., 1844).

Houghton, Walter E. (ed.), *The Wellesley Index to Victorian Periodicals 1824–1900*, 5 vols (London: Routledge and Kegan Paul, 1966).

—*The Victorian Frame of Mind* (New Haven: Yale, 1957.

House, Humphry, *The Dickens World* (Oxford: Oxford UP, 1960).

House, Madeline, and Storey, Graham (eds), *The Letters of Charles Dickens*, 8 vols (Oxford: Clarendon Press, 1969).

Hugo, Victor Marie, *Notre Dame de Paris*, trans. I.G. Burnham. (London: J.M. Dent, 1965).

Irving, Washington, *The Legend of Sleepy Hollow and Other Stories*, ed. Lauriat Lane, Jr (1819 New York: Airmont, 1964).

'Jack Sheppard: a Romance', rev. of *Jack Sheppard*, *Athenaeum*, October 26, 1839.

Jackson, Rosemary, *Fantasy: the Literature of Subversion* (London: Routledge, 1981).

James, G[eorge] P[ayne] R[ainsford], *Corse de Leon; or, The Brigand* (New York: Farmer and Daggers, 1845).

—*Dark Scenes of History* (London: T.C. Newby, 1849).

Jardine, David, *Criminal Trials* (1835–40) (London: M.A. Nattali, 1846).

James, Louis, *Fiction for the Working Man 1830–50* (London: Penguin, 1973).

Jerrold, Blanchard, *Life of George Cruikshank. Special copy enlarged to four volumes and illustrated with hundreds of additional engravings, portraits, autographs &c. &c. &c.*, 4 vols (Manchester, 1880).

John, Juliet (ed.), *Cult Criminals, The Newgate Novels 1830–1847*, 8 vols (London: Routledge, 1998).

Joline, Adrian H., *At the Library Table* (Boston: Badger, 1910.

Joyce, James, *Ulysses* (London: Penguin, 1998).

Kenyon, John, *The History Men: The Historical Profession in England since the Renaissance* (London: Weidenfeld and Nicolson 1983).

Knox, E.A., *The Tractarian Movement, 1833–1845* (London: Putnam, 1933).

Kuhn, Thomas S., *The Structure of Scientific Revolutions* (Chicago: Chicago UP, 1962).

Lamb, Charles, *Poetical and Dramatic Tales, Essays and Criticisms*, Charles Kent (ed.) (London: George Routledge and Sons, 1889).

Le Fanu, J. Sheridan, *Madam Crowl's Ghost and other Stories*, M.R. James (ed.) (London: Wordsworth, 1994).

Lewis, Matthew, *The Monk*, Howard Anderson (ed.) (Oxford: Oxford UP, 1973).

Ligocki, Llewellyn, 'William Harrison Ainsworth's Use of History: The Tower of London and other Tudor Novels'. Diss., University of Kansas, 1968.

Linebaugh, Peter, *The London Hanged, Crime and Society in the Eighteenth Century* (London: Penguin, 1991.

Lingard, John, *The History of England from the First Invasion of the Romans to the Accession of William and Mary*, 10 vols (London: Charles Dolman, 1830).

Lloyd Smith, Allan, and Sage, Victor (eds), *Gothick Origins and Innovations* (Amsterdam: Rodopi, 1994).

Locke, Harold, *A Bibliographical Catalogue of the Published Novels and Ballads of William Harrison Ainsworth* (London: Matthews, 1925).

Lockhart, J[ohn] G[ibson], *Memoirs of the Life of Sir Walter Scott* (Edinburgh: Robert Cadell, 1838).

Low, Donald A., *The Regency Underworld* (London, J.M. Dent, 1982).

Lukács, Georg, *The Historical Novel*, trans. Hannah and Stanley Mitchell (London: Merlin Press, 1974)

Lytton, Edward George Earle Bulwer-Lytton, *Collected Works*, 32 vols (London: George Routledge and Sons, 1863).

Macaulay, James, *The Gothic Revival: 1745–1845* (London: Blackie, 1975).

MacCulloch, Diarmaid, *Thomas Cranmer* (New Haven: Yale UP, 1996).

MacKay, Charles, *Memoirs of Extraordinary Popular Delusions and the Madness of Crowds*, 2nd edn (1851; London: Wordsworth, 1995).

Maclellan, Alec, *The Lost World of Agharti, The Mystery of Vril Power* (London: Souvenir Press, 1996).

Macquarrie, John, *Principles of Christian Theology* (London: SCM Press, 1977).

Maginn, William, 'The Man in the Bell', *Blackwood's Edinburgh Magazine*, November 1821.

Marlowe, Christopher, *Doctor Faustus*, John D. Jump (ed.) (Manchester: Manchester UP, 1988).

Marriott, Sir John, *English History and English Fiction* (London: Blackie and Son, 1944).

Martin, Philip and Jarvis, Robin (eds), *Reviewing Romanticism* (London: Macmillan, 1992).

Mason, Leo, 'William Harrison Ainsworth', *The Dickensian* XXXV (1939)

Maturin, Charles, *Melmoth the Wanderer*, Douglas Grant (ed.) (Oxford: Oxford UP, 1989).

Mayhead, Robin. *Walter Scott*. Cambridge: Cambridge UP, 1973.

Mayhew, Henry, *London Labour and the London Poor*, Victor Neuburg (ed.) (London: Penguin, 1985).

Meredith, Michael, 'A Fine Distancing: Browning's Debt to Harrison Ainsworth', *Browning Society Notes*, 21 (1991–2).

Moers, Ellen, *The Dandy, Brummell to Beerbohm* (New York: Viking, 1960).

Monod, Paul Kléber, *Jacobitism and the English People: 1688–1788* (Cambridge: UP 1989).

Moore, Lucy, *The Thieves' Opera* (London: Penguin, 1997).

Morrison, Robert, and Baldick, Chris (eds), *Tales of Terror from Blackwood's Magazine* (Oxford: Oxford UP, 1995).

—(eds) *The Vampyre and Other Tales of the Macabre* (Oxford: Oxford UP, 1997).

Nathan, George Jean, *Another Book on the Theatre* (New York: B.W. Huebsch, 1915).

Neale, J.E., *Queen Elizabeth I* (London: Pimlico, 1934).

Newton, H. Chance, *Crime and the Drama or, Dark Deeds Dramatised* (London: Stanley Paul and Co, 1927).

Nicholls, Mark, *Investigating Gunpowder Plot* (Manchester: Manchester UP, 1991).

Nietzsche, Friedrich, *Thus Spoke Zarathustra*, trans. R.J. Hollingdale (London: Penguin, 1969).

Nord, Deborah Epstein, *Walking the Victorian Streets: Women, Representation and the City* (London: Cornell UP, 1995).

O'Neill, Edward H. (ed.), *The Complete Tales and Poems of Edgar Allan Poe* (New York: Dorset, 1989).

Oliphant, Margaret, *Annals of a Publishing House: William Blackwood and His Sons: Their Magazine and Friends*, 2 vols, vol. 2 (Edinburgh, William Blackwood and Sons, 1898)

Olmsted, John Charles, *A Victorian Art of Fiction* (New York: Garland, 1979).

Parrish, Stephen M., 'The Whig Interpretation of Literature', *Text*, 4 (1988),

Parsons, Coleman O., *Witchcraft and Demonology in Scott's Fiction* (Edinburgh: Oliver and Boyd, 1964).

Parsons, Gerald (ed.), *Religion in Victorian Britain*, 4 vols (Manchester: Manchester UP, 1991).

Partridge, Eric, *A Dictionary of the Underworld* (London: Routledge and Kegan Paul, 1950).

Paton, James, III, 'The Historical Novels of William Harrison Ainsworth'. Diss., Western Reserve University, 1954.

Patten, Robert L., *George Cruikshank's Life, Times, and Art*, 2 vols, vol. 2 (Cambridge: The Lutterworth Press, 1996).

Paulson, Ronald, *Hogarth: High Art and Low* (Cambridge: The Lutterworth Press, 1992).

Pawling, Christopher (ed.), *Popular Fiction and Social Change* (London: Macmillan, 1984).

Peacock, Thomas Love, *Crotchet Castle*, Raymond Wright (ed.) (London: Penguin, 1969).

Pearson, Hesketh, *Walter Scott: His Life and Personality* (London: Hamish Hamilton, 1987).

Peel, Edgar, and Southern, Pat, *The Trials of the Lancashire Witches, A Study of Seventeenth-Century Witchcraft* (Newton Abbot: David and Charles, 1969).

Poe, Edgar Allen, *The Essays and Reviews of Edgar Allan Poe*, (ed.) G.R. Thompson (New York: Penguin, 1984).

Praz, Mario, *The Romantic Agony*, trans. Angus Davidson (Oxford: Oxford UP, 1970).

Priestley, J.B., *Charles Dickens and his World* (London: Thames and Hudson, 1978).

Propp, Vladimir, *The Morphology of the Folktale*, trans. Laurence Scott (Austin: University of Texas, 1998)

Pugin, Augustus Welby, *Contrasts; or A Parallel Between the Noble Edifices of the Fourteenth and Fifteenth Centuries, and Similar Buildings of the Present Day; Shewing the Present Decay of Taste* (London, 1836).

Punter, David, *The Literature of Terror, A History of Gothic Fictions from 1765 to the Present Day*, 2nd edn, 2 vols (London: Longman, 1996).

Radcliffe, Ann, *The Italian*, Frederick Garber (ed.) (1797 Oxford: Oxford UP, 1968).

—*The Mysteries of Udolpho*, Bonamy Dobrée (ed.) (1794 Oxford: Oxford UP, 1966).

Raines, F.R. (ed.), *The Journal of Nicholas Assheton of Downham, in the county of Lancaster, esq. for part of the year 1617, and a part of the year following: interspersed with notes from the life of his contemporary, John Bruen Stapleford, in the county of Chester, esq.* (New York: Johnson Reprint, 1969).

Rance, Nicholas, *The Historical Novel and Popular Politics in Nineteenth Century England* (London: Vision, 1975).

Rawlings, Philip, *Drunks, Whores and Idle Apprentices, Criminal Biographies of the Eighteenth Century* (London: Routledge, 1992).

Reed, John R., *Victorian Conventions* (Ohio: Ohio UP, 1975).

Reynolds, G[eorge] W[illiam] M[acArthur], *The Mysteries of London*, Trefor Thomas (ed.) (Keele: Keele UP, 1996).

Richardson, Ruth, *Death, Dissection and the Destitute* (London: Penguin, 1988).

Richter, David H., 'From Medievalism to Historicism: Representations of History in the Gothic Novel and Historical Romance', *Studies in Medievalism*, 4 (1992).

Ricks, Beatrice, 'Characteristics of the Gothic Historical Novel in the Works of William Harrison Ainsworth'. Diss., University of Oklahoma, 1954.

Rigby, Elizabeth, rev. of *Jane Eyre*, by Currer Bell, *The Quarterly Review*, 84, December 1848.

Roberts, Marie, *Gothic Immortals, The Fiction of the Brotherhood of the Rosy Cross* (London: Routledge, 1990).

Robertson, Fiona, *Legitimate Histories: Scott, Gothic, and the Authorities of Fiction* (Oxford, Clarendon Press, 1994).

Rosa, Matthew Whiting, *The Silver-Fork School* (New York: Kennikat, 1936).

Rousseau, Jean-Jacques, *The Social Contract and Discourses*, trans. G.D.H. Cole (London: Everyman, 1988).

Rowse, A.L., *The Tower of London in the History of the Nation* (London: Weidenfeld and Nicolson, 1972).

Rumbelow, Donald, *The Triple Tree: Newgate, Tyburn and The Old Bailey* (London: Harrap, 1982).

Sabin, Roger, *Adult Comics: An Introduction* (London, Routledge, 1993).

Sadleir, Michael, *Blessington – D'Orsay: A Masquerade* (London: Constable, 1933).

Sage, Victor, *Horror Fiction in the Protestant Tradition* (London: Macmillan, 1988).

Sales, Roger, 'Pierce Egan and the Representation of London', *Reviewing Romanticism*, Philip Martin and Robin Jarvis (eds) (London, Macmillan, 1992).

Sanders, Andrew, *The Victorian Historical Novel, 1840–1880* (London: Macmillan, 1978).

Schiller, Friedrich, *The Robbers*, trans. F.J. Lamport (London: Penguin, 1979).

Schroeder, Natalie, 'Jack Sheppard and Barnaby Rudge: Yet More "Humbug" from a "Jolter Head"', *Studies in the Novel*, 18(1) (1986).

Scott, Sir Walter, *Letters on Demonology and Witchcraft, Addressed to J.G. Lockhart, Esq.* (London: George Routledge and Sons, 1884).

—*The Poetical Works*, Francis Turner Palgrave (ed.) (London: Macmillan, 1928).

—*The Waverley Novels*, 47 vols (Edinburgh: Robert Cadell, 1838).

—'Remarks on Frankenstein: or, The Modern Prometheus', *Blackwood's Magazine*, II, 1818. (Edinburgh: Ballantyne's Novelists Library, Vol. X, 1824)

Shadwell, Thomas, *Complete Works*, Montague Summers (ed.), 5 vols (London: The Fortune Press, 1927).

Shakespeare, William, *The Tragedy of Macbeth*, Nicholas Brooke (ed.) (Oxford: Oxford UP, 1998).

Sharpe, J.A., *Crime in Early Modern England 1550–1750* (London: Longman, 1984).

Shelley, Mary, *Frankenstein* (1818), ed. Peter Fairclough, *Three Gothic Novels* (London: Penguin, 1968).

Smith, J.T., *Vagabondiana, or The Anecdotes of Mendicant Wanderers through the Streets of London, with Portraits of the Most Remarkable* (London, 1817).

Spink, Henry Hawkes, *The Gunpowder Plot and Lord Mounteagle's Letter; Being a Proof, with Moral Certitude, of the Authorship of the Document Together with Some Account of the Whole Thirteen Gunpowder Conspirators, Including Guy Fawkes* (London: Simpkin, Marshall, Hamilton, Kent and Co, 1902).

Sprenger, James and Kramer, Heinrich, *Malleus Maleficarum*, trans. Montague Summers (London: Dover, 1978).

Springhall, John, *Youth, Popular Culture and Moral Panics: Penny Gaffs to Gansta-Rap, 1830–1996* (London: Routledge, 1998).

Stanton, Phoebe, *Pugin* (London: Thames and Hudson, 1971).

Steer, F.W., *The History of the Dunmow Flitch Ceremony* (Chelmsford: Essex County Council, 1951).

Stoker, Bram, *Dracula*, Maurice Hindle (ed.) (London: Penguin, 1993).

Sucksmith, H.P., 'The Secret of Immediacy: Dickens' Debt to the Tale of Terror in *Blackwood's*', *Nineteenth-Century Fiction*, 26 (1971).

Summers, Montague, *The History of Witchcraft* (London: Senate, 1994).

Sutherland, John, *Victorian Fiction: Writers, Publishers, Readers* (London: Macmillan, 1995).

Swifte, Edmund Lenthal, 'The Reply to the Question "Is there not a ghost story connected with the Tower of London?"' *Notes and Queries*, September 8 1860.

Thackeray, William Makepeace, *Collected Works*, 25 vols (London: Caxton, 1920).

—*The Letters and Private Papers of William Makepeace Thackeray*, Gordon N. Ray (ed.), 4 vols (London: Oxford UP, 1945).

Thomas, Donald, *The Victorian Underworld* (London: John Murray, 1998).

Thomas, Keith, *Religion and the Decline of Magic* (London: Penguin, 1991) 1971 in Chap Five n39.

Thompson, E.P., *The Making of the English Working Class* (London: Pelican, 1968).

Thompson, G.R. (ed.), *The Essays and Reviews of Edgar Allan Poe* (New York: Penguin, 1984).

Tobias, John J., *Prince of Fences: The Life and Crimes of Ikey Solomons* (London: Valentine, 1974).

Tristan, Flora, *London Journal 1840*, trans. Dennis Palmer and Giselle Pincetl (Charlestown: Charles River Books, 1980).

Truffaut, François, and Scott, Helen G., *Hitchcock* (London: Paladin, 1986).

Turner, E.S., *Boys Will Be Boys* (London: Michael Joseph, 1948).

Uglow, Jenny, *Hogarth* (London: Faber and Faber, 1998).

Vaux, James Hardy, *Memoirs of a Transport* (London, 1819).

Walkowitz, Judith R., *The City of Dreadful Delight* (London: Virago, 1992–4).

Walpole, Horace, *The Castle of Otranto* (1764), ed. Peter Fairclough, *Three Gothic Novels* (London: Penguin, 1968).

Walpole, Hugh, 'The historical novel in England since Sir Walter Scott', *Sir Walter Scott Today*, ed. H.J.C. Grierson (London: 1932)

Ward, Kenneth, *The Fortunes of Victor Hugo in England* (New York: Columbia UP, 1938).

Watkin, David, *English Architecture* (London: Thames and Hudson, 1994).

Warner, Philip, *The Best of British Pluck: The Boy's Own Paper* (London: MacDonald and Jane's, 1976).

Warren, Russell, 'Journey to the Centre of the Earth', *Encounters*, 2 (1995).

Washington, Peter, *Madame Blavatsky's Baboon, Theosophy and the Emergence of the Western Guru* (London: Secker and Warburg, 1993).

Wertham, Fredric, *The Seduction of the Innocent* (London: Museum Press, 1955)

Wheatley, Dennis, *The Devil and All His Works* (London: Hutchinson, 1971).

Wilde, Oscar, *The Picture of Dorian Gray* (1891 Oxford: OUP, 1998).

Wilkinson, George Theodore, *The Newgate Calendar* (London: Wordsworth, 1997).

Williams, Ioan (ed.), *Sir Walter Scott on Novelists and Fiction* (London: Routledge and Kegan Paul, 1968).

Williams, Raymond, *Culture and Society, 1780–1950* (London: Penguin, 1963).

Wills, Gary, *Witches and Jesuits, Shakespeare's Macbeth* (Oxford: Oxford UP, 1995).

Wilson, Angus, *The World of Charles Dickens* (London: Penguin, 1970).

Wilson, Edmund, *The Wound and the Bow, Seven Studies in Literature* (New York: Farrar Straus Giroux, 1978).

Wilson, Harriette, *Memoirs of Herself and Others* (London: Peter Davies, 1930).

Worth, George J., *William Harrison Ainsworth* (New York: Twayne, 1972).

Yates, Edmund, 'Celebrities at Home. No. LXXXXIV. Mr. W. Harrison Ainsworth at Little Rockley', *The World,* March 27 1878.

INDEX

Abbot, Edwin, 239

Ackroyd, Peter, *Dickens*, 14–15; *Hawksmoor*, 239n

Acton, Dr. William, 207

Adam and the Ants, 157n

Adelphi Theatre, London, 178, 201

Agincourt, Battle of, 368

Ainsworth, Ann (*née* Harrison), 5, 150n, 286–287

Ainsworth, Captain John, 346

Ainsworth, Dr. William Francis, 368, 382, 385, 400

Ainsworth, Frances 'Fanny' (*née* Ebers), 97, 121, 130–131, 171

Ainsworth, Thomas Gilbert, 5n, 150n, 346, 384, 387

Ainsworth, Thomas, 4–5, 48, 95

Ainsworth, William Harrison (please also refer to Chronology, xi–xv), abandons Newgate writing, 19, 24, 230; becomes editor of *Bentley's Miscellany*, 21–22, 232; bicycles, 387; birth and childhood, 4–5, 47, 58, 80–81; birth of daughter, Clara, by Sarah Wells, 381; birth of daughters, 5, 123, 125, 381; black-balled at the Trinity Club, 19, 228; buys *Bentley's Miscellany*, 371–372; buys Hill View Lodge, Reigate, for brother, 384; buys the *New Monthly Magazine*, 296; Catholic sympathies, 50n, 60, 79–80, 98–99, 126, 174n, 233, 235–236, 238, 250, 255–259, 267, 299, 373; celebrates completion of *The Tower of London*, 231, 270–271, 396–397; child custody battle, 171–173; comments on Forster's biography of Dickens, 15; considers taking Chetham Librarianship, 386; contemporary critical responses, 1, 3, 5–7, 10–11, 17–20, 23–27, 29–34, 39–42, 44–45, 97–98, 100–103, 129–130, 153, 155, 169–170, 195, 219–230, 239–240, 246, 275–278, 337,

STUDIES IN BRITISH LITERATURE